QUANTITATIVE METHODS FOR BUSINESS

FOURTH EDITION

David R. Anderson
UNIVERSITY OF CINCINNATI

Dennis J. Sweeney
UNIVERSITY OF CINCINNATI

Thomas A. Williams
ROCHESTER INSTITUTE OF TECHNOLOGY

West Publishing Company

St. Paul   New York   Los Angeles   San Francisco

Cover Photo: Morton Beebe, The Image Bank
Text Design: Rita Naughton
Project Management: Maureen P. Conway, Spectrum Publisher Services
Compositor: Harper Graphics

96 95 94 93 92 91 90 89   8 7 6 5 4 3 2 1

Library of Congress Cataloging-in-Publication Data

Anderson, David Ray, 1941—
    Quantitative methods for business.

    Bibliography: p.
    Includes index.
    1. Management science.   I. Sweeney, Dennis J.
II. Williams, Thomas Arthur, 1944–   . III. Title.
T56.A63   1989   658.4′033   88-26085
ISBN 0-314-46935-4
ISBN 0-314-51347-7
ISBN 0-314-51348-5

TO:
Krista and Mark
Mark, Linda, Brad, Tim, Scott, and Lisa
Cathy, David, and Kristin

Contents

Preface

The purpose of this fourth edition, as with previous editions, is to provide students with a sound conceptual understanding of the role that quantitative methods play in the decision-making process. The text describes the many quantitative methods that have been developed over the years, explains how they work, and shows how they can be applied and interpreted by the decision maker.

We have written this book with the needs of the nonmathematician in mind; it is applications oriented. In each chapter a problem is described in conjunction with the quantitative procedure being introduced. The development of the quantitative technique or model includes applying it to the problem in order to generate a solution or recommendation. We have found that this approach helps to motivate the student by demonstrating not only how the procedure works, but also how it can contribute to the decision-making process.

CHANGES IN THE FOURTH EDITION

In preparing the fourth edition we have been careful to maintain the overall format and approach of the previous editions. However, based on our own classroom experience and suggestions from users of previous editions, a number of significant changes have been made to enhance the content, organization, and readability of the text.

Complete Revision of Linear Programming

Chapters 7–9 now provide an earlier focus on problem formulation, sensitivity analysis, and the use of computer software in solving linear programming problems. Chapter 7 introduces the graphical method for solving linear programming problems; a new Chapter 8 provides a complete integration of modeling, computer solution, sensitivity analysis, and the interpretation of computer output; and Chapter 9 describes how selected decision-making problems can be formulated and solved as linear programs. Chapter 10 then shows how the simplex method is used to solve linear programs and to develop the standard sensitivity analysis. This new organization provides greater flexibility for instructors who do not want to teach the simplex method, since Chapters 7–9 now provide a complete introduction to linear programming without discussing the simplex solution procedure.

On the other hand, those who want to include the simplex method have a chapter devoted to this topic.

Transportation, Assignment, and Transshipment Problems

In this edition the material on the transportation, assignment, and transshipment problems has been combined into one chapter. For each problem, the discussion begins by showing how to develop a linear programming model. Special-purpose solution procedures are then presented for the transportation and assignment problems to demonstrate the streamlined solution process that is possible because of the special problem structure. Users who want simply to treat these problems as special cases of the general linear programming approach can do so by skipping the sections on the special-purpose algorithms.

Case Problems

Another significant new feature of this edition is the addition of case problems to 11 of the chapters. These case problems provide the student with the opportunity to attempt a larger-scale problem for which a computer solution is generally required. A managerial report is required, and questions at the end of each of the cases suggest important issues to be addressed in the student's analysis and recommendations.

Decision Analysis and Utility

This edition of the text further expands on the importance of decision analysis. A section discussing sensitivity analysis with respect to state-of-nature probabilities has been added, as well as a section describing marginal analysis for problems involving many decision alternatives and many states of nature. The material on the analytic hierarchy process has been combined with the goal programming material in a new chapter entitled "Multicriteria Decision Problems" (Chapter 17).

Other Major Changes

Many of the other chapters in the text have been carefully revised in order to take advantage of the input we have had from users of previous editions. Some of the specific changes are as follows:

1. The presentation of computer output has been expanded. LINDO/PC is used to solve linear and integer programming problems. Output from *The Management Scientist* software package is presented in the other chapters. A section has been added to Chapter 1 describing the use of *The Management Scientist*.
2. A new section has been added to Chapter 1 describing mathematical models of cost, volume, and profit.
3. A new section has been added to Chapter 13 to introduce the student to the critical path procedure without the complication of probabilistic activity times.
4. Chapter 16 has been revised to explain in more detail the difference between single-channel and multiple-channel waiting lines.
5. New problems have been added and existing ones revised. As was true in previous editions, the problems are suggestive of the types of situations in which the methods can be applied. Many are scaled-down versions of real-life problems.

PREREQUISITE

The mathematical prerequisite for this text is a course in algebra. Two chapters on probability and probability distributions have been included to provide the necessary background for the use of probability in the later chapters.

Throughout the text we have utilized generally accepted notation for the topic being covered. In this regard students who pursue study beyond the level of this text will find the difficulties of reading more advanced material minimized. To assist in further study, a bibliography is included in the backmatter of the book.

COURSE OUTLINE FLEXIBILITY

The text has been designed so that the instructor has substantial flexibility in terms of selecting topics to meet specific course needs. While many variations are possible, the single-quarter and single-semester outlines that follow are illustrative of the options available.

Possible One-Quarter Outline
Introduction (Chapter 1)
Decision Analysis (Chapters 4 and 5)
Forecasting (Chapter 6)
Linear Programming (Chapters 7, 8, and 9)
PERT/CPM (Chapter 13)
Inventory Models (Chapter 14)
Computer Simulation (Chapter 15)

Possible One-Semester Outline
Introduction (Chapter 1)
Probability Concepts (Chapters 2 and 3)
Decision Analysis (Chapters 4 and 5)
Forecasting (Chapter 6)
Linear Programming (Chapters 7, 8, and 9)
Transportation, Assignment, and Transshipment Problems (Chapter 11)
Integer Linear Programming (Chapter 12)
Computer Simulation (Chapter 15)
Waiting-Line Models (Chapter 16)

Many other possibilities exist for such a course, depending on course objectives and the background of the students.

ANCILLARIES

A complete package of support materials accompanies the text: an Instructor's Manual; a Study Guide, coauthored by John A. Lawrence and Barry Alan Pasternack, California State University at Fullerton; a Test Bank, prepared by Constance McClaren, Indiana State University; transparency masters; and *The Management Scientist*, an IBM-compatible software package, capable of solving a variety of problems. This menu-driven software package is new to the fourth edition and has been designed to provide a high degree of user flexibility, including the ability to easily save and modify problems. For a small extra charge, a copy of the software may be ordered shrinkwrapped with the text.

We believe that the applications orientation of the text, combined with this package of support materials, provides a solid framework for introducing students to quantitative methods and their application.

ACKNOWLEDGMENTS

We owe a debt to many of our colleagues and friends for their helpful comments and suggestions during the development of this and previous editions. Among these are Donald Adolphson, Shiv Kumar Aggarwah, E. Leonard Arnoff, Uttarayan Bagchi, Edward Baker, Norman Baker, James Bartos, Stephen Becktold, Richard Beckwith, George Bohlen, Stanley Brooking, Randall Byers, Jeffrey Camm, Thomas Case, Dennis E. Drinka, John Eatman, Ron Ebert, Margaret Eggers, Candice Elliott, Peter Ellis, Lawrence Ettkin, Jim Evans, Edward Fox, John Flueck, Edward Fisher, Richard Flood, Robert Garfinkel, Roger Glaser, Fabienna Godlewski, Stephen Goodman, Jack Goodwin, Barry Griffin, Richard Gunther, Ellie Hakak, David Hott, Raymond Jackson, Edward Kao, Rebecca Klemm, Bharat Kolluri, Darlene Lanier, John Lawrence, Jr., Phillip Lowery, Cynthia Ma, Wiley Mangum, Prem Mann, R. Kipp Martin, Kamlesh Mathur, Joseph Mazzola, Richard McCready, Patrick McKeown, Constance McLaren, Edward Minieka, Alan Neebe, Susan Pariseau, Barnett Parker, David Pentico, Gary Pickett, Leonard Presby, B. Madhusudan Rao, Jeffrey L. Ringuest, Douglas Rippy, Richard Rosenthal, Wayland Smith, Jayavel Sounderpandian, Carol Stamm, Willban Terpening, Richard A. Toelle, Pitner Traughber, William Truscott, William Verdini, James Vigen, Robert Winkler, Ed Winkofsky, Bruce Woodworth, M. Zafer Yakin, and Cathleen Zucco.

Our associates from organizations who supplied the Quantitative Methods in Practice applications made a major contribution to the text. These individuals are cited in a credit line on the first page of each application.

We are also indebted to our editor, Mary C. Schiller, and others at West Publishing Company for their editorial counsel and support during the preparation of this text. Finally, we would like to express our appreciation to Lois Creech for her typing and secretarial support.

David R. Anderson
Dennis J. Sweeney
Thomas A. Williams

CHAPTER

1

Introduction

This book is concerned with quantitative approaches to decision making. In recent years, many new and important quantitative methods have been developed to assist in the decision-making process. The emphasis of this book is not on the methods per se, but rather on showing how the methods can be used to contribute to a better decision-making process. Our approach is to describe decision-making situations in which quantitative methods have been successfully applied and then show how the appropriate methods can be used to help the manager make better decisions. While a variety of names exists for the body of knowledge and methodology involving quantitative approaches to decision making, two of the most widely known and accepted names are *management science* (MS) and *operations research* (OR).

The foundation for quantitative approaches to decision making was laid during the scientific management revolution of the early 1900s initiated by Frederic W. Taylor. But the origin of modern management science/operations research is generally attributed to the World War II period, when operations research teams were formed to deal with strategic and tactical problems faced by the military. These teams, which often consisted of people with diverse specialties (mathematicians, engineers, behavioral scientists, etc.), were joined together to solve a common problem through the utilization of the scientific method. After the war, many of these team members continued their research on quantitative approaches to decision making.

Two developments, which occurred during the post-World War II period, led to the growth and use of quantitative methods in nonmilitary organizations. Probably the most significant development was the discovery by George Dantzig, in 1947, of the simplex method for solving linear programming problems. Many more methodological developments followed and, in 1957, the first book on operations research was published by

1

Churchman, Ackoff, and Arnoff.[1] Concurrently with these methodological developments there was a virtual explosion in computing power made available through digital computers. Computers enabled practitioners to implement the methodological advances successfully to solve a large variety of industrial problems. The computer technology explosion continues; microcomputers are more powerful than the mainframe computers of the 1960s. Today, variants of the post-World War II methodological developments are being used on microcomputers to solve problems larger than those solved on mainframe computers 15 years ago.

DOMINANCE OF THE PROBLEM

A central theme in the quantitative approach to decision making is a problem orientation. A problem may be as specific as improving the efficiency of a production line or as broad as establishing a long-range corporate strategy involving a combination of financial, marketing, and manufacturing operations. Nearly all projects begin with the recognition of a problem that does not have an obvious solution. Quantitative analysts may then be asked to assist in identifying the "best" decision or solution for the problem. Reasons why a quantitative approach might be used in the decision-making process include the following:

1. The problem is complex, and the manager cannot develop a good solution without the aid of quantitative specialists.
2. The problem is very important (for example, a great deal of money is involved), and the manager desires a thorough analysis before attempting to make a decision.
3. The problem is new, and the manager has no previous experience to draw upon.
4. The problem is repetitive, and the manager saves time and effort by relying on quantitative procedures to make the routine decision recommendations.

A survey by Thomas and DaCosta[2] showed the application (problem) areas in Table 1.1 as the ones most frequently the subject of quantitative analysis in large corporations. As the survey shows, nearly all large corporations (88%) are involved in forecasting and over 50% are utilizing quantitative approaches to production scheduling, inventory control, capital budgeting, and transportation.

Another survey by Gaither[3] reported a variety of manufacturing-related applications that have utilized quantitative techniques. The three problem areas most frequently cited were production planning and control, project planning and control, and inventory analysis. The problem areas mentioned in both the Thomas and DaCosta and Gaither surveys by no means comprise a complete list of the applications. However, they do indicate the wide variety of problems in which quantitative methods have been successfully applied.

[1]Churchman, C.W., R.L. Ackoff, and E.L. Arnoff, *Introduction to Operations Research.* New York, John Wiley & Sons, 1957.

[2]Thomas, G., and J. DaCosta, "A Sample Survey of Corporate Operations Research," *Interfaces*, vol. 9, no. 4, pp. 102–111, 1979.

[3]Gaither, N., "The Adoption of Operations Research Techniques by Manufacturing Organizations," *Decision Sciences*, vol. 6, no. 4, pp. 797–813, 1975.

Table 1.1
Application Areas for Quantitative Methods

Area of Application	Percentage of Companies Reporting Applications in Area
Forecasting	88
Production scheduling	70
Inventory control	70
Capital budgeting	56
Transportation	51
Plant location	42
Quality control	40
Advertising and sales research	35
Equipment replacement	33
Maintenance and repair	28
Accounting procedures	27
Packaging	9

1.2
QUANTITATIVE ANALYSIS AND THE DECISION-MAKING PROCESS

The role of quantitative analysis in the managerial decision-making process is perhaps best understood by considering the flowchart in Figure 1.1. Note that the process is initiated by the appearance of a problem. The manager responsible for making a decision, or selecting a course of action, will probably make an analysis of the problem, which includes a statement of the specific goals or objectives, an identification of constraints, an evaluation of alternative decisions, and a selection of the apparent "best" decision or solution for the problem.

The analysis process employed by the manager may take two basic forms: qualitative and quantitative. The qualitative analysis is based primarily on the manager's judgment

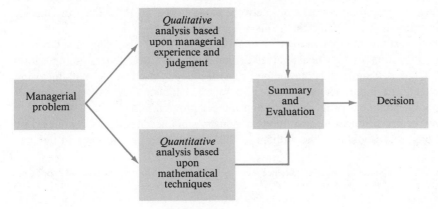

Figure 1.1
The Decision-Making Process

and experience. This type of analysis includes the manager's intuitive "feel" for the problem and is more an art than a science. If the manager has had experience with similar problems, or if the problem is relatively simple, heavy emphasis may be placed on a qualitative analysis. However, if the manager has had little experience with similar problems, or if the problem is sufficiently important and complex, then a quantitative analysis of the problem can be a very important consideration in the manager's final decision. In the quantitative approach to the problem, an analyst will concentrate on the quantitative facts or data associated with the problem and develop mathematical expressions that describe the objectives, constraints, and relationships that exist in the problem. Then, by using one or more quantitative methods, the analyst will provide a recommendation based on the quantitative aspects of the problem.

Both the qualitative and the quantitative analyses of a problem provide important information for the manager or decision maker. In many cases a manager will draw on both sources and, through a comparison and evaluation of the information, make a final decision.

While skills in the qualitative approach are inherent in the manager and usually increase with experience, the skills of the quantitative approach can be learned only by studying the assumptions and methods of quantitative analysis. A manager can increase decision-making effectiveness by learning more about quantitative methodology and by better understanding its contribution to the decision-making process. The manager who is knowledgeable in quantitative decision-making procedures is in a much better position to compare and evaluate the qualitative and quantitative sources of recommendations and ultimately combine the two sources in order to make the best possible decision.

The section of Figure 1.1 entitled "Quantitative analysis based upon mathematical techniques" encompasses most of the subject matter of this text. We will consider a managerial problem, introduce the appropriate quantitative methodology, and then develop and evaluate the recommended decision.

There are several important tools, or methods, that have been found useful in the quantitative analysis phase of the decision-making process. One of your objectives in studying this book should be to develop an understanding of what these methods are, how they are used, and, most important, how they can assist the manager in making better decisions. The most frequently used quantitative methods as determined in a survey of corporate executives conducted by Forgionne[4] are listed in Table 1.2. The Forgionne findings are consistent with those in the earlier Thomas and DaCosta study. A survey by Ledbetter and Cox[5] lends further support to these findings by ranking regression (statistical analysis), linear programming, simulation, network models (PERT/CPM), queueing theory, dynamic programming, and game theory in order of usage.

The Gaither study of applications in manufacturing firms also supports the high frequency of utilization for statistical analysis, simulation, and linear programming. However, PERT/CPM is identified as the method most frequently used in the manufacturing firms surveyed. The manufacturing firms also report a higher than average usage of queueing theory, nonlinear programming, and integer programming.

A survey of practitioners in government, industry, and academia was conducted by Shannon, Long, and Buckles.[6] The authors of this study asked practitioners to indicate

[4]Forgionne, G.A., "Corporate Management Science Activities: An Update," *Interfaces*, vol. 13, no. 3, pp. 20–23, 1983.

[5]Ledbetter, W., and J. Cox, "Are OR Techniques Being Used?" *Industrial Engineering*, vol. 9, no. 2, pp. 19–21, 1977.

[6]Shannon, R.E., S.S. Long, and B.P. Buckles, "Operations Research Methodologies in Industrial Engineering: A Survey," *AIIE Transactions*, vol. 12, no. 4, pp. 364–367, 1980.

Table 1.2
The Utilization of Quantitative Methods

	Frequency of Use (% of respondents)		
	Never	**Moderate**	**Frequent**
Statistical	1.6	38.7	59.7
Computer simulation	12.9	53.2	33.9
PERT/CPM	25.8	53.2	21.0
Linear programming	25.8	59.7	14.5
Queueing theory	40.3	50.0	9.7
Nonlinear programming	53.2	38.7	8.1
Dynamic programming	61.3	33.9	4.8
Game theory	69.4	27.4	3.2

whether or not they were familiar with the various quantitative methods and whether or not they had actually used the methods in specific applications. The results of this study are shown in Table 1.3.

Table 1.3
Familiarity with and Use of Various Quantitative Methods by Practitioners

Method	**Familiarity Rank**	**Usage (%)**
Linear programming	1	83.8
Simulation	2	80.3
Network analysis	3	58.1
Queueing theory	4	54.7
Decision trees	5	54.7
Integer programming	6	38.5
Dynamic programming	7	32.5
Nonlinear programming	8	30.7
Markov processes	9	31.6
Replacement analysis	10	38.5
Game theory	11	13.7
Goal programming	12	20.5

Since nearly every student takes a separate course in statistical analysis, we have restricted our coverage of statistical topics in this text to probability, decision analysis, and forecasting. However, we do describe and present applications for the other major quantitative methods most frequently used in decision making. Before proceeding with the study of the specific quantitative methods, let us look more closely at the general steps involved in carrying out the quantitative analysis of a managerial problem.

1.3

THE QUANTITATIVE ANALYSIS PROCESS

We begin our study of quantitative approaches to decision making by considering a five-step procedure: (1) problem definition, (2) model development, (3) data preparation, (4) model solution, and (5) report generation.

1 Problem Definition

The problem definition step is the most critical phase of the quantitative analysis process. It usually takes imagination, teamwork, and considerable effort to transform a rather general problem description into a well-defined problem that can be approached quantitatively. For example, a broadly described "excessive inventory" problem must be clearly defined in terms of specific objectives and operating constraints before an analyst can proceed to the next step in the quantitative analysis process. User involvement is essential during the problem definition step. The quantitative analyst must work closely with the manager or user of the results.

2 Model Development

Models are representations of real objects or situations. These representations, or models, can be presented in various forms. For example, a scale model of an airplane is a representation of a real airplane. Similarly, a child's toy truck is a model of a real truck. The model airplane and toy truck are examples of models that are physical replicas of real objects. In modeling terminology, physical replicas are referred to as *iconic models*.

A second classification of models includes those that are physical in form but do not have the same physical appearance as the object being modeled. Such models are referred to as *analog models.* The speedometer of an automobile is an analog model; the position of the needle on the dial represents the speed of the automobile. A thermometer is an analog model representing temperature.

A third classification of models—the primary type of model we will be studying—includes those that represent a problem by a system of symbols and mathematical relationships or expressions. Such models are referred to as *mathematical models* and are a critical part of any quantitative approach to decision making. For example, the total profit from the sale of a product can be determined by multiplying the profit per unit by the quantity sold. If we let x represent the number of units sold and P the total profit, then, with a profit of $10 per unit, the following mathematical model defines the total profit earned by selling x units:

$$P = 10x \qquad (1.1)$$

The purpose, or value, of any model is that it enables us to draw conclusions about the real situation by studying and analyzing the model. For example, an airplane designer might test an iconic model of a new airplane in a wind tunnel in order to learn about the potential flying characteristics of the full-size airplane. Similarly, a mathematical model may be used to draw conclusions about how much profit will be earned if a specified quantity of a particular product is sold. According to the mathematical model of equation (1.1), we would expect to obtain a $30 profit by selling three units of the product.

In general, experimenting with models requires less time and is less expensive than experimenting with the real object or situation. Certainly, a model airplane is quicker and less expensive to build and study than the full-size airplane. Similarly, the above mathematical model allows a quick identification of profit expectations without requiring the manager actually to produce and sell x units. Models also have the advantage of reducing the risk associated with experimenting with the real situation. In particular, bad designs or bad decisions that cause the model airplane to crash or a mathematical model to show a $10,000 loss can be avoided in the real situation.

The accuracy of the conclusions and decisions based on a model are dependent on how well the model represents the real situation. The more closely the model of the airplane represents the real airplane, the more accurate the conclusions and predictions about the airplane's flight characteristics will be. Similarly, the closer the mathematical model represents the company's true profit–volume relationship, the more accurate the profit projections will be.

Since this text deals with mathematical models, let us look more closely at the mathematical modeling process. When initially considering a managerial problem, we usually find that the problem definition phase leads to a specific objective, such as maximization of profits or minimization of costs, and possibly a set of restrictions or constraints, such as production capacities. The success of the mathematical model and quantitative approach will depend heavily on how accurately the objective and constraints can be expressed in terms of mathematical equations or relationships.

A mathematical expression that describes the problem's objective is referred to as the *objective function*. For example, the profit equation $P = 10x$ would be an objective function for a firm attempting to maximize profit. A production capacity *constraint* would be necessary if, for instance, 5 hours are required to produce each unit and there are only 40 hours available per week. Let x indicate the number of units produced each week. The production capacity constraint is given by

$$5x \leq 40 \tag{1.2}$$

The value of $5x$ is the total time required to produce the x units; the symbol $\leq$ indicates that the production time required must be less than or equal to the 40 hours available.

The question or decision problem is the following: How many units of the product should be scheduled each week in order to maximize profit? A complete mathematical model for this simple production problem is

$$\text{maximize} \qquad P = 10x \quad \text{objective function}$$
$$\text{subject to (s.t.)}$$
$$\left. \begin{array}{r} 5x \leq 40 \\ x \geq 0 \end{array} \right\} \quad \text{constraints}$$

The $x \geq 0$ constraint requires the production quantity x to be greater than or equal to zero, which simply recognizes the fact that it is not possible to manufacture a negative number of units. This model is an example of a linear programming model.

In the above mathematical model the profit per unit ($10), the production time per unit (5 hours), and the production capacity (40 hours) are environmental factors that are not under the control of the manager or decision maker. Such environmental factors, which can affect both the objective function and the constraints, are referred to as the *uncontrollable inputs* to the model. The inputs that are controlled or determined by the decision maker are referred to as the _controllable inputs_ to the model. In the above example the production quantity x is the controllable input to the model. The controllable inputs are the decision alternatives specified by the manager and thus are also referred to as the decision variables of the model.

Once all controllable and uncontrollable inputs are specified, the objective function and constraints can be evaluated and the output of the model determined. In this sense the output of the model is simply the projection of what would happen if those particular environmental factors and decisions occurred in the real situation. A flowchart of how controllable and uncontrollable inputs are transformed by the mathematical model into output is shown in Figure 1.2. A similar flowchart showing the specific details of the production model is shown in Figure 1.3.

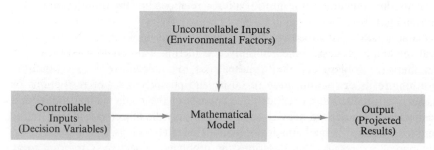

Figure 1.2
Flowchart of the Process of Transforming Model Inputs into Output

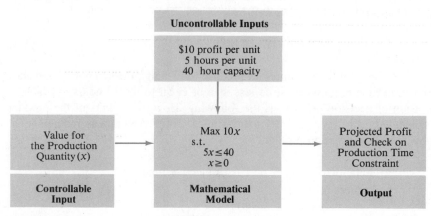

Figure 1.3
Flowchart for the Production Model

As stated earlier, the uncontrollable inputs are those the decision maker cannot influence. The specific controllable and uncontrollable inputs of a model depend on the particular problem or decision-making situation. In the production problem the production time available, 40 hours, is an uncontrollable input. However, if it were possible to hire more employees or use overtime, the number of hours of production time would become a controllable input and therefore a decision variable in the model.

Uncontrollable inputs either can be known exactly or can be uncertain and subject to variation. If all uncontrollable inputs to a model are known and cannot vary, the model is referred to as a *deterministic model*. Corporate income tax rates are not under the influence of the manager and thus constitute an uncontrollable input in many decision models. Since these rates are known and fixed (at least in the short run), a mathematical model with corporate income tax rates as the only uncontrollable input would be a deterministic model. The distinguishing feature of a deterministic model is that the uncontrollable input values are known in advance.

If any of the uncontrollable inputs are uncertain and subject to variation, the model is referred to as a *stochastic model*. An uncontrollable input to many production planning models is demand for the product. Since future demand may be any of a range of values, a mathematical model that treats demand with uncertainty would be called a stochastic model. In the production model the number of hours of production time required per unit, the total hours available, and the unit profit were all uncontrollable inputs. Since the uncontrollable inputs were all known to take on fixed values, the model is deterministic. If, however, the number of hours of production time per unit could vary from 3 to 6 hours depending on the quality of the raw material, the model would be stochastic. The distinguishing feature of a stochastic model is that the value of the output cannot be determined even if the value of the controllable input is known because the specific values of the uncontrollable inputs are unknown. In this respect, stochastic models are often more difficult to analyze.

3 Data Preparation

The third step in the process of quantitative analysis is the preparation of the data required by the model. Data in this sense refer to the values of the uncontrollable inputs to the model. All uncontrollable inputs or data must be specified before we can analyze the model and select a recommended decision or solution for the problem.

In the production model the values of the uncontrollable inputs or data were $10 per unit for profit, 5 hours per unit for production time, and 40 hours for production capacity. In the development of the model these data values were known and were incorporated into the model as it was being developed. If the model is relatively small and the uncontrollable input values or data required are few, the quantitative analyst will probably combine model development and data preparation into one step. That is, in these situations the data values are inserted as the equations of the mathematical model are developed.

However, in many mathematical modeling situations the data, or uncontrollable input values, are not readily available. In these situations the quantitative analyst may know that the model will need profit per unit, production time, and production capacity data, but the values are not known until the accounting, production, and engineering departments can be consulted. Rather than attempting to collect the required data as the model is being developed, the analyst will usually adopt a general notation for the model development step and then perform a separate data preparation step to obtain the uncontrollable input values required by the model.

Using the general notation

$$c = \text{profit per unit}$$
$$a = \text{production time in hours per unit}$$
$$b = \text{production capacity in hours}$$

the model development step of the production problem would have resulted in the following general model:

$$\max \ cx$$
$$\text{s.t.}$$
$$ax \leq b$$
$$x \geq 0$$

Then a separate data preparation step to identify the values for c, a, and b would be necessary in order to complete the model.

Many inexperienced quantitative analysts assume that once the problem has been defined and a general model developed, the problem is essentially solved. These individuals tend to believe that data preparation is a trivial step in the process and can be easily handled by clerical staff. Actually, especially with large-scale models that have numerous data input values, this assumption could not be further from the truth. For example, a moderate-size linear programming model with 50 decision variables and 25 constraints will have over 1300 data elements that must be identified in the data preparation step. The time required to prepare these data and the possibility of data collection errors will make the data preparation step a critical part of the quantitative analysis process. Often a fairly large database is needed to support a mathematical model, and information systems specialists assist in the data preparation step.

Model Solution

Once the model development and data preparation steps have been completed, we can proceed to the model solution step. In this step the analyst will attempt to identify the values of the decision variables that provide the "best" output for the model. The specific decision-variable value or values providing the "best" output will be referred to as the optimal solution for the model. For the production problem the model solution step involves finding the value of the production quantity decision variable x that maximizes profit while not causing a violation of the production capacity constraint.

One procedure that might be used in the model solution step involves a trial-and-error approach, where the model is used to test and evaluate various decision alternatives. In the production model this would mean testing and evaluating the model under various production quantities or values of x. Referring to Figure 1.3, note that we could input trial values for x and check the corresponding output for projected profit and satisfaction of the production capacity constraint. If a particular decision alternative does not satisfy one or more of the model constraints, the decision alternative is rejected as being *infeasible*, regardless of the objective function value. If all constraints are satisfied, the decision alternative is *feasible* and is a candidate for the "best" solution or recommended decision. Through this trial-and-error process of evaluating selected decision alternatives, a decision maker can identify a good—and possibly the best—feasible solution to the problem. This solution would then be the recommended decision for the problem.

Table 1.4 shows the results of a trial-and-error approach to solving the production model of Figure 1.3. The recommended decision is a production quantity of 8, since the feasible solution with the highest projected profit occurs at $x = 8$.

While the trial-and-error solution process is often acceptable and can provide valuable information for the manager, it has the drawbacks of not necessarily providing the best

Table 1.4
Trial-and-Error Solution for the Production Model of Figure 1.3

Decision Alternative (production quantity) x	Projected Profit	Total Hours of Production	Feasible Solution? (capacity = 40)
0	0	0	Yes
2	20	10	Yes
4	40	20	Yes
6	60	30	Yes
8	80	40	Yes
10	100	50	No
12	120	60	No

solution and of being inefficient in terms of requiring numerous calculations if many decision alternatives are tried. Thus quantitative analysts have developed special solution procedures for many models that are much more efficient than the trial-and-error approach. Throughout this text you will be introduced to solution procedures that are applicable to the specific mathematical models that will be formulated. While some relatively small models or problems can be solved by hand computations, most practical applications require the use of a computer.

It is important to realize that the model development and model solution steps are not completely separable. While an analyst will want to develop an accurate model or representation of the actual problem situation, the analyst also wants to be able to find a solution to the model. If we approach the model development step by attempting to find the most accurate and realistic mathematical model, we may find the model so large and complex that it is impossible to obtain a solution. In this case a simpler and perhaps more easily understood model with a readily available solution procedure is preferred, even if the recommended solution is only a rough approximation of the best decision. As you learn more about quantitative solution procedures, you will have a better idea of the types of mathematical models that can be developed and solved.

After a model solution has been obtained, both the quantitative analyst and the manager will be interested in determining how good the solution really is. While the analyst has undoubtedly taken many precautions to develop a realistic model, often the goodness or accuracy of the model cannot be assessed until model solutions are generated. Model testing and validation are frequently conducted with relatively small "test" problems that have known or at least expected solutions. If the model generates the expected solutions, and if other output information appears correct, the go-ahead may be given to the use of the model on the full-scale problem. However, if the model test and validation identifies potential problems or inaccuracies inherent in the model, corrective action such as model modification and/or the collection of more accurate input data may be taken. Whatever the corrective action, the model solution will not be used in practice until the model has satisfactorily passed testing and validation.

5 Report Generation

The final step in the quantitative analysis process is the preparation of managerial reports based on the model's solution. Referring to Figure 1.1, we see that the solution based on the quantitative analysis of a problem is one of the inputs that is considered by the manager before making a final decision. Thus it is essential that the results of the model appear in a report that can be easily understood by the decision maker. The report will include the recommended decision and other pertinent information about the model results that may be helpful to the decision maker. Figure 1.4 summarizes the five-step quantitative analysis process.

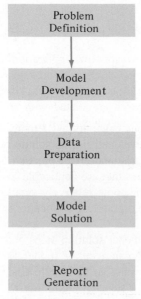

Figure 1.4
Steps of the Quantitative Analysis Process

1.4

IMPLEMENTATION

Although the generation of a managerial report is the final step in the quantitative analysis process, the implementation of the information contained in the report is a final action that remains to be taken by the manager or decision maker. As discussed in Section 1.2, it is the responsibility of the manager to integrate the quantitative solution with qualitative considerations in order to make the best possible decision. After doing this, the manager must oversee the implementation and follow-up evaluation of the decision. During the implementation and follow-up, the manager should continue to monitor the contribution of the model. At times this process may lead to requests for model expansion or refinement that will cause the analyst to return to one of the earlier steps of the quantitative analysis process.

Successful implementation of results is of critical importance to the quantitative analyst as well as the manager. If the results of the quantitative analysis process are not implemented, the entire effort may be of no value. Because implementation often requires people to do things differently (and more effectively, one hopes), it often meets with resistance. People want to know, ''What's wrong with the way I've been doing it?'' and so on. One of the most effective ways to ensure a successful implementation is to secure as much user involvement as possible throughout the modeling process. If the user feels that he or she has been involved in identifying the problem and developing the solutions, then he or she is much more likely to implement the results. The success rate for implementing the results of a project is much greater for those projects in which there has been substantial user involvement.

1.5

MODELS OF COST, REVENUE, AND PROFIT

Some of the most basic quantitative models arising in business and economic applications are those involving the relationship between a volume variable—such as production volume or sales volume—and cost, revenue, or profit. Through the use of these models a manager can determine the projected cost, revenue, and/or profit associated with an established production quantity or a forecasted sales volume. Financial planning, production planning, sales quotas, and other areas of decision making can benefit from such cost, revenue, and profit models.

Cost and Volume Models

The cost of manufacturing or producing a particular product is a function of the volume produced. This cost can usually be defined as a sum of two costs: fixed cost and variable cost. The *fixed cost* is the portion of the total cost that does not depend on the production volume; this cost remains the same no matter how much is produced. The *variable cost*, on the other hand, is the portion of the total cost that is dependent on and varies with the production volume. For example, suppose that the setup cost for a production line operation is $3000. This is a fixed cost that is incurred regardless of the number of units eventually produced. In addition, suppose that variable labor and material costs are $2 for each unit produced. The cost–volume model for a production run of x units would be written as

$$C(x) = 3000 + 2x \tag{1.3}$$

where

$$x = \text{production volume in units}$$
$$C(x) = \text{total cost of producing } x \text{ units}$$

Use of the model in (1.3) will allow determination of the total production costs once the production volume is established. For example, a production volume of $x = 1200$ units would result in a total cost of $C(1200) = 3000 + 2(1200) = \$5400$.

Marginal cost is defined as the rate of change of the total cost with respect to volume. That is, it is the cost increase associated with a one-unit increase in the production volume. In the cost model of (1.3), we see that the total cost $C(x)$ will increase by $2 for each unit increase in the production volume. Thus, the marginal cost is $2. With more complex total cost models, marginal cost may depend on the production volume. In such cases, we could have marginal cost increasing or decreasing with the production volume x.

Revenue and Volume Models

A manager will also want information on the projected revenue associated with selling a specified number of units. Thus, a model of the relationship between revenue and volume is also needed. Suppose that the product referred to above sells for $5 per unit. The model for total revenue can be written as

$$R(x) = 5x \qquad (1.4)$$

where

$$x = \text{sales volume in units}$$
$$R(x) = \text{total revenue associated with selling } x \text{ units}$$

Marginal revenue is defined as the rate of change of total revenue with respect to sales volume. That is, it is the increase in total revenue resulting from a one-unit increase in sales volume. In the model of equation (1.4) we see that the marginal revenue is $5. In this case marginal revenue is constant and does not vary with the sales volume. With more complex models we may find that marginal revenue increases or decreases as the sales volume, x, increases.

Profit and Volume Models

One of the most important criteria for managerial decision making is profit. Managers need to be able to know the profit implications of their decisions. If we assume that we will only produce what can be sold, the production volume and sales volume will be equal. We can combine (1.3) and (1.4) to develop a profit–volume model that will determine profit associated with a specified production–sales volume. Since total profit is total revenue minus total cost, the following model provides the profit associated with producing and selling x units:

$$P(x) = R(x) - C(x) \qquad (1.5)$$
$$= 5x - (3000 + 2x) = -3000 + 3x$$

Thus, the model for profit, $P(x)$, can be derived from the models of the revenue–volume and cost–volume relationships.

Break-Even Analysis

Using (1.5) we can now determine the profit associated with any production–sales volume, x. For example, suppose a demand forecast indicates that 500 units of the product can be sold. The decision to produce and sell the 500 units results in a projected profit of

$$P(500) = -3000 + 3(500) = -1500$$

In other words, a loss of $1500 is predicted. If sales are expected to be 500 units, the manager may decide against producing the product. However, a demand forecast of 1800 units would show a projected profit of

$$P(1800) = -3000 + 3(1800) = 2400$$

This profit may be enough to justify proceeding with the production and sale of the product.

We see that a volume of 500 units will yield a loss, whereas a volume of 1800 provides a profit. The volume that results in total revenue equaling total cost (providing $0 profit) is called the *break-even point.* If the break-even point is known, a manager can quickly infer that a volume above the break-even point will result in a profit, while a volume below the break-even point will result in a loss. Thus the break-even point for a product provides valuable information for a manager who must make a yes/no decision concerning production of the product.

Let us now return to the example above and show how the profit model in equation (1.5) can be used to compute the break-even point. The break-even point can be found by setting the profit expression equal to zero and solving for the volume. Using (1.5), we have

$$P(x) = -3000 + 3x = 0$$
$$3x = 3000$$
$$x = 1000$$

With this information, we know that production and sales of the product must be at least 1000 units before a profit can be expected. The graph of the total cost model, the total revenue model, and the location of the break-even point is shown in Figure 1.5.

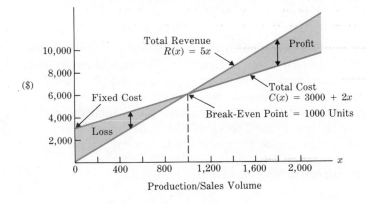

Figure 1.5
Graph of the Break-even Analysis for the Production Example

1.6

A MICROCOMPUTER SOFTWARE PACKAGE

As stated earlier, developments in computer technology have been a major factor in making quantitative methods available to decision makers. Currently microcomputer software packages of quantitative methods are making many techniques easier to use. A software package called *The Management Scientist* has been prepared to accompany this text. It can be used to solve problems in the text as well as small-scale problems encountered in practice. Working with this software package will give you an understanding of the role of the computer in applying quantitative methods to decision problems.

The Management Scientist software package contains modules, or programs, that will enable you to solve problems in the following chapters and topical areas:

Chapter 4	Decision analysis
Chapter 5	Utility and decision making
Chapter 6	Forecasting
Chapters 7–10	Linear programming
Chapter 11	Transportation problem
Chapter 11	Assignment problem
Chapter 12	Integer linear programming
Chapter 13	Project management: PERT/CPM
Chapter 14	Inventory models
Chapter 16	Waiting-line models

Use of *The Management Scientist* with this text is optional. Occasionally we will insert a figure in the text that will show the output *The Management Scientist* would have provided for the problem being solved. But, familiarity with the software is not necessary to understand the figure. In the linear and integer programming chapters, the LINDO/PC software package is illustrated. But, again, familiarity with the software is not necessary to understand the material. If you decide to use *The Management Scientist* software package, first load DOS on an IBM compatible microcomputer. At A⟩, insert Disk 1 in drive A and type MS. The remainder of this section provides an introductory description of the software package.

Top Level Menu

After installing and starting to run (by typing MS) *The Management Scientist* software, you will encounter the Top Level Menu shown in Figure 1.6. The choices on the menu provide access to the corresponding modules, or programs. Simply enter the number of your selection, press ''Return,'' and the requested module will be loaded into the computer's memory. When you have obtained the solution information from the module selected, the program will return you to the Top Level Menu. At this point you may select another module or select menu choice 13, which will let you exit the package.

```
                    THE MANAGEMENT SCIENTIST

                        Top Level Menu

1   Linear Programming           7    PERT/CPM

2   Transportation               8    Inventory Models

3   Assignment                   9    Waiting Lines

4   Integer Linear Programming  10    Decision Analysis

5   Shortest Route              11    Forecasting

6   Minimal Spanning Tree       12    Markov Processes

             13    EXIT PROGRAM
```

Figure 1.6
Top-Level Menu of *The Management Scientist* Software Package

All of the programs in *The Management Scientist* are menu-driven. At various steps of all modules, menus will appear on the screen. By entering the number corresponding to your choice, you will be able to proceed as desired with the analysis and solution.

Opening Menu

After you make a module selection from the Top Level Menu, the module will load into the computer's memory and a title screen for the module will be displayed. The title screen contains a brief description of the types of problems the module can be used to solve.

After the title screen appears, you may press "Return," to obtain an opening menu such as the one shown for the assignment problem in Figure 1.7. From the opening menu you may choose to create a new problem, retrieve a previously saved problem from a data disk, delete a previously saved problem on a data disk, or exit the module by returning to the Top Level Menu.

```
ASSIGNMENT PROBLEM MENU
Choices
   1   Create a New Problem
   2   Retrieve a Previously Saved Problem
   3   Delete a Previously Saved Problem
   4   Return to the Top Level Menu
```

Figure 1.7
Opening Menu for the Assignment Problem Module of *The Management Scientist* Software Package

Data Input

Anytime a problem is being considered for the first time, you must select the option to create a new problem from the opening menu shown in Figure 1.7. The module will then guide you through the data input process by displaying prompts that indicate the information or data to be entered. By first studying the quantitative method in the text, you should easily understand the information or data prompts displayed by the module.

Data Editing

Occasionally during the data input process you may strike the wrong key or numerical value and then press "Return." This will enter the incorrect value into the program. However, all modules will display the input data at the end of the data input process. From this display you will be given the opportunity to modify or change any of the original input data before requesting the model solution.

Saving, Retrieving, and/or Deleting Problems

The Management Scientist allows you to save problems for future use on a data disk. You will be given the opportunity to specify the disk drive to be used for problem saving when you initially start up the software package. The problem saving option for most modules appears after you have entered and verified the accuracy of the input data. At this point, if you wish to save the problem for future use, you will be provided with instructions for naming the problem. The problem will be saved automatically, using the name specified.

When reentering the module at a later date, the Retrieve option from the opening menu will let you recall a previously saved problem. Simply enter the name of the saved problem, and it will be loaded and become active in the module. When you no longer need access to a particular problem, the Delete option from the opening menu can be used to erase the problem from your data disk.

Solution and Output Information

After *The Management Scientist* has solved the problem, the solution will appear on the screen. The type of information provided and its interpretation varies with the module selected. By reading the corresponding chapter in the text, you should be able to interpret the output information. After the solution and other output information have been displayed on the screen, you will be provided with the option of deciding whether or not to send the information to the printer. If you choose to obtain printed output, input data as well as the solution information will be printed.

Further Advice about Data Input

When using *The Management Scientist*, you may find the following data input suggestions helpful.

1. Do not enter commas (,) with your input data. For example, to enter the numerical value of 104,000, simply type the six digits 104000.
2. Do not enter the dollar sign ($) for profit or cost data. For example, a cost of $20.00 should be entered as 20.
3. Do not enter the percent sign (%) if percentage input is requested. For a percentage of 25%, simply enter 25. Do not enter 25% or 0.25.
4. If the computer did not interpret your input correctly (for example, you tried to input a comma), the message ''Redo from start'' may appear. This message refers to the input question or prompt you are currently responding to. The message means to respond to the same question or prompt again.
5. For data values containing the digit zero, be sure to enter the numeric 0 rather than the letter O.
6. Occasionally a quantitative model will be formulated with fractional values such as ¼, ⅔, ⅚, and so on. The data input for the computer must be in decimal form. The fraction of ¼ can be entered as .25. However, the fractions ⅔ and ⅚ have repeating decimal forms. In cases such as these we recommend the convention of rounding to five places. Thus, the corresponding decimal values of .66667 and .83333 should be entered.
7. Finally, we recommend that in general you attempt to scale extremely large input data so that smaller numbers may be input and operated on by the computer. For example, a cost of $2,500,000 may be scaled to 2.5 with the understanding that the data used in the problem reflect millions of dollars.

Summary

This is a book about how quantitative approaches to decision problems may be used to help managers make better decisions. The focus of the text is on the decision-making process and on the role of quantitative methods in that process. We have discussed the problem orientation of this process and in an overview have shown how mathematical models can be used in this type of analysis.

The difference between the model and the situation or managerial problem it represents is an important point. Mathematical models are abstractions of real-world situations and, as such, cannot capture all the aspects of the real situation. However, if a model can capture the major relevant aspects of the problem and provide a solution recommendation, it can be a valuable aid to decision making. One of the characteristics of quantitative analysis that will become increasingly apparent as we proceed through the text is the search for a best solution to the problem. In carrying out the analysis, we will be attempting to develop procedures for finding the ''best'' or optimal solution.

We showed how relatively simple quantitative models of cost–volume and revenue–volume could be combined to provide a profit model and a break-even point. Finally, we concluded the chapter by describing the features of *The Management Scientist*, a microcomputer software package developed to accompany this text.

Glossary

Model   Representation of a real object or situation.

Iconic model   Physical replica or representation of a real object.

Analog model   While physical in form, an analog model does not have a physical appearance similar to the real object or situation it represents.

Mathematical model   Mathematical symbols and expressions used to represent a real situation.

Objective function   A mathematical expression used to identify the objective of a problem.

Constraints   Restrictions or limitations imposed on the problem.

Uncontrollable input   The environmental factors or inputs that cannot be specified by the decision maker.

Controllable input   The decision alternatives or inputs that can be specified by the decision maker.

Deterministic model   A model where all uncontrollable inputs are known and cannot vary.

Stochastic model   A model where at least one uncontrollable input is uncertain and subject to variation.

Infeasible solution   A decision alternative or solution that violates one or more constraints.

Feasible solution   A decision alternative or solution that satisfies all constraints.

Fixed cost   The portion of total cost that does not depend on volume.

Variable cost   The portion of total cost that varies with volume.

Marginal cost   The rate of change of total cost with respect to volume.

Marginal revenue   The rate of change of total revenue with respect to volume.

Break-even point   The volume where total revenue equals total cost and profit is zero.

Problems

1. Discuss the different roles played by the qualitative and quantitative approaches to managerial decision making. Why is it important for a manager or decision maker to have a good understanding of both of these approaches to decision making?

2. A firm has just completed a new plant that will produce over 500 different products using over 50 different production lines and machines. The product scheduling decisions are critical in that sales will be lost if customer demands are not met on time. If no individual in the firm has had experience with this production operation, and if new production schedules must be generated each week, why should the firm consider a quantitative approach to the production scheduling problem?

3. List and discuss the five steps of the quantitative analysis process.

4. Give an example of the three types of models discussed in this chapter: iconic, analog, and mathematical.

5. What are the advantages of analyzing and experimenting with a model as opposed to a real object or situation?

6. Recall the production model from Figure 1.3:

$$\max 10x$$

$$\text{s.t.}$$

$$5x \le 40$$

$$x \ge 0$$

Suppose that the firm in this example considers a second product that has a profit of $5 per unit and requires 2 hours for each unit produced. Use x_1 to denote the number of units of product 1 and x_2 to denote the number of units of product 2.
a. Show the mathematical model when both products are considered simultaneously.
b. Identify the controllable and uncontrollable inputs for this model.
c. Draw the flowchart of the input-output process for this model (see Figure 1.3).
d. What are the optimal solution values of x_1 and x_2?

7. Is the model developed in problem 6 a deterministic or a stochastic model? Explain.

8. Suppose that we modify the model in Figure 1.3 to obtain the following mathematical model:

$$\max 10x$$

$$\text{s.t.}$$

$$ax \le 40$$

$$x \ge 0$$

where a is the number of hours required for each unit produced. With $a = 5$, the optimal solution is $x = 8$. If we have a stochastic model with $a = 3$, $a = 4$, $a = 5$, or $a = 6$ as the possible values for the number of hours required per unit, what is the optimal value for x? What problems does this stochastic model cause?

9. A retail store in Des Moines, Iowa, receives shipments of a particular product from Kansas City and Minneapolis. Let

$$x_1 = \text{units of product received from Kansas City}$$

$$x_2 = \text{units of product received from Minneapolis}$$

   a. Write an expression for the total units of product received by the retail store in Des Moines.
   b. Shipments from Kansas City cost $0.20 per unit, and shipments from Minneapolis cost $0.25 per unit. Develop an objective function representing the total cost of shipments to Des Moines.
   c. Assuming that the monthly demand at the retail store is 5000 units, develop a constraint that requires 5000 units to be shipped to Des Moines.
   d. No more than 4000 units can be shipped from Kansas City and no more than 3000 units can be shipped from Minneapolis in a month. Develop constraints to model this situation.
   e. Of course, negative amounts cannot be shipped. Combine the objective function and constraints developed to state a mathematical model for satisfying the demand at the Des Moines retail store at minimum cost.

10. Suppose that you are going on a weekend trip to a city that is d miles away. Develop a model that determines your round-trip gasoline costs. What assumptions or approximations do you have to make in order to treat this model as a deterministic model? Are these assumptions or approximations acceptable to you?

11. Suppose that a manager has a choice between the following two mathematical models (a) a relatively simple model that is a reasonable approximation of the real situation and (b) a thorough and complex model that is the most accurate mathematical representation of the real situation possible. Why might the model described in (a) be preferred by the manager?

12. For most products, higher prices result in a decreased demand whereas lower prices result in an increased demand. Let

$$x = \text{annual demand for a product in units}$$

$$p = \text{price per unit}$$

Assume that a firm accepts the following price–demand relationship as being realistic:

$$x = 800 - 10p$$

where the price p must be between $20 and $70.
   a. How many units can the firm sell at the $20 per unit price? At the $70 per unit price?
   b. Show the mathematical model for the total revenue, which is the annual demand multiplied by the unit price.
   c. Based on other considerations, the firm's management will only consider price alternatives of $30, $40, and $50. Use your model from part (b) to determine the price alternative that will maximize the total revenue.

d. What are the annual demand and total revenue corresponding to your recommended price?

13. Financial Analysts, Inc. is an investment firm that manages stock portfolios for a number of clients. A new client has just requested that the firm handle an $80,000 portfolio. As an initial investment strategy the client would like to restrict the portfolio to a mix of the following two stocks:

Stock	Price/ Share	Estimated Annual Return/Share	Maximum Possible Investment
Oil Alaska	$50	$6	$50,000
Southwest Petroleum	$30	$4	$45,000

Let

$$x_1 = \text{number of shares of Oil Alaska}$$

$$x_2 = \text{number of shares of Southwest Petroleum}$$

a. Develop the objective function, assuming that the client desires to maximize the total annual return.
b. Show the mathematical expression for each of the following three constraints:
   (1) Total investment funds available is $80,000.
   (2) Maximum Oil Alaska investment is $50,000.
   (3) Maximum Southwest Petroleum investment is $45,000.
Note: Adding the $x_1 \geq 0$ and $x_2 \geq 0$ constraints provides a linear programming model for the investment problem. A solution procedure for this model will be discussed in Chapter 7.

14. Models of inventory systems frequently consider the relationship between a beginning inventory, a production quantity, a demand or sales, and an ending inventory. For a given production period j, let

$$s_{j-1} = \text{ending inventory from the previous period}$$
$$\text{(beginning inventory for period } j\text{)}$$

$$x_j = \text{production quantity in period } j$$

$$d_j = \text{demand in period } j$$

$$s_j = \text{ending inventory for period } j$$

a. Write the mathematical relationship or model that describes how the above four variables are related.
b. What constraint should be added if production capacity for period j is given by C_j?
c. What constraint should be added if safety stock requirements for period j require an ending inventory of at least I_j?

15. The O'Neill Shoe Company will produce a special style shoe if the order size is large enough to provide a reasonable profit. For each special style order the company incurs a fixed cost of $1000 for the production setup. The variable cost is $30 per pair, and each pair sells for $40.
    a. Let x indicate the number of pairs of shoes produced. Develop a mathematical model for the total cost of producing x pairs of shoes.
    b. Let P indicate the total profit. Develop a mathematical model for the total profit realized from an order for x pairs of shoes.
    c. How large must the shoe order be before O'Neill will break even?

16. Martin Publishers produces and markets textbooks for the college market. Martin is considering publishing a new textbook. The fixed cost associated with the design and preparation of the book is $250,000. Once the book is ready for production there will be an added labor and materials cost of $4.50 for each book produced. The books will be sold to college and university bookstores for $28 each.
    a. Develop the cost–volume, revenue–volume, and profit–volume models that are appropriate for this problem.
    b. What is the break-even point for the sales of the textbook?
    c. If the forecasted sales for the textbook are 15,000 copies, what decision would you recommend? What is the projected profit or loss?

17. Sea Castle Resorts has an option to purchase ocean-front property for $2 million. Preparation of the land for development of a high-rise condominium building will cost an additional $800,000. Individual condominium units in the building can be built at a cost of $30,000 per unit. Design plans for the condominium show that a total of 56 units can be built on the property.
    a. What is the selling price per condominium unit for the project to break even?
    b. What is the number of units that must be sold for the project to break even if management uses a price of $98,000 per unit?
    c. What is the projected profit if all 56 units are sold at the $98,000 per unit sales price?

18. The MS company produces a product that sells 1000 units per month. The monthly production setup has a fixed cost of $4000. The variable production cost is $4.40 per unit. The revenue is $10 per unit.
    a. Show the cost–volume, revenue–volume, and profit–volume relationships that are appropriate in this situation.
    b. What is the projected monthly profit from this production operation?
    c. A major national discount chain has offered MS a contract to buy 500 additional units per month. MS has the capacity and can extend the production run to 1500 units with no problem. However, the discount chain will purchase the 500 additional units only if the price is $7.50 per unit for the special order. Should MS accept the contract to sell 500 units at the $7.50 price? Use the concepts of marginal cost and marginal revenue to justify your answer. What is the projected monthly profit if this contract order is accepted?

Introduction to Chapter-Ending Quantitative Methods in Practice

Quantitative Methods in Practice applications prepared by practitioners are presented at the end of 13 chapters. We feel that these provide a meaningful extension to the text material. The purpose is to provide the reader with a better appreciation for the types of companies that use quantitative methods and the types of problems these companies are able to solve.

Each Quantitative Methods in Practice section begins with a description of the company involved and continues with a discussion of the areas where the company has successfully applied quantitative methods. The remainder deals with an application that is closely related to the preceding chapter and/or part of the book. An effort has been made to avoid unnecessary technical detail and to focus on the managerial aspects and the value of the results to the company.

Since Chapter 1 is designed to provide an introduction, we have selected the Mead Corporation Quantitative Methods in Practice application because it provides an overview of several areas in which quantitative methods can be used effectively. It is evidence of the impact quantitative approaches to decision making are having at some companies.

Quantitative Methods in Practice

Mead Corporation*
Dayton, Ohio

Mead Corporation is basically a forest products company that manufactures paper, pulp, and lumber; converts paperboard into shipping containers and beverage carriers; and distributes paper, school supplies, and stationery. Mead is also a major distributor of pipe, valves, and other industrial materials to refineries, petrochemical and power plants, and oil-well drillers. Mead is the nation's leading independent producer of ductile iron castings for automobiles and construction equipment. The company also makes rubber products for the exploration and production of gas and oil. Mead's Advanced Systems Group develops businesses for the future, including storing, retrieving, printing, and reproducing data through the innovative application of digital technology.

Quantitative Methods at Mead Corporation

Quantitative applications at Mead are developed and implemented by the company's Operations Research (OR) Department. The OR department provides timely, efficient internal consulting services to the operating groups and corporate staff in the functional areas of operations, finance, marketing, and human resources. The department assists decision makers by providing analytical tools of quantitative analysis as well as personal analysis and recommendations. Through conversations and observations, the department recognizes needs where quantitative methods are applicable and recommends appropriate projects. In addition, the department provides a resource reservoir for information and assistance on quantitative methodology and assumes responsibility for keeping current in techniques that could produce efficiencies at Mead. This charter results in a variety of projects and applications that span the corporation. Four examples of quantitative methods applications at Mead are described below.

A Corporate Planning System

The OR department built and maintains a corporate planning system. This system allows business units to create and evaluate their 5-year plans in an interactive computer environment.

---

*The authors are indebted to Dr. Edward P. Winkofsky, Mead Corporation, Dayton, Ohio, for providing this application.

Once the individual business units have finished their planning, the system consolidates the information at a group level. The assumptions of the units and the group are evaluated and reconciled. The use of this computer model facilitates the process by ensuring uniformity of calculations and reporting by all the planning units. Ultimately, the information is consolidated and evaluated at a corporate level.

A Timberland Financing Model

Another example of a quantitative methods application involves the development of a timberland financing model. Working directly with financial management, analysts assisted in the creation of a deterministic model that considered the major factors in a timberland financing arrangement. The model was used to examine the liability and profitability of timberland acquisition under various assumptions concerning forest growth rates, the inflation rate, and other financial considerations. By using the model, management was able to examine fully the acquisition and modify the financial arrangement as operating conditions warranted. The model is currently operated and modified by financial management and is considered a major tool in the examination of timberland financing.

Inventory Analysis

Inventory analysis is an area in which more sophisticated quantitative tools have been used. Simulation models have been used to describe the major factors (demand or usage rates, lead times, production rates, etc.) in an inventory system. Typical costs included in an inventory model are purchase, storage, ordering, stockout, and degradation costs. The simulation model is used to evaluate reorder points, safety stocks, customer service levels, review periods, and the response time of the inventory system to extraordinary events.

Once developed and in place, the model can be updated as economic and operating conditions change. Thus the model can be used by management to evaluate its inventory system on an ongoing basis and to ensure that it is operating in a cost-efficient manner. These inventory simulation models are user friendly and can be operated and maintained by management with little formal computer training.

A Timber-Harvesting Model

Mead has also used models to assist with the long-range management of the company's timberland. Through the use of large-scale linear programs, timber-harvesting plans have been developed to cover a substantial time horizon. These models consider wood market conditions, mill pulpwood requirements, harvesting capacities, and general forest management principles. Within these constraints the model develops an optimal harvesting and purchasing schedule based on discounted cash flow. Alternative schedules are developed to reflect various assumptions concerning forest growth, wood availability, and general economic conditions.

Quantitative methods are also used in the development of the inputs for the linear programming models described above. Timber prices and supplies as well as mill requirements must be forecast over the time horizon. Advanced sampling techniques are used to evaluate land holdings and to project forest growth. The harvest schedule is developed through the use of a number of quantitative methods.

Summary

The applications described above—although only a few of the many projects at Mead—convey the breadth of the activities currently in use within the company. The quantitative analyst at Mead must be able to work in a number of different environments and be proficient in a wide range of quantitative methods. In addition the analyst must possess exceptional oral and written communication skills. Only with this background will the analyst be able to achieve the major objective of quantitative methods at Mead—the development and implementation of user-friendly quantitative models that will support and enhance management decision making throughout the organization.

Questions

1. Which techniques listed in Table 1.2 are being used in the four applications described at the Mead Corporation?
2. Which of the Mead applications used a deterministic model and which used a stochastic model? What were the conditions in the applications that indicated a stochastic model was necessary?
3. Discuss how the five steps of the quantitative analysis process described in Section 1.3 occurred in Mead's inventory analysis application.
4. Discuss the benefits associated with the quantitative analysis applications at Mead.

CHAPTER

2

Introduction to Probability

Throughout our lives we are faced with decision-making situations that involve an uncertain future. Perhaps you will be asked for an analysis of one of the following situations involving uncertainty:

1. What is the chance that sales will decrease if the price of the product is increased?
2. What is the likelihood that the new assembly method will increase productivity?
3. How likely is it that the project will be completed on time?
4. What are the odds that the new investment will be profitable?

The subject matter most useful in dealing effectively with the above uncertainties is contained under the heading of probability. In everyday terminology, *probability* is a numerical measure of the "chance" or "likelihood" that a particular event will occur. For example, if we consider the event "rain tomorrow," we understand that when the television weather report indicates a near-zero probability of rain, there is almost no chance of rain. However, if a 90% probability of rain is reported, we know that it is very likely or almost certain that rain will occur. A 50% probability indicates that rain is just as likely to occur as not.

Probability values are always assigned on a scale from 0 to 1. A probability near 0 indicates that the event is very unlikely to occur; a probability near 1 indicates that the event is almost certain to occur. Other probabilities between 0 and 1 represent varying degrees of likelihood that the event will occur. Figure 2.1 depicts this view of probability.

Probability is important in decision making because it provides a basis for measuring, expressing, and analyzing the uncertainties associated with future events. In this chapter we introduce the fundamental concepts of probability and begin to illustrate their use as decision-making tools. In subsequent chapters we will extend these basic notions of probability and demonstrate the important role that probability plays in quantitative approaches to decision making.

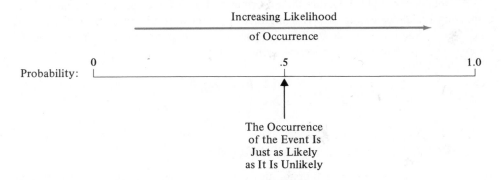

Figure 2.1
Probability as a Numerical Measure of the Likelihood of Occurrence

2.1

EXPERIMENTS AND SAMPLE SPACE

Using the terminology of probability, we define an *experiment* to be any process that generates well-defined outcomes. By this we mean that on any single repetition of the experiment, *one and only one* of the possible experimental outcomes will occur. Several examples of experiments and their associated outcomes are as follows:

Experiment	Experimental Outcomes
Toss a coin	Head, tail
Select a part for inspection	Defective, nondefective
Conduct a sales call	Purchase, no purchase
Roll a die	1, 2, 3, 4, 5, 6
Play a football game	Win, lose, tie

The first step in analyzing a particular experiment is to define carefully the experimental outcomes. When we have defined *all* possible experimental outcomes, we have identified the *sample space* for the experiment. That is, the sample space is the set of all possible experimental outcomes. Any one particular experimental outcome is referred to as a *sample point* and is an element of the sample space.

Let us consider the experiment of rolling a die, with the experimental outcomes defined as the number of dots appearing on the upward face of the die. In this experiment, the numerical values 1, 2, 3, 4, 5, and 6 represent the possible experimental outcomes or sample points for the experiment. If we let S denote the sample space, we can describe the sample space and sample points for the die-rolling experiment with the following set notation:

$$S = \{1, 2, 3, 4, 5, 6\}$$

As another example, consider the experiment of a customer purchasing one of four competing brands of toothpaste. Assume that the brands are identified by the letters A, B, C, and D. Letting S denote the sample space for this experiment, we can describe the sample space by listing its four sample points as follows:

$$S = \{A, B, C, D\}$$

2.2

ASSIGNING PROBABILITIES TO EXPERIMENTAL OUTCOMES

We are now ready to see how probabilities can be assigned to experimental outcomes (sample points). Recall the discussion of probability at the beginning of this chapter. The probability of an experimental outcome is a numerical measure of the likelihood that the experimental outcome will occur. In assigning probabilities to the experimental outcomes there are various acceptable approaches; however, regardless of the approach taken, the following two *basic requirements of probability* must be satisfied:

1. The probability values assigned to each experimental outcome (sample point) must be between 0 and 1. That is, if we let E_i indicate the experimental outcome and $P(E_i)$ indicate the probability of the experimental outcome, we must have

$$0 \le P(E_i) \le 1 \qquad \text{for all } i \tag{2.1}$$

2. The sum of *all* of the experimental outcome probabilities must be 1. For example, if a sample space has k experimental outcomes, we must have

$$P(E_1) + P(E_2) + \cdots + P(E_k) = \sum P(E_i) = 1 \tag{2.2}$$

Any method of assigning probability values to the experimental outcomes that satisfies these two requirements and results in a reasonable numerical measure of the likelihood of the outcome is acceptable. In practice, the classical, relative frequency, and subjective methods are used most often.

Classical Method

To illustrate the classical method of assigning probabilities, let us consider the experiment of flipping a coin. On any one flip, we will observe one of two experimental outcomes, head or tail. It would seem reasonable to assume that the two possible outcomes are equally likely. Therefore, since one of the two equally likely outcomes is a head, we logically should conclude that the probability of observing a head is ½, or 0.50. Similarly, the probability of observing a tail is also 0.50. When the assumption of equally likely outcomes is used as a basis for assigning probabilities, the approach is referred to as the *classical method*. If an experiment has n possible outcomes, the classical approach assigns a probability of $1/n$ to each outcome.

The classical method was developed originally in the analysis of gambling problems, where the assumption of equally likely outcomes often is reasonable. In many business problems, however, this assumption is not valid. Hence alternative methods of assigning probabilities are required.

Relative Frequency Method

Suppose that a firm is considering marketing a new product and is interested in the probability of a customer making a purchase. When a sales call is conducted there are two possible outcomes: the customer purchases the product or the customer does not purchase the product. However, in this case we usually would not be willing to make the assumption that the experimental outcomes are equally likely. Thus the classical method of assigning probabilities would be inappropriate. Furthermore, suppose that in a test market evaluation of the product, 400 potential customers were contacted; 100 actually purchased the product, but 300 did not. In effect, then, we have repeated the experiment of contacting a customer 400 times and have found that 100 times the product was purchased. Thus we might decide to assign a probability of $100/400 = 0.25$ to the experimental outcome of purchasing the product. Similarly, $300/400 = 0.75$ could be assigned to the experimental outcome of not purchasing the product. This approach to the assigning of probabilities is referred to as the *relative frequency method*.

Subjective Method

The classical and relative frequency methods cannot be applied to all situations where probability assessments are desired. For example, there are many situations where the experimental outcomes are not equally likely and where relative frequency data are unavailable. For example, consider the next football game that the Pittsburgh Steelers will play. What is the probability that the Steelers will win? The experimental outcomes of a win, a loss, or a tie are not necessarily equally likely. Also, since the teams involved have not played several times previously this year, there are no relative frequency data available that are relevant to this upcoming game. Thus if we want an estimate of the probability of the Steelers winning, we must use a subjective opinion of its value.

Using the subjective method to assign probabilities to the experimental outcomes, we may use any data available, our experience, intuition, etc. However, after we consider all available information, a probability value that expresses the degree of belief that the experimental outcome will occur must be specified. This method of assigning probability is referred to as the *subjective method*. Since subjective probability expresses a person's degree of belief, it is personal. Different people can be expected to assign different probabilities to the same outcome.

Even in situations where either the classical or relative frequency approach can be applied, management may want to provide subjective probability estimates. In such cases, the best probability estimates often are obtained by combining the estimates from the classical or relative frequency approaches with the subjective probability estimates.

2.3

EVENTS AND THEIR PROBABILITIES

An *event* is a collection of sample points (experimental outcomes). For example, consider the experiment of rolling a die; the sample space has six sample points and is denoted by $S = \{1, 2, 3, 4, 5, 6\}$. Now consider the event that the number of dots shown on the upward face of the die is an even number. There are three sample points in this event: 2, 4, or 6. Using the letter A to denote this event, we can write A as a collection of sample points:

$$A = \{2, 4, 6\}$$

Thus if the experimental outcome or sample point were either 2, 4, or 6, we would say that the event A has occurred.

Much of the focus of probability analysis is involved with computing probabilities for various events that are of interest to a decision maker. If the probabilities of the sample points are defined, the following definition may be used to compute the probability of any event:

> The probability of an event is equal to the sum of the probabilities of the sample points in the event.

Returning to the experiment of rolling a die, we could use the classical method of assigning probabilities to conclude that the probability associated with each sample point is $\frac{1}{6}$. Thus the probability of rolling a 2 is $\frac{1}{6}$, the probability of rolling a 4 is $\frac{1}{6}$, and the probability of rolling a 6 is $\frac{1}{6}$. The probability of event A—an even number of dots on the upward face of the die—is

$$P(A) = P(2) + P(4) + P(6)$$
$$= \frac{1}{6} + \frac{1}{6} + \frac{1}{6} = \frac{3}{6} = \frac{1}{2}$$

Any time that we can identify all the sample points of an experiment and assign the corresponding sample point probabilities, we can use the above approach to compute the probability of any event of interest to a decision maker. However, in many experiments the number of sample points is large and the identification of the sample points, as well as determining their associated probabilities, becomes extremely cumbersome if not impossible. In the remainder of this chapter we present some basic probability relationships that can be used to compute the probability of an event without requiring knowledge of sample point probabilities. These probability relationships require a knowledge of the probabilities for some events in the experiment. Probabilities of other events are then computed from these known probabilities using one or more of the probability relationships.

2.4

SOME BASIC RELATIONSHIPS OF PROBABILITY

Complement of an Event

Given an event A, the *complement of event A* is defined to be the event consisting of all sample points that are *not* in A. The complement of A is denoted by $\overline{A}$. Figure 2.2 provides a diagram, known as a *Venn diagram*, that illustrates the concept of a complement. The rectangular area represents the sample space for the experiment and as such contains all possible sample points. The circle represents event A and contains only the sample points that belong to A. The shaded region of the diagram contains all sample points not in event A, which is by definition the complement of A.

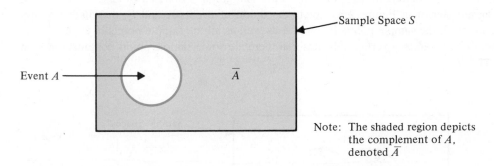

Note: The shaded region depicts the complement of A, denoted $\overline{A}$

Figure 2.2
Complement of Event A

In any probability application, event A and its complement A must satisfy the following condition

$$P(A) + P(\overline{A}) = 1$$

Solving for $P(A)$, we have

$$P(A) = 1 - P(\overline{A}) \qquad (2.3)$$

Equation (2.3) shows that the probability of an event A can be easily computed if the probability of its complement, $P(\overline{A})$, is known.

As an example, consider the case of a sales manager who, after reviewing sales reports, states that 80% of new customer contacts result in no sale. By letting A denote the event of a sale and $\overline{A}$ denote the event of no sale, the manager is stating that $P(\overline{A}) = 0.80$. Using equation (2.3), we see that

$$P(A) = 1 - P(\overline{A}) = 1 - 0.80 = 0.20$$

which shows that there is a 0.20 probability that a sale will be made on a new customer contact.

In another example, a purchasing agent states that there is a 0.90 probability that a supplier will send a shipment that is free of defective parts. Using the complement, we can conclude that there is a $1 - 0.90 = 0.10$ probability that the shipment will contain some defective parts.

Addition Law

The addition law is a helpful probability relationship when we have two events and are interested in knowing the probability that at least one of the events occurs. That is, with events A and B, we are interested in knowing the probability that event A or event B or both occur.

Before we present the addition law, we need to discuss two concepts concerning the combination of events: the *union* of events and the *intersection* of events.

Given two events A and B, the *union of events A and B* is the event containing all sample points belonging to *A or B or both*. The union is denoted by $A \cup B$. The Venn diagram shown in Figure 2.3 depicts the union of events A and B; the shaded region contains all the sample points in event A as well as all the sample points in event B. The fact that the circles overlap indicates that there are some sample points contained in both A and B.

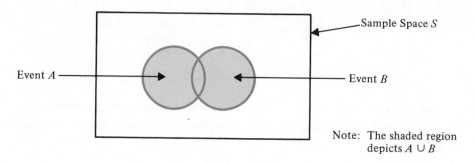

Figure 2.3
Union of Events A and B

Given two events A and B, the *intersection of events A and B* is the event containing the sample points belonging to *both A and B*. The intersection is denoted by $A \cap B$. The Venn diagram depicting the intersection of the two events is shown in Figure 2.4. The area where the two circles overlap is the intersection; it contains the sample points that are in both A and B.

Let us now continue with a discussion of the addition law. The addition law provides a way to compute the probability of event A or B or both occurring. In other words, the addition law is used to compute the probability of the union of two events, $A \cup B$. The *addition law* is formally stated as follows:

$$P(A \cup B) = P(A) + P(B) - P(A \cap B) \tag{2.4}$$

To obtain an intuitive understanding of the addition law, note that the first two terms in the addition law, $P(A) + P(B)$, account for all the sample points in $A \cup B$. However,

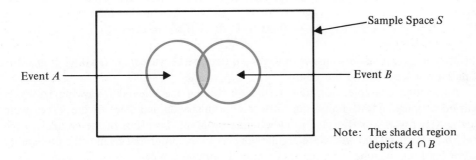

Figure 2.4
Intersection of Events A and B

since the sample points in the intersection $A \cap B$ are in both A and B, when we compute $P(A) + P(B)$ we are in effect counting each of the sample points in $A \cap B$ twice. We correct for this by subtracting $P(A \cap B)$.

As an example of the application of the addition law, consider the following grades obtained in a college course in quantitative methods for decision making. Of 200 students taking the course, 160 passed the midterm examination and 140 passed the final examination; 124 students passed both exams. Let

$$A = \text{event of passing the midterm exam}$$
$$B = \text{event of passing the final exam}$$

The above relative frequency information leads to the following probabilities:

$$P(A) = \frac{160}{200} = 0.80$$

$$P(B) = \frac{140}{200} = 0.70$$

$$P(A \cap B) = \frac{124}{200} = 0.62$$

After reviewing the grades, the professor of the course decided to give a passing grade to any student who passed at least one of the two exams. That is, a passing grade is given to any student who passes the midterm, to any student who passes the final, and to any student who passes both exams. What is the probability of receiving a passing grade in this course?

While your first reaction may be to try to count how many of the 200 students passed at least one exam, note that the probability question is about the union of the events A and B. That is, we want to know the probability that a student passes the midterm (A), passes the final (B), or passes both. Thus we want to know $P(A \cup B)$. Using the addition law (2.4) for the events A and B, we have

$$P(A \cup B) = P(A) + P(B) - P(A \cap B)$$

Knowing the three probabilities on the right-hand side of this expression, we can write

$$P(A \cup B) = 0.80 + 0.70 - 0.62 = 0.88$$

This tells us there is an 88% chance of passing the course because there is a 0.88 probability of passing at least one of the exams.

As another example, consider a study involving the television-viewing habits of married couples. It was found that 30% of the husbands and 20% of the wives were regular viewers of a particular Friday evening program. For 12% of the couples in the study both husband and wife were regular viewers of the program. What is the probability that at least one member of a married couple is a regular viewer of the program?

Let

$$H = \text{husband is a regular viewer}$$

$$W = \text{wife is a regular viewer}$$

We have $P(H) = 0.30$, $P(W) = 0.20$, and $P(H \cap W) = 0.12$; thus, using the addition law,

$$P(H \cup W) = P(H) + P(W) - P(H \cap W) = 0.30 + 0.20 - 0.12 = 0.38$$

This shows that there is a 0.38 probability that at least one member of a given married couple is a regular viewer of the program.

Before going on, let us see how the addition law is applied to *mutually exclusive events*. Two or more events are said to be mutually exclusive if the events do not have any sample points in common—that is, there are no sample points in the intersection of the events. For two events A and B to be mutually exclusive, we must have $P(A \cap B) = 0$. Figure 2.5 provides a Venn diagram depicting two mutually exclusive events. Since $P(A \cap B) = 0$, for the *special case of mutually exclusive events* the addition law becomes

$$P(A \cup B) = P(A) + P(B) \tag{2.5}$$

To compute the probability of the union of two mutually exclusive events, we simply add the corresponding probabilities.

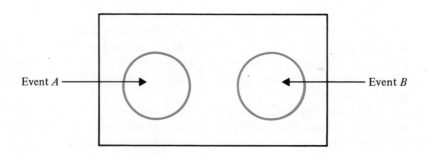

Figure 2.5
Mutually Exclusive Events

Conditional Probability

In many probability situations it is important to be able to determine the probability of one event given that another event is known to have occurred. Suppose that we have an event A with probability $P(A)$. If we obtain new information or learn that another event, denoted B, has occurred, we will want to take advantage of this information in computing a new or revised probability for event A.

This new probability of event A is written $P(A \mid B)$. The "$\mid$" is used to denote the fact that we are considering the probability of event A *given the condition that event B has occurred*. Thus the notation $P(A \mid B)$ is read "the probability of A *given B*."

With two events A and B, the general definitions of *conditional probability* for A given B and for B given A are as follows:

$$P(A \mid B) = \frac{P(A \cap B)}{P(B)} \tag{2.6}$$

$$P(B \mid A) = \frac{P(A \cap B)}{P(A)} \tag{2.7}$$

Note that for these expressions to have meaning, $P(B)$ cannot equal 0 in equation (2.6) and $P(A)$ cannot equal 0 in equation (2.7).

To obtain an intuitive understanding of the use of equation (2.6), consider the Venn diagram in Figure 2.6. The lightly shaded region denotes that event B has occurred; the

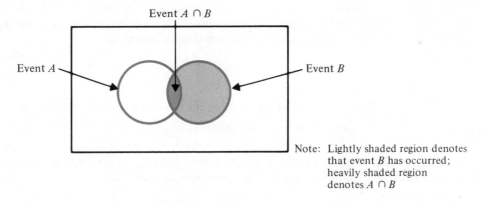

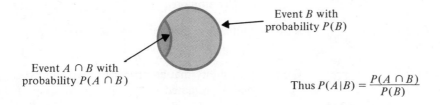

Figure 2.6
Venn Diagram for Illustrating Conditional Probability

heavily shaded region denotes that the event $(A \cap B)$ has occurred. We know that once B has occurred, the only way that we can also observe event A is for the event $(A \cap B)$ to occur. Thus the ratio $P(A \cap B)/P(B)$ provides the probability that we will observe event A given the fact that event B has already occurred.

As an illustration of the application of conditional probability, consider the situation of the promotional status of male and female officers of a major metropolitan police force in the eastern United States. The police force consists of 1200 officers: 960 men and 240 women. Over the past 2 years, 324 officers on the police force have been awarded promotions. The specific breakdown of promotions for male and female officers is shown in Table 2.1.

Table 2.1
Promotional Status of Police Officers over the Past 2 Years

	Promoted	Not Promoted	Total
Men	288	672	960
Women	36	204	240
Total	324	876	1200

After reviewing the promotional record, a committee of female officers raised a discrimination case on the basis that only 36 women officers had received promotions over the past 2 years. The police administration has argued that the relatively low number of promotions for female officers is due not to discrimination but to the fact that there are not very many female officers on the police force. Let us show how conditional probability could be used to evaluate the discrimination charge.

Let

$$M = \text{event an officer is a man}$$
$$W = \text{event an officer is a woman}$$
$$B = \text{event an officer is promoted}$$

Dividing the data values in Table 2.1 by the total of 1200 officers permits us to summarize the available information in the following probability values:

$$P(M \cap B) = \frac{288}{1200} = 0.24 = \text{probability that an officer is a man } and \text{ is promoted}$$

$$P(M \cap \overline{B}) = \frac{672}{1200} = 0.56 = \text{probability that an officer is a man } and \text{ is not promoted}$$

$$P(W \cap B) = \frac{36}{1200} = 0.03 = \text{probability that an officer is a woman } and \text{ is promoted}$$

$$P(W \cap \overline{B}) = \frac{204}{1200} = 0.17 = \text{probability that an officer is a woman } and \text{ is not promoted}$$

Since each of these values gives the probability of the intersection of two events, the probabilities are given the name of *joint probabilities*. Table 2.2, which provides a summary of the probability information for the police officer promotion situation, is referred to as a *joint probability table*.

Table 2.2
Joint Probability Table for Police Officer Promotions

Joint probabilities
appear in the body
of the table

	Promoted	**Not Promoted**	**Total**
Men	0.24	0.56	0.80
Women	0.03	0.17	0.20
Total	0.27	0.73	1.00

Marginal probabilities
appear in the margins
of the table

The values in the margins of the joint probability table provide the probabilities of each event separately. That is, $P(M) = 0.80$, $P(W) = 0.20$, $P(B) = 0.27$, and $P(\overline{B}) = 0.73$. Thus we see that 80% of the force is male, 20% of the force is female, 27% of all officers received promotions, and 73% were not promoted. These probabilities are referred to as *marginal probabilities* because of their locations in the margins of the joint probability table. Returning to the issue of discrimination against the female officers, we see that the probability of promotion of an officer is $P(B) = 0.27$ (regardless of whether that officer is male or female). However, the critical issue in the discrimination case involves the two conditional probabilities $P(B \mid M)$ and $P(B \mid W)$. That is, what is the probability of a promotion *given* that the officer is a man and what is the probability of a promotion *given* that the officer is a woman? If these two probabilities are equal, there is no basis for a discrimination argument, since the chances of a promotion are the same for male and female officers. However, if the two conditional probabilities differ, there will be support for the position that male and female officers are treated differently when it comes to promotions.

Using (2.6), the conditional probability relationship, we obtain

$$P(B \mid M) = \frac{P(M \cap B)}{P(M)} = \frac{0.24}{0.80} = 0.30$$

$$P(B \mid W) = \frac{P(W \cap B)}{P(W)} = \frac{0.03}{0.20} = 0.15$$

What conclusions do you draw? The probability of a promotion given that the officer is a man is 0.30. This is twice the 0.15 probability of a promotion given that the officer is a woman. While the use of conditional probability does not in itself prove that discrimination exists in this case, the conditional probability values are strong support for the argument presented by the female officers.

In this illustration $P(B) = 0.27$, $P(B \mid M) = 0.30$, and $P(B \mid W) = 0.15$. This shows clearly that the probability of a promotion (event B) is affected or influenced by whether the officer is male or female. In particular, since $P(B \mid M) \neq P(B)$, we would say that events B and M are *dependent events*. That is, the probability of event B (promotion) is altered or affected by knowing whether or not M (the officer is male) occurs. Similarly, with $P(B \mid W) \neq P(B)$, we would say that events B and W are dependent events. On the other hand, if the probability of event B was not changed by the existence of event M, that is, $P(B \mid M) = P(B)$, we would say that events B and M are *independent events*. This leads us to the following definition of the independence of events:

Two events A and B are *independent* if

$$P(B \mid A) = P(B)$$

or

$$P(A \mid B) = P(A)$$

otherwise, the events are *dependent*.

Multiplication Law

The *multiplication law* can be used to find the probability of an intersection (simultaneous occurrence) of two events. The multiplication law is derived from the definition of conditional probability. Using (2.6) and (2.7) and solving for $P(A \cap B)$, we obtain the multiplication law:

$$P(A \cap B) = P(A \mid B)P(B) \tag{2.8}$$
$$P(A \cap B) = P(B \mid A)P(A) \tag{2.9}$$

The multiplication law is useful in situations where probabilities such as $P(A)$, $P(B)$, $P(A \mid B)$, and/or $P(B \mid A)$ are known but where $P(A \cap B)$ is not. For example, consider the case where a newspaper circulation department knows that 84% of its customers subscribe to the daily edition of the paper. Let D denote the event that a customer subscribes to the daily edition; we have $P(D) = 0.84$. In addition, it is known that the conditional probability that a customer who already holds a daily subscription also subscribes to the Sunday edition (event S) is 0.75; that is, $P(S \mid D) = 0.75$. What is the probability that a customer subscribes to both the daily and Sunday editions of the newspaper? Using (2.9), we compute $P(D \cap S)$ as follows:

$$P(D \cap S) = P(S \mid D)P(D) = 0.75(0.84) = 0.63$$

This tells us that 63% of the newspaper's customers take both the daily and Sunday editions.

Before concluding this section, let us consider the special case of the multiplication law when the events involved are independent. Recall that independent events exist whenever $P(B \mid A) = P(B)$ or $P(A \mid B) = P(A)$. Returning to the multiplication law, equations (2.8) and (2.9), we see that we can substitute $P(A)$ for $P(A \mid B)$ and $P(B)$ for $P(B \mid A)$. Hence for the *special case of independent events*, the multiplication law becomes

$$P(A \cap B) = P(A)P(B) \qquad (2.10)$$

Thus to compute the probability of the intersection of two independent events we simply multiply the corresponding probabilities. For example, a service station manager knows from past experience that 80 percent of the customers use a credit card when purchasing gasoline. What is the probability that the next two customers purchasing gasoline will both use a credit card? If we let

A = event that the first customer uses a credit card

B = event that the second customer uses a credit card

then the event of interest is $A \cap B$. Given no other information, it seems reasonable to assume that A and B are independent events. Thus

$$P(A \cap B) = P(A)P(B) = (0.80)(0.80) = 0.64$$

2.5

BAYES' THEOREM

In discussing conditional probability we indicated that it is possible to revise probabilities given new information. Often we begin probability analysis with initial or *prior probability* estimates for specific events of interest. Then from sources such as a sample, a special report, a product test, and so on we obtain additional information about the events. Given this new information, we want to revise or update the prior probability values. The new or revised probabilities for the events are referred to as *posterior probabilities*. Bayes' theorem provides a means for computing these posterior probabilities. The steps of the probability revision process are shown in Figure 2.7.

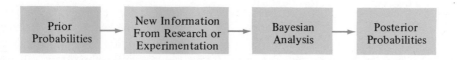

Figure 2.7
Probability Revision Using Bayes' Theorem

In cases where we have two events of interest, say A_1 and A_2, we begin the analysis with the prior probabilities $P(A_1)$ and $P(A_2)$. If the new information available is that event B has occurred, the following expressions—known as *Bayes' theorem*—can be used to compute the posterior probabilities $P(A_1 \mid B)$ and $P(A_2 \mid B)$:[1]

---

[1]In this application of Bayes' theorem, events A_1 and A_2 must be mutually exclusive and must be the only two events that can possibly occur.

$$P(A_1 \mid B) = \frac{P(B \mid A_1)P(A_1)}{P(B \mid A_1)P(A_1) + P(B \mid A_2)P(A_2)} \tag{2.11}$$

and

$$P(A_2 \mid B) = \frac{P(B \mid A_2)P(A_2)}{P(B \mid A_1)P(A_1) + P(B \mid A_2)P(A_2)} \tag{2.12}$$

As an application of Bayes' theorem, consider a manufacturing firm that receives parts from two different suppliers. Let A_1 denote the event that a part is from supplier 1 and A_2 denote the event that a part is from supplier 2. Currently, 65% of the parts purchased by the company are from supplier 1, while the remaining 35% are from supplier 2. Thus if a part is selected at random, we would assign the prior probabilities $P(A_1) = 0.65$ and $P(A_2) = 0.35$.

The quality of the purchased parts varies with the source of supply. Based on historical data, the quality ratings of the two suppliers are as shown in Table 2.3. Thus if we let G denote the event that a part is good and B denote the event that a part is defective or bad, the information in Table 2.3 provides the following conditional probability values:

$$P(G \mid A_1) = 0.98 \qquad P(B \mid A_1) = 0.02$$
$$P(G \mid A_2) = 0.95 \qquad P(B \mid A_2) = 0.05$$

Table 2.3
Historical Quality Level of Two Parts Suppliers

	Percentage Good Parts (G)	Percentage Bad Parts (B)
Supplier A_1	98%	2%
Supplier A_2	95%	5%

With the prior probabilities $P(A_1) = 0.65$ and $P(A_2) = 0.35$ and the given conditional probability information, we are ready to show how Bayes' theorem can be used to revise the prior probabilities in light of new information. For example, assume that the parts from the two suppliers are used in the firm's manufacturing process and that a machine breaks down because it attempts to process a bad part. Given the information that the part causing the problem is bad, what is the probability that the part is from each of the suppliers? That is, what are the posterior probabilities $P(A_1 \mid B)$ and $P(A_2 \mid B)$? In the first case we use equation (2.11) to show that

$$P(A_1 \mid B) = \frac{P(B \mid A_1)P(A_1)}{P(B \mid A_1)P(A_1) + P(B \mid A_2)P(A_2)}$$

$$= \frac{(0.02)(0.65)}{(0.02)(0.65) + (0.05)(0.35)} = \frac{0.0130}{0.0130 + 0.0175}$$

$$= \frac{0.0130}{0.0305} = 0.426$$

Using equation (2.12) we find $P(A_2 \mid B)$ as follows:

$$P(A_2 \mid B) = \frac{P(B \mid A_2)P(A_2)}{P(B \mid A_1)P(A_1) + P(B \mid A_2)P(A_2)}$$

$$= \frac{(0.05)(0.35)}{(0.02)(0.65) + (0.05)(0.35)} = \frac{0.0175}{0.0130 + 0.0175}$$

$$= \frac{0.0175}{0.0305} = 0.574$$

Note that initially we had a probability of 0.65 that a part selected at random was from supplier 1. However, given information that the part is bad, the probability that the part is from supplier 1 drops to 0.426. In fact, if the part is bad, there is a better than 50–50 chance that the part came from supplier 2; that is, $P(A_2 \mid B) = 0.574$. Problem 19 at the end of the chapter asks you to use Bayes' theorem to revise the prior probabilities if a part inspected is found to be good. In that problem you are asked to compute the posterior probabilities $P(A_1 \mid G)$ and $P(A_2 \mid G)$.

Tabular Approach

A tabular approach helpful in conducting the Bayes' theorem calculations is shown in Table 2.4. The computations shown there are conducted as follows:

Table 2.4
Summary of Bayes' Theorem Calculations for the Two-Supplier Problem

Events A_i	Prior Probabilities $P(A_i)$	Conditional Probabilities $P(B \mid A_i)$	Joint Probabilities $P(A_i \cap B)$	Posterior Probabilities $P(A_i \mid B)$
A_1	0.65	0.02	0.0130	0.0130/0.0305 = 0.426
A_2	0.35	0.05	0.0175	0.0175/0.0305 = 0.574
	1.00		$P(B) = 0.0305$	1.000

Step 1 Prepare the following three columns:

Column 1—The list of all mutually exclusive events that can occur in the problem
Column 2—The prior probabilities for the events
Column 3—The conditional probabilities of the new information *given* each event

Step 2 In column 4 compute the joint probabilities for each event A_i and the new information B. These joint probabilities are found by multiplying the values in column 2 by the corresponding values in column 3—that is, $P(A_i \cap B) = P(A_i)P(B \mid A_i)$.

Step 3 Sum the joint probability column to find the probability of the new information, $P(B)$. Thus we see that in this example there is a 0.0130 probability of a bad part and supplier 1 and there is a 0.0175 probability of a bad part and supplier 2. Thus, since these are the only two ways in which a bad part can be obtained, the sum 0.0130 + 0.0175 shows that there is an overall probability of 0.0305 of finding a bad part from the combined shipments of both suppliers.

Step 4 In column 5 compute the posterior probabilities using the basic relationship of conditional probability

$$P(A_i \mid B) = \frac{P(A_i \cap B)}{P(B)}$$

Note that the joint probabilities $P(A_i \cap B)$ are found in column 4, while the probability $P(B)$ appears as the sum of column 4.

Figure 2.8 provides a tree diagram that may help you better understand how Bayes' theorem works to obtain the desired posterior probabilities. Proceeding from left to right, the tree diagram shows that the parts come from the two suppliers with the prior probabilities $P(A_1) = 0.65$ and $P(A_2) = 0.35$. Then the tree diagram shows that for each supplier a part may be good or bad; the conditional probabilities $P(G \mid A_i)$ and $P(B \mid A_i)$

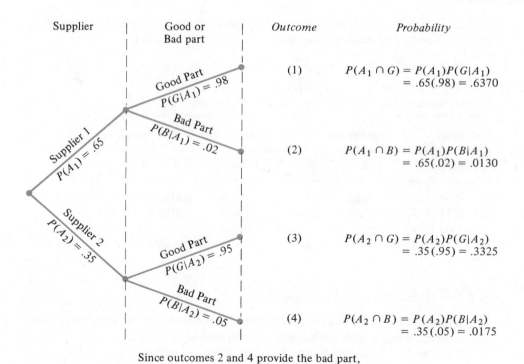

Since outcomes 2 and 4 provide the bad part,
$$P(B) = P(A_1 \cap B) + P(A_2 \cap B) = .0130 + .0175 = .0305$$

Figure 2.8
Tree Diagram of the Bayes Theorem Computations for the Two-Supplier Problem

show the probability of obtaining good (G) and bad (B) parts from each of the suppliers. Note that the tree diagram shows four outcomes, indicated by the joint probabilities $P(A_1 \cap G)$, $P(A_1 \cap B)$, $P(A_2 \cap G)$, and $P(A_2 \cap B)$. Thus we see that for the case of observing a bad part we must be at outcome 2 or outcome 4 of the tree diagram. At outcome 2 we have $P(A_1 \cap B) = 0.0130$, and at outcome 4 we have $P(A_2 \cap B) = 0.0175$. Since these are the only two outcomes that provide a bad part, we see that the probability of a bad part must be $0.0130 + 0.0175 = 0.0305$. Since outcome 4 has the larger joint probability (that is, 0.0175), there is a greater chance that the bad part is observed because outcome 4 occurred than because outcome 2 occurred. Note that the source of the supply providing outcome 4 is supplier 2. Thus on a relative basis the probability of the bad part coming from supplier 2 is $0.0175/0.0305 = 0.574$; that is, $P(A_2 \mid B) = 0.574$. Similarly, using outcome 2 we see that $P(A_1 \mid B) = 0.0130/0.0305 = 0.426$. Thus in applying Bayes' theorem we have conducted the analysis shown in the tree diagram whether we actually use the tree diagram itself, do the computations using the tabular approach of Table 2.4, or use the Bayes' theorem formulas (2.11) and (2.12).

As a final note, we can generalize Bayes' theorem to the case where there are n mutually exclusive events $A_1, A_2, \ldots, A_n$ and where one of the n events must occur when the experiment is conducted. In such a case Bayes' theorem for the computation of any posterior probability $P(A_i \mid B)$ appears as follows:

$$P(A_i \mid B) = \frac{P(B \mid A_i)P(A_i)}{P(B \mid A_1)P(A_1) + P(B \mid A_2)P(A_2) + \cdots + P(B \mid A_n)P(A_n)} \quad (2.13)$$

$$\text{for} \quad A_i = A_1, A_2, \ldots, A_n$$

With prior probabilities $P(A_1)$, $P(A_2)$, $\ldots$, $P(A_n)$ and the appropriate conditional probabilities $P(B \mid A_1)$, $P(B \mid A_2)$, $\ldots$, $P(B \mid A_n)$, equation (2.13) can be used to compute the posterior probability of an event $A_1, A_2, \ldots, A_n$.

Summary

In this chapter we have introduced basic probability concepts and illustrated how probability analysis can be used to provide helpful decision-making information. We described how probability can be interpreted as a numerical measure of the likelihood that an event will occur. In addition, we saw that the probability of an event could be computed either by summing the probabilities of the experimental outcomes (sample points) comprising the event or by using the basic relationships of probability. For cases where additional information is available, we showed how conditional probability and Bayes' theorem could be used to obtain revised or posterior probabilities.

The probability concepts that have been covered in this chapter will be helpful in future chapters when we describe quantitative methods based on the use of probability information. Specific chapters and quantitative methods that make use of probability are

Chapter 3   Probability distributions
Chapter 4   Decision analysis
Chapter 5   Utility and decision making
Chapter 13   Project management: PERT/CPM

Glossary

Probability   A numerical measure of the likelihood that an event will occur.

Experiment   Any process that generates well-defined outcomes.

Sample space   The set of all possible sample points (experimental outcomes).

Sample points   The individual outcomes of an experiment.

Basic requirements of probability   Two principles or requirements that restrict the manner in which probability assignments can be made:
1. For each experimental outcome E_i we must have $0 \leq P(E_i) \leq 1$.
2. If there are k experimental outcomes, then $\Sigma P(E_i) = 1$.

Classical method   A method of assigning probabilities which assumes that the experimental outcomes are equally likely.

Relative frequency method   A method of assigning probabilties based on experimentation or historical data.

Subjective method   A method of assigning probabilities based on judgment.

Event   A collection of sample points or experimental outcomes.

Complement of event A   The event containing all sample points that are not in A.

Venn diagram   A graphical device for representing the sample space and operations involving events.

Union of events A and B   The event containing all sample points that are in A, in B, or in both.

Intersection of events A and B   The event containing all sample points that are in both A and B.

Addition law   A probability law used to compute the probability of a union, $P(A \cup B)$. It is $P(A \cup B) = P(A) + P(B) - P(A \cap B)$. For mutually exclusive events, since $P(A \cap B) = 0$, it reduces to $P(A \cup B) = P(A) + P(B)$.

Mutually exclusive events   Events that have no sample points in common; that is, $A \cap B$ is empty and $P(A \cap B) = 0$.

Conditional probability   The probability of an event given that another event has occurred. The conditional probability of A given B is $P(A \mid B) = P(A \cap B)/P(B)$.

Joint probabilities   The values that provide the probability of the intersection of two events.

Joint probability table   A table used to display the joint and marginal probabilities.

Marginal probabilities   The values in the margins of the joint probability table; these values provide the probability of each event separately.

Dependent events   Two events A and B, where $P(A \mid B) \neq P(A)$ or $P(B \mid A) \neq P(B)$; that is, the probability of one event is altered or affected by knowing whether or not the other event occurs.

Independent events   Two events A and B, where $P(A \mid B) = P(A)$ and $P(B \mid A) = P(B)$; that is, the events have no influence on each other.

Multiplication law   A probability law used to compute the probability of an intersection, $P(A \cap B)$. It is $P(A \cap B) = P(A)P(B \mid A)$ or $P(A \cap B) = P(B)P(A \mid B)$. For independent events it reduces to $P(A \cap B) = P(A)P(B)$.

Prior probabilities   Initial probabilities of events.

Posterior probabilities   Revised probabilities of events based on additional information.
Bayes' theorem   A method used to compute posterior probabilities.

Problems

1. Consider the experiment of rolling a die and observing the number of dots appearing
   on the upward face of the die. The sample space is $S = \{1, 2, 3, 4, 5, 6\}$.
   a. Which method (classical, relative frequency, or subjective) would you recommend
   for assigning probabilities to the experimental outcomes?
   b. What are your probability assignments?
   c. Show that your probability assignments satisfy the two basic requirements for
   assigning probabilities.

2. A small-appliance store in Madeira has collected data on refrigerator sales for the
   past 50 weeks:

Number of Refrigerators Sold	Number of Weeks
0	6
1	12
2	15
3	10
4	5
5	2
	50

Suppose that we are interested in the experiment of observing the number of refrigerators sold in one week of store operation.
a. How many sample points (experimental outcomes) are possible?
b. Which approach would you recommend for assigning probabilities to the sample
points?
c. Assign probabilities to the sample points and verify that your assignments satisfy
the two basic requirements.

3. The manager of a furniture store sells from zero to four china hutches each week.
   Based on past experience, the following probabilities are assigned to sales of zero,
   one, two, three, or four hutches:

$$P(0) = 0.08$$
$$P(1) = 0.18$$
$$P(2) = 0.32$$
$$P(3) = 0.30$$
$$P(4) = 0.12$$

a. Are these valid probability assignments? Why or why not?
b. Let A be the event that two or fewer are sold in the one week. Find $P(A)$.
c. Let B be the event that three or more are sold in one week. Find $P(B)$.

4. Suppose that a manager of a large apartment complex provides the following subjective probability estimates about the number of vacancies that will exist next month:

Vacancies	Probability
0	0.05
1	0.15
2	0.35
3	0.25
4	0.10
5	0.10

List the sample points in each of the following events and provide the probability of the event.
   a. No vacancies
   b. At least four vacancies
   c. Two or fewer vacancies

5. Let A be an event that a person's primary method of transportation to and from work is an automobile and B be an event that a person's primary method of transportation to and from work is a bus. Suppose that in a large city we find $P(A) = 0.45$ and $P(B) = 0.35$.
   a. Are events A and B mutually exclusive? What is the probability that a person uses an automobile or a bus in going to and from work?
   b. Find the probability that a person's primary method of transportation is something other than a bus.

6. During winter in Cincinnati, Mr. Krebs experiences difficulty in starting his two cars. The probability that the first car starts is 0.80, and the probability that the second car starts is 0.40. There is a probability of 0.30 that both cars start.
   a. Define the events involved and use probability notation to show the probability information given above.
   b. What is the probability that at least one car starts?
   c. What is the probability that Mr. Krebs cannot start either of the two cars?

7. Suppose that $P(A) = 0.30$, $P(B) = 0.25$, and $P(A \cap B) = 0.20$.
   a. Find $P(A \cup B)$, $P(A \mid B)$, and $P(B \mid A)$.
   b. Are events A and B independent events? Why or why not?

8. A large consumer goods company has been running a television advertisement for one of its soap products. A survey was conducted. On the basis of this survey probabilities were assigned to the following events:

$$A = \text{individual purchased the product}$$
$$B = \text{individual sees the advertisement}$$
$$A \cap B = \text{individual purchased the product and sees the advertisement}$$

The probabilities assigned were $P(A) = 0.20$, $P(B) = 0.40$, and $P(A \cap B) = 0.12$. The following questions relate to this situation.
   a. What is the probability of an individual purchasing the product given that the individual saw the advertisement? Does seeing the advertisement increase the probability that the individual will purchase the product? As a decision maker,

would you recommend continuing the advertisement (assuming that the cost is reasonable)?

b. Assume that those individuals who do not purchase the company's soap product buy from a competitor. What would be your estimate of the company's market share? Would you expect that expanding the advertisement to a larger audience will increase the company's market share? Why or why not?

9. Suppose that $P(A) = 0.60$, $P(B) = 0.30$, and events A and B are mutually exclusive.
   a. Find $P(A \cup B)$ and $P(A \cap B)$.
   b. Are events A and B independent? Explain.
   c. Can you make a general statement about whether or not mutually exclusive events can be independent?

10. A research study investigating the relationship between smoking and heart disease in a sample of 1000 men over 50 years of age provided the following data:

	Smoker	Nonsmoker	Total
Record of Heart Disease	100	80	180
No Record of Heart Disease	200	620	820
Total	300	700	1000

   a. Show a joint probability table that summarizes the results of this study.
   b. What is the probability that a man over 50 years of age is a smoker and has a record of heart disease?
   c. Compute and interpret the marginal probabilities.
   d. Given that a man over 50 years of age is a smoker, what is the probability that he has heart disease?
   e. Given that a man over 50 years of age is a nonsmoker, what is the probability that he has heart disease?
   f. Does the research show that heart disease and smoking are independent events? Use probability to justify your answer.
   g. What conclusion would you draw about the relationship between smoking and heart disease?

11. A Daytona Beach nightclub has the following data on the age and marital status of 140 customers:

		Marital Status	
		Single	Married
Age	Under 30	77	14
	30 or over	28	21

   a. Develop a joint probability table using the above data.
   b. Use the marginal probabilities to comment on the age of customers attending the club.
   c. Use the marginal probabilities to comment on the marital status of customers attending the club.

d. What is the probability of finding a customer who is under the age of 30 and single?

e. If a customer is under 30, what is the probability that he or she is single?

f. Is marital status independent of age? Explain, using probabilities.

12. A market survey of 800 people found the following facts about the ability to recall a television commercial for a particular product and the actual purchase of the product:

	Could Recall Television Commercial	Could Not Recall Television Commercial	Total
Purchased the Product	160	80	240
Had Not Purchased the Product	240	320	560
Total	400	400	800

Let A be the event of purchasing the product and B be the event of recalling the television commercial.

a. Find $P(A)$, $P(B)$, and $P(A \cap B)$.

b. Are A and B mutually exclusive events? Use probability values to explain.

c. What is the probability that a person who could recall seeing the television commercial purchased the product?

d. Are A and B independent events? Use probability values to explain.

e. Comment on the value of the commercial in terms of its relationship to purchasing the product.

13. A survey of automobile ownership was conducted for 200 families in Houston. The results of the study showing ownership of automobiles of United States and foreign manufacture are summarized:

		Do You Own a U.S. Car?		Total
		Yes	No	Total
Do You Own a Foreign Car?	Yes	30	10	40
	No	150	10	160
Total		180	20	

a. Show the joint probability table for the given data.

b. Use the marginal probabilities to compare U.S. and foreign car ownership.

c. What is the probability that a family will own both a foreign car and a U.S. car?

d. What is the probability that a family owns a car, U.S. or foreign?

e. If a family owns a U.S. car, what is the probability that it also owns a foreign car?

f. If a family owns a foreign car, what is the probability that it also owns a U.S. car?

g. Are U.S. and foreign car ownership independent events? Explain.

14. Shown below are data from a sample of 80 families in a Midwestern city. The data shows the record of college attendance by fathers and their oldest sons.

		Son	
		Attended College	*Did Not Attend College*
Father	*Attended College*	18	7
	Did Not Attend College	22	33

   a. Show the joint probability table.
   b. Use the marginal probabilities to comment on the comparison between fathers and sons in terms of attending college.
   c. What is the probability that a son attends college given that his father attended college?
   d. What is the probability that a son attends college given that his father did not attend college?
   e. Is attending college by the son independent of whether or not his father attended college? Explain, using probability values.

15. The probability that Ms. Smith will receive an offer on the first job she applies for is 0.5, and the probability that she will receive an offer on the second job she applies for is 0.6. She thinks that the probability that she will receive an offer on both jobs is 0.30.
   a. Define the events involved, and use probability notation to show the probability information given above.
   b. What is the probability that Ms. Smith receives an offer on the second job given that she receives an offer for the first job?
   c. What is the probability that Ms. Smith receives an offer on at least one of the jobs she applies for?
   d. What is the probability that Ms. Smith does not receive an offer on either of the two jobs she applies for?
   e. Are the job offers independent? Explain.

16. In the evaluation of a sales training program, a firm found that of 50 salespersons making a bonus last year, 20 had attended a special sales training program. The firm has 200 salespersons. Let A be the event a salesperson attends the sales training program and B be the event a salesperson makes a bonus.
   a. Find $P(A \mid B)$ and $P(B)$.
   b. What is the probability of finding a salesperson who both attended the training program and made a bonus? That is, find $P(A \cap B)$.
   c. Assume that 40% of the salespersons have attended the training program. What is the probability that a salesperson makes a bonus given that the salesperson attended the sales training program $P(B \mid A)$?
   d. If the firm evaluates the training program in terms of the effect it has on the probability of a salesperson's making a bonus, what is your evaluation of the training program? Comment on whether A and B are dependent or independent events.

17. A purchasing agent has placed two rush orders for a particular raw material from two different suppliers, A and B. If neither order arrives in 2 weeks the production process must be shut down until at least one of the orders arrives. The probability that supplier A can deliver the material in 2 weeks is 0.40. The probability that supplier B can deliver the material in 2 weeks is 0.50.
   a. What is the probability that both suppliers deliver the material in 2 weeks? Since two separate suppliers are involved, we are willing to assume independence.
   b. What is the probability that at least one supplier delivers the material in 2 weeks?
   c. What is the probability the production process is shut down in 2 weeks because of a shortage in raw material (that is, both orders are late)?

18. In a study of television viewing habits among married couples, a researcher found that for a popular Saturday night program, 25% of the husbands viewed the program regularly and 30% of the wives viewed the program regularly. The study found that for couples where the husband watches the program regularly, 80% of the wives also watch regularly.
   a. What is the probability that both a husband and wife watch the program regularly?
   b. What is the probability that at least one—husband or wife—watches the program regularly?
   c. What percentage of married couples do not have at least one regular viewer of the program?

19. Refer to the two-supplier problem in Section 2.5.
   a. Letting A_1 = supplier 1, A_2 = supplier 2, and G = a good part, what are $P(A_1)$, $P(A_2)$, $P(G \mid A_1)$ and $P(G \mid A_2)$?
   b. Assume that a part inspected during the manufacturing process is found to be good (G). What is the probability that this part is from supplier 1? From supplier 2? That is, compute $P(A_1 \mid G)$ and $P(A_2 \mid G)$.

20. In a major eastern city, 60% of the automobile drivers are 30 years of age or older, and 40% of the drivers are under 30 years of age. Of all drivers 30 years of age or older, 4% will have a traffic violation during a 12-month period. Of all drivers under 30 years of age, 10% will have a traffic violation during a 12-month period. Assume that a driver has had a traffic violation during the past 12 months; what is the probability that the driver is under 30 years of age?

21. A certain college football team plays 55% of its games at home and 45% of its games away. Given that the team has a home game, there is a 0.80 probability that it will win. Given that the team has an away game, there is a 0.65 probability that it will win. If the team wins on a particular Saturday, what is the probability that the game was played at home?

22. At the C&H Savings and Loan Association 50% of the individuals holding a loan are college graduates and 50% are not college graduates. C&H finds that 90% of the loans held by college graduates are repaid without late penalties; 10% incur late penalties. Furthermore, 60% of the loans held by the individuals who are not college graduates are repaid without late penalties; 40% incur late penalties.
   a. If we find that a loan has just been repaid that did not incur a late penalty, what is the probability this loan was to a college graduate?
   b. Show a tree diagram that describes this situation. Use the format of Figure 2.8
   c. What percentage of C&H loans are repaid without late penalties being incurred? What percentage are repaid with late penalties?

23. A consulting firm has submitted a bid for a large research project. The firm's management initially felt there was a 50–50 chance of getting the bid. However, the agency to which the bid was submitted has subsequently requested additional information on the bid. Past experience indicates that on 75% of the successful bids and 40% of the unsuccessful bids additional information is requested.

    a. What is the prior probability the bid will be successful (that is, prior to receiving the request for additional information)?

    b. What is the conditional probability of a request for additional information given that the bid will ultimately be successful?

    c. Compute a posterior probability that the bid will be successful given that a request for additional information has been received.

24. A salesperson for Business Communication Systems, Inc. sells automatic envelope-addressing equipment to medium- and small-size businesses. The probability of making a sale to a new customer is 0.10. During the initial contact with a customer, sometimes the salesperson will be asked to call back later. Of the 30 most recent sales, 12 were made to customers who requested a call back later. Of 100 customers who did not make a purchase, 17 had requested a call back later. If a customer asks the salesperson to call back later, should the salesperson do so? What is the probability of making a sale to a customer who has requested a call back later?

25. An oil company has purchased an option on land in Alaska. Preliminary geologic studies have assigned the following prior probabilities:

$$P(\text{high-quality oil}) = 0.50$$
$$P(\text{medium-quality oil}) = 0.20$$
$$P(\text{no oil}) = 0.30$$

    a. What is the probability of finding oil?

    b. After 200 feet of drilling on the first well, a soil test is taken. The probabilities of finding this particular type of soil are as follows:

$$P(\text{soil} \mid \text{high-quality oil}) = 0.20$$
$$P(\text{soil} \mid \text{medium-quality oil}) = 0.80$$
$$P(\text{soil} \mid \text{no oil}) = 0.20$$

    How should the firm interpret the soil test? What are the revised probabilities for high-quality oil, medium-quality oil, and no oil? What is the new probability of finding oil?

26. The Wayne Manufacturing Company purchases a certain part from three suppliers, A_1, A_2, and A_3. Supplier A_1 supplies 60% of the parts; A_2, 30%; and A_3, 10%. The quality of parts is known to vary among suppliers, with A_1, A_2, and A_3 parts having 0.25%, 1%, and 2% defective rates, respectively. The parts are used in one of the company's major products.

    a. When a defective part is found, which supplier is the most likely source? Find the revised probabilities for each of the three suppliers.

    b. What is the probability that the company's major product is assembled with a defective part?

Quantitative Methods in Practice

Morton Thiokol, Inc.*
Chicago, Illinois

Morton Norwich combined with Thiokol Corporation in 1982 to form the current company, Morton Thiokol, Inc. From a salt business first started in Chicago in 1848, Jay Morton named his firm the Morton Salt Company in 1910. In 1914 the Morton Girl and slogan, "When it rains, it pours," established Morton Salt as a recognized name to the consumer. In the following years, Morton added specialty chemicals businesses and Texize, a manufacturer of consumer household products, to its rapidly growing salt business.

Thiokol Corporation began in 1928 as a manufacturer of specialty polysuflide polymers that found widespread use as sealants. Other specialty chemical buisnesses that serve plastic, electronic, and other industries were added later. As an outgrowth of the expanding chemical business, the company became involved in the manufacture of solid rocket propellants and today builds a variety of rocket motors including the boosters for the Space Shuttle and satellites used in the U.S. space programs.

The combination of Morton and Thiokol has resulted in a company with strong businesses in salt and household products, rocket motors, and specialty chemicals. In particular, the specialty chemicals group now consists of several decentralized manufacturing operations serving their particular market segment.

Probability Analysis Guides Management Decision Making

Managers at the various divisions throughout Morton Thiokol make decisions in light of uncertain outcomes. Often the managers' feel for the chances associated with the outcomes and/or subjective estimates of probabilities suggest a specific decision or course of action. Issues such as how much inventory to maintain, forecasts of demand, and estimates about order quantities from specific customers are instances where managers use probability considerations as part of the decision-making process. In the following example we describe how probability considerations aided a customer service decision at Carstab Corporation, a subsidiary of Morton Thiokol.

Carstab Corporation provides a variety of specialty chemical products for its customers. Because of the diversity of customer applications, customers differ substantially in terms of the unique specifications they require for the product. One approach to servicing customers would be for Carstab to wait until a customer order is received and then make

---

*The authors are indebted to Michael Haskell of Morton Thiokol's Carstab subsidiary for providing this application.

54

the product to the exact customer specifications. A disadvantage of this approach is that the customer's order would have to wait until Carstab could schedule production for the special order. In some instances this would require an undesirable waiting period for the customer. In addition, this approach also has the disadvantage of requiring Carstab to make relatively short production runs for specific customer orders, thus losing the economic advantage of larger production runs. In order to avoid these disadvantages, Carstab makes relatively large production runs for many of its products and holds goods in inventory awaiting customers' orders. In doing this the company realizes that not all of its inventory will meet the unique specification requirements for all customers.

In one instance, a customer made small but repeated orders for an expensive catalyst product used in its chemical processing. Because of the nature of its operation, the customer placed unique specifications on the product. Some, but not all of the lots produced by Carstab would meet the customer's exact specifications.

The customer agreed to test each lot as it was received to determine whether or not the catalyst would perform the desired function. Carstab agreed to ship lots to the customer with the understanding that the customer would perform the test and return the lots that did not pass the customer's specification test. The problem encountered was that only 60% of the lots sent to the customer would pass the customer's test. This meant that although the product was still good and usable to other customers, approximately 40% of the shipments sent to this customer were being returned.

Carstab explored the possibility of duplicating the customer's test and shipping only lots that passed the test. However, the test was unique to this one customer, and it was infeasible to purchase the expensive testing equipment needed to perform the customer's test.

Therefore, in order to improve the customer service Carstab chemists designed a new test, one that was believed to indicate whether nor not the lot would eventually pass the customer's test. The question was: would the Carstab test increase the probability that a lot shipped to the customer would pass the customer's test? The probability information sought was the probability that a lot will pass the customer's test given it has passed the company's test.

A sample of lots was tested under both the customer's procedure and the company's proposed procedure. Results were that 55% of the lots passed the company's test and 50% of the lots passed both the customer's test and the company's test. In probability notation, we have

$$A = \text{the event the lot passes the customer's test}$$
$$B = \text{the event the lot passes the company's test}$$

where

$$P(B) = 0.55 \quad \text{and} \quad P(A \cap B) = 0.50$$

The probability information sought was the conditional probability $P(A \mid B)$, which was given by

$$P(A \mid B) = \frac{P(A \cap B)}{P(B)} = \frac{0.50}{0.55} = 0.909$$

Prior to the company's test, the probability a lot would pass the customer's test was 0.60. However, the new results showed that given a lot passed the company's test, it had a 0.909 probability of passing the customer's test. This was good supporting evidence for the use of the company's test prior to shipment. Based on this probability analysis, the preshipment testing procedure was implemented at the company. Immediate results showed an improved level of customer service. A few lots were still being returned; however, the percentage was greatly reduced. The customer was more satisfied and return shipping costs were reduced.

As seen in this example, probability did not make the decision for the manager. However, some basic probability considerations provided important decision-making information and were a significant factor in the decision to implement the new testing procedure which resulted in improved service to the customer.

Questions

1. Why didn't Carstab produce a product that would meet customer specifications 100% of the time?

2. What probability information was helpful to Carstab in identifying its ability to produce a product that would meet the customer's specifications?

3. For the testing procedure described in this application, how would the results have changed if $P(B) = 0.40$ and $P(A \cap B) = 0.30$? Explain.

CHAPTER

3

Probability Distributions

In this chapter we continue the study of probability as a decision-making tool by introducing the concepts of random variables and probability distributions. In our study we consider the probability distributions of both discrete and continuous random variables. Of particular interest will be five special probability distributions: the binomial, the Poisson, the uniform, the normal, and the exponential distributions. These probability distributions are important because they have been used extensively in practice. Special formulas and/or tables are available that make probability information easily available to the decision maker.

3.1

RANDOM VARIABLES

Recall that in Chapter 2 we defined an experiment as any process that generates well-defined outcomes. We now want to concentrate on the process of assigning *numerical values* to the outcomes. This is where the notion of a random variable comes into play.

For any particular experiment a random variable can be defined such that each possible experimental outcome generates exactly one numerical value for the random variable. For example, if we consider the experiment of selling automobiles for one day at a particular dealership, we could describe the experimental outcomes in terms of the *number* of cars sold. In this case, if x = number of cars sold, x is called a random variable. The particular numerical value that the random variable takes on depends on the outcome of the experiment.[1] That is, we will not know the specific value of the random variable until we have observed the experimental outcome. For example, if on a given day three cars are sold, the value of the random variable is 3; if on another day (a repeat of the experiment) four cars are sold, the value is 4. We define a random variable as follows:

A *random variable* is a numerical description of the outcome of an experiment.

Some additional examples of experiments and their associated random variables are given in Table 3.1. While many experiments have experimental outcomes that lend themselves quite naturally to numerical values, others do not. For example, for the experiment of tossing a coin one time, the experimental outcome will be either a head or a tail, neither of which has a natural numerical value. However, we still may want to express the outcomes in terms of a random variable. Thus we need a rule that can be used to assign a numerical value to each of the experimental outcomes. One possibility is to let the random variable $x = 1$ if the experimental outcome is a head and $x = 0$ if the experimental outcome is a tail. While the numerical values for x are arbitrary, x is a random variable because it describes the experimental outcomes numerically.

A random variable may be classified as either discrete or continuous depending on the numerical values it can have. A random variable that may only take on a finite or countable number of different values is referred to as a *discrete random variable*. The number of units sold, the number of defects observed, the number of customers that enter a bank during one day of operation, and so on, are examples of discrete random variables. On the other hand, random variables such as weight, time, temperature, and so forth, which may take on any value in a certain interval or collection of intervals, are referred to as *continuous random variables*. For instance, the third random variable in Table 3.1 (percentage of project completed after 6 months) is a continuous random variable because it may take on any value in the interval from 0 to 100 (for example, 56.33, or 64.22).

Table 3.1
Examples of Random Variables

Experiment	Random Variable (x)	Possible Values for the Random Variable
Make 100 sales calls	Total number of sales	$0, 1, 2, \ldots, 100$
Inspect a shipment of 70 radios	Number of defective radios	$0, 1, 2, \ldots, 70$
Build a new library	Percentage of project completed after 6 months	$0 \leq x \leq 100$

3.2

DISCRETE RANDOM VARIABLES

In order to demonstrate the use of a discrete random variable, let us consider the sales of automobiles at DiCarlo Motors, Inc. in Saratoga, New York. The owner of DiCarlo

---

[1]More advanced texts on probability make a distinction between the random variable, denoted by X, and the values it can take on, denoted by x. In this text we will use x for both purposes.

Motors is interested in the daily sales volume for automobiles. Suppose that we let x be a random variable denoting the number of cars sold on a given day. Sales records show that five is the maximum number of cars that DiCarlo has ever sold during one day. Since the owner believes that the previous history of sales adequately represents what will occur in the future, we would expect the random variable x to take on one of the numerical values 0, 1, 2, 3, 4, or 5. The possible values of the random variable are finite; thus we would classify x as a discrete random variable.

The Probability Distribution of a Discrete Random Variable

Once we have defined an appropriate discrete random variable for a particular situation, we can turn our attention to determining the probability associated with each possible value of the random variable. In the DiCarlo Motors problem we are interested in determining the probabilities of x being 0, 1, 2, 3, 4, or 5. In other words, we would like to know the probabilities associated with each possible daily sales volume for automobiles.

Suppose that in checking DiCarlo's sales records we find that over the past year the firm has been open for business on exactly 300 days. The sales volumes generated and the frequency of their occurrence are summarized in Table 3.2. With these historical data available, the owner of DiCarlo Motors feels that the relative frequency method will provide a reasonable means of assessing the probabilities for the random variable x. Using common notation, the *probability function*, denoted by $f(x)$, provides the probability that the random variable x takes on some specific value. Since on 54 of the 300 days of historical data DiCarlo Motors did not sell any cars and since no sales corresponds to $x = 0$, we assign to $f(0)$ the value $54/300 = 0.18$. Similarly, since $f(1)$ denotes the probability that x takes on the value 1, we assign to $f(1)$ the value $117/300 = 0.39$. After computing the relative frequencies for the other possible values of x, we can develop a table of x and $f(x)$ values, as shown in Table 3.3. This table is one way of representing the *probability distribution* of the random variable x.

Table 3.2
Cars Sold per Day at DiCarlo Motors

Sales Volume	Number of Days
No sales	54
Exactly one car	117
Exactly two cars	72
Exactly three cars	42
Exactly four cars	12
Exactly five cars	3
Total	300

We can also represent the probability distribution of x graphically. In Figure 3.1 the values of the random variable x are shown on the horizontal axis. The probability that x takes on these values is shown on the vertical axis. For many discrete random variables the probability distribution can also be represented as a formula that provides $f(x)$ for every possible value of x. We will illustrate this approach in the next section.

Table 3.3
Probability Distribution for the
Number of Cars Sold per Day

x	$f(x)$
0	0.18
1	0.39
2	0.24
3	0.14
4	0.04
5	0.01
Total	1.00

In the development of a *discrete probability distribution*, the following two conditions must always be satisfied:

$$f(x) \geq 0 \tag{3.1}$$
$$\sum f(x) = 1 \tag{3.2}$$

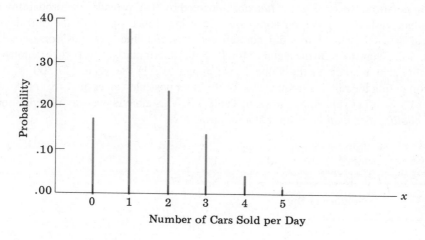

Figure 3.1
Graphical Representation of the Probability
Distribution for Number of Cars Sold per Day

Condition (3.1) is the requirement that the probabilities associated with each value of x must be greater than or equal to zero, whereas (3.2) indicates that the sum of the probabilities for all values of the random variable x must be equal to 1. Referring to Table 3.3 for the DiCarlo Motors probability distribution, we see that (3.1) and (3.2) are satisfied. Thus, the probability distribution developed for DiCarlo Motors is a valid discrete probability distribution.

Once a random variable and its probability distribution have been established, a variety of additional probability information can be developed, depending on the needs and interests of the decision maker. For example, for the DiCarlo Motors problem the probability distribution shown in Table 3.3 can be used to provide the following information:

1. There is a 0.18 probability that no cars will be sold in a day.
2. The most probable sales volume is 1, with $f(1) = 0.39$.
3. There is a 0.05 probability of an outstanding sales day with four or five cars being sold.

Using probability information such as that just given, DiCarlo's management can better understand the uncertainties associated with the car sales operation. Perhaps this improved understanding can serve as the basis for a new policy or decision that will increase the effectiveness of the firm.

Expected Value

Once we have constructed the probability distribution for a random variable, we often want to compute the mean or expected value of the random variable. The *expected value* of a discrete random variable is a weighted average of all possible values of the random variable, where the weights are the probabilities associated with the values. The mathematical formula for computing the expected value of a discrete random variable x is

$$E(x) = \mu = \sum x f(x) \tag{3.3}$$

As can be seen from the above expression, both the notations $E(x)$ and μ are used to refer to the expected value of a random variable.

Equation (3.3) shows us that in order to compute the expected value of a discrete random variable we must multiply each value of the random variable by the corresponding value of its probability function. We then add the resulting terms. The calculation of the expected value of the random variable (number of daily sales) for DiCarlo Motors is shown in Table 3.4. The first column contains the values of the random variable x, while the second column contains their associated probabilities, $f(x)$. Multiplying each value of x by its probability $f(x)$ provides the $xf(x)$ values, as shown in column 3 of Table 3.4. Following equation (3.3), we sum this column, $\Sigma x f(x)$, to find the expected value of 1.50 cars sold per day.

Table 3.4
Expected Value Calculation

x	$f(x)$	$xf(x)$
0	0.18	$0(0.18) = 0.00$
1	0.39	$1(0.39) = 0.39$
2	0.24	$2(0.24) = 0.48$
3	0.14	$3(0.14) = 0.42$
4	0.04	$4(0.04) = 0.16$
5	0.01	$5(0.01) = \underline{0.05}$
		$E(x) = 1.50$

The expected value of a random variable can be thought of as a mean, or average, value. That is, for experiments that can be repeated numerous times, the expected value can be interpreted as the "long-run" average value for the random variable. However, the expected value is not necessarily the number that we think the random variable will take on the next time the experiment is conducted. In fact, it is impossible for DiCarlo to sell exactly 1.50 cars on any given day. But if we envision selling cars at DiCarlo Motors for many days into the future, the expected value of 1.50 cars provides a good estimate of the mean, or average, daily sales volume.

The expected value can be important to the manager from both planning and decision-making points of view. For example, suppose that DiCarlo Motors will be open 60 days during the next 3 months. How many cars will be sold during this time? While we cannot specify the exact sales for any given day, the expected value of 1.50 cars per day provides an expected or average sales estimate of $60(1.50) = 90$ cars for the next 3-month period. In terms of setting sales quotas and/or planning orders, the expected value may provide helpful decision-making information.

Variance

While the expected value gives us an idea of the average or central value for the random variable, often we would also like a measure of the dispersion, or variability, of the possible values of the random variable. For example, if the values of the random variable range from quite large to quite small, we would want a large value for our measure of variability. On the other hand, if the values of the random variable show only modest variation, we would want a relatively small value. We now want to use the variance measure to summarize the variability in the values of a random variable. The mathematical expression for the *variance* of a discrete random variable is

$$\text{Var}(x) = \sigma^2 = \sum (x - \mu)^2 f(x) \tag{3.4}$$

As equation (3.4) shows, an essential part of the variance formula is a *deviation*, $x - \mu$, which measures how far a particular value of the random variable is from the expected value or mean, μ. In computing the variance of a random variable, the deviations are squared and then weighted by the corresponding value of the probability function. The sum of these weighted squared deviations for all values of the random variable is referred to as the variance. Thus the variance is a weighted average of the squared deviations.

The calculation of the variance for the number of daily sales in the DiCarlo Motors problem is summarized in Table 3.5. We see that the variance for the number of cars sold per day is 1.25. A related measure of variability is the *standard deviation*, σ, which is defined as the positive square root of the variance. For DiCarlo Motors the standard deviation of the number of cars sold per day is

$$\sigma = \sqrt{1.25} = 1.118$$

For the purpose of easier managerial interpretation, the standard deviation may be preferred over the variance because it is measured in the same units as the random variable ($\sigma = 1.118$ cars sold per day). The variance (σ^2) is measured in squared units and is thus more difficult for a manager to interpret.

Table 3.5
Calculation of Variance

x	$x - \mu$	$(x - \mu)^2$	$f(x)$	$(x - \mu)^2 f(x)$
0	$0 - 1.50 = -1.50$	2.25	0.18	$2.25(0.18) = 0.4050$
1	$1 - 1.50 = -0.50$	0.25	0.39	$0.25(0.39) = 0.0975$
2	$2 - 1.50 = 0.50$	0.25	0.24	$0.25(0.24) = 0.0600$
3	$3 - 1.50 = 1.50$	2.25	0.14	$2.25(0.14) = 0.3150$
4	$4 - 1.50 = 2.50$	6.25	0.04	$6.25(0.04) = 0.2500$
5	$5 - 1.50 = 3.50$	12.25	0.01	$12.25(0.01) = \underline{0.1225}$
				$\sigma^2 = 1.2500$

At this point our interpretation of the variance and the standard deviation is limited to comparisons of the variability of different random variables. For example, if the daily sales data from a second DiCarlo dealership in Albany, New York, reported $\sigma^2 = 2.56$ and $\sigma = 1.6$, we can conclude that the number of cars sold per day at this dealership exhibits more variability than at the first DiCarlo dealership, where $\sigma^2 = 1.25$ and $\sigma = 1.118$. Later in this chapter we will discuss the normal distribution. At that time we will show that the variance and the standard deviation of a random variable are essential for making probability calculations.

3.3

THE BINOMIAL DISTRIBUTION

In this section we consider a class of experiments possessing the following characteristics:

1. The overall experiment can be described in terms of a sequence of n identical experiments called *trials*.
2. Two outcomes are possible on each trial. We refer to one outcome as a *success* and the other as a *failure*.
3. The probabilities of the two outcomes do not change from one trial to the next.
4. The trials are independent (i.e., the outcome of one trial does not affect the outcome of any other trial).

Experiments that satisfy conditions 2, 3, and 4 are said to be generated by a *Bernoulli process*. In addition, if condition 1 is satisfied (there are n trials), we say we have a *binomial experiment*. An important discrete random variable associated with the binomial experiment is the number of successful outcomes in the n trials. If we let x denote the value of this random variable, then x can have a value of $0, 1, 2, 3, \ldots, n$, depending on the number of successes observed in the n trials. The probability distribution associated with this random variable is called the *binomial probability distribution*.

In cases where the binomial distribution is applicable, the following mathematical formula can be used to compute the probability of any possible value for the random variable:

$$f(x) = \frac{n!}{x!(n - x)!} p^x (1 - p)^{n-x} \qquad x = 0, 1, \ldots, n \qquad (3.5)$$

where

$$n = \text{number of trials}$$
$$p = \text{probability of success on one trial}$$
$$x = \text{number of successes in } n \text{ trials}$$
$$f(x) = \text{probability of } x \text{ successes in } n \text{ trials}$$

The term $n!$ in the above expression is referred to as *n factorial*. It is defined as follows:

$$n! = n(n - 1)(n - 2) \cdots (2)(1)$$

For example, $4! = (4)(3)(2)(1) = 24$. Also, by definition, the special case of zero factorial is $0! = 1$.

The Nastke Clothing Store Problem

As an illustration of the binomial probability distribution, let us consider the experiment of customers entering the Nastke Clothing Store. To keep the problem relatively small, let us restrict our attention to the next three customers who enter the store. If, based on past experience, the store manager estimates the probability that any one customer will make a purchase to be 0.30, what is the probability that exactly two of the next three customers make a purchase?

We first want to demonstrate that three customers entering the clothing store and electing whether or not to make a purchase can be viewed as a binomial experiment. Checking the four requirements for a binomial experiment, we see the following:

1. The experiment can be described as a sequence of three identical trials, one trial for each of the three customers who will enter the store.
2. Two outcomes—the customer makes a purchase (success) or the customer does not make a purchase (failure)—are possible for each trial.
3. The probabilities of the purchase (0.30) and no purchase (0.70) outcomes are assumed to be the same for all customers.
4. The purchase decision of each customer is independent of the decisions of the other customers.

Thus if we define the random variable x as the number of customers making a purchase (i.e., the number of successes in the three trials), we see that the requirements of the binomial probability distribution have been satisfied.

With $n = 3$ trials and the probability of a purchase $p = 0.30$ for each customer, equation (3.5) can be used to compute the probability of two customers making a purchase. This probability, denoted $f(2)$, is

$$f(2) = \frac{3!}{2!1!} (0.30)^2 (0.70)^1$$
$$= \frac{3 \times 2 \times 1}{2 \times 1 \times 1} (0.30)^2 (0.70)^1 = 0.189$$

Similarly, the probability of no customers making a purchase, denoted $f(0)$, is

$$f(0) = \frac{3!}{0!3!}(0.30)^0(0.70)^3$$

$$= \frac{3 \times 2 \times 1}{1 \times 3 \times 2 \times 1}(0.30)^0(0.70)^3 = 0.343$$

Use equation (3.5) to show that the probabilities of one and three purchases are $f(1) = 0.441$ and $f(3) = 0.027$. The binomial probability distribution for the Nastke Clothing Store problem is summarized in Table 3.6 and Figure 3.2.

Table 3.6
Probability Distribution for the Number
of Customers Making a Purchase

x	$f(x)$
0	0.343
1	0.441
2	0.189
3	0.027
Total	1.000

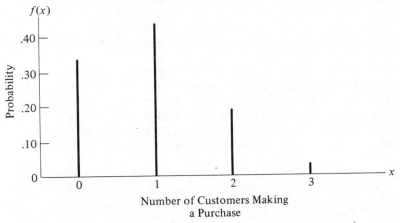

Figure 3.2
Graphical Representation of the Probability Distribution
of x for the Nastke Clothing Store Problem

If we consider any variation of the Nastke problem, such as ten customers rather than three entering the store, the binomial probability function given by equation (3.5) is still applicable. For example, the probability that exactly four of the ten customers making a purchase is

$$f(4) = \frac{10!}{4!6!}(0.30)^4(0.70)^6 = 0.2001$$

With the use of equation (3.5), tables have been developed that provide the probability of x successes in n trials for a binomial experiment. These tables are generally easier and quicker to use than equation (3.5), especially when the number of trials involved is large.

Table 3.7
Selected Values from the Binomial Probability Tables
Example: $n = 10$, $x = 4$, $p = 0.30$; $f(4) = 0.2001$

							p				
n	x	0.05	0.10	0.15	0.20	0.25	0.30	0.35	0.40	0.45	0.50
9	0	0.6302	0.3874	0.2316	0.1342	0.0751	0.0404	0.0207	0.0101	0.0046	0.0020
	1	0.2985	0.3874	0.3679	0.3020	0.2253	0.1556	0.1004	0.0605	0.0339	0.0176
	2	0.0629	0.1722	0.2597	0.3020	0.3003	0.2668	0.2162	0.1612	0.1110	0.0703
	3	0.0077	0.0446	0.1069	0.1762	0.2336	0.2668	0.2716	0.2508	0.2119	0.1641
	4	0.0006	0.0074	0.0283	0.0661	0.1168	0.1715	0.2194	0.2508	0.2600	0.2461
	5	0.0000	0.0008	0.0050	0.0165	0.0389	0.0735	0.1181	0.1672	0.2128	0.2461
	6	0.0000	0.0001	0.0006	0.0028	0.0087	0.0210	0.0424	0.0743	0.1160	0.1641
	7	0.0000	0.0000	0.0000	0.0003	0.0012	0.0039	0.0098	0.0212	0.0407	0.0703
	8	0.0000	0.0000	0.0000	0.0000	0.0001	0.0004	0.0013	0.0035	0.0083	0.0176
	9	0.0000	0.0000	0.0000	0.0000	0.0000	0.0000	0.0001	0.0003	0.0008	0.0020
10	0	0.5987	0.3487	0.1969	0.1074	0.0563	0.0282	0.0135	0.0060	0.0025	0.0010
	1	0.3151	0.3874	0.3474	0.2684	0.1877	0.1211	0.0725	0.0403	0.0207	0.0098
	2	0.0746	0.1937	0.2759	0.3020	0.2816	0.2335	0.1757	0.1209	0.0763	0.0439
	3	0.0105	0.0574	0.1298	0.2013	0.2503	0.2668	0.2522	0.2150	0.1665	0.1172
	4	0.0010	0.0112	0.0401	0.0881	0.1460	**0.2001**	0.2377	0.2508	0.2384	0.2051
	5	0.0001	0.0015	0.0085	0.0264	0.0584	0.1029	0.1536	0.2007	0.2340	0.2461
	6	0.0000	0.0001	0.0012	0.0055	0.0162	0.0368	0.0689	0.1115	0.1596	0.2051
	7	0.0000	0.0000	0.0001	0.0008	0.0031	0.0090	0.0212	0.0425	0.0746	0.1172
	8	0.0000	0.0000	0.0000	0.0001	0.0004	0.0014	0.0043	0.0106	0.0229	0.0439
	9	0.0000	0.0000	0.0000	0.0000	0.0000	0.0001	0.0005	0.0016	0.0042	0.0098
	10	0.0000	0.0000	0.0000	0.0000	0.0000	0.0000	0.0000	0.0001	0.0003	0.0010
11	0	0.5688	0.3138	0.1673	0.0859	0.0422	0.0198	0.0088	0.0036	0.0014	0.0005
	1	0.3293	0.3835	0.3248	0.2362	0.1549	0.0932	0.0518	0.0266	0.0125	0.0054
	2	0.0867	0.2131	0.2866	0.2953	0.2581	0.1998	0.1395	0.0887	0.0531	0.0269
	3	0.0137	0.0710	0.1517	0.2215	0.2581	0.2568	0.2254	0.1774	0.1259	0.0806
	4	0.0014	0.0158	0.0536	0.1107	0.1721	0.2201	0.2428	0.2365	0.2060	0.1611
	5	0.0001	0.0025	0.0132	0.0388	0.0803	0.1321	0.1830	0.2207	0.2360	0.2256
	6	0.0000	0.0003	0.0023	0.0097	0.0268	0.0566	0.0985	0.1471	0.1931	0.2256
	7	0.0000	0.0000	0.0003	0.0017	0.0064	0.0173	0.0379	0.0701	0.1128	0.1611
	8	0.0000	0.0000	0.0000	0.0002	0.0011	0.0037	0.0102	0.0234	0.0462	0.0806
	9	0.0000	0.0000	0.0000	0.0000	0.0001	0.0005	0.0018	0.0052	0.0126	0.0269
	10	0.0000	0.0000	0.0000	0.0000	0.0000	0.0000	0.0002	0.0007	0.0021	0.0054
	11	0.0000	0.0000	0.0000	0.0000	0.0000	0.0000	0.0000	0.0000	0.0002	0.0005

Such a table of binomial probability values is provided in Appendix A. We have included a portion of this table in Table 3.7. In order to use this table it is necessary to specify the values of n, p, and x for the binomial experiment of interest. Check the use of this table by employing it to verify the probability of four successes in ten trials for the Nastke Clothing Store problem. Note that the value of $f(4) = 0.2001$ can be read directly from the table of binomial probabilities, making it unnecessary to perform the calculations required by equation (3.5).

The Expected Value and Variance for the Binomial Probability Distribution

Given the probability distribution in Table 3.6, we can use equation (3.3) to compute the expected value or expected number of customers making a purchase:

$$\mu = \sum xf(x) = 0(0.343) + 1(0.441) + 2(0.189) + 3(0.027) = 0.9$$

Note that we could have obtained this same expected value simply by multiplying n (the number of trials) by p (the probability of success on any one trial):

$$np = 3(0.30) = 0.9$$

For the special case of a binomial probability distribution, the expected value of the random variable is given by

$$\mu = np \tag{3.6}$$

Thus, if the probability distribution is known to be binomial, it is not necessary to carry out the detailed calculations required by equation (3.3) in order to compute the expected value.

Suppose that during the next month Nastke's Clothing Store expects 1000 customers to enter the store. What is the expected number of customers who will make a purchase? Using equation (3.6) the answer is $\mu = np = (1000)(0.3) = 300$. Thus, in order to increase the expected number of sales, Nastke's must induce more customers to enter the store and/or somehow increase the probability that any individual customer will make a purchase after entering.

For the special case of a binomial distribution the variance of the random variable is

$$\sigma^2 = np(1 - p) \tag{3.7}$$

For the Nastke Clothing Store problem with three customers, we see that the variance and standard deviation for the number of customers making a purchase are

$$\sigma^2 = np(1 - p) = 3(0.3)(0.7) = 0.63$$
$$\sigma = \sqrt{0.63} = 0.79$$

3.4

THE POISSON DISTRIBUTION

In this section we will consider a discrete random variable that is often useful when dealing with the number of occurrences of an event over a specified interval of time or space. For example, the random variable of interest might be the number of arrivals at a carwash in 1 hour, the number of repairs needed in 10 miles of highway, or the number of leaks in 100 miles of pipeline. If the two assumptions listed below are satisfied, it can be shown that the probability function of the random variable is given by equation (3.8). It is referred to as the *Poisson probability function*.

1. The probability of an occurrence of the event is the same for any two intervals of equal length.
2. The occurrence or nonoccurrence of the event in any interval is independent of the occurrence or nonoccurrence in any other interval.

$$f(x) = \frac{\lambda^x e^{-\lambda}}{x!} \quad \text{for } x = 0,1,2,\ldots \tag{3.8}$$

where

$$\lambda = \text{mean or average number of occurrences in an interval}$$
$$e = 2.71828$$
$$x = \text{number of occurrences of the event}$$
$$f(x) = \text{probability of } x \text{ occurrences}$$

Before we consider a specific example to see how the Poisson distribution can be applied, note that equation (3.8) shows that there is no upper limit to the number of possible values that a Poisson random variable can take on. That is, although x is still a discrete random variable with $x = 0,1,2,\ldots$, the Poisson random variable ha s no specific upper limit.

An Example Involving Time Intervals

Suppose that we are interested in the number of arrivals at the drive-in teller window of a bank during a 15-minute period on weekday mornings. If we can assume that the probability of a car arriving is the same for any two time periods of equal length and that the arrival or nonarrival of a car in any time period is independent of the arrival or nonarrival in any other time period, the Poisson probability function is applicable. Assuming that these conditions are satisfied and that an analysis of historical data shows that the average number of cars arriving in a 15-minute period of time is 10, the Poisson probability function with $\lambda = 10$ applies:

$$f(x) = \frac{\lambda^x e^{-\lambda}}{x!} = \frac{10^x e^{-10}}{x!} \quad \text{for } x = 0,1,2,\ldots$$

If we wanted to know the probability of exactly five arrivals in 15 minutes, we would set $x = 5$ and obtain[2]

---

[2]Values of $e^{-\lambda}$ can be found in Appendix D.

$$f(5) = \frac{10^5 e^{-10}}{5!} = 0.0378$$

Although this probability was determined by evaluating the probability function with $\lambda = 10$ and $x = 5$, it is often easier to refer to tables for the Poisson probability distribution. These tables provide probabilities for specific values of x and λ. We have included such a table as Appendix B. For convenience we have reproduced a portion of this table as Table 3.8. Note that in order to use the table of Poisson probabilities we need know only the values of x and λ. Thus from Table 3.8 we see that the probability of five arrivals in a 15-minute period is found by locating the value in the row of the table corresponding to $x = 5$ and the column of the table corresponding to $\lambda = 10$. Hence we obtain $f(5) = 0.0378$.

Table 3.8
Selected Values from the Poisson Probability Tables
Example: $\lambda = 10$, $x = 5$; $f(5) = 0.0378$

x	9.1	9.2	9.3	9.4	9.5	9.6	9.7	9.8	9.9	10
0	0.0001	0.0001	0.0001	0.0001	0.0001	0.0001	0.0001	0.0001	0.0001	0.0000
1	0.0010	0.0009	0.0009	0.0008	0.0007	0.0007	0.0006	0.0005	0.0005	0.0005
2	0.0046	0.0043	0.0040	0.0037	0.0034	0.0031	0.0029	0.0027	0.0025	0.0023
3	0.0140	0.0131	0.0123	0.0115	0.0107	0.0100	0.0093	0.0087	0.0081	0.0076
4	0.0319	0.0302	0.0285	0.0269	0.0254	0.0240	0.0226	0.0213	0.0201	0.0189
5	0.0581	0.0555	0.0530	0.0506	0.0483	0.0460	0.0439	0.0418	0.0398	**0.0378**
6	0.0881	0.0851	0.0822	0.0793	0.0764	0.0736	0.0709	0.0682	0.0656	0.0631
7	0.1145	0.1118	0.1091	0.1064	0.1037	0.1010	0.0982	0.0955	0.0928	0.0901
8	0.1302	0.1286	0.1269	0.1251	0.1232	0.1212	0.1191	0.1170	0.1148	0.1126
9	0.1317	0.1315	0.1311	0.1306	0.1300	0.1293	0.1284	0.1274	0.1263	0.1251
10	0.1198	0.1210	0.1219	0.1228	0.1235	0.1241	0.1245	0.1249	0.1250	0.1251
11	0.0991	0.1012	0.1031	0.1049	0.1067	0.1083	0.1098	0.1112	0.1125	0.1137
12	0.0752	0.0776	0.0799	0.0822	0.0844	0.0866	0.0888	0.0908	0.0928	0.0948
13	0.0526	0.0549	0.0572	0.0594	0.0617	0.0640	0.0662	0.0685	0.0707	0.0729
14	0.0342	0.0361	0.0380	0.0399	0.0419	0.0439	0.0459	0.0479	0.0500	0.0521
15	0.0208	0.0221	0.0235	0.0250	0.0265	0.0281	0.0297	0.0313	0.0330	0.0347
16	0.0118	0.0127	0.0137	0.0147	0.0157	0.0168	0.0180	0.0192	0.0204	0.0217
17	0.0063	0.0069	0.0075	0.0081	0.0088	0.0095	0.0103	0.0111	0.0119	0.0128
18	0.0032	0.0035	0.0039	0.0042	0.0046	0.0051	0.0055	0.0060	0.0065	0.0071
19	0.0015	0.0017	0.0019	0.0021	0.0023	0.0026	0.0028	0.0031	0.0034	0.0037
20	0.0007	0.0008	0.0009	0.0010	0.0011	0.0012	0.0014	0.0015	0.0017	0.0019
21	0.0003	0.0003	0.0004	0.0004	0.0005	0.0006	0.0006	0.0007	0.0008	0.0009
22	0.0001	0.0001	0.0002	0.0002	0.0002	0.0002	0.0003	0.0003	0.0004	0.0004
23	0.0000	0.0001	0.0001	0.0001	0.0001	0.0001	0.0001	0.0001	0.0002	0.0002
24	0.0000	0.0000	0.0000	0.0000	0.0000	0.0000	0.0000	0.0001	0.0001	0.0001

An Example Involving Length or Distance Intervals

Let us illustrate the variety of applications where the Poisson probability distribution is useful. Suppose that we are concerned with the occurrence of major defects in a section of highway 1 month after resurfacing. We assume that the probability of a defect is the same for any two intervals of equal length, and that the occurrence or nonoccurrence of a defect in any one interval is independent of the occurrence or nonoccurrence in any other interval. Thus the Poisson probability distribution can be applied.

Suppose we learn that major defects 1 month after resurfacing occur at the average rate of two per mile. Let us find the probability that there will be no major defects in a particular 3-mile section of the highway. Since we are interested in an interval with a length of 3 miles, λ = (2 defects/mile)(3 miles) = 6 represents the expected number of major defects over the 3-mile section of highway. Thus by using equation (3.8) or Appendix B with λ = 6 and x = 0 we see that the probability of no major defects is 0.0025. Thus it is very unlikely that there will be no major defects in the 3-mile section. In fact, there is a $1 - 0.0025 = 0.9975$ probability of at least one major defect in the highway section.

3.5

CONTINUOUS RANDOM VARIABLES

In this section we will introduce probability distributions for continuous random variables. Recall from Section 3.1 that random variables which can take on any value in a certain interval or collection of intervals are said to be continuous. Some examples of continuous random variables are as follows:

1. The *number of ounces* of soup placed in a can labeled ''8 ounces''
2. The *flight time* of an airplane traveling from Chicago to New York
3. The *lifetime* of the picture tube in a new television set
4. The *drilling depth* required to reach oil in an offshore drilling operation

In order to understand the nature of continuous random variables more fully, suppose that in the first example we find that one can of soup has 8.2 ounces and another 8.3 ounces. Other cans could weigh 8.25 ounces, 8.225 ounces, etc. In fact, the actual weight can be any numerical value from 0 ounces for an empty can to, say, 10.00 ounces for a can filled to capacity. Since there are an infinite number of values in this interval, we can no longer list each value of the random variable and then identify its associated probability. In fact, for continuous random variables we will need to introduce a new method for computing the probabilities associated with the values of the random variable.

An Example Using the Uniform Distribution

Let x denote the flight time of an airplane traveling from Chicago to New York. Assume that the minimum time is 2 hours and that the maximum time is 2 hours and 20 minutes. Thus, in terms of minutes, the flight time can be any value in the interval from 120 minutes to 140 minutes (e.g., 124 minutes, 125.48 minutes, etc.). Since the random variable x can take on any value from 120 to 140 minutes, x is a continuous rather than a discrete random variable. Assume that sufficient actual flight data are available to conclude that the probability of a flight time between 120 and 121 minutes is the same as the probability of a flight time within any other 1-minute interval up to and including 140 minutes. With every 1-minute interval being equally likely, the random variable x is said to have *a uniform probability distribution*. The following function, referred to as a *probability density function*, describes the uniform probability distribution for the flight time random variable:

$$f(x) = \begin{cases} \dfrac{1}{20} & \text{for } 120 \leq x \leq 140 \\ \\ 0 & \text{elsewhere} \end{cases} \tag{3.9}$$

A graph of this probability density function is shown in Figure 3.3. In general, the uniform probability density function for a random variable x is

$$f(x) = \begin{cases} \dfrac{1}{b - a} & \text{for } a \leq x \leq b \\ \\ 0 & \text{elsewhere} \end{cases} \tag{3.10}$$

In the flight time example, $a = 120$ and $b = 140$.

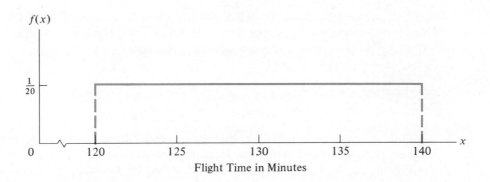

Figure 3.3
Uniform Probability Density
Function for Flight Time

In the graph of a probability density function, $f(x)$ shows the height or value of the function at any particular value of x. Because we have a *uniform* probability density function for flight time the height or value of the function is the same for each value of x between 120 and 140. That is, $f(x) = \frac{1}{20}$ for all values of x between 120 and 140. The probability density function $f(x)$, unlike the probability function for a discrete random variable, represents the height of the function at any particular value of x and *not* probability. Recall that for each value of a discrete random variable (say, $x = 2$), the probability function yielded the probability of x having *exactly* that value [for example, $f(2)$]. However, since a continuous random variable has an infinite number of possible values, we can no longer identify the probability for each specific value of x. Rather, we must consider probability in terms of the likelihood that a random variable has a value within a *specified interval*. For example, in the flight time problem an acceptable probability question is, What is the probability that the flight time is between 120 and 130 minutes? That is, what is $P(120 \leq x \leq 130)$? Since the flight time must be between 120 and 140 minutes and since the probability is uniform over this interval, we feel comfortable saying that $P(120 \leq x \leq 130) = 0.50$. Indeed, as we shall see, this is correct.

Area as a Measure of Probability

Refer to Figure 3.4. Specifically, consider the *area under the graph of $f(x)$* in the interval from 120 to 130. Note that the region is rectangular in shape, and that the area of a rectangle is simply the width times the height. With the width of the interval equal to $130 - 120 = 10$ and the height of the graph $f(x) = \frac{1}{20}$, we have area = width × height = $10(\frac{1}{20}) = \frac{10}{20} = 0.50$.

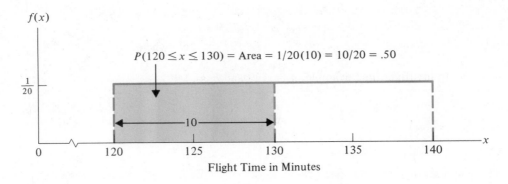

Figure 3.4
Area Provides Probability
of Flight Time

What observation can you make about the area under the graph of $f(x)$ and probability? They are identical! Indeed, this is true for all continuous random variables. Namely, once a probability density function $f(x)$ has been identified for a continuous random variable, then the probability that x takes on a value between some lower value a and some higher value b can be found by computing the *area* under the graph of $f(x)$ over the interval a to b.

Once we have the appropriate probability distribution and accept the interpretation of area as probability, we can answer any number of probability questions. For example, what is the probability of a flight time between 128 and 136 minutes? The width of the interval is $136 - 128 = 8$. With the uniform height of $\frac{1}{20}$, we see $P(128 \leq x \leq 136) = \frac{8}{20} = 0.40$.

Note that $P(120 \leq x \leq 140) = 20(\frac{1}{20}) = 1$. That is, the total area under the $f(x)$ graph is equal to 1. This property holds for all continuous probability distributions and is the analog of the condition that the sum of the probabilities has to equal 1 for a discrete probability distribution. For a continuous probability distribution we must also require that $f(x) \geq 0$ for all values of x. This is the analog of the requirement that $f(x) \geq 0$ for discrete probability distributions.

When we deal with continuous random variables and probability distributions, two major differences stand out as compared to the treatment of their discrete counterparts:

1. We no longer talk about the probability of the random variable taking on a particular value. Instead we talk about the probability of the random variable taking on a value within some given interval.
2. The probability of the random variable taking on a value within some given interval is defined to be the area under the graph of the probability density function over the interval. This implies that the probability that a continuous random variable takes on any particular value is zero, since the area under the graph of $f(x)$ at a single point is zero.

3.6

THE NORMAL DISTRIBUTION

Perhaps the most important probability distribution used to describe a continuous random variable is the *normal probability distribution*. The normal probability distribution is applicable in a great many practical problem situations. Its probability density function has the form of the bell-shaped curve shown in Figure 3.5.

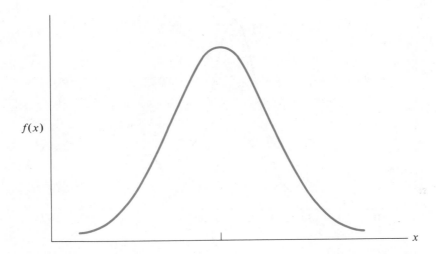

Figure 3.5
Bell-Shaped Curve of the
Normal Probability Distribution

The mathematical form of the probability density function for the uniform distribution was fairly simple: $f(x) = 1/(b - a)$ for $a \leq x \leq b$. The mathematical function that provides the bell-shaped curve of the normal probability density function is more complex. The mathematical formula is

$$f(x) = \frac{1}{\sigma \sqrt{2\pi}} e^{-(x-\mu)^2/2\sigma^2} \qquad \text{for } -\infty < x < \infty \qquad (3.11)$$

where

μ = mean or expected value of the random variable x

σ^2 = variance of the random variable x

σ = standard deviation of the random variable x

π = 3.14159

e = 2.71828

Recall from the discussion of continuous random variables in the preceding section that $f(x)$ is the height of the curve at a particular value of x. Thus once the mean (μ) and either the standard deviation (σ) or variance (σ^2) are specified, equation (3.11) can be used to determine the graph for the corresponding normal distribution. Figure 3.6 shows two normal distributions, one with μ = 50 and σ = 15 and another with μ = 50 and σ = 7.5. Note in particular the effect that the standard deviation σ has on the general shape of the normal curve. A larger standard deviation tends to flatten and broaden the curve. This of course, is what we should expect, since larger values of σ indicate a larger variability in the values of the random variable.

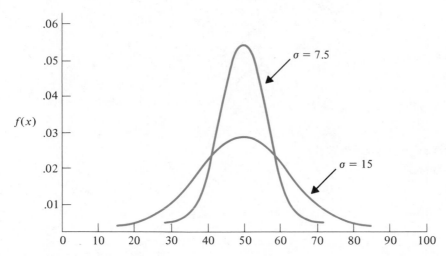

Figure 3.6
Other Normal Distributions
with μ = 50

Fortunately, whenever we use the normal distribution to answer probability questions, we do not have to use the probability density function as shown in equation (3.11). In fact, when we use the normal distribution we will have tables of probability values [areas under the $f(x)$ curve] that can provide the desired probability information. In order to learn how to use the tables of areas or probabilities for the normal distribution, we must first introduce the standard normal distribution.

The Standard Normal Distribution

A random variable that has a normal distribution with a mean of 0 and a standard deviation of 1 is said to have a *standard normal distribution*. We use the letter z to designate this particular normal random variable. The graph of the standard normal distribution is shown in Figure 3.7. Note that it has the same general appearance as other normal distributions,

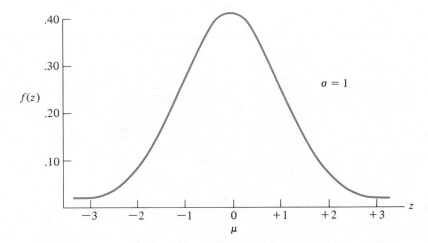

Figure 3.7
Standard Normal
Distribution

but with the special properties of $\mu = 0$ and $\sigma = 1$. The units on the horizontal axis (z) measure the number of standard deviations from the mean.

Recall the procedure for finding probabilities associated with a continuous random variable. We wish to determine the probability of the random variable having a value in a specified interval from a to b. Thus we have to find the area under the curve in the interval from a to b. In the previous section we saw that finding probabilities, or areas under the curve, for a uniform distribution was relatively easy. All we had to do was multiply the width of the interval by the height of the graph. However, finding areas under the normal distribution curve appears at first glance to be much more difficult, since the height of the curve varies. The mathematical technique for obtaining these areas is beyond the scope of the text, but fortunately tables are available that provide the areas or probability values for the standard normal distribution. Table 3.9 is such a table of areas. This table is also available as Appendix C.

Let us see how Table 3.9 is used to find probabilities. First note that values of z appear in the left-hand column, with the second decimal value of z appearing in the top row. For example, for a z value of 1.00 we find the 1.0 in the left-hand column and 0.00 in the top row. Then by looking in the body of the table we find a value of 0.3413 corresponding to the 1.00 value for z. The value 0.3413 is the area under the curve between the mean ($z = 0.00$) and $z = 1.00$. This is shown graphically in Figure 3.8.

Thus we see that the values in Table 3.9 provide *the area under the curve between the mean ($z = 0.00$) and any specified positive value of z. For another example, we can use the table to find that the area or probability of a z value in the interval $z = 0.00$ to $z = 1.25$ is 0.3944.

Suppose that we want the probability of obtaining a z value between $z = -1.00$ and $z = 1.00$. We already have used Table 3.9 to find that the probability of a z value between $z = 0.00$ and $z = 1.00$ is 0.3413. Note now that the normal distribution is symmetric. That is, the shape of the curve to the left of the mean is the mirror image of the shape of the curve to the right of the mean. Thus the probability of a z value between $z = 0.00$ and $z = -1.00$ is the same as that between $z = 0.00$ and $z = 1.00$; that is,

Table 3.9
Areas or Probabilities for the Standard Normal Distribution

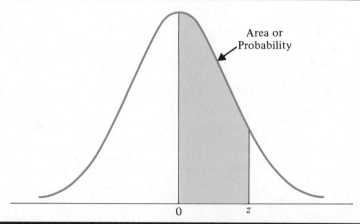

z	0.00	0.01	0.02	0.03	0.04	0.05	0.06	0.07	0.08	0.09
0.0	0.0000	0.0040	0.0080	0.0120	0.0160	0.0199	0.0239	0.0279	0.0319	0.0359
0.1	0.0398	0.0438	0.0478	0.0517	0.0557	0.0596	0.0636	0.0675	0.0714	0.0753
0.2	0.0793	0.0832	0.0871	0.0910	0.0948	0.0987	0.1026	0.1064	0.1103	0.1141
0.3	0.1179	0.1217	0.1255	0.1293	0.1331	0.1368	0.1406	0.1443	0.1480	0.1517
0.4	0.1554	0.1591	0.1628	0.1664	0.1700	0.1736	0.1772	0.1808	0.1844	0.1879
0.5	0.1915	0.1950	0.1985	0.2019	0.2054	0.2088	0.2123	0.2157	0.2190	0.2224
0.6	0.2257	0.2291	0.2324	0.2357	0.2389	0.2422	0.2454	0.2486	0.2518	0.2549
0.7	0.2580	0.2612	0.2642	0.2673	0.2704	0.2734	0.2764	0.2794	0.2823	0.2852
0.8	0.2881	0.2910	0.2939	0.2967	0.2995	0.3023	0.3051	0.3078	0.3106	0.3133
0.9	0.3159	0.3186	0.3212	0.3238	0.3264	0.3289	0.3315	0.3340	0.3365	0.3389
1.0	0.3413	0.3438	0.3461	0.3485	0.3508	0.3531	0.3554	0.3577	0.3599	0.3621
1.1	0.3643	0.3665	0.3686	0.3708	0.3729	0.3749	0.3770	0.3790	0.3810	0.3830
1.2	0.3849	0.3869	0.3888	0.3907	0.3925	0.3944	0.3962	0.3980	0.3997	0.4015
1.3	0.4032	0.4049	0.4066	0.4082	0.4099	0.4115	0.4131	0.4147	0.4162	0.4177
1.4	0.4192	0.4207	0.4222	0.4236	0.4251	0.4265	0.4279	0.4292	0.4306	0.4319
1.5	0.4332	0.4345	0.4357	0.4370	0.4382	0.4394	0.4406	0.4418	0.4429	0.4441
1.6	0.4452	0.4463	0.4474	0.4484	0.4495	0.4505	0.4515	0.4525	0.4535	0.4545
1.7	0.4554	0.4564	0.4573	0.4582	0.4591	0.4599	0.4608	0.4616	0.4625	0.4633
1.8	0.4641	0.4649	0.4656	0.4664	0.4671	0.4678	0.4686	0.4693	0.4699	0.4706
1.9	0.4713	0.4719	0.4726	0.4732	0.4738	0.4744	0.4750	0.4756	0.4761	0.4767
2.0	0.4772	0.4778	0.4783	0.4788	0.4793	0.4798	0.4803	0.4808	0.4812	0.4817
2.1	0.4821	0.4826	0.4830	0.4834	0.4838	0.4842	0.4846	0.4850	0.4854	0.4857
2.2	0.4861	0.4864	0.4868	0.4871	0.4875	0.4878	0.4881	0.4884	0.4887	0.4890
2.3	0.4893	0.4896	0.4898	0.4901	0.4904	0.4906	0.4909	0.4911	0.4913	0.4916
2.4	0.4918	0.4920	0.4922	0.4925	0.4927	0.4929	0.4931	0.4932	0.4934	0.4936
2.5	0.4938	0.4940	0.4941	0.4943	0.4945	0.4946	0.4948	0.4949	0.4951	0.4952
2.6	0.4953	0.4955	0.4956	0.4957	0.4959	0.4960	0.4961	0.4962	0.4963	0.4964
2.7	0.4965	0.4966	0.4967	0.4968	0.4969	0.4970	0.4971	0.4972	0.4973	0.4974
2.8	0.4974	0.4975	0.4976	0.4977	0.4977	0.4978	0.4979	0.4979	0.4980	0.4981
2.9	0.4981	0.4982	0.4982	0.4983	0.4884	0.4984	0.4985	0.4985	0.4986	0.4986
3.0	0.4986	0.4987	0.4987	0.4988	0.4988	0.4989	0.4989	0.4989	0.4990	0.4990

0.3413. Hence the probability of a z value between $z = -1.00$ and $z = 1.00$ is $0.3413 + 0.3413 = 0.6826$. This is shown graphically in Figure 3.9.

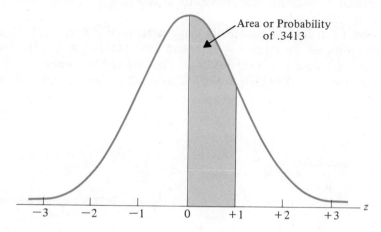

Figure 3.8
Probability of z between
0.00 and +1.00

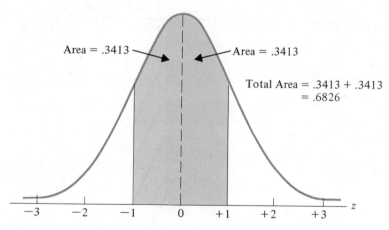

Figure 3.9
Probability of z between
−1.00 and +1.00

Similarly, we can find that the probability of a z value between -2.00 and $+2.00$ is $0.4772 + 0.4772 = 0.9544$, whereas the probability of a z value between -3.00 and $+3.00$ is $0.4986 + 0.4986 = 0.9972$. Since we know that the total probability or total area under the curve for any continuous random variable must be 1.0000, the probability of 0.9972 tells us the value of z will almost always fall between -3.00 and $+3.00$. Note that the figures depicting the standard normal distribution show this graphically.

Look now at two final examples of computing areas for the standard normal distribution. First let us find the probability that z is greater than 2.00. We see from Table

3.9 that the area between $z = 0.00$ and $z = 2.00$ is 0.4772. Since 0.5000 is the total area above the mean, the area above $z = 2.00$ must be $0.5000 - 0.4772 = 0.0228$. This is shown graphically in Figure 3.10. Again, because of the fact that the normal distribution is symmetric, the probability of obtaining a value of z less than $z = -2.00$ is also 0.0228.

Now let us find the probability that z is between 1.00 and 2.00. We first note that the area between the mean $z = 0.00$ and $z = 2.00$ is 0.4772. The area between the mean $z = 0.00$ and $z = 1.00$ is 0.3413. Thus the area between $z = 1.00$ and $z = 2.00$ must be $0.4772 - 0.3413 = 0.1359$. This result is shown graphically in Figure 3.11.

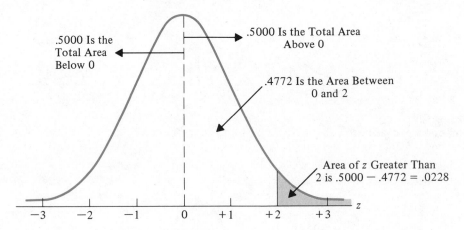

Figure 3.10
Probability of z
Greater than 2.00

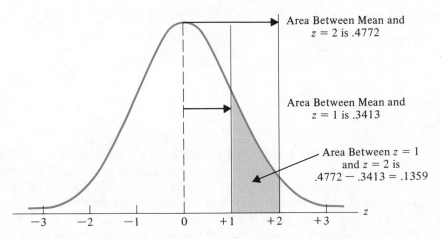

Figure 3.11
Probability of z between
1.00 and 2.00

Computing Probabilities for Any Normal Distribution by Converting to the Standard Normal Distribution

The reason that we have been discussing the standard normal distribution so extensively is that probabilities for any normal distribution can be computed by first converting to the standard normal distribution. Thus when we have a normal distribution with any mean μ and any standard deviation σ, we can answer probability questions about this distribution by converting to the standard normal distribution. We then use Table 3.9 and the appropriate z values to find the probability. The formula used to convert any normal random variable x with mean μ and standard deviation σ to the standard normal distribution is

$$z = \frac{x - \mu}{\sigma} \qquad (3.12)$$

When used in this way z is a measure of the number of standard deviations that x is from μ.

In order to see how the conversion to the z value allows us to use the standard normal distribution to compute probabilities for any normal distribution, let us consider an example. Suppose that we have a normal distribution with $\mu = 10$ and $\sigma = 2$. This normal distribution is shown graphically in Figure 3.12. Note that in addition to the values of the random variable shown on the x axis, we have included a second axis (the z axis) to show that for each value of x there is a corresponding value of z. For example, when $x = 10$ the corresponding z value (the number of standard deviations away from the mean) is $z = (x - \mu)/\sigma = (10 - 10)/2 = 0$. Similarly, for $x = 14$ we have $z = (x - \mu)/\sigma = (14 - 10)/2 = 4/2 = 2$.

Now suppose we want to know the probability that the random variable x is between 10 and 14—that is, $P(10 \leq x \leq 14)$. We do not have tables that provide this probability

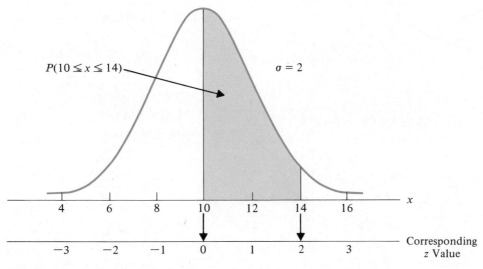

Figure 3.12
Normal Distribution with $\mu = 10$ and $\sigma = 2$
Also Shows Corresponding z Values

directly. However, note that in Figure 3.12 the area under the curve (probability) for x between 10 and 14 is the *same* as the area under the curve for z between 0 and 2. Using $z = 2.00$ and Table 3.9, we find that the area or probability of z being between 0 and 2 is 0.4772. Thus we conclude that the probability of x being between 10 and 14 is also 0.4772.

The above procedure applies to any normal distribution problem. That is, for any x value there is a corresponding z value given by equation (3.12). To find the probability that x is in a specified interval, simply convert the x interval to its corresponding z interval. Then the table for the standard normal distribution can be used to answer the probability question.

The Grear Tire Company Problem

Suppose that the Grear Tire Company has just developed a new steel-belted radial tire that will be sold through a national chain of discount stores. Since the tire is a new product, Grear's management believes that the mileage guarantee offered with the tire will be an important factor in the acceptance of the product. Before finalizing the tire mileage guarantee policy, Grear's management would like some probability information concerning the number of miles the tires will last.

From actual road tests with the tires, Grear's engineering group has estimated the mean tire mileage at $\mu = 36{,}500$ miles and the standard deviation at $\sigma = 5000$ miles. In addition, the data collected indicate that a normal distribution is a reasonable assumption.

Using the normal distribution, what percentage of the tires can be expected to last more than 40,000 miles? In other words, what is the probability that the tire mileage will exceed 40,000? This question can be interpreted as trying to find the area of the shaded region in Figure 3.13.

At $x = 40{,}000$ we have

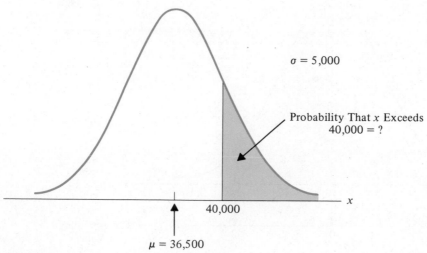

Figure 3.13
Grear Tire Company
Tire Mileage

$$z = \frac{x - \mu}{\sigma} = \frac{40{,}000 - 36{,}500}{5{,}000} = \frac{3{,}500}{5{,}000} = 0.70$$

Thus the probability that the normal distribution for tire mileage will have an x value greater than 40,000 is the same as the probability that the standard normal distribution will have a z value greater than 0.70. Using Table 3.9, we find that the area corresponding to $z = 0.70$ is 0.2580. However, remember that the table always provides the area between the mean and the z value. Thus we know there is a 0.2580 area between the mean and $z = 0.70$. Since the total area above the mean is 0.5000, we must have $0.5000 - 0.2580 = 0.2420$ as the area above $z = 0.70$. In terms of the tire mileage x, we can conclude that there is a 0.2420 probability that x will be above 40,000. Thus about 24.2% of the tires manufactured by Grear can be expected to last more than 40,000 miles.

Let us now assume that Grear is considering a guarantee that will provide a discount on a new set of tires if the mileage on the original tires does not exceed the mileage stated on the guarantee. What should the guarantee mileage be if Grear would like no more than 10% of the tires to be eligible for the discount? This question is interpreted graphically in Figure 3.14. Note that 10% of the area is below the unknown guarantee mileage. With this information we know that 40% of the area must be between the mean and the unknown guarantee mileage. The question is, how many standard deviations (z value) do we have to be *below* the mean to find 40% of the area? If we look up 0.4000 in the *body* of Table 3.9, we see that a 0.4000 area occurs at $z = 1.28$. Since the area is below the mean, we know the z value of interest must be -1.28. This tells us we must be 1.28 standard deviations less than the mean to find the desired guarantee mileage. This mileage is then computed as follows:

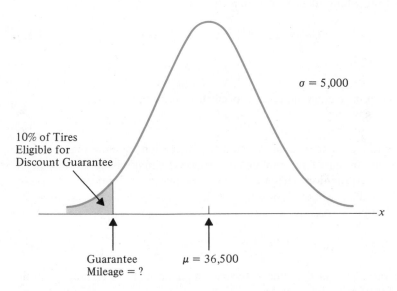

10% of Tires
Eligible for
Discount Guarantee

$\sigma = 5{,}000$

Guarantee
Mileage = ?

$\mu = 36{,}500$

x

Figure 3.14
Grear's Discount
Guarantee

$$\text{Guarantee mileage} = \mu - 1.28\sigma$$
$$= 36,500 - 1.28(5000) = 30,100$$

We see that a guarantee of 30,100 miles will meet the requirement that approximately 10% of the tires will be eligible for the discount. Perhaps with this information the firm will set its tire mileage guarantee policy at 30,000 miles.

Again we see the important role that probability distributions play in providing decision-making information. Namely, once a probability distribution is established for a particular problem situation, it can be used rather quickly and easily to provide probability data about the problem. While the data do not make a decision recommendation directly, they do provide information that helps the decision maker better understand the problem. Ultimately this information may assist the decision maker in reaching a good decision.

3.7

THE EXPONENTIAL DISTRIBUTION

A continuous probability distribution that is useful in computing the probability of the time to complete a task is the exponential distribution. For example, the exponential random variable can refer to the time required to load or unload a truck, the time required to provide service to a customer at a bank teller window, or the time between car arrivals at a carwash. Probability questions in the above examples could be, What is the probability that the time required to load or unload a truck is 30 minutes or less? What is the probability that the time required to service a customer at the bank teller window is 2 minutes or less? What is the probability that the time between car arrivals at a carwash is 1 minute or less? In these instances, the *exponential probability distribution* may be used to provide the requested probability information.

The exponential probability density function is

$$f(x) = \mu e^{-\mu x} \qquad x > 0 \tag{3.13}$$

where

$$\mu = \text{mean or average number of occurrences per time period}$$
$$e = 2.71828$$

As an illustration of the exponential probability distribution, assume that the time between telephone calls for emergency ambulance service at a major hospital follows an exponential probability distribution. Historical data show that the calls occur at a mean or average rate of 1.2 calls per hour. Using $\mu = 1.2$, the appropriate exponential probability density function is

$$f(x) = 1.2e^{-1.2x} \qquad x > 0 \tag{3.14}$$

where the random variable x is the time between telephone calls. The graph of this probability density function is shown in Figure 3.15.

Recall that for any continuous random variable, the area under the curve corresponding to an interval provides the probability that the random variable takes on a value in

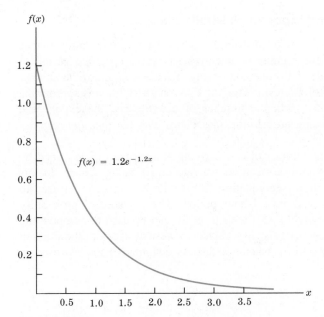

Figure 3.15
Probability Density Function for the
Exponential Distribution with $\mu = 1.2$

that interval. In computing probabilities (areas) for the exponential probability distribution, equation (3.15) can be used to compute the probability that the random variable x is *less than or equal to* some specific value t.

$$P(x \leq t) = 1 - e^{-\mu t} \tag{3.15}$$

For example, in the emergency ambulance service example we use (3.15) with $\mu = 1.2$ and $t = 1$ in order to compute the probability that the time between calls is 1 hour or less.

$$P(x \leq 1) = 1 - e^{-1.2(1)} = 1 - e^{-1.2}$$

Since $e^{-1.2} = 0.3012$ (see Appendix D), the probability that the time between calls is 1 hour or less is

$$P(x \leq 1) = 1 - 0.3012 = 0.6988$$

The probabilities associated with other times t can be computed. For example, what is the probability that the time between calls is 30 minutes or less? Since the mean rate of calls ($\mu = 1.2$ per hour) was expressed in terms of an hourly period, the probability question must be stated on an hourly basis. Thus, the probability that the time between calls is 30 minutes or less is equivalent to the time between calls being 0.5 hours or less. Using equation (3.15) this probability is

$$P(x \leq 0.5) = 1 - e^{-1.2(0.5)}$$
$$= 1 - e^{-0.6} = 1 - 0.5488 = 0.4512$$

Relationship between the Poisson and Exponential Distributions

In Section 3.4 we introduced the Poisson distribution as a discrete distribution that is often useful when dealing with the number of occurrences over a specified period of time. The Poisson random variable is discrete and simply provides a count of the number of occurrences in the time period of interest. When the Poisson distribution is appropriate for finding probabilities associated with the number of occurrences, the exponential distribution is appropriate for finding probabilities associates with the *time between occurrences*.

For example, suppose that the number of cars arriving at a carwash is described by a Poisson probability distribution with a mean arrival rate of 10 cars per hour. In this case the Poisson probability function [see equation (3.8)] with $\lambda = 10$ can be used to compute the probability of x arrivals in a 1-hour period. The exponential probability distribution [see equations (3.14) and (3.15)] with $\mu = 10$ can be used to compute the probability of the time between car arrivals. In Chapter 16 we will use both the Poisson and exponential probability distributions when we discuss quantitative models used to analyze waiting-line systems.

Summary

In this chapter we have continued the study of probability by introducing the important concepts of random variables and probability distributions. We saw that random variables are used to provide numerical descriptions of the outcomes of experiments. When random variables are used, computations of the expected value, variance, and standard deviation can help the decision maker understand characteristics of the problem under study. We discussed the probability distributions for both discrete and continuous random variables.

Of particular interest were the special probability distributions, such as the binomial, Poisson, uniform, normal, and exponential distributions. These distributions are important because they have wide applicability and because they have special formulas and/or tables that make the probability information easily available to a decision maker.

Through a variety of problems and applications we illustrated the role that probability distributions play in providing decision-making information. While the probability values generated by the techniques and methods of this chapter do not by themselves make decision recommendations, they do provide assistance to the decision maker in terms of understanding the uncertainties inherent in the problem. Ultimately, this better understanding may lead to new and better decisions.

Glossary

Random variable   A numerical description of the outcome of an experiment.

Discrete random variable   A random variable that can take on only a finite or countable number of values.

Continuous random variable   A random variable that may take on any value in an interval or collection of intervals.

Probability function   A function, denoted $f(x)$, which provides the probability that a discrete random variable x takes on some specific value.

Discrete probability distribution   A table, graph, or equation describing the values of the random variable and the associated probabilities.

Expected value   A weighted average of the values of the random variable, where the probability function provides the weights. If an experiment can be repeated a large number of times, the expected value can be interpreted as the "long-run average."

Variance   A measure of the dispersion or variability in the random variable. It is a weighted average of the squared deviations from the mean μ.

Standard deviation   The positive square root of the variance.

Binomial probability distribution   The probability distribution for a discrete random variable. It is used to compute the probability of x successes in n trials.

Poisson probability distribution   The probability distribution for a discrete random variable. It is used to compute the probability of x occurrences of an event over a specified interval.

Uniform probability distribution   A continuous probability distribution where the probability that the random variable will assume a value in any interval of equal length is the same for each interval.

Probability density function   The function that describes the probability distribution of a continuous random variable.

Normal probability distribution   A continuous probability distribution. Its probability density function is bell-shaped and determined by the mean μ and standard deviation σ.

Standard normal distribution   A normal distribution with a mean of 0 and a standard deviation of 1.

Exponential probability distribution   A continuous probability distribution that is useful in describing the time to complete a task or the time between occurrences of an event.

Problems

1. Listed below is a series of experiments and associated random variables. In each case identify the values that the random variable can take on and state whether the random variable is discrete or continuous.

Experiment	Random Variable (x)
a. Take a 20-question examination	Number of questions answered correctly
b. Observe cars arriving at a tollbooth for 1 hour	Number of cars arriving at the tollbooth
c. Audit 50 tax returns	Number of returns containing errors
d. Observe an employee's work	Number of nonproductive hours
e. Weigh a shipment of goods	Number of pounds

2. The McCormick Hardware Store places an order for riding lawn mowers each February. The following probability distribution for the demand is assumed:

Handwritten table (top left):

x	f(x)	xf(x)	x−μ	(x−μ)²
0	.10	.00	2.45	6.0025
1	.15	.15	−1.45	2.1025
2	.30	.60	−.45	.2025
3	.20	.60	.55	.3025
4	.15	.60	1.55	2.4025
5	.10	.50	2.55	6.5025

(b.) 2.45

Demand	Probability
0	0.10
1	0.15
2	0.30
3	0.20
4	0.15
5	0.10

Handwritten (right):

(x−μ)²x

.600250
.315375
.060750
.060500
.360375
.65025

σ = 1.4309

© σ² = 2.047500

a. If the store orders three riding lawn mowers, what is the probability of selling all three?

b. What is the expected demand for the lawn mowers?

c. What is the variance in the demand for the lawn mowers? What is the standard deviation?

3. The probability distribution for collision insurance claims paid by the Newton Automobile Insurance Company is as follows:

Handwritten (left):

(4) a+b,

Outcome	Payoff(x)	f(x)	xf(x)
Player Wins	+5	(a.) 19/38	+2.37
Player Loses	−5	20/38	−2.63

(b.) −.26

E(x) = $.26 tells us that on avg, the player can anticipate a loss of $.26 per bet.

Claim	Probability
$ 0	0.90
$ 500	0.04
$1000	0.03
$2000	0.01
$3000	0.01
$4000	0.01

Handwritten (right):

(c.)

x	f(x)	x−μ	(x−μ)²	(x−μ)²f(x)
5	18/38	5.26	27.6676	13.1052
−5	20/38	−4.74	22.4676	11.8251

σ² = 24.9308

σ = 4.993)

(d.) E(Payoff) = 100 E(x)
= 100(−.26)
= −$26

a. Use the expected collision claim amount to determine the collision insurance premium that would allow the company to break even on the collision portion of the policy.

b. The insurance company charges an annual rate of $250 for the collision coverage. What is the expected value of the collision policy for the policyholder? Why does the policyholder purchase a collision policy with this expected value?

4. A roulette wheel at a Las Vegas casino has 18 red numbers, 18 black numbers, and 2 green numbers. Assume that a $5 bet is placed on the black numbers. If a black number comes up, the player wins $5; otherwise the player loses $5.

a. Let x be a random variable indicating the player's *net* winnings on one bet. Show the probability distribution for x.

b. What is the expected winnings? What is your interpretation of this value?

c. What is the variance in the winnings? What is the standard deviation?

d. If a player places 100 bets of $5 each, what is the expected winnings? Comment on why casinos like a high volume of betting.

5. The Hub Real Estate Investment stock is currently selling for $16 per share. An investor plans to buy shares and hold the stock for 1 year. Let x be the random variable indicating the price of the stock after 1 year. The probability distribution for x is shown below:

Handwritten (bottom):

a. 0 ≤ f(x) & Σf(x)=1

b. E(x) = Σxf(x)
= 16(.35)+ 17(.25)+ 18(.25)+ 19(.10) + 20(.05)
= 17.25

c. E(Gain) = E(x) − 16
= 17.25 − 16
= $1.25

1.25/16 = .078 ≈ 7.8%

(d)

x	f(x)	(x-μ)	(x-μ)²	(x-μ)²f(x)
16	.35	-1.25	1.5625	.5469
17	.25	-.25	.0625	.0156
18	.25	.75	.5625	.1406
19	.10	1.75	3.0625	.3063
20	.05	2.75	7.5625	.3781

$\sigma^2 = 1.3875$

$\sigma = 1.1779$

Price of Stock (x)	f(x)
16	0.35
17	0.25
18	0.25
19	0.10
20	0.05

a. Show that the given probability distribution possesses the properties of all probability distributions.

b. What is the expected price of the stock after 1 year?

c. What is the expected gain per share of the stock over the 1-year period? What percent return on the investment is reflected by this expected value?

d. What is the variance in the price of the stock over the 1-year period?

e. Another stock with a similar expected return has a variance of 3. Which stock appears to be the better investment in terms of minimizing risk or uncertainty associated with the investment? Explain.

e. The stock w/ the lower variance is the preferred stock. In this case the stock with the variance of 1.3875

6. The J. R. Ryland Computer Company is considering a plant expansion that will enable the company to begin production of a new computer product. The company's president must determine whether to make the expansion a medium-scale or large-scale project. An uncertainty involves the demand for the new product, which for planning purposes may be low demand, medium demand, or high demand. The probability estimates for the demands are 0.20, 0.50, and 0.30, respectively. Letting x indicate the annual profit in $1000's, the firm's planners have developed profit forecasts for the medium-scale and large-scale expansion projects:

Demand	Medium-Scale Expansion Profits		Large-Scale Expansion Profits	
	x	f(x)	x	f(x)
Low	$ 50	0.20	$ 0	0.20
Medium	$150	0.50	$100	0.50
High	$200	0.30	$300	0.30

a. Compute the expected value for the profit associated with the two expansion alternatives. Which decision is preferred for the objective of maximizing the expected profit?

b. Compute the variance for the profit associated with the two expansion alternatives. Which decision is preferred for the objective of minimizing the risk or uncertainty?

7. At a particular university it has been found that 20% of the students withdraw without completing the introductory statistics course. Assume that 20 students have registered for the course this term. Use Appendix A p.731

a. f(2) = .1369

b. F(4) = .2182

c. $P(x \geq 3) = 1 - [F(0) + f(1) + f(2)]$ where

f(0) = .0115

f(1) = .0576

f(2) = .369

$P(x \geq 3) = 1 - [.0115 + .0576 + .1369] = .7940$

a. What is the probability that exactly two students will withdraw?

b. What is the probability that exactly four students will withdraw?

c. What is the probability that three or more students will withdraw?

d. What is the expected number of withdrawals? $E(x) = np$ ⟶ $20(.20) = 4$

8. When a particular machine is functioning properly, only 1% of the items produced are defective. Assume that the machine is functioning properly in answering the following questions:

a. If two items are examined, what is the probability that exactly one is defective?

b. If five items are examined, what is the probability that none are defective?

c. What is the expected number of defective items in a sample of 200?

d. What is the standard deviation of the number of defective items in a sample of 200?

Appendix A p.731
n=8 x=2 p=10%

9. A salesperson contacts eight potential customers per day. From past experience we know that the probability of a potential customer making a purchase is 0.10.

b) P(at least 2) = 1-(f(0)+f(1))
= 1-(.4305+.3826)
= .1869

a. What is the probability the salesperson makes *exactly* two sales in a day? $f(2) = .1488$

b. What is the probability the salesperson makes *at least* two sales in a day?

c. What percentage of days will the salesperson not make a sale?

c) f(0) = .4305 = 43.05%

d. What is the expected number of sales per day? Over a 5-day week, how many sales are expected?

d) E(x) = np = 8 × .10
= .8 sales per day
.8×5 = 4.0 sales per week
or 40×.1 = 4

10. Assume that the binomial distribution applies for the case of a college basketball player shooting free throws. Late in a basketball game, a team will sometimes foul intentionally in the hope that the player shooting the free throws will miss and the team committing the foul will get the ball. Assume that the best player on the opposing team has a 0.82 probability of making a free throw and that the worst player has a 0.56 probability of making a free throw.

a. What are the probabilites that the best player makes, 0, 1, and 2 points if fouled and given two free throws?

b. What are the probabilities that the worst player makes 0, 1, and 2 points if fouled and given two free throws?

c. Does it make sense for a coach to have a preset plan as to which player to foul intentionally late in a basketball game? Explain.

11. In an audit of a company's billings, an auditor randomly selects five bills. If 3% of all bills contain an error, what is the probability that the auditor will find the following:

a. Exactly one bill in error?

b. At least one bill in error?

12. The arrivals of customers at a bank follow the Poisson distribution. Answer the following questions assuming a mean arrival rate of three per minute.

a. What is the probability of exactly three arrivals in a 1-minute period?

b. What is the probability of at least three arrivals in a 1-minute period?

13. A certain restaurant has a reputation for good food. Restaurant management boasts that on a Saturday night groups of customers arrive at the rate of 15 groups every half-hour. $\lambda = \frac{15}{30 min}$ $\lambda = .5/min.$

Table p.737
a) λ=5·.5=2.5
f(0) = .0821

a. What is the probability that 5 minutes will pass with no customers arriving?

b) λ=10·.5=5
f(8) = .0653

b. What is the probability that eight groups of customers will arrive in 10 minutes?

c) λ=10(.5)=5

c. What is the probability that three or more groups will arrive in a 10-minute period of time?

f ≥ 3 = 1-(.0067+.0337+.0812)
= .8654

14. During the registration period at a local university, students consult advisors with questions about course selection. A particular advisor noted that during the registration period an average of eight students per hour ask questions, although the exact arrival times of the students were random in nature. Use the Poisson distribution to answer the following questions:

 a. What is the probability that exactly eight students come in for consultation during a particular 1-hour period?

 b. What is the probability that exactly three students come in for consultation during a particular ½-hour period?

15. During rush hours accidents occur in a particular metropolitan area at the rate of two per hour. The morning rush period lasts for 1 hour 30 minutes and the evening rush period lasts for 2 hours.

 a. On a particular day, what is the probability that there will be no accidents during the morning rush period?

 b. What is the probability of two accidents during the evening rush period?

 c. What is the probability of four or more accidents during the morning rush period?

 d. On a particular day what is the probability there will be no accidents during both the morning and evening rush periods?

16. Airline passengers arrive randomly and independently at the passenger screening facility at a major international airport. The mean arrival rate is 10 passengers per minute.

 a. What is the probability of no arrivals in a 1-minute period?

 b. What is the probability three or fewer passengers arrive in a 1-minute period?

 c. What is the probability of no arrivals in a 15-second period?

 d. What is the probability of at least one arrival in a 15-second period?

17. In an office building the waiting time for an elevator is found to be uniformly distributed between 0 minutes and 5 minutes.

 a. What is the probability density function $f(x)$ for this uniform distribution?

 b. What is the probability of waiting longer than 3.5 minutes?

 c. What is the probability that the elevator arrives in the first 45 seconds?

 d. What is the probability of a waiting time between 1 and 3 minutes?

18. The travel time for a truck traveling from Davenport to Iowa City is uniformly distributed between 70 and 90 minutes.

 a. State the mathematical expression for the probability density function.

 b. Compute the probability that the truck will make the trip in 75 minutes or less.

 c. What is the probability that the trip will take longer than 82 minutes?

 d. What is the probability that the trip will take exactly 80 minutes?

19. Bus arrival times at a particular location are uniformly distributed between 2:10 and 2:25 P.M., with 2:10 listed as the scheduled arrival time.

 a. The bus is considered delayed if it arrives after 2:15 P.M.. What is the probability that the bus will be considered delayed?

 b. If a person arrives at the bus stop at 2:17, what is the probability that the person will still catch the bus?

20. The time required to complete a particular assembly operation is uniformly distributed between 30 and 40 minutes.

 a. What is the mathematical expression for the probability density function?

b. Compute the probability that the assembly operation will require more than 38 minutes to complete.

c. If management wants to set a time standard for this operation, what time should be selected such that 70% of the time the operation will be completed within the time specified?

21. The demand for a new product is assumed to be normally distributed with $\mu = 200$ and $\sigma = 40$. Letting x be the number of units demanded, find the following:
   a. $P(180 \leq x \leq 220)$
   b. $P(x \geq 250)$
   c. $P(x \leq 100)$
   d. $P(225 \leq x \leq 250)$

22. The Webster National Bank is reviewing its service charge and interest-paying policies on checking accounts. The bank has found that the average daily balance on personal checking accounts is $550.00, with a standard deviation of $150.00. In addition, the average daily balances have been found to be normally distributed.
   a. What is the probability that a personal checking account customer carries an average daily balance in excess of $800.00?
   b. What is the probability that a customer carries an average daily balance below $200.00?
   c. What is the probability that a customer carries an average daily balance between $300.00 and $700.00?
   d. The bank is considering paying interest to customers carrying average daily balances in excess of a certain amount. If the bank wants to pay interest to 5% of its customers, what is the minimum average daily balance it should be willing to pay interest on?

23. A soup company markets eight varieties of homemade soups throughout the Eastern states. The standard-size soup can holds a maximum of 11 ounces, while the label on each can advertises contents of $10\frac{3}{4}$ ounces. The extra $\frac{1}{4}$ ounce is to allow for the possibility of the automatic filling machine placing more soup than the company actually wants in a can. Past experience shows that the number of ounces placed in a can is approximately normally distributed, with a mean of 10.75 ounces and a standard deviation of 0.1 ounces. What is the probability that the machine will attempt to place more than 11 ounces in a can, causing an overflow to occur?

24. Assume that the test scores from a college admissions test are normally distributed, with a mean of 450 and a standard deviation of 100.
   a. What is the probability that a person taking the test scores between 400 and 500?
   b. Suppose that someone receives a score of 630. What is the probability that another person taking the test scores better than 630?
   c. If a particular university will not admit anyone scoring below 480, what percentage of the persons taking the test would be acceptable to the university?

25. The lifetime of a color television picture tube is normally distributed, with a mean of 7.8 years and a standard deviation of 2 years.
   a. What is the probability that a picture tube will last more than 10 years?
   b. If the firm guarantees the picture tube for 2 years, what percentage of the television sets sold will have to be replaced because of picture tube failure?

c. If the firm is willing to replace the picture tubes in a maximum of 1% of the television sets sold, what guarantee period can be offered for the television picture tubes?

26. General Hospital's patient account division has compiled data on the age of accounts receivable. The data collected indicate that the age of the accounts follows a normal distribution, with $\mu = 28$ days and $\sigma = 8$ days.
    a. What is the probability that an account is between 20 and 40 days old $[P(20 \leq x \leq 40)]$?
    b. The hospital administrator is interested in sending reminder letters to the oldest 15% of accounts. How many days old should an account be before a reminder letter is sent?
    c. The hospital administrator would like to give a discount to the accounts that pay their balance by the 21st day. What percentage of the accounts will receive the discount?

27. The time required to complete a final examination in a particular college course is normally distributed, with a mean of 80 minutes and a standard deviation of 10 minutes. Answer the following questions.
    a. What is the probability of completing the exam in 1 hour or less?
    b. What is the probability that a student will complete the exam in more than 60 minutes but less than 75 minutes?
    c. Assume that the class has 60 students and that the examination period is 90 minutes in length. How many students do you expect will be unable to complete the exam in the allotted time?

28. From past experience, the management of a well-known fast-food restaurant estimates that the number of weekly customers at a particular location is normally distributed, with a mean of 5000 customers and a standard deviation of 800 customers.
    a. What is the probability that in a given week the number of customers will be 4760 to 5800?
    b. What is the probability of more than 6500 customers?
    c. For 90% of the weeks the number of customers should exceed what amount?

29. Vehicles arrive at a particular intersection at the mean rate of three per minute. If the time between vehicle arrivals follows the exponential probability distribution, answer the following questions:
    a. What is the probability that the time between vehicle arrivals is 1 minute or less?
    b. What is the probability that the time between vehicle arrivals is more than 1 minute?
    c. What is the probability that a vehicle arrives within 12 seconds (0.2 minutes) of the previous vehicle?

30. Computer programs are processed at a computer center at the rate of six per hour. Using the assumption that the time required by the computer programs follows an exponential probability distribution, answer the following questions:
    a. What is the probability a computer program will take 15 minutes (0.25 hours) or less to run?
    b. What is the probability a computer program will take more than 6 minutes?
    c. What is the probability a computer program will require at least 3 minutes but less than 12 minutes?

31. The film manufacturing industry finds that flaws or defects in film processing occur at the mean rate of one defect per 100 feet of film. Use the exponential probability distribution to answer the following questions.
    a. What is the probability that the first defect will occur during the first 100 feet of film manufactured?
    b. What is the probability that the first defect will occur after the first 100 feet, but before a total of 200 feet of film have been manufactured?
    c. What is the probability that at least 200 feet of film can be manufactured before a defect is found?

32. A machine breaks down an average of three times during a normal 40-hour work week. The time between breakdowns follows the exponential probability distribution.
    a. What is the probability of a breakdown during the first 4 hours of the work week?
    b. What is the probability of a breakdown during the first day of the week (8 hours)?
    c. What is the probability of a breakdown between the fourth and eighth hour of the first day of the week?
    d. What is the probability that the machine can operate at least 20 hours without a breakdown?

33. A police patrol car receives requests for police action at the mean rate of 2 requests per hour. Assume that the exponential probability distribution applies.
    a. What is the probability that a police patrol car will receive a request for police action within 15 minutes of a previous request?
    b. What is the probability that a police patrol car will not receive a request for police action during a 1-hour period?

34. Customers arrive at a bank at the mean rate of 20 per hour. The exponential probability distribution describes the time between customer arrivals.
    a. What is the probability that a customer arrives within 3 minutes of a previous customer?
    b. What is the probability that the bank will go 6 minutes without a customer arrival?

Quantitative Methods in Practice

Burroughs Corporation*
Rochester, New York

The business of the Burroughs Corporation is information management. The company was founded on the invention of one of the first information processing devices—the Burroughs adding machine—and has grown to serve all the major aspects associated with the recording, computation, editing, processing, and communication of information. Established as the American Arithmometer Company in St. Louis, Missouri, in 1886, the company moved its operations to Detroit, Michigan, in 1904 and changed its name to Burroughs 1 year later. Through decades or marketing growth and technological developments, Burroughs has evolved as a multinational corporation with a full range of products and a reputation for innovation and reliability in information management. Burroughs employs nearly 67,000 people worldwide.

The Office Products Group (OPG) is one of the major operating groups of the corporation and is headquartered in Rochester, New York. The Office Products Group designs, engineers, manufactures, and markets a range of business forms, checks, office supplies, and document encoding, signing, and protective equipment, as well as accounting systems and credit cards.

The Quality Assurance Department, located in the Office Products Group, makes extensive use of the concepts involving probability and probability distributions in order to establish tolerances for new manufacturing processes and to determine probabilities that existing manufacturing processes exceed known tolerances. This type of analysis frequently involves the application of the normal probability distribution. One such application is described below.

Credit Cards for Banking

One of the products manufactured by OPG is a plastic credit card that is used in Burroughs automatic bank teller machines. Some of the banks that were using these machines were having problems with the credit cards being rejected in the equipment. An analysis of the rejected credit cards showed that these cards did not meet the product specifications for length and height as shown in Table A3.1. A process study was started in an attempt to determine the cause of the credit card rejection problem.

---

*The authors are indebted to Frank C. Garcia of Burroughs Corporation, Rochester, New York, for providing this application.

Table A3.1
Credit Card Specifications

	Minimum Dimension	Maximum Dimension
Length	3.365 in.	3.375 in.
Height	2.123 in.	2.127 in.

Results of Process Study

In the manufacturing process, the plastic cards are cut to their final dimensions from larger plastic sheets using a die cutting machine. Four different dies can be used, but all dies are designed to produce cards that meet the same product specifications. Approximately 250 cards from each of the four dies were sampled during typical manufacturing runs. The height and length of each card were accurately measured. The results of this study are presented in Table A3.2.

Table A3.2
Height and Length Characteristics
of Cards Produced by Four Dies

		Mean	Standard Deviation
Die 1	Length	3.367 in.	0.0010 in.
	Height	2.123 in.	0.0018 in.
Die 2	Length	3.368 in.	0.0014 in.
	Height	2.125 in.	0.0021 in.
Die 3	Length	3.367 in.	0.0010 in.
	Height	2.128 in.	0.0032 in.
Die 4	Length	3.366 in.	0.0007 in.
	Height	2.124 in.	0.0015 in.

The height and length of the cards produced by each die were assumed to follow a normal distribution. The probabilities that the height and length of the cards produced by these dies would not meet product specifications were calculated. For example, the probability of die 1 producing a card with a length less than the minimum acceptable length of 3.365 inches was calculated as follows:

1. Assume a normal distribution for length of cards produced by die 1 with a mean of 3.367 inches and a standard deviation of 0.0010 inches (see Table A3.2).
2. The minimum acceptable length is 3.365 inches; the z value corresponding to 3.365 is

$$z = \frac{x - \mu}{\sigma} = \frac{3.365 - 3.367}{0.001} = -2$$

3. Using the table for the standard normal distribution, the corresponding probability of a length as small as 3.365 inches or smaller is $0.5000 - 0.4772 = 0.0228$, or approximately 0.023.

Thus, approximately 2.3% of the cards manufactured using die 1 have a length less than the minimum length specification. The probability values for the four dies are summarized in Table A3.3.

Table A3.3
Probabilites of Not Meeting Product
Specifications for the Four Dies

	Minimum Length	Maximum Length	Minimum Height	Maximum Height
Die 1	0.023	°	0.500	0.013
Die 2	0.016	°	0.171	0.171
Die 3	0.023	°	0.059	0.622
Die 4	0.076	°	0.251	0.023

°Denotes a probability value less than 0.01.

The probabilities that the length of the cards would not meet specifications were relatively low for all four dies. However, probabilities that the cards would not meet height specifications were unacceptably large for all four dies. For example, die 3 showed a 0.622 probability of exceeding the maximum height specification. Inspection of die 3 revealed that the cutting edges were dull; thus, this die was removed from production for sharpening. Although the inspection of the other three dies indicated that they were in good physical condition, they still could not meet the required height specifications. Further investigation revealed that the entire die cutting operation had to be upgraded to meet the height dimension specifications. As a result, new process equipment was installed. Tests and probability calculations showed that the new equipment would be able to produce cards that met all dimensional specifications.

Questions

1. Using the information in Table A3.2, compute the probability of die 4 producing a card with a length less than the minimum acceptable length of 3.365 inches.
2. Table A3.3 shows that the probability of die 1 producing a card with a height of less than the minimum acceptable height of 2.123 inches is 0.500. Explain how this value was computed.

CHAPTER

4

Decision Analysis

Decision analysis can be used to determine optimal strategies when a decision maker is faced with several decision alternatives and an uncertain or risk-filled pattern of future events. For example, a manufacturer of a new style or line of seasonal clothing would like to manufacture large quantities of the product if consumer acceptance and consequently demand for the product are going to be high. However, the manufacturer would like to produce much smaller quantities if consumer acceptance and demand for the product are going to be low. Unfortunately, seasonal clothing items require the manufacturer to make a production quantity decision before the demand is actually known. Actual consumer acceptance of the new product will not be determined until the items have been placed in the stores and buyers have had the opportunity to purchase them. Selection of the best production volume decision from among several production volume alternatives when the decision maker is faced with the uncertainty of future demand is a problem suited for decision analysis.

We begin the study of decision analysis by considering problems in which there are reasonably few decision alternatives and possible future events. The concepts of a payoff table and a decision tree are introduced to provide a structure for this type of decision situation and to illustrate the fundamentals involved in decision analysis. The discussion is then extended to show how additional information obtained through experimentation can be combined with the decision maker's preliminary information in order to develop an optimal decision strategy. The chapter concludes with a discussion of how marginal analysis can be used in situations involving numerous decision alternatives and numerous states of nature.

4.1

STRUCTURING THE DECISION PROBLEM

In order to illustrate the decision analysis approach, let us consider the case of Political Systems, Inc. (PSI), a newly formed computer service firm specializing in information services such as surveys and data analysis for individuals running for political office. PSI is in the final stages of selecting a computer system for its Midwest branch, located in Chicago. While the firm has decided on a computer manufacturer, it is currently attempting to determine the size of the computer system that would be the most economical to lease. We will use decision analysis to help PSI make its computer leasing decision.

The first step in the decision analysis approach is to identify the alternatives considered by the decision maker. For PSI, the final decision will be to lease one of three computer systems, which differ in size and capacity. The three *decision alternatives*, denoted d_1, d_2, and d_3, are as follows:

$$d_1 = \text{lease the large computer system}$$
$$d_2 = \text{lease the medium-sized computer system}$$
$$d_3 = \text{lease the small computer system}$$

Obviously, the selection of the *best* decision alternative will depend on what PSI management foresees as the possible market acceptance of the service and consequently the possible demand or load on the PSI computer system. Often the future events associated with a decision situation are uncertain. That is, while a decision maker may have an idea of the variety of possible future events, the decision maker will often be unsure as to which particular event will occur. Thus the second step in a decision analysis approach is to identify the future events that might occur. These future events, which are not under the control of the decision maker, are referred to as the *states of nature*. It is assumed that the list of possible states of nature includes everything that can happen and that the individual states of nature do not overlap; that is, the states of nature are defined so that one and only one of the listed states of nature will occur.

When asked about the states of nature for the PSI decision problem, management viewed the possible acceptance of the PSI service as an either-or situation. That is, management believed that the firm's overall level of acceptance in the market place would be one of two possibilities: high acceptance or low acceptance. Thus the PSI states of nature, denoted s_1 and s_2, are as follows:

Future events not under the control of the decision maker

$$s_1 = \text{high customer acceptance of PSI services}$$
$$s_2 = \text{low customer acceptance of PSI services}$$

Given the three decision alternatives and the two states of nature, which computer system should PSI lease? In order to answer this question, we will need information on the profit associated with each combination of a decision alternative and a state of nature. For example, what profit would PSI experience if the firm decided to lease the large computer system (d_1) and market acceptance was high (s_1)? What profit would PSI experience if the firm decided to lease the large computer system (d_1) and market acceptance was low (s_2)? And so on.

Payoff Tables

In decision analysis terminology, we refer to the outcome resulting from making a certain decision and the occurrence of a particular state of nature as the *payoff*. Using the best information available, management has estimated the payoffs or profits for the PSI computer leasing problem. These estimates are presented in Table 4.1. A table of this form is referred to as a *payoff table*. In general, entries in a payoff table can be stated in terms of profits, costs, or any other measure of output that may be appropriate for the particular situation being analyzed. The notation we will use for the entries in the payoff table is $V(d_i, s_j)$, which denotes the payoff associated with decision alternative d_i and state of nature s_j. Using this notation we see that $V(d_3, s_1) = \$100,000$.

Table 4.1
Payoff Table for the PSI Computer Leasing Problem

| | | States of Nature | |
| | | High Acceptance | Low Acceptance |
Decision Alternatives		s_1	s_2
Lease a large system	d_1	200,000	−20,000
Lease a medium-sized system	d_2	150,000	20,000
Lease a small system	d_3	100,000	60,000

Profit or
payoff in $

Decision Trees

A *decision tree* provides a graphical representation of the decision-making process. Figure 4.1 shows a decision tree for the PSI computer leasing problem. Note that the tree shows the natural or logical progression that will occur. First the firm must make its decision (d_1, d_2, or d_3); then, once the decision is implemented, the state of nature (s_1 or s_2) will occur. The number at each end point of the tree represents the payoff associated with a particular chain of events. For example, the topmost payoff of 200,000 arises whenever management makes the decision to purchase a large system (d_1) and customer acceptance turns out to be high (s_1). The next lower terminal point of −20,000 is reached when management has made the decision to lease the large system (d_1) and the state of nature turns out to be a low degree of customer acceptance (s_2). Thus we see that each possible sequence of events for the PSI problem is represented in the decision tree.

 Using the general terminology associated with decision trees, we will refer to the intersection or junction points of the tree as *nodes* and the arcs or connectors between the nodes as *branches*. Figure 4.1 shows the PSI decision tree with the nodes numbered 1 to 4. When the branches *leaving* a given node are decision branches, we refer to the node as a *decision node*. Decision nodes are denoted by squares. Similarly, when the branches leaving a given node are state-of-nature branches, we refer to the node as a *state-of-nature node*. State-of-nature nodes are denoted by circles. Using this node-labeling procedure, node 1 is a decision node, whereas nodes 2, 3, and 4 are state-of-nature nodes.

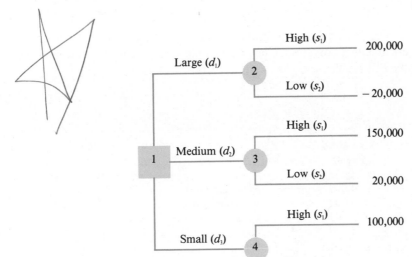

Figure 4.1
Decision Tree for the PSI Problem

The identification of the decision alternatives, the states of nature, and the determination of the payoff associated with each decision alternative and state of nature combination are the first three steps in the decision analysis process. The question we now turn to is the following: How can the decision maker best utilize the information presented in the payoff table or the decision tree to arrive at a decision? As we will see, there are several approaches that may be used.

4.2

DECISION MAKING WITHOUT PROBABILITIES

In this section we consider approaches to decision making that do not require knowledge of the probabilities of the states of nature. These approaches are appropriate in situations where the decision maker has very little confidence in his or her ability to assess the probabilities of the various states of nature, or where it is desirable to consider best- and worst-case analyses that are independent of state-of-nature probabilities. Because different approaches sometimes lead to different decision recommendations, it is important for the decision maker to understand the approaches available and then select the specific approach that, according to the decision maker's judgment, is the most appropriate.

Optimistic Approach

The *optimistic approach* evaluates each decision alternative in terms of the *best* payoff that can occur. The decision alternative that is recommended is the one that provides the best possible payoff. For a problem in which it is desired to maximize profit, as it is in the PSI leasing problem, the optimistic approach would lead the decision maker to choose the alternative corresponding to the largest profit. For problems involving minimization, this approach leads to choosing the alternative with the smallest payoff.

To illustrate the use of the optimistic approach we will show how it can be used to develop a recommendation for the PSI leasing problem. First we determine the maximum payoff possible for each of the decision alternatives; then we select the decision alternative that provides the overall maximum profit. This is just a systematic way of identifying the decision alternative that provides the largest possible profit. Table 4.2 illustrates this calculation for the PSI problem.

Table 4.2
PSI Maximum Payoff ($) for Each Decision Alternative

Decision Alternatives		Maximum Payoff	
Large system	d_1	200,000	⟵—— Maximum of the
Medium system	d_2	150,000	maximum payoff
Small system	d_3	100,000	values

Since $200,000, corresponding to d_1, yields the maximum of the maximum payoffs, the decision to lease a large system is the recommended decision alternative using the optimistic approach. It is easy to see why this is called an optimistic approach. It simply recommends the decision alternative that provides the best of all payoffs, $200,000.

Conservative Approach

The *conservative approach* evaluates each decision alternative in terms of the *worst* payoff that can occur. The decision alternative recommended is the one that provides the best of the worst possible payoffs. For a problem in which the output measure is profit, as it is in the PSI leasing problem, the conservative approach would lead the decision maker to choose the alternative that maximizes the minimum possible profit that could be obtained. For problems involving minimization, this approach identifies the alternative that will minimize the maximum payoff.

To illustrate the use of the conservative approach, we will show how it can be used to develop a recommendation for the PSI leasing problem. First the decision maker would identify the minimum payoff for each of the decision alternatives; then, the decision maker would select the alternative that maximizes the minimum payoff. Table 4.3 illustrates this approach for the PSI problem.

Table 4.3
PSI Minimum Payoff ($) for Each Decision Alternative

Decision Alternatives		Minimum Payoff	
Large system	d_1	$-20,000$	Maximum of the
Medium system	d_2	20,000	minimum payoff
Small system	d_3	60,000 ⟵	values

Since $60,000, corresponding to d_3, yields the maximum of the minimum payoffs, the decision alternative to lease a small system is recommended. This decision approach is considered conservative because it concentrates on the worst possible payoffs and then recommends the decision alternative that avoids the possibility of extremely "bad" payoffs. In using the conservative approach, PSI is guaranteed a profit of at least $60,000. While PSI may still make more, it *cannot* make less than $60,000.

Minimax Regret Approach

Minimax regret is another approach to decision making without probabilities. This approach is neither purely optimistic or purely conservative. Let us illustrate the minimax regret approach by showing how it can be used to select a decision alternative for the PSI leasing problem.

Suppose that we make the decision to lease the small system (d_3) and afterwards learn that customer acceptance of the PSI service is high (s_1). Table 4.1 shows the resulting profit to be $100,000. However, now that we know that state of nature s_1 has occurred, we see that the large system decision (d_1), yielding a profit of $200,000, would have been the optimal decision. The difference between the optimal payoff ($200,000) and the payoff experienced ($100,000) is referred to as the *opportunity loss* or *regret* associated with the d_3 decision when state of nature s_1 occurs ($200,000 - $100,000 = $100,000). If we had made decision d_2 and state of nature s_1 had occurred, the opportunity loss or regret would have been $200,000 - $150,000 = $50,000.

In maximization problems the general expression for opportunity loss or regret is given by

$$R(d_i, s_j) = V^*(s_j) - V(d_i, s_j) \tag{4.1}$$

where

$R(d_i, s_j) =$ regret associated with decision alternative d_i and state of nature s_j

$V^*(s_j) =$ best payoff value[1] under state of nature s_j

$V(d_i, s_j) =$ payoff associated with decision alternative d_i and state of nature s_j

Using equation (4.1) and the payoffs in Table 4.1, we can compute the regret associated with all combinations of decision alternatives d_i and states of nature s_j. We simply replace each entry in the payoff table with the value found by subtracting the entry from the largest entry in its column. Table 4.4 shows the regret, or opportunity loss, table for the PSI problem.

Table 4.4
Regret or Opportunity Loss ($) for the PSI Problem

		States of Nature	
		High Acceptance s_1	Low Acceptance s_2
Decision Alternatives			
Large system	d_1	0	80,000
Medium system	d_2	50,000	40,000
Small system	d_3	100,000	0

[1] In cost minimization problems $V^*(s_j)$ will be the smallest entry in column j. Thus for minimization problems, equation (4.1) must be changed to $R(d_i, s_j) = V(d_i, s_j) - V^*(s_j)$.

The next step in applying the minimax regret approach requires the decision maker to identify the maximum regret for each decision alternative. These data are shown in Table 4.5. The choice of a best decision is made by selecting the alternative corresponding to the *mini*mum of the *max*imum *regret* values; hence the name *minimax regret*. For the PSI problem the decision to lease a medium-sized computer system, with a corresponding regret of $50,000, is the recommended minimax regret decision.

Table 4.5
PSI Maximum Regret or Opportunity Loss ($) for Each Decision Alternative

Decision Alternatives		Maximum Regret or Opportunity Loss	
Large system	d_1	80,000	
Medium system	d_2	50,000	⟵—————— Minimum of the
Small system	d_3	100,000	maximum regret

Note that the three approaches discussed in this section have provided different recommendations. This is not in itself bad. It simply reflects the difference in decision-making philosophies that underlie the various approaches. Ultimately, the decision maker will have to choose the most appropriate approach and then make the final decision accordingly. The major criticism of the approaches discussed in this section is that they do not consider any information about the probabilities of the various states of nature. In the next section we discuss an approach that utilizes probability information in selecting a decision alternative.

4.3

DECISION MAKING WITH PROBABILITIES

In many decision-making situations it is possible to obtain probability estimates for each of the possible states of nature. When such probabilities are available, the *expected value approach* can be used to identify the best decision alternative. The expected value approach evaluates each decision alternative in terms of its expected value. The decision alternative that is recommended is the one that provides the best expected value. Let us first define the expected value of a decision alternative and then show how it can be used for the PSI decision problem.

Let

$$N = \text{the number of possible states of nature}$$
$$P(s_j) = \text{the probability of state of nature } s_j$$

Since one and only one of the N states of nature can occur, the associated probabilities must satisfy the following two conditions:

$$P(s_j) \geq 0 \qquad \text{for all states of nature} \tag{4.2}$$

$$\sum_{j=1}^{N} P(s_j) = P(s_1) + P(s_2) + \cdots + P(s_N) = 1 \tag{4.3}$$

The expected value (EV) of decision alternative d_i is

$$EV(d_i) = \sum_{j=1}^{N} P(s_j)V(d_i, s_j) \tag{4.4}$$

In words, the expected value of a decision alternative is the sum of weighted payoffs for the alternative. The weight for a payoff is the probability of the associated state of nature and therefore the probability that the payoff occurs. Let us now return to the PSI problem to see how the expected value approach can be applied.

Suppose that PSI management believes that s_1, the high-acceptance state of nature, has a 0.3 probability of occurrence and that s_2, the low-acceptance state of nature, has a 0.7 probability. Thus $P(s_1) = 0.3$ and $P(s_2) = 0.7$. Using the payoff values $V(d_i, s_j)$ shown in Table 4.1 and equation (4.4), expected values for the three decision alternatives can be calculated:

$$EV(d_1) = 0.3(200,000) + 0.7(-20,000) = \$46,000$$
$$EV(d_2) = 0.3(150,000) + 0.7(\;20,000) = \$59,000$$
$$EV(d_3) = 0.3(100,000) + 0.7(\;60,000) = \$72,000$$

Thus, according to the expected value approach, since d_3 has the highest expected value (\$72,000), d_3 is the recommended decision.

The calculations required to identify the decision alternative with the best expected value can be conveniently carried out on a decision tree. Figure 4.2 shows the decision tree for the PSI problem with state-of-nature branch probabilities. We will now use the branch probabilities and the expected value approach to arrive at the optimal decision for PSI.

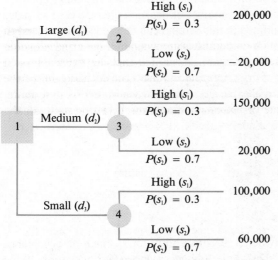

Figure 4.2
PSI Decision Tree with State-of-Nature Branch Probabilities

Working backward through the decision tree, we first compute the expected value at each state-of-nature node. That is, at each state-of-nature node we weight each possible payoff by its chance of occurrence. By doing this we obtain the expected values for nodes 2, 3, and 4 as shown in Figure 4.3.

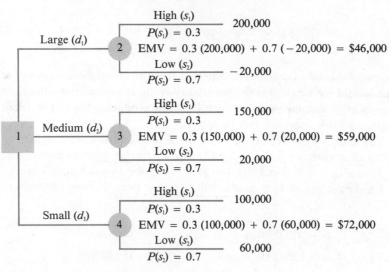

Figure 4.3
Applying the Expected Value Approach Using Decision Trees

Since the decision maker controls the branch leaving decision node 1 and since we are trying to maximize expected profits, the best decision branch at node 1 is d_3. Thus the decision tree analysis leads us to recommend d_3 with an expected value of $72,000. Note that this is the same recommendation that was obtained using the expected value approach in conjunction with the payoff table.

We have seen how decision trees can be used to analyze decisions with state-of-nature probabilities. While other decision problems may be substantially more complex than the PSI problem, if there are a reasonable number of decision alternatives and states of nature, the decision tree approach outlined in this section can be used. First the analyst must draw a decision tree consisting of decision and state-of-nature nodes and branches that describe the sequential nature of the problem. Assuming that the expected value approach is to be used, the next step is to determine the probabilities for each of the state-of-nature branches and compute the expected value at each state-of-nature node. The decision branch leading to the state-of-nature node with the best expected value is then selected. The decision alternative associated with this branch is the decision recommended.

4.4

SENSITIVITY ANALYSIS

For the PSI problem, management provided a 0.3 probability for s_1, the high-acceptance state of nature, and a 0.7 probability for s_2, the low-acceptance state of nature. Using these probabilities we found that decision alternative d_3 had the highest expected value and was the recommended decision. In this section we consider how changes in the probability estimates for the states of nature affect or alter the recommended decision. The study of the effect of such changes is referred to as *sensitivity analysis*.

One approach to sensitivity analysis is to consider different probabilities for the states of nature and then recompute the expected value for each of the decision alternatives. Repeating this several times, we can begin to learn how changes in the probabilities for the states of nature affect the recommended decision. For example, suppose that we consider a change in the probabilities for the states of nature such that $P(s_1) = 0.6$ and $P(s_2) = 0.4$. Using these probabilities and repeating the expected value computations, we find the following:

$$EV(d_1) = 0.6(200,000) + 0.4(-20,000) = \$112,000$$
$$EV(d_2) = 0.6(150,000) + 0.4(20,000) = \$98,000$$
$$EV(d_3) = 0.6(100,000) + 0.4(60,000) = \$84,000$$

Thus, with these probabilities, the recommended decision alternative is d_1, with an expected value of \$112,000.

Obviously, we could continue to modify the probabilities of the states of nature and begin to learn more about how such changes affect the recommended decision. The only drawback to this approach is that there will be numerous calculations required to evaluate the effect of several possible changes in the state of nature probabilities.

For the special case of decision analysis with two states of nature, the sensitivity analysis computations can be eased substantially through the use of a graphical procedure. Let us demonstrate this procedure by further analyzing the PSI problem. We begin by denoting the probability of state of nature s_1 by p. That is,

$$P(s_1) = p$$

and thus

$$P(s_2) = 1 - P(s_1) = 1 - p$$

The expected value for decision alternative d_1 can then be written as a function of p.

$$
\begin{aligned}
EV(d_1) &= P(s_1)(200,000) + P(s_2)(-20,000) \\
&= p(200,000) + (1 - p)(-20,000) \\
&= 220,000p - 20,000
\end{aligned}
\tag{4.5}
$$

Repeating the expected value computation for decision alternatives d_2 and d_3, we obtain the following expressions for expected value as a function of p:

$$EV(d_2) = 130,000p + 20,000 \tag{4.6}$$
$$EV(d_3) = 40,000p + 60,000 \tag{4.7}$$

Thus we have developed three linear equations that express the expected value of the three decision alternatives as a function of the probability of state of nature s_1.

Let us continue by developing a graph with values of p on the horizontal axis and the associated expected values on the vertical axis. Since expressions (4.5), (4.6), and (4.7) are all linear equations, we can graph each equation, or line, by finding any two points on the line and drawing the line through the points. Using $EV(d_1)$ in (4.5) as an example, we first let $p = 0$ and find that $EV(d_1) = -20{,}000$. Then, letting $p = 1$, we find that $EV(d_1) = 200{,}000$. Connecting these two points, $(0, -20{,}000)$ and $(1, 200{,}000)$, provides the line labeled $EV(d_1)$ in Figure 4.4. This figure also shows a line labeled $EV(d_2)$ and a line labeled $EV(d_3)$; these are the graphs of (4.6) and (4.7), respectively.

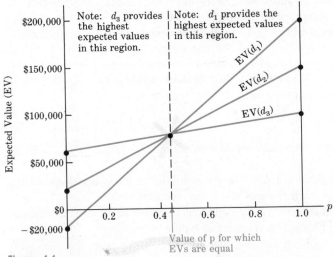

Figure 4.4
Expected Value as a Function of p

Figure 4.4 can now be used for sensitivity analysis. Recall that PSI is seeking to maximize profit. Note that for small values of p, decision alternative d_3 provides the largest expected value and is thus the recommended decision. Similarly, for large values of p, we see that decision alternative d_1 provides the largest expected value and is thus the recommended decision. Further, note that there is no section of the graph for which decision alternative d_2 provides the largest expected value. Thus, with the exception of the point where the three expected value lines intersect and all three expected values are equal, decision alternative d_2 can never be the decision alternative recommended by the expected value approach.

Referring to Figure 4.4 again, we see that the three lines intersect at a value of p between 0.4 and 0.5. In other words, at some point between 0.4 and 0.5, all three decision alternatives provide the same expected value.

Whenever two or more lines intersect on a sensitivity analysis graph, we can set the equations for two of the intersecting lines equal to each other and solve for the value of p. Using the equations for decision alternative d_1 and decision alternative d_3, we obtain

$$220{,}000p - 20{,}000 = 40{,}000p + 60{,}000$$

Thus,

$$180{,}000p = 80{,}000$$

$$p = \frac{80{,}000}{180{,}000} = 0.44$$

Hence, whenever $p = 0.44$, each decision alternative will provide the same expected value. Using this value of p in Figure 4.4, we can now conclude that for $p < 0.44$, decision alternative d_3 provides the largest expected value; and that for $p > 0.44$, decision alternative d_1 provides the largest expected value. Since p is simply the probability of state of nature s_1 and $(1 - p)$ is the probability of state of nature s_2, we now have the sensitivity analysis information that tells us how changes in the state-of-nature probabilities affect the recommended decision alternative.

The benefit of performing sensitivity analysis is that it can provide a better perspective on management's original judgment regarding the state-of-nature probabilities. Management originally estimated the probability of high customer acceptance as $P(s_1) = 0.3$. As a result, decision alternative d_3 was recommended. After carrying out the sensitivity analysis, we can now tell management that the original estimate of $P(s_1)$ is not extremely critical in order for d_3 to be the recommended decision. In fact, as long as $P(s_1) < 0.44$, the d_3 decision alternative remains optimal.

Note that in the PSI problem the three lines for the three decision alternatives graphed in Figure 4.4 intersect at the same point ($p = 0.44$). Similar sensitivity analysis computations for other decision analysis problems with two states of nature and three decision alternatives should not be expected to result in the same type of graph. With a different sensitivity analysis graph, d_1 could be the best decision alternative for certain values of p, d_2 the best decision alternative of other values of p, and d_3 the best decision alternative for the remaining values of p. This situation is demonstrated in the sensitivity analysis computation for problem 5 at the end of the chapter.

The graphical sensitivity analysis procedure we have described for the PSI problem applies only to decision analysis problems with two states of nature. However, sensitivity analysis is important in problems with more than two states of nature. In these cases a computer software package such as *The Management Scientist* can be used to assist with the computations. Basically, we return to the approach of testing a variety of likely changes for the state-of-nature probabilities. The software package is helpful in making the necessary expected value computations and providing the decision alternative recommendations with a minimum of time and effort on the part of the analyst.

4.5

EXPECTED VALUE OF PERFECT INFORMATION

Suppose that PSI had the opportunity to conduct a market research study that would evaluate consumer needs for the PSI service. Such a study could help by improving the current probability assessments for the states of nature. However, if the cost of obtaining the market research information exceeds its value, PSI should not conduct the market research study.

To determine the maximum possible value that PSI should pay for additional information, let us suppose that PSI could obtain perfect information regarding the states of nature; that is, we will assume that PSI could determine with certainty which state of nature will occur. To make use of perfect information we need to develop a decision strategy for PSI to follow. As we will show, a decision strategy is simply a policy or decision rule that is to be followed by the decision maker. In computing the *expected value of perfect information* (*EVPI*), the decision strategy is a rule that specifies which decision alternative should be selected given each state of nature.

To help determine the optimal decision strategy for PSI we have reproduced PSI's payoff table as Table 4.6. We see that if state of nature s_1 occurs, then the best decision alternative is d_1 with a profit of \$200,000. Similarly, if state of nature s_2 occurs, then

Table 4.6
Payoff Table for the PSI Problem

		States of Nature	
		High Acceptance s_1	Low Acceptance s_2
Decision Alternatives			
Large system	d_1	200,000	−20,000
Medium system	d_2	150,000	20,000
Small system	d_3	100,000	60,000

the best decision alternative is d_3 with a profit of $60,000. Thus the optimal decision strategy PSI should follow if perfect information were available can be stated as follows:

> **Optimal Decision Strategy with Perfect Information**
>
> If s_1 occurs, then select d_1.
> If s_2 occurs, then select d_3.

What is the expected value for this decision strategy? Since $P(s_1) = 0.3$ and $P(s_2) = 0.7$, we see that there is a 0.3 probability that PSI will make $200,000 and a 0.7 probability PSI will make $60,000. Thus the expected value of the decision strategy that uses perfect information is

$$(0.3)(\$200,000) + (0.7)(\$60,000) = \$102,000$$

Recall that when perfect information was not available, the expected value approach resulted in recommending decision alternative d_3 with an expected value of $72,000. Since $72,000 is the expected value without perfect information and $102,000 is the expected value with perfect information, $102,000 − $72,000 = $30,000 represents the expected value of perfect information (EVPI); that is,

$$EVPI = \$102,000 - \$72,000 = \$30,000$$

In other words, $30,000 represents the additional expected value that can be obtained if perfect information were available about the states of nature. Figure 4.5 provides a summary of the computation of the EVPI for the PSI problem.

Generally speaking, a market research study will not provide "perfect" information; however, the information provided might be worth a good portion of the $30,000. In any case, PSI's management knows it should never pay more than $30,000 for any information, no matter how good. Provided the market survey cost is reasonably small—say, $5000 to $10,000—it appears economically desirable for PSI to consider the market research study.

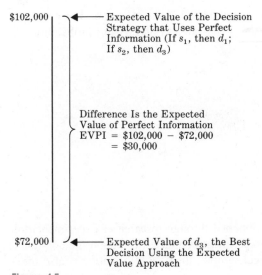

$102,000 ◄──── Expected Value of the Decision
Strategy that Uses Perfect
Information (If s_1, then d_1;
If s_2, then d_3)

Difference Is the Expected
Value of Perfect Information
EVPI = $102,000 − $72,000
= $30,000

$72,000 ◄──── Expected Value of d_3, the Best
Decision Using the Expected
Value Approach

Figure 4.5
The Expected Value of Perfect Information

4.6

DECISION ANALSYSIS WITH SAMPLE INFORMATION

In applying the expected value approach, we have seen how probability information about the states of nature affects the expected value calculations and thus the decision recommendation. Frequently decision makers have preliminary or prior probability estimates for the states of nature that are initially the best probability values available. However, in order to make the best possible decision, the decision maker may want to seek additional information about the states of nature. This new information can be used to revise or update the prior probabilities so that the final decision is based on more accurate probability estimates for the states of nature.

The seeking of additional information is most often accomplished through experiments designed to provide sample information or more current data about the states of nature. Raw material sampling, product testing, and test market research are examples of experiments that may enable a revision or updating of the state-of-nature probabilities. In the following discussion we will reconsider the PSI computer leasing problem and show how sample information can be used to revise the state-of-nature probabilities. We will then show how the revised probabilities can be used to develop an optimal decision strategy for PSI.

Recall that management had assigned a probability of $P(s_1) = 0.3$ to state of nature s_1 and a probability of $P(s_2) = 0.7$ to state of nature s_2. At this point we will refer to these initial probability estimates, $P(s_1)$ and $P(s_2)$, as the *prior probabilities* for the states of nature. Using these prior probabilities we found that d_3, the decision to lease the small system was optimal, yielding an expected value of $72,000. Recall also that we showed that the expected value of new information about the states of nature could potentially be worth as much as EVPI = $30,000.

Suppose that PSI decides to consider hiring a market research firm to study the potential acceptance of the PSI service. The market research study will provide new information that can be combined with the prior probabilities through a Bayesian procedure to obtain updated or revised probability estimates for the states of nature. These *revised* probabilities are called *posterior probabilities*. The process of revising probabilities is depicted in Figure 4.6.

INDICATOR

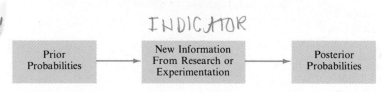

| Prior Probabilities | New Information From Research or Experimentation | Posterior Probabilities |

Figure 4.6
Probability Revision Based on New Information

We will refer to the new information obtained through research or experimentation as an *indicator*. Since in many cases the experiment conducted to obtain the additional information will consist of taking a statistical sample, the new information is also often referred to as *sample information*.

Using the indicator terminology, we can denote the outcomes of the PSI marketing research study as follows:

I_1 = favorable market research report (i.e., in the market research study the individuals contacted generally express interest in PSI's services)

I_2 = unfavorable market research report (i.e., in the market research study the individuals contacted generally express little interest in PSI's services)

Given one of these possible indicators, our objective is to provide improved estimates of the probabilities of the two states of nature. The end result of the *Bayesian revision* process depicted in Figure 4.6 is a set of posterior probabilities of the form $P(s_j|I_k)$, where $P(s_j|I_k)$ represents the conditional probability that state of nature s_j will occur given that the outcome of the market research study was indicator I_k.

To make effective use of this indicator information, we must know something about the probability relationships between the indicators and the states of nature. For example, in the PSI problem, given that the state of nature ultimately turns out to be high customer acceptance, what is the probability that the market research study will result in a favorable report? In this case we are asking about the conditional probability of indicator I_1 given state of nature s_1, written $P(I_1|s_1)$. In order to carry out the analysis, we will need conditional probabilities for all indicators given all states of nature, that is, $P(I_1|s_1)$, $P(I_1|s_2)$, $P(I_2|s_1)$, and $P(I_2|s_2)$.

In the PSI example the past record of the marketing research company on similar studies has led to the following estimates of the relevant conditional probabilities:

States of Nature	Market Research Report	
	Favorable I_1	Unfavorable I_2
High acceptance s_1	$P(I_1|s_1) = 0.8$	$P(I_2|s_1) = 0.2$
Low acceptance s_2	$P(I_1|s_2) = 0.1$	$P(I_2|s_2) = 0.9$

Note that these probability estimates indicate that a good degree of confidence can be placed in the market research report. When the true state of nature is s_1, the market research report will be favorable 80% of the time and unfavorable only 20%. When the true state is s_2, the report will make the correct indication 90% of the time. Now let us see how this additional information can be incorporated into the decision-making process.

4.7

DEVELOPING A DECISION STRATEGY

A decision strategy is a policy or decision rule that is to be followed by the decision maker. In the PSI case, with the market research study, a decision strategy is a rule that recommends a particular decision based on whether the market research report is favorable or unfavorable. We will employ a decision tree analysis to find the optimal decision strategy for PSI.

Figure 4.7 shows the decision tree for the PSI computer leasing problem provided that a market research study is conducted. Note that as you move from left to right, the tree shows the natural or logical order that will occur in the decision-making process. First the firm will obtain the market research report indicator (I_1 or I_2); then a decision (d_1, d_2, or d_3) will be made; finally, the state of nature (s_1 or s_2) will occur. The decision and the state of nature combine to provide the final profit or payoff.

Using decision tree terminology, we have now introduced an *indicator node*, node 1, and *indicator branches*, I_1 and I_2. Since the branches emanating from indicator nodes are not under the control of the decision maker but are determined by chance, these nodes are depicted by a circle just like the state-of-nature nodes. We see that nodes 2 and 3 are decision nodes, while nodes 4, 5, 6, 7, 8, and 9 are state-of-nature nodes. For decision nodes the decision maker must select the specific branch d_1, d_2, or d_3 that will be taken. Selecting the best decision branch is equivalent to making the best decision. However, since the indicator and state-of-nature branches are not controlled by the decision maker, the specific branch leaving an indicator or a state-of-nature node will depend on the probability associated with the branch. Thus, before we can carry out an analysis of the decision tree and develop a decision strategy, we must compute the probability of each indicator branch and the probability of each state-of-nature branch. Note from the decision tree that the state-of-nature branches occur *after* the indicator branches. Thus when we attempt to compute state-of-nature branch probabilities, we will need to consider which indicator was previously observed. That is, we will express state-of-nature probabilities in terms of the probability of state of nature s_j *given* indicator I_k was observed. Thus all state-of-nature probabilities will be expressed in a $P(s_j|I_k)$ form.

Computing Branch Probabilities

The prior probabilities for the states of nature in the PSI problem were given as $P(s_1) = 0.3$ and $P(s_2) = 0.7$. In Section 4.6 we identified the relationships between the market research indicators and states of nature with the conditional probabilities

$$P(I_1|s_1) = 0.8 \qquad P(I_2|s_1) = 0.2$$
$$P(I_1|s_2) = 0.1 \qquad P(I_2|s_2) = 0.9$$

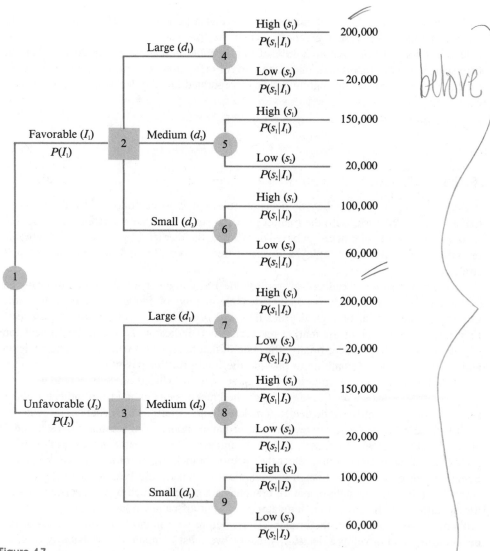

Figure 4.7
The PSI Decision Tree Incorporating the Results of the Market Research Study

In order to develop a decision strategy utilizing the decision tree in Figure 4.7, we need indicator branch probabilities $P(I_k)$ and state-of-nature branch probabilities $P(s_j|I_k)$. The problem now facing us is determining how to use the given prior probability estimates $P(s_j)$ and conditional probability estimates $P(I_k|s_j)$ to calculate the branch probabilities $P(I_k)$ and $P(s_j|I_k)$. In this section we will show how the Bayesian revision process discussed in Section 2.5 and referred to in Figure 4.6 can be used to calculate the branch probabilities $P(I_k)$ and $P(s_j|I_k)$.

In order to see how this Bayesian procedure is applied and at the same time understand how the procedure works, let us look closely at the calculation of the indicator branch probability, $P(I_1)$, for the PSI market research study. First, note that there are only two ways in which the outcome I_1 can occur:

1. The market research report is favorable (I_1) *and* the state of nature turns out to be high acceptance (s_1), written ($I_1 \cap s_1$).

2. The market research report is favorable (I_1) *and* the state of nature turns out to be low acceptance (s_2), written ($I_1 \cap s_2$).

The probabilities of these two outcomes are written $P(I_1 \cap s_1)$ and $P(I_1 \cap s_2)$, respectively. We can now add these two probabilities to obtain the following branch probability:

$$P(I_1) = P(I_1 \cap s_1) + P(I_1 \cap s_2) \qquad (4.8)$$

The multiplication law of probability provides the following formulas for $P(I_1 \cap s_1)$ and $P(I_1 \cap s_2)$:

$$P(I_1 \cap s_1) = P(I_1|s_1) P(s_1) \qquad (4.9)$$

$$P(I_1 \cap s_2) = P(I_1|s_2) P(s_2) \qquad (4.10)$$

Finally, substituting the above expressions for $P(I_1 \cap s_1)$ and $P(I_1 \cap s_2)$ in equation (4.8), we obtain

$$P(I_1) = P(I_1|s_1) P(s_1) + P(I_1|s_2) P(s_2) \qquad (4.11)$$

Generalizing the above expression for any indicator branch probability, $P(I_k)$, and N states of nature, $s_1, s_2, \ldots s_N$, we have

$$P(I_k) = P(I_k|s_1)P(s_1) + P(I_k|s_2)P(s_2) + \cdots + P(I_k|s_N)P(s_N) \qquad (4.12)$$

or

$$P(I_k) = \sum_{j=1}^{N} P(I_k|s_j)P(s_j) \qquad (14.13)$$

Returning to the PSI problem with the two prior probabilities $P(s_1) = 0.3$ and $P(s_2) = 0.7$ and the conditional probabilities $P(I_1|s_1) = 0.8$, $P(I_1|s_2) = 0.1$, $P(I_2|s_1) = 0.2$, and $P(I_2|s_2) = 0.9$, we can use equation (4.13) to compute the two indicator branch probabilities. These calculations are as follows:

$$P(I_1) = P(I_1|s_1)P(s_1) + P(I_1|s_2)P(s_2)$$
$$= (0.8)(0.3) + (0.1)(0.7) = 0.31$$

and

$$P(I_2) = P(I_2|s_1)P(s_1) + P(I_2|s_2)P(s_2)$$
$$= (0.2)(0.3) + (0.9)(0.7) = 0.69$$

The above probabilities indicate that the probability of I_1, a favorable market research report, is 0.31 and the probability of I_2, an unfavorable market research report, is 0.69.

Now that we know the indicator branch probabilities, let us show how the Bayesian process enables us to compute the revised, or posterior, state-of-nature branch probabilities $P(s_j|I_k)$. We will illustrate this procedure by considering the state-of-nature branch probability $P(s_1|I_1)$, the probability the market acceptance is high (s_1) given that the market research report is favorable (I_1). The fundamental conditional probability relationship as presented in Chapter 2 can be written

$$P(s_1|I_1) = \frac{P(I_1 \cap s_1)}{P(I_1)} \tag{4.14}$$

Using equation (4.9) for $P(I_1 \cap s_1)$, we have

$$P(s_1|I_1) = \frac{P(I_1|s_1)P(s_1)}{P(I_1)} \tag{4.15}$$

With known probabilities $P(I_1|s_1) = 0.8$, $P(s_1) = 0.3$, and $P(I_1) = 0.31$, the revised state-of-nature probability, $P(s_1|I_1)$, becomes

$$P(s_1|I_1) = \frac{(0.8)(0.3)}{0.31} = \frac{0.24}{0.31} = 0.7742$$

Recall that the prior probability of a high market acceptance was $P(s_1) = 0.3$. The above probability information now tells us that if the market research indicator is favorable, the probability of a high market acceptance should be revised to $P(s_1|I_1) = 0.7742$.

Generalizing (4.15) for any state of nature s_j and any indicator I_k provides

$$P(s_j|I_k) = \frac{P(I_k|s_j)P(s_j)}{P(I_k)} \tag{4.16}$$

Thus, we can use (4.16) to compute the revised or posterior state-of-nature branch probabilities. For example, the revised probability of low market acceptance, s_2, given the market research indicator is favorable, I_1, becomes

$$P(s_2|I_1) = \frac{P(I_1|s_2)P(s_2)}{P(I_1)} = \frac{(0.1)(0.7)}{0.31} = \frac{0.07}{0.31} = 0.2258$$

Similar calculations for an unfavorable market research indicator, I_2, will provide the revised state-of-nature branch probabilities $P(s_1|I_2) = 0.0870$ and $P(s_2|I_2) = 0.9130$. Figure 4.8 shows the PSI decision tree after all indicator and all revised state-of-nature branch probabilities have been computed.

Although the above procedure can be used to compute branch probabilities, the calculations can become quite cumbersome as the problem size grows larger. Thus in order to assist in applying Bayes' theorem to compute branch probabilities, we present the following tabular procedure that will make it easier to carry out the computations, especially for large decision analysis problems.

Computing Branch Probabilities: A Tabular Procedure

The procedure used for computing the probabilities of the indicator and state-of-nature branches can be carried out by utilizing the tabular approach for Bayes' theorem discussed in Section 2.5. First, for each indicator I_k we form a table consisting of the following five column headings:

Column 1 States of nature s_j

Column 2 Prior probabilities $P(s_j)$

Column 3 Conditional probabilities $P(I_k|s_j)$

Column 4 Joint probabilities $P(I_k \cap s_j)$

Column 5 Posterior probabilities $P(s_j|I_k)$

Then, given any indicator I_k, the following procedure can be used to calculate $P(I_k)$ and the $P(s_j|I_k)$ values.

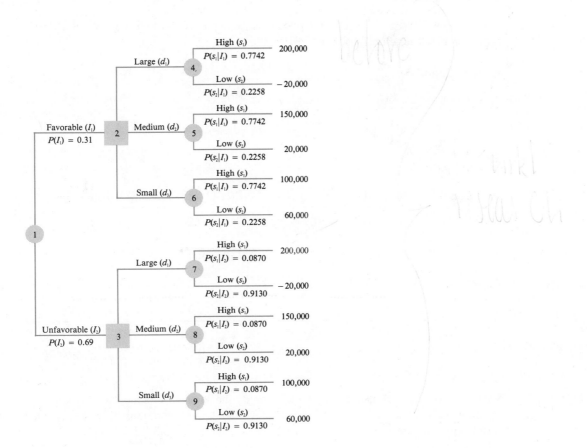

Figure 4.8
The PSI Decision Tree with Branch Probabilities

Step 1 In column 1 list the states of nature appropriate to the problem being analyzed.

Step 2 In column 2 enter the prior probability corresponding to each state of nature listed in column 1.

Step 3 In column 3 enter the appropriate value of $P(I_k|s_j)$ for each state of nature specified in column 1.

Step 4 To compute each entry in column 4, multiply each entry in column 2 by the corresponding entry in column 3.

Step 5 Add the entries in column 4. The sum is the value of $P(I_k)$. For convenience, write the sum below column 4.

Step 6 To compute each entry in column 5 divide the corresponding entry in column 4 by $P(I_k)$.

We will now illustrate the above procedure to compute $P(I_1)$ and the revised state-of-nature probabilities $P(s_j|I_1)$ for the PSI problem.

Steps 1, 2, and 3

s_j	$P(s_j)$	$P(I_1|s_j)$	$P(I_1 \cap s_j)$	$P(s_j|I_1)$
s_1	0.3	0.8		
s_2	0.7	0.1		

Steps 4 and 5

s_j	$P(s_j)$	$P(I_1|s_j)$	$P(I_1 \cap s_j)$	$P(s_j|I_1)$
s_1	0.3	0.8	0.24	
s_2	0.7	0.1	0.07	
			$P(I_1) = 0.31$	

Step 6

s_j	$P(s_j)$	$P(I_1|s_j)$	$P(I_1 \cap s_j)$	$P(s_j|I_1)$
s_1	0.3	0.8	0.24	$0.24/0.31 = 0.7742$
s_2	0.7	0.1	0.07	$0.07/0.31 = 0.2258$
			$P(I_1) = 0.31$	

Note that $P(I_1)$, $P(s_1|I_1)$, and $P(s_2|I_1)$ are exactly the same as we calculated by applying equations (4.13) and (4.16) directly. The above tabular computations could be repeated in order to compute $P(I_2)$ and the revised state-of-nature probabilities $P(s_j|I_2)$.

An Optimal Decision Strategy

Regardless of the method used to compute the branch probabilities, we can now use the branch probabilities and the expected value approach to arrive at the optimal decision strategy for PSI. Working *backward* through the decision tree, we first compute the expected value at each state-of-nature node. That is, at each state-of-nature node the possible payoffs are weighted by their chance of occurrence. Thus the expected values for nodes 4 through 9 are computed as follows:

$$EV(\text{node } 4) = (0.7742)(200,000) + (0.2258)(-20,000) = 150,324$$
$$EV(\text{node } 5) = (0.7742)(150,000) + (0.2258)(\ 20,000) = 120,646$$
$$EV(\text{node } 6) = (0.7742)(100,000) + (0.2258)(\ 60,000) = \ 90,968$$
$$EV(\text{node } 7) = (0.0870)(200,000) + (0.9130)(-20,000) = \ -860$$
$$EV(\text{node } 8) = (0.0870)(150,000) + (0.9130)(\ 20,000) = \ 31,310$$
$$EV(\text{node } 9) = (0.0870)(100,000) + (0.9130)(\ 60,000) = \ 63,480$$

Figure 4.9 shows the above calculations directly on the decision tree. Since the decision maker controls the branch leaving a decision node, and since we are trying to maximize expected profits, the optimal decision at node 2 is d_1. Thus since d_1 leads to an expected value of \$150,324, we say that $EV(\text{node } 2) = \$150,324$.

A similar analysis of decision node 3 shows that the optimal decision branch at this node is d_3. Thus $EV(\text{node } 3)$ becomes \$63,480, provided that the optimal decision of d_3 is made.

As a final step, we can continue working backward to the indicator node and establish its expected value. We see that since node 1 has probability branches, we cannot select the best branch. Rather we must compute the expected value over all possible branches. Thus we have

$$EV(\text{node } 1) = (0.31)\ EV(\text{node } 2) + (0.69)\ EV(\text{node } 3)$$
$$= (0.31)(\$150,324) + (0.69)(\$63,480) = \$90,402$$

The value of \$90,402 is viewed as the expected value of the optimal decision strategy when the market research study is used. In other words, it is the expected value using the sample information provided by the market research report.

Note that the final decision has not yet been determined. We will need to know the results of the market research study before deciding to lease a large system (d_1) or a small system (d_3). The results of the decision analysis at this point, however, have provided us with the following optimal *decision strategy* if the market research study is conducted.

Decision Strategy	
If	*Then*
Report favorable (I_1)	Lease large system (d_1)
Report unfavorable (I_2)	Lease small system (d_3)

Thus we have seen how the decision tree approach can be used to develop optimal decision strategies when sample information is available. While other decision analysis problems may not be as simple as the PSI problem, the approach we have outlined is still applicable. First draw a decision tree consisting of indicator, decision, and state-of-nature nodes and branches such that the tree describes the specific decision-making process. Posterior probability calculations must be made in order to establish indicator and state-of-nature branch probabilities. Then, by working backward through the tree,

□ = decision
    nodes

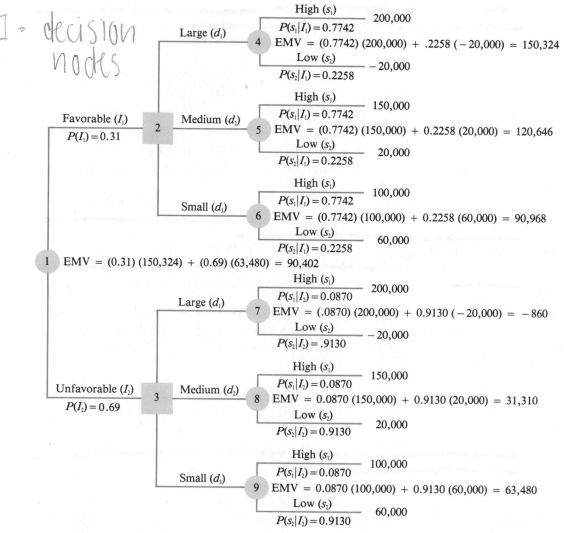

Figure 4.9
Developing a Decision Strategy for the PSI Problem

computing expected values at state-of-nature and indicator nodes, and selecting the best decision branch at decision nodes, the analyst can determine an optimal decision strategy and its associated expected value.

4.8

EXPECTED VALUE OF SAMPLE INFORMATION

In the PSI problem, management now has a decision strategy of leasing the large computer system if the market research report is favorable and leasing the small computer system if the market research report is unfavorable. Since the additional information provided by the market research firm will result in an added cost for PSI in terms of the fee paid to the research firm, PSI management may question the value of this market research information.

The value of sample information is often measured by calculating what is referred to as the *expected value of sample information (EVSI)*. For maximization problems,[2]

$$
\text{EVSI} = \begin{bmatrix} \text{expected value of the} \\ \text{optimal decision } with \\ \text{sample information} \end{bmatrix} - \begin{bmatrix} \text{expected value of the} \\ \text{optimal decision } without \\ \text{sample information} \end{bmatrix} \quad (4.17)
$$

For PSI the market research information is considered the "sample" information. The decision tree calculations indicated that the expected value of the optimal decision with the market research information is $90,402, while the expected value of the optimal decision without the market research information is $72,000. Using equation (4.17), the expected value of the market research report is

$$
\text{EVSI} = \$90,402 - \$72,000 = \$18,402
$$

Thus PSI should be willing to pay up to $18,402 for the market research information.

Efficiency of Sample Information

In Section 4.5 we saw that the expected value of perfect information (EVPI) for the PSI problem was $30,000. While we never expected the market research report to obtain perfect information, we can use an *efficiency* measure to express the value of the report. With perfect information having an efficiency rating of 100%, the efficiency rating E for sample information is computed as follows:

$$
E = \frac{\text{EVSI}}{\text{EVPI}} \times 100 \quad (4.18)
$$

For our PSI example,

$$
E = \frac{18,402}{30,000} \times 100 = 61.3\%
$$

In other words, the information from the market research firm is 61.3% as "efficient" as perfect information.

Low efficiency ratings for sample information might lead the decision maker to look for other types of information. On the other hand, high efficiency ratings indicate that the sample information is almost as good as perfect information, and additional sources of information should not be worthwhile.

The calculations associated with developing a decision strategy can be very time consuming as the problem size increases. Consequently, computer packages have been developed to perform the calculations for decision analysis problems. Figure 4.10 shows a portion of the computer output from the decision analysis module of *The Management*

---

[2]In minimization problems the expected value of the optimal decision with sample information will be less than or equal to the expected value of the optimal decision without sample information. Thus in minimization problems,

$$
\text{EVSI} = \begin{bmatrix} \text{expected value of the} \\ \text{optimal decision } without \\ \text{sample information} \end{bmatrix} - \begin{bmatrix} \text{expected value of the} \\ \text{optimal decision } with \\ \text{sample information} \end{bmatrix}
$$

```
BEST DECISION RECOMMENDATION
*****************************

USING THE EXPECTED VALUE CRITERION


    DECISION           CRITERION        RECOMMENDED
    ALTERNATIVE          VALUE           DECISION
    ***********         *********        **********

        1              46,000.00

        2              59,000.00

        3              72,000.00            YES


EXPECTED VALUE OF PERFECT INFORMATION IS   30,000.00



OPTIMAL DECISION STRATEGY
*****************************

                                                        PROB OF
        IF              BEST         EXPECTED           INDICATOR
     INDICATOR        DECISION         VALUE            OUTCOME
     *********        ********       ********          *********

        1                1          150,322.59           0.310

        2                3           63,478.26           0.690


    EXPECTED VALUE OF THE ABOVE STRATEGY          90,400.00

    EXPECTED VALUE OF THE SAMPLE INFORMATION      18,400.00

    EFFICIENCY OF THE SAMPLE INFORMATION             61.3%
```

Figure 4.10
Computer Output for the PSI Problem using *The Management Scientist Software Package*

Scientist. The slight difference that you see between the results presented in Figure 4.10 and the results in this chapter are simply due to the fact that in the chapter presentation we rounded some of the probability values in order to simplify the computations.

4.9

DECISION ANALYSIS INVOLVING NUMEROUS DECISION ALTERNATIVES AND NUMEROUS STATES OF NATURE

In the previous sections of this chapter we have considered decision situations where the decision alternatives and the states of nature are finite and can be listed. In this section we consider situations where both the decision alternatives and the states of nature are so numerous that it would be impractical, if not impossible, to use the payoff table or decision tree approach.

As an example of such a situation, consider the problem faced by the Kremer Chemical Company, which has a contract with one of its customers to supply a liquid chemical product. Historically, the customer places orders approximately every 6 months. Since an aging process of 2 months is required for the product, Kremer will have to decide how many pounds of the chemical to produce before the customer places an order.

Although the orders placed by the customer are always for an integral number of pounds, previous experience with the customer's orders has shown that the quantity ordered ranges from 700 to 1300 pounds. Thus, since the states of nature correspond to the levels of demand for the chemical, we would have to set up a payoff table consisting of approximately 600 states of nature (s_1 = demand of 700 pounds, s_2 = demand of 701 pounds, etc.). In addition, since the number of pounds to produce depends on the demand, we would need approximately 600 decision alternatives (d_1 = produce 700 pounds, d_2 = produce 701 pounds, etc.). Clearly, the number of decision alternatives and the number of states of nature are too large to practically consider a payoff table or decision tree approach.

Kremer's manufacturing costs for the chemical are $15 per pound, and the product sells at the fixed contract price of $20 per pound. If Kremer does not produce enough of the chemical to satisfy demand (''underproduces''), Kremer has agreed to absorb the added cost of filling the order by purchasing a higher-quality substitute product from another chemical firm. The substitute product, including transportation expenses, will cost Kremer $24 per pound. Since the product cannot be stored more than 4 months without spoilage, if Kremer produces too much of the chemical (''overproduces''), Kremer cannot inventory excess production until the customer's next 6-month order. As a result, Kremer sells the excess production to a chemical reprocessing firm for $13 per pound.

After further analysis of previous customer orders, Kremer believes that the customer's demand can be approximated by a normal probability distribution with a mean of 1000 pounds and a standard deviation of 100 pounds; this distribution is shown in Figure 14.11. Given Kremer's price and cost data, as well as the probability distribution of demand shown in Figure 14.11, how much production should Kremer plan for in anticipation of the customer's order for the chemical product?

The approach we will use to solve the Kremer Chemical problem is referred to as *marginal analysis*. Before presenting the details of the marginal analysis approach, however, we need to develop a better understanding of the costs involved in underproducing or overproducing. For example, let us assume that Kremer Chemical had to choose between just two possible production quantities or decision alternatives: (1) d_1 = produce 1000 pounds of the chemical; or (2) d_2 = produce 1001 pounds of the chemical. Obviously, the choice of which of these two decision alternatives is best will depend on the size of the customer's order. Thus, consider the following two states of nature: (1) s_1 = demand is less than or equal to 1000 pounds; and (2) s_2 = demand is greater than 1000

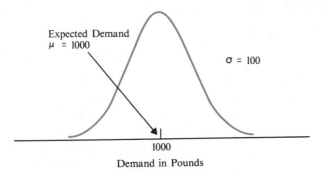

Figure 4.11
Normal Probability Distribution of Demand for Kremer Chemical Company

pounds. The payoff table for the problem expressed with two decision alternatives and two states of nature would appear as follows:

Decision Alternatives		States of Nature	
		Demand $\leq$ 1000 s_1	Demand $>$ 1000 s_2
Produce 1000 lbs	d_1		
Produce 1001 lbs	d_2		

In Section 4.2 we introduced the concept of opportunity loss. Let us now consider how we can develop an opportunity loss table for the modified Kremer Chemical problem in which Kremer must choose between a production quantity of 1000 pounds and a production quantity of 1001 pounds. First we note that if the state of nature turns out to be s_1 (demand $\leq$ 1000 pounds), then the decision to produce 1000 pounds (d_1) would always be preferred as compared to the decision to produce 1001 pounds. Thus, the opportunity loss associated with the d_1 decision when state of nature s_1 occurs is 0. Similarly, if the state of nature turns out to be s_2 (demand $>$ 1000), then the decision to produce 1001 pounds (d_2) would have been the optimal decision; hence, the opportunity loss associated with the d_2 decision when state of nature s_2 occurs is 0.

If Kremer decides to produce 1000 pounds and the actual demand turned out to be exactly 1001 pounds, then the best decision would have been d_2. In this case d_1 would have resulted in underestimating demand by one unit. The cost or loss of not ordering one additional unit and finding that it could have been sold is referred to as the cost per unit of *underestimating* demand. We refer to this cost as c_u.

Recall that if Kremer underproduces, it will have to purchase a substitute product at a higher cost per unit in order to satisfy the customer's demand for the product. Since the substitute product costs Kremer $24 per pound and Kremer sells the product to the customer for $20 per pound, a cost of $c_u = \$24 - \$20 = \$4$ is incurred for every pound of underestimated demand. Table 4.7 shows what the cost of underestimating demand would be for each decision and several possible demand levels.

Table 4.7
Cost of Underestimating Demand for Selected Demand Levels

Demand	Cost of Underestimating Demand	
	d_1 (1000 lb)	d_2 (1001 lb)
1001 lb	$4(1) = \$ 4$	$4(0) = \$0$
1002 lb	$4(2) = \$ 8$	$4(1) = \$4$
1003 lb	$4(3) = \$12$	$4(2) = \$8$
.	.	.
.	.	.
.	.	.

As Table 4.7 shows, if the demand turns out to be greater than 1000 pounds, then the total cost of underestimating demand will always be $4 less for decision d_2. Thus, if d_1 is selected and s_2 occurs, Kremer would incur a \$4 loss as compared to the best decision d_2. Thus the opportunity loss associated with the d_1 decision if state of nature s_2 occurs is $c_u = \$4$.

To determine the opportunity loss associated with the d_2 decision if state of nature s_1 occurs, let us consider what would happen if Kremer produced 1001 pounds and demand turned out to be exactly 1000 pounds. In this case Kremer would have overestimated demand by one unit. The cost or loss of ordering one additional unit and finding that it cannot be sold is referred to as the cost per unit of *overestimating* demand; we refer to this cost as c_o.

If Kremer overestimates demand by 1 pound, the company incurs a cost of \$15 to manufacture the one additional pound; this surplus is reprocessed and sold for \$13. Thus, Kremer has a cost of $c_o = \$15 - \$13 = \$2$ associated with overestimating demand by 1 pound. Table 4.8 shows what the cost of overestimating demand would be for each decision and several possible demand levels.

Table 4.8
Cost of Overestimating Demand for Selected Demand Levels

	Cost of Overestimating Demand	
Demand	d_1 (1000 lb)	d_2 (1001 lb)
1000 lb	\$2(0) = \$0	\$2(1) = \$2
999 lb	\$2(1) = \$2	\$2(2) = \$4
998 lb	\$2(2) = \$4	\$2(3) = \$6
.	.	.
.	.	.
.	.	.

As Table 4.8 shows, if the demand turns out to be less than or equal to 1000 pounds, then the total cost of overestimating demand will always be \$2 less for decision d_1. Thus, if d_2 is selected and s_1 occurs, Kremer would incur a \$2 loss as compared to the best decision d_1. Thus the opportunity loss associated with the d_2 decision if state of nature s_1 occurs is $c_o = \$2$. A summary of the opportunity losses that can occur corresponding to decision alternatives d_1 and d_2 and states of nature s_1 and s_2 is shown in Table 4.9.

Table 4.9
Opportunity Loss Table for the Kremer Chemical Company Problem

		States of Nature	
Decision Alternatives		Demand ≤ 1000 s_1	Demand > 1000 s_2
Produce 1000 lb	d_1	\$0	\$4
Produce 1001 lb	d_2	\$2	\$0

Since the exact level of demand for the chemical product is unknown, we will have to consider the probability of demand and thus the probability of obtaining the above losses. By looking at the demand probability distribution in Figure 4.10, we see that $P(\text{demand} \leq 1000) = 0.50$ and that $P(\text{demand} > 1000) = 0.5$. Thus, the expected loss (EL) for each decision alternative is

$$EL(d_1) = \$0(0.5) + \$4(0.5) = \$2$$
$$EL(d_2) = \$2(0.5) + \$0(0.5) = \$1$$

Note that because the opportunity loss associated with the best decision for each state of nature is 0, we can compute the expected loss by simply multiplying the possible losses, $c_u = \$4$ and $c_o = \$2$, by the probability of obtaining the loss.

Based on the above expected losses, do you prefer a production level of 1000 or 1001 pounds? Since the expected loss is greater for d_1, and since we want to avoid this higher loss, we should make d_2 (1001 pounds) the preferred decision alternative. We could now consider increasing the production level to 1002 pounds in order to compare the expected loss associated with producing 1002 pounds with the expected loss of producing 1001 pounds.

The problem with continuing this type of analysis is that it would be very time consuming and cumbersome. As indicated, we would next have to compare production quantities of 1001 and 1002. If the expected loss of 1002 is less than the expected loss of 1001, we would then compare production quantities of 1002 and 1003, then 1003 and 1004, and so on; in general, at each step we would compare the expected loss of some production level Q with the expected loss of $Q + 1$. This process would continue until we found the value of Q where the expected loss of producing Q pounds equaled the expected loss of producing $Q + 1$ pounds.

If we denote the optimal production quantity by Q^*, the optimal production quantity occurs when the marginal analysis shows that

$$EL(Q^* + 1) = EL(Q^*) \tag{4.19}$$

When the above relationship holds, there is no economic advantage to increasing the production size by one additional pound. Following the logic that we used to compute the expected losses for the production quantities 1000 and 1001, the general expression for $EL(Q^* + 1)$ and $EL(Q^*)$ can be written

$$EL(Q^* + 1) = c_o\, P(\text{demand} \leq Q^*) \tag{4.20}$$
$$EL(Q^*) = c_u\, P(\text{demand} > Q^*) \tag{4.21}$$

Since we know from basic probability that

$$P(\text{demand} \leq Q^*) + P(\text{demand} > Q^*) = 1 \tag{4.22}$$

we can write

$$P(\text{demand} > Q^*) = 1 - P(\text{demand} \leq Q^*) \tag{4.23}$$

Using this expression, (4.21) can be rewritten as

$$EL(Q^*) = c_u\, [1 - P(\text{demand} \leq Q^*)] \tag{4.24}$$

Expressions (4.20) and (4.24) can be used to show that $EL(Q^* + 1) = EL(Q^*)$ whenever

$$c_o\, P(\text{demand} \leq Q^*) = c_u\, [1 - P(\text{demand} \leq Q^*)] \qquad (4.25)$$

Solving for $P(\text{demand} \leq Q^*)$, we have

$$P(\text{demand} \leq Q^*) = \frac{c_u}{c_u + c_o} \qquad (4.26)$$

The above expression provides the general condition for the optimal production quantity Q^*.

Applying equation (4.26) to the Kremer Chemical problem indicates that the optimal order quantity must satisfy the following condition:

$$P(\text{demand} \leq Q^*) = \frac{c_u}{c_u + c_o} = \frac{4}{4 + 2} = 0.67$$

Now we can use the normal probability distribution for demand as shown in Figure 4.12 to find the order quantity that satisfies the condition that $P(\text{demand} \leq Q^*) = 0.67$.

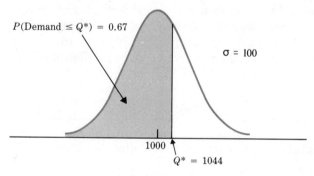

Figure 4.12
Probability Distribution of Demand for Kremer Chemical Company Showing the Location of the Optimal Production Quantity Q*

From Appendix C we see that the area between the mean of the standard normal distribution and $z = 0.44$ standard deviations above the mean is 0.17. Since the area below the mean is 0.50, the area below a value of $z = 0.44$ standard deviations above the mean is 0.67. For the Kremer Chemical Company, the mean or expected demand is given by $\mu = 1000$ and the standard deviation is $\sigma = 100$; thus, the optimal order quantity is

$$Q^* = \mu + z\sigma$$
$$= 1000 + 0.44(100) = 1044$$

We see that with the assumed normal probability distribution of demand, the Kremer Chemical Company should produce 1044 pounds of the chemical in anticipation of the customer's order. Note that in this case the cost of underestimation is more than the cost of overestimation. Thus Kremer is willing to risk a higher probability of overestimation and hence a higher probability of a surplus. In fact, Kremer's optimal production quantity has a 0.67 probability of having a surplus and a $1 - 0.67 = 0.33$ probability of a stockout.

Summary

In this chapter we have emphasized how decision analysis can be used to solve problems with a limited number of decision alternatives and a limited number of possible states of nature. The goal of decision analysis is to identify the best decision alternative given an uncertain or risk-filled pattern of future events (that is, states of nature).

We presented three approaches to decision making without probabilities, and discussed the use of the expected value approach for solving problems with probabilities. Then we showed how additional information about the states of nature can be used to revise or update the probability estimates and develop an optimal decision strategy for the problem. The notions of expected value of sample information, expected value of perfect information, and efficiency were used to evaluate the contribution of the sample information. The chapter concluded with a discussion of how marginal analysis can be used in situations involving numerous decision alternatives and numerous states of nature.

In the example which we used to introduce decision analysis, we expressed the payoffs associated with the problem in terms of monetary values; thus, the best decision was the one with the largest expected monetary value. While decision analysis applications are often based on the expected value of monetary payoffs, there are other measures of payoff that can be used. In Chapter 5 we introduce utility as another measure of payoff.

Glossary

States of nature   The uncontrollable future events that can affect the outcome of a decision.

Payoff   The outcome measure, such as profit, cost, time, and so on. Each combination of a decision alternative and a state of nature has an associated payoff.

Payoff table   A tabular representation of the payoffs for a decision problem.

Optimistic approach   An approach to choosing a decision alternative without using probabilities. For a maximization problem it leads to choosing the alternative corresponding to the largest payoff; for a minimization problem it leads to choosing the alternative corresponding to the smallest payoff.

Conservative approach   An approach to choosing a decision alternative without using probabilities. For a maximization problem it leads to choosing the alternative that maximizes the minimum payoff; for a minimization problem it leads to choosing the alternative that minimizes the maximum payoff.

Minimax regret   An approach to choosing a decision alternative without using probabilities. For each alternative, the maximum regret is computed. This approach leads to choosing the alternative that minimizes the maximum regret.

Opportunity loss or regret   The amount of loss (lower profit or higher cost) due to not making the best decision for each state of nature.

Decision tree   A graphical representation of the decision-making situation from decision to state-of-nature to payoff.

Nodes   The intersection or junction points of the decision tree.

Branches   Lines or arcs connecting nodes of the decision tree.

Expected value   For a decision alternative, it is the weighted average of the payoffs. The weights are the state-of-nature probabilities.

Expected value of perfect information (EVPI)   The expected value of information that would tell the decision maker exactly which state of nature was going to occur (that is, perfect information).

Prior probabilities   The probabilities of the states of nature prior to obtaining sample information.

Posterior (revised) probabilities   The probabilities of the states of nature after using Bayes' theorem to adjust the prior probabilities based on given indicator information.

Indicators   Information about the states of nature. An indicator may be the result of a sample.

Bayesian revision   The process of adjusting prior probabilities to create the posterior probabilities based on sample information.

Expected value of sample information (EVSI)   The difference between the expected value of an optimal strategy based on new information and the "best" expected value without any new information. It is a measure of the value of new information.

Efficiency   The ratio of EVSI to EVPI; perfect information is 100% efficient.

Marginal analysis   A procedure for solving decision analysis problems involving numerous decision alternatives and numerous states of nature.

Problems

1. Suppose that a decision maker faced with four decision alternatives and four states of nature develops the following profit payoff table:

		States of Nature		
	s_1	s_2	s_3	s_4
d_1	14	9	10	5
Decision d_2	11	10	8	7
Alternative d_3	9	10	10	11
d_4	8	10	11	13

   a. If the decision maker knows nothing about the chances or probability of occurrence of the four states of nature, what is the recommended decision using the optimistic, conservative, and minimax regret approaches?

   b. Which aproach do you prefer? Explain. Is it important for the decision maker to establish the most appropriate approach before analyzing the problem? Explain.

   c. Assume that the payoff table provides *cost* rather than profit payoffs. What is the recommended decision using the optimistic, conservative, and minimax regret approaches?

2. Suppose that the decision maker in problem 1 obtains information that enables the following probability estimates to be made: $P(s_1) = 0.5$, $P(s_2) = 0.2$, $P(s_3) = 0.2$, $P(s_4) = 0.1$.

a. Use the expected value approach to determine the optimal decision.

b. Now assume that the entries in the payoff table are costs; use the expected value approach to determine the optimal decision.

3. Southland Corporation's decision to produce a new line of recreational products has resulted in the need to construct either a small plant or a large plant. The decision as to which plant size to select depends on how the marketplace reacts to the new product line. In order to conduct an analysis, marketing management has decided to view the possible long-run demand as either low, medium, or high. The following payoff table shows the projected profit in millions of dollars.

		Low	Medium	High
		Long-Run Demand		
Decision Alternatives	Small plant	150	200	200
	Large plant	50	200	500

Handwritten annotations:
0   0   300   —   300
100   0   0   —   100

200   150 C
500   0   50

a. Construct a decision tree for this problem and determine the recommended decision using the optimistic, conservative, and minimax regret approaches.

b. Assume that the best estimate of the probability of a low long-run demand is 0.20, a medium long-run demand is 0.15, and a high long-run demand is 0.65. What is the recommended decision using the expected value approach?

4. In order to save on gasoline expenses, Rona and Jerry agreed to form a carpool for traveling to and from work. After limiting the travel routes to two alternatives, Rona and Jerry could not agree on the best way to travel to work. Jerry preferred the expressway, since it was usually the fastest; however, Rona pointed out that traffic jams on the expressway sometimes led to long delays. Rona preferred the somewhat longer, but more consistent, Queen City Avenue. While Jerry still preferred the expressway, he agreed with Rona that they should take Queen City Avenue if the expressway had a traffic jam. Unfortunately, they do not know the state of the expressway ahead of time. The following payoff table provides the one-way time estimates for traveling to or from work:

		Expressway Open s_1	Expressway Jammed s_2
		States of Nature	
Expressway	d_1	25	45
Queen City Avenue	d_2	30	30

Travel time in minutes

a. After driving to work on the expressway for 1 month (20 days), they found the expressway jammed three times. Assuming that these days are representative of future days, should they continue to use the expressway for traveling to work? Explain.

$\frac{3}{20}$

b. Use graphical sensitivity analysis to determine the values of the probability of state of nature s_1 for which d_1 has the best expected value.

c. Would it make sense not to adopt the expected value approach for this particular problem? Explain.

5. The payoff table showing profit for a decision problem with two states of nature and three decision alternatives is presented below:

		States of Nature	
		s_1	s_2
Decision Alternatives	d_1	80	50
	d_2	65	85
	d_3	30	100

Use graphical sensitivity analysis to determine the values of the probability of state of nature s_1 for which each of the decision alternatives has the largest expected value.

6. Milford Trucking, located in Chicago, has requests to haul two shipments, one to St. Louis and one to Detroit. Because of a scheduling problem, Milford will be able to accept only one of these assignments. The St. Louis customer has guaranteed a return shipment, but the Detroit customer has not. Thus if Milford accepts the Detroit shipment and cannot find a Detroit-to-Chicago return shipment, the truck will return to Chicago empty. The payoff table showing profit is as follows:

		Return Shipment from Detroit	No Return Shipment from Detroit
		s_1	s_2
St. Louis	d_1	2000	2000
Detroit	d_2	2500	1000

a. If the probability of a Detroit return shipment is 0.4, what should Milford do?

b. Use graphical sensitivity analysis to determine the values of the probability of state of nature s_1 for which d_1 has the largest expected value.

c. What is the expected value of perfect information that would tell Milford whether or not Detroit had a return shipment?

7. Hale's TV Productions is considering producing a pilot for a comedy series for a major television network. While the network may reject the pilot and the series, it may also purchase the program for 1 or 2 years. Hale may decide to produce the pilot or transfer the rights for the series to a competitor for $100,000. Hale's profits are summarized in the following payoff table:

		States of Nature		
		Reject	1 Year	2 Years
Produce pilot	d_1	-100	50	150
Sell to competitor	d_2	100	100	100

Profit in $\$ \times 10^3$

a. If the probability estimates for the states of nature are $P(\text{reject}) = 0.2$, $P(1\ \text{year}) = 0.3$, $P(2\ \text{years}) = 0.5$, what should the company do?

b. What is the maximum that Hale should be willing to pay for information on what the network will do?

8. McHuffter Condominiums, Inc. of Pensacola, Florida, recently purchased land near the Gulf of Mexico and is attempting to determine the size of the condominium development it should build. Three sizes of developments are being considered: small d_1, medium d_2, and large d_3. At the same time an uncertain economy makes it difficult to ascertain the demand for the new condominiums. McHuffter's management realizes that a large development followed by a low demand could be very costly to the company. However, if McHuffter makes a conservative small development decision and then finds a high demand, the firm's profits will be lower than they might have been. With the three levels of demand—low, medium, and high—McHuffter's management has prepared the following payoff table:

		S_1	S_2 Demand	S_3
		Low	Medium	High
Decision Alternatives	Small d_1	400	400	400
	Medium d_2	100	600	600
	Large d_3	−300	300	900

Profit in $ × 10^3

a. If nothing is known about the demand probabilities, what are the decision recommendations using the optimistic, conservative, and minimax regret approaches?

b. If $P(\text{low}) = 0.20$, $P(\text{medium}) = 0.35$, and $P(\text{high}) = 0.45$, what decision is recommended using the expected value approach?

c. What is the expected value of perfect information?

9. Construct a decision tree for the McHuffter Condominiums problem (problem 8). What is the expected value at each state-of-nature node? What is the optimal decision?

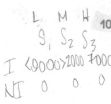

10. Martin's Service Station is considering investing in a heavy-duty snowplow this fall. Martin has analyzed the situation carefully and feels that this would be a very profitable investment if the snowfall is heavy. A small profit could still be made if the snowfall is moderate, but Martin would lose money if snowfall is light. Specifically, Martin forecasts a profit of $7000 if snowfall is heavy and $2000 if it is moderate, and a $9000 loss if it is light. Based on the weather bureau's long-range forecast, Martin estimates that $P(\text{heavy snowfall}) = 0.4$, $P(\text{moderate snowfall}) = 0.3$, and $P(\text{light snowfall}) = 0.3$.

a. Prepare a decision tree for Martin's problem.

b. Using the expected value approach, would you recommend that Martin invest in the snowplow?

11. Refer again to the investment problem faced by Martin's Service Station (problem 10). Martin can purchase a blade to attach to his service truck that can also be used to plow driveways and parking lots. Since this truck must also be available to start cars, etc., Martin will not be able to generate as much revenue plowing snow if he elects this alternative. But he will keep his loss smaller if there is light snowfall.

Under this alternative Martin forecasts a profit of $3500 if snowfall is heavy and $1000 if it is moderate, and a $1500 loss if snowfall is light.

a. Prepare a new decision tree showing all three alternatives.

b. Using the expected value approach, what is the optimal decision?

c. What is the expected value of perfect information?

12. The Gorman Manufacturing Company must decide whether it should purchase a component part from a supplier or manufacture the component at its Milan, Michigan, plant. If demand is high, it would be to Gorman's advantage to manufacture the component. However, if demand is low, Gorman's unit manufacturing cost will be high due to underutilization of equipment. The projected profit in thousands of dollars for Gorman's make or buy decision is shown below:

	Demand		
	Low	Medium	High
Manufacture component	−20	40	100
Purchase component	10	45	70

The states of nature have the following probabilities: $P(\text{low demand}) = 0.35$, $P(\text{medium demand}) = 0.35$, and $P(\text{high demand}) = 0.30$.

a. Use a decision tree to recommend a decision.

b. Use EVPI to determine whether Gorman should attempt to obtain a better estimate of demand.

13. In problem 4, suppose that Rona and Jerry wished to determine the best way to return home in the evenings. In 20 days of traveling home on the expressway, they found the expressway jammed six times.

a. Using the travel time table shown in problem 4, what route would you recommend they take on their way home in the evening?

b. If they had perfect information about the traffic condition of the expressway, what would be their savings in terms of expected travel time?

14. A firm produces a perishable food product at a cost of $10 per case. The product sells for $15 per case. For planning purposes the company is considering possible demands of 100, 200, or 300 cases. If the demand is less than production, the excess production is lost. If demand is more than production, the firm, in an attempt to maintain a good service image, will satisfy the excess demand with a special production run at a cost of $18 per case. The product, however, always sells at $15 per case.

a. Set up the payoff table for this problem.

b. If $P(100) = 0.2$, $P(200) = 0.2$, and $P(300) = 0.6$, should the company produce 100, 200, or 300 cases?

c. What is the EVPI?

15. Sealcoat, Inc. has a contract with one of its customers to supply a unique liquid chemical product that will be used by the customer in the manufacture of a lubricant for airplane engines. Because of the chemical process used by Sealcoat, batch sizes for the liquid chemical product must be 1000 pounds. The customer has agreed to adjust manufacturing to the full batch quantities and will order either one, two, or

three batches every 3 months. Since an aging process of 1 month exists for the product, Sealcoat will have to make its production (how much to make) decision before the customer places an order. Thus Sealcoat can list the product demand alternatives of 1000, 2000, or 3000 pounds, but the exact demand is unknown.

Sealcoat's manufacturing costs are $150 per pound, and the product sells at the fixed contract price of $200 per pound. If the customer orders more than Sealcoat has produced, Sealcoat has agreed to absorb the added cost of filling the order by purchasing a higher-quality substitute product from another chemical firm. The substitute product, including transportation expenses, will cost Sealcoat $240 per pound. Since the product cannot be stored more than 2 months without spoilage, Sealcoat cannot inventory excess production until the customer's next 3-month order. Therefore, if the customer's current order is less than Sealcoat has produced, the excess production will be reprocessed and is valued at $50 per pound.

The inventory decision in this problem is how much should Sealcoat produce given the above costs and the possible demands of 1000, 2000, or 3000 pounds? Based on historical data and an analysis of the customer's future demands, Sealcoat has assessed the following probability distribution for demand:

Demand	Probability
1000	0.3
2000	0.5
3000	0.2
Total	1.0

a. Develop a payoff table for the Sealcoat problem.
b. How many batches should Sealcoat produce every 3 months?
c. How much of a discount should Sealcoat be willing to allow the customer for specifying in advance exactly how many batches will be purchased?

16. A quality control procedure involves 100% inspection of parts received from a supplier. Historical records show that the following defective rates have been observed.

Percent Defective	Probability
0	0.15
1	0.25
2	0.40
3	0.20

The cost to inspect 100% of the parts received is $250 for each shipment of 500 parts. If the shipment is not 100% inspected, defective parts will cause rework problems later in the production process. The rework cost is $25 for each defective part.

a. Complete the following payoff table, where the entries represent the total cost of inspection and reworking:

	Percent Defective			
	0	1	2	3
100% inspection	$250	$250	$250	$250
No inspection				

b. The plant manager is considering eliminating the inspection process in order to save the $250 inspection cost per shipment. Do you support this action? Use expected value to justify your answer.

c. Show the decision tree for this problem.

17. Suppose that you are given a decision situation with three possible states of nature: s_1, s_2, and s_3. The prior probabilities are $P(s_1) = 0.2$, $P(s_2) = 0.5$, and $P(s_3) = 0.3$. Indicator information I is obtained and it is known that $P(I|s_1) = 0.1$, $P(I|s_2) = 0.05$, and $P(I|s_3) = 0.2$. Compute the revised or posterior probabilities: $P(s_1|I)$, $P(s_2|I)$, and $P(s_3|I)$.

18. The payoff table showing profit for a decision problem with two states of nature and three decision alternatives is presented below:

	s_1	s_2
d_1	15	10
d_2	10	12
d_3	8	20

The prior probabilities for s_1 and s_2 are $P(s_1) = 0.8$ and $P(s_2) = 0.2$.

a. Using only the prior probabilities and the expected value approach, find the optimal decision.

b. Use graphical sensitivity analysis to determine the values of the probability of state of nature s_1 for which each of the decision alternatives has the largest expected value.

c. Find the EVPI.

d. Suppose that some indicator information I is obtained with $P(I|s_1) = 0.2$ and $P(I|s_2) = 0.75$. Find the posterior probabilities $P(s_1|I)$ and $P(s_2|I)$. Recommend a decision alternative based on these probabilities.

19. Consider the following decision tree representation of a decision analysis problem with two indicators, two decision alternatives, and two states of nature:

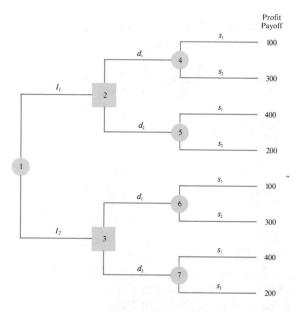

Assume that the following probability information is given:

$$P(s_1) = 0.4 \qquad P(I_1|s_1) = 0.8 \qquad P(I_2|s_1) = 0.2$$
$$P(s_2) = 0.6 \qquad P(I_1|s_2) = 0.4 \qquad P(I_2|s_2) = 0.6$$

a. What are the values for $P(I_1)$ and $P(I_2)$?
b. What are the values of $P(s_1|I_1)$, $P(s_2|I_1)$, $P(s_1|I_2)$, and $P(s_2|I_2)$?
c. Use the decision tree approach and determine the optimal decision strategy. What is the expected value of your solution?

20. The payoff table for problem 19 is as follows:

	s_1	s_2
d_1	100	300
d_2	400	200

a. What is your decision without the indicator information?
b. What is the expected value of the indicator or sample information, EVSI?
c. What is the expected value of perfect information, EVPI?
d. What is the efficiency of the indicator information?

21. The payoff table for Hale's TV Productions (problem 7) is as follows:

		States of Nature		
		s_1	s_2	s_3
Produce pilot	d_1	−100	50	150
Sell to competitor	d_2	100	100	100
Probability of states of nature		0.2	0.3	0.5

For a consulting fee of $2500, an agency will review the plans for the comedy series and indicate the overall chances of a favorable network reaction to the series. If the special agency review results in a favorable (I_1) or an unfavorable (I_2) evaluation, what should Hale's decision strategy be? Assume Hale believes the following conditional probabilities are realistic appraisals of the agency's evaluation accuracy:

$$P(I_1|s_1) = 0.3 \quad P(I_2|s_1) = 0.7$$
$$P(I_1|s_2) = 0.6 \quad P(I_2|s_2) = 0.4$$
$$P(I_1|s_3) = 0.9 \quad P(I_2|s_3) = 0.1$$

a. Show the decision tree for this problem.
b. What is the recommended decision strategy and the expected value, assuming that the agency information is obtained?
c. What is the EVSI? Is the $2500 consulting fee worth the information? What is the maximum Hale should be willing to pay for the consulting information?

22. McHuffter Condominiums (problem 8) is conducting a survey that will help evaluate the demand for the new condominium development. McHuffter's payoff table (profit) is as follows:

			States of Nature		
			Low s_1	Medium s_2	High s_3
Decision Alternatives	Small	d_1	400	400	400
	Medium	d_2	100	600	600
	Large	d_3	−300	300	900
Probability of states of nature			0.20	0.35	0.45

The survey will result in three indicators of demand [weak (I_1), average (I_2), or strong (I_3)], where the conditional probabilities are as follows:

	$P(I_k|s_k)$		
	I_1	I_2	I_3
s_1	0.6	0.3	0.1
s_2	0.4	0.4	0.2
s_3	0.1	0.4	0.5

a. What is McHuffter's optimal strategy?
b. What is the expected value of the survey information?
c. What are the EVPI and the efficiency of the survey information?

23. The payoff table for Martin's Service Station (problems 10 and 11) is as follows:

		Snowfall		
		Heavy s_1	Moderate s_2	Light s_3
Purchase snowplow	d_1	7000	2000	−9000
Do not invest	d_2	0	0	0
Purchase snowplow with blade	d_3	3500	1000	−1500
Probabilities of states of nature		0.4	0.3	0.3

Suppose that Martin decides to wait to check the September temperature pattern before making a final decision. Estimates of the probabilities associated with an unseasonably cold September (I_1) are as follows: $P(I_1|s_1) = 0.30$, $P(I_1|s_2) = 0.20$, $P(I_1|s_3) = 0.05$. If Martin observes an unseasonably cold September, what is the recommended decision? If Martin does not observe an unseasonably cold September (I_2), what is the recommended decision?

24. A food processor considers daily production runs of 100, 200, or 300 cases. Possible demands for the product are 100, 200, or 300 cases. The payoff table is as follows:

			Demand		
			100 s_1	200 s_2	300 s_3
	d_2	100	500	200	−100
Production	d_2	200	−400	800	700
	d_3	300	−1000	−200	1600

a. If $P(s_1) = 0.20$, $P(s_2) = 0.20$, and $P(s_3) = 0.60$, what is your recommended production quantity?
b. On some days the firm receives phone calls for advance orders and on some days it does not. Let I_1 = advance orders are received and I_2 = no advance orders are received. If $P(I_2|s_1) = 0.80$, $P(I_2|s_2) = 0.40$, and $P(I_2|s_3) = 0.10$, what is your recommended production quantity for days the company does not receive any advance orders?

25. The Gorman Manufacturing Company (problem 12) has the following payoff table for a make-or-buy decision:

		Demand		
		Low s_1	Medium s_2	High s_3
Manufacture component	d_1	−20	40	100
Purchase component	d_2	10	45	70
Probabilities of states of nature		0.35	0.35	0.30

A test market study of the potential demand for the product is expected to report either a favorable (I_1) or unfavorable (I_2) condition. The relevant conditional probabilities are as follows:

$$P(I_1|s_1) = 0.10 \qquad P(I_2|s_1) = 0.90$$
$$P(I_1|s_2) = 0.40 \qquad P(I_2|s_2) = 0.60$$
$$P(I_1|s_3) = 0.60 \qquad P(I_2|s_3) = 0.40$$

a. What is the probability that the market research report will be favorable?
b. What is Gorman's optimal decision strategy?
c. What is the expected value of the market research information?
d. What is the efficiency of the information?

26. The traveling time to work for Rona and Jerry has the following time payoff table (problem 4):

		States of Nature for Expressway	
		Open s_1	Jammed s_2
Expressway	d_1	25	45
Queen City Avenue	d_2	30	30
Probabilities of states of nature		0.85	0.15

After a period of time Rona and Jerry noted that the weather seemed to affect the traffic conditions on the expressway. They identified three weather conditions (indicators) with the following conditional probabilities:

I_1 = clear
I_2 = overcast
I_3 = rain
$P(I_1|s_1) = 0.8 \qquad P(I_2|s_1) = 0.2 \qquad P(I_3|s_1) = 0$
$P(I_1|s_2) = 0.1 \qquad P(I_2|s_2) = 0.3 \qquad P(I_3|s_2) = 0.6$

a. Show the decision tree for the problem of traveling to work.
b. What is the optimal decision strategy and the expected travel time?
c. What is the efficiency of the weather information?

27. The research and development manager for Beck Company is trying to decide whether or not to fund a project to develop a new lubricant. It is assumed that the project will be either a major technical success, a minor technical success, or a failure. The company has estimated that the value of a major technical success is $150,000, since the lubricant can be used in a number of products the company is making. If the project is a minor technical success, its value is $10,000, since Beck feels that the knowledge gained will benefit some other ongoing projects. If the project is a failure, it will cost the company $100,000.

Based on the opinion of the scientists involved and the manager's own subjective assessment, the assigned prior probabilities are as follows:

$$P(\text{major success}) = 0.15$$
$$P(\text{minor success}) = 0.45$$
$$P(\text{failure}) = 0.40$$

a. Using the expected value approach, should the project be funded?
b. Suppose that a group of expert scientists from a research institute could be hired as consultants to study the project and make a recommendation. If this study will cost $30,000, should the Beck Company consider hiring the consultants?

28. Consider again the problem faced by the R&D manager of Beck Company (problem 27). Suppose that an experiment can be conducted to shed some light on the technical feasibility of the project. There are three possible outcomes for the experiment:

I_1 = prototype lubricant works well at all temperatures
I_2 = prototype lubricant works well only at temperatures above 10°F
I_3 = prototype lubricant does not work well at any temperature

Suppose that we can determine the following conditional probabilities:

$$P(I_1|\text{major success}) = 0.70$$
$$P(I_1|\text{minor success}) = 0.10$$
$$P(I_1|\text{failure}) = 0.10$$

$$P(I_2|\text{major success}) = 0.25$$
$$P(I_2|\text{minor success}) = 0.70$$
$$P(I_2|\text{failure}) = 0.30$$

$$P(I_3|\text{major success}) = 0.05$$
$$P(I_3|\text{minor success}) = 0.20$$
$$P(I_3|\text{failure}) = 0.60$$

a. Assuming that the experiment is conducted and the prototype lubricant works well at all temperatures, should the project be funded?
b. Assuming that the experiment is conducted and the prototype lubricant works well only at temperatures above 10°F, should the project be funded?
c. Develop a decision strategy that Beck's R&D manager can use to recommend a funding decision based on the outcome of the experiment.
d. Find the EVSI for the experiment. How efficient is the information in the experiment?

29. The payoff table for Sealcoat, Inc. (problem 15) is as follows:

		Demand		
Production		1,000	2,000	3,000
Quantity		s_1	s_2	s_3
1,000	d_1	50,000	10,000	30,000
2,000	d_2	$-50,000$	100,000	60,000
3,000	d_3	$-150,000$	0	150,000
Probabilities		0.30	0.50	0.20

Sealcoat has identified a pattern in the demand for the product based on the customer's previous order quantity. Let

I_1 = customer's last order was 1000 pounds

I_2 = customer's last order was 2000 pounds

I_3 = customer's last order was 3000 pounds

The conditional probabilities are as follows:

$$P(I_1|s_1) = 0.10 \quad P(I_2|s_1) = 0.40 \quad P(I_3|s_1) = 0.50$$
$$P(I_1|s_2) = 0.22 \quad P(I_2|s_2) = 0.68 \quad P(I_3|s_2) = 0.10$$
$$P(I_1|s_3) = 0.80 \quad P(I_2|s_3) = 0.20 \quad P(I_3|s_3) = 0.00$$

a. Develop an optimal decision strategy for Sealcoat.
b. What is the EVSI?
c. What is the efficiency of the information for the most recent order?

30. Milford Trucking Company (problem 6) has the following payoff table:

		Return Shipment from Detroit	No Return Shipment from Detroit
		s_1	s_2
St. Louis	d_1	2000	2000
Detroit	d_2	2500	1000
Probabilities		0.40	0.60

a. Milford can phone a Detroit truck dispatch center and determine if the general Detroit shipping activity is busy (I_1) or slow (I_2). If the report is busy, the chances of obtaining a return shipment will increase. Suppose that the following conditional probabilities are given:

$$P(I_1|s_1) = 0.6 \quad P(I_2|s_1) = 0.4$$
$$P(I_1|s_2) = 0.3 \quad P(I_2|s_2) = 0.7$$

What should Milford do?

b. If the Detroit report is busy (I_1), what is the probability that Milford will obtain a return shipment if it makes the trip to Detroit?

c. What is the efficiency of the phone information?

31. The quality control inspection process (problem 16) has the following payoff table:

		\multicolumn{4}{c}{**Percent Defective**}
		0	1	2	3
		s_1	s_2	s_3	s_4
100% inspection	d_1	250	250	250	250
No inspection	d_2	0	125	250	375
Probabilities		0.15	0.25	0.40	0.20

Suppose that a sample of five parts is selected from the shipment and one defect is found.

a. Let I = one defect in a sample of five. Use the binomial probability distribution to compute $P(I|s_1)$, $P(I|s_2)$, $P(I|s_3)$, and $P(I|s_4)$, where the state of nature identifies the value for p.

b. If I occurs, what are the revised probabilities for the states of nature?

c. Should the entire shipment be 100% inspected whenever one defect is found in a sample of size 5?

d. What is the cost saving associated with the sample information?

32. Based upon an analysis of historical data, the production manager of the *Carolina Times* has determined that the demand distribution for non-subscription copies of the Sunday edition is approximately normally distributed with a mean of 30,000 copies and a standard deviation of 4000 copies. Consequently, in order to satisfy the average demand for non-subscription copies, the *Carolina Times* has been printing 30,000 copies each week. The Sunday edition sells for $1.50 per copy, and the costs associated with producing and distributing each copy are approximately $1.10. Although the paper from copies returned by the newsstands is recycled, the costs associated with handling returns offsets any gains due to recycling; thus, unsold copies result in a loss of $1.50 per copy. Should the *Carolina Times* continue to print 30,000 copies of the Sunday edition to satisfy the non-subscription demand? If not, what do you recommend.

33. Gerald Reed has been selling shirts at the Newport Jazz Festival for several years; each shirt has printed on it "Newport Jazz" and the date of the festival. He purchases the shirts for $4.99 each, and sells them at the festival for $14.99. At the end of the festival, any unsold shirts are sold to a discount department store for $2.99. If demand for the shirts is normally distributed with a mean of 2500 shirts and a standard deviation of 200 shirts, how many shirts should Gerald order?

34. Mississippi River Tours (MRT) operates tour boats in New Orleans. During the 11:30 A.M.–1:30 P.M. tour MRT sells box lunches for $8.95 each; the box lunches are ordered one day in advance from a local caterer for $3.95. The demand for lunches is approximately normally distributed with a mean of 210 lunches per tour and a

standard deviation of 65 lunches. Unsold lunches are discarded at the end of each tour.

a. How many lunches should MRT order each day?

b. A local street vendor has offered to purchase the leftover box lunches from MRT for $1.95 each. If MRT accepts this offer, how many box lunches should be ordered each day?

35. The Chicken House is a fast-food restaurant that specializes in fried chicken. At various times throughout the day a batch of chicken is fried and transferred to warmers, from which customer orders are satisfied. Demand after 7:00 P.M. is highly variable, and can be approximated by a normal distribution with a mean of 180 pieces per day and a standard deviation of 50 pieces. To provide adequate time for cleaning the kitchen, the last batch of chicken is prepared at 7:00 P.M.; thus, the amount of chicken currently in the warmers plus the amount prepared at 7:00 P.M. is what will be available to satisfy the after 7:00 P.M. demand. Each piece of chicken prepared costs $0.80 and is sold for $1.25. Because of the concern for quality, any pieces that are leftover at closing are discarded.

a. If there are 40 pieces of chicken in the warmer at 7:00 P.M., how many additional pieces of chicken should The Chicken House prepare?

b. Assume that The Chicken House has accepted the offer made by a local convenience market to purchase all leftover chicken for 50 cents a piece. If there are 40 pieces of chicken in the warmer at 7:00 P.M., how many additional pieces of chicken should The Chicken House prepare?

problems due friday
12, 14, 19, 21, 22, 33

Case Problem
Property Purchase Strategy

Glenn Foreman, president of Oceanview Development Corporation, is considering submitting a bid to purchase property that will be sold by sealed bid at a county tax foreclosure. Glenn's initial judgment is to submit a bid of $5 million. From past experience Glenn estimates that a bid of $5 million will have a 0.20 probability of being the highest bid and securing the property for Oceanview. The current date is June 1. Sealed bids for the property must be submitted by August 15. The winning bid will be announced on September 1.

If Oceanview submits the highest bid and obtains the property, the firm plans to build and sell a complex of luxury condominiums. However, a complicating factor is that the property is currently zoned for single-family residences only. Glenn feels that a referendum could be placed on the voting ballot in time for the November election. Passage of the referendum would change the zoning of the property and permit construction of the condominiums.

The sealed-bid procedure requires the bid to be submitted with a certified check for 10% of the amount bid. If the bid is rejected, the deposit is refunded. If the bid is accepted, the deposit is the down payment for the property. However, if the bid is accepted and the bidder does not follow through with the purchase and meet the remainder of the financial obligation within 6 months, the deposit will be forfeited. In this case the county will offer the property to the next highest bidder.

In order to determine whether or not to submit the $5 million bid, Glenn has done some preliminary analysis. This preliminary work provided an estimate of 0.3 for the probability that the referendum for a zoning change will be approved and resulted in estimates of the costs and revenues that will be incurred if the condominiums are built. The data obtained are shown below:

Cost and Revenue Estimates

Revenue from condominum sales	$15,000,000
Expenses	
Property	$ 5,000,000
Construction expenses	$ 8,000,000

If Oceanview obtains the property and the zoning change is not approved in November, Glenn feels that the best option would be for the firm not to complete the purchase of the property. In this case Oceanview would forfeit the 10% deposit that accompanied the bid.

Because the likelihood of the zoning referendum being approved is such an important factor in the decision process, Glenn has suggested that the firm hire a market research service to conduct a survey of voters. The survey would provide a better estimate of the likelihood that the referendum for a zoning change would be approved. The market research firm that Oceanview Development has worked with in the past has agreed to do the study for $15,000. The results of the study will be available August 1, so that Oceanview will have this information before the August 15 bid deadline. The results of the survey will either be a prediction that the zoning change will be approved or a prediction that the zoning change will not be approved. After considering the record of the market research service in previous studies conducted for Oceanview, Glenn has developed the following probability estimates concerning the accuracy of the market research information:

$$P(I_1|s_1) = 0.9 \qquad P(I_2|s_1) = 0.1$$
$$P(I_1|s_2) = 0.2 \qquad P(I_2|s_2) = 0.8$$

where

I_1 = prediction that the zoning change will be approved

I_2 = prediction that the zoning change will not be approved

s_2 = the zoning change is approved by the voters

s_2 = the zoning change is not approved by the voters

Managerial Report

Perform an analysis of the problem facing the Oceanview Development Corporation and prepare a report that summarizes your findings and recommendations. Include information on an analysis of the following:

1. A decision tree that shows the logical sequence of the decision problem.
2. A recommendation regarding what Oceanview should do if the market research information is not available.
3. A decision strategy that Oceanview should follow if the market research is conducted.
4. A recommendation as to whether Oceanview should employ the market research firm. What is the value of the information provided by the market research firm?

Include a copy of the details of your analysis in the appendix to your report.

Quantitative Methods in Practice

Ohio Edison Company*
Akron, Ohio

Ohio Edison Company is an investor-owned electric utility headquartered in northeastern Ohio. Ohio Edison and a Pennsylvania subsidiary provide electrical service to over 2 million people. Most of this electricity is generated by coal-fired power plants. In order to meet evolving air-quality standards, Ohio Edison has embarked on a program to replace existing pollution control equipment on most of its generating plants with more efficient equipment. The combination of this program to upgrade air-quality control equipment with the continuing need to construct new generating plants to meet future power requirements has resulted in a large capital investment program.

Quantitative analysis activities at Ohio Edison are distributed throughout the company rather than centralized in a specific department. The usage of quantitative methods is more or less evenly divided among the following areas: fossil and nuclear fuel planning, environmental studies, capacity planning, large equipment evaluation, and corporate planning. Applications include decision analysis, optimal ordering strategies, computer modeling, and simulation.

A Decision Analysis Application

The flue gas emitted by coal-fired power plants contains small ash particles and sulfur dioxide (SO_2). Federal and state regulatory agencies have established emission limits for both particulates and sulfur dioxide. Recently, Ohio Edison developed a plan to comply with new air-quality standards at one of its largest power plants. This plant consists of seven coal-fired units and constitutes about one-third of the generating capacity of Ohio Edison and the subsidiary company. Most of these units had been constructed in the 1960s. Although all the units had initially been constructed with equipment to control particulate emissions, that equipment was not capable of meeting new particulate emission requirements.

A decision had already been made to burn low-sulfur coal in four of the smaller units (units 1 to 4) at the plant in order to meet SO_2 emission standards. Fabric filters were to be installed on these units to control particulate emissions. Fabric filters, also

---

*The authors are indebted to Thomas J. Madden and M. S. Hyrnick of Ohio Edison Company, Akron, Ohio, for providing this application.

known as baghouses, use thousands of fabric bags to filter out the particulates; they function in much the same way as a household vacuum cleaner.

It was considered likely, although not certain, that the three larger units (units 5 to 7) at this plant would burn medium- to high-sulfur coal. A method of controlling particulate emissions at these units had not yet been selected. Preliminary studies had narrowed the particulate control equipment choice to a decision between fabric filters and electrostatic precipitators (which remove particulates suspended in the flue gas as charged particles by passing the flue gas through a strong electric field). This decision was affected by a number of uncertainties, including the following:

Uncertainty in the way some air-quality laws and regulations might be interpreted.
Certain interpretations could require that either low-sulfur coal or high-sulfur Ohio coal (or neither) be burned in units 5 to 7.
Potential future changes in air quality laws and regulations.
An overall plant reliability improvement program was underway at this plant.
The outcome of this program would affect the operating costs of whichever pollution control technology was installed in these units.
Construction costs of the equipment were uncertain, particularly since limited space at the plant site made it necessary to install the equipment on a massive bridge deck over a four-lane highway immediately adjacent to the power plant.
The costs associated with replacing the electrical power required to operate the particulate control equipment were uncertain.
Various uncertain factors, including potential accidents and chronic operating problems that could increase the costs of operating the generating units, were identified. The degree to which each of these factors affected operating costs varied with the choice of technology and with the sulfur content of the coal.

Decision Analysis

The decision to be made involved a choice between two types of particulate control equipment (fabric filters or electrostatic precipitators) for units 5 to 7. Because of the complexity of the problem, the high degree of uncertainty associated with factors affecting the decision, and the importance (because of potential reliability and cost impact on Ohio Edison) of the choice, decision analysis was used in the selection process.

The decision measure used to evaluate the outcomes of the particulate technology decision analysis was the annual revenue requirements for the three large units over their remaining lifetime. Revenue requirements are the monies that would have to be collected from the utility customers in order to recover costs resulting from the decision. They include not only direct costs but also the cost of capital and return on investment.

A decision tree was constructed to represent the particulate control decision, its uncertainties and costs. A simplified version of this decision tree is shown in Figure A4.1. The decision and state-of-nature nodes are indicated. Note that to conserve space, a type of shorthand notation is used. The coal sulfur content state-of-nature node should actually be located at the end of each branch of the capital cost state-of-nature node, as the dotted lines indicate. Each of the indicated state-of-nature nodes actually represents several probabilistic cost models or submodels. The total revenue requirements calculated are the sum of the revenue requirements for capital and operating costs. Costs associated with these models were obtained from engineering calculations or estimates. Probabilities were obtained from existing data or the subjective assessments of knowledgeable persons.

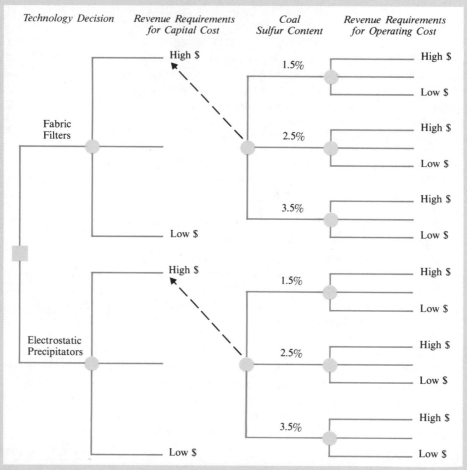

Figure A4.1
Simplified Particulate Control Equipment Decision Tree

Results

A decision tree similar to that shown in Figure A4.1 was used to generate cumulative probability distributions for the annual revenue requirements outcomes calculated for each of the two particulate control alternatives. Careful study of these results led to the following conclusions:

The expected value of annual revenue requirements for the electrostatic precipitator technology was approximately $1 million lower than that for the fabric filters.

The fabric filter alternative had a higher ''upside risk''—that is, a higher probability of high revenue requirements—than did the precipitator alternative.

The precipitator technology had nearly an 80% probability of having lower annual revenue requirements than the fabric filters.

Although the capital cost of the fabric filter equipment (the cost of installing the equipment) was lower than for the precipitator, this was more than offset by the higher operating costs associated with the fabric filter.

These results led Ohio Edison to select the electrostatic precipitator technology for the generating units in question. Had the decision analysis not been performed, the particulate control decision might have been based chiefly on capital cost, a decision measure that would have favored the fabric filter equipment. Decision analysis offers a means for effectively analyzing the uncertainties involved in a decision. Because of this, it is felt that the use of decision analysis methodology in this application resulted in a decision that yielded both lower expected revenue requirements and lower risk.

Questions

1. Why was decision analysis used in the selection of particulate control equipment for units 5, 6, and 7?
2. List the decision alternatives for the decision analysis problem developed by Ohio Edison.
3. What were the benefits of using decision analysis in this application?

CHAPTER

5

Utility and Decision Making

In the previous chapter we frequently expressed the payoffs in terms of monetary values. When probability information was available about the states of nature, we recommended selecting the decision alternative with the best expected monetary value. However, there are situations in which the decision alternative with the best expected monetary value is not the most desirable decision.

By the most desirable decision we mean the one that is preferred by the decision maker, taking into account not only monetary value but also many other factors, such as the possibility of making a very large profit and/or incurring a very large loss. Examples of situations in which selecting the decision alternative with the best expected monetary value may not lead to the selection of the most preferred alternative are numerous. One such example is the decision made by most people to buy insurance. Clearly, the decision to buy insurance for a house does not provide a higher expected monetary value than not buying such insurance. Otherwise insurance companies could not pay expenses and make a profit. Similarly, many people buy tickets for state lotteries even though the expected monetary value of such a decision is negative.

Should we conclude that persons or businesses that buy insurance or participate in lotteries do so because they are unable to determine which decision alternative leads to the best expected monetary value? On the contrary, we take the view that in these cases monetary value is not the sole measure of the true worth of the outcome to the decision maker.

We will see that in cases where the expected monetary value approach does not lead to the most preferred decision alternative, expressing the value (or worth) of an outcome in terms of its *utility* will permit the use of *expected utility* to identify the most desirable decision.

5.1

THE MEANING OF UTILITY

Utility is a measure of the total worth of a particular outcome; it reflects the decision maker's attitude toward a collection of factors such as profit, loss, and risk. Researchers have found that as long as the monetary value of payoffs stay within a range that is considered reasonable to the decision maker, selecting the decision alternative with the best expected monetary value usually leads to selection of the most preferred decision. However, when the payoffs become extreme, most decision makers are not satisfied with the decision that simply provides the best expected monetary value.

As an example of a case where utility can help in selecting the best decision alternative, let us consider the problem faced by Swofford, Inc., a relatively small real estate investment firm located in Atlanta, Georgia. Swofford currently has two investment opportunities, which require approximately the same cash outlay. The cash requirements necessary prohibit Swofford from making more than one investment at this time. Consequently there are three possible decision alternatives that may be considered.

The three decision alternatives, denoted by d_1, d_2, and d_3, are as follows:

$$d_1 = \text{make investment } A$$
$$d_2 = \text{make investment } B$$
$$d_3 = \text{do not invest}$$

The monetary payoffs associated with the investment opportunities depend largely on what happens to the real estate market during the next 6 months. Either real estate prices will go up, remain stable, or go down. Thus the Swofford states of nature, denoted by s_1, s_2, and s_3, are as follows:

$$s_1 = \text{real estate prices go up}$$
$$s_2 = \text{real estate prices remain stable}$$
$$s_3 = \text{real estate prices go down}$$

Using the best information available, Swofford has estimated the profits or payoffs associated with each decision alternative and state-of-nature combination. The resulting payoff table is shown in Table 5.1.

The best estimate of the probability that prices will go up is 0.30; the best estimate of the probability that prices will remain stable is 0.50; and the best estimate of the probability that real estate prices will go down is 0.20. Thus the expected values for the three decision alternatives are

$$\text{EV}(d_1) = 0.3(30,000) + 0.5(20,000) \quad + 0.2(-50,000) = \quad 9,000$$
$$\text{EV}(d_2) = 0.3(50,000) + 0.5(-20,000) + 0.2(-30,000) = -1,000$$
$$\text{EV}(d_3) = 0.3(0) \quad\quad + 0.5(0) \quad\quad + 0.2(0) \quad\quad\quad = \quad 0$$

Table 5.1
Payoff Table for Swofford, Inc.

Decision Alternatives		States of Nature		
		Prices Up s_1	Prices Stable s_2	Prices Down s_3
Investment A	d_1	$30,000	$20,000	−$50,000
Investment B	d_2	$50,000	−$20,000	−$30,000
Do not invest	d_3	0	0	0

Using the expected value approach, the optimal decision is to select investment A with an expected monetary value of $9000. Is this really the best decision alternative? Let us consider some other relevant factors that relate to Swofford's capability for absorbing the loss of $50,000 if investment A is made and prices actually go down.

It turns out that Swofford's current financial position is very weak. This was partly reflected in Swofford's ability to undertake at most one investment at the current time. More important, however, the firm's president feels that if the next investment results in substantial losses, Swofford's future will be in jeopardy. Although the expected value approach leads to a recommendation for d_1, do you think this is the decision the firm's president would prefer? We suspect that d_2 or d_3 would be selected in order to avoid the possibility of incurring a $50,000 loss. In fact, it is reasonable to believe that if a loss as great as even $30,000 could drive Swofford out of business, the president would select d_3, feeling that both investment A and investment B are too risky for Swofford's current financial position.

The way we can resolve Swofford's dilemma is first to determine Swofford's utility for the various monetary outcomes. Recall that the utility of any outcome is the total worth of that outcome taking into account the risks and payoffs involved. If the utilities for the various outcomes are assessed correctly, then the decision alternative with the highest expected utility is the most preferred or best alternative. In the next section we will see how to determine the utility of the monetary outcomes in such a fashion that the alternative with the highest expected utility is most preferred.

5.2

DEVELOPING UTILITIES FOR MONETARY PAYOFFS

The procedure we will use to establish utility values for the payoffs in Swofford's problem requires that we first assign a utility value to the best and worst possible payoffs in the decision situation. Any values will work as long as the utility assigned to the best payoff is greater than the utility assigned to the worst payoff. In this case, $50,000 is the best payoff and −$50,000 is the worst. Suppose, then, that we arbitrarily make the following assignments to these two payoffs:

$$\text{Utility of} \ -\$50,000 \ = \ U(-50,000) \ = \ 0$$
$$\text{Utility of} \ \ \ \ \$50,000 \ = \ U(50,000) \ \ \ = \ 10$$

Now let us see how we can determine the utility associated with every other payoff.

Consider the process of establishing the utility of a payoff of $30,000. First we ask Swofford's president to state a preference between a guaranteed $30,000 payoff and the opportunity to engage in the following *lottery*, or bet:

Lottery: Swofford's obtains a payoff of $50,000 with probability p
and a payoff of $-$50,000$ with probability $(1 - p)$.

Obviously, if p is very close to 1, Swofford's president would prefer the lottery to the certain payoff of $30,000, since the firm would virtually guarantee itself a payoff of $50,000. On the other hand, if p is very close to 0, Swofford's president would clearly prefer the guarantee of $30,000. In any event, as p changes continuously from 0 to 1, the preference for the guaranteed payoff of $30,000 will change at some point into a preference for the lottery. At this value of p, Swofford's president would have no greater preference for the guaranteed payoff of $30,000 than for the lottery. For example, let us assume that when $p = 0.95$, Swofford's president is indifferent between the certain payoff of $30,000 and the lottery. Given this value of p, we can compute the utility of a $30,000 payoff as follows:

$$U(30,000) = pU(50,000) + (1 - p)U(-50,000)$$
$$= 0.95(10) + (0.05)(0)$$
$$= 9.5$$

Obviously, if we had started with a different assignment of utilities for a payoff of $50,000 and $-$50,000$, we would have ended up with a different utility for $30,000. For example, if we had started with an assignment of 100 for $50,000 and 10 for $-$50,000$, the utility of a $30,000 payoff would be

$$U(30,000) = 0.95(100) + 0.05(10)$$
$$= 95 + 0.5$$
$$= 95.5$$

Hence we must conclude that the utility assigned to each payoff is not unique but merely depends on the initial choice of utilities for the best and worst payoffs. We will discuss this further at the end of this section. For now, however, we will continue to use a value of 10 for the utility of $50,000 and a value of 0 for the utility of $-$50,000$.

Before computing the utility for the other payoffs, let us consider the significance of Swofford's president assigning a utility of 9.5 to a payoff of $30,000. Clearly, when $p = 0.95$, the expected value of the lottery is

$$EV(lottery) = 0.95(\$50,000) + 0.05(-\$50,000)$$
$$= \$47,500 - \$2,500$$
$$= \$45,000$$

We see that although the expected value of the lottery when $p = 0.95$ is $45,000, Swofford's president would just as soon take a guaranteed payoff of $30,000. Thus Swofford's president is taking a conservative, or risk-avoiding, viewpoint. The president would rather have $30,000 for certain than risk anything greater than a 5% chance of incurring a loss of $50,000. One can view the difference between the EV of $45,000 and the $30,000 amount for certain as the risk premium that Swofford's president would be willing to pay to avoid the 5% chance of losing $50,000.

To compute the utility associated with a payoff of −$20,000, we must ask Swofford's president to state a preference between a guaranteed −$20,000 payoff and the opportunity to engage in the following lottery.

> Lottery: Swofford's obtains a payoff of $50,000 with probability p
> and a payoff of −$50,000 with probability $(1 − p)$.

Note that this is exactly the same lottery we used to establish the utility of a payoff of $30,000. In fact, this will be the lottery used to establish the utility for any monetary value in the Swofford payoff table. Using this lottery, then, we must ask Swofford's president to state the value of p that would make the president indifferent between a guaranteed payoff of −$20,000 and the lottery. For example, we might begin by asking the president to choose between a certain loss of $20,000 and the lottery with a payoff of $50,000 with probability $p = 0.90$ and a payoff of −$50,000 with probability $(1 − p) = 0.10$. What answer do you think we would get? Surely, with this high probability of obtaining a payoff of $50,000, the president would elect the lottery. Next we might ask if $p = 0.85$ would result in indifference between the loss of $20,000 for certain and the lottery. Again the president might tell us that the lottery would be preferred. Suppose that we continue in this fashion until we get to $p = 0.55$, where we find that with this value of p, the president is indifferent between the payoff of −$20,000 and the lottery. That is, for any value of p less than 0.55, the president would rather take a loss of $20,000 for certain than risk the potential loss of $50,000 with the lottery; and for any value of p above 0.55, the president would elect the lottery. Thus the utility assigned to a payoff of −$20,000 is

$$\begin{aligned} U(-\$20,000) &= pU(50,000) + (1 − p)U(-\$50,000) \\ &= 0.55(10) + 0.45(0) \\ &= 5.5 \end{aligned}$$

Again let us examine the significance of this assignment as compared with the expected value approach. When $p = 0.55$, the expected value of the lottery is

$$\begin{aligned} \text{EV(lottery)} &= 0.55(\$50,000) + 0.45(-\$50,000) \\ &= \$27,500 − \$22,500 \\ &= \$5,000 \end{aligned}$$

Thus Swofford's president would just as soon absorb a loss of $20,000 for certain as take the lottery, even though the expected value of the lottery is $5000. Once again we see the conservative, or risk-avoiding, point of view of Swofford's president.

In the above two examples where we computed the utility for a specific monetary payoff, M, we first found the probability p where the decision maker was indifferent between a guaranteed payoff of M and a lottery with a payoff of $50,000 with probability p and −$50,000 with probability $(1 − p)$. The utility of M was then computed as

$$U(M) = pU(\$50,000) + (1 - p)U(-\$50,000)$$
$$= p(10) + (1 - p)0$$
$$= 10p$$

Using the above procedure, utility values for the rest of the payoffs in Swofford's problem were developed. The results are presented in Table 5.2.

Table 5.2
Utility of Monetary Payoffs for the Swofford, Inc. Problem

Monetary Value	Indifference Value of p	Utility Value
$50,000	Does not apply	10.0
30,000	0.95	9.5
20,000	0.90	9.0
0	0.75	7.5
−20,000	0.55	5.5
−30,000	0.40	4.0
−50,000	Does not apply	0

Now that we have determined the utility value of each of the possible monetary values, we can write the original payoff table in terms of utility values. Table 5.3 shows the utility for the various outcomes in the Swofford problem. The notation we will use for the entries in the utility table is $U(d_i, s_j)$, which denotes the utility associated with decision alternative d_i and state of nature s_j. Using this notation, we see that $U(d_2, s_3) = 4.0$.

Table 5.3
Utility Table for Swofford, Inc.

Decision Alternatives		States of Nature		
		Prices Up s_1	Prices Stable s_2	Prices Down s_3
Investment A	d_1	9.5	9.0	0
Investment B	d_2	10.0	5.5	4.0
Do not invest	d_3	7.5	7.5	7.5

The Expected Utility Approach

We can now apply the expected value computations introduced in Chapter 4 to the payoffs in Table 5.3 in order to select an optimal decision alternative for Swofford, Inc. However, since utility values represent such a special case of expected value, we will refer to the expected value when applied to utility values as the *expected utility (EU)*. In this way we will avoid any possible confusion between the expected value for the original payoff table and the expected value for the payoff table consisting of *utility values*. Thus, the expected utility approach requires the analyst to compute the expected utility for each decision alternative and then select the alternative yielding the best expected utility. If there are N possible states of nature, the expected utility of a decision alternative d_i is given by

$$EU(d_i) = \sum_{j=1}^{N} P(s_j)U(d_i, s_j) \qquad (5.1)$$

The expected utility for each of the decision alternatives in the Swofford problem is computed as follows:

$$EU(d_1) = 0.3(9.5) + 0.5(9.0) + 0.2(0) = 7.35$$
$$EU(d_2) = 0.3(10) + 0.5(5.5) + 0.2(4.0) = 6.55$$
$$EU(d_3) = 0.3(7.5) + 0.5(7.5) + 0.2(7.5) = 7.50$$

We see that the optimal decision using the expected utility approach is d_3, do not invest. The ranking of alternatives according to the president's utility assignments and the associated monetary values are as follows:

Ranking of Decision Alternatives	Expected Utility	Expected Monetary Value
Do not invest	7.50	0
Investment A	7.35	9000
Investment B	6.55	−1000

Note that whereas investment A had the highest expected monetary value of $9000, the analysis indicates that Swofford should decline this investment. The rationale behind not selecting investment A is that the 0.20 probability of a $50,000 loss was considered to involve a very serious risk by Swofford's president. The seriousness of this risk and its associated impact on the company were not adequately reflected by the expected monetary value of investment A. It was necessary to assess the utility for each payoff in order to adequately take this risk into account.

In the Swofford problem we have been using a utility of 10 for the largest possible payoff and 0 for the smallest. Since the choice of values could have been anything, we might have chosen 1 for the utility of the largest payoff and 0 for the utility of the smallest. Had we made this choice, the utility for any monetary value M would have been the value of p at which the decision maker was indifferent between a payoff of M for certain and a lottery in which the best payoff is obtained with probability p and the worst payoff is obtained with probability $(1 - p)$. Thus the utility for any monetary value would have been equal to the probability of earning the best payoff. Often this choice is made because of the ease in computation. We chose not to do so to emphasize the distinction between the utility values and the indifference probabilities for the lottery.

5.3

SUMMARY OF STEPS FOR DETERMINING THE UTILITY OF MONEY

Before considering other aspects of utility, let us summarize the steps involved in determining the utility for a monetary value and using it within the decision analysis framework. The steps outlined below state in general terms the procedure used to solve the Swofford, Inc. investment problem. The steps are as follows:

Step 1 Develop a payoff table using monetary values.

Step 2 Identify the best and worst payoff values in the table and assign each a utility value, with U(best payoff) $>$ U(worst payoff).

Step 3 For every other monetary value M in the original payoff table, perform steps a through c below in order to determine its utility value.
    a. Define the following lottery: The best payoff is obtained with probability p and the worst payoff is obtained with probability $(1 - p)$.
    b. Determine the value of p such that the decision maker is indifferent between a payoff of M for certain and the lottery defined in step a.
    c. Calculate the utility of M as follows: $U(M) = pU$(best payoff) $+ (1 - p)U$(worst payoff).

Step 4 Convert the payoff table from monetary values to the calculated utility values.

Step 5 Apply the expected utility approach to the utility table and select the decision alternative with the highest expected utility.

5.4

RISK AVOIDERS VERSUS RISK TAKERS

The financial position of Swofford, Inc. was such that the firm's president evaluated investment opportunities from a conservative, or risk-avoiding, point of view. However, if the firm had had a surplus of cash and a very stable future, we might have found Swofford's president looking for investment alternatives that, although perhaps risky, contained a potential for substantial profit. If the president had behaved in this manner, the president would have been classified as a *risk taker*. In this section we analyze the decision problem faced by Swofford from the point of view of a decision maker who would be classified as a risk taker. We then compare the conservative, or risk-avoiding, point of view of Swofford's president with the behavior of a decision maker who is a risk taker.

Given the decision problem faced by Swofford, Inc. and using the general procedure for developing utilities as discussed in Section 5.3, a risk taker might express the utility for the various payoffs as shown in Table 5.4. As before, we have taken $U(50,000)$ $= 10$ and $U(-50,000) = 0$. Note carefully the difference in behavior reflected in Table 5.4 and Table 5.2. That is, in determining the value of p at which the decision maker is indifferent between a payoff of M for certain and a lottery in which \$50,000 is obtained with probability p and $-$\$50,000 with probability $(1 - p)$, the risk taker is willing to accept a greater risk of incurring a loss of $50,000 in order to gain the opportunity to realize a profit of $50,000.

Table 5.4
Revised Utility Values for the Swofford, Inc. Problem Assuming a Risk Taker

Monetary Value	Indifference Value of p	Utility Value
$50,000	Does not apply	10.0
30,000	0.50	5.0
20,000	0.40	4.0
0	0.25	2.5
−20,000	0.15	1.5
−30,000	0.10	1.0
−50,000	Does not apply	0

To help develop the utility table for the risk taker, we have reproduced the Swofford, Inc. payoff table in Table 5.5. Using these payoffs and the risk taker's utility values given in Table 5.4, we can write the risk taker's utility table as shown in Table 5.6. Using the state-of-nature probabilities $P(s_1) = 0.3$, $P(s_2) = 0.5$, and $P(s_3) = 0.2$, the expected utility for each decision alternative is:

Table 5.5
Payoff Table for Swofford, Inc. Problem

Decision Alternatives		States of Nature		
		Prices Up s_1	Prices Stable s_2	Prices Down s_3
Investment A	d_1	$30,000	$20,000	−$50,000
Investment B	d_2	$50,000	−$20,000	−$30,000
Do not invest	d_3	0	0	0

Table 5.6
Utility Table of a Risk Taker for the Swofford, Inc. Problem

Decision Alternatives		States of Nature		
		Prices Up s_1	Prices Stable s_2	Prices Down s_3
Investment A	d_1	5.0	4.0	0
Investment B	d_2	10.0	1.5	1.0
Do not invest	d_3	2.5	2.5	2.5

$$EU(d_1) = 0.3(5.0) + 0.5(4.0) + 0.2(0) = 3.50$$
$$EU(d_2) = 0.3(10) + 0.5(1.5) + 0.2(1.0) = 3.95$$
$$EU(d_3) = 0.3(2.5) + 0.5(2.5) + 0.2(2.5) = 2.50$$

What is the recommended decision? Perhaps somewhat to your surprise, the analysis recommends investment B, with the highest expected utility of 3.95. Recall that this investment has a $-\$1000$ expected monetary value; why is it now the recommended decision? Remember that the decision maker in this revised problem is a risk taker. Thus although the expected value of investment B is negative, utility analysis has shown that this decision maker is enough of a risk taker to prefer investment B and its potential for the \$50,000 profit.

Using the expected utility values, the order of preference of the decision alternatives for the risk taker and the associated expected monetary values are as follows:

Ranking of Decision Alternatives	Expected Utility	Expected Monetary Value
Investment B	3.95	$-\$1000$
Investment A	3.50	\$9000
Do not invest	2.50	0

When we compare the above utility analysis for a risk taker with the more conservative, *risk-avoider* preferences of the president of Swofford, Inc., we see that, even with the same decision problem, different attitudes toward risk can lead to different recommended decisions. The utility values established by Swofford's president indicated that the firm should not invest at this time, whereas the utilities established by the risk taker showed a preference for investment B. Note that both of these decisions differ from the best expected value decision, which was investment A.

We can obtain another perspective of the difference between behaviors of a risk avoider and a risk taker by developing a graph that depicts the relationship between monetary value and utility. The horizontal axis of the graph will be used to represent monetary values, and the vertical axis will represent the utility associated with each monetary value. Now, consider the data in Table 5.2, with a utility value corresponding to each monetary value for the original Swofford, Inc. problem. These values can be plotted on a graph such as in Figure 5.1, and a curve can be drawn through the observed points. The resulting curve is the *utility function for money* for Swofford's president. Recall that these points reflected the conservative or risk-avoiding nature of Swofford's president. Hence we refer to the curve in Figure 5.1 as a utility function for a risk avoider. Using the data in Table 5.4, developed for a risk taker, we can plot these points on a graph such as in Figure 5.2. The resulting curve depicts the utility function for a risk taker.

By looking at the utility functions of Figures 5.1 and 5.2, we can begin to generalize about the utility functions for risk avoiders and risk takers. Although the exact shape of the utility function will vary from one decision maker to another, we can see the general shape of these two classifications of utility functions. The utility function for the risk-

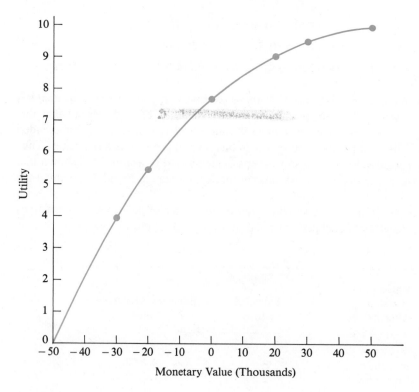

Figure 5.1
Utility Function for Money for the Risk Avoider

avoider class shows a diminishing marginal return for money. For example, the increase in utility going from a monetary value of −$30,000 to $0 is 7.5 − 4.0 = 3.5, whereas the increase in utility in going from $0 to $30,000 is only 9.5 − 7.5 = 2.0. On the other hand, the utility function for a risk taker shows an increasing marginal return for money. For example, in Figure 5.2, we see that the increase in utility in going from −$30,000 to $0 is 2.5 − 1.0 = 1.5, whereas the increase in utility in going from $0 to $30,000 is 5.0 − 2.5 = 2.5. Note also that in either case the utility function is always increasing. That is, more money leads to more utility. This is a property possessed by all utility functions.

We concluded above that the utility function for a risk avoider shows a diminishing marginal return for money and that the utility function for a risk taker shows an increasing marginal return. When the marginal return for money is neither decreasing nor increasing but remains constant, the corresponding utility function describes the behavior of a decision maker who is neutral to risk. The following characteristics are associated with a *risk-neutral decision maker*.

1. The utility function can be drawn as a straight line connecting the ''best'' and the ''worst'' points.
2. The expected utility approach and the expected value approach applied to monetary payoffs result in the same action.

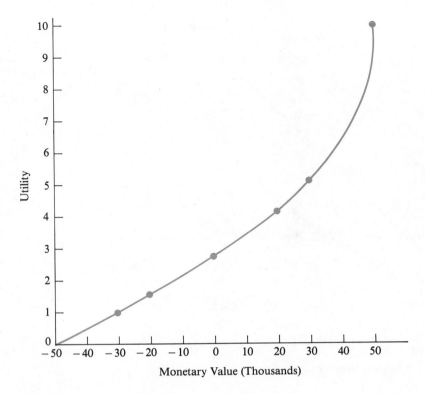

Figure 5.2
Utility Function for Money for the Risk Taker

Figure 5.3 depicts the utility function of a risk-neutral decision maker using the Swofford, Inc. problem data. For comparison purposes, we also show the utility functions for the cases where the decision maker is either a risk taker or a risk avoider.

5.5

EXPECTED VALUE VERSUS EXPECTED UTILITY AS AN APPROACH TO DECISION MAKING

In many decision-making problems, expected monetary value and expected utility will lead to identical recommendations. In fact, this will always be true if the decision maker is risk neutral. In general, if the decision maker is almost risk-neutral over the range of payoffs (from lowest to highest) for a particular decision problem, the decision alternative with the best expected monetary value leads to selection of the most preferred decision alternative. The trick lies in recognizing the range of monetary values over which a decision maker's utility function is risk-neutral.

It is generally agreed that when the payoffs for a particular decision-making problem fall into a reasonable range—the best is not too good and the worst is not too bad—decision makers tend to express preferences in agreement with the expected monetary value approach. Thus as a general guideline we suggest asking the decision maker to

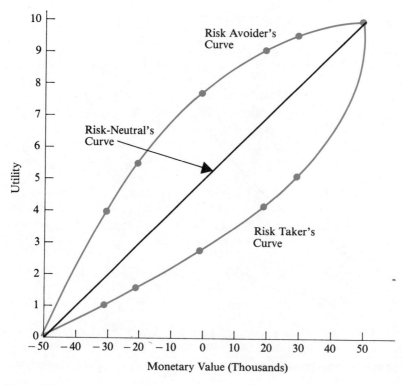

Figure 5.3
Utility Functions for Risk Avoider, Risk Taker, and Risk-Neutral Decision Makers

consider the best and worst possible payoffs for a problem and assess their reasonableness. If the decision maker believes they are in the reasonable range, then the decision alternative with the best expected monetary value can be used. However, if the payoffs appear unreasonably large or unreasonably small (for example, a huge loss) and if the decision maker feels monetary values do not adequately reflect her or his true preferences for the payoffs, a utility analysis of the problem should be considered.

Unfortunately, determination of the appropriate utilities is not a trivial task. As we have seen, measuring utility requires a degree of subjectivity on the part of the decision maker, and different decision makers will have different utility functions. This aspect of utility often causes decision makers to feel uncomfortable about using the expected utility approach. However, if we encounter a decision situation in which we are convinced that monetary value is not the primary measure of performance, and if we agree that a quantitative analysis of the decision problem is desirable, then some form of utility analysis should be performed.

Summary

In this chapter we have suggested that expected utility should be used in decision situations in which an analysis based on expected monetary value would lead to unacceptable decisions. Unlike monetary value, utility is a measure of the total worth of an outcome resulting from the choice of a decision alternative and the occurrence of a state of nature. As such, utility takes into account the decision maker's attitude toward the profit, loss, and risk associated with an outcome. In our examples we have seen how the use of utility analysis can lead to decision recommendations that differ from those that would be selected based upon expected monetary value.

While admittedly a decision maker's utility can be difficult to measure, we have offered a step-by-step procedure that can be used to determine a decision maker's utility for any payoff value. Using the decision maker's evaluation of a lottery involving only the best and worst payoffs, the procedure provides a method whereby each entry in the payoff table can be converted to a utility value. Then expected utility can be used to select the best decision alternative.

Even with utility as a measure of worth, we saw how the analysis for a conservative, or risk-avoiding, decision maker could lead to different decision recommendations than for a risk taker. In cases where the decision maker is risk-neutral, however, we saw that the recommendations using expected utility are identical to the recommendations using expected monetary value.

Glossary

Utility   A measure of the total worth of an outcome reflecting a decision maker's attitude toward considerations such as profit, loss, and risk.

Lottery   A hypothetical investment alternative with a probability p of obtaining the best possible payoff and a probability of $(1 - p)$ of obtaining the worst possible payoff.

Expected utility approach (EU)   A decision approach that requires the analyst to compute the expected utility for each decision alternative and then select the alternative yielding the highest expected utility.

Risk taker   A decision maker who tends to prefer decisions that, although risky, have a possibility for a high or extremely good payoff.

Risk avoider   A decision maker who tends to avoid decisions that have the risk of a low or extremely bad payoff.

Utility function for money   A curve that depicts the relationship between monetary value and utility.

Risk-neutral decision maker   A decision maker who is neutral to risk. For this decision maker the decision alternative with the best expected monetary value is identical to the alternative with the highest expected utility.

Problems

1. A firm has three investment alternatives. The payoff table and associated probabilities are as follows:

		Economic Conditions		
		Up	Stable	Down
Investments	d_1	100	25	0
	d_2	75	50	25	← Thousands of dollars
	d_3	50	50	50
Probabilities		0.40	0.30	0.30

a. Using the expected value approach, which decision is preferred?

b. For the lottery having a payoff of $100,000 with probability p and $0 with probability $(1 - p)$, two decision makers expressed the following indifference probabilities:

	Indifference Probability (p)	
Profit	Decision Maker A	Decision Maker B
$75,000	0.80	0.60
$50,000	0.60	0.30
$25,000	0.30	0.15

Find the most preferred decision for each decision maker using the expected utility approach.

c. Why don't decision makers A and B select the same decision alternative?

2. Alexander Industries is considering purchasing an insurance policy for its new office building in St. Louis, Missouri. The policy has an annual cost of $10,000. If Alexander Industries does not purchase the insurance and minor fire damage occurs to the office building, a cost of $100,000 is anticipated; the cost if a major or total destruction occurs is $200,000. The payoff table, including the state-of-nature probabilities, is as follows:

			Damage		
			s_1 None	s_2 Minor	s_3 Major
Decision	Purchase insurance	d_1	10,000	10,000	10,000
Alternatives	Do not purchase insurance	d_2	0	100,000	200,000 ← Cost
	Probabilities		0.96	0.03	0.01

a. Using the expected value approach, what decision do you recommend?

b. What lottery would you use to assess utilities? (Note that since the data are costs, the best payoff is $0.)

c. Assume that we found the following indifference probabilities for the lottery defined in part (b):

Cost	Indifference Probability
10,000	$p = 0.99$
100,000	$p = 0.60$

What decision would you recommend?

d. Do you favor using expected value or expected utility for this decision problem? Why?

3. In a certain state lottery, a lottery ticket costs $2. In terms of the decision to purchase or not to purchase a lottery ticket, suppose that the following payoff table applies:

			States of Nature	
			s_1 Win	s_2 Lose
Decision Alternatives	Purchase lottery ticket	d_1	300,000	-2
	Do not purchase lottery ticket	d_2	0	0

.000004   .999996

a. If a realistic estimate of the chances of winning are 1 in 250,000, use the expected value approach to recommend a decision.

b. If a particular decision maker assigns an indifference probability of 0.000001 to the $0 payoff, would this individual purchase a lottery ticket? Use expected utility to justify your answer.

4. There are two different routes for traveling between two cities. Route A normally takes 60 minutes, while route B normally takes 45 minutes. If traffic problems are encountered on route A, the travel time increases to 70 minutes; traffic problems on route B increase travel time to 90 minutes. The probability of the delay is 0.20 for route A and 0.30 for route B.

a. Using the expected value approach, what is the recommended route?

b. If utilities are to be assigned to the travel times, what is the appropriate lottery? Note that the smaller times should reflect higher utilities.

c. Using the lottery of part (b), assume that the decision maker expresses indifference probabilities of

$$p = 0.80 \quad \text{for 60 minutes}$$
$$p = 0.60 \quad \text{for 70 minutes}$$

What route should this decision maker select? Is the decision maker a risk taker or a risk avoider?

5. Three decision makers have assessed utilities for the following decision problem:

		States of Nature		
		s_1	s_2	s_3
Decision Alternatives	d_1	20	50	-20
	d_2	80	100	-100 ← Payoff in dollars

The indifference probabilities are as follows:

	Indifference Probabilties (p)		
Payoffs	Decision Maker A	Decision Maker B	Decision Maker C
100	1.00	1.00	1.00
80	0.95	0.70	0.90
50	0.90	0.60	0.75
20	0.70	0.45	0.60
-20	0.50	0.25	0.40
-100	0.00	0.00	0.00

a. Plot the utility function for money for each decision maker.

b. Classify each decision maker as a risk avoider, a risk taker, or risk-neutral.

c. For the payoff of 20, what is the premium that the risk avoider will pay to avoid risk? What is the premium that the risk taker will pay to have the opportunity of the high payoff?

6. In problem 5, if $P(s_1) = 0.25$, $P(s_2) = 0.50$, and $P(s_3) = 0.25$, find a recommended decision for each of the three decision makers. Note that for the same decision problem, different utilities can lead to different decisions.

7. Suppose that the point spread for a particular sporting event is 10 points and that with this spread you are convinced you would have a 0.60 probability of winning a bet on your team. However, the local bookie will accept only a $1000 bet. Assuming that such bets are legal, would you bet on your team? (Disregard any commission charged by the bookie.) Remember that *you* must pay losses out of your own pocket. Your payoff table is as follows:

			States of Nature	
			s_1 You Win	s_2 You Lose
Decision	Bet	d_1	1,000	$-1,000$
Alternatives	Don't bet	d_2	0	0

a. What decision does the expected value approach recommend?

b. What is *your* indifference probability for the $0 payoff? (While this is not easy, be as realistic as possible. Remember, this is required if we are to do an analysis that reflects your attitude toward risk.)

c. What decision would you make based on the expected utility approach? In this case are you a risk taker or risk avoider?

d. Would other individuals assess the same utility values you do? Explain.

e. If your decision in part (c) was to place the bet, repeat the analysis assuming a minimum bet of $10,000.

8. A Las Vegas roulette wheel has 38 different numerical values. If an individual bets on one number and wins, the payoff is 35 to 1.

a. Show a payoff table for a $10 bet on one number using decision alternatives of bet and do not bet.

b. What is the recommended decision using the expected value approach?

c. Do the Las Vegas casinos want risk-taking or risk-avoiding customers? Explain.

d. What range of utility values would a decision maker have to assign to the $0 payoff in order to have expected utility justify his or her decision to place the $10 bet?

9. A new product has the following profit projections and associated probabilities:

Profit	Probability
$150,000	0.10
$100,000	0.25
$ 50,000	0.20
0	0.15
−$ 50,000	0.20
−$100,000	0.10

a. Use the expected value approach to make the decision of whether to market the new product.

b. Because of the high dollar values involved, especially the possibility of a $100,000 loss, the marketing vice-president has expressed some concern about the use of the expected value approach. As a consequence, if a utility analysis is performed, what is the appropriate lottery?

c. Assume that the following indifference probabilities are assigned:

Profit	Indifference Probability (*p*)
$100,000	0.95
$ 50,000	0.70
$ 0	0.50
−$ 50,000	0.25

c. Do the utilities reflect the behavior of a risk taker or a risk avoider?

d. Use expected utility to make a recommended decision.

e. Should the decision maker feel comfortable with the final decision recommended by the analysis?

10. A television network has been receiving low ratings for its programs. Currently, management is considering two alternatives for the Monday night 8:00 P.M.–9:00 P.M. time slot: a Western program with a well-known star, or a musical variety program with a relatively unknown husband-and-wife team. The percentages of viewing audience estimates depend on the degree of program acceptance. The relevant data are as follows:

Program Acceptance	Percentage of Viewing Audience	
	Western	Musical Variety
High	30%	40%
Moderate	25%	20%
Poor	20%	15%

The probabilities associated with program acceptance levels are as follows:

Program Acceptance	Probability	
	Western	Musical Variety
High	0.30	0.30
Moderate	0.60	0.40
Poor	0.10	0.30

a. Using the expected value approach, which program should the network choose?
b. Assuming a utility analysis is desired, what is the appropriate lottery?
c. Using the appropriate lottery in part (b), assume that the network's program manager has assigned the following indifference probabilities:

Percentage of Audience	Indifference Probability (p)
30%	0.40
25%	0.30
20%	0.10

Using utility measures, which program would you recommend? Is the manager in this problem a risk taker or a risk avoider?

CHAPTER

6

Forecasting

A critical aspect of managing any organization is planning for the future. Indeed, the long-run success of an organization is closely related to how well management is able to foresee the future and develop appropriate strategies. Good judgment, intuition, and an awareness of the state of the economy may give a manager a rough idea or "feeling" of what is likely to happen in the future. However, it is often difficult to convert this "feeling" into hard data such as next quarter's sales volume or next year's raw-material cost per unit. The purpose of this chapter is to introduce several methods that can help predict many future aspects of a business operation.

Let us suppose for a moment that we have been asked to provide quarterly estimates of the sales volume for a particular product during the coming 1-year period. Production schedules, raw-material purchasing plans, inventory policies, and sales quotas will all be affected by the quarterly estimates we provide. Consequently, poor estimates may result in poor planning and hence result in increased costs for the firm. How should we go about providing the quarterly sales volume estimates?

We will certainly want to review the actual sales data for the product in past periods. Suppose that we have actual sales data for each quarter over the past 3 years. From these historical data we can identify the general level of sales and determine whether or not there is any trend such as an increase or decrease in sales volume over time. A further review of the data might reveal a seasonal pattern, such as peak sales occurring in the third quarter of each year and sales volume bottoming out during the first quarter. By reviewing historical data we are in a better position to understand the pattern of past sales and are hence better able to predict future sales for the product.

The historical sales data referred to form what is called a *time series*. Specifically, a time series is a set of observations measured at successive points in time or over successive periods of time. In this chapter we will introduce several procedures that can be used to analyze time series data. The objective of this analysis will be to provide good *forecasts* or predictions of future values of the time series.

Forecasting methods can be classified as quantitative or qualitative. Quantitative forecasting methods are based on an analysis of historical data concerning a time series and possibly other related time series. If the historical data used are restricted to past values of the series we are trying to forecast, the forecasting procedure is called a time series method. In this chapter we discuss three time series methods: smoothing (moving averages and exponential smoothing), trend projection, and trend projection adjusted for seasonal influences. If the historical data used in a quantitative forecasting method involve other time series that are believed to be related to the time series we are trying to forecast, we say that we are using a causal method. We discuss the use of regression analysis as a causal forecasting method. Qualitative forecasting methods generally utilize the judgment of experts to make forecasts. An advantage of these procedures is that they can be applied in situations where no historical data are available. We discuss some of these approaches in Section 6.6. Figure 6.1 provides an overview of the different types of forecasting methods.

6.1

THE COMPONENTS OF A TIME SERIES

In order to explain the pattern or behavior of the data in a time series it is often helpful to think of the time series as consisting of several components. The usual assumption is that four separate components—trend, cyclical, seasonal, and irregular—combine to make the time series take on specific values. Let us look more closely at each of these components of a time series.

Trend Component

In time series analysis the measurements may be taken every hour, day, week, month, or year or at any other regular interval.[1] Although time series data generally exhibit

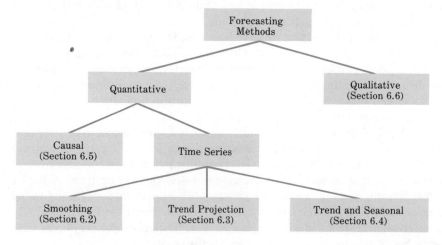

Figure 6.1
An Overview of Forecasting Methods

[1]We restrict our attention here to time series where the values of the series are recorded at equal intervals. Treatment of cases where the observations are not made at equal intervals is beyond the scope of this text.

random fluctuations, the time series may still show gradual shifts or movements to relatively higher or lower values over a longer period of time. This gradual shifting of the time series, which is usually due to long-term factors such as changes in the population, changes in demographic characteristics of the population, changes in technology, and changes in consumer preferences, is referred to as the *trend* in the time series.

For example, a manufacturer of photographic equipment may see substantial month-to-month variability in the number of cameras sold. However, in reviewing the sales over the past 10 to 15 years, this manufacturer may find a gradual increase in the annual sales volume. Suppose that the sales volume was approximately 1800 cameras per month in 1975, 2200 cameras per month in 1980, and 2600 cameras per month in 1985. While actual month-to-month sales volumes may vary substantially, this gradual growth in sales over time shows an upward trend for the time series. Figure 6.2 shows a straight line that may be a good approximation of the trend in the sales data. While the trend for camera sales appears to be linear and increasing over time, sometimes the trend in a time series is better described by other patterns.

Figure 6.3 shows some other possible time series trend patterns. In (a) we see a nonlinear trend. This curve describes a time series showing very little growth initially, followed by a period of rapid growth, and then a leveling off. This might be a good approximation to sales for a product from introduction through a growth period and into a period of market saturation. The linear decreasing trend in (b) is useful for time series displaying a steady decrease over time. The horizontal line in (c) is used for a time series that does not show any consistent increase or decrease over time. It is actually the case of no trend.

Cyclical Component

While a time series may exhibit a gradual shifting or trend pattern over long periods of time, we cannot expect all future values of the time series to be exactly on the trend line.

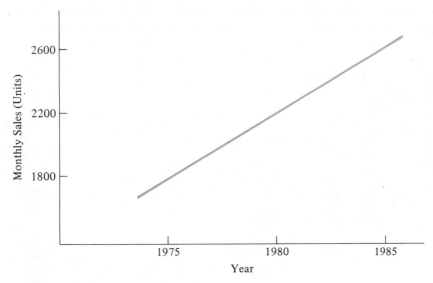

Figure 6.2
Linear Trend of Camera Sales

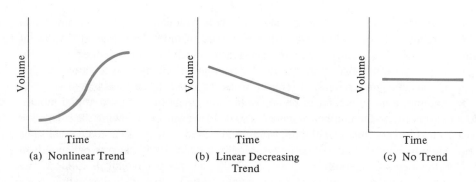

(a) Nonlinear Trend   (b) Linear Decreasing   (c) No Trend
                                 Trend

Figure 6.3
Examples of Some Possible Time Series Trend Patterns

In fact, time series often show alternating sequences of points below and above the trend line. Any regular pattern or sequences of points above and below the trend line is attributable to the *cyclical component* of the time series. Figure 6.4 shows the graph of a time series with an obvious cyclical component. The observations are taken at intervals 1 year apart.

Many time series exhibit cyclical behavior with regular runs of observations below and above the trend line. The general belief is that this component of the time series often reflects multiyear cyclical movements in the economy. For example, periods of moderate inflation followed by periods of rapid inflation can lead to many time series that alternate below and above a generally increasing trend line (e.g., housing costs). Many time series in the late 1970s and early 1980s displayed this type of behavior.

Seasonal Component

While the trend and cyclical components of a time series are identified by analyzing multiyear movements in historical data, many time series show a regular pattern of variability within 1-year periods. For example, a manufacturer of swimming pools expects

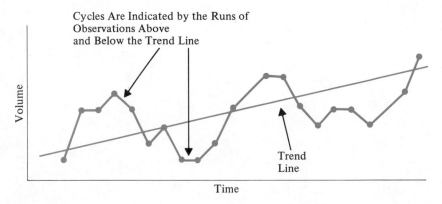

Figure 6.4
Trend and Cyclical Components of a Time Series
Data Points Are 1 Year Apart

low sales activity in the fall and winter months, with peak sales occurring in the spring and summer months. Manufacturers of snow removal equipment and heavy clothing, however, expect just the opposite yearly pattern. It should not be surprising that the component of the time series that represents the variability in the data due to seasonal influences is called the *seasonal component*. While we generally think of seasonal movement in a time series as occurring within 1 year, the seasonal component can also be used to represent any repeating pattern that is less than 1 year in duration. For example, daily traffic volume data show within-the-day ''seasonal'' behavior, with peak levels during rush hours, moderate flow during the rest of the day and early evening, and light flow from midnight to early morning.

Irregular Component

The *irregular component* of the time series is the residual or ''catch-all'' factor that accounts for the deviation of the actual time series value from what we would expect given the effects of the trend, cyclical, and seasonal components. It accounts for the random variability in the time series. The irregular component is caused by the short-term, unanticipated, and nonrecurring factors that affect the time series. Since this component accounts for the random variability in the time series, it is unpredictable. We cannot attempt to predict its impact on the time series in advance.

6.2

FORECASTING USING SMOOTHING METHODS

In this section we discuss forecasting techniques that are appropriate for a time series that exhibits no significant trend, cyclical, or seasonal effects. In such situations the objective of the forecasting method is to ''smooth out'' the irregular component of the time series through some type of averaging process. We begin with a consideration of the method known as moving averages.

Moving Averages

The *moving averages* method consists of computing an average of the *most recent n* data values in the time series. This average is then used as the forecast for the next period. Mathematically, the moving average calculation is made as follows:

$$\text{Moving average} = \frac{\Sigma \text{ (most recent } n \text{ data values)}}{n} \tag{6.1}$$

The term ''moving'' average is based on the fact that as a new observation becomes available for the time series, it replaces the oldest observation in equation (6.1), and a new average is computed. As a result the average will change or ''move'' as new observations become available.

To illustrate the moving averages method, consider the 12 weeks of data presented in Table 6.1 and Figure 6.5. These data show the number of gallons of gasoline sold by a gasoline distributor in Bennington, Vermont, over the past 12 weeks.

Table 6.1
Gasoline Sales Time Series

Week	Sales (1000s of gallons)
1	17
2	21
3	19
4	23
5	18
6	16
7	20
8	18
9	22
10	20
11	15
12	22

In order to use moving averages to forecast the gasoline sales time series, we must first select the number of data values to be included in the moving average. As an example, let us compute forecasts based on a 3-week moving average. The moving average calculation for the first 3 weeks of the gasoline sales time series is as follows:

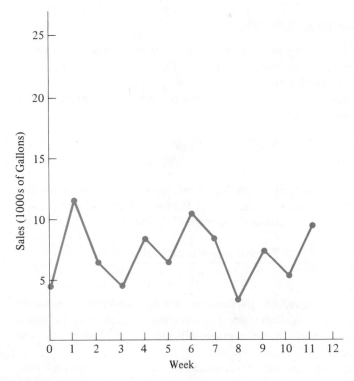

Figure 6.5
Graph of Gasoline Sales Time Series

$$\text{Moving average (weeks 1–3)} = \frac{17 + 21 + 19}{3} = 19$$

This moving average value is then used as the forecast for week 4. Since the actual value observed in week 4 is 23, we see that the *forecast error* in week 4 is $23 - 19 = 4$. In general, the forecast error is the difference between the observed value of the time series and the forecast.

The calculation for the second 3-week moving average is shown below:

$$\text{Moving average (weeks 2–4)} = \frac{21 + 19 + 23}{3} = 21$$

This moving average provides a forecast for week 5 of 21. The error associated with this forecast is $18 - 21 = -3$. Thus we see that the forecast error can be positive or negative depending on whether the forecast is too low or too high.

A complete summary of the 3-week moving average calculations for the gasoline sales time series is shown in Table 6.2 and Figure 6.6.

Table 6.2
Summary of 3-Week Moving Average Calculations

Week	Time Series Value	Moving Average Forecast	Forecast Error	(Error)
1	17			
2	21			
3	19			
4	23	19	4	16
5	18	21	-3	9
6	16	20	-4	16
7	20	19	1	1
8	18	18	0	0
9	22	18	4	16
10	20	20	0	0
11	15	20	-5	25
12	22	19	3	9
			Totals 0	92

An important consideration in using any forecasting method is the accuracy of the forecast. Clearly, we would like the forecast errors to be small. The last two columns of Table 6.2, which contain the forecast errors and the forecast errors squared, can be used to develop measures of accuracy.

One measure of forecast accuracy you might think of using would be to simply sum the forecast errors over time. The problem with this measure is that if the errors are random (as they should be if our choice of forecasting method is appropriate), some errors will be positive and some errors will be negative, resulting in a sum near zero regardless of the size of the individual errors. Referring to Table 6.2, we see that the sum of forecast errors for the gasoline sales time series is zero. This difficulty can be avoided by squaring each of the individual forecast errors.

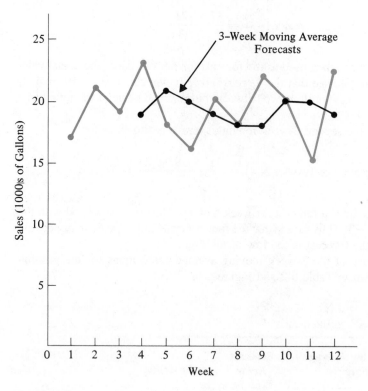

Figure 6.6
Graph of Gasoline Sales Time Series and 3-Week Moving Average Forecasts

For the gasoline sales time series we can use the last column of Table 6.2 to compute the average of the sum of the squared errors. Doing so, we obtain

$$\text{Average of the sum of squared errors} = \frac{92}{9} = 10.22$$

This average of the sum of squared errors is commonly referred to as the *mean squared error* (MSE). The mean squared error is an often-used measure of the accuracy of a forecasting method and the one we will use in this chapter.

As we indicated previously, in order to use the moving averages method we must first select the number of data values to be included in the moving average. It should not be too surprising that, for a particular time series, different-length moving averages will differ in their ability to forecast the time series accurately. One possible approach to choosing the best length is to use trial and error to identify the length that minimizes the MSE measure of forecast accuracy. Then, if we are willing to assume that the length which is best for the past will also be best for the future, we would forecast the next value in the time series using the number of data values that minimized the MSE for the historical time series. Problem 1 at the end of the chapter will ask you to consider 4-week and 5-week moving averages for the gasoline sales data. A comparison of the mean square error for each will indicate the number of weeks of data you may want to include in the moving average calculation.

Weighted Moving Averages

In the moving averages method each observation in the moving average calculation receives the same weight. One possible variation, known as *weighted moving averages*, involves selecting different weights for each data value and then computing a weighted mean as the forecast. In most cases the most recent observation receives the most weight, and the weight decreases for older data values. For example, using the gasoline sales time series, let us illustrate the computation of a weighted 3-week moving average, where the most recent observation receives a weight three times as great as that given the oldest observation, and the next oldest observation receives a weight twice as great as the oldest. The weighted moving average forecast for week 4 would be computed as follows:

$$
\begin{aligned}
\text{Weighted moving} & \\
\text{average forecast} & \\
\text{for week 4} \quad &= \tfrac{3}{6}(19) + \tfrac{2}{6}(21) + \tfrac{1}{6}(17) \\
&= 19.33
\end{aligned}
$$

Note that for the weighted moving average the sum of the weights is equal to 1. This was also true for the simple moving average, where each weight was $\tfrac{1}{3}$. However, recall that the simple or unweighted moving average provided a forecast of 19. Problem 2 at the end of the chapter asks you to calculate the remaining values for the 3-week weighted moving average and compare the forecast accuracy with what we have obtained for the unweighted moving average.

Exponential Smoothing

Exponential smoothing is a forecasting technique that uses a weighted average of past time series values in order to forecast the value of the time series in the next period. The basic exponential smoothing model is as follows:

$$
F_{t+1} = \alpha Y_t + (1 - \alpha)F_t \tag{6.2}
$$

where

$$
\begin{aligned}
F_{t+1} &= \text{forecast of the time series for period } t + 1 \\
Y_t &= \text{actual value of the time series in period } t \\
F_t &= \text{forecast of the time series for period } t \\
\alpha &= \textit{smoothing constant } (0 \le \alpha \le 1)
\end{aligned}
$$

To see that the forecast for any period is a weighted average of *all the previous actual values* for the time series, suppose that we have a time series consisting of three periods of data: Y_1, Y_2, and Y_3. To get the exponential smoothing calculations started, we let F_1 equal the actual value of the time series in period 1; that is, $F_1 = Y_1$. Hence the forecast for period 2 is written as follows:

$$
\begin{aligned}
F_2 &= \alpha Y_1 + (1 - \alpha)F_1 \\
&= \alpha Y_1 + (1 - \alpha)Y_1 \\
&= Y_1
\end{aligned}
$$

In general, then, the exponential smoothing forecast for period 2 is equal to the actual value of the time series in period 1.

To obtain the forecast for period 3, we substitute $F_2 = Y_1$ in the expression for F_3; the result is

$$F_3 = \alpha Y_2 + (1 - \alpha)Y_1$$

Finally, substituting this expression for F_3 in the expression for F_4, we obtain

$$
\begin{aligned}
F_4 &= \alpha Y_3 + (1 - \alpha)[\alpha Y_2 + (1 - \alpha)Y_1] \\
&= \alpha Y_3 + \alpha(1 - \alpha)Y_2 + (1 - \alpha)^2 Y_1
\end{aligned}
$$

Hence we see that F_4 is a weighted average of the first three time series values. The sum of the coefficients or weights for Y_1, Y_2, and Y_3 will always equal 1. A similar argument can be made to show that any forecast F_{t+1} is a weighted average of the previous t time series values.

An advantage of exponential smoothing is that it is a simple procedure and requires very little historical data for its use. Once the smoothing constant α has been selected, only two pieces of information are required in order to compute the forecast for the next period. Referring to equation (6.2), we see that with a given α we can compute the forecast for period $t + 1$ simply by knowing the actual and forecast time series values for period t, that is, Y_t and F_t.

To illustrate the exponential smoothing approach to forecasting, consider the gasoline sales time series presented previously in Table 6.1 and Figure 6.5. As we indicated in the discussion above, the exponential smoothing forecast for period 2 is equal to the actual value of the time series in period 1. Thus, with $Y_1 = 17$, we will set $F_2 = 17$ to get the exponential smoothing computations started. Referring to the time series data in Table 6.1, we find an actual time series value in period 2 of $Y_2 = 21$. Thus period 2 has a forecast error of $21 - 17 = 4$.

Continuing with the exponential smoothing computations provides the following forecast for period 3:

$$F_3 = 0.2Y_2 + 0.8F_2 = 0.2(21) + 0.8(17) = 17.8$$

Once the actual time series value in period 3, $Y_3 = 19$, is known, we can generate a forecast for period 4 as follows:

$$F_4 = 0.2Y_3 + 0.8F_3 = 0.2(19) + 0.8(17.8) = 18.04$$

By continuing the exponential smoothing calculations we are able to determine the weekly forecast values and the corresponding weekly forecast errors, as shown in Table 6.3. Note that we have not shown an exponential smoothing forecast or the forecast error for period 1, because F_1 was set equal to Y_1 in order to begin the smoothing computations. For week 12, we have $Y_{12} = 22$ and $F_{12} = 18.48$. Can you use this information to generate a forecast for week 13 before the actual value of week 13 becomes known? Using the exponential smoothing model, we have

$$F_{13} = 0.2Y_{12} + 0.8F_{12} = 0.2(22) + 0.8(18.48) = 19.18$$

Table 6.3
Summary of the Exponential Smoothing Forecasts and Forecast Errors for
Gasoline Sales with Smoothing Constant $\alpha = 0.2$

Week t	Time Series Value Y_t	Exponential Smoothing Forecast F_t	Forecast Error $Y_t - F_t$
1	17		
2	21	17.00	4.00
3	19	17.80	1.20
4	23	18.04	4.96
5	18	19.03	−1.03
6	16	18.83	−2.83
7	20	18.26	1.74
8	18	18.61	−0.61
9	22	18.49	3.51
10	20	19.19	0.81
11	15	19.35	−4.35
12	22	18.48	3.52

Thus the exponential smoothing forecast of the amount sold in week 13 is 19.18, or 19,180 gallons of gasoline. With this forecast the firm can make plans and decisions accordingly. The accuracy of the forecast will not be known until the firm conducts its business through week 13. However, the exponential smoothing model has provided a good forecast for the unknown 13th-week gasoline sales volume. Figure 6.7 shows the plot of the actual and the forecast time series values. Note in particular how the forecasts "smooth out" the irregular fluctuations in the time series.

In the preceding smoothing calculations we used a smoothing constant of $\alpha = 0.2$, although any value of α between 0 and 1 is acceptable. However, some values will yield better forecasts than others. Some insight into choosing a good value for α can be obtained by rewriting the basic exponential smoothing model as follows:

$$F_{t+1} = \alpha Y_t + (1 - \alpha)F_t$$
$$F_{t+1} = \alpha Y_t + F_t - \alpha F_t \qquad (6.3)$$
$$F_{t+1} = \underset{\substack{\uparrow \\ \text{Forecast} \\ \text{in period } t}}{F_t} + \alpha \underset{\substack{\uparrow \\ \text{Forecast error} \\ \text{in period } t}}{\underbrace{(Y_t - F_t)}}$$

Thus we see that the new forecast F_{t+1} is equal to the previous forecast F_t plus an adjustment, which is α times the most recent forecast error, $Y_t - F_t$. That is, the forecast in period $t + 1$ is obtained by adjusting the forecast in period t by a fraction of the forecast error. If the time series is very volatile and contains substantial random variability, a small value of the smoothing constant is preferred. The reason for this choice is that since much of the forecast error is due to random variability, we do not want to overreact and adjust the forecasts too quickly. For a fairly stable time series with relatively little

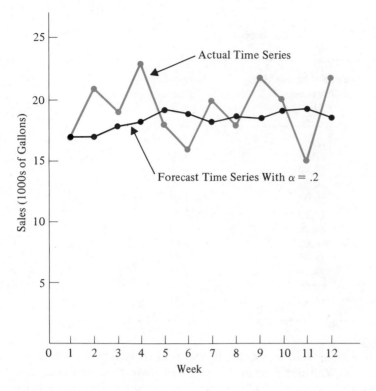

Figure 6.7
Graph of Actual and Forecast Gasoline Sales Time Series with Smoothing Constant $\alpha = 0.2$

random variability, larger values of the smoothing constant have the advantage of quickly adjusting the forecasts when forecasting errors occur and therefore allowing the forecast to react faster to changing conditions.

The criterion we will use to determine a desirable value for the smoothing constant α is the same as the criterion we proposed earlier for determining the number of periods of data to include in the moving averages calculation. That is, we choose the value of α that minimizes the mean square error (MSE).

A summary of the mean square error calculations for the exponential smoothing forecast of gasoline sales with $\alpha = 0.2$ is shown in Table 6.4. Note that there is one less squared error term than the number of time periods, because we had no past values with which to make a forecast for period 1.

Microcomputer programs of exponential smoothing models can be very helpful in terms of identifying a good value for the smoothing constant. Such programs enable the user to input the historical data once and then check the forecasting accuracy for a variety of values for the smoothing constant. In Figure 6.8 we show the results obtained for $\alpha = 0.2$ using the forecasting module of *The Management Scientist* software package. In addition to the forecast and forecast error for each time series value, the output provides the mean square error measure of accuracy and the forecast for the next period in the time series.

Would a different value of α have provided better results in terms of a lower MSE value? Perhaps the most straightforward way to answer this question is simply to try another value for α. We will then compare its mean square error with the MSE value of 8.98 obtained using a smoothing constant of 0.2.

The exponential smoothing results with $\alpha = 0.3$ are shown in Table 6.5. With MSE $= 9.35$, we see that for the current data set a smoothing constant of $\alpha = 0.3$ results in

Table 6.4
Mean Square Error Computations for Forecasting Gasoline Sales with $\alpha = 0.2$

Week t	Time Series Value Y_t	Forecast F_t	Forecast Error $Y_t - F_t$	Squared Error $(Y_t - F_t)^2$
1	17			
2	21	17.00	4.00	16.00
3	19	17.80	1.20	1.44
4	23	18.04	4.96	24.60
5	18	19.03	-1.03	1.06
6	16	18.83	-2.83	8.01
7	20	18.26	1.74	3.03
8	18	18.61	-0.61	0.37
9	22	18.49	3.51	12.32
10	20	19.19	0.81	0.66
11	15	19.35	-4.35	18.92
12	22	18.48	3.52	12.39
			Total	98.80

$$\text{Mean square error (MSE)} = \frac{98.80}{11} = 8.98$$

FORECASTING WITH EXPONENTIAL SMOOTHING
****

THE SMOOTHING CONSTANT IS .2

TIME PERIOD	TIME SERIES VALUE	FORECAST	FORECAST ERROR
1	17		
2	21	17.00	4.00
3	19	17.80	1.20
4	23	18.04	4.96
5	18	19.03	-1.03
6	16	18.83	-2.83
7	20	18.26	1.74
8	18	18.61	-0.61
9	22	18.49	3.51
10	20	19.19	0.81
11	15	19.35	-4.35
12	22	18.48	3.52

THE MEAN SQUARE ERROR   8.98

THE FORECAST FOR PERIOD 13   19.18

Figure 6.8
Exponential Smoothing Output from *The Management Scientist* Software Package

less forecast accuracy than a smoothing constant of $\alpha = 0.2$. Thus we would be inclined to prefer the original smoothing constant of 0.2. With a trial-and-error calculation with other values of α, a "good" value for the smoothing constant can be found. This value can be used in the exponential smoothing model to provide forecasts for the future. At a later date, after a number of new time series observations have been obtained, it is good practice to analyze the newly collected time series data to see if the smoothing constant should be revised to provide better forecasting results.

Table 6.5
Mean Square Error Computations for Forecasting Gasoline Sales with $\alpha = 0.3$

Week t	Time Series Value Y_t	Forecast F_t	Forecast Error $Y_t - F_t$	Squared Error $(Y_t - F_t)^2$
1	17	17.00		
2	21	17.00	4.00	16.00
3	19	18.20	0.80	0.64
4	23	18.44	4.56	20.79
5	18	19.81	-1.81	3.28
6	16	19.27	-3.27	10.69
7	20	18.29	1.71	2.92
8	18	18.80	-0.80	0.64
9	22	18.56	3.44	11.83
10	20	19.59	0.41	0.17
11	15	19.71	-4.71	22.18
12	22	18.30	3.70	13.69
			Total	102.83

$$\text{Mean square error (MSE)} = \frac{102.83}{11} = 9.35$$

6.3

FORECASTING A TIME SERIES USING TREND PROJECTION

In this section we will see how to forecast the values of a time series that exhibits a long-term linear trend. Specifically, let us consider the time series data for bicycle sales of a particular manufacturer over the past 10 years, as shown in Table 6.6 and Figure 6.9. Note that 21,600 bicycles were sold in year 1, 22,900 were sold in year 2, and so on; in year 10, the most recent year, 31,400 bicycles were sold. Although the graph in Figure 6.9 shows some up-and-down movement over the past 10 years, the time series seems to have an overall increasing or upward trend in the number of bicycles sold.

We do not want the trend component of a time series to follow each and every "up" and "down" movement. Rather, the trend component should reflect the gradual shifting— in this case, growth—of the time series values. After we view the time series data in Table 6.6 and the graph in Figure 6.9, we might agree that a linear trend as shown in Figure 6.10 has the potential of providing a reasonable description of the long-run movement in the series. Thus we can now concentrate on finding the linear function that best approximates the trend.

Table 6.6
Bicycle Sales Data

Year t	Sales in Thousands Y_t
1	21.6
2	22.9
3	25.5
4	21.9
5	23.9
6	27.5
7	31.5
8	29.7
9	28.6
10	31.4

For a linear trend the estimated sales volume expressed as a function of time can be written as

$$T_t = b_0 + b_1 t \tag{6.4}$$

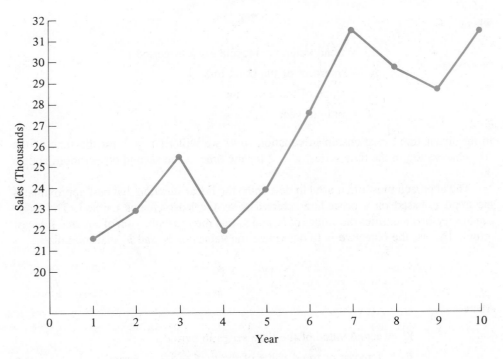

Figure 6.9
Graph of the Bicycle Sales Time Series

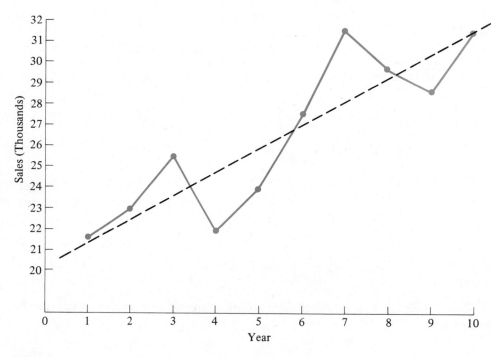

Figure 6.10
Trend Represented by a Linear Function for Bicycle Sales

where

$$T_t = \text{trend value for bicycle sales in period } t$$
$$b_0 = \text{intercept of the trend line}$$
$$b_1 = \text{slope of the trend line}$$
$$t = \text{time in years}$$

In the linear trend relationship in equation (6.4) we will let $t = 1$ for the time of the first observation in the time series, $t = 2$ for the time of the second observation, and so on.

The approach most often used to determine the linear function that best approximates the trend is based on a procedure referred to as the least-squares method. The least-squares method identifies the values of b_0 and b_1 that minimize the sum of squared forecast errors. That is, the objective is to determine the values of b_0 and b_1 that minimize

$$\sum_{t=1}^{n} (Y_t - T_t)^2 \tag{6.5}$$

where

$$Y_t = \text{actual value of the time series in period } t$$
$$T_t = \text{forecast or trend value of the time series in period } t$$
$$n = \text{number of periods}$$

The least-squares method, which is also used for the statistical technique known as regression analysis, is described in most elementary books on statistics. Shown below are the formulas that can be used to compute the value of b_0 and the value of b_1 using this approach:

$$b_1 = \frac{\Sigma \, tY_t - (\Sigma \, t \, \Sigma \, Y_t)/n}{\Sigma \, t^2 - (\Sigma \, t)^2/n} \tag{6.6}$$

$$b_0 = \overline{Y} - b_1 \overline{t} \tag{6.7}$$

where

$\overline{Y}$ = average value of the time series; that is, $\overline{Y} = \dfrac{\Sigma \, Y_t}{n}$

$\overline{t}$ = average value of t; that is, $\overline{t} = \dfrac{\Sigma \, t}{n}$

The above summations are for values of t from 1 through n. Using the above relationships for b_0 and b_1 and the bicycle sales data of Table 6.6, we have the following calculations:

	t	Y_t	tY_t	t^2
	1	21.6	21.6	1
	2	22.9	45.8	4
	3	25.5	76.5	9
	4	21.9	87.6	16
	5	23.9	119.5	25
	6	27.5	165.0	36
	7	31.5	220.5	49
	8	29.7	237.6	64
	9	28.6	257.4	81
	10	31.4	314.0	100
Totals	55	264.5	1545.5	385

$$\overline{t} = \frac{55}{10} = 5.5 \text{ years}$$

$$\overline{Y} = \frac{264.5}{10} = 26.45 \text{ thousands}$$

$$b_1 = \frac{1545.5 - (55)(264.5)/10}{385 - (55)^2/10} = \frac{90.75}{82.5} = 1.10$$

$$b_0 = 26.45 - 1.10(5.5) = 20.4$$

Therefore,

$$T_t = 20.4 + 1.1t \tag{6.8}$$

is the expression for the linear trend component of the bicycle sales time series.

Trend Projections

The slope of 1.1 indicates that over the past 10 years the firm has experienced an average growth in sales of around 1100 units per year. If we assume that the past 10-year trend in sales is a good indicator of the future, then equation (6.8) can be used to project the trend component of the time series. For example, substituting $t = 11$ into equation (6.8) yields next year's trend projection, T_{11}:

$$T_{11} = 20.4 + 1.1(11) = 32.5$$

Thus, using the trend component, we would forecast sales of 32,500 bicycles next year.

The use of a linear function to model the trend is common. However, as we discussed earlier, sometimes time series exhibit a nonlinear trend. Figure 6.11 shows two common nonlinear trend functions. More advanced texts discuss in detail how to solve for the trend component when a nonlinear function is used and how to decide when to use such a function. For our purposes it is sufficient to note that the analyst should choose the function that provides the best fit to the time series data.

6.4

FORECASTING A TIME SERIES WITH TREND AND SEASONAL COMPONENTS

In the previous section we showed how to forecast a time series that had a trend component. In this section we expand our discussion by showing how to forecast a time series that has both trend and seasonal components. The approach we will take is first to remove the seasonal effect or seasonal component from the time series. This step is referred to as *deseasonalizing* the time series. After deseasonalizing, the time series will have only a trend component. As a result we can use the least-squares method described in the previous section to identify the trend component of the time series. Then, using a trend projection calculation, we will be able to forecast the trend component of the time series in future periods. The final step in developing the forecast will be to incorporate the seasonal component by using a seasonal factor to adjust the trend projection. In this manner we will be able to identify the trend and seasonal components and consider both in forecasting the time series.

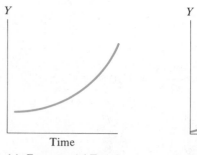

(a) Exponential Trend

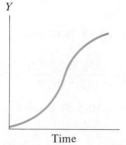

(b) Gompertz Growth Curve

Figure 6.11
Some Possible Functional Forms for Nonlinear Trend Patterns

In addition to a trend component (T) and a seasonal component (S), we will assume that the time series also has an irregular component (I). The irregular component accounts for any random effects in the time series that cannot be explained by the trend and seasonal components. Using T_t, S_t, and I_t to identify the trend, seasonal, and irregular components at time t, we will assume that the actual time series value, denoted by Y_t, can be described by the following *multiplicative time series model*:

$$Y_t = T_t \times S_t \times I_t \qquad (6.9)$$

In this model T_t is the trend measured in units of the item being forecast. However, the S_t and I_t components are measured in relative terms, with values above 1.00 indicating effects above the normal or average level. Values below 1.00 indicate below-average levels for each component. In order to illustrate the use of (6.9) to model a time series, suppose that we have a trend projection of 540 units. In addition, suppose that $S_t = 1.10$ shows a seasonal effect 10% above average and $I_t = 0.98$ shows an irregular effect 2% below average. Using these values in (6.9), the time series value would be $Y_t = 540(1.10)(0.98) = 582$.

In this section we will illustrate the use of the multiplicative model with trend, seasonal, and irregular components by working with the quarterly data presented in Table 6.7 and Figure 6.12. These data show the television set sales (in thousands of units) for a particular manufacturer over the past 4 years. We begin by showing how to identify the seasonal component of the time series.

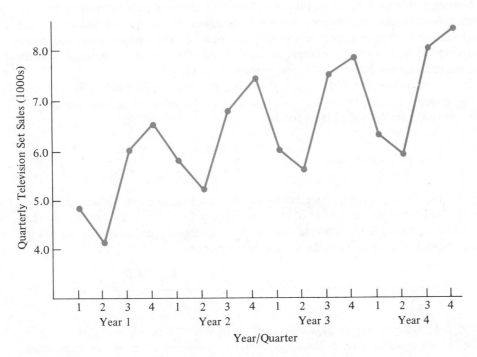

Figure 6.12
Graph of Quarterly Television Set Sales Time Series

Table 6.7
Quarterly Data for Television Set Sales

Year	Quarter	Sales (1000s)
1	1	4.8
	2	4.1
	3	6.0
	4	6.5
2	1	5.8
	2	5.2
	3	6.8
	4	7.4
3	1	6.0
	2	5.6
	3	7.5
	4	7.8
4	1	6.3
	2	5.9
	3	8.0
	4	8.4

Calculating the Seasonal Indexes

By referring to Figure 6.12 we can begin to identify a seasonal pattern for the television set sales. Specifically, we observe that sales are lowest in the second quarter of each year, followed by higher sales levels in quarters 3 and 4. The computational procedure used to identify each quarter's seasonal influence begins with the use of moving averages to isolate the seasonal and irregular components, S_t and I_t.

Since we are working with a quarterly series, we will use four data values (1 year of data) in each moving average. The moving average calculation for the first four quarters of the television set sales data is as follows:

$$\text{First moving average} = \frac{4.8 + 4.1 + 6.0 + 6.5}{4} = \frac{21.4}{4} = 5.35$$

Note that the moving average calculation for the first four quarters yields the average quarterly sales over the first year of the time series. Continuing the moving average calculation, we next add the 5.8 value for the first quarter of year 2 and drop the 4.8 for the first quarter of year 1. Thus the second moving average is

$$\text{Second moving average} = \frac{4.1 + 6.0 + 6.5 + 5.8}{4} = \frac{22.4}{4} = 5.6$$

Similarly, the third moving average calculation is $(6.0 + 6.5 + 5.8 + 5.2)/4 = 5.875$.

Before we proceed with the moving average calculations for the entire time series, let us return to the first moving average calculation, which resulted in a value of 5.35. The 5.35 value represents an average quarterly sales volume (across all seasons) for year

1. As we look back at the calculation of the 5.35 value, perhaps it makes sense to associate 5.35 with the "middle" quarter of the moving average group. However, note that some difficulty in identifying the middle quarter is encountered; with four quarters in the moving average, there is no middle quarter. The 5.35 value corresponds to the end of quarter 2 and the beginning of quarter 3. Similarly, if we go to the next moving average value of 5.60, the middle corresponds to the end of quarter 3 and the beginning of quarter 4.

Recall that the reason for computing moving averages is to isolate the combined seasonal irregular components. However, the moving average values we have computed do not correspond directly to the original quarters of the time series. We can resolve this difficulty by using the midpoints between successive moving average values. For example, since 5.35 corresponds to the beginning of quarter 3 and 5.60 corresponds to the end of quarter 3, we will use $(5.35 + 5.60)/2 = 5.475$ as the moving average value for quarter 3. Similarly, we associate a moving average value of $(5.60 + 5.875)/2 = 5.738$ with quarter 4. What results is called a centered moving average. A complete summary of the centered moving average calculations for the television set sales data is shown in Table 6.8.

TABLE 6.8
Centered Moving Average Calculations for the Television Set Sales Time Series

Year	Quarter	Sales (1000s)	Four-Quarter Moving Average	Centered Moving Average
1	1	4.8		
	2	4.1		
	3	6.0	5.350	5.475
	4	6.5	5.600	5.738
2	1	5.8	5.875	5.975
	2	5.2	6.075	6.188
	3	6.8	6.300	6.325
	4	7.4	6.350	6.400
3	1	6.0	6.450	6.538
	2	5.6	6.625	6.675
	3	7.5	6.725	6.763
	4	7.8	6.800	6.838
4	1	6.3	6.875	6.938
	2	5.9	7.000	7.075
	3	8.0	7.150	
	4	8.4		

Let us pause for a moment to consider what the moving averages in Table 6.8 tell us about this time series. A plot of the actual time series values and the corresponding centered moving average is shown in Figure 6.13. Note particularly how the centered moving average values tend to "smooth out" the fluctuations in the time series. Since the moving average values are for four quarters of data, they do not include the fluctuations due to seasonal influences. Each point in the centered moving average represents what the value of the time series would be if there were no seasonal or irregular influence.

By dividing each time series observation by the corresponding centered moving average value, we can identify the seasonal-irregular effect in the time series. For example,

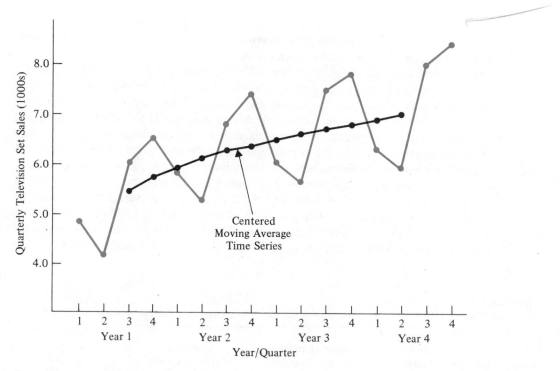

Figure 6.13
Graph of Quarterly Television Set Sales Time Series and Centered Moving Average

the third quarter of year 1 shows 6.0/5.475 = 1.096 as the combined seasonal-irregular component. The resulting seasonal-irregular values for the entire time series values are summarized in Table 6.9.

Consider the third quarter. The results from years 1, 2, and 3 show third-quarter values of 1.096, 1.075, and 1.109, respectively. Thus in all cases the seasonal-irregular component appears to have an above average influence in the third quarter. Since the year-to-year fluctuations in the seasonal-irregular component can be attributed primarily to the irregular component, we can average the computed values to eliminate the irregular influence and obtain an estimate of the third-quarter seasonal influence:

$$\text{Seasonal effect of third quarter} = \frac{1.096 + 1.075 + 1.109}{3} = 1.09$$

We refer to 1.09 as the *seasonal index* for the third quarter. In Table 6.10 we summarize the calculations involved in computing the seasonal indexes for the television set sales time series. Thus we see that the seasonal indexes for all four quarters are as follows: quarter 1, 0.93; quarter 2, 0.84; quarter 3, 1.09; and quarter 4, 1.14.

Table 6.9
Seasonal-Irregular Factors for the Television Set Sales Time Series

Year	Quarter	Sales (1000s)	Centered Moving Average	Seasonal-Irregular Component
1	1	4.8		
	2	4.1		
	3	6.0	5.475	1.096
	4	6.5	5.738	1.133
2	1	5.8	5.975	0.971
	2	5.2	6.188	0.840
	3	6.8	6.325	1.075
	4	7.4	6.400	1.156
3	1	6.0	6.538	0.918
	2	5.6	6.675	0.839
	3	7.5	6.763	1.109
	4	7.8	6.838	1.141
4	1	6.3	6.938	0.908
	2	5.9	7.075	0.834
	3	8.0		
	4	8.4		

Table 6.10
Seasonal Index Calculations for the Television Set Sales Time Series

Quarter	Seasonal-Irregular Component Values $(S_t I_t)$	Seasonal Index (S_t)
1	0.971, 0.918, 0.908	0.93
2	0.840, 0.839, 0.834	0.84
3	1.096, 1.075, 1.109	1.09
4	1.133, 1.156, 1.141	1.14

Interpretation of the values in Table 6.10 provides some observations about the "seasonal" component in television set sales. The best sales quarter is the fourth quarter, with sales averaging 14% above the average quarterly level. The worst, or slowest, sales quarter is the second quarter; its seasonal index of 0.84 shows that sales average 16% below the average quarterly sales. The seasonal component corresponds nicely to the intuitive expectation that television-viewing interest and thus television purchase patterns tend to peak in the fourth quarter, with its coming winter season and fewer outdoor activities. The low second-quarter sales reflect the reduced television interest resulting from the spring and presummer activities of the potential customers.

One final adjustment is sometimes necessary in computing the seasonal index. The multiplicative model requires that the average seasonal index equal 1.00; that is, the sum of the four seasonal indexes in Table 6.10 should equal 4.00. This is necessary if the seasonal effects are to even out over the year, as they must. The average of the seasonal indexes in our example is equal to 1.00, and hence this type of adjustment is not necessary. In other cases a slight adjustment may be necessary. The adjustment can be made by simply multiplying each seasonal index by the number of seasons divided by the sum of the unadjusted seasonal indexes. For example, for quarterly data we would multiply each seasonal index by 4/(sum of the unadjusted seasonal indexes). Some of the problems at the end of the chapter will require this adjustment in order to obtain the appropriate seasonal indexes.

Deseasonalizing the Time Series

Often the purpose of finding seasonal indexes is to remove the seasonal effects from a time series. This process is referred to as *deseasonalizing* the time series. Economic time series adjusted for seasonal variations (deseasonalized time series) are often reported in publications such as the *Survey of Current Business* and *The Wall Street Journal*. Using the notation of the multiplicative model, we have

$$Y_t = T_t \times S_t \times I_t$$

By dividing each time series observation by the corresponding seasonal index, we have removed the effect of season from the time series. The deseasonalized time series for television set sales is summarized in Table 6.11. A graph of the deseasonalized television set sales time series is shown in Figure 6.14.

Table 6.11
Deseasonalized Time Series for Television Set Sales

Year	Quarter	Sales (1000s) (Y_t)	Seasonal Index (S_t)	Deseasonalized Sales $(Y_t/S_t = T_tI_t)$
1	1	4.8	0.93	5.16
	2	4.1	0.84	4.88
	3	6.0	1.09	5.50
	4	6.5	1.14	5.70
2	1	5.8	0.93	6.24
	2	5.2	0.84	6.19
	3	6.8	1.09	6.24
	4	7.4	1.14	6.49
3	1	6.0	0.93	6.45
	2	5.6	0.84	6.67
	3	7.5	1.09	6.88
	4	7.8	1.14	6.84
4	1	6.3	0.93	6.77
	2	5.9	0.84	7.02
	3	8.0	1.09	7.34
	4	8.4	1.14	7.37

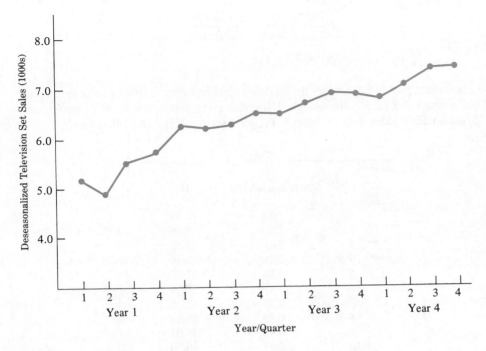

Figure 6.14
Deseasonalized Television Set Sales Time Series

Using the Deseasonalized Time Series to Identify Trend

Looking at Figure 6.14, we see that while the graph shows some up-and-down movement over the past 16 quarters, the time series seems to have an upward linear trend. Now, to identify this trend we can use the same procedure we introduced for identifying trend when forecasting with annual data; in this case, since we have deseasonalized the data, quarterly sales values can be used. Thus for a linear trend the estimated sales volume expressed as a function of time can be written

$$T_t = b_0 + b_1 t$$

where

T_t = trend value for television set sales in period t

b_0 = intercept of the trend line

b_1 = slope of the trend line

As before, we will let $t = 1$ for the time of the first observation in the time series, $t = 2$ for the time of the second observation, and so on. Thus for the deseasonalized television set sales time series, $t = 1$ corresponds to the first deseasonalized quarterly sales value and $t = 16$ corresponds to the most recent deseasonalized quarterly sales value. The formulas for computing the value of b_0 and the value of b_1 are shown again as

$$b_1 = \frac{\Sigma\, tY_t - (\Sigma\, t\, \Sigma\, Y_t)/n}{\Sigma\, t^2 - (\Sigma\, t)^2/n}$$

$$b_0 = \overline{Y} - b_1\overline{t}$$

Note, however, that Y_t now refers to the deseasonalized time series value at time t and not the actual value of the time series. Using the given relationships for b_0 and b_1 and the deseasonalized sales data of Table 6.11, we have the following calculations:

t	Y_t (deseasonalized)	tY_t	t^2
1	5.16	5.16	1
2	4.88	9.76	4
3	5.50	16.50	9
4	5.70	22.80	16
5	6.24	31.20	25
6	6.19	37.14	36
7	6.24	43.68	49
8	6.49	51.92	64
9	6.45	58.05	81
10	6.67	66.70	100
11	6.88	75.68	121
12	6.84	82.08	144
13	6.77	88.01	169
14	7.02	98.28	196
15	7.34	110.10	225
16	7.37	117.92	256
Totals 136	101.74	914.98	1496

$$\overline{t} = \frac{136}{16} = 8.5$$

$$\overline{Y} = \frac{101.74}{16} = 6.359$$

$$b_1 = \frac{914.98 - (136)(101.74)/16}{1496 - (136)^2/16} = \frac{50.19}{340} = 0.148$$

$$b_0 = 6.359 - 0.148(8.5) = 5.101$$

Therefore,

$$T_t = 5.101 + 0.148t$$

is the expression for the linear trend component of the time series.

The slope of 0.148 indicates that over the past 16 quarters, the firm has experienced an average deseasonalized growth in sales of around 148 sets per quarter. If we assume that the past 16-quarter trend in sales data is a reasonably good indicator of the future, then this equation can be used to project the trend component of the time series for future quarters. For example, substituting $t = 17$ into the equation yields next quarter's trend projection, T_{17}:

$$T_{17} = 5.101 + 0.148(17) = 7.617$$

Using the trend component only, we would forecast sales of 7617 television sets for the next quarter. In a similar fashion, if we were to use the trend component only, we would forecast sales of 7765, 7913, and 8061 television sets in quarters 18, 19, and 20, respectively.

Seasonal Adjustments

Now that we have a forecast of sales for each of the next four quarters based on trend, we must adjust these forecasts to account for the effect of season. For example, since the seasonal index for the first quarter is 0.93, the forecast for the first quarter of year 5 can be obtained by multiplying the forecast based on trend ($T_{17} = 7617$) times the seasonal index (0.93). Thus the forecast for the next quarter is 7617(0.93) = 7084. Table 6.12 shows the quarterly forecast for quarters 17, 18, 19, and 20. The quarterly forecasts show the high-volume fourth quarter with a 9190 unit forecast, while the low-volume second quarter has a 6523-unit forecast.

Table 6.12
Quarter-by-Quarter Short-Range Forecasts for the Television Set Sales Time Series

Year	Quarter	Trend Forecast	Seasonal Index (see Table 6.10)	Quarterly Forecast
5	1	7617	0.93	(7617)(0.93) = 7084
	2	7765	0.84	(7765)(0.84) = 6523
	3	7913	1.09	(7913)(1.09) = 8625
	4	8061	1.14	(8061)(1.14) = 9190

Models Based on Monthly Data

The television set sales example provided in this section used quarterly data to illustrate the computation of seasonal indexes with relatively few computations. Many businesses use monthly rather than quarterly forecasts. In such cases the procedures introduced in this section can be applied with minor modifications. First, a 12-month moving average replaces the four-quarter moving average; second, 12 monthly seasonal indexes, rather than four quarterly seasonal indexes, will need to be computed. Other than these changes, the computational and forecasting procedures are identical. Problem 18 at the end of the chapter asks you to develop monthly seasonal indexes for a situation requiring monthly forecasts.

Cyclical Component

Mathematically the multiplicative model of (6.9) can be expanded to include a cyclical component as follows:

$$Y_t = T_t \times C_t \times S_t \times I_t \qquad (6.10)$$

Just as with the seasonal component, the cyclical component is expressed as a percent of trend. As mentioned in Section 6.1, this component is attributable to multiyear cycles in the time series. It is analogous to the seasonal component, but over a longer period of time. However, because of the length of time involved and the varying length of cycles, it is often difficult to obtain enough relevant data to estimate the cyclical component. We leave further discussion of the cyclical component to texts on forecasting methods.

6.5

FORECASTING USING REGRESSION MODELS

Regression analysis is a statistical technique that can be used to develop forecasts based on the relationship between two or more variables. In regression notation and terminology, we let y indicate the *dependent* or *response* variable. This is the variable whose value we wish to forecast. The forecast of y will be based on one or more *independent* or *predictor* variables denoted by $x_1, x_2, \ldots, x_n$. If we can obtain a sample of data for all variables involved, regression analysis will provide an equation that can be used to forecast the value of y given the values of $x_1, x_2, \ldots, x_n$. In this section we restrict our attention to regression models involving one independent variable.

To demonstrate the use of regression analysis in forecasting, let us consider the sales forecasting problem faced by Armand's Pizza, Inc. Armand's Pizza, Inc. is a chain of Italian-food restaurants located in a five-state area. The most successful locations for Armand's have been near college campuses. Prior to opening a new restaurant, Armand's management requires a forecast of the yearly sales revenues. Such an estimate is used in planning the appropriate restaurant capacity, making initial staffing decisions, and deciding whether the potential revenue justifies the cost of operation. Since no past data are available on sales at a new store, Armand's cannot use time series data to develop the forecast.

Armand's management believes that annual sales revenue is related to the size of the student population on the nearby campus. On an intuitive basis, management believes that restaurants located near large campuses generate more revenue than those located near small campuses. If a relationship can be established between sales revenue and the size of the campus population, Armand's can use the size of the campus population to predict revenues for the new restaurant. To evaluate the relationship between annual sales y and student population x, Armand's collected data from a sample of 10 of its restaurants located near college campuses. These data are summarized in Table 6.13. For example, we see that restaurant 1, with $y = 58$ and $x = 2$, had $58,000 in sales revenue and was located near a campus with 2000 students.

Figure 6.15 shows graphically the data presented in Table 6.13. The size of the student population is shown on the horizontal axis, with annual sales on the vertical axis. A graph such as this is known as a *scatter diagram*. The usual practice is to plot the independent variable on the horizontal axis and the dependent variable on the vertical axis. The advantage of a scatter diagram is that it provides an overview of the data and enables us to draw preliminary conclusions about a possible relationship between the variables.

Table 6.13
Data on Student Population and Annual Sales for 10 Armand's
Restaurants

Restaurant	y = Annual Sales ($1000s)	x = Student Population (1000s)
1	58	2
2	105	6
3	88	8
4	118	8
5	117	12
6	137	16
7	157	20
8	169	20
9	149	22
10	202	26

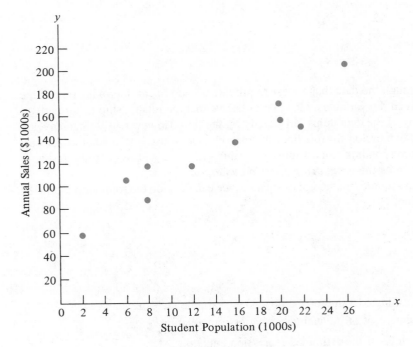

Figure 6.15
Scatter Diagram of Annual Sales versus Student Population

What preliminary conclusions can we draw from Figure 6.15? It appears that low sales volumes are associated with small student populations and higher sales volumes are associated with larger student populations. It also appears that the relationship between the two variables can be approximated by a straight line. In Figure 6.16 we have drawn

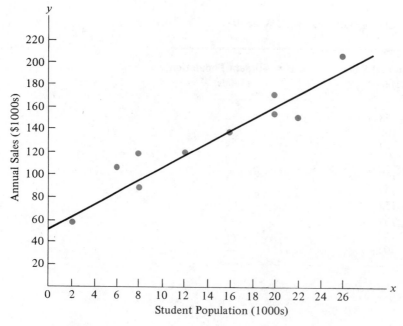

Figure 6.16
Straight-Line Approximation

a straight line through the data that appear to provide a good linear approximation of the relationship between the variables. However, observe that the relationship is not perfect. Indeed, few if any of the data items fall exactly on the line. However, if we can develop the mathematical expression for this line, we may be able to use it to predict or forecast the value of y corresponding to each possible value of x. We will refer to the resulting equation of the line as the *estimated regression equation*.

Using the least-squares method of estimation, we can develop the following estimated regression equation:

$$\hat{y} = b_0 + b_1 x \tag{6.11}$$

where

$\hat{y}$ = estimated value of the dependent variable (sales revenue $)
b_0 = intercept of the estimated regression equation
b_1 = slope of the estimated regression equation
x = value of the independent variable (student population)

Using the sample data, the intercept b_0 and slope b_1 can be computed using the following expressions:

$$b_1 = \frac{\sum x_i y_i - (\sum x_i \sum y_i)/n}{\sum x_i^2 - (\sum x_i)^2/n} \tag{6.12}$$

$$b_0 = \bar{y} - b_1\bar{x} \tag{6.13}$$

where

x_i = value of the independent variable for the ith observation

y_i = value of the dependent variable for the ith observation

$\bar{x}$ = mean value for the independent variable

$\bar{y}$ = mean value for the dependent variable

n = total number of observations

Some of the calculations necessary to develop the least-squares estimated regression equation for the Armand's Pizza problem are shown in Table 6.14. In our example there are 10 restaurants or observations; hence $n = 10$. Using (6.12) and (6.13), we can now compute the slope and intercept of the estimated regression equation for Armand's Restaurants. The calculation of the slope b_1 proceeds as follows:

$$b_1 = \frac{\Sigma \, x_i y_i - (\Sigma \, x_i \, \Sigma \, y_i)/n}{\Sigma \, x_i^2 - (\Sigma \, x_i)^2/n}$$

$$= \frac{21{,}040 - (140)(1{,}300)/10}{2{,}528 - (140)^2/10}$$

$$= \frac{2{,}840}{568}$$

$$= 5$$

Table 6.14
Calculations Necessary to Develop the Least-Squares Estimated
Regression Equation for Armand's Pizza

Restaurant (i)	y_i	x_i	$x_i y_i$	x_i^2
1	58	2	116	4
2	105	6	630	36
3	88	8	704	64
4	118	8	944	64
5	117	12	1,404	144
6	137	16	2,192	256
7	157	20	3,140	400
8	169	20	3,380	400
9	149	22	3,278	484
10	202	26	5,252	676
Totals	1,300	140	21,040	2,528

The calculation of the y intercept b_0 is as follows:

$$\bar{x} = \frac{\Sigma x_i}{n} = \frac{140}{10} = 14$$

$$\bar{y} = \frac{\Sigma y_i}{n} = \frac{1,300}{10} = 130$$

$$b_0 = \bar{y} - b_1\bar{x}$$

$$= 130 - 5(14)$$

$$= 60$$

Thus the estimated regression equation found by using the method of least squares is

$$\hat{y} = 60 + 5x$$

In Figure 6.17 we show the graph of this equation.

The slope of the estimated regression equation ($b_1 = 5$) is positive, implying that as student population increases, annual sales increase. In fact we can conclude (since sales are measured in $1000s and student population in 1000s) that an increase in the student population of 1000 is associated with an increase of $5000 in expected annual sales; that is, sales are expected to increase by $5.00 per student.

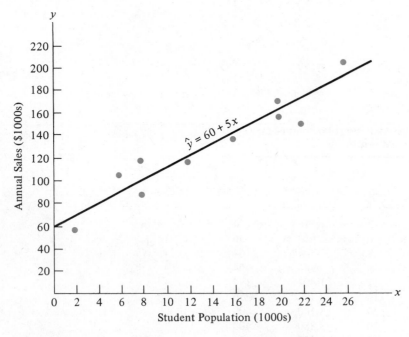

Figure 6.17

Graph of the Estimated Regression Equation for Armand's Pizza: $\hat{y} = 60 + 5x$

If we believe that the least-squares estimated regression equation adequately describes the relationship between x and y, then it would seem reasonable to use the estimated regression equation to forecast the value of y for a given value of x. For example, if we wanted to forecast annual sales for a new restaurant location near a campus with 16,000 students, we would compute

$$\hat{y} = 60 + 5(16)$$
$$= 140$$

Hence we would forecast sales of $140,000 per year.

6.6
QUALITATIVE APPROACHES TO FORECASTING

In the previous sections we have discussed several types of quantitative forecasting methods. Since each of these techniques requires historical data on the variable of interest, these techniques cannot be applied in situations where no historical data are available. Furthermore, even when historical data are available, a significant change in environmental conditions affecting the time series may make the use of past data questionable in predicting future values of the time series. For example, a government-imposed gas rationing program would cause one to question the validity of a gas sales forecast based on past data. Qualitative forecasting techniques offer an alternative in these, and other, cases.

One of the most commonly used qualitative forecasting methods is the *Delphi approach*. This technique, originally developed by a research group at the Rand Corporation, attempts to obtain forecasts through "group consensus." In the usual application of this technique, the members of a panel of experts—all of whom are physically separated from and unknown to each other—are asked to respond to a series of questionnaires. The responses from the first questionnaire are tabulated and used to prepare a second questionnaire, which contains information and opinions of the whole group. Each respondent is then asked to reconsider and possibly revise his or her previous response in light of the group information that has been provided. This basic process continues until the coordinator feels that some degree of consensus has been reached. Note that the goal of the Delphi approach is not to produce a single answer as output but to produce instead a relatively narrow spread of opinions within which the "majority" of experts concur.

The qualitative procedure referred to as *scenario writing* consists of developing a conceptual scenario of the future based on a well-defined set of assumptions. Thus by starting with a different set of assumptions, many different future scenarios can be presented. The job of the decision maker is to decide which scenario is most likely to occur in the future and then to make decisions accordingly.

Subjective or intuitive qualitative approaches are based on the ability of the human mind to process a variety of information that is, in most cases, difficult to quantify. These techniques are often used in group work, wherein a committee or panel seeks to develop new ideas or solve complex problems through a series of "brainstorming sessions." In such sessions individuals are freed from the usual group restrictions of peer pressure and criticism, since any idea or opinion can be presented without regard to its relevancy and, even more important, without fear of criticism.

Summary

The purpose of this chapter has been to provide an introduction to the basic methods of time series analysis and forecasting. First we showed that in order to explain the behavior of a time series, it is often helpful to think of the time series as consisting of four separate components: trend, cyclical, seasonal, and irregular. By isolating these components and measuring their apparent effect, it is possible to forecast future values of the time series.

We discussed how smoothing methods can be used to forecast a time series that exhibits no significant trend, seasonal, or cyclical effect. The moving averages approach consists of computing an average of past data values and then using this average as the forecast for the next period. The exponential smoothing method uses a weighted average of past time series values to compute a forecast.

When the time series exhibits only a long-term trend, we showed how the least-squares method could be used to make trend projections. When both trend and seasonal influences are significant, we showed how a multiplicative model could be used to isolate the effects of the two factors and prepare better forecasts. Finally, regression analysis was described as a procedure for developing so-called causal forecasting methods. A *causal forecasting method* is one that relates the time series value (dependent variable) to other independent variables that are believed to explain (cause) the time series behavior.

Qualitative forecasting methods were discussed as approaches that could be used when little or no historical data were available. These methods are also considered most appropriate when the past pattern of the time series is not expected to continue into the future.

Glossary

Time series   A set of observations measured at successive points in time or over successive periods of time.

Forecast   A projection or prediction of future values of a time series.

Trend   The long-run shift or movement in the time series observable over several periods of time.

Cyclical component   The component of the time series model that accounts for the periodic above-trend and below-trend behavior of the time series lasting more than 1 year.

Seasonal component   The component of the time series model that shows a periodic pattern over 1 year or less.

Irregular component   The component of the time series model that reflects the random variation of the actual time series values beyond what can be explained by the trend, cyclical, and seasonal components.

Moving averages   A method of forecasting or smoothing a time series by averaging each successive group of data points.

Forecast error   The difference between the observed value of the time series and the forecast.

Mean square error (MSE)   One approach to measuring the accuracy of a forecasting model. This measure is the average of the sum of the squared differences between the forecast values and the actual time series values.

Weighted moving averages   A method of forecasting or smoothing a time series by computing a weighted average of past data values. The sum of the weights must equal 1.

Exponential smoothing   A forecasting technique that uses a weighted average of past time series values in order to forecast the value of the time series in the next period.

Smoothing constant   A parameter of the exponential smoothing model that provides the weight given to the most recent time series value in the calculation of the forecast.

Deseasonalized time series   A time series that has had the effect of season removed by dividing each original time series observation by the corresponding seasonal index.

Multiplicative time series model   A model that assumes that the separate components can be multiplied together to identify the time series value. When the components of trend, seasonal, and irregular are assumed present, we obtain $Y_t = T_t \times S_t \times I_t$.

Delphi approach   A qualitative forecasting method that obtains forecasts through "group consensus."

Scenario writing   A qualitative forecasting method that consists of developing a conceptual scenario of the future based on a well-defined set of assumptions.

Causal forecasting methods   Forecasting methods that relate a time series value to other variables that are believed to explain or cause its behavior. Regression analysis is a commonly used causal forecasting method.

Problems

1. Refer to the gasoline sales time series data in Table 6.1.
    a. Compute 4- and 5-week moving averages for the time series.
    b. Compute the mean square error (MSE) for the 4- and 5-week moving average forecasts.
    c. What appears to be the best number of weeks of past data to use in the moving average computation? Remember that the MSE for the 3-week moving average is 10.22.

2. Refer again to the gasoline sales time series data in Table 6.1.
    a. Using a weight of $\frac{1}{2}$ for the most recent observation, $\frac{1}{3}$ for the second most recent, and $\frac{1}{6}$ for the third most recent, compute a 3-week weighted moving average for the time series.
    b. Compute the mean square error for the weighted moving average in part (a). Do you prefer this weighted moving average to the unweighted moving average? Remember that the MSE for the unweighted moving average is 10.22.

3. Use the gasoline sales time series data from Table 6.1 to compute the exponential smoothing forecasts using $\alpha = 0.1$. Using the mean square error criterion, would you prefer a smoothing constant of $\alpha = 0.1$ or $\alpha = 0.2$ for the gasoline sales time series?

4. Using a smoothing constant of $\alpha = 0.2$, equation (6.2) shows that the forecast for the 13th week of the gasoline sales data from Table 6.1 is given by $F_{13} = 0.2Y_{12} + 0.8F_{12}$. However, the forecast for week 12 is given by $F_{12} = 0.2Y_{11} + 0.8F_{11}$. Thus we could combine these two results to show that the forecast for the 13th week can be written

$$F_{13} = 0.2Y_{12} + 0.8(0.2Y_{11} + 0.8F_{11}) = 0.2Y_{12} + 0.16Y_{11} + 0.64F_{11}$$

a. Making use of the fact that $F_{11} = 0.2Y_{10} + 0.8F_{10}$ (and similar expressions for F_{10} and F_9), continue to expand the expression for F_{13} until it is written in terms of the past data values Y_{12}, Y_{11}, Y_{10}, Y_9, Y_8, and the forecast for period 8.

b. Refer to the coefficients or weights for the past data Y_{12}, Y_{11}, Y_{10}, Y_9, and Y_8; what observation do you make about how exponential smoothing weights past data values in arriving at new forecasts? Compare this weighting pattern with the weighting pattern of the moving averages method.

5. The following time series shows the sales of a particular product over the past 12 months:

Month	Sales
1	105
2	135
3	120
4	105
5	90
6	120
7	145
8	140
9	100
10	80
11	100
12	110

Use $\alpha = 0.3$ to compute the exponential smoothing values for the time series.

6. Analyze the forecasting errors for the time series in problem 5 by using a smoothing constant of 0.5. Does a smoothing constant of 0.3 or 0.5 appear to provide the better forecasts?

7. The number of component parts used in a production process each week in the last 10 weeks showed the following:

Week	Parts	Week	Parts
1	200	6	210
2	350	7	280
3	250	8	350
4	360	9	290
5	250	10	320

Use a smoothing constant of 0.25 to develop the exponential smoothing values for this time series. Indicate your forecast for next week.

8. A chain of grocery stores experienced the following weekly demand (cases) for a particular brand of automatic-dishwasher detergent:

Week	Demand
1	22
2	18
3	23
4	21
5	17
6	24
7	20
8	19
9	18
10	21

Use exponential smoothing with $\alpha = 0.2$ in order to develop a forecast for week 11.

9. United Dairies, Inc. supplies milk to several independent grocers throughout Dade County in Florida. Management of United Dairies would like to develop a forecast of the number of half-gallons of milk sold per week. Sales data for the past 12 weeks are as follows:

Week	Sales (units)
1	2750
2	3100
3	3250
4	2800
5	2900
6	3050
7	3300
8	3100
9	2950
10	3000
11	3200
12	3150

Use the above 12 weeks of data and exponential smoothing with $\alpha = 0.4$ to develop a forecast of demand for the 13th week.

10. Average attendance figures at home football games for a major university show the following 7-year pattern:

Year	Attendance
1	28,000
2	30,000
3	31,500
4	30,400
5	30,500
6	32,200
7	30,800

Develop the trend expression shown in equation (6.4) for this time series. Use the trend expression to forecast attendance for year 8.

11. Automobile sales at B. J. Scott Motors, Inc. provided the following 10-year time series:

Year	Sales
1	400
2	390
3	320
4	340
5	270
6	260
7	300
8	320
9	340
10	370

Plot the time series and comment on the appropriateness of a linear trend. What type of functional form do you believe would be most appropriate for the trend pattern of this time series?

12. The president of a small manufacturing firm has been concerned about the continual growth in manufacturing costs over the past several years. Shown below is a time series of the cost per unit for the firm's leading product over the past 8 years:

Year	Cost/Unit ($)
1	20.00
2	24.50
3	28.20
4	27.50
5	26.60
6	30.00
7	31.00
8	36.00

a. Show a graph of this time series. Does a linear trend appear to exist?

b. Develop a linear trend expression for the above time series. What is the average cost increase that the firm has been realizing per year?

13. The enrollment data for a state college for the past 6 years are shown below:

Year	Enrollment
1	20,500
2	20,200
3	19,500
4	19,000
5	19,100
6	18,800

Develop a linear trend expression and comment on what is happening to enrollment at this institution. Use the trend expression to forecast enrollment for year 7.

14. Canton Supplies, Inc. is a service firm that employs approximately 100 individuals. Because of the necessity of meeting monthly cash obligations, management of Canton Supplies would like to develop a forecast of monthly cash requirements. Due to a recent change in operating policy, only the past 7 months of data were considered to be relevant. Develop a linear trend expression for the historical data shown below. Use the trend expression to develop a forecast of cash requirements for each of the next 2 months.

Month	1	2	3	4	5	6	7
Cash Required ($1000)	205	212	218	224	230	240	246

15. The Costello Music Company has been in business for 5 years. During this time the sale of electric organs has grown from 12 units in the first year to 76 units in the most recent year. Fred Costello, the firm's owner, would like to develop a forecast of organ sales for the coming year. The historical data are shown below:

Year	1	2	3	4	5
Sales	12	28	34	50	76

a. Show a graph of this time series. Does a linear trend appear to exist?

b. Develop a linear trend expression for the above time series. What is the average increase in sales that the firm has been realizing per year?

16. Hudson Marine has been an authorized dealer for C&D marine radios for the past 7 years. The number of radios sold each year is shown below:

	1	2	3	4	5	6	7
Number Sold	35	50	75	90	105	110	130

a. Show a graph of this time series. Does a linear trend appear to exist?

b. Develop a linear trend for the above time series.

c. Use the linear trend developed in part (b) and prepare a forecast for annual sales in year 8.

17. The quarterly sales data for a college textbook over the past 3 years are as follows:

	Year 1	Year 2	Year 3
Quarter 1	1690	1800	1850
Quarter 2	940	900	1100
Quarter 3	2625	2900	2930
Quarter 4	2500	2360	2615

a. Show the four-quarter moving average values for this time series. Plot both the original time series and the moving averages on the same graph.

b. Compute seasonal indexes for the four quarters.

c. When does the textbook publisher experience the largest seasonal effect? Does this appear reasonable? Explain.

18. Identify the monthly seasonal indexes for the following 3 years of expenses for a six-unit apartment house in southern Florida. Use a 12-month moving average calculation.

Month	Year 1	Year 2	Year 3
January	170	180	195
February	180	205	210
March	205	215	230
April	230	245	280
May	240	265	290
June	315	330	390
July	360	400	420
August	290	335	330
September	240	260	290
October	240	270	295
November	230	255	280
December	195	220	250

19. Refer to the Hudson Marine problem presented in problem 16. Suppose that the quarterly sales values for the 7 years of historical data are as follows:

	Quarter 1	Quarter 2	Quarter 3	Quarter 4	Total Sales
Year 1	6	15	10	4	35
Year 2	10	18	15	7	50
Year 3	14	26	23	12	75
Year 4	19	28	25	18	90
Year 5	22	34	28	21	105
Year 6	24	36	30	20	110
Year 7	28	40	35	27	130

a. Show the four-quarter moving average values for this time series. Plot both the original time series and the moving average series on the same graph.
b. Compute the seasonal indexes for the four quarters.
c. When does Hudson Marine experience the largest seasonal effect? Does this seem reasonable? Explain.

20. Consider the Costello Music Company problem presented in problem 15. The quarterly sales data are shown below:

	Quarter 1	Quarter 2	Quarter 3	Quarter 4	Total Yearly Sales
Year 1	4	2	1	5	12
Year 2	6	4	4	14	28
Year 3	10	3	5	16	34
Year 4	12	9	7	22	50
Year 5	18	10	13	35	76

a. Compute the seasonal indexes for the four quarters.
b. When does Costello Music experience the largest seasonal effect? Does this appear reasonable? Explain.

21. Refer to the Hudson Marine data presented in problem 19.
   a. Deseasonalize the data and use the deseasonalized time series to identify the trend.
   b. Use the results of part (a) to develop a quarterly forecast for next year based on trend.
   c. Use the seasonal indexes developed in problem 19 to adjust the forecasts developed in part (b) to account for the effect of season.

22. Consider the Costello Music Company time series presented in problem 20.
   a. Deseasonalize the data and use the deseasonalized time series to identify the trend.
   b. Use the results of part (a) to develop a quarterly forecast for next year based on trend.
   c. Use the seasonal indexes developed in problem 20 to adjust the forecasts developed in part (b) to account for the effect of season.

23. Eddie's Restaurants collected the following data on the relationship between advertising and sales at a sample of five restaurants:

Advertising Expenditures ($1000s)	Sales ($1000s)
1.0	19.0
4.0	44.0
6.0	40.0
10.0	52.0
14.0	53.0

a. Let x equal advertising expenditures ($1000s) and y equal sales ($1000s). Use the method of least squares to develop a straight-line approximation to the relationship between the two variables.
b. Use the equation developed in part (a) to forecast sales for an advertising expenditure of $8000.

24. The management of a chain of fast-food restaurants would like to investigate the relationship between the daily sales volume of a company restaurant and the number of competitor restaurants within a 1-mile radius of the firm's restaurant. The following data have been collected:

Number of Competitors within 1 Mile	Sales ($)
1	3600
1	3300
2	3100
3	2900
3	2700
4	2500
5	2300
5	2000

a. Develop the least-squares estimated regression equation that relates daily sales volume to the number of competitor restaurants within a 1-mile radius.

b. Use the estimated regression equation developed in part (a) to forecast the daily sales volume for a particular company restaurant that has four competitors within a 1-mile radius.

25. In a manufacturing process the assembly-line speed (feet/minute) was thought to affect the number of defective parts found during the inspection process. To test this theory, management devised a situation where the same batch of parts was inspected visually at a variety of line speeds. The following data were collected:

Line Speed	Number of Defective Parts Found
20	21
20	19
40	15
30	16
60	14
40	17

a. Develop the estimated regression equation that relates line speed to the number of defective parts found.

b. Use the equation developed in part (a) to forecast the number of defective parts found for a line speed of 50 feet per minute.

Case Problem
Forecasting Sales

The Vintage Restaurant is located on Captiva Island, a resort community near Fort Meyers, Florida. The restaurant, which is owned and operated by Karen Payne, has just completed its third year of operation. During this period of time Karen has sought to establish a reputation for the restaurant as a high-quality dining establishment that specializes in fresh seafood. The efforts made by Karen and her staff have proved successful, and her restaurant has become one of the best and fastest-growing restaurants on the island.

Karen has concluded that in order to plan better for the growth of the restaurant in the future, it is necessary to develop a system that will enable her to forecast food and beverage sales by month for up to 1 year in advance. Karen has available data on the total food and beverage sales that were realized during the previous 3 years of operation. These data are provided below:

Food and Beverage Sales for the Vintage Restaurant ($1000s)

Month	First Year	Second Year	Third Year
January	242	263	282
February	235	238	255
March	232	247	265
April	178	193	205
May	184	193	210
June	140	149	160
July	145	157	166
August	152	161	174
September	110	122	126
October	130	130	148
November	152	167	173
December	206	230	235

Managerial Report

Perform an analysis of the sales data for the Vintage Restaurant. Prepare a report for Karen that summarizes your findings, forecasts, and recommendations. Include information on the following:

1. A graph of the time series.
2. An analysis of the seasonality of the data. Include the seasonal indexes for each month and comment on the high seasonal and low seasonal sales months. Do the seasonal indexes make intuitive sense? Discuss.

3. Forecast sales for January through December of the fourth year.

4. Assume that the January sales for the fourth year turned out to be $295,000. What was your forecast error? If this is a large error, Karen may be puzzled as to why there is such a difference between your forecast and the actual sales value. What can you do to resolve her uncertainty in the forecasting procedure?

5. Develop recommendations as to when the system you have developed should be updated to account for new sales data that will occur.

6. Include any detailed calculations of your analysis in the appendix of your report.

Quantitative Methods in Practice

The Cincinnati Gas & Electric Company*

Cincinnati, Ohio

The Cincinnati Gas Light and Coke Company was chartered by the State of Ohio on April 3, 1837. Under this charter the company manufactured gas by distillation of coal and sold it for lighting purposes. During the last quarter of the nineteenth century the company successfully marketed gas for lighting, heating, and cooking and as fuel for gas engines.

In 1901 the Cincinnati Gas Light and Coke Company and the Cincinnati Electric Light Company merged to form The Cincinnati Gas & Electric Company (CG&E). This new company was able to shift from manufactured gas to natural gas and adopt the rapidly emerging technologies in generating and distributing electricity. CG&E operated as a subsidiary of the Columbia Gas Electric Company from 1909 until 1944.

Today CG&E is a privately owned public utility serving approximately 370,000 gas customers and 600,000 electric customers. The company's service area covers approximately 3000 square miles in and around the Greater Cincinnati area.

Forecasting at CG&E

As in any modern company, forecasting at CG&E is an integral part of operating and managing the business. Depending on the decision to be made, the forecasting techniques used range from judgment and graphical trend projections to sophisticated multiple regression models.

Forecasting in the utility industry offers some unique perspectives compared to other industries. Since there are no finished-goods or in-process inventories of electricity, this product must be generated to meet the instantaneous requirements of the customers. Electrical shortages are not just lost sales, but "brownouts" or "blackouts." This situation places an unusual burden on the utility forecaster. On the positive side, the demand for energy and the sale of energy is more predictable than for many other products. Also, unlike the situation in a multiproduct firm, a great amount of forecasting effort and expertise can be concentrated on the two products: gas and electricity.

---

*The authors are indebted to Dr. Richard Evans, The Cincinnati Gas & Electric Company, Cincinnati, Ohio, for providing this application.

Forecasting Electric Energy and Peak Loads

The two types of forecasts discussed in this section are the long-range forecasts of electric peak load and electric energy. The largest observed electric demand for any given period, such as an hour, a day, a month, or a year, is defined as the peak load. The cumulative amount of energy generated and used over the period of an hour is referred to as electric energy.

Until the mid-1970s the seasonal pattern of both electric energy and electric peak load were very regular; the time series for both of these exhibited a fairly steady exponential growth. Business cycles had little noticeable effect on either. Perhaps the most serious shift in the behavior of these time series came from the increasing installation of air conditioning units in the Greater Cincinnati area. This fact caused an accelerated growth in the trend component and also in the relative magnitude of the summer peaks. Nevertheless, the two time series were very regular and generally quite predictable.

Trend projection was the most popular method used to forecast electric energy and electric peak load. The forecast accuracy was quite acceptable and even enviable when compared to forecast errors experienced in other industries.

A New Era in Forecasting

In the mid-1970s a variety of actions by the government, the off-and-on energy shortages, and price signals to the consumer began to affect the consumption of electric energy. As a result the behavior of the peak load and electric energy time series became more and more unpredictable. Hence a simple trend projection forecasting model was no longer adequate. As a result a special forecasting model—referred to as an econometric model— was developed by CG&E to better account for the behavior of these time series.

The purpose of the econometric model is to forecast the annual energy consumption by residential, commercial, and industrial classes of service. These forecasts are then used to develop forecasts of summer and winter peak loads. First energy consumption in the industrial and commercial classes is forecast. For an assumed level of economic activity, the projection of electric energy is made along with a forecast of employment in the area. The employment forecast is converted to a forecast of adult population through the use of unemployment rates and labor force participation rates. Household forecasts are then developed through the use of demographic statistics on the average number of persons per household. The resulting forecast of households is used as an indicator of residential customers.

At this point a comparison is made with the demographic projections for the area population. The differences between the residential customers forecast and the population forecast are reconciled to produce the final forecast of residential customers. This forecast becomes the principal independent variable in forecasting residential electric energy.

Summer and winter peak loads are then forecast by applying class peak contribution factors to the energy forecasts. The contributions that each class makes toward the peak are summed to establish the peak forecast.

A number of economic and demographic time series are used in the construction of the above econometric model. Simply speaking, the entire forecasting system is a compilation of several statistically verified multiple regression equations.

Impact and Value of the Forecasts

The forecast of the annual electric peak load guides the timing decisions for constructing future generating units. The financial impact of these decisions is great. For example, the last generating unit built by the company cost nearly $600 million, and the interest rate on a recent first mortgage bond was 16%. At this rate, annual interest costs would be nearly $100 million. Obviously, a timing decision that leads to having the unit available no sooner than necessary is crucial.

The energy forecasts are important in other ways also. For example, purchases of coal and nuclear fuel for the generating units are based on the forecast levels of energy needed. The revenue from the electric operations of the company is determined from forecasted sales, which in turn enters into the planning of rate changes and external financing. These planning and decision-making processes are among the most important management activities in the company. It is imperative that the decision makers have the best forecast information available to assist them in arriving at these decisions.

Questions

1. Describe some of the unique perspectives associated with forecasting in the utility industry as compared with other industries.
2. Until the mid-1970s, what type of forecasting procedure was used by CG&E? What necessitated a change?
3. Briefly describe CG&E's current approach to forecasting.
4. What are the benefits of accurate forecasts for CG&E?

CHAPTER

7

Linear Programming: The Graphical Method

Linear programming is a problem-solving approach that has been developed to help managers make decisions. Some typical applications where linear programming has been used are described below:

1. A manufacturer wants to develop a production schedule and an inventory policy that will satisfy sales demand in future periods. Ideally the schedule and policy will enable the company to satisfy demand and at the same time *minimize* the total production and inventory costs.

2. A financial analyst must select an investment portfolio from a variety of stock and bond investment alternatives. The analyst would like to establish the portfolio that *maximizes* the return on investment.

3. A marketing manager wants to determine how best to allocate a fixed advertising budget among alternative advertising media such as radio, television, newspaper, and magazines. The manager would like to determine the media mix that *maximizes* advertising effectiveness.

4. A company has warehouses in a number of locations throughout the United States. Given a set of customer demands for its products, the company would like to determine which warehouse should ship how much product to which customers so that the total transportation costs are *minimized*.

These are only a few examples of situations where linear programming has been used successfully, but the examples illustrate the diversity of linear programming applications. A close scrutiny reveals one basic property that all of these examples have in common. In each example we were concerned with *maximizing* or *minimizing* some quantity. In example 1 we wanted to minimize costs; in example 2 we wanted to maximize return on investment; in example 3 we wanted to maximize advertising effectiveness; and in example 4 we wanted to minimize total transportation costs. *In all linear programming problems the maximization or minimization of some quantity is the objective*.

A second property of all linear programming problems is that there are restrictions or *constraints* that limit the degree to which the objective can be pursued. In example 1 the manufacturer is restricted by constraints requiring product demand to be satisfied and by the constraints limiting production capacity. The financial analyst's portfolio problem is constrained by the total amount of investment funds available and the maximum amounts that can be invested in each stock or bond. The marketing manager's media selection decision is constrained by a fixed advertising budget and the availability of the various media. In the transportation problem the minimum cost shipping schedule is constrained by the supply of product available at each warehouse. *Thus constraints are another general feature of every linear programming problem*.

7.1

A SIMPLE MAXIMIZATION PROBLEM

Let us consider the problem currently being faced by RMC, Inc., a small firm that produces a variety of chemical-based products. In a particular production process, three raw materials are used to produce two products: a fuel additive and a solvent base. The fuel additive is sold to oil companies and is used in the production of gasoline and related fuels. The solvent base is sold to a variety of chemical firms and is used in both home and industrial cleaning products. The three raw materials are blended to form the fuel additive and solvent base as shown in Table 7.1. From the table we see that a ton of fuel additive is a mixture of $2/5$ ton of material 1 and $3/5$ ton of material 3. A ton of solvent base is a mixture of $1/2$ ton of material 1, $1/5$ ton of material 2, and $3/10$ ton of material 3.

Table 7.1
Material Requirements per Ton for the RMC Problem

Product	Material 1	Material 2	Material 3
Fuel additive	$2/5$	0	$3/5$
Solvent base	$1/2$	$1/5$	$3/10$

Example: $1/2$ ton of material 1 is used in each ton of solvent base.

RMC's production is constrained by a limited availability of the three raw materials. For the current production period, RMC has available the following quantities of each raw material:

Material	Amount Available for Production
Material 1	20 tons
Material 2	5 tons
Material 3	21 tons

Because of spoilage and the nature of the production process, any materials not used for current production are useless and must be discarded.

RMC's management, after an analysis of potential demand, has established prices that will ensure the sale of all the fuel additive and solvent base produced. After deducting all relevant costs, the accounting department has determined that the company will make $40 for every ton of fuel additive produced and $30 for every ton of solvent base produced. RMC's problem is: Given the limited availability of the raw materials, how many tons of each product should be produced in order to maximize profit?

7.2

THE OBJECTIVE FUNCTION

As pointed out earlier, every linear programming problem has a maximization or minimization objective. For the RMC problem the objective is to maximize profit. We can write this objective in mathematical form with the introduction of some simple notation. Let

x_1 = the number of tons of fuel additive that RMC produces

x_2 = the number of tons of solvent base that RMC produces

RMC's profit will come from two sources: (1) the profit made by producing x_1 tons of fuel additive and (2) the profit made by producing x_2 tons of solvent base. Since RMC makes $40 for every ton of fuel additive produced, the company will make $40x_1$ if x_1 tons of fuel additive are produced. Also, since RMC makes $30 for every ton of solvent base produced, the company will make $30x_2$ if x_2 tons of solvent base are produced. Denoting the total profit by z, and deleting the dollar sign, we have

$$\text{Total profit} = z = 40x_1 + 30x_2 \qquad (7.1)$$

The optimal solution to RMC's problem is the production combination that will maximize total profit. That is, RMC must determine the values of the variables x_1 and x_2 that will yield the highest possible value of z. In linear programming terminology we refer to x_1 and x_2 as the *decision variables*. Since the objective—maximize total profit—is a *function* of these decision variables, we refer to $40x_1 + 30x_2$ as the *objective function*. Using "max" as an abbreviation for maximize, the objective is written as follows:

$$\text{max } z = \text{max } 40x_1 + 30x_2. \qquad (7.2)$$

In the RMC problem, any particular production combination of fuel additive and solvent base is referred to as a *solution* to the problem. However, only those solutions that satisfy *all* the constraints are referred to as *feasible solutions*. The particular feasible production combination or feasible solution that results in the largest profit will be referred to as the *optimal* production combination or, equivalently, the *optimal solution*. At this point, however, we have no idea what the optimal solution will be. In fact, we have not even developed a procedure for identifying feasible solutions. The procedure for determining the feasible solutions requires us first to identify all the constraints of the problem.

7.3

THE CONSTRAINTS

Since there are limited amounts of three raw materials available, we have three conditions or restrictions that limit the amount of fuel additive and solvent base RMC can produce. From the production information (see Table 7.1), we know that every ton of fuel additive will use $\frac{2}{5}$ ton of material 1. Thus the total number of tons of material 1 used in the production of x_1 tons of fuel additive will be $\frac{2}{5}x_1$. In addition, every ton of solvent base will use $\frac{1}{2}$ ton of material 1. As a result, x_2 tons of solvent base will use $\frac{1}{2}x_2$ tons of material 1. The total number of tons of material 1 required to produce x_1 tons of fuel additive and x_2 tons of solvent base is given by

$$\text{Total tons of material 1 required} = \tfrac{2}{5}x_1 + \tfrac{1}{2}x_2$$

Since RMC has a maximum of 20 tons of material 1 available, it follows that the production combination we select must satisfy the requirement

$$\tfrac{2}{5}x_1 + \tfrac{1}{2}x_2 \le 20 \tag{7.3}$$

Relationship (7.3) is referred to as an inequality and denotes the fact that the total number of tons of material 1 used in the production of x_1 tons of fuel additive and x_2 tons of solvent base must be less than or equal to the amount of material 1 that RMC has available.

From Table 7.1 we see that while the fuel additive does not require material 2, every ton of solvent base produced requires $\frac{1}{5}$ ton of material 2. Since there are 5 tons of material 2 available, it follows that

$$0x_1 + \tfrac{1}{5}x_2 \le 5$$

or, simply,

$$\tfrac{1}{5}x_2 \le 5 \tag{7.4}$$

Inequality (7.4) is the material 2 constraint for RMC. Verify for yourself that the material 3 constraint is

$$\tfrac{3}{5}x_1 + \tfrac{3}{10}x_2 \le 21 \tag{7.5}$$

We now have specified the mathematical relationships for the constraints associated with the three materials. Are there any other constraints that we have forgotten? Can

RMC produce a negative number of tons of fuel additive or solvent base? Clearly, the answer is no. Thus, in order to prevent the decision variables x_1 and x_2 from having negative values, two constraints,

$$x_1 \geq 0 \quad \text{and} \quad x_2 \geq 0 \tag{7.6}$$

must be added. These constraints ensure that the solution to our problem will contain nonnegative values for the decision variables and are thus referred to as the *nonnegativity constraints*. Nonnegativity constraints are a general feature of all linear programming problems and will be written in the abbreviated form

$$x_1, x_2 \geq 0$$

7.4

THE MATHEMATICAL STATEMENT OF THE RMC PROBLEM

The mathematical statement, or mathematical formulation, of the RMC problem is now complete. We have succeeded in translating the objective and constraints of the real-world problem into a set of mathematical relationships referred to as a *mathematical model*. The complete mathematical model for the RMC problem is as follows:

$$\begin{aligned}
\max \quad & 40x_1 + 30x_2 \\
\text{subject to (s.t.)} \quad & \\
& \tfrac{2}{5}x_1 + \tfrac{1}{2}x_2 \leq 20 \qquad \text{Material 1} \\
& \qquad\quad \tfrac{1}{5}x_2 \leq 5 \qquad \text{Material 2} \\
& \tfrac{3}{5}x_1 + \tfrac{3}{10}x_2 \leq 21 \qquad \text{Material 3} \\
& x_1, x_2 \geq 0
\end{aligned}$$

Our job now is to find the product mix (i.e., the combination of x_1 and x_2) that satisfies all the constraints and, at the same time, yields a value for the objective function that is greater than or equal to the value given by any other feasible solution. Once this is done, we will have found the optimal solution to the problem.

This mathematical model of the RMC problem is a *linear program*. The problem has the objective function and constraints that we said earlier were common properties of all linear programs. But what is the special feature of this mathematical model that makes it a *linear* program? The special feature that makes it a linear program is that the objective function and all *constraint functions* (the left-hand sides of the constraint inequalities) are linear functions of the decision variables.

Mathematical functions in which each variable appears in a separate term and is raised to the first power are called *linear functions*. The cbjective function $40x_1 + 30x_2$ is linear, since each decision variable appears in a separate term and has an exponent of 1. If the objective function had appeared as $40x_1^2 + 30\sqrt{x_2}$, it would not have been a linear function and we would not have had a linear program. The number of tons of material 1 required, $\tfrac{2}{5}x_1 + \tfrac{1}{2}x_2$, is also a linear function of the decision variables for the same reasons. Similarly, the functions on the left-hand side of all the constraint inequalities (the constraint functions) are linear functions. Thus the mathematical formulation of the RMC problem is referred to as a linear program.

7.5

GRAPHICAL SOLUTION

A linear programming problem involving only two decision variables can be solved with a graphical solution procedure. Let us begin the graphical solution procedure by developing a graph that displays the possible solutions (x_1 and x_2 values) for the RMC problem. The graph (Figure 7.1) will have values of x_1 on the horizontal axis and values of x_2 on the vertical axis. Any point on the graph can be identified by the x_1 and x_2 values, which indicate the position of the point along the x_1 and x_2 axes, respectively. Since every point (x_1, x_2) corresponds to a possible solution, every point on the graph is called a *solution*. The solution where $x_1 = 0$ and $x_2 = 0$ is referred to as the *origin*.

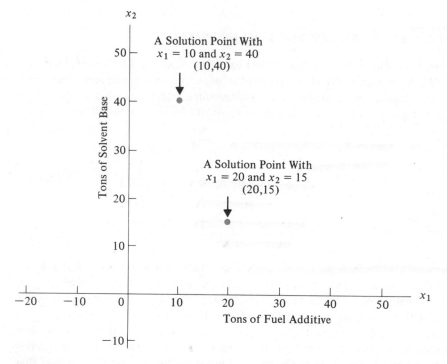

Figure 7.1
Graph of Solution Points for the Two-Variable RMC Problem

The next step is to show which of the solutions correspond to feasible solutions for the linear program. Both x_1 and x_2 must be nonnegative, so we need only consider that portion of the graph where $x_1 \geq 0$ and $x_2 \geq 0$. In Figure 7.2 the arrows point to the portion of the solution region where these nonnegativity requirements are satisfied.

Earlier we saw that the inequality representing the material 1 constraint was of the form

$$\tfrac{2}{5}x_1 + \tfrac{1}{2}x_2 \leq 20$$

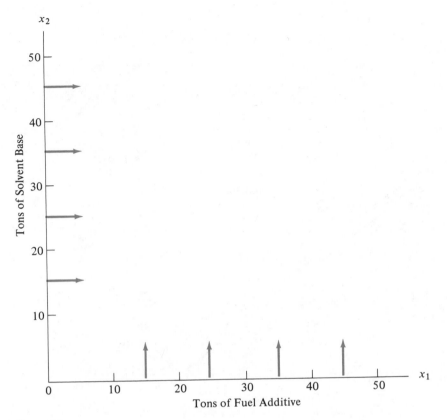

Figure 7.2
The Nonnegativity Constraints

To show all solution points that satisfy this relationship, we start by graphing the line corresponding to the equation

$$\tfrac{2}{5} x_1 + \tfrac{1}{2} x_2 = 20$$

The graph of this equation is found by identifying two points that lie on the line and then drawing a line through the points. Setting $x_1 = 0$ and solving for x_2, we see that $\tfrac{1}{2}x_2 = 20$ or $x_2 = 40$, and hence the point ($x_1 = 0$, $x_2 = 40$) satisfies the above equation. To find a second point satisfying this equation, we set $x_2 = 0$ and solve for x_1. By doing this we obtain $\tfrac{2}{5}x_1 = 20$, or $x_1 = 50$. Thus a second point satisfying the equation is ($x_1 = 50$, $x_2 = 0$). Given these two points, we can now graph the line. This line, which will be called the material 1 constraint line, is shown in Figure 7.3.

Recall that the inequality representing the material 1 constraint is

$$\tfrac{2}{5} x_1 + \tfrac{1}{2} x_2 \le 20$$

Can you identify all of the solutions that satisfy this constraint? Well, since we have the line where $\tfrac{2}{5}x_1 + \tfrac{1}{2}x_2 = 20$, we know that any point on this line must satisfy the constraint. But where are the solutions satisfying $\tfrac{2}{5}x_1 + \tfrac{1}{2}x_2 < 20$? Consider two solution

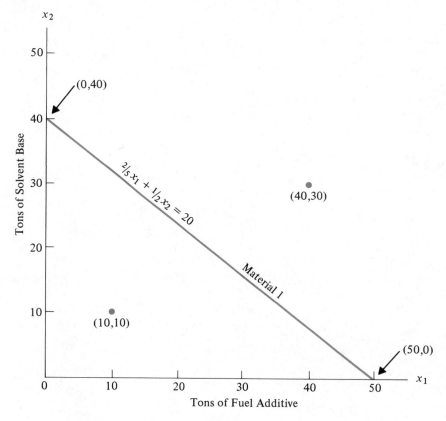

Figure 7.3
The Material 1 Constraint Line

points ($x_1 = 10$, $x_2 = 10$) and ($x_1 = 40$, $x_2 = 30$). We can see from Figure 7.3 that the first solution is below the constraint line and the second is above the constraint line. Which of these solutions will satisfy the material 1 constraint? For the point ($x_1 = 10$, $x_2 = 10$) we have

$$\tfrac{2}{5} x_1 + \tfrac{1}{2} x_2 = \tfrac{2}{5}(10) + \tfrac{1}{2}(10) = 9$$

Since 9 tons is less than the 20 tons of material 1 available, the ($x_1 = 10$, $x_2 = 10$) production combination, or solution, satisfies the constraint. For $x_1 = 40$ and $x_2 = 30$ we have

$$\tfrac{2}{5} x_1 + \tfrac{1}{2} x_2 = \tfrac{2}{5}(40) + \tfrac{1}{2}(30) = 31$$

The 31 tons is greater than the 20 tons available, so the $x_1 = 40$, $x_2 = 30$ solution does not satisfy the constraint and is thus not feasible.

It turns out that if a particular solution is not feasible, then all other solutions on the same side of the constraint line are not feasible. If a particular solution is feasible, then all other solutions on the same side of the constraint line are feasible. Thus, one needs only to evaluate one solution point to determine which side of a constraint line provides feasible solutions. In Figure 7.4 we show all the points that satisfy the material 1 constraint by shading the feasible area.

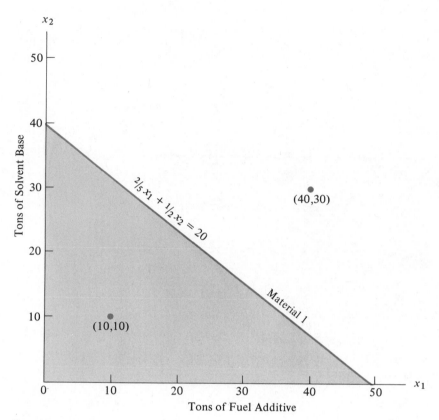

Figure 7.4
Feasible Region for the Material 1 Constraint

Next let us identify all solution points that satisfy the material 2 constraint:

$$\tfrac{1}{5} x_2 \leq 5$$

We start by drawing the constraint line corresponding to the equation $\tfrac{1}{5}x_2 = 5$. Since this equation is equivalent to the equation $x_2 = 25$, we simply draw a line whose x_2 value is 25 for every value of x_1; this is a line that is parallel to and 25 units above the horizontal axis. In Figure 7.5 we have drawn the line corresponding to the material 2 constraint. Following the approach we used for the material 1 constraint, we realize that only points on or below the line will satisfy the material 2 constraint. Thus in Figure 7.5 the shaded region corresponds to all feasible production combinations or feasible solutions for the material 2 constraint.

In a similar manner we can determine the set of all feasible production combinations for the material 3 constraint. The result is shown in Figure 7.6. For practice, try to graph the feasible region for the material 3 constraint and see if your result agrees with that shown in Figure 7.6.

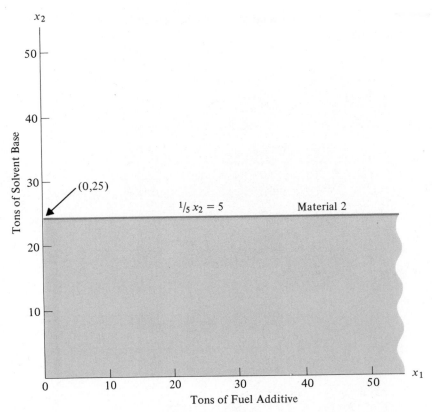

Figure 7.5
Feasible Region for the Material 2 Constraint

We now have three separate graphs showing the feasible solutions for each of the three constraints. In a linear programming problem we need to identify the solutions that satisfy *all* the constraints *simultaneously*. To find these solutions we can draw the three constraints on one graph and observe the region containing the points that do in fact satisfy all the constraints simultaneously.

The graphs in Figures 7.4–7.6 can be superimposed to obtain one graph with all three constraints. This combined constraint graph is shown in Figure 7.7. The shaded region in this figure includes every solution point that satisfies all the constraints simultaneously. Since solutions that satisfy all the constraints simultaneously are termed feasible solutions, the shaded region is called the feasible solution region, or simply the *feasible region*. Any point on the boundary of the feasible region, or within the feasible region, is a feasible solution.

Now that we have identified the feasible region, we are ready to proceed with the graphical solution method and find the optimal solution to the RMC problem. Recall that the optimal solution for a linear programming problem is the feasible solution that provides the best possible value of the objective function. Thus, one approach to finding the optimal solution would be to evaluate the objective function for each feasible solution and pick the one yielding the best value. The difficulty with this approach is that there are too many feasible solutions (actually an infinite number), and so it would not be

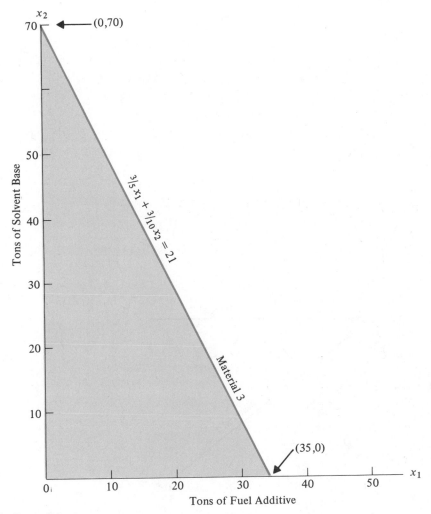

Figure 7.6
Feasible Region for the Material 3 Constraint

possible to evaluate all feasible solutions. We need a better way of identifying the feasible solution that will maximize RMC's profit.

Let us start the optimizing step of the graphical solution procedure by redrawing the feasible region on a separate graph. The graph is shown in Figure 7.8. Rather than selecting a feasible solution and computing the associated profit, let us select a value for profit and find all the feasible solution points (x_1, x_2) that yield the selected value. For example, what feasible solutions provide a profit of $240? To answer this, we must find the values of x_1 and x_2 in the feasible region that will make the objective function

$$40x_1 + 30x_2 = 240$$

This expression is simply the equation of a line. Thus all feasible solutions (x_1, x_2) yielding a profit of $240 must be on the line. We learned earlier in this section how to graph a constraint line. The procedure for graphing the profit or objective function line

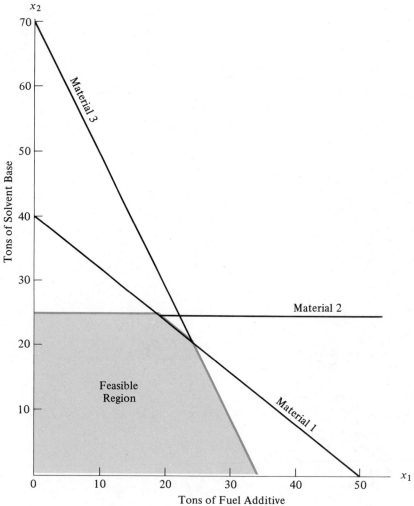

Figure 7.7
Feasible Solution Region for the RMC Problem

is the same. Letting $x_1 = 0$, we see that x_2 must be 8; thus the solution point ($x_1 = 0$, $x_2 = 8$) is on the line. Similarly, by letting $x_2 = 0$ we see that the solution point ($x_1 = 6$, $x_2 = 0$) is also on the line. Drawing the line through these two points identifies all the solutions that have a profit of $240. A graph of this profit line is presented in Figure 7.9. From this graph you can see that there are an infinite number of feasible production combinations that will provide a $240 profit.

Since the objective is to find the feasible solution that has the highest profit, let us proceed by selecting higher profit values and finding the solutions that yield the stated values. For example, what solutions provide a $720 profit? What solutions provide a $1200 profit? To answer these questions we must find the x_1 and x_2 values that are on the following lines:

$$40x_1 + 30x_2 = 720$$

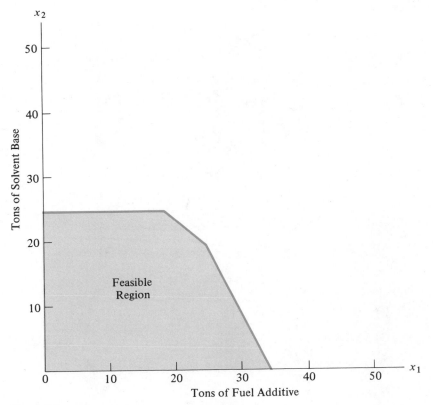

Figure 7.8
Feasible Solution Region for the RMC Problem

and

$$40x_1 + 30x_2 = 1200$$

Using the previous procedure for graphing profit and constraint lines, we have drawn the $720 and $1200 profit lines on the graph in Figure 7.10. While not all solution points on the $1200 profit line are in the feasible region, at least some points on the line are, and thus it is possible to obtain a feasible production combination that provides a $1200 profit.

Can we find a feasible solution yielding an even higher profit? Look at Figure 7.10 and see what general observations you can make about the profit lines. You should be able to identify the following properties: (1) the profit lines are *parallel* to each other; and (2) higher profit lines occur as we move farther from the origin. This can also be seen algebraically. With z representing total profit, the objective function is

$$z = 40x_1 + 30x_2$$

Solving for x_2 in terms of x_1 and z, we obtain

$$30x_2 = -40x_1 + z$$

$$x_2 = -^{40}/_{30}\, x_1 + ^{1}/_{30}\, z \qquad (7.7)$$

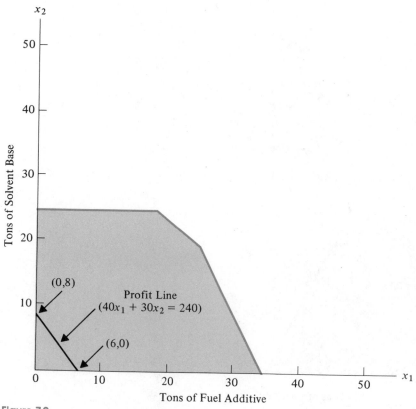

Figure 7.9
$240 Profit Line for the RMC Problem

Equation (7.7) is the *slope-intercept form* of the linear equation relating x_1 and x_2. The coefficient of x_1, $-{}^{40}\!/_{30}$, is the slope of the line, and the term $^1\!/_{30}z$ is the x_2 intercept [that is, the value of x_2 where the graph of equation (7.7) crosses the x_2 axis]. Substituting the profit values of $z = 240$, $z = 720$, and $z = 1200$ into equation (7.7) yields the following slope-intercept equations for the profit lines shown in Figure 7.10:

For $z = 240$,

$$x_2 = -{}^{40}\!/_{30}\, x_1 + 8$$

For $z = 720$,

$$x_2 = -{}^{40}\!/_{30}\, x_1 + 24$$

For $z = 1200$,

$$x_2 = -{}^{40}\!/_{30}\, x_1 + 40$$

The slope $(-{}^{40}\!/_{30})$ is the same for each profit line since the profit lines are parallel. Further, we see that the x_2 intercept increases with larger values of profit. Thus higher profit lines are farther from the origin.

Because the profit lines are parallel and higher profit lines are farther from the origin, we can obtain solutions that yield increasingly higher values for the objective function by continuing to move the profit line farther from the origin in such a fashion that it

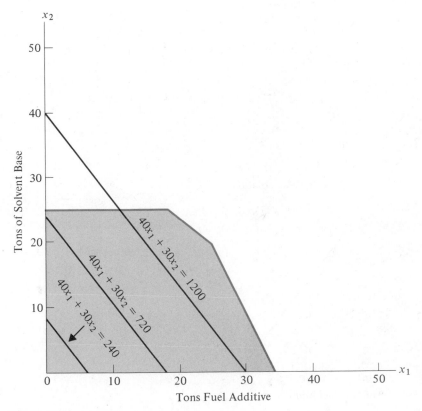

Figure 7.10
Selected Profit Lines for the RMC Problem

remains parallel to the other profit lines. However, at some point we will find that any further outward movement will place the profit line entirely outside the feasible region. Since points outside the feasible region are unacceptable, the point in the feasible region that lies on the highest profit line is an optimal solution to the linear program.

You should now be able to identify the optimal solution point for the RMC problem. Use a ruler and move the profit line as far from the origin as you can. What is the last point in the feasible region that you reach? This point, which is the optimal solution, is shown graphically in Figure 7.11. The optimal values for the decision variables are the x_1 and x_2 values at this point.

Depending on the accuracy of your graph, you may or may not be able to determine the exact optimal values of x_1 and x_2 directly from the graph. However, referring to Figure 7.7, we note that the optimal solution point for the RMC example is at the *intersection* of the material 1 constraint line and the material 3 constraint line. That is, the optimal solution is on both the material 1 constraint line,

$$\tfrac{2}{5} x_1 + \tfrac{1}{2} x_2 = 20 \tag{7.8}$$

and the material 3 constraint line,

$$\tfrac{3}{5} x_1 + \tfrac{3}{10} x_2 = 21 \tag{7.9}$$

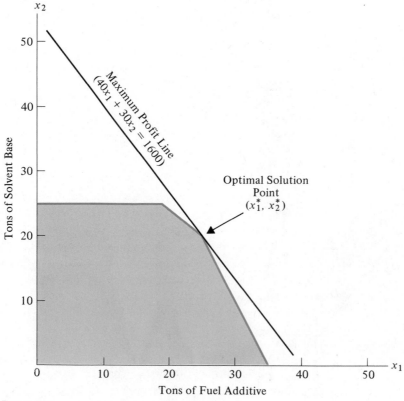

Figure 7.11
Optimal Solution for the RMC Problem

Thus the values of the decision variables x_1 and x_2 must satisfy both equations (7.8) and (7.9) simultaneously. Using (7.8) and solving for x_1 gives

$$\tfrac{2}{5} x_1 = 20 - \tfrac{1}{2} x_2$$

or

$$x_1 = 50 - \tfrac{5}{4} x_2 \qquad (7.10)$$

Substituting this expression for x_1 into equation (7.9) and solving for x_2 provides the following:

$$\tfrac{3}{5}(50 - \tfrac{5}{4} x_2) + \tfrac{3}{10} x_2 = 21$$
$$30 - \tfrac{3}{4} x_2 + \tfrac{3}{10} x_2 = 21$$
$$30 - \tfrac{30}{40} x_2 + \tfrac{12}{40} x_2 = 21$$
$$-\tfrac{18}{40} x_2 = -9$$
$$x_2 = (\tfrac{40}{18})(9) = 20$$

Substituting $x_2 = 20$ in equation (7.10) and solving for x_1 provides

$$x_1 = 50 - \tfrac{5}{4}(20)$$
$$= 50 - 25 = 25$$

Thus the exact location of the optimal solution point is $x_1 = 25$ and $x_2 = 20$. This solution point provides the optimal production quantities for RMC at 25 tons of fuel additive and 20 tons of solvent base and yields a profit of $40(25) + 30(20) = \$1600$.

In any graphical solution of a two-decision-variable linear programming problem the exact values of the decision variables at the optimal solution can be determined by first using the graphical procedure to identify the optimal solution point and then solving the two simultaneous equations associated with this point.

A Note on Graphing Lines

As can be seen from the graphical solution of the RMC problem, an important aspect of the graphical method is the ability to graph lines showing the constraints and the objective function of the linear program. The simplest procedure for graphing the equation of a line is to find any two points that satisfy the equation and then draw the line through the two points. For the material 1 constraint line of the RMC problem,

$$\tfrac{2}{5}x_1 + \tfrac{1}{2}x_2 = 20$$

this procedure identified the two points ($x_1 = 0$, $x_2 = 40$) and ($x_1 = 50$, $x_2 = 0$). The material 1 constraint line was then graphed by drawing a line through these two points.

When only one variable appears in a constraint equation, such as the material 2 constraint in the RMC problem ($\tfrac{1}{5}x_2 \leq 5$), it is easy to find two points on the line. First, solve for the value of the variable that appears in the equation (for the material 2 constraint, we get $x_2 = 25$), then choose any two values for the other variable. For instance, we could choose the two points ($x_1 = 0$, $x_2 = 25$) and ($x_1 = 10$, $x_2 = 25$).

All constraint and objective function lines in two-variable linear programs can be graphed if two points on the line can be identified. However, finding the two points on the line is not always as easy as it was in the RMC problem. For example, consider the following constraint:

$$2x_1 - 1x_2 \leq 100$$

Using the equality form and setting $x_1 = 0$, we find that the point ($x_1 = 0$, $x_2 = -100$) is on the constraint line. Setting $x_2 = 0$, we find a second point ($x_1 = 50$, $x_2 = 0$) on the constraint line. If we have drawn only the nonnegative ($x_1 \geq 0$, $x_2 \geq 0$) portion of the graph, the first point ($x_1 = 0$, $x_2 = -100$) cannot be plotted because $x_2 = -100$ is not on the graph. Whenever we have two points on the line but one or both of the points cannot be plotted in the nonnegative portion of the graph, the simplest approach is to enlarge the graph to include the negative x_1 and/or x_2 axes. In this example, the point ($x_1 = 0$, $x_2 = -100$) can be plotted by extending the graph to include the negative x_2 axis. Once both points satisfying the constraint equation have been located, the line can be drawn. The constraint line and the feasible solutions for the constraint $2x_1 - 1x_2 \leq 100$ are shown in Figure 7.12.

As another example, let us consider a constraint of the form

$$1x_1 - 1x_2 \geq 0$$

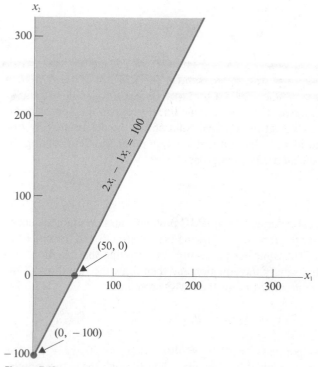

Figure 7.12
Feasible Solutions for the Constraint $2x_1 - 1x_2 \leq 100$

To find all solutions satisfying the constraint as an equality, we first set $x_1 = 0$ and solve for x_2. This shows that the origin ($x_1 = 0$, $x_2 = 0$) is on the constraint line. Setting $x_2 = 0$ and solving for x_1 provides the same point. However, we can obtain a second point on the line by setting x_2 equal to any value other than zero and then solving for x_1. For instance, setting $x_2 = 100$ and solving for x_1, we find that the point ($x_1 = 100$, $x_2 = 100$) is on the line. With the two points ($x_1 = 0$, $x_2 = 0$) and ($x_1 = 100$, $x_2 = 100$), the constraint line $1x_1 - 1x_2 = 0$ and the feasible solutions for $1x_1 - 1x_2 \geq 0$ can be plotted as shown in Figure 7.13.

Summary of the Graphical Solution Procedure for Maximization Problems

The graphical solution procedure is one method of solving two-variable linear programming problems such as the RMC problem. The steps of the graphical solution procedure for a maximization problem are outlined below.

1. Prepare a graph of the feasible solutions for each of the constraints.
2. Determine the feasible region by identifying the solutions that satisfy all the constraints simultaneously.
3. Draw an objective function line showing all values of the x_1 and x_2 variables that yield a specified value of the objective function.

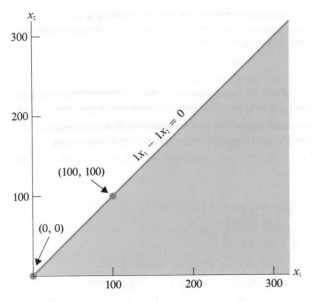

Figure 7.13
Feasible Solutions for the Constraint $1x_1 - 1x_2 \geq 0$

4. Move parallel objective function lines toward larger values (usually away from the origin) until further movement would take the line completely outside the feasible region.
5. Any feasible solution on the objective function line with the largest value is an optimal solution.

Slack Variables

In addition to the optimal solution and the expected profit, the management of RMC will probably want information about the production requirements for the three materials. We can determine this information by substituting the optimal solution values ($x_1 = 25$, $x_2 = 20$) into the constraints of our linear program as follows:

Material	Tons Required for $x_1 = 25$, $x_2 = 20$	Tons Available	Unused Tons
Material 1	$\frac{2}{5}(25) + \frac{1}{2}(20) = 20$	20	0
Material 2	$0(25) + \frac{1}{5}(20) = 4$	5	1
Material 3	$\frac{3}{5}(25) + \frac{3}{10}(20) = 21$	21	0

Thus the complete solution tells management that the production of 25 tons of fuel additive and 20 tons of solvent base will require all available material 1 and material 3, but only 4 of the 5 tons of material 2. The 1 ton of unused material 2 is referred to as *slack*. In linear programming terminology, any unused or idle capacity for a $\leq$ constraint is referred to as the slack associated with the constraint. Thus the material 2 constraint is shown to have a slack of 1 ton.

Often variables are added to the formulation of a linear programming problem to represent the slack, or idle capacity. Such variables are called *slack variables*, and since the unused capacity makes no contribution to profit, they have coefficients of zero in the objective function. More generally, slack variables can be thought of as representing the difference between the right-hand side and the left-hand side of a $\leq$ constraint. After addition of slack variables to the mathematical statement of the RMC problem, the mathematical model appears as follows:

$$\max \quad 40x_1 + 30x_2 + 0s_1 + 0s_2 + 0s_3$$
$$\text{s.t.}$$
$$\tfrac{2}{5}x_1 + \tfrac{1}{2}x_2 + 1s_1 \qquad\qquad\qquad = 20$$
$$\tfrac{1}{5}x_2 \qquad + 1s_2 \qquad = 5$$
$$\tfrac{3}{5}x_1 + \tfrac{3}{10}x_2 \qquad\qquad + 1s_3 = 21$$
$$x_1, x_2, s_1, s_2, s_3 \geq 0$$

Whenever a linear program is written in a form with all the constraints expressed as equalities, it is said to be written in *standard form*.

Referring to the standard form of the RMC problem, we see that at the optimal solution ($x_1 = 25$, $x_2 = 20$) the values for the slack variables are as follows:

Constraint	Value of Slack Variable
Material 1	$s_1 = 0$
Material 2	$s_2 = 1$
Material 3	$s_3 = 0$

Could we have used the graphical analysis to provide some of the above information? The answer is yes. By finding the optimal solution in Figure 7.7, we see that the material 1 constraint and the material 3 constraint restrict, or *bind*, the feasible region at this point. Thus the solution requires the use of all of these two resources. In other words, the graph shows us that material 1 and material 3 will have zero slack. On the other hand, since the material 2 constraint is not binding the feasible region at the optimal solution, we can expect some slack for this resource.

As a final comment, we point out that some linear programs may have one or more constraints that do not affect the feasible region. That is, the feasible region remains the same whether or not the constraint is included in the problem. Since such a constraint does not affect the feasible region and thus cannot affect the optimal solution, it is called a *redundant constraint*. Redundant constraints can be dropped from the problem without having any effect on the optimal solution. However, in most linear programming problems redundant constraints are not discarded because they are not immediately recognizable as being redundant. There were no redundant constraints in the RMC problem, since each constraint had an effect on the feasible region. Problem 12 at the end of the chapter concerns a linear program with a redundant constraint.

7.6
EXTREME POINTS AND THE OPTIMAL SOLUTION

Suppose that the profit for 1 ton of solvent base is increased from \$30 to \$60 while the profit for 1 ton of fuel additive and all the constraints remain unchanged. The complete linear programming model of this new problem is identical to the mathematical model in Section 7.4, except for the revised objective function:

$$\max \quad 40x_1 + 60x_2$$

How does this change in the objective function affect the optimal solution to the RMC problem? Figure 7.14 shows the graphical solution of the RMC problem with the revised objective function. Note that since the constraints have not changed, the feasible region has not changed. However, the profit lines have been altered to reflect the new objective function.

By moving the profit line in a parallel manner away from the origin, we find the optimal solution as shown in Figure 7.14. The values of the decision variables at this

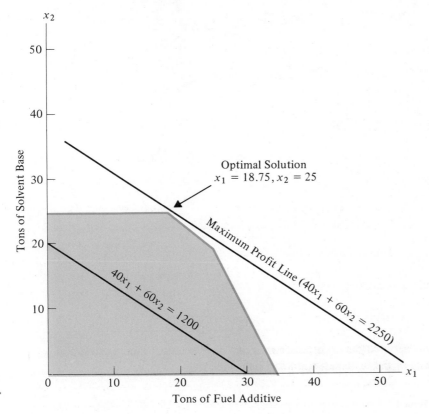

Figure 7.14
Optimal Solution for the RMC Problem with an Objective Function of $40x_1 + 60x_2$

point are $x_1 = 18.75$ and $x_2 = 25$. The increased profit for the solvent base has caused a change in the optimal solution. In fact, as you may have suspected, we are cutting back the production of the lower-profit fuel additive and increasing the production of the higher-profit solvent base.

What have you noticed about the location of the optimal solutions in the linear programming problems that we have solved thus far? Look closely at the graphical solutions in Figures 7.11 and 7.14. An important observation that you should be able to make is that the optimal solutions occur at one of the vertices or ''corners'' of the feasible region. In linear programing terminology these vertices are referred to as the *extreme points* of the feasible region. Thus, the RMC problem has five vertices or five extreme points for its feasible region (see Figure 7.15). We can now state our observation about the location of optimal solutions as follows:[1]

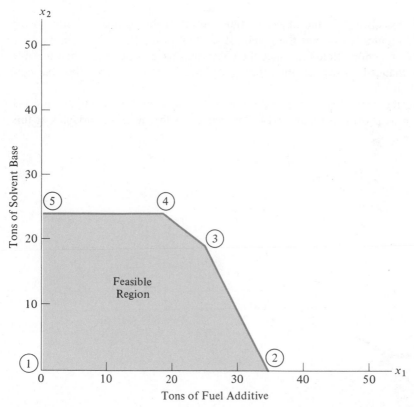

Figure 7.15
The Five Extreme Points of the Feasible Region for the RMC Problem

> The optimal solution to a linear programming problem can be found at an extreme point of the feasible region for the problem.

[1] We will see in Section 7.8 that there are two special cases (infeasibility and unboundedness) in linear programming where there is no optimal solution. The above statement does not apply to these cases.

This property means that if you are looking for the optimal solution to a linear programming problem, you do not have to evaluate all feasible solution points. In fact, you have to consider *only* the feasible solutions that occur at the extreme points of the feasible region. Thus, for the RMC problem, instead of computing and comparing the profit for all feasible solutions, we can find the optimal solution by evaluating the five extreme-point solutions and selecting the one that provides the highest profit. Actually, the graphical solution procedure is nothing more than a convenient way of identifying an optimal extreme point for two-variable problems.

Alternate Optimal Solutions

What happens if the highest profit line coincides with one of the constraint lines on the boundary of the feasible region? This case is shown for a $40x_1 + 50x_2$ objective function in Figure 7.16. Does an optimal solution still occur at an extreme point? The answer is yes. In fact, in this case an optimal solution occurs at extreme point ③, extreme point ④, and any point on the line segment joining these two points. This is the special case of alternate optimal solutions, or *alternate optima*. As you can see, whenever alternate optima occur, there will be an infinite number of optimal solutions lying on the line segment joining two extreme points. A linear programming problem having alternate

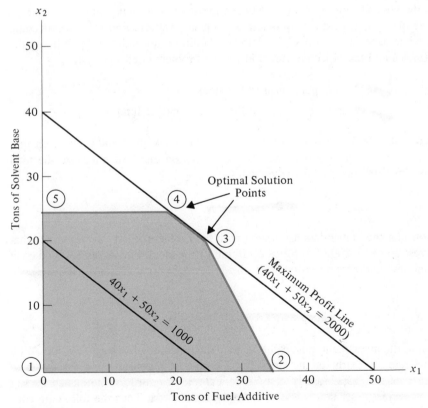

Figure 7.16
Optimal Solutions for the RMC Problem with an Objective Function of $40x_1 + 50x_2$

optima is a good situation for the manager attempting to implement the solution. It means that multiple solutions exist and the manager can select the specific solution that is most appropriate.

7.7
A SIMPLE MINIMIZATION PROBLEM

Innis Investments manages funds for a number of companies and wealthy clients. The investment strategy is tailored to each client's needs. For a new client, Innis has been authorized to invest up to $1.2 million in two investment funds: a stock fund and a money market fund. Each unit of the stock fund costs $50 and provides an annual rate of return of 10%; each unit of the money market fund costs $100 and provides an annual rate of return of 4%.

The client wants to minimize risk subject to the requirement that the annual income from the investment be at least $60,000. According to Innis's risk measurement system, each unit invested in the stock fund has a risk index of 8, and each unit invested in the money market fund has a risk index of 3; the higher risk index associated with the stock fund simply indicates that it is the riskier investment. Innis's client has also specified that at least $300,000 be invested in the money market fund. How many units of each fund should Innis purchase for the client if the objective is to minimize the total risk index for the portfolio?

To find the best allocation of funds between the stock and money market funds, we will formulate the Innis Investments problem as a linear program. Following a procedure similar to the one used for the RMC problem, we begin the formulation by defining the decision variables and the objective function for the problem. Let

$$x_1 = \text{units purchased in the stock fund}$$
$$x_2 = \text{units purchased in the money market fund}$$

Since the risk index is 8 for each unit invested in the stock fund and 3 for each unit invested in the money market fund, the objective function that will minimize the total risk index for the portfolio can be written as

$$\min \; 8x_1 + 3x_2$$

Next, consider the constraints associated with the problem. First, we recognize that Innis can invest up to $1,200,000. Since each unit of the stock fund costs $50 and each unit of the money market fund costs $100, the following constraint on funds available is needed:

$$50x_1 + 100x_2 \leq 1,200,000$$

In addition, the investment must result in an annual income of at least $60,000. With a 10% annual rate of return for the stock fund, each unit purchased in the stock fund will earn 0.10 ($50) = $5; similarly, the 4% annual rate of return for the money market fund results in earnings per unit invested of 0.04($100) = $4. Thus the following constraint is required to ensure an annual income of at least $60,000:

$$5x_1 + 4x_2 \geq 60,000$$

Finally, since each unit purchased in the money market fund costs $100, the requirement that at least $300,000 be invested in the money market fund means that at least 3000 units of the money market fund must be purchased; thus we must add the constraint

$$x_2 \geq 3000$$

After adding the nonnegativity constraints ($x_1, x_2 \geq 0$), we obtain the following linear programming model of the Innis Investments problem:

min $8x_1 + 3x_2$

s.t.

$50x_1 +$	$100x_2 \leq$	$1,200,000$	Funds available
$5x_1 +$	$4x_2 \geq$	$60,000$	Annual income
	$x_2 \geq$	$3,000$	Minimum units in money market
$x_1, x_2 \geq 0$			

Since the linear programming model has only two decision variables, the graphical solution procedure can be used to find the optimal investment plan. The graphical method for this problem, just as in the RMC problem, requires us first to graph the constraint lines in order to find the feasible region. By graphing each constraint line separately and then checking points on either side of the constraint line, the feasible solutions for each constraint can be identified. By combining the feasible solutions for each constraint on the same graph, we obtain the feasible region shown in Figure 7.17.

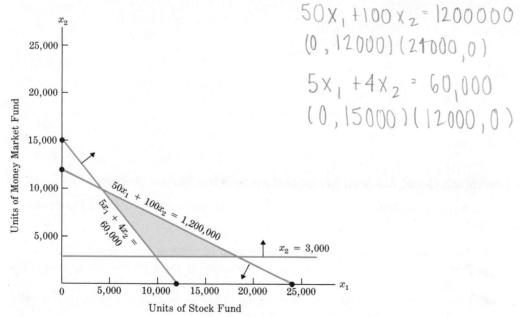

Figure 7.17
Feasible Region for Innis Investments Problem

To find the optimal solution (the one that will minimize the total risk index for the portfolio), we now draw the objective function line corresponding to a particular total risk value. For example, we might start by drawing the line $8x_1 + 3x_2 = 120,000$. This line is shown in Figure 7.18. Clearly there are points in the feasible region that would provide a total risk value of 120,000. To find the values of x_1 and x_2 that provide smaller total portfolio risk values, we move the objective function line in a lower left direction until, if we moved it any farther, it would be entirely outside the feasible region. Note that the objective function line $8x_1 + 3x_2 = 62,000$ intersects the feasible region at the extreme point $x_1 = 4000$ and $x_2 = 10,000$. This extreme point provides the minimum portfolio risk solution with an objective function value of 62,000. From Figures 7.17 and 7.18 we can see that the funds available and the annual income constraints are binding.

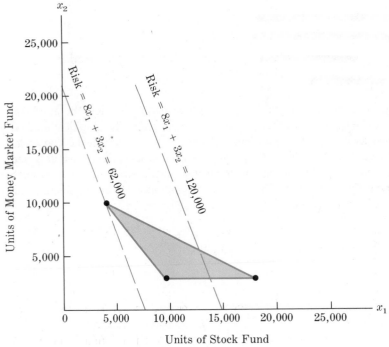

Figure 7.18
Graphical Solution for Innis Investments Problem

Summary of the Graphical Solution Procedure for Minimization Problems

The steps of the graphical solution procedure for a minimization problem are summarized below.

1. Prepare a graph of the feasible solution region for each of the constraints.
2. Determine the feasible solution region by identifying the solutions that satisfy all the constraints simultaneously.
3. Draw an objective function line showing all values of the x_1 and x_2 variables that yield a specified value of the objective function.
4. Move parallel objective function lines toward smaller objective function values until further movement would take the line completely outside the feasible region.

5. Any feasible solution on the objective function line with the smallest value is an optimal solution.

Surplus Variables

A complete analysis of the optimal solution to the Innis Investments problem shows that the total risk index for the optimal portfolio ($8x_1 + 3x_2 = 8(4,000) + 3(10,000) = 62,000$) is achieved by using all the available funds. That is, $50x_1 + 100x_2 = 50(4,000) + 100(10,000) = 1,200,000$. The required annual income is achieved exactly, since $5(4,000) + 4(10,000) = 60,000$. Note, however, that the purchase of 10,000 units of the money market fund exceeds the minimum requirement of 3,000 by 7,000 units. This excess investment in the money market fund is referred to as *surplus*. In linear programming terminology, any excess quantity corresponding to a $\geq$ constraint is referred to as surplus.

Recall that with a $\leq$ constraint, a slack variable can be added to the left-hand side of the constraint in order to convert the constraint to equality form. With a $\geq$ constraint, a *surplus variable* can be subtracted from the left-hand side to convert the constraint to equality form. Just as with slack variables, surplus variables are given a coefficient of zero in the objective function because they have no effect on its value. After including one slack variable for the $\leq$ constraint and two surplus variables for the $\geq$ constraints, the linear programming model of the Innis Investments problem appears as follows:

$$\min \quad 8x_1 + 3x_2 + 0s_1 + 0s_2 + 0s_3$$

s.t.

$$
\begin{aligned}
50x_1 + 100x_2 + 1s_1 \qquad\qquad &= 1,200,000 \\
5x_1 + 4x_2 \qquad - 1s_2 \qquad &= 60,000 \\
1x_2 \qquad\qquad - 1s_3 &= 3,000 \\
x_1, x_2, s_1, s_2, s_3 &\geq 0
\end{aligned}
$$

All the constraints are now equalities. Hence the above formulation is the standard form representation of the Innis Investments problem. At the optimal solution of $x_1 = 4000$ and $x_2 = 10,000$, the values of the slack and surplus variables are as follows:

Constraint	Value of Slack or Surplus Variable
Funds available	$s_1 = 0$
Annual income	$s_2 = 0$
Minimum units in money market	$s_3 = 7,000$

Refer to Figures 7.17 and 7.18. Note that the zero slack and surplus variables are associated with the constraints that are binding at the optimal solution: that is, the constraints on funds available and annual income. The surplus of 7,000 units is associated with the nonbinding constraint on the minimum allowable investment in the money market fund.

Note that in the RMC problem all the constraints were of the $\leq$ type and that in the Innis Investments problem the constraints were a mixture of $\leq$ and $\geq$ types. In general, linear programming problems may have some $\leq$ constraints, some $\geq$ constraints, and some $=$ constraints. For an equality constraint, feasible solutions must lie directly on the constraint line.

An example of a linear program with all three constraint forms is given below.

$$\min\ 2x_1 + 2x_2$$
$$\text{s.t.}$$
$$1x_1 + 3x_2 \leq 12$$
$$3x_1 + 1x_2 \geq 13$$
$$1x_1 - 1x_2 = 3$$
$$x_1,\ x_2 \geq 0$$

The standard-form representation of this problem is

$$\min\ 2x_1 + 2x_2 + 0s_1 + 0s_2$$
$$\text{s.t.}$$
$$1x_1 + 3x_2 + 1s_1 \qquad\quad = 12$$
$$3x_1 + 1x_2 \qquad - 1s_2 = 13$$
$$1x_1 - 1x_2 \qquad\qquad\quad = 3$$
$$x_1,\ x_2,\ s_1,\ s_2 \geq 0$$

This standard-form representation requires a slack variable for the $\leq$ constraint and a surplus variable for the $\geq$ constraint. However, neither a slack nor a surplus variable is required for the third constraint, since it is already in equality form.

The graphical solution method is a convenient way to find the optimal solution for two-variable linear programming problems. When solving linear programs graphically, it is not necessary to rewrite the problem in its standard form. Nevertheless, we should be able to compute the values of the slack and surplus variables and understand what they mean. In Chapter 8 we will see that the values of slack and surplus variables are included in the computer solution of linear programs. In Chapter 10 we will introduce an algebraic solution procedure, the simplex method, which can be used to find optimal extreme-point solutions for linear programming problems having as many as several thousand decision variables. The mathematical steps of the simplex method involve solving simultaneous equations that represent the constraints of the linear program. Thus, in setting up a linear program for solution by the simplex method, we must have one linear equation for each constraint in the problem; therefore the problem must be in its standard form.

As a final point, it is important to realize that the standard form of the linear programming problem is equivalent to the original formulation of the problem. That is, the optimal solution to any linear programming problem is the same as the optimal solution to the standard form of the problem. The standard form has not changed the basic problem; it has only changed how we write the constraints for the problem.

7.8

INFEASIBILITY AND UNBOUNDEDNESS

In this section we discuss two special situations that can arise when we attempt to solve linear programming problems.

Infeasibility

Infeasibility comes about when there is no solution to the linear programming problem that satisfies all the constraints, including the nonnegativity conditions x_1, $x_2 \geq 0$. Graphically, infeasibility means that a feasible region does not exist; that is, there are no points that satisfy all the constraint equations and the nonnegativity conditions simultaneously. To illustrate this situation, let us look again at the problem faced by RMC.

Suppose that management had specified that at least 30 tons of fuel additive and 15 tons of solvent base must be produced. The graph of our solution region may now be constructed to reflect these requirements (see Figure 7.19). The shaded area in the lower left-hand portion of the graph depicts those points satisfying the less-than-or-equal-to constraints on the amount of materials available. The shaded area in the upper right-hand

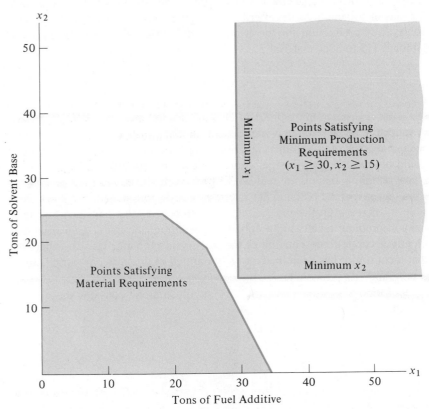

Figure 7.19
No Feasible Region for the RMC Problem with Minimum Production Requirements

portion depicts those points satisfying the minimum production requirements of 30 tons of fuel additive and 15 tons of solvent base. But there are no points satisfying both sets of constraints. Thus we see that if management imposes these minimum production requirements, there will be no feasible solution to the linear programming model.

How should we interpret this infeasibility in terms of our current problem? First, we should tell management that, given the available amounts of the three materials, it is not possible to produce 30 tons of fuel additive and 15 tons of solvent base. Moreover, we can tell management exactly how much more of each material is needed, as follows:

Material	Minimum Tons Required for $x_1 = 30, x_2 = 15$	Tons Available	Additional Tons Required
Material 1	$\frac{2}{5}(30) + \frac{1}{2}(15) = 19.5$	20	—
Material 2	$0(30) + \frac{1}{5}(15) = 3$	5	—
Material 3	$\frac{3}{5}(30) + \frac{3}{10}(15) = 22.5$	21	1.5

Thus, RMC has a sufficient supply of materials 1 and 2 but will need 1.5 additional tons of material 3 in order to meet management's production requirements of 30 tons of fuel additive and 15 tons of solvent base. If, after reviewing the above analysis, management still wants this level of production for the two products, RMC will somehow have to obtain the additional 1.5 tons of material 3.

Unboundedness

The solution to a linear programming problem is *unbounded* if the value of the solution may be made infinitely large without violating any of the constraints. This condition might be termed *managerial utopia*. If this condition were to occur in a profit maximization problem, it would be true that the manager could achieve an unlimited profit.

In linear programming models of real-world problems, the occurrence of an unbounded solution means that the problem has been improperly formulated. We know that it is not possible to increase profits indefinitely. Therefore we must conclude that if a profit maximization problem results in an unbounded solution, the mathematical model is not a sufficiently accurate representation of the real-world problem. Usually what has happened is that a constraint has been inadvertently omitted in the problem formulation.

If a linear programming problem has an unbounded solution, the graph of the feasible region extends to infinity in some direction. As an illustration, consider the simple numerical example

$$\max\ 2x_1 + 1x_2$$
$$\text{s.t.}$$
$$1x_1 \qquad\ \geq 2$$
$$\qquad 1x_2 \leq 5$$
$$x_1,\ x_2 \geq 0$$

In Figure 7.20 we have graphed the feasible region associated with this problem. Note that we can only indicate part of the feasible region, since the feasible region extends infinitely in the direction of the x_1 axis. Looking at the profit lines in Figure 7.20, we see that the solution to this problem may be made as large as desired. That is, no matter what solution we pick, there will always be another feasible solution with a larger value. Thus we say that the solution to this linear program is unbounded.

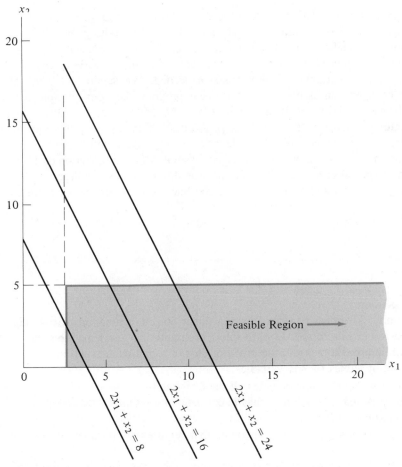

Figure 7.20
Example of an Unbounded Problem

Summary

Two problems, the RMC and Innis Investments problems, were formulated as linear programs and solved by a graphical procedure. In studying the graphical solution procedure we noted that if an optimal solution to a linear programming problem exists, it occurs at one of the extreme points of the feasible region.

In the process of formulating a mathematical model of these problems, a general definition of a linear program was developed.

A linear program is a mathematical model with the following properties:

1. A linear objective function that is to be maximized or minimized
2. A set of linear constraints
3. Variables that are all restricted to nonnegative values

We have seen how slack variables can be used to write less-than-or-equal-to constraints in equality form and how surplus variables can be used to write greater-than-or-equal-to constraints in equality form. The value of a slack variable can usually be interpreted as the amount of unused resource, while the value of a surplus variable indicates the amount by which a minimum requirement is exceeded. We stated that when all constraints have been written as equalities, the linear program has been written in its standard form. In the special cases of infeasibility and unboundedness, we showed that there was no optimal solution to the problem. In the case of infeasibility there are no feasible solutions, while in the case of unboundedness the objective function can be made infinitely large for a maximization problem or infinitely small for a minimization problem. In addition, a third special case, alternate optima, was discussed. In this case we have two optimal extreme points, and all the points on the line segment connecting them are also optimal.

Glossary

Constraint An equation or inequality that rules out certain combinations of variables as feasible solutions.

Objective function All linear programs have a linear objective function that is either to be maximized or minimized. In most linear programming problems the objective function will be used to measure the profit or cost of a particular solution.

Solution Any set of values for the variables.

Feasible solution A solution that satisfies all the constraints.

Optimal solution A feasible solution that maximizes or minimizes the value of the objective function.

Nonnegativity constraints A set of constraints that requires all variables to be nonnegative.

Mathematical model A representation of a problem where the objective and all constraint conditions are described by mathematical expressions.

Linear program A mathematical model with a linear objective function, a set of linear constraints, and nonnegative variables.

Constraint function The left-hand side of a constraint (i.e., the portion of the constraint containing the variables).

Linear equations or functions Mathematical expressions in which the variables appear in separate terms and are raised to the first power.

Feasible region The set of all possible feasible solutions.

Decision variable A variable used to represent the decisions that must be made by a manager in order to obtain the optimal solution.

Slack variable A variable added to the left-hand side of a less-than-or-equal-to constraint to convert the constraint into an equality.

Surplus variable   A variable subtracted from the left-hand side of a greater-than-or-equal-to constraint to convert the constraint into an equality.

Standard form   A linear program in which all of the constraints are written as equalities. The optimal solution of the standard form of a linear program is the same as the optimal solution of the original formulation of the linear program.

Redundant constraint   A constraint that does not affect the feasible region. If a constraint is redundant, it could be removed from the problem without affecting the feasible region.

Extreme point   Extreme points are the feasible solution points occurring at the vertices or "corners" of the feasible region. With two variables, extreme points are determined by the intersection of the constraint lines.

Alternate optima   The situation when a linear program has two or more optimal solutions.

Infeasibility   The situation in which there is no solution to the linear programming problem that satisfies all the constraints.

Unboundedness   A maximization linear programming problem is said to be unbounded if the value of the solution may be made infinitely large without violating any of the constraints. A minimization problem is unbounded if the value of the solution may be made infinitely small.

Problems

1. Which of the following mathematical relationships could be found in a linear programming model and which could not? For the relationships that are unacceptable for linear programs, state your reasons.
   a. $-1x_1 + 2x_2 - 1x_3 \leq 70$
   b. $2x_1 - 2x_3 = 50$
   c. $1x_1 - 2x_2^2 + 4x_3 \leq 10$
   d. $3\sqrt{x_1} + 2x_2 - 1x_3 \geq 15$
   e. $1x_1 + 1x_2 + 1x_3 = 6$
   f. $2x_1 + 5x_2 + 1x_1x_2 \leq 25$

2. Find the feasible solution points for the following constraints:
   a. $4x_1 + 2x_2 \leq 16$
   b. $4x_1 + 2x_2 \geq 16$
   c. $4x_1 + 2x_2 = 16$

3. Graphing constraint lines is an essential step in the graphical method. Show a separate graph of the constraint lines and feasible solutions for each of the following constraints:
   a. $3x_1 + 2x_2 \leq 18$
   b. $12x_1 + 8x_2 \geq 480$
   c. $5x_1 + 10x_2 = 200$

4. Show a separate graph of the constraint lines and feasible solutions for each of the following constraints:
   a. $3x_1 - 4x_2 \geq 60$
   b. $-6x_1 + 5x_2 \leq 60$
   c. $5x_1 - 2x_2 \leq 0$

5. Given below are three objective functions for linear programming problems:

$$z = 7x_1 + 10x_2$$
$$z = 6x_1 + 4x_2$$
$$z = -4x_1 + 7x_2$$

Determine the slope of each objective function. Show the graph of each of the three objective functions for $z = 420$.

6. Solve the following linear program:

$$\max \quad 5x_1 + 5x_2$$
$$\text{s.t.}$$
$$1x_1 \qquad\qquad \le 100$$
$$1x_2 \le 80$$
$$2x_1 + 4x_2 \le 400$$
$$x_1, x_2 \ge 0$$

7. Identify the feasible region for the following set of constraints:

$$\tfrac{1}{2}x_1 + \tfrac{1}{4}x_2 \ge 30$$
$$1x_1 + 5x_2 \ge 250$$
$$\tfrac{1}{4}x_1 + \tfrac{1}{2}x_2 \le 50$$
$$x_1, x_2 \ge 0$$

8. Identify the feasible region for the following set of constraints:

$$2x_1 - 1x_2 \le 0$$
$$-1x_1 + 1.5x_2 \le 200$$
$$x_1, x_2 \ge 0$$

9. Identify the feasible region for the following set of constraints:

$$3x_1 - 2x_2 \ge 0$$
$$2x_1 - 1x_2 \le 200$$
$$1x_1 \qquad\quad \le 150$$
$$x_1, x_2 \ge 0$$

10. Consider the following linear programming problem:

$$\max \quad 2x_1 + 3x_2$$
$$\text{s.t}$$
$$1x_1 + 2x_2 \le 6$$
$$5x_1 + 3x_2 \le 15$$
$$x_1, x_2 \ge 0$$

Find the optimal solution. What is the value of the objective function at the optimal solution?

11. Consider the following linear programming problem:

$$\max \quad 3x_1 + 3x_2$$

$$\text{s.t.}$$

$$2x_1 + 4x_2 \leq 12$$

$$6x_1 + 4x_2 \leq 24$$

$$x_1, x_2 \geq 0$$

a. Find the optimal solution.
b. If the objective function were changed to $2x_1 + 6x_2$, what would the optimal solution be?
c. How many extreme points are there? What are the values of x_1 and x_2 at each extreme point?

12. Consider the following linear programming problem:

$$\max \quad 3x_1 + 2x_2$$

$$\text{s.t.}$$

$$2x_1 + 2x_2 \leq 8$$

$$3x_1 + 2x_2 \leq 12$$

$$1x_1 + .5x_2 \leq 3$$

$$x_1, x_2 \geq 0$$

a. Find the optimal solution. What is the value of the objective function?
b. Does this problem have a redundant constraint? If so, what is it? Does the solution change if the redundant constraint is removed from the problem? Explain.

13. Par, Inc. is a small manufacturer of golf equipment and supplies. Par has been convinced by its distributor that there is an existing market for both a medium-priced golf bag, referred to as a standard model, and a high-priced golf bag, referred to as a deluxe model. The distributor is so confident of the market that if Par can make the bags at a competitive price, the distributor has agreed to purchase all the bags that Par can manufacture over the next three months. A careful analysis of the manufacturing requirements resulted in the following table, which shows the production time requirements for the four required manufacturing operations and the accounting department's estimate of the profit contribution per bag:

| Product | Production Time (hours) | | | | Profit per Bag |
	Cutting and Dyeing	Sewing	Finishing	Inspection and Packaging	
Standard	$7/10$	$1/2$	1	$1/10$	$10
Deluxe	1	$5/6$	$2/3$	$1/4$	$ 9

The director of manufacturing estimates that 630 hours of cutting and dyeing time, 600 hours of sewing time, 708 hours of finishing time, and 135 hours of inspection and packaging time will be available for the production of golf bags during the next 3 months.

   a. Assuming that the company wants to maximize profit, how many bags of each model should Par manufacture?

   b. What is the profit Par can earn with the above production quantities?

   c. How many hours of production time will be scheduled for each operation?

   d. What is the slack time in each operation?

14. Refer to problem 13. Suppose that the selling price for the Par, Inc. standard bag must be reduced by $7 due to competitive pressures. No other costs or prices are affected.

   a. What are the optimal production quantities for Par, Inc.?

   b. What constraint lines combine to form the optimal extreme point?

15. Suppose that the management of Par, Inc. (problem 13) encounters each of the following situations:

   a. The accounting department revises its estimate of profit contribution for the deluxe bag to $18 per bag.

   b. A new low-cost material is available for the standard bag, and the profit contribution per standard bag can be increased to $20 per bag. (Assume that the profit contribution of the deluxe bag is the original $9 value.)

   c. New sewing equipment is available that would increase the sewing operation capacity to 750 hours. (Assume that $10x_1 + 9x_2$ is the appropriate objective function.)

   If each of the above conditions is encountered separately, what are the optimal solution and profit contribution for each situation?

16. Refer to the feasible region for the RMC problem in Figure 7.15.

   a. Develop an objective function that will make extreme point ② the optimal extreme point.

   b. What is the optimal solution using the objective function you selected in part (a)?

   c. What are the values of the slack variables associated with this solution?

17. Kelson Sporting Equipment, Inc. makes two different types of baseball gloves: a regular model and a catcher's model. The firm has 900 hours of production time available in its cutting and sewing department, 300 hours of production time available in its finishing department, and 100 hours of production time available in its packaging and shipping department. The production time requirements and the profit per glove are given below:

	Production Time (hours)			
Model	Cutting and Sewing	Finishing	Packaging and Shipping	**Profit/Glove**
Regular model	1	$\frac{1}{2}$	$\frac{1}{8}$	$5
Catcher's model	$\frac{3}{2}$	$\frac{1}{3}$	$\frac{1}{4}$	$8

  a. Assuming that the company wants to maximize profit, how many gloves of each model should Kelson manufacture?

  b. What profit can Kelson earn with the above production quantities?

  c. How many hours of production time will be scheduled in each department?

  d. What is the slack time in each department?

18. The Erlanger Manufacturing Company makes two products. The profit estimates are $25 for each unit of product 1 sold and $30 for each unit of product 2 sold. The labor-hour requirements for the products in each of three production departments are summarized below:

	Product 1	**Product 2**
Department *A*	1.50	3.00
Department *B*	2.00	1.00
Department *C*	.25	.25

The production supervisors in the departments have estimated that the following number of labor-hours will be available during the next month: 450 hours in department *A*, 350 hours in department *B*, and 50 hours in department *C*. Assuming that the company is interested in maximizing profits, answer the following:

  a. What is the linear programming model for this problem?

  b. Find the optimal solution. How much of each product should be produced, and what is the projected profit?

  c. What is the scheduled production time and slack time in each department?

19. Yard Care, Inc. manufactures a variety of lawn care products, including two well-known lawn fertilizers. Each fertilizer product is a blend of two raw materials known as K40 and K50. During the current production period, 900 pounds of K40 and 400 pounds of K50 are available. Each pound of the product known as Green Lawn uses $3/5$ pound of K40 and $2/5$ pound of K50. Each pound of the product known as Lawn Care uses $3/4$ pound of K40 and $1/4$ pound of K50. In addition, a current limit on the availability of packaging materials restricts the production of Lawn Care to a maximum of 500 pounds.

  a. If the profit contribution for both products is $3 per pound, how many pounds of each product should the company manufacture?

  b. Should it be a concern to the company that the availability of packaging materials is restricting the production of Lawn Care? What would happen to the production quantities and the projected profit if the firm were able to remove the restriction on the amount of Lawn Care that could be produced?

20. Investment Advisors, Inc. is a brokerage firm that manages stock portfolios for a number of clients. A new client has requested that the firm handle an $80,000 investment portfolio. As an initial investment strategy the client would like to restrict the portfolio to a mix of the following stocks:

Stock	Price/Share	Estimated Annual Return/Share	Risk Index/Share
U.S. Oil	$25	$3	0.50
Hub Properties	$50	$5	0.25

The risk index for the stock is a rating of the relative risk of the two investment alternatives. For the data given, U.S. Oil is judged to be the riskier investment. By constraining the total risk for the portfolio, the investment firm avoids placing excessive amounts of the portfolio in potentially high-return but also high-risk investments. For the current portfolio an upper limit of 700 has been set for the total risk index of all investments. In addition, the firm has set an upper limit of 1000 shares for the more risky U.S. Oil stock. How many shares of each stock should be purchased in order to maximize the total annual return?

21. Consider the following linear program:

$$\min \quad 3x_1 + 4x_2$$
$$\text{s.t.}$$
$$1x_1 + 3x_2 \geq 6$$
$$1x_1 + 1x_2 \geq 4$$
$$x_1, x_2 \geq 0$$

Identify the feasible region and find the optimal solution. What is the value of the objective function?

22. M&D Chemicals produces two products that are sold as raw materials to companies manufacturing bath soaps, laundry detergents, and other soap products. Based on an analysis of current inventory levels and potential demand for the coming month, M&D's management has specified that the total production for products 1 and 2 combined must be at least 350 gallons. Also, a major customer's order for 125 gallons of product 1 must be satisfied. Product 1 requires 2 hours of processing time per gallon and product 2 requires 1 hour of processing time per gallon; for the coming month, 600 hours of processing time are available. Production costs are $2 per gallon for product 1 and $3 per gallon for product 2.

   a. Determine the production quantities that will satisfy the requirements specified above at minimum cost.
   b. What is the total product cost?
   c. Identify the amount of any surplus production.

23. Refer again to the M&D Chemicals problem (problem 22). Suppose, due to the use of some new equipment, that the production cost for product 2 is reduced to $1.50 per gallon.

   a. What are the optimal production quantities for M&D Chemicals?
   b. What constraint lines combine to form the optimal extreme point?

24. Identify the three extreme point solutions for the M&D Chemicals problem (problem 22). Identify the value of the objective function and the values of the slack and surplus variables at each extreme point.

25. Greentree Kennels, Inc. provides overnight lodging for a variety of pets. A particular feature at Greentree's is the quality of care the pets receive, including excellent food. The kennel's dog food is made by mixing two brand-name dog food products to obtain what the kennel calls the "well-balanced dog diet." The data for the two dog foods are as follows:

Dog Food	Cost/ Ounce	Protein (%)	Fat (%)
Bark Bits	$.06	30	15
Canine Chow	$.05	20	30

   If Greentree wants to be sure that the dogs receive at least 5 ounces of protein and at least 3 ounces of fat per day, what is the minimum cost mix of the two dog food products?

26. Jack Kammer has been trying to figure out the correct amount of fertilizer that should be applied to his lawn. After getting his soil analyzed at the local agricultural agency, he was advised to put at least 60 pounds of nitrogen, 24 pounds of phosphorus compounds, and 40 pounds of potassium compounds on the lawn this season. One-third of the mixture is to be applied in May, one-third in July, and one-third in late September. After checking the local discount stores, Jack finds that one store is currently having a sale on packaged fertilizer. One type on sale is a 20-5-20 mixture containing 20% nitrogen, 5% phosphorus compounds, and 20% potassium compounds, and selling at $4 for a 20-pound bag. The other type on sale is a 10-10-5 mixture selling for $5 for a 40-pound bag. Jack would like to know how many bags of each type he should purchase so he can combine the ingredients to form a mixture that will meet the minimum agricultural agency requirements. Jack would like to spend as little as possible to keep his lawn healthy. What should he do?

27. Car Phones, Inc. sells two models of car telephones: model x and model y. Records show that 3 hours of sales time are used for each model x phone that is sold, and 5 hours of sales time for each model y phone. A total of 600 hours of sales time is available for the next 4-week period. In addition, management planning policies call for minimum sales goals of 25 units for both model x and model y.
   a. Show the feasible region for the Car Phones, Inc. problem.
   b. Assuming the company makes a $40 profit contribution for each model x sold and a $50 profit contribution for each model y sold, what is the optimal sales goal for the company for the next 4-week period?
   c. Develop a constraint and show the feasible region if management adds the restriction that Car Phones must sell at least as many model y phones as model x phones.
   d. What is the new optimal solution if the constraint in part (c) is added to the problem?

28. Kats is a new pet food product. Each 16-ounce can of Kats consists of a blend, or mixture, of two pet food ingredients. Let

$$x_1 = \text{the number of ounces of ingredient } A \text{ in a 16-ounce can}$$
$$x_2 = \text{the number of ounces of ingredient } B \text{ in a 16-ounce can}$$

Each ounce of ingredient A contains $\frac{1}{2}$ ounce of protein and $\frac{1}{8}$ ounce of fat. Each ounce of ingredient B contains $\frac{1}{10}$ ounce of protein and $\frac{1}{3}$ ounce of fat. Restrictions are that a 16-ounce can of Kats must have at least 4 ounces of protein and 2.5 ounces of fat. If ingredient A costs $0.04 per ounce and ingredient B costs $0.03 per ounce, what is the minimum cost blend of ingredients A and B in each 16-ounce can of Kats? Identify and interpret the values of the surplus variables for the problem.

29. Photo Chemicals produces two types of photograph developing fluids. Both products cost Photo Chemicals $1 per gallon to produce. Based on an analysis of current inventory levels and outstanding orders for the next month, Photo Chemicals' management has specified that at least 30 gallons of product 1 and at least 20 gallons of product 2 must be produced during the next 2 weeks. Management has also stated that an existing inventory of highly perishable raw material required in the production of both fluids must be used within the next 2 weeks. The current inventory of the perishable raw material is 80 pounds. While more of this raw material can be ordered if necessary, any of the current inventory that is not used within the next 2 weeks will spoil; hence the management requirement that at least 80 pounds be used in the next 2 weeks. Furthermore, it is known that product 1 requires 1 pound of this perishable raw material per gallon and product 2 requires 2 pounds of the raw material per gallon. Since Photo Chemicals' objective is to keep its production costs at the minimum possible level, the firm's management is looking for a minimum cost production plan that uses all the 80 pounds of perishable raw material and provides at least 30 gallons of product 1 and at least 20 gallons of product 2. What is the minimum cost solution?

30. Bryant's Pizza, Inc. is a producer of frozen pizza products. The company makes a profit of $1.00 for each regular pizza it produces and $1.50 for each deluxe pizza produced. Each pizza includes a combination of dough mix and topping mix. Currently the firm has 150 pounds of dough mix and 50 pounds of topping mix. Each regular pizza uses 1 pound of dough mix and 4 ounces of topping mix. Each deluxe pizza uses 1 pound of dough mix and 8 ounces of topping mix. Based on past demand Bryant can sell at least 50 regular pizzas and at least 25 deluxe pizzas. How many regular and deluxe pizzas should the company make in order to maximize profits?
    a. Show the above problem in standard form.
    b. What are the values and interpretations of all slack and surplus variables?
    c. Which constraints are binding the optimal solution?

31. Wilkinson Motors, Inc. sells standard automobiles and station wagons. The firm makes a $400 profit for each automobile it sells and at $500 profit for each station wagon it sells. The company is planning next quarter's order, which the manufacturer says cannot exceed 300 automobiles and 150 station wagons. Dealer preparation time requires 2 hours for each automobile and 3 hours for each station wagon. Next quarter the company has 900 hours of shop time available for new car preparation. How many automobiles and station wagons should be ordered so that profit is maximized?

a. Show the linear programming model of the above problem.
b. Show the standard form and identify the slack variables.
c. Identify the extreme points of the feasible region.
d. Find the optimal solution.
e. Which constraints are binding?

32. Ryland Farms in northwestern Indiana grows soybeans and corn on its 500 acres of land. An acre of soybeans brings a $100 profit and an acre of corn brings a $200 profit. Because of a government program, no more than 200 acres may be planted in soybeans. During the planting season 1200 hours of planting time will be available. Each acre of soybeans requires 2 hours, while each acre of corn requires 6 hours. How many acres of soybeans and how many acres of corn should be planted in order to maximize profits?
    a. Show the linear programming model of the above problem.
    b. Show the standard form and identify all slack variables.
    c. Find the optimal solution.
    d. Identify all the extreme points of the feasible region.
    e. If the farm could get either more hours of labor for planting or additional land, which should it attempt to obtain? Why?

33. Reconsider the Par, Inc. situation in problem 13. Suppose that management adds the requirements that at least 500 standard bags and at least 360 deluxe bags must be produced.
    a. Graph the constraints for this revised Par, Inc. problem. What happens to the feasible region? Explain.
    b. If there are no feasible solutions, explain what is needed to produce 500 standard bags and 360 deluxe bags.

34. Consider the following linear program:

$$\max \quad 1x_1 + 2x_2$$
$$\text{s.t.}$$
$$1x_1 \qquad\qquad \leq 5$$
$$1x_2 \leq 4$$
$$2x_1 + 2x_2 = 12$$
$$x_1, x_2 \geq 0$$

a. Show the feasible region.
b. What are the extreme points of the feasible region?
c. Find the optimal solution using the graphical procedure.

35. Consider the following linear program:

$$\min \quad 2x_1 + 2x_2$$
$$\text{s.t.}$$
$$1x_1 + 3x_2 \leq 12$$
$$3x_1 + 1x_2 \geq 13$$
$$1x_1 - 1x_2 = 3$$
$$x_1, x_2 \geq 0$$

a. Show the feasible region.

b. What are the extreme points of the feasible region?

c. Find the optimal solution using the graphical procedure.

36. Write the following linear program in standard form:

$$\max \quad 5x_1 + 2x_2 + 8x_3$$

s.t.

$$1x_1 - 2x_2 + \tfrac{1}{2}x_3 \le 420$$
$$2x_1 + 3x_2 - 1x_3 \le 610$$
$$6x_1 - 1x_2 + 3x_3 \le 125$$

$$x_1, x_2, x_3 \ge 0$$

37. Given the linear program

$$\max \quad 4x_1 + 1x_2$$

s.t.

$$10x_1 + 2x_2 \le 30$$
$$3x_1 + 2x_2 \le 12$$
$$2x_1 + 2x_2 \le 10$$

$$x_1, x_2 \ge 0$$

a. Write this problem in standard form.

b. Solve the problem.

c. What are the values of the three slack variables at the optimal solution?

38. Given the linear program

$$\max \quad 3x_1 + 4x_2$$

s.t.

$$-1x_1 + 2x_2 \le 8$$
$$1x_1 + 2x_2 \le 12$$
$$2x_1 + 1x_2 \le 16$$

$$x_1, x_2 \ge 0$$

a. Write the problem in standard form.

b. Solve the problem.

c. What are the values of the three slack variables at the optimal solution?

39. Given the linear program

$$\min \quad 6x_1 + 4x_2$$

s.t.

$$2x_1 + 1x_2 \ge 12$$
$$1x_1 + 1x_2 \ge 10$$
$$1x_2 \le 4$$

$$x_1, x_2 \ge 0$$

   a. Write the problem in standard form.
   b. Solve the problem using the graphical solution procedure.
   c. What are the values of the slack and surplus variables?

40. Does the following linear program involve infeasibility, unboundedness, and/or alternate optimal solutions? Explain.

$$\begin{aligned} \max \quad & 4x_1 + 8x_2 \\ \text{s.t} \quad & \\ & 2x_1 + 2x_2 \leq 10 \\ & -1x_1 + 1x_2 \geq 8 \\ & x_1, x_2 \geq 0 \end{aligned}$$

41. Does the following linear program involve infeasibility, unboundedness, and/or alternate optimal solutions? Explain.

$$\begin{aligned} \max \quad & 1x_1 + 1x_2 \\ \text{s.t.} \quad & \\ & 8x_1 + 6x_2 \geq 24 \\ & 4x_1 + 6x_2 \geq -12 \\ & 2x_2 \geq 4 \\ & x_1, x_2 \geq 0 \end{aligned}$$

42. Consider the following linear program:

$$\begin{aligned} \max \quad & 1x_1 + 1x_2 \\ \text{s.t.} \quad & \\ & 5x_1 + 3x_2 \leq 15 \\ & 3x_1 + 5x_2 \leq 15 \\ & x_1, x_2 \geq 0 \end{aligned}$$

   a. What is the optimal solution for this problem?
   b. Suppose that the objective function is changed to $1x_1 + 2x_2$. Find the new optimal solution.
   c. By adjusting the coefficient of x_2 in the objective function, develop a new objective function that will make the solutions found in parts (a) and (b) above alternate optimal solutions.

43. Consider the following linear program:

$$\begin{aligned} \max \quad & 1x_1 - 2x_2 \\ \text{s.t.} \quad & \\ & -4x_1 + 3x_2 \leq 3 \\ & 1x_1 - 1x_2 \leq 3 \\ & x_1, x_2 \geq 0 \end{aligned}$$

    a. Graph the feasible region for the problem.
    b. Is the feasible region unbounded? Explain.
    c. Find the optimal solution.
    d. Does an unbounded feasible region imply that the optimal solution to the linear program will be unbounded?

44. Discuss what happens to the Innis Investments problem (see Section 7.7) if the risk measure for the money market fund is increased to 6.4. What would you recommend? Explain.

45. Reconsider the Kelson Sporting Equipment, Inc. production example (problem 17). Discuss the concepts of infeasibility, unboundedness, and alternate optima as they occur in each of the following situations:
    a. Management has requested that the production of baseball gloves (regular model plus catcher's model) be such that the total number of gloves produced is at least 750. That is, $1x_1 + 1x_2 \geq 750$.
    b. The original problem has to be solved again because the profit for the regular model is adjusted downward to $4 per glove.
    c. What would have to happen for this problem to be unbounded?

46. Management of High Tech Services (HTS) would like to develop a model that will help allocate technicians' time between service calls to regular contract customers and new customers. A maximum of 80 hours of technician time is available over the 2-week planning period. In order to satisfy cash flow requirements, at least $800 in revenue (per technician) must be generated during the 2-week period. Technician time for regular customers generates $25 per hour. However, technician time for new customers only generates an average of $8 per hour because in many cases a new customer contact does not provide billable services. To ensure that new customer contacts are being maintained, the time technicians spend on new customer contacts must be at least 60% of the time technicians spend on regular customer contacts. Given the above revenue and policy requirements, HTS would like to determine how to allocate technicians' time between regular customers and new customers so that the total number of customers contacted during the 2-week period will be maximized. Technicians require an average of 50 minutes for each regular customer contact and 1 hour for each new customer contact.
    a. Develop a linear programming model that will enable HTS to determine how to allocate technicians' time between regular customers and new customers.
    b. Graph the feasible region.
    c. Solve the appropriate simultaneous linear equations to determine the values of x_1 and x_2 at each extreme point of the feasible region.
    d. Find the optimal solution.

Case Problem
Advertising Strategy

Midtown Motors, Inc. has hired a marketing services firm to develop an advertising strategy for promoting Midtown's used car sales. The marketing firm has recommended that Midtown use spot announcements on both television and radio as the advertising media for the proposed promotional campaign. Advertising strategy guidelines are expressed as follows:

1. Use at least 30 announcements for combined television and radio coverage.
2. Do not use more than 25 radio announcements.
3. The number of radio announcements cannot be less than the number of television announcements.

The television station has quoted a cost of $1200 per spot announcement and the radio station has quoted a cost of $300 per spot announcement. Midtown's advertising budget has been set at $25,500. The marketing services firm has rated the various advertising media in terms of audience coverage and recall power of the advertisement. For Midtown's media alternatives, the television announcement is rated at 600 and the radio announcement is rated at 200. Midtown's president would like to know how many television and how many radio spot announcements should be used in order to maximize the overall rating of the advertising campaign.

Midtown's president believes that the televison station will consider running the Midtown spot announcement on its highly rated evening news program (at the same cost) if Midtown will consider using additional television announcements.

Managerial Report

Perform an analysis of advertising strategy for Midtown Motors and a report to Midtown's president presenting your findings and recommendations. Include (but do not limit your discussion to) a consideration of the following:

a. The recommended number of television and radio spot announcements.
b. The relative merits of each advertising medium.
c. The rating that would be necessary for the news program before it would make sense to increase the number of television spots.
d. The number of television spots that should be purchased if the news program is rated highly enough to make increasing the number of television spots advisable.

e. The restrictions placed on the advertising strategy that Midtown might want to consider relaxing or altering.
f. The best use of any possible increase in the advertising budget.
g. Any other information that may help Midtown's president make the advertising strategy decision.

Include a copy of your linear programming model and graphical solution in the appendix to your report.

CHAPTER

8

Linear Programming: Sensitivity Analysis and Computer Solution

In this chapter we provide an introduction to sensitivity analysis and the use of computers for solving linear programming problems. Sensitivity analysis associated with the optimal solution provides valuable supplementary information for the decision maker. After showing how sensitivity analysis can be conducted using a graphical approach, we demonstrate how LINDO/PC, a software package for solving linear programming problems on a microcomputer, can be used to solve the RMC and Innis Investments problems presented in Chapter 7. In discussing the computer solution for these problems we will focus on the interpretation of the computer output, which includes the optimal solution and sensitivity analysis information. The chapter concludes with a discussion of the formulation, computer solution, and sensitivity analysis for a linear programming problem involving more than two decision variables.

8.1

INTRODUCTION TO SENSITIVITY ANALYSIS

Sensitivity analysis is the study of how changes in the coefficients of a linear program affect the optimal solution. Using sensitivity analysis we can answer questions such as the following:

1. How will a *change in a coefficient of the objective function* affect the optimal solution?
2. How will a *change in the right-hand-side value for a constraint* affect the optimal solution?

Since sensitivity analysis is concerned with how the above changes affect the optimal solution, the analysis does not begin until the optimal solution to the original linear programming problem has been obtained. For this reason, sensitivity analysis is often referred to as *postoptimality analysis*.

One of the primary reasons that sensitivity analysis is important to decision makers is that real-world problems exist in a changing environment. Prices of raw materials change, product demand changes, companies purchase new machinery to replace old, stock prices fluctuate, employee turnover occurs, and so on. If a linear programming model has been used in such an environment, we can expect some of the coefficients to change over time. As a result we will want to determine how these changes affect the optimal solution to the original linear programming problem. Sensitivity analysis provides us with the information needed to respond to such changes without requiring the complete solution of a revised linear program.

Recall the RMC problem introduced in Chapter 7.

$$\max \; 40x_1 \; + \; 30x_2$$

s.t.

$$\frac{2}{5}x_1 \; + \; \frac{1}{2}x_2 \le 20 \qquad \text{Material 1}$$
$$\frac{1}{5}x_2 \le \;\; 5 \qquad \text{Material 2}$$
$$\frac{3}{5}x_1 \; + \; \frac{3}{10}x_2 \le 21 \qquad \text{Material 3}$$
$$x_1, x_2 \ge 0$$

The optimal solution, 25 tons of fuel additive (x_1) and 20 tons of solvent base (x_2), was based on profit figures of \$40 per ton of fuel additive and \$30 per ton of solvent base. However, suppose we later learn that because of a price reduction the profit for the fuel additive is reduced from \$40 to \$35 per ton. Sensitivity analysis can be used to determine whether or not the production schedule calling for 25 tons of fuel additive and 20 tons of solvent base is still best. If it is, there will be no need to solve a modified linear programming problem with $35x_1 + 30x_2$ as the new objective function.

Sensitivity analysis can also be used to determine which coefficients in a linear programming model are most critical. For example, suppose that the RMC management believes that the \$30 per ton profit for the solvent base is only a rough estimate of the profit that will actually be obtained. If sensitivity analysis shows that 25 tons of fuel additive and 20 tons of solvent base will be the optimal solution as long as the profit for the solvent base is between \$20 and \$40, management should feel comfortable with the \$30 per ton estimate and the recommended production quantities. However, if sensitivity analysis shows that 25 tons of fuel additive and 20 tons of solvent base will be the optimal solution only if the profit for the solvent base is between \$29.90 and \$32.00 per ton, management may want to review the accuracy of the \$30 per ton profit estimate. Management would especially want to consider how the optimal production quantities should be revised if the profit per ton for the solvent base were to drop.

Another aspect of sensitivity analysis is concerned with changes in the right-hand-side values of the constraints. Recall that in the RMC problem the optimal solution used all available material 1 and material 3. What would happen to the optimal solution and total profit if RMC could obtain additional quantities of either of these resources? Sensitivity analysis can help determine how much each added ton of material is worth and how many tons can be added before diminishing returns set in.

8.2

GRAPHICAL SENSITIVITY ANALYSIS

For linear programming problems with two decision variables, graphical solution methods can be used to perform sensitivity analysis on the objective function coefficients and the right-hand-side values for the constraints.

Objective Function Coefficients

Let us first consider how changes in the objective function coefficients might affect the optimal solution to the RMC problem. For instance, what range of values can the profit per ton of the fuel additive take on without causing RMC Corporation to change from the solution of 25 tons of fuel additive and 20 tons of solvent base? Such a range of values is called the *range of optimality* for the objective function coefficient.

Figure 8.1 shows the graphical solution to the RMC problem. A careful inspection of this graph shows that as long as the slope of the objective function is between the slope of line A (which coincides with the material 1 constraint line) and the slope of line B (which coincides with the material 3 constraint line), extreme point ③ with $x_1 = 25$ and $x_2 = 20$ will be optimal. Changing an objective function coefficient for x_1 or x_2 will cause the slope of the objective function to change. In Figure 8.1, we see that such a change causes the objective function line to rotate about extreme point ③. However, as long as the objective function line stays within the shaded region, extreme point ③ will remain optimal.

Rotating the objective function line *counterclockwise* increases the slope. Thus when the objective function line has been rotated counterclockwise (slope increased) enough to coincide with line A, we obtain alternate optima between extreme points ③ and ④. Any further counterclockwise rotation of the objective function line will cause extreme point ③ to be nonoptimal. Hence the slope of line A provides an upper limit for the slope of the objective function line.

Rotating the objective function line *clockwise* decreases the slope. Thus when the objective function line has been rotated clockwise (slope decreased and becoming more negative) enough to coincide with line B, we obtain alternate optima between extreme points ③ and ②. Any further clockwise rotation of the objective function line will cause extreme point ③ to be nonoptimal. Hence the slope of line B provides a lower limit for the slope of the objective function line.

From the above discussion it should be clear that extreme point ③ will be the optimal solution as long as

upper limit CC

$$\text{Slope of line } B \leq \text{slope of objective function line} \leq \text{slope of line } A$$

In Figure 8.1 we see that the equation for line A, the material 1 constraint line, is

$$\tfrac{2}{5} x_1 + \tfrac{1}{2} x_2 = 20$$

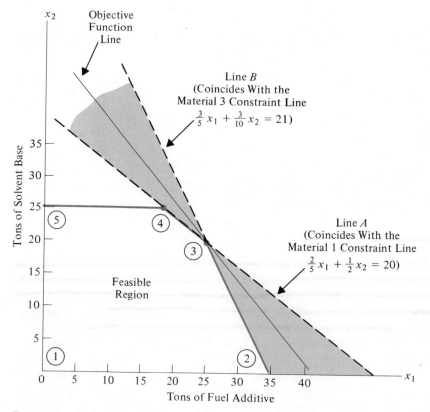

Figure 8.1

Graphical Solution of RMC Problem with Slope of Objective Function Between Slopes of Line *A* and Line *B*. Extreme Point ③ Is Optimal

By solving this equation for x_2, we can write the equation for line *A* in its slope-intercept form (see Section 7.5). This is done as follows:

$$\tfrac{1}{2}x_2 = -\tfrac{2}{5}x_1 + 20$$
$$x_2 = -\tfrac{4}{5}x_1 + 40$$

Slope of →   Intercept of
line *A*   line *A* on x_2 axis

Thus the slope for line *A* is $-\tfrac{4}{5}$ and its intercept on the x_2 axis is 40.

Again referring to Figure 8.1, we see that the equation for line *B*, the material 3 constraint line, is

$$\tfrac{3}{5}x_1 + \tfrac{3}{10}x_2 = 21$$

Solving for x_2 provides the slope-intercept form for line *B*:

$$\tfrac{3}{10}x_2 = -\tfrac{3}{5}x_1 + 21$$
$$x_2 = -2x_1 + 70$$

Thus the slope for line B is -2 and its intercept on the x_2 axis is 70.

Now that the slopes of line A and line B have been computed, we see that in order for extreme point ③ to be optimal, we must have

$$-2 \le \text{slope of the objective function line} \le -\tfrac{4}{5} \qquad (8.1)$$

Let us now consider the general form of the slope of the objective function line. Let c_1 denote the profit per ton of fuel additive, c_2 the profit per ton of solvent base, and z the value of the objective function. Using this notation, the objective function can be written

$$z = c_1 x_1 + c_2 x_2$$

Solving for x_2 provides the following slope-intercept form for the objective function line:

$$x_2 = -\left(\frac{c_1}{c_2}\right) x_1 + \frac{z}{c_2}$$

Thus we see that in general the slope of the objective function line is $-c_1/c_2$. Substituting $-c_1/c_2$ into expression (8.1) shows that extreme point ③ will be optimal as long as the following expression is satisfied:

$$-2 \le -\frac{c_1}{c_2} \le -\tfrac{4}{5} \qquad (8.2)$$

To compute the range of optimality for the fuel additive profit coefficient c_1, we will hold the profit coefficient for the solvent base fixed at its initial value $c_2 = 30$. Doing so in inequality (8.2), we obtain

$$-2 \le -\frac{c_1}{30} \le -\tfrac{4}{5}$$

$$-2 \le -\frac{40}{c_2} \le -\frac{1}{5}$$

From the left-hand inequality, we have

$$-2 \le -\frac{c_1}{30}$$

$$\frac{1}{40} \cdot \frac{-2}{1} = -\frac{40}{c_2} \cdot \frac{1}{40}$$

Thus

$$-60 \le -c_1 \qquad \text{or} \qquad c_1 \le 60$$

$$\frac{-1}{20} = \frac{-1}{c_2}$$

From the right-hand inequality, we have

$$-\frac{c_1}{30} \le -\tfrac{4}{5}$$

$$-1c_2 = -20$$

$$\boxed{c_2 = 20}$$

Thus

$$-c_1 \le -\frac{120}{5} = -24 \qquad \text{or} \qquad c_1 \ge 24$$

$$\frac{1}{40} - \frac{40}{c_2} \le -\frac{4}{5} \cdot \frac{1}{40}$$

$$-\frac{1}{c_2} \le \frac{-1}{50}$$

$$\boxed{c_2 = 50}$$

Combining the above limits for c_1 provides the following range of optimality for the fuel additive profit coefficient:

$$24 \le c_1 \le 60$$

In the original RMC problem, fuel additive had a profit coefficient of $40 per ton. The resulting optimal solution was 25 tons of fuel additive and 20 tons of solvent base. The range of optimality for c_1 tells RMC's management that, with other coefficients unchanged, the profit coefficient for the fuel additive can be anywhere between $24 per ton and $60 per ton and the production quantities of 25 tons of fuel additive and 20 tons of solvent base will remain optimal. Note here that while the production quantities will not change, the total profit will vary due to the change in the profit per ton of fuel additive.

The above computations can be repeated holding the profit per ton of fuel additive constant at $c_1 = 40$. The range of optimality for the profit per ton of solvent base can then be determined. Check to see that this range is $20 \le c_2 \le 50$.

In cases where the rotation of the objective function line about an optimal extreme point causes the objective function line to become *vertical*, there will be either no upper limit or no lower limit for the slope as it appears in the form of expression (8.2). To see how this special situation can happen in graphical sensitivity analysis, assume that the objective function for the RMC problem had been such that extreme point ② in Figure 8.2 provided the optimal solution. Rotating the objective function line counterclockwise around extreme point ② provides an upper limit for the slope when the objective function line coincides with line B. Since we have previously seen that the slope of line B is -2, the upper limit for the slope of the objective function line must be -2. However, rotating the objective function line clockwise causes the line to become vertical. In this case the slope becomes more and more negative, approaching a value of minus infinity, and hence there is no lower limit for the slope of the objective function. Using the upper limit of -2, we can write

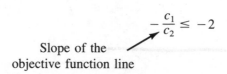

$$-\frac{c_1}{c_2} \le -2$$

Slope of the
objective function line

Following our previous procedure of holding c_2 constant at its original value, $c_2 = 30$, we have

$$-\frac{c_1}{30} \le -2$$

Solving for c_1 provides the following result:

$$-c_1 \le -60 \qquad \text{or} \qquad c_1 \ge 60$$

In reviewing Figure 8.2 we note that extreme point ② remains optimal for all values of c_1 above 60. Thus we obtain the following range of optimality for c_1 at extreme point ②:

$$60 \le c_1 < \infty$$

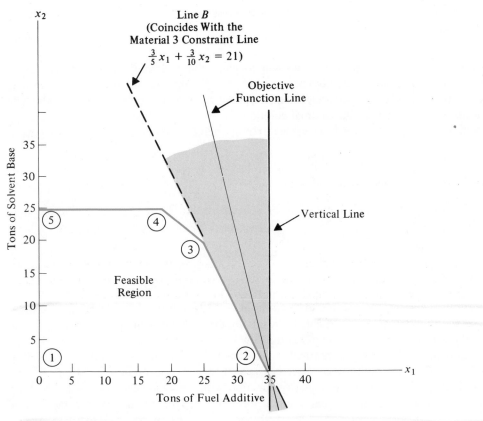

Figure 8.2
Graphical Solution of RMC Problem With Optimal Solution at Extreme Point ②

Simultaneous Changes

The range of optimality for objective function coefficients is applicable only for changes made to one coefficient at a time. All other coefficients are assumed fixed at their initial values. If two or more objective function coefficients are changed simultaneously, further analysis is necessary to determine if the optimal solution will change. However, when solving two-variable problems graphically, inequality (8.2) suggests an easy way to determine whether or not simultaneous changes in both objective function coefficients will cause a change in the optimal solution. Simply compute the slope of the objective function $(-c_1/c_2)$ for the new coefficient values. If this ratio is greater than or equal to the lower limit on the slope of the objective function and less than or equal to the upper limit, then the changes made will not cause a change in the optimal solution.

Let us illustrate this approach by considering changes in both of the objective function coefficients for the RMC problem. Suppose that the profit per ton of fuel additive is increased to $55 and simultaneously the profit contribution per ton of solvent base is reduced to $25. Recall that the ranges of optimality for c_1 and c_2 (both computed in a one-at-a-time manner) are

$$24 \leq c_1 \leq 60 \tag{8.3}$$

$$20 \leq c_2 \leq 50 \tag{8.4}$$

Given these ranges of optimality, we can conclude that changing either c_1 to \$55 or c_2 to \$25 (but not both) would not cause a change in the optimal solution of $x_1 = 25$ and $x_2 = 20$. But we cannot conclude that changing both coefficients simultaneously will not result in a change in the optimal solution.

In expression (8.2) we showed that extreme point ③ remains optimal as long as

$$-2 \leq -\frac{c_1}{c_2} \leq -\tfrac{4}{5}$$

If c_1 is changed to 55 and simultaneously c_2 is changed to 25, the new objective function slope will be given by

$$-\frac{c_1}{c_2} = -\frac{55}{25} = -2.2$$

Since this value is less than the lower limit of -2, the current solution of $x_1 = 25$ and $x_2 = 20$ will no longer be optimal. By resolving the problem with $c_1 = 55$ and $c_2 = 25$ we will find that extreme point ② is the new optimal solution.

Looking at the ranges of optimality, we concluded that changing either c_1 to \$55 or c_2 to \$25 (but not both) would not cause a change in the optimal solution. But in recomputing the slope of the objective function with simultaneous changes for both c_1 and c_2, we saw that the optimal solution did change. This emphasizes the fact that a range of optimality can only be used to draw a conclusion about changes made to one *objective function coefficient at a time*.

Right-Hand Sides

Let us now consider how a change in the right-hand-side value for a constraint may affect the feasible region and perhaps cause a change in the optimal solution to the problem. To illustrate this aspect of sensitivity analysis, let us consider what happens if an additional 3 tons of material 3 becomes available. In this case, the right-hand side of the third constraint is changed from 21 to 24, and the constraint is rewritten as

$$\tfrac{3}{5} x_1 + \tfrac{3}{10} x_2 \leq 24$$

By obtaining an additional 3 tons of material 3 we have expanded the feasible region for the RMC problem; the new feasible region is shown in Figure 8.3. Since the feasible region has been enlarged, we now want to determine whether or not one of the new feasible solutions provides an improvement in the value of the objective function. Application of the graphical solution procedure to the problem with the enlarged feasible region shows that the extreme point with $x_1 = \tfrac{100}{3}$ and $x_2 = \tfrac{40}{3}$ now provides the optimal solution. The new value for the objective function is $40(\tfrac{100}{3}) + 30(\tfrac{40}{3}) = 1733.33$, providing an increase in profit of \$1733.33 $-$ 1600 = \$133.33. Thus the increased profit occurs at a rate of \$133.33/3 = \$44.44 per ton of material 3 added.

The change in the value of the objective function per unit increase in the value of the right-hand side is called the *shadow price*. Thus the shadow price for material 3 is

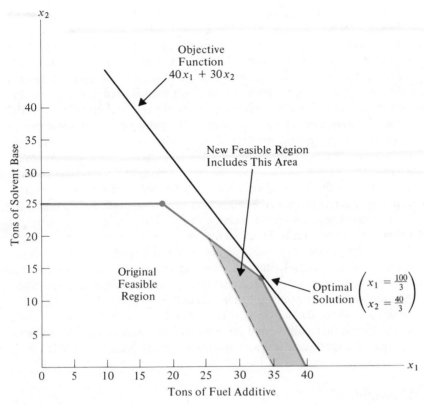

Figure 8.3
Effect of a 3-Unit Increase in the Right-Hand Side of the Material 3 Constraint

$44.44. In the RMC problem, if it were possible to purchase more of material 3, management should be willing to pay up to $44.44 per ton for it.

We caution here that the value of the shadow price may be applicable only for small changes in the right-hand side. As more and more resources are obtained and the right-hand-side value continues to increase, other constraints will become binding and limit the change in the value of the objective function. For example, in the RMC problem we would eventually reach a point where more material 3 would be of no value. This would occur in the RMC problem at the point where the material 3 constraint becomes nonbinding. Clearly, at this point the shadow price would equal zero. In the next section, we show how to determine the range of values for a right-hand side over which the shadow price will accurately predict the change in the objective function. Finally, we note that the shadow price for any nonbinding constraint will be zero because a change in the right-hand side of such a constraint will affect only the value of the slack or surplus variable for that constraint.

Cautionary Note on Interpretation of Shadow Prices

As stated previously, the shadow price represents the change in value of the objective function per unit increase in the right-hand side of a linear programming constraint. When the constraint right-hand side represents an amount of resources available, the shadow price is usually interpreted as the value of one additional unit of the resource. Such an interpretation is not always correct. It is correct when the amount of resources represents a fixed quantity that must be paid for even if all of the resources are not used. In this case, the cost of such a resource is not relevant (i.e., it is a sunk cost and will remain the same regardless of the decision made) and should not be deducted in computing the objective function coefficients. This was the situation for the material costs in the RMC problem and hence we interpreted the shadow price as the value of an additional unit of the resource. However, there are other situations when such an interpretation is not correct.

In some formulations it is appropriate to view the right-hand side as the maximum amount of a resource available and not a fixed amount that must be paid for no matter what. In this type of situation it would be appropriate to deduct the resource cost in computing objective function coefficients. The resource cost would then be relevant (i.e., the amount of cost incurred depends on the decision made). The correct interpretation of the shadow price in such a situation is the maximum premium (over the normal price) a company should be willing to pay to obtain one additional unit of the resource.

As an illustration of this second situation, suppose that in the RMC problem the right-hand sides of the constraints represented quantities available from a supplier. RMC would be free to purchase any amount up to that quantity at a normal price. In such a case it would be appropriate to deduct the cost of materials in computing the objective function coefficients for the fuel additive and solvent base. The shadow price for material 3 would then represent the maximum premium (over the normal price) that RMC should be willing to pay to obtain more than 21 tons of material 3.

Coefficients of the Constraints

A change in one of the coefficients of the constraints can have a significant effect on the optimal solution to a linear programming problem. A complete discussion of the ramifications of making changes in these coefficients is beyond the scope of this text. However, we can make some general comments about this aspect of sensitivity analysis.

For example, suppose that we have an optimal solution to a linear programming problem and variable x_j has a positive value. Let us also assume that constraint i is of the less-than-or-equal-to type. If the coefficient associated with x_j in constraint i is increased and constraint i is binding, the value of the objective function will get worse. That is, in a maximization problem the objective function will decrease; in a minimization problem it will increase. On the other hand, if the coefficient associated with x_j in constraint i is decreased and constraint i is binding, the value of the optimal solution will improve and the amount of x_j will increase. The converse of the above is true if constraint i is of the greater-than-or-equal-to type. For the case of equality constraints, additional analysis is necessary to determine the effect on the optimal solution. Finally, we note that if there is a small change in one of the coefficients of a nonbinding constraint, there will be no effect on the optimal solution.

8.3

COMPUTER SOLUTION USING LINDO/PC: A MICROCOMPUTER SOFTWARE PACKAGE

Computer programs designed to solve linear programming problems are now widely available. Most large companies, as well as most universities, have access to these computer programs. The developmental effort for large-scale "software packages" has come primarily from computer manufacturers and/or software service companies such as IBM, Control Data, and Ketron. Usually, after a short period of familiarization with the specific features of the package, users can solve linear programming problems with few difficulties. Problems involving thousands of variables and thousands of constraints can now be solved routinely through the use of computer packages. Most large linear programs can be solved with just a few minutes of computer time; small linear programs usually require only a few seconds.

More recently there has been a virtual explosion of software for microcomputers. A large number of "user-friendly" computer programs that can be used to solve linear programs on microcomputers are now available. These programs, developed by academicians and small software companies, are almost all easy to use.[1] Most of these programs are designed to solve smaller linear programs (a few hundred variables at most). To solve large-scale linear programs involving several thousand variables and constraints, software packages designed for mainframe computers should be used.

LINDO/PC, developed by Linus E. Schrage at the University of Chicago, is a microcomputer version of the popular LINDO computer package that is widely available on mainframe computers. LINDO/PC allows the user to interact with the computer in a conversational mode. By this we mean that once the program has been loaded in the microcomputer, the user inputs the objective function and constraints as requested by the computer program. When satisfied that all data have been entered correctly, the user enters the command "GO" and the LINDO/PC system solves the problem. The optimal solution and its related information are available at the user's computer monitor.

We will use the RMC problem to demonstrate the use of LINDO/PC. Since computer input must utilize decimal rather than fractional data values, the RMC problem is restated below with decimal coefficients:

$$\max \quad 40x_1 + 30x_2$$

s.t.

$$
\begin{array}{llll}
0.4x_1 + 0.5x_2 & \leq 20 & \text{Material 1} \\
 0.2x_2 & \leq 5 & \text{Material 2} \\
0.6x_1 + 0.3x_2 & \leq 21 & \text{Material 3} \\
\end{array}
$$

$$x_1, x_2 \geq 0$$

An example of the data input portion of a LINDO/PC computer session on an IBM Personal Computer is shown in Figure 8.4. The information keyed in by the user is shown in color, and the response from the computer package is shown in black. Note in particular the interactive nature of the system, with the alternating user input and LINDO/PC response. Specific commands and symbols shown in Figure 8.4 are described as follows:

1. The "A>" is the user prompt for the IBM Personal Computer. The user command "LINDO" causes the LINDO/PC program to be loaded and some copyright information to be printed.
2. LINDO/PC begins by sending the symbol ":" to indicate that it is waiting for an instruction from the user.

---

[1] The *Management Scientist* software package that is available with this textbook includes a user-friendly linear programming routine.

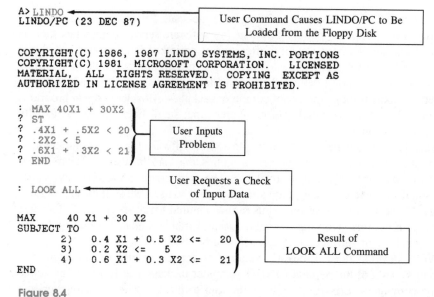

```
A> LINDO
LINDO/PC (23 DEC 87)
```

User Command Causes LINDO/PC to Be
Loaded from the Floppy Disk

```
COPYRIGHT(C) 1986, 1987 LINDO SYSTEMS, INC. PORTIONS
COPYRIGHT(C) 1981 MICROSOFT CORPORATION.  LICENSED
MATERIAL, ALL RIGHTS RESERVED. COPYING EXCEPT AS
AUTHORIZED IN LICENSE AGREEMENT IS PROHIBITED.
```

```
:  MAX 40X1 + 30X2
?  ST
?  .4X1 + .5X2 < 20
?  .2X2 < 5
?  .6X1 + .3X2 < 21
?  END
```

User Inputs
Problem

```
:  LOOK ALL
```

User Requests a Check
of Input Data

```
MAX     40 X1 + 30 X2
SUBJECT TO
       2)   0.4 X1 + 0.5 X2 <=   20
       3)   0.2 X2 <=   5
       4)   0.6 X1 + 0.3 X2 <=   21
END
```

Result of
LOOK ALL Command

Figure 8.4
Data Input Session with the LINDO/PC Microcomputer Package. Note: User Input Shown in Color,
Computer Response Shown in Black

3. The user keys in the objective function as it appears in the mathematical statement of the problem.
4. LINDO/PC then sends the symbol ''?'' to indicate that it is waiting for additional input concerning the linear program being solved.
5. The user input ''ST'' stands for ''subject to,'' notifying the program that information about the constraints is to follow.
6. After inputting each of the constraints with the symbol $<$, which is interpreted as $\leq$ by LINDO/PC, the user inputs ''END'' to signal that the data input is complete.
7. LINDO/PC again responds with '':'' to indicate that it is waiting for an instruction.
8. The user inputs the optional instruction ''LOOK ALL,'' which results in the computer printing the linear programming problem that LINDO/PC is ready to solve. ''LOOK ALL'' is not a required instruction, but using it provides an easy check on the accuracy of the input data. In the computer package the objective function is identified as row 1. Thus, under the ''SUBJECT TO'' heading we see the material 1 constraint identified as row 2, the material 2 constraint as row 3, and the material 3 constraint as row 4.

With the input data complete, the LINDO/PC package proceeds to develop the solution of the problem when given the command ''GO.'' The output from LINDO/PC is shown in Figure 8.5.

Interpretation of Computer Output

Let us look more closely at the LINDO/PC output in Figure 8.5 and interpret the computer solution provided for the RMC problem. First note the number 1600.00000, which appears under the heading ''OBJECTIVE FUNCTION VALUE.'' From this value, we can conclude that the optimal solution to the RMC problem will provide a profit of $1600. Directly below the objective function value we find the values of the decision variables

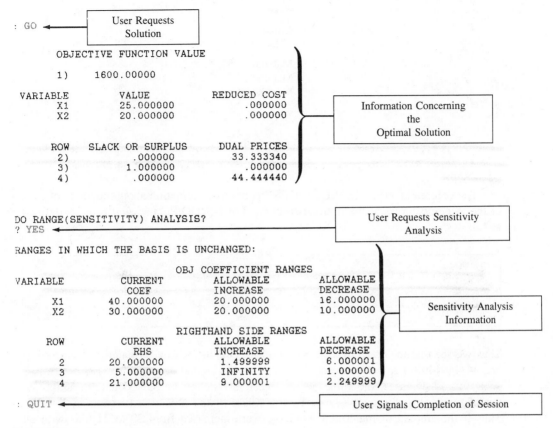

```
: GO  ◄────         User Requests
                    Solution

         OBJECTIVE FUNCTION VALUE

      1)      1600.00000

    VARIABLE          VALUE          REDUCED COST
        X1          25.000000           .000000
        X2          20.000000           .000000            Information Concerning
                                                                   the
                                                            Optimal Solution
        ROW    SLACK OR SURPLUS        DUAL PRICES
        2)          .000000           33.333340
        3)         1.000000             .000000
        4)          .000000           44.444440


    DO RANGE(SENSITIVITY) ANALYSIS?                    User Requests Sensitivity
    ? YES  ◄────                                              Analysis

    RANGES IN WHICH THE BASIS IS UNCHANGED:

                          OBJ COEFFICIENT RANGES
    VARIABLE          CURRENT      ALLOWABLE      ALLOWABLE
                       COEF        INCREASE       DECREASE
        X1          40.000000     20.000000      16.000000
        X2          30.000000     20.000000      10.000000          Sensitivity Analysis
                                                                      Information
                          RIGHTHAND SIDE RANGES
        ROW           CURRENT      ALLOWABLE      ALLOWABLE
                       RHS         INCREASE       DECREASE
         2          20.000000      1.499999       6.000001
         3           5.000000      INFINITY       1.000000
         4          21.000000      9.000001       2.249999

    : QUIT  ◄────                             User Signals Completion of Session
```

Figure 8.5
RMC Solution Using the LINDO/PC Microcomputer Package. Note: User Commands Shown in
Color; Computer Response Shown in Black

at the optimal solution. Thus, we have $x_1 = 25$ tons of fuel additive and $x_2 = 20$ tons
of solvent base as the optimal production quantities.

The information in the column labeled "REDUCED COST" indicates how much
the objective function coefficient of each decision variable would have to improve[2] before
it would be possible for that variable to assume a positive value in the optimal solution.
Thus if a decision variable is already positive in the optimal solution, its reduced cost is
zero. For the RMC problem the optimal solution is $x_1 = 25$ and $x_2 = 20$. With both
variables already having positive values, their corresponding reduced costs are zero. In
Section 8.4 we will interpret the reduced cost for a decision variable that does not have
a positive value in the optimal solution.

Immediately following the optimal x_1 and x_2 values and the reduced cost information,
the computer output provides information about the status of the constraints. Recall that
the RMC problem had three less-than-or-equal-to constraints corresponding to the three
materials available. The information shown in the column labeled "SLACK OR SUR-
PLUS" provides the value of the slack variable for each of the departments. This information is summarized below:

[2]For a maximization problem, "improve" means get bigger; for a minimization problem, "improve" means
get smaller.

Row	Constraint	Slack
2	Material 1	0
3	Material 2	1
4	Material 3 ·	0

From the above information we see that the binding constraints (the material 1 and material 3 constraints) have zero slack at the optimal solution. There is a surplus of 1 ton of material 2.

The column labeled "DUAL PRICES" contains information about the value of each of the three resources at the optimal solution. For LINDO/PC the *dual price* is defined as follows:

> The dual price associated with a constraint is the *improvement* in the optimal value of the objective function per unit increase in the right-hand-side value for the constraint.

Thus we see that the nonzero dual prices of 33.333340 for row 2 (material 1 constraint) and 44.444440 for row 4 (material 3 constraint) tell us that an additional ton of material 1 improves (increases) the value of the objective function by $33.33 and an additional ton of material 4 improves (increases) the value of the objective function by $44.44. Thus if the amount of material 1 available were increased from 20 to 21 tons with all other coefficients in the problem remaining the same, RMC's profit would be increased by $33.33, from $1600 to $1633.33. A similar interpretation for the material 3 constraint implies that an increase in available material 3 from 21 to 22 tons, with all other coefficients in the problem remaining the same, would increase RMC's profit to $1600 + $44.44 = $1644.44. Since the material 2 constraint has slack or unused capacity available, the dual price of zero shows that additional material 2 will not improve the value of the objective function.

As you may recall from the discussion of shadow prices in Section 8.2, the information in the "DUAL PRICES" column provides the shadow prices for RMC's three resources. In fact, in the case of a *maximization* linear program, the LINDO/PC dual price is the *same* as the shadow price. However, as we will discuss later, in a minimization linear program the dual price provided by the LINDO/PC output is the *negative* of the corresponding shadow price.

Referring again to the computer output in Figure 8.5, we see that after providing the constraint information on slack/surplus variables and dual prices, LINDO/PC asks the user the following question: "DO RANGE (SENSITIVITY) ANALYSIS?" The user response of "YES" requests ranges on the objective function coefficients and the right-hand sides of the constraints.

Considering the information provided under the computer output heading labeled "OBJ COEFFICIENT RANGES," we see that variable x_1, which has a current profit coefficient of 40, has an allowable increase of 20 and an allowable decrease of 16. Adding 20 to and subtracting 16 from the current coefficient of 40 provides the following range of optimality for c_1:

$$24 \leq c_1 \leq 60$$

This tells us that as long as the profit contribution associated with the fuel additive is between $24 and $60, the production of $x_1 = 25$ tons of fuel additive and $x_2 = 20$ tons of solvent base will remain the optimal solution. Note that this is the range of optimality that we obtained when we performed graphical sensitivity analysis for c_1 in Section 8.2.

Using the objective function coefficient range information for solvent base, we can use the allowable increase and allowable decrease values for c_2 to compute the following range of optimality:

$$20 \leq c_2 \leq 50$$

This tells us that as long as the profit contribution associated with a ton of solvent base is between $20 and $50, the production of $x_1 = 25$ tons of fuel additive and $x_2 = 20$ tons of solvent base will remain the optimal solution.

The final section of the computer printout ("RIGHTHAND SIDE RANGES") contains ranging information for the constraint right-hand sides. As long as the constraint right-hand side value stays within this range, the associated dual price gives the improvement in value of the objective function per unit increase in the right-hand side. For example, let us consider the material 1 constraint with a current right-hand-side value of 20 tons. Since the dual price for this constraint is $33.33, we can conclude that additional material 1 will increase the objective function by $33.33 per ton. It is also true that a reduction in the material 1 available will reduce the value of the objective function by $33.33 per ton. From the range information given, we see that the dual price of $33.33 is valid for increases up to 1.499999 and decreases up to 6.000001. A similar interpretation for the material 3 constraint right-hand side (row 4) shows that the dual price of $44.44 is applicable for increases of up to 9 tons and decreases up to 2.25 tons.

As mentioned, the right-hand-side ranges provide limits within which the dual prices are applicable. For changes outside the range, the problem must be resolved to find the new optimal solution and new dual price. We will call the range over which the dual price is applicable the *range of feasibility*.

By adding the allowable increase to and subtracting the allowable decrease from the current right-hand-side value of each constraint, we obtain the *ranges of feasibility* for the RMC problem. These computations provide the following ranges of feasibility for the right-hand-side values:

Constraint	Min RHS	Max RHS
Material 1	14.0	21.5
Material 2	4	∞
Material 3	18.75	30.0

As long as the values of the right-hand sides are within the above ranges, the dual prices shown on the computer output will not change. Values of the right-hand sides outside these limits will result in changes in the dual price information.

Note in Figure 8.5 that at the completion of the sensitivity analysis LINDO/PC sends "::" and waits for another instruction. In this case the user selected "QUIT" to signal the end of the LINDO/PC session. An optional instruction at this point would be "ALT," which would have enabled the user to alter or modify one or more aspects of the problem and seek additional solution information.

Simultaneous Changes

At this point we reemphasize that the sensitivity analysis presented in computer output is based on the assumption that coefficients are changed *one at a time*, with all other coefficients of the problem remaining as stated in the original problem. The sensitivity analysis information provided in computer output does not apply to two or more simultaneous changes in the problem. However, with the help of the *100% rule*,[3] some analysis of simultaneous changes is possible.

If simultaneous changes in two or more objective function coefficients are made, the solution will not change as long as the 100% rule is satisfied. Similarly, if simultaneous changes are made in two or more right-hand sides, the dual prices will not change as long as the 100% rule is satisfied.

To apply the 100% rule, for each coefficient changed we must compute the percentage of the allowable increase or allowable decrease represented by the change. *If the sum of the percentages over all changes does not exceed 100%, then we say that the simultaneous changes satisfy the 100% rule.* Let us illustrate by considering simultaneous changes in the right-hand sides for the RMC problem.

Suppose, for instance, that in the RMC problem we could obtain 1 additional ton of material 1 and 2 additional tons of material 3. The 1 additional ton of material 1 is $(1/1.499999)(100) = 66.67\%$ of the allowable increase in the constraint right-hand side. The 2 additional tons of material 3 are $(2/9.000001)(100) = 22.22\%$ of the allowable increase in the material 3 constraint right-hand side. The accumulated percentage of change is $66.67\% + 22.22\% = 88.89\%$. Since the cumulative percentage change does not exceed 100%, we can conclude that the dual prices are applicable and that the objective function will improve by $(1)(33.33) + 2(44.44) = 122.21$.

Interpretation of Computer Output—A Second Example

As another example of interpreting computer output, let us reconsider the Innis Investments minimization problem introduced in Section 7.7. The linear programming model for this problem is restated below, where x_1 = units purchased in the stock fund and x_2 = units purchased in the money market fund.

$$\min \quad 8x_1 + 3x_2$$
s.t.
$$50x_1 + 100x_2 \leq 1,200,000 \quad \text{Funds available}$$
$$5x_1 + 4x_2 \geq 60,000 \quad \text{Annual income}$$
$$x_2 \geq 3,000 \quad \text{Minimum units in money market}$$
$$x_1, x_2 \geq 0$$

[3]See *Applied Mathematical Programming*. By S.P. Bradley, Hax, A.C., and Magnanti, T.L., Addison-Wesley, 1977.

The LINDO/PC solution for the Innis Investments problem is presented in Figure 8.6. The computer output shows that the optimal solution has an objective function value of 62,000. The values of the decision variables show that 4000 units of the stock fund ($x_1 = 4000$) and 10,000 units of the money market fund ($x_2 = 10,000$) provide the minimum total risk solution.

```
      OBJECTIVE FUNCTION VALUE

   1)     62000.0000

VARIABLE         VALUE          REDUCED COST
   X1        4000.000000           .000000
   X2       10000.000000           .000000


  ROW    SLACK OR SURPLUS      DUAL PRICES
   2)          .000000            .056667
   3)          .000000          -2.166667
   4)         7000.000000         .000000


DO RANGE(SENSITIVITY) ANALYSIS?
? YES

RANGES IN WHICH THE BASIS IS UNCHANGED:

                           OBJ COEFFICIENT RANGES
VARIABLE         CURRENT       ALLOWABLE       ALLOWABLE
                 COEF          INCREASE        DECREASE
   X1          8.000000        INFINITY        4.250000
   X2          3.000000        3.400000        INFINITY

                           RIGHTHAND SIDE RANGES
  ROW          CURRENT        ALLOWABLE       ALLOWABLE
               RHS            INCREASE        DECREASE
   2     1200000.000000     300000.000000    420000.000000
   3       60000.000000      42000.000000     12000.000000
   4        3000.000000       7000.000000     INFINITY
```

Figure 8.6
LINDO/PC Output for Innis Investments Problem

The "SLACK or SURPLUS" information shows that the $\geq$ constraint for the money market minimum (see row 4) has a surplus of 7000 units. This tells us that the number of units of the money market fund exceeds the minimum requirement by 7000 units. The "SLACK or SURPLUS" values are zero for the other two constraints; this indicates that these constraints are binding at the optimal solution.

The "DUAL PRICE" column again shows us the *improvement* in the objective function for a one-unit increase in the right-hand side of the constraint. Focusing first on the dual price of 0.056667 for the funds available constraint (row 2), we see that if we can increase the funds available by $1, the objective function value will *improve* by 0.056667 units of risk. Since the objective is to minimize risk, improvement in this case means a lowering of portfolio risk. Thus if $1 is available, the value of the optimal solution will improve (decrease) to 61,999.943. The "RIGHTHAND SIDE RANGES" section of the output shows that the allowable increase for the funds available constraint (row 2) is 300,000. Thus the dual price of 0.056667 per unit would be applicable for every additional dollar up to a total of $1,500,000.

Let us again return to the "DUAL PRICE" section of the output and consider the dual price for the annual income constraint (row 3). The *negative dual price* tells us that the objective function *will not improve* if the value of the right-hand side is increased by one unit. In fact the dual price of -2.166667 tells us that if the right-hand side of the annual income constraint is increased from $60,000 to $60,001, the value of the objective function will not improve, but will get worse by the amount of 2.166667. Since becoming worse means an increase in risk, the value of the objective function will become 62,002.167 if the one-unit increase in the annual income requirement is made.

Since the dual price refers to improvement in the value of the objective function per unit increase in the right-hand side, a constraint with a negative dual price should not have its right-hand side increased. In fact if the dual price is negative, efforts should be made to reduce the right-hand side of the constraint. If the right-hand side of the annual income constraint were decreased from $60,000 to $59,999, the dual price tells us the total portfolio risk could be lowered by 2.166667 to 61,997.833.

The interpretation of the dual price from the LINDO/PC output is the improvement in the value of the objective function per unit increase in the right-hand side of a constraint. However, as we have seen, the interpretation of an *improvement* in the value of an objective function depends on whether we are solving a maximization or a minimization problem. The following table summarizes the approach to interpreting the value of a dual price:

Problem Type	Interpretation of Dual Price
Maximization	Amount of improvement (*increase*) in the value of the objective function per unit *increase* in the right-hand side of the constraint.
Minimization	Amount of improvement (*decrease*) in the value of the objective function per unit *increase* in the right-hand side of the constraint.

The dual price for a $\leq$ constraint will always be greater than or equal to 0 because increasing the right-hand side cannot make the value of the objective function worse. Similarly, the dual price for a $\geq$ constraint will always be less than or equal to 0 because increasing the right-hand side cannot improve the value of the objective function.

We caution that the interpretation of dual prices here is based on LINDO/PC's sign convention. Recall that for maximization problems dual prices and shadow prices are the same; for minimization problems they have opposite signs. If you are using a different software package, you should check to see what convention and terminology are being used for this type of sensitivity analysis information.[4]

Finally, consider the right-hand-side ranges provided in Figure 8.6. Adding the allowable increase to and subtracting the allowable decrease from the current right-hand side of each constraint provides the *ranges of feasibility* for the Innis Investments problem. These computations provide the following ranges of feasibility for the right-hand sides:

[4] *The Management Scientist* software prepared by the authors of this text follows the same convention as LINDO/ PC.

Constraint	Min RHS	Max RHS
Funds available	780,000	1,500,000
Annual income	48,000	102,000
Minimum money market	0	10,000

As long as the right-hand sides are within the above ranges, the dual prices shown on the computer output are applicable. Let us now consider the computer solution and interpretation of the computer output for a linear program involving more than two decision variables.

8.4

MORE THAN TWO DECISION VARIABLES

The graphical solution procedure is useful only for linear programs involving two decision variables. Computer software packages are designed to handle linear programs involving large numbers of variables and constraints. In this section we discuss the formulation and computer solution of a linear program involving four decision variables. As we will see, the approach to problem formulation and computer solution is essentially the same as for problems with two decision variables. After obtaining a verbal statement of the problem, we define the decision variables that will enable us to write the objective function and constraints associated with the problem as a linear program. Once the problem has been formulated, we can use a computer software package such as LINDO/PC to obtain the optimal solution.

The Electronic Communications, Inc. Problem

Electronic Communications, Inc. manufactures portable radio systems that can be used for two-way communications. The company's new product, which has a range of up to 25 miles, is particularly suitable for use in a variety of business and personal applications. The distribution channels for the new radio are as follows:

1. Marine equipment distributors
2. Business equipment distributors
3. National retail chain
4. Mail order

Because of differing distribution and promotional costs, the profitability of the product will vary with the distribution channel. In addition, the advertising cost and the personal sales effort required will also vary with the distribution channels. Table 8.1 summarizes the profit, advertising cost, and personal sales effort data pertaining to the Electronic Communications problem. Additional facts are that the firm has set the advertising budget at $5000 and that there is a maximum of 1800 hours of sales force time available for allocation to the sales effort. Management has also decided to produce exactly 600 units

Table 8.1
Profit, Advertising Cost, and Personal Sales Time Data for the Electronic Communications, Inc. Problem

Distribution Channel	Profit per Unit Sold	Advertising Cost per Unit Sold	Personal Sales Effort per Unit Sold
Marine distributor	$90	$10	2 hours
Business distributor	$84	$ 8	3 hours
National retail chain	$70	$ 9	3 hours
Mail order	$60	$15	None

for the current production period. Finally, an ongoing contract with the national chain of retail stores requires that at least 150 units be distributed through this distribution channel.

Electronic Communications, Inc. is now faced with the problem of establishing a strategy that will provide for the distribution of the radios in such a way that overall profitability of the new radio production will be maximized. Decisions must be made as to how many units should be allocated to each of the four distribution channels, as well as how to allocate the advertising budget and sales force effort to each of the four distribution channels.

Formulation of the Electronic Communications, Inc. Problem

To formulate a linear programming model for the Electronic Communications, Inc. problem, we introduce the following four decision variables:

x_1 = the number of units produced for the marine equipment distribution channel
x_2 = the number of units produced for the business equipment distribution channel
x_3 = the number of units produced for the national retail chain distribution channel
x_4 = the number of units produced for the mail order distribution channel

Using the data in Table 8.1, the objective function for maximizing the profit associated with the radios can be written as follows:

$$\max 90x_1 + 84x_2 + 70x_3 + 60x_4$$

Let us now proceed to formulate the constraints for the problem. Since the advertising budget has been set at $5000, the constraint that limits the amount of advertising expenditure can be written as follows:

$$10x_1 + 8x_2 + 9x_3 + 15x_4 \leq 5000$$

Similarly, since the sales time is limited to 1800 hours, we obtain the constraint

$$2x_1 + 3x_2 + 3x_3 \leq 1800$$

Management's decision to produce exactly 600 units during the current production period is expressed as

$$1x_1 + 1x_2 + 1x_3 + 1x_4 = 600$$

Finally, to account for the fact that the number of units distributed by the national retail chain stores must be at least 150, we add the constraint

$$1x_3 \geq 150$$

Combining all of the constraints with the nonnegativity requirements enables us to write the complete linear programming model for the Electronic Communications, Inc. problem as follows:

$$\max \quad 90x_1 + 84x_2 + 70x_3 + 60x_4$$

s.t.

$10x_1 +$	$8x_2 +$	$9x_3 +$	$15x_4$	≤ 5000	Advertising budget
$2x_1 +$	$3x_2 +$	$3x_3$		≤ 1800	Sales force availability
$1x_1 +$	$1x_2 +$	$1x_3 +$	$1x_4 =$	600	Production level
		$1x_3$		≥ 150	Retail stores requirement

$$x_1, x_2, x_3, x_4 \geq 0$$

Computer Solution and Interpretation for the Electronic-Communications, Inc. Problem

A portion of the output from the LINDO/PC computer solution of the Electronic Communications problem is shown in Figure 8.7. The OBJECTIVE FUNCTION VALUE

```
              OBJECTIVE FUNCTION VALUE

       1)         48450.0000

       VARIABLE         VALUE          REDUCED COST
           X1         25.000000            .000000
           X2        425.000000            .000000
           X3        150.000000            .000000
           X4           .000000          45.000000

          ROW    SLACK OR SURPLUS      DUAL PRICES
            2)          .000000          3.000000
            3)        25.000000           .000000
            4)          .000000         60.000000
            5)          .000000        -17.000000
```

Figure 8.7
A Portion of the Computer Output for the Electronic Communications, Inc. Problem

section shows that the optimal solution to the problem will provide a maximum profit of $48,450. The optimal values of the decision variables are given by $x_1 = 25$, $x_2 = 425$, $x_3 = 150$, and $x_4 = 0$. Thus, the optimal strategy for Electronic Communications is to concentrate on the business equipment distribution channel with $x_2 = 425$ units. In addition, the firm should allocate 25 units to the marine equipment distribution channel ($x_1 = 25$) and meet its 150-unit commitment to the national retail chain distribution channel ($x_3 = 150$). With $x_4 = 0$, the optimal solution indicates that the firm should not use the mail order distribution channel.

Let us now look at the information contained in the column labeled "REDUCED COST." Recall that the reduced costs indicate how much each objective function coefficient would have to improve before the corresponding decision variable could assume a positive value in the optimal solution. As the computer output shows, the first three reduced costs are zero since the corresponding decision variables already have positive values in the optimal solution. However, the reduced cost of 45 for decision variable x_4 tells us that the profit for the new radios distributed via the mail order distribution channel would have to increase from its current value of $60 per unit to at least $60 + $45 = $105 per unit before it would be profitable to begin using the mail order distribution channel.

The computer output information on the slack/surplus variables and the dual prices is restated below.

Row	Constraint	Type of Constraint	Slack or Surplus	Dual Price
2	Advertising budget	$\leq$	0	3
3	Sales force availability	$\leq$	25	0
4	Production level	$=$	0	60
5	Retail chain requirement	$\geq$	0	-17

We see that the advertising budget constraint has a slack of zero, indicating that the entire budget of $5000 has been used. The corresponding dual price of 3 tells us that an additional dollar added to the advertising budget will improve the objective function (increase the profit) by $3. Thus the possibility of increasing the advertising budget should be seriously considered by the firm. The slack of 25 hours for the sales force availability constraint shows that the allocated 1800 hours of sales time are adequate to distribute the radios produced and that 25 hours of sales force time will remain unused. Since the production level constraint is an equality, the zero slack/surplus shown on the output is expected. However, the dual price of 60 associated with this constraint shows that if the firm will consider increasing the production level for the radios, the value of the objective function, or profit, will improve at the rate of $60 per radio produced. Finally, the surplus of zero associated with the retail chain distribution channel commitment is a result of this constraint being binding. The negative dual price indicates that increasing the commitment from 150 to 151 units will actually decrease the profit by $17. Thus Electronic Communications may want to consider reducing its commitment to the retail chain distribution channel. A *decrease* in the commitment will actually improve profit at the rate of $17 per unit.

Let us now consider the additional sensitivity analysis information provided by the computer output shown in Figure 8.8. Adding the ALLOWABLE INCREASE and subtracting the ALLOWABLE DECREASE values from the current objective function coefficients provides the following ranges of optimality for the objective function coefficients:

$$84 \leq c_1 < \infty$$
$$50 \leq c_2 \leq 90$$
$$-\infty < c_3 \leq 87$$
$$-\infty < c_4 \leq 105$$

Thus the current solution, or strategy, remains optimal, provided that the objective function coefficients remain in the above ranges of optimality. Note in particular the range of optimality associated with the mail order distribution channel coefficient c_4. This information is consistent with the earlier observation for the REDUCED COST portion of the output. In both instances we see that the per-unit profit would have to increase to \$105 before the mail order distribution channel could be in the optimal solution with a positive value.

```
                        OBJ COEFFICIENT RANGES
    VARIABLE        CURRENT        ALLOWABLE       ALLOWABLE
                     COEF          INCREASE        DECREASE
       X1          90.000000       INFINITY         6.000000
       X2          84.000000       6.000000        34.000000
       X3          70.000000      17.000000        INFINITY
       X4          60.000000      45.000000        INFINITY

                        RIGHTHAND SIDE RANGES
     ROW           CURRENT        ALLOWABLE       ALLOWABLE
                     RHS          INCREASE        DECREASE
       2         5000.000000      850.000000       50.000000
       3         1800.000000      INFINITY         25.000000
       4          600.000000       3.571429        85.000000
       5          150.000000      50.000000       150.000000
```

Figure 8.8
Objective Function Coefficient and Right-Hand Side Ranges for the Electronic Communications, Inc. Problem

Finally, the sensitivity analysis information on RIGHTHAND SIDE RANGES, as shown in Figure 8.8, can be used to compute the ranges of feasibility for the right-hand-side values. Adding the ALLOWABLE INCREASE and subtracting the ALLOWABLE DECREASE from the current right-hand-side values provides the following ranges of feasibility:

Constraint	Min RHS	Max RHS
Advertising budget	4950	5850
Sales force	1775	∞
Production level	515	603.57
Retail chain requirement	0	200

Several interpretations of the above ranges are possible. In particular, recall that the dual price for advertising budget enabled us to conclude that each $1 increase in the budget would improve the profit by $3. The above range for the advertising budget shows that this statement about the value of increasing the budget is appropriate up to an advertising budget of $5850. Increases above this level would not necessarily be beneficial. Also note that the dual price of -17 for the retail chain requirement suggested the desirability of reducing this commitment. The above range of feasibility for this constraint shows that the commitment could be reduced to zero and the value of the reduction would be at the rate of $17 per unit.

Let us again point out that the sensitivity analysis or postoptimality analysis provided by computer software packages for linear programming problems considers only *one change at a time*, with all other coefficients of the problem remaining as originally specified. As mentioned earlier, simultaneous changes can sometimes be analyzed without resolving the problem, provided that the cumulative changes are not large enough to violate the 100 percent rule.

Finally, recall that the complete solution to the Electronic Communications problem requested information not only on the number of units to be distributed over each channel but also the allocation of the advertising budget and the sales force effort to each distribution channel. Since the optimal solution is $x_1 = 25$, $x_2 = 425$, $x_3 = 150$, and $x_4 = 0$, we can simply evaluate each term in a given constraint to determine how much of the constraint resource is allocated to each distribution channel. For example, the advertising budget constraint of

$$10x_1 + 8x_2 + 9x_3 + 15x_4 \leq 5000$$

shows $10x_1 = 10(25) = \$250$, $8x_2 = 8(425) = \$3400$, $9x_3 = 9(150) = \$1350$, and $15x_4 = 15(0) = \$0$. Thus the advertising budget allocations are, respectively, $250, $3400, $1350, and $0 for each of the four distribution channels. Making similar calculations for the sales force constraint enables the managerial summary of the Electronic Communications optimal solution as shown in Table 8.2.

Summary

In this chapter we have presented the important concepts of sensitivity analysis and the computer solution of linear programming problems. We first considered graphical sensitivity analysis in order to demonstrate how a change in a coefficient of the objective function or in the right-hand-side value for a constraint can affect the optimal solution to the problem. Methods were introduced for finding the ranges of optimality for the

Table 8.2
Profit Maximizing Strategy for the Electronic Communications, Inc. Problem

Distribution Channel	Volume	Advertising Allocation	Sales Force Allocation (hours)
Marine distributor	25	$ 250	50
Business distributor	425	$3400	1275
National retail chain	150	$1350	450
Mail order	0	0	0
Totals	600	$5000	1775

Projected total profit = $48,450

objective function coefficients and the ranges of feasibility for the right-hand sides of the constraints. The concept of a shadow price was introduced as a measure of the change in the value of the objective function per unit increase in the right-hand side of a constraint. In cases where the constraint involves a limit on an available resource, the shadow price provides important information that helps to determine the desirability of obtaining additional units of the resource.

Sensitivity analysis is conducted after the optimal solution to the original linear programming problem has been obtained. For this reason sensitivity analysis is often referred to as postoptimality analysis. The standard sensitivity analysis procedures are based on the assumption that only one of the coefficients of the problem changes; all other coefficients are assumed to be held constant at their initial values. It is possible to do some limited sensitivity analysis on the effect of changing more than one coefficient at a time. For two-variable problems the effect of both objective function coefficients changing can be determined by recomputing the slope $(-c_1/c_2)$. For larger problems the effect of simultaneous changes can be determined by using the 100% rule.

Since the graphical method and graphical sensitivity analysis are limited to linear programs with two decision variables, a computer solution procedure was presented as a practical method of solving linear programming problems with any number of decision variables. Although many software packages are available for computer solution (including the authors' *The Management Scientist*), we selected the LINDO/PC package to illustrate linear programming solutions on a microcomputer. We demonstrated the ''user-friendly'' aspect of the data input. Then we showed the computer output for three example problems in order to demonstrate the use and interpretation of the results. In addition to the value of the objective function and the optimal values of the decision variables, the computer output provides a variety of additional information concerning slack variables, surplus variables, and dual prices, as well as objective function coefficient and right-hand-side ranges.

Glossary

Sensitivity analysis The evaluation of how changes in the coefficients of a linear programming problem affect the optimal solution to the problem.

Postoptimality analysis Another name for sensitivity analysis, indicating that the analysis is performed after the optimal solution to the original linear programming problem has been obtained.

Range of optimality The range of values over which an objective function coefficient may vary without causing any change in the values of the decision variables in the optimal solution.

Shadow price The change in the value of the objective function per unit increase in the value of the right-hand side associated with a constraint.

Dual price The improvement in the value of the objective function per unit increase in a constraint right-hand-side value. In a maximization problem the dual price is the same as the shadow price. In a minimization problem the dual price is the negative of the shadow price.

Range of feasibility The range over which a right-hand-side value may vary without changing the value and interpretation of the dual or shadow price.

100% rule A rule indicating when simultaneous changes in two or more objective function coefficients will not cause a change in the optimal values for the decision variables. It can also be applied to indicate when two or more right-hand-side changes will not cause a change in any of the dual prices.

Problems

1. Recall the Par, Inc. problem (Chapter 7, problem 13). Letting

$$x_1 = \text{number of standard bags produced}$$
$$x_2 = \text{number of deluxe bags produced}$$

leads to the following formulation of the Par, Inc. problem:

$$
\begin{array}{lll}
\max & 10x_1 + 9x_2 & \\
\text{s.t.} & & \\
& \tfrac{7}{10}x_1 + 1x_2 \leq 630 & \text{Cutting and dyeing time} \\
& \tfrac{1}{2}x_1 + \tfrac{5}{6}x_2 \leq 600 & \text{Sewing time} \\
& 1x_1 + \tfrac{2}{3}x_2 \leq 708 & \text{Finishing time} \\
& \tfrac{1}{10}x_1 + \tfrac{1}{4}x_2 \leq 135 & \text{Inspection and packaging time} \\
& x_1, \; x_2 \geq 0 &
\end{array}
$$

Use the graphical sensitivity analysis approach to determine the range of optimality for the objective function coefficients.

2. Refer to the Par, Inc. situation in problem 1. Suppose that an additional 10 hours of cutting and dyeing time becomes available. Determine the new optimal solution and the value of the shadow price for the constraint.

3. Consider the linear program given below.

$$\max \quad 2x_1 + 3x_2$$

s.t.

$$x_1 + x_2 \leq 10$$
$$2x_1 + x_2 \geq 4$$
$$x_1 + 3x_2 \leq 24$$
$$2x_1 + x_2 \leq 16$$
$$x_1, x_2 \geq 0$$

a. Solve this problem using the graphical solution procedure.
b. Compute the range of optimality for c_1.
c. Compute the range of optimality for c_2.
d. Suppose that c_1 is increased from 2 to 2.5. What is the new optimal solution?
e. Suppose that c_2 is decreased from 3 to 1. What is the new optimal solution?

4. Refer again to problem 3.
a. Compute the shadow prices for constraints 1 and 2 and interpret them.
b. What are the dual prices for constraints 1 and 2? Interpret them.

5. Consider the linear program given below.

$$\min \quad x_1 + x_2$$

s.t.

$$x_1 + 2x_2 \geq 7$$
$$2x_1 + x_2 \geq 5$$
$$x_1 + 6x_2 \geq 11$$
$$x_1, x_2 \geq 0$$

a. Solve this problem using the graphical solution procedure.
b. Compute the range of optimality for c_1.
c. Compute the range of optimality for c_2.
d. Suppose that c_1 is increased to 1.5. Find the new optimal solution.
e. Suppose that c_2 is decreased to $1/3$. Find the new optimal solution.

6. Refer again to problem 5.
a. Compute and interpret the shadow prices for the constraints.
b. What are the dual prices? Interpret them.

7. Consider the linear program given below.

$$\max \quad 5x_1 + 7x_2$$

s.t.

$$2x_1 + x_2 \geq 3$$
$$-x_1 + 5x_2 \geq 4$$
$$2x_1 - 3x_2 \leq 6$$
$$3x_1 + 2x_2 \leq 35$$
$$3/7 x_1 + x_2 \leq 10$$
$$x_1, x_2 \geq 0$$

a. Solve this problem using the graphical solution procedure.
b. Compute the range of optimality for c_1.
c. Compute the range of optimality for c_2.
d. Suppose that c_1 is decreased to 2. What is the new optimal solution?
e. Suppose that c_2 is increased to 10. What is the new optimal solution?

8. Refer again to problem 7 and suppose that the objective function coefficient for c_2 is reduced to 3.
   a. Resolve using the graphical solution procedure.
   b. Compute the dual prices for constraints 2 and 3.

9. Refer again to problem 3.
   a. Suppose that c_1 is increased to 3 and c_2 is increased to 4. Find the new optimal solution.
   b. Suppose that c_1 is increased to 3 and c_2 is decreased to 2. Find the new optimal solution.

10. Refer again to problem 7.
    a. Suppose that c_1 is decreased to 4 and c_2 is increased to 10. Find the new optimal solution.
    b. Suppose that c_1 is decreased to 4 and c_2 is increased to 8. Find the new optimal solution.

11. Recall the Kelson Sporting Equipment problem (Chapter 7, problem 17). Letting

$$x_1 = \text{number of regular gloves}$$
$$x_2 = \text{number of catcher's mitts}$$

leads to the following formulation:

$$\max \quad 5x_1 + 8x_2$$

s.t.

$x_1 + \tfrac{3}{2}x_2 \leq 900$	Cutting and sewing
$\tfrac{1}{2}x_1 + \tfrac{1}{3}x_2 \leq 300$	Finishing
$\tfrac{1}{8}x_1 + \tfrac{1}{4}x_2 \leq 100$	Packaging and shipping
$x_1, x_2 \geq 0$	

The LINDO/PC computer solution of this problem is shown in Figure 8.9.
   a. What is the optimal solution and what is the value of the profit contribution?
   b. Which constraints are binding?
   c. What are the dual prices for the resources? Interpret each.
   d. If overtime can be scheduled in one of the departments, where would you recommend doing so?

12. Refer again to the computer solution of the Kelson Sporting Equipment problem in Figure 8.9 (see problem 11 above).
    a. Compute the ranges of optimality for the objective function coefficients.
    b. Interpret the ranges in part (a) for the Kelson problem.
    c. Compute the range of feasibility for the right-hand sides.
    d. How much will the value of the optimal solution improve if 20 extra hours of packaging and shipping time are made available?

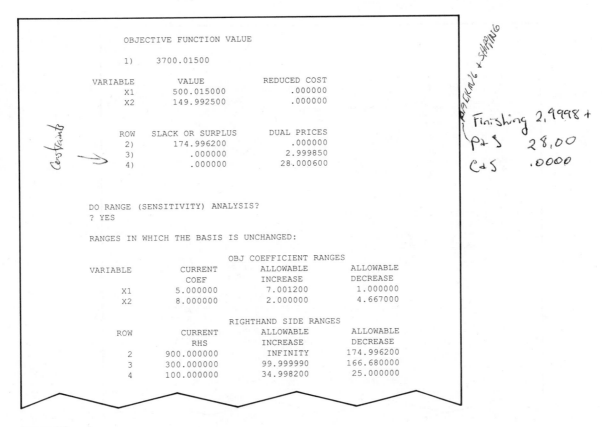

Figure 8.9
LINDO/PC Solution of Kelson Sporting Equipment Problem

13. Recall the Investment Advisors problem (Chapter 7, problem 20). Letting

$$x_1 = \text{shares of U.S. Oil}$$
$$x_2 = \text{shares of Hub Properties}$$

leads to the following formulation:

max	$3x_1 +$	$5x_2$	Maximize annual return
s.t.			
	$25x_1 +$	$50x_2 \leq 80{,}000$	Funds available
	$0.50x_1 +$	$0.25x_2 \leq 700$	Risk maximum
	$1x_1$	$\leq 1{,}000$	U.S. Oil maximum
	$x_1, x_2 \geq 0$		

The LINDO/PC computer solution of this problem is shown in Figure 8.10.
a. What is the optimal solution and what is the value of the total estimated annual return?

```
            OBJECTIVE FUNCTION VALUE

        1)     8400.00000

   VARIABLE          VALUE           REDUCED COST
       X1        800.000000            .000000
       X2       1200.000000            .000000


     ROW    SLACK OR SURPLUS       DUAL PRICES
      2)          .000000            .093333
      3)          .000000           1.333333
      4)        200.000000            .000000



  DO RANGE (SENSITIVITY) ANALYSIS?
  ? YES

  RANGES IN WHICH THE BASIS IS UNCHANGED:

                        OBJ COEFFICIENT RANGES
   VARIABLE         CURRENT        ALLOWABLE         ALLOWABLE
                     COEF          INCREASE          DECREASE
       X1          3.000000        7.000000           .500000
       X2          5.000000        1.000000          3.500000

                        RIGHTHAND SIDE RANGES
     ROW          CURRENT         ALLOWABLE         ALLOWABLE
                    RHS           INCREASE          DECREASE
      2        80000.000000     60000.000000     15000.000000
      3          700.000000        75.000000       300.000000
      4         1000.000000       INFINITY         200.000000
```

Figure 8.10
LINDO/PC Solution of Investment Advisors Problem

    b. Which constraints are binding? What is your interpretation of this in terms of the problem?

    c. What are the dual prices for the constraints? Interpret each.

    d. Would it be beneficial to relax the constraint on the amount invested in U.S. Oil? Why or why not?

14. Refer again to Figure 8.10, which shows the computer solution of problem 13.

    a. How much would the estimated per-share return for U.S. Oil have to increase before it would be beneficial to increase the investment in this stock?

    b. How much would the estimated per-share return for Hub Properties have to decrease before it would be beneficial to reduce the investment in this stock?

    c. How much would the total annual return be reduced if the U.S. Oil maximum were reduced to 900 shares?

15. Recall the Wilkinson Motors problem (Chapter 7, problem 31). Letting

$$x_1 = \text{number of automobiles}$$
$$x_2 = \text{number of station wagons}$$

leads to the following formulation:

$$\max \quad 400x_1 + 500x_2 \qquad \text{Maximize profit contribution}$$

s.t.

$$
\begin{aligned}
2x_1 + 3x_2 &\leq 900 &\quad \text{Dealer preparation time}\\
1x_1 \quad\quad &\leq 300 &\quad \text{Auto limit}\\
1x_2 &\leq 150 &\quad \text{Wagon limit}
\end{aligned}
$$

$$x_1, x_2 \geq 0$$

The LINDO/PC computer solution of this problem is shown in Figure 8.11.

a. How many regular automobiles and station wagons should Wilkinson order? What will the profit contribution be if all the units ordered are sold?

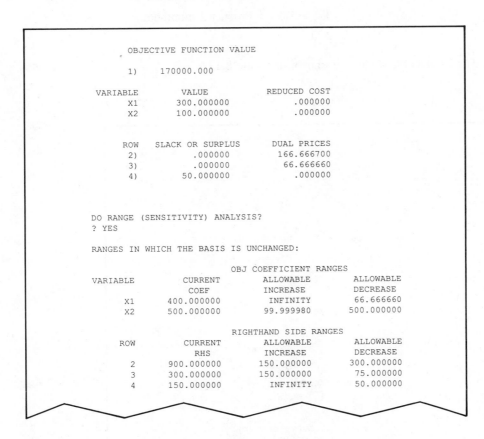

Figure 8.11
LINDO/PC Solution of Wilkinson Motors Problem

b. How much would the profit contribution of the regular automobiles have to decrease before Wilkinson would consider modifying its optimal solution?   *more than 66.67*

c. Should Wilkinson consider raising the limit on the number of station wagons ordered beyond 150?

d. If the profit contribution for regular automobiles is reduced by $30 and the profit contribution for station wagons is increased by $50, should Wilkinson consider changing the order? Explain.

16. Recall the Photo Chemicals problem (Chapter 7, problem 29). Letting

$$x_1 = \text{gallons of product 1 produced}$$
$$x_2 = \text{gallons of product 2 produced}$$

leads to the following formulation:

$$\min \quad 1x_1 + 1x_2 \qquad \text{Minimize production cost}$$

s.t.

$$1x_1 + 2x_2 \geq 80 \qquad \text{Raw material}$$
$$1x_1 \qquad\quad \geq 30 \qquad \text{Product 1 minimum}$$
$$1x_2 \geq 20 \qquad \text{Product 2 minimum}$$
$$x_1, \; x_2 \geq 0$$

The LINDO/PC solution is shown in Figure 8.12.

```
        OBJECTIVE FUNCTION VALUE

    1)      55.0000000

VARIABLE         VALUE          REDUCED COST
    X1          30.000000          .000000
    X2          25.000000          .000000


    ROW    SLACK OR SURPLUS      DUAL PRICES
    2)           .000000          -.500000
    3)           .000000          -.500000
    4)          5.000000           .000000




DO RANGE (SENSITIVITY) ANALYSIS?
? YES

RANGES IN WHICH THE BASIS IS UNCHANGED:

                      OBJ COEFFICIENT RANGES
VARIABLE         CURRENT        ALLOWABLE      ALLOWABLE
                  COEF          INCREASE       DECREASE
    X1          1.000000        INFINITY        .500000
    X2          1.000000        1.000000       1.000000

                      RIGHTHAND SIDE RANGES
    ROW          CURRENT        ALLOWABLE      ALLOWABLE
                  RHS           INCREASE       DECREASE
     2          80.000000       INFINITY       10.000000
     3          30.000000       10.000000      30.000000
     4          20.000000        5.000000       INFINITY
```

Figure 8.12
LINDO/PC Solution of Photo Chemicals Problem

a. What is the optimal solution and what is minimum production cost?
b. Compute the range of optimality for the objective function coefficients.
c. What are the dual prices for each constraint? Interpret each.
d. What are the shadow prices for each constraint?
e. If the amount of raw material to be processed were increased from 80 to 85 gallons, how would the optimal solution change?
f. Compute the range of feasibility for each of the right-hand-side values.

17. Recall the M&D Chemicals problem (Chapter 7, problem 22). Letting

$$x_1 = \text{gallons of product 1 produced}$$
$$x_2 = \text{gallons of product 2 produced}$$

leads to the following formulation:

$$\min 2x_1 + 3x_2$$

s.t.

$1x_1$		≥ 125	Demand for product 1
$1x_1 + 1x_2$		≥ 350	Total production requirement
$2x_1 + 1x_2$		≤ 600	Processing time limitation
$x_1, x_2 \geq 0$			

The LINDO/PC solution is shown in Figure 8.13.
a. What is the optimal solution and what is the minimum production cost?
b. Compute the range of optimality for the objective function coefficients.
c. What are the dual prices for each constraint? Interpret each.
d. What are the shadow prices for each constraint?
e. If the total production requirement were increased from 350 to 450 gallons, how would the value of the optimal solution change?
f. Compute the range of feasibility for the right-hand-side values.

18. Suppose that in a product-mix problem $x_1, x_2, x_3,$ and x_4 indicate the units of products 1, 2, 3, and 4, respectively, and the linear program is

$$\max \quad 4x_1 + 6x_2 + 3x_3 + 1x_4$$

s.t.

$1.5x_1 + 2x_2 + 4x_3 + 3x_4 \leq 550$		Machine A hours
$4x_1 + 1x_2 + 2x_3 + 1x_4 \leq 700$		Machine B hours
$2x_1 + 3x_2 + 1x_3 + 2x_4 \leq 200$		Machine C hours
$x_1, x_2, x_3, x_4 \geq 0$		

The computer solution developed using LINDO/PC is shown in Figure 8.14.
a. What is the optimal solution and what is the value of the objective function?
b. Which constraints are binding?
c. Which machines have excess capacity available? How much?
d. If the objective function coefficient of x_1 is increased by 0.50, will the optimal solution change?

```
              OBJECTIVE FUNCTION VALUE

   1)          800.000000

   VARIABLE          VALUE        REDUCED COST
       X1          250.000000        .000000
       X2          100.000000        .000000


       ROW     SLACK OR SURPLUS     DUAL PRICES
        2)        125.000000          .000000
        3)           .000000        -4.000000
        4)           .000000         1.000000



   DO RANGE (SENSITIVITY) ANALYSIS?
   ? YES


   RANGES IN WHICH THE BASIS IS UNCHANGED:

                           OBJ COEFFICIENT RANGES
   VARIABLE        CURRENT       ALLOWABLE        ALLOWABLE
                    COEF         INCREASE         DECREASE
       X1         2.000000       1.000000         INFINITY
       X2         3.000000       INFINITY         1.000000

                           RIGHTHAND SIDE RANGES
   ROW             CURRENT       ALLOWABLE        ALLOWABLE
                     RHS         INCREASE         DECREASE
        2         125.000000     125.000000       INFINITY
        3         350.000000     125.000000       50.000000
        4         600.000000     100.000000       125.000000
```

Figure 8.13
LINDO/PC Solution of M & D Chemicals Problem

19. Refer again to the LINDO/PC solution of problem 18 in Figure 8.14.
   a. Compute the range of optimality for each objective function coefficient.
   b. Suppose that the objective function coefficient for x_1 is decreased by 3, the objective function coefficient of x_2 is increased by 1.5, and the objective function coefficient for x_4 is increased by 1. What will the new optimal solution be?
   c. Compute the range of feasibility for the right-hand-side values.
   d. If the number of hours available on machine A is increased by 300, will the dual price for that constraint change?

20. Consider the following linear program and the LINDO/PC computer solution shown in Figure 8.15.

$$\min \quad 15x_1 + 15x_2 + 16x_3$$
$$\text{s.t.}$$
$$1x_1 \qquad + \quad 1x_3 \leq 30$$
$$0.5x_1 - \quad 1x_2 + \quad 6x_3 \geq 15$$
$$3x_1 + \quad 4x_2 - \quad 1x_3 \geq 20$$
$$x_1, x_2, x_3 \geq 0$$

```
        OBJECTIVE FUNCTION VALUE

    1)     525.000000

 VARIABLE          VALUE          REDUCED COST
       X1          .000000           .050000
       X2        25.000000           .000000
       X3       125.000000           .000000
       X4          .000000          3.500000


   ROW    SLACK OR SURPLUS       DUAL PRICES
    2)          .000000             .300000
    3)       425.000000             .000000
    4)          .000000            1.800000



DO RANGE (SENSITIVITY) ANALYSIS?
? YES

RANGES IN WHICH THE BASIS IS UNCHANGED:

                          OBJ COEFFICIENT RANGES
 VARIABLE          CURRENT         ALLOWABLE        ALLOWABLE
                   COEF            INCREASE         DECREASE
       X1        4.000000           .050000         INFINITY
       X2        6.000000          3.000000          .076923
       X3        3.000000          9.000000          .999999
       X4        1.000000          3.500000         INFINITY

                          RIGHTHAND SIDE RANGES
   ROW            CURRENT         ALLOWABLE        ALLOWABLE
                   RHS             INCREASE         DECREASE
    2            550.000000       250.000000       416.666700
    3            700.000000        INFINITY        425.000000
    4            200.000000       625.000000        62.500000
```

Figure 8.14
LINDO/PC Solution of Problem 18

a. What is the optimal solution and what is the optimal value for the objective function?
b. Which constraints are binding?
c. What are the dual prices? Interpret each.
d. What are the shadow prices?
e. If you could change the right-hand side of one constraint by 1 unit, which one would you choose? What would be the new value of the right-hand side?

21. Refer again to the LINDO/PC solution of problem 20 in Figure 8.15.
   a. Develop and interpret the ranges of optimality for the objective function coefficients.
   b. Suppose that c_1 is increased by 0.25. What is the new optimal solution?
   c. Suppose that c_1 is increased by 0.25 and c_2 is decreased by 0.25. What is the new optimal solution?

22. Supersport Footballs, Inc. has the problem of determining the best number of All-Pro (x_1), College (x_2), and High-School (x_3) models of footballs to produce in order

```
                OBJECTIVE FUNCTION VALUE

        1)     139.729700

   VARIABLE          VALUE          REDUCED COST
     X1            7.297297            .000000
     X2             .000000            .675674
     X3            1.891892            .000000


     ROW    SLACK OR SURPLUS       DUAL PRICES
      2)        20.810810            .000000
      3)          .000000          -3.405405
      4)          .000000          -4.432433



DO RANGE (SENSITIVITY) ANALYSIS?
? YES

RANGES IN WHICH THE BASIS IS UNCHANGED:

                         OBJ COEFFICIENT RANGES
   VARIABLE        CURRENT        ALLOWABLE        ALLOWABLE
                     COEF         INCREASE         DECREASE
     X1          15.000000         .543477        13.666670
     X2          15.000000        INFINITY          .675674
     X3          16.000000       164.000000        2.499995

                         RIGHTHAND SIDE RANGES
     ROW         CURRENT        ALLOWABLE        ALLOWABLE
                   RHS          INCREASE         DECREASE
      2          30.000000       INFINITY        20.810810
      3          15.000000       96.249990       11.666670
      4          20.000000       70.000000       22.500000
```

Figure 8.15
LINDO/PC Solution of Problem 20

to maximize profits. Constraints include production capacity limitations in each of three departments (cutting and dyeing, sewing, and inspection and packaging) as well as a constraint that requires production of at least 1000 All-Pro footballs. The linear programming model of Supersport's problem is shown below:

$$\max \quad 3x_1 + 5x_2 + 4x_3$$

s.t.

$$12x_1 + 10x_2 + 8x_3 \leq 18{,}000 \quad \text{Cutting and dyeing time}$$
$$15x_1 + 15x_2 + 12x_3 \leq 18{,}000 \quad \text{Sewing time}$$
$$3x_1 + 4x_2 + 2x_3 \leq 9{,}000 \quad \text{Inspection and packaging time}$$
$$1x_1 \qquad\qquad\qquad \geq 1{,}000 \quad \text{All-Pro model}$$
$$x_1, x_2, x_3 \geq 0$$

The LINDO/PC solution to the Supersport problem is shown in Figure 8.16.

a. How many footballs of each type should Supersport produce in order to maximize the profit contribution?

```
              OBJECTIVE FUNCTION VALUE

         1)     4000.00000

    VARIABLE         VALUE          REDUCED COST
         X1       1000.000000          .000000
         X2           .000000          .000000
         X3        250.000000          .000000


      ROW     SLACK OR SURPLUS     DUAL PRICES
       2)       4000.000000          .000000
       3)           .000000          .333333
       4)       5500.000000          .000000
       5)           .000000        -2.000000



    DO RANGE (SENSITIVITY) ANALYSIS?
    ? YES

    RANGES IN WHICH THE BASIS IS UNCHANGED:

                          OBJ COEFFICIENT RANGES
    VARIABLE         CURRENT        ALLOWABLE       ALLOWABLE
                      COEF          INCREASE        DECREASE
       X1          3.000000        2.000000        INFINITY
       X2          5.000000         .000000        INFINITY
       X3          4.000000        INFINITY         .000000

                          RIGHTHAND SIDE RANGES
      ROW         CURRENT          ALLOWABLE       ALLOWABLE
                   RHS             INCREASE        DECREASE
       2        18000.000000       INFINITY       4000.000000
       3        18000.000000      6000.000000     3000.000000
       4         9000.000000       INFINITY       5500.000000
       5         1000.000000       200.000000     1000.000000
```

Figure 8.16
LINDO/PC Solution of Supersport Footballs Problem

b. Which constraints are binding?

c. Interpret the slack and/or surplus in each constraint.

d. Compute and interpret the range of optimality for the profit contribution of the three footballs.

23. Refer again to the computer solution of problem 22 (see Figure 8.16).

   a. Overtime rates in the sewing department are $12 per hour. Would you recommend that the company consider using overtime in that department? Explain.

   b. What is the shadow price for the fourth constraint? Interpret its value for management.

   c. Note that the reduced cost for x_2 is zero, but x_2 is not in solution at a positive value. What is your interpretation of this?

   d. Suppose that the profit contribution of the College ball is increased by $1. How do you expect the solution to change?

Note: Problems 24 and 25 and the case problem require computer solution and interpretation of the results.

24. A manufacturer makes three components for sale to refrigeration companies. The components are processed on two machines: a shaper and a grinder. The times (in minutes) required on each machine are given below.

	Machine	
Component	Shaper	Grinder
1	6	4
2	4	5
3	4	2

The shaper is available for 120 hours and the grinder is available for 110 hours. No more than 200 units of component 3 can be sold, but up to 1000 units of each of the other components can be sold. In fact the company already has orders for 600 units of component 1 that must be satisfied. The profit contribution for components 1, 2, and 3 are $8, $6, and $9, respectively.

   a. Formulate and solve for the recommended production quantities. Use any computer code available.

   b. What is the range of optimality for the profit contributions of the three components? Interpret these ranges for company management.

   c. What is the range of feasibility for the right-hand sides? Interpret these ranges for company management.

   d. If more time could be made available on the grinder, how much would it be worth?

   e. If more units of component 3 can be sold by reducing the sales price by $4, should the company reduce the price?

25. The Pfeiffer Company manages approximately $15 million for clients. For each client Pfeiffer chooses a mix of three investment vehicles: a growth stock fund, an income fund, and a money market fund. Each client has different investment objectives and tolerance for risk. In order to accommodate these differences, Pfeiffer places limits on the percentage of each portfolio that may be invested in the three funds and assigns a portfolio risk index to each client.

   Here's how the system works for Dennis Hartmann, one of Pfeiffer's clients. Based on an evaluation of Hartmann's risk tolerance, Pfeiffer has assigned Hartmann's portfolio a risk index of 0.05. Furthermore, to maintain diversity, the fraction of Hartmann's portfolio invested in the growth and income funds must be at least 10% for each, and at least 20% must be in the money market fund.

   The risk ratings for the growth, income, and money market funds are 0.10, 0.05, and 0.01, respectively. A portfolio risk index is computed as a weighted average of the risk ratings for the three funds where the weights are the fraction of the portfolio invested in each of the funds. Hartmann has given Pfeiffer $300,000 to manage. Pfeiffer is currently forecasting a yield of 20% on the growth fund, 10% on the income fund, and 6% on the money market fund.

   a. Develop a linear programming model to select the best mix of investments for Hartmann's portfolio.

   b. Use any linear programming computer code to solve the model you developed in part (a).

c. How much may the yields on the three funds vary before it will be necessary for Pfeiffer to modify Hartmann's portfolio?

d. If Hartmann were more risk-tolerant, how much of a yield increase could he expect? For instance, what if his portfolio risk index is increased to 0.06?

e. If Pfeiffer revised his yield estimate for the growth fund downward to 0.10, how would you recommend modifying Hartmann's portfolio?

f. What information must Pfeiffer maintain on each client in order to use this system to manage client portfolios?

g. On a weekly basis Pfeiffer revises the yield estimates for the three funds. Suppose that Pfeiffer has 50 clients. Describe how you would envision Pfeiffer making weekly modifications in each client's portfolio and deciding how to allocate the total funds managed among the three investment funds.

Case Problem
Product Mix

TJ's, Inc. makes three nut mixes for sale to grocery chains located in the Southeast. The three mixes, referred to as the Regular Mix, the Deluxe Mix, and the Holiday Mix, are made by mixing together different percentages of five types of nuts.

In preparation for the fall season, TJ's has just purchased the following shipments of nuts at the prices shown:

Type of Nut	Amount (pounds)	Cost per Shipment
Almonds	6000	$7500
Brazil	7500	$7125
Filberts	7500	$6750
Pecans	6000	$7200
Walnuts	7500	$7875

The Regular Mix consists of 15% almonds, 25% Brazil, 25% filberts, 10% pecans, and 25% walnuts. The Deluxe Mix consists of 20% of each type of nut, and the Holiday Mix consists of 25% almonds, 15% Brazil, 15% filberts, 25% pecans, and 20% walnuts.

TJ's accountant has analyzed the cost of packaging materials, sales price per pound, etc., and determined that the contribution to profit is $1.65 per pound for the Regular Mix, $2.00 per pound for the Deluxe Mix, and $2.25 per pound for the Holiday Mix. These figures do not include the cost of the nuts included in the different mixes because that cost can vary greatly in the commodity markets.

Customer orders already received are summarized below:

Type of Mix	Orders (pounds)
Regular	10,000
Deluxe	3,000
Holiday	5,000

Because demand is running high, it is expected that TJ's will receive many more orders than can be satisfied.

TJ's is committed to using the nuts available to maximize profit over the fall season. But, even if it is not profitable to do so, TJ's president has indicated that the orders already received must be satisfied.

Managerial Report

Perform an analysis of TJ's product mix problem and prepare a report for TJ's president that summarizes your findings. Be sure to include information and analysis on the following:

1. The cost per pound of the nuts included in the Regular, Deluxe, and Holiday mixes.
2. The optimal product mix and profit contribution.
3. Recommendations regarding how profit contribution can be increased if additional quantities of nuts can be purchased.
4. Suppose that an additional 1000 pounds of almonds is available for $1000 from a supplier who overbought. Should TJ's purchase these almonds?
5. Recommendations regarding how profit contribution could be increased (if at all) if TJ's does not satisfy all existing orders.

CHAPTER

9

Linear Programming Applications

Our study thus far has been directed toward understanding linear programming in terms of the graphical solution method, sensitivity analysis, and the interpretation of computer solutions to linear programs. This background is essential for knowing when linear programming is an appropriate problem-solving tool and for interpreting the results of a linear programming solution to a problem. However, the benefits of this study will be realized only by learning how linear programming can be used to solve practical decision-making problems. The purpose of this chapter is to show how a variety of problems can be formulated and solved using linear programming.

There are two ways in which one may develop skills in model building. (In this chapter model building should be taken to mean formulating a linear program that is a "model" of the real-world decision-making problem for which a solution is desired.) The first way is by on-the-job experience. This is essentially a trial-and-error approach and obviously could not be attempted in a textbook. The second way in which one may develop these skills is by studying how others have developed successful models. In this chapter we attempt to help you develop skills along these lines by presenting several reasonably detailed examples of successful linear programming applications. Relatively small problems will be used in the examples, but the principles being demonstrated are applicable to much larger problems.

In practice, linear programming has proved to be one of the most successful quantitative aids for managerial decision making. Numerous applications have been reported in the chemical, airline, steel, paper, petroleum, and other industries. The specific problems studied have included production scheduling, capital budgeting, plant location, transportation, media selection, among many others.

As the variety of the applications mentioned would suggest, linear programming is a flexible problem-solving tool with applications in many disciplines. In this chapter we present introductory applications from the areas of marketing, finance, and production management, as well as other common linear programming applications. Computer solutions, obtained using LINDO/PC, are presented and interpreted for most of the problems.

9.1

MARKETING APPLICATIONS

Media Selection

Media selection applications of linear programming are designed to help marketing managers allocate a fixed advertising budget across various advertising media. Potential media include newspaper, magazine, radio, television, and direct mail. In most of these applications the objective is the maximization of audience exposure. Restrictions on the allowable allocation usually arise through considerations such as company policy, contract requirements, and availability of media. In the application that follows, we illustrate how a media selection problem might be formulated and solved using a linear programming model.

Consider the case of the Relax-and-Enjoy Lake Development Corporation. Relax-and-Enjoy is developing a lakeside community at a privately owned lake and is in the business of selling property for vacation and/or retreat cottages. The primary market for these lakeside lots includes all middle- and upper-income families within approximately 100 miles of the development. Relax-and-Enjoy has employed the advertising firm of Boone, Phillips and Jackson to design the promotional campaign for the project.

After considering possible advertising media and the market to be covered, Boone has made the preliminary recommendation to restrict the first month's advertising to five sources. At the end of the month, Boone will then reevaluate its strategy based on the month's results. Boone has collected data on the number of potential purchase families reached, the cost per advertisement, the maximum number of times each medium is available, and the expected exposure for each of the five media. The expected exposure is measured in terms of an exposure unit, a measure of the relative value of one advertisement in each of the media. These measures, based on Boone's experience in the advertising business, take into account such factors as audience profile (age, income, and education of the audience reached), image presented, and quality of the advertisement. The information collected is presented in Table 9.1.

Relax-and-Enjoy has provided Boone with an advertising budget of $30,000 for the first month's campaign. In addition, Relax-and-Enjoy has imposed the following restrictions on how Boone may allocate these funds: At least 10 television commercials must be used, and at least 50,000 potential purchasers must be reached during the month. In addition, no more than $18,000 may be spent on television advertisements. What advertising media selection plan should the advertising firm recommend?

The first step in formulating a linear programming model of this problem is to define the decision variables. We let

$$x_1 = \text{number of times daytime TV is used}$$
$$x_2 = \text{number of times evening TV is used}$$
$$x_3 = \text{number of times daily newspaper is used}$$

$$x_4 = \text{number of times Sunday newspaper is used}$$
$$x_5 = \text{number of times radio is used}$$

Table 9.1
Advertising Media Alternatives for the Relax-and-Enjoy Lake Development Corporation

Advertising Media	Number of Potential Purchase Families Reached	Cost per Advertisement	Maximum Times Available per Month*	Expected Exposure Units
1. Daytime TV (1 min), station WKLA	1000	$1500	15	65
2. Evening TV (30 sec), station WKLA	2000	$3000	10	90
3. Daily newspaper (full page), *The Morning Journal*	1500	$ 400	25	40
4. Sunday newspaper magazine (½ page color), *The Sunday Press*	2500	$1000	4	60
5. Radio, 8:00 A.M. or 5:00 P.M. news (30 sec), station KNOP	300	$ 100	30	20

*The maximum number of times the medium is available is either the maximum number of times the advertising medium occurs (e.g., four Sundays for medium 4) or the maximum number of times Boone will allow the medium to be used.

With the overall goal of maximizing the expected exposure, the objective function becomes

$$\max 65x_1 + 90x_2 + 40x_3 + 60x_4 + 20x_5$$

The constraints for the model can now be formulated from the information given:

$$
\begin{aligned}
x_1 &\leq 15 \\
x_2 &\leq 10 \\
x_3 &\leq 25 \\
x_4 &\leq 4 \\
x_5 &\leq 30
\end{aligned}
\left.\right\} \text{Availability of media}
$$

$$1500x_1 + 3000x_2 + 400x_3 + 1000x_4 + 100x_5 \leq 30{,}000 \qquad \text{Budget}$$

$$
\begin{aligned}
x_1 + x_2 &\geq 10 \\
1500x_1 + 3000x_2 &\leq 18{,}000
\end{aligned}
\left.\right\} \text{Television restrictions}
$$

$$1000x_1 + 2000x_2 + 1500x_3 + 2500x_4 + 300x_5 \geq 50{,}000 \qquad \text{Audience coverage}$$

$$x_1, x_2, x_3, x_4, x_5 \geq 0$$

The solution to this five-variable, nine-constraint linear programming model is presented in Table 9.2.

Table 9.2
Advertising Plan for the Relax-and-Enjoy Lake Development Corporation

Media	Frequency	Budget
Daytime TV	10	$15,000
Daily newspaper	25	10,000
Sunday newspaper	2	2,000
Radio	30	3,000
		$30,000

Total audience contacted = 61,500
Expected exposure = 2,370

We point out that the above media selection model, probably more than most other linear programming models, requires crucial subjective evaluations as input. The most critical of these inputs is the expected exposure rating measure. While marketing managers may have substantial data concerning expected advertising exposure, the final coefficient that includes image and quality considerations is based primarily on managerial judgment. However, judgment input is a very acceptable way of obtaining necessary data for a linear programming model.

A possible shortcoming of this model is that even if the expected exposure measure were not subject to error, there is no guarantee that maximization of total expected exposure will lead to a maximization of profit or of sales (a common surrogate for profit). However, this is not a shortcoming of linear programming; rather it is a shortcoming of the use of exposure as a criterion. Certainly if we were able to measure directly the effect of an advertisement on profit, we would use total profit as the objective to be maximized.

In addition, you should be aware that the media selection model as formulated in this section does not include considerations such as the following:

1. Reduced exposure value for repeat media usage
2. Cost discounts for repeat media usage
3. Audience overlap by different media
4. Timing recommendations for the advertisements

A more complex formulation—more variables and constraints—can often be used to overcome some of these limitations, but it will not always be possible to overcome all of them with a linear programming model. However, even in these cases a linear programming model can often be used to arrive at an approximation of the best decision. Management evaluation combined with the linear programming solution should then make possible the selection of an overall effective advertising strategy.

Marketing Research

Marketing research is conducted by a variety of organizations in order to learn about consumer characteristics, attitudes, and preferences toward products and/or services offered by an organization. Often the actual research is performed by a marketing research firm that specializes in providing client organizations with the desired market information. Typical services offered by a marketing research firm include designing the study, conducting market surveys, analyzing the data collected, and providing summary reports and recommendations for the client. In the research design phase, targets or quotas may be established for the number and types of respondents to be reached by a survey. With quota guidelines established, the objective of the marketing research firm is to conduct the survey so as to meet the client's needs at a minimum cost.

Market Survey, Inc. (MSI) is a marketing research firm that specializes in evaluating consumer reaction to new products, services, and advertising campaigns. A client firm has requested assistance from MSI in ascertaining consumer reaction to a recently marketed product for household use. During meetings with the client it was agreed that door-to-door, personal interviews would be used to obtain information from both households with children and households without children. In addition, it was agreed that both day and evening interviews would be necessary in order to allow for a variety of household work schedules. Specifically, the client's contract called for MSI to conduct 1000 interviews with the following quota guidelines:

1. At least 400 households with children would be interviewed.
2. At least 400 households without children would be interviewed.
3. The total number of households interviewed during the evening would be at least as great as the number of households interviewed during the day.
4. At least 40% of the interviews for households with children would be conducted during the evening.
5. At least 60% of the interviews for households without children would be conducted during the evening.

Since the interviews of households with children take additional interviewer time, and since evening interviewers are paid more than daytime interviewers, the cost of an interview varies with the type of interview. Based on previous research studies, estimates of the interview costs are as follows:

Household	Interview Cost	
	Day	Evening
Children	$20	$25
No children	$18	$20

What is the household, time-of-day interview plan that will satisfy the contract requirements at a minimum total interviewing cost?

The formulation of a linear programming model for the Market Survey problem is a good opportunity to introduce the use of double-subscripted decision variables. Using x to represent the decision variables, we will use two subscripts for x, with the first subscript indicating whether the interview involves children or not and the second subscript indicating whether the interview is in the day or evening. Using 1 for children and 2 for no children, and 1 for day and 2 for evening, double subscripts can be used to identify the following four decision variables:

$$x_{11} = \text{the number of interviews for households with children to be conducted during the day}$$

$$x_{12} = \text{the number of interviews for households with children to be conducted during the evening}$$

$$x_{21} = \text{the number of interviews for households without children to be conducted during the day}$$

$$x_{22} = \text{the number of interviews for households without children to be conducted during the evening}$$

We begin the linear programming model formulation by using the cost-per-interview data to develop the following objective function:

$$\min 20x_{11} + 25x_{12} + 18x_{21} + 20x_{22}$$

The constraint requiring a total of 1000 interviews is written:

$$x_{11} + x_{12} + x_{21} + x_{22} = 1000$$

The five specifications concerning the types of interviews lead to the following constraints:

1. Households with children:

$$x_{11} + x_{12} \geq 400$$

2. Households without children:

$$x_{21} + x_{22} \geq 400$$

3. At least as many evening interviews as day interviews:

$$x_{12} + x_{22} \geq x_{11} + x_{21}$$

The usual format for linear programming model formulation and computer input places all decision variables on the left-hand side of the inequality and a constant (possibly zero) on the right-hand side. Thus, we will rewrite this constraint as

$$-x_{11} + x_{12} - x_{21} + x_{22} \geq 0$$

4. At least 40% of interviews for households with children during the evening:

$$x_{12} \geq 0.4(x_{11} + x_{12})$$

or

$$-0.4x_{11} + 0.6x_{12} \geq 0$$

5. At least 60% of interviews for households without children during the evening:

$$x_{22} \geq 0.6(x_{21} + x_{22})$$

or

$$-0.6x_{21} + 0.4x_{22} \geq 0$$

By adding the nonnegativity requirements, the four-variable, six-constraint linear programming model becomes

$$\min \quad 20x_{11} + 25x_{12} + 18x_{21} + 20x_{22}$$

s.t.

$$
\begin{array}{llll}
x_{11} + & x_{12} + & x_{21} + & x_{22} = 1000 \qquad \text{Total interviews} \\
x_{11} + & x_{12} & & \geq 400 \qquad \text{Households with children} \\
& & x_{21} + & x_{22} \geq 400 \qquad \text{Households without children} \\
-x_{11} + & x_{12} - & x_{21} + & x_{22} \geq \quad 0 \qquad \text{More evening interviews} \\
-0.4x_{11} + & 0.6x_{12} & & \geq \quad 0 \qquad \text{Evening households with children} \\
& & -0.6x_{21} + & 0.4x_{22} \geq \quad 0 \qquad \text{Evening households without children} \\
\end{array}
$$

$$x_{11}, x_{12}, x_{21}, x_{22} \geq 0$$

The computer solution to the above linear program is shown in Figure 9.1. Using the results of the computer solution, we see that the minimum cost of $20,320 occurs with the following interview schedule:

| | Number of Interviews | | |
Household	Day	Evening	Totals
Children	240	160	400
No children	240	360	600
Totals	480	520	1000

As can be seen, 480 interviews will be scheduled during the day and 520 during the evening. Households with children will be covered by 400 interviews and households without children will be covered by 600 interviews.

As mentioned in Chapter 8, when using LINDO/PC, row 1 refers to the objective function, row 2 refers to constraint 1, row 3 refers to constraint 2, and so on. Dual price information for each constraint is provided in the column labeled DUAL PRICES.

Selected sensitivity analysis information from Figure 9.1 shows a dual price of -19.2 for row 2. This tells us that the objective function will get worse (cost increase) by $19.20 if the number of interviews is increased from 1000 to 1001. Thus $19.20 is the incremental cost of obtaining additional interviews. It is also the savings that could be realized by reducing the number of interviews from 1000 to 999. The dual price for the requirement of 400 households with children (row 3) is -2.799999. This dual price indicates that requesting additional interviews of households with children will not improve the objective function. In fact, additional interviews of households with children will add to the total cost at a rate of approximately $2.80 per additional interview.

The surplus variable with a value of 200 for row 4 shows that 200 more households without children will be interviewed than required. Similarly, the surplus variable with a value of 40 for row 5 shows that the number of evening interviews exceeds the number of daytime interviews by 40. The zero values for the surplus variables in rows 6 and 7 indicate that the more expensive evening interviews are being held at a minimum.

```
                    OBJECTIVE FUNCTION VALUE

        1)          20320.0000

        VARIABLE              VALUE          REDUCED COST
           X11           240.000000             .000000
           X12           160.000000             .000000
           X21           240.000000             .000000
           X22           360.000000             .000000


           ROW        SLACK OR SURPLUS        DUAL PRICES
           2)               .000000         -19.200000
           3)               .000000          -2.799999
           4)            200.000000            .000000
           5)             40.000000            .000000
           6)               .000000          -5.000000
           7)               .000000          -2.000000
```

Figure 9.1
Computer Solution of the Marketing Research Problem Using LINDO/PC

9.2

FINANCIAL APPLICATIONS

Portfolio Selection

Portfolio selection problems involve situations in which a financial manager must select specific investments—for example, stocks, bonds—from a variety of investment alternatives. This type of problem is frequently encountered by managers of mutual funds, credit unions, insurance companies, and banks. The objective function for portfolio selection problems is usually maximization of expected return or minimization of risk. The constraints usually take the form of restrictions on the type of permissible investments, state laws, company policy, maximum permissible risk, and so on.

Problems of this type have been formulated and solved using a variety of mathematical programming techniques. However, if in a particular portfolio selection problem it is possible to formulate a linear objective function and linear constraints, then linear programming can be used to solve the problem. In this section we show how a portfolio selection problem can be formulated and solved as a linear program.

Consider the case of Welte Mutual Funds, Inc., located in New York City. Welte has just obtained $100,000 by converting industrial bonds to cash and is now looking for other investment opportunities for these funds. Considering Welte's current investments, the firm's top financial analyst recommends that all new investments should be made in the oil industry, steel industry, or government bonds. Specifically, the analyst has identified five investment opportunities and projected their annual rates of return.

The investments and rates of return are shown in Table 9.3.

Management of Welte has imposed the following investment guidelines:

Table 9.3
Investment Opportunities for Welte
Mutual Funds

Investment	Projected Rate of Return (%)
Atlantic Oil	7.3
Pacific Oil	10.3
Midwest Steel	6.4
Huber Steel	7.5
Government bonds	4.5

1. Neither industry (oil or steel) should receive more than 50% of the total new investment.
2. Government bonds should be at least 25% of the steel industry investments.
3. The investment in Pacific Oil, the high-return but high-risk investment, cannot be more than 60% of the total oil industry investment.

What portfolio recommendations—investments and amounts—should be made for the available $100,000? Given the objective of maximizing projected return subject to the budgetary and managerially imposed constraints, we can answer this question by formulating a linear programming model of the problem. The solution to this linear programming model will then provide investment recommendations for the management of Welte Mutual Funds.

Let

$$x_1 = \text{dollars invested in Atlantic Oil}$$
$$x_2 = \text{dollars invested in Pacific Oil}$$
$$x_3 = \text{dollars invested in Midwest Steel}$$
$$x_4 = \text{dollars invested in Huber Steel}$$
$$x_5 = \text{dollars invested in government bonds}$$

Using the projected rates of return shown in Table 9.3, the objective function for maximizing the total rate of return for the portfolio can be written as

$$\max 0.073x_1 + 0.103x_2 + 0.064x_3 + 0.075x_4 + 0.045x_5$$

The constraint specifying the investment of $100,000 is written as

$$x_1 + x_2 + x_3 + x_4 + x_5 = 100{,}000$$

The requirements that neither the oil nor the steel industry should receive more than 50% of the $100,000 investment are as follows:

$$x_1 + x_2 \leq 50,000 \quad \text{Oil industry}$$
$$x_3 + x_4 \leq 50,000 \quad \text{Steel industry}$$

The requirement that government bonds be at least 25% of the steel industry investment is expressed as follows:

$$x_5 \geq 0.25 (x_3 + x_4)$$

or

$$-0.25x_3 - 0.25x_4 + x_5 \geq 0$$

Finally, the constraint that Pacific Oil cannot be more than 60% of the total oil industry investment becomes

$$x_2 \leq 0.60(x_1 + x_2)$$

or

$$-0.60x_1 + 0.40x_2 \leq 0$$

By adding the nonnegativity restrictions, the complete linear programming model for the Welte Mutual Fund investment problem is as follows:

max $0.073x_1 + 0.103x_2 + 0.064x_3 + 0.075x_4 + 0.045x_5$

s.t.

$x_1 +$	$x_2 +$	$x_3 +$	$x_4 +$	$x_5 = 100,000$	Available funds
$x_1 +$	x_2			$\leq 50,000$	Oil industry maximum
		$x_3 +$	x_4	$\leq 50,000$	Steel industry maximum
	$- 0.25x_3 -$	$0.25x_4 +$	$x_5 \geq$	0	Government bonds minimum
$-0.6x_1 +$	$0.4x_2$		$\leq$	0	Pacific Oil restriction

$$x_1, x_2, x_3, x_4, x_5 \geq 0$$

This problem was solved using LINDO/PC. The output is shown in Figure 9.2. In Table 9.4 we show how the funds are divided among the securities. Note that the optimal solution indicates that the portfolio should be diversified among all the investment opportunities except Midwest Steel. The projected annual return for this portfolio is $8000, which is an overall return rate of 8%.

Using the computer printout for the Welte investment problem as shown in Figure 9.2, we see that the dual price for row 4 is zero. This is because constraint 3 (steel industry maximum) is not a binding constraint; increases in the steel industry limit of $50,000 will not improve the value of the objective function. Indeed, the slack variable for this constraint shows that the current steel industry investment is $10,000 below its limit of $50,000. The dual prices for the other constraints are nonzero, indicating that they are binding constraints at the optimal solution.

```
                        OBJECTIVE FUNCTION VALUE

          1)           8000.00000

          VARIABLE            VALUE           REDUCED COST
              X1        20000.000000             .000000
              X2        30000.000000             .000000
              X3             .000000             .011000
              X4        40000.000000             .000000
              X5        10000.000000             .000000


          ROW        SLACK OR SURPLUS        DUAL PRICES
              2)             .000000            .069000
              3)             .000000            .022000
              4)        10000.000000            .000000
              5)             .000000           -.024000
              6)             .000000            .030000
```

Figure 9.2
Computer Solution of Welte Mutual Funds Problem Using LINDO/PC

Table 9.4
Optimal Portfolio Selection for Welte Mutual Funds

Investment	Amount	Expected Annual Return
Atlantic Oil	$ 20,000	$1,460
Pacific Oil	30,000	3,090
Huber Steel	40,000	3,000
Government bonds	10,000	450
	$100,000	$8,000

Expected annual return of $8,000 = 8%

The dual price of 0.069 for row 2 (constraint 1) shows that the objective function can be increased by 0.069 if one more dollar can be made available for the portfolio investment. If more funds can be obtained at a cost of less than 6.9%, management should consider obtaining them. On the other hand, if a return in excess of 6.9% can be obtained by investing funds elsewhere (other than in these five securities), management should question the wisdom of investing the entire $100,000 in this portfolio.

Similar interpretations can be given to the other dual prices. Note, however, that the dual price for row 5 (constraint 4) is negative; its value is -0.024. This indicates that increasing the value on the right-hand side of the constraint by one unit can be expected to cause a change in the objective function of -0.024. In terms of the optimal portfolio, this means that if Welte invests one more dollar in government bonds, the total return will decrease by 2.4 cents. To see why this is so, note again from the dual price for constraint 1 that the marginal return on the funds invested in the portfolio is 6.9% (the average return is 8%). The rate of return on government bonds is 4.5%. Thus the cost of investing one more dollar in government bonds is the difference between the marginal return on the portfolio and the marginal return on government bonds: 6.9% − 4.5% = 2.4%.

Note that the optimal solution with $x_3 = 0$ shows that Midwest Steel should not be included in the portfolio. The associated REDUCED COST for x_3 of 0.011 tells us that the objective function coefficient for Midwest Steel would have to increase by 0.011 before it would be desirable to consider the Midwest Steel investment alternative. With this increase the Midwest Steel return would be $0.064 + 0.011 = 0.075$, making this investment just as desirable as the currently used Huber Steel investment alternative.

Two other points concerning this problem are worth mentioning. First, a simple modification of this model permits determining the fraction of available funds invested in each security. That is, we divide each of the right-hand-side values by 100,000. Then the optimal values for the variables will give the fraction of funds that should be invested in each security for a portfolio of any size. Second, a shortcoming of the linear programming approach to the portfolio selection problem is that we may not be able to invest the exact amount specified in each of the securities. For example, if Atlantic Oil sold for $75 a share, we would have to purchase exactly 266⅔ shares in order to spend exactly the recommended $20,000. One way to avoid this difficulty is to purchase the largest possible whole number of shares with the amount of funds recommended (for example, 266 shares of Atlantic Oil). This guarantees that the budget constraint will not be violated. This, of course, introduces the possibility that the solution will no longer be optimal, but the danger is slight if large numbers of securities are involved.

Financial-Mix Strategy

Financial-mix strategies involve the selection of means for financing company projects, inventories, production operations, and various other activities. In this section we illustrate how linear programming can be used to solve problems of this type by formulating and solving a problem involving the financing of production operations. In this particular application a financial decision must be made with regard to how much production is to be supported by internally generated funds and how much is to be supported by external funds.

The Jefferson Adding Machine Company will begin production of two new models of electronic calculators during the next 3 months. Since these models require an expansion of the current production operation, the company will need operating funds to cover material, labor, and other expenses during the initial production period. Revenue from this initial production period will not be available until after the end of the period. Thus the company must arrange financing for these operating expenses before production can begin.

Jefferson has set aside $3000 in internal funds to cover expenses of this operation. If additional funds are needed, they will have to be generated externally. A local bank has offered a line of short-term credit in an amount not to exceed $10,000. The interest rate over the life of the loan will be 12% per year on the average amount borrowed. One stipulation set by the bank requires that the remainder of the company cash set aside for this operation plus the accounts receivable for this product line be at least twice as great as the outstanding loan plus interest at the end of the initial production period.

In addition to the financial restrictions placed on this operation, labor capacity is also a factor for Jefferson to consider. Only 2500 hours of assembly time and 150 hours of packaging and shipping time are available for the new product line during the initial

3-month production period. Relevant cost, price, and production time requirements for the two models, referred to as models Y and Z, are shown in Table 9.5.

Table 9.5
Cost, Price, and Labor Data for the Jefferson Adding Machine Company

Model	Unit Cost (materials and other variable expenses)	Selling Price	Profit Margin	Labor Hours Required	
				Assembly	Packaging and shipping
Y	$ 50	$ 58	$ 8	12	1
Z	$100	$120	$20	25	2

Additional restrictions have been imposed by company management in order to guarantee that the market reaction to both products can be tested; that is, at least 50 units of model Y and at least 25 units of model Z must be produced in this first production period.

Since the cost of the units produced using borrowed funds will in effect experience an interest charge, the profit contributions for the units of models Y and Z produced on borrowed funds will be reduced. Hence we adopt the following notation for the decision variables in this problem:

x_1 = units of model Y produced with company funds

x_2 = units of model Y produced with borrowed funds

x_3 = units of model Z produced with company funds

x_4 = units of model Z produced with borrowed funds

How much will the profit contribution be reduced for units produced on borrowed funds? To answer this question, one must know for how long the loan will be outstanding. We assume that all units of each model are sold as they are produced to independent distributors and that the average rate of turnover of accounts receivable is 3 months. Since company management has specified that the loan is to be repaid by funds generated by the units produced on borrowed funds, the funds borrowed to produce one unit of model Y or Z will be repaid approximately 3 months later. Hence the profit contribution for each unit of model Y produced on borrowed funds is reduced from $8 to $8 − ($50 × 0.12 × ¼ yr) = $6.50, and the profit contribution for each unit of model Z produced on borrowed funds is reduced from $20 to $20 − ($100 × 0.12 × ¼ yr) = $17. With this information we can now formulate the objective function for Jefferson's financial mix problem:

$$\max 8x_1 + 6.5x_2 + 20x_3 + 17x_4$$

We can also specify the following constraints for the model:

$$12x_1 + 12x_2 + 25x_3 + 25x_4 \leq 2{,}500 \quad \text{Assembly capacity}$$
$$x_1 + x_2 + 2x_3 + 2x_4 \leq 150 \quad \text{Packaging and shipping capacity}$$

$$50x_1 \qquad + \; 100x_3 \qquad\qquad \leq \; 3{,}000 \qquad \text{Internal funds available}$$
$$50x_2 \qquad\quad + \; 100x_4 \leq 10{,}000 \qquad \text{External funds available}$$
$$x_1 + \quad x_2 \qquad\qquad\qquad\qquad \geq \qquad 50 \qquad \text{Model } Y \text{ requirement}$$
$$x_3 + \quad x_4 \geq \quad 25 \qquad \text{Model } Z \text{ requirement}$$

In addition, the following constraint must be included to satisfy the bank loan requirement:

$$\text{Cash} \; + \; \text{accounts receivable} \geq 2(\text{loan} \; + \; \text{interest})$$

This restriction must be satisfied at the end of the period. Recalling that accounts receivable are outstanding for an average of 3 months, the following relationships can be used to derive a mathematical expression for the above inequality at the end of the period:

$$\text{Cash} = 3000 \qquad - \quad 50x_1 - 100x_3$$
$$\text{Accounts receivable} = \quad 58x_1 \; + \; 58x_2 + 120x_3 + 120x_4$$
$$\text{Loan} = \quad 50x_2 \; + \; 100x_4$$
$$\text{Interest} = \quad (0.12 \times \tfrac{1}{4} \text{ yr})(50x_2 + 100x_4) = 1.5x_2 + 3x_4$$

Therefore the constraint resulting from the bank restriction can be written as

$$3000 - 50x_1 - 100x_3 + 58x_1 + 58x_2 + 120x_3 + 120x_4 \geq 2(51.5x_2 + 103x_4)$$

or

$$3000 \geq -8x_2 + 45x_2 - 20x_2$$

which is equivalent to

$$-8x_1 + 45x_2 - 20x_3 + 86x_4 \leq 3000$$

Adding the nonnegativity constraints, the complete linear programming model for the Jefferson Adding Machine Company can now be stated:

$$\max \quad 8x_1 + 6.5x_2 + \; 20x_3 + \; 17x_4$$
$$\text{s.t.}$$
$$12x_1 + \; 12x_2 + \; 25x_3 + \; 25x_4 \leq \; 2500$$
$$x_1 + \quad x_2 + \quad 2x_3 + \quad 2x_4 \leq \quad 150$$
$$50x_1 + \qquad\qquad 100x_3 \qquad\qquad \leq \quad 3000$$
$$50x_2 \qquad\quad + \; 100x_4 \leq 10{,}000$$
$$x_1 + \quad x_2 \qquad\qquad\qquad\qquad \geq \qquad 50$$
$$x_3 + \quad x_4 \geq \quad 25$$
$$-8x_1 + \; 45x_2 - \; 20x_3 + \; 86x_4 \leq \; 3000$$
$$x_1, x_2, x_3, x_4 \geq 0$$

The computer solution to this four-variable, seven-constraint financial-mix problem is shown in Figure 9.3. The profit of $1191.86 is realized with the optimal solution of $x_1 = 50$, $x_2 = 0$, $x_3 = 5$, and $x_4 = 40.7$. Note that the reduced cost of zero for x_2 tells us that the objective function coefficient *does not have to increase* in order to consider bringing x_2 into the optimal solution. This is an indication that alternate optimal solutions exist for the problem. Figure 9.4 shows a computer solution yielding an alternate optimal solution. The profit of $1191.86 is now associated with the solution $x_1 = 0$, $x_2 = 50$, $x_3 = 30$, and $x_4 = 15.7$.

```
              OBJECTIVE FUNCTION VALUE

     1)          1191.86000

       VARIABLE           VALUE          REDUCED COST
          X1            50.000000          .000000
          X2              .000000          .000000
          X3             5.000000          .000000
          X4            40.697670          .000000

        ROW       SLACK OR SURPLUS       DUAL PRICES
         2)           757.558200          .000000
         3)             8.604652          .000000
         4)              .000000          .239535
         5)          5930.232000          .000000
         6)              .000000        -2.395350
         7)            20.697670          .000000
         8)              .000000          .197674
```

Figure 9.3
Computer Solution of Jefferson Adding Machine Problem Using LINDO/PC

Obviously management could implement either of the solutions shown in the figures and maximize profit. The solution in Figure 9.4 is rounded and summarized in Table 9.6 along with the expected profit and borrowed funds for each model of calculator. This solution requires the company to use all its internal funds ($3000), but only slightly more than $4000 of the available $10,000 line of credit.

Some additional interpretations from the computer solution in Figure 9.4 show that assembly capacity (row 2, slack = 757.6 hours) and packaging and shipping capacity (row 3, slack = 8.6 hours) are adequate to meet the production requirements. Additional hours of these resources will not improve the value of the optimal solution. The dual price of 0.239535 associated with the internal funds constraint (row 4) shows that a profit improvement of approximately $0.24 can be made from an additional dollar of internal funds. With this high return on the internal funds investment, Jefferson may want to consider seriously allocating additional internal funds to this project. The negative dual price of -2.39535 for row 6 tells us that increases in the model Y production requirement will reduce the profit margin. In fact, the negative dual price shows that reducing the current 50-unit requirement for model Y will actually increase profits at the rate of approximately $2.40 per unit reduction in the requirement.

```
                    OBJECTIVE FUNCTION VALUE

        1)          1191.86000

        VARIABLE         VALUE          REDUCED COST
           X1           .000000           .000000
           X2         50.000000           .000000
           X3         30.000000           .000000
           X4         15.697670           .000000

          ROW     SLACK OR SURPLUS       DUAL PRICES
           2)        757.558100           .000000
           3)          8.604650           .000000
           4)           .000000           .239535
           5)       5930.232000           .000000
           6)           .000000         -2.395349
           7)         20.697670           .000000
           8)           .000000           .197674
           9)           .000000           .000000
```

Figure 9.4
Alternate Optimal Solution to Jefferson Adding Machine Problem Using LINDO/PC

Table 9.6
Optimal Financial Mix for the Production of Jefferson Adding Machines

	Units	Expected Profit	Amount of Borrowed Funds
Model Y			
Borrowed funds (x_2)	50 × 6.5	$ 325	$2500 50 × 50
Model Z			
Company funds (x_3)	30	600	—
Borrowed funds (x_4)	15.7	267	1570 15.7 × 100
Totals		$1192	$4070

9.3

PRODUCTION MANAGEMENT APPLICATIONS

Production Scheduling

One of the most important areas of linear programming deals with multiperiod planning applications such as production scheduling. The solution to a production scheduling problem enables the manager to establish an efficient low-cost production schedule for one or more products over several time periods, such as weeks, months, and so on. Essentially, a production scheduling problem can be viewed as a product-mix problem for each of several periods in the future. The manager must determine the production levels that will allow the company to meet product demand requirements, given limitations on production capacity, labor capacity, and storage space. At the same time, it is desired to minimize the total cost of carrying out this task.

One major reason for the widespread application of linear programming to production scheduling problems is that these problems are of a recurring nature. A production schedule must be established for the current month, then again for the next month, the month after that, and so on. When the production manager looks at the problem each month, he or she will find that while demands for the products have changed, production times, production capacities, storage space limitations, and so on, are roughly the same. Thus the production manager is basically resolving the same problem handled in previous months. Hence a general linear programming model of the production scheduling procedure may be frequently applied. Once the model has been formulated, the manager can simply supply the data—demands, capacities, and so on—for the given production period, and the linear programming model can then be used to develop the production schedule. Thus one linear programming formulation may have many repeat applications.

Let us consider the case of the Bollinger Electronics Company, which produces two different electronic components for a major airplane engine manufacturer. The airplane engine manufacturer notifies the Bollinger sales office each quarter as to what the monthly requirements for components will be during each of the next 3 months. The monthly requirements for the components may vary considerably depending on the type of engine the airplane engine manufacturer is producing. The order shown in Table 9.7 has just been received for the next 3-month period.

Table 9.7
Three-Month Demand Schedule for Bollinger Electronics
Company

Component	April	May	June
322A	1000	3000	5000
802B	1000	500	3000

After the order is processed, a demand statement is sent to the production control department. The production control department must then develop a 3-month production plan for the components. Knowing the preference of the production department manager for constant demand levels that result in balanced workloads and constant machine and labor utilization, the production scheduler might consider the alternative of producing at a constant rate for all 3 months. This would set monthly production quotas at 3000 units per month for component 322A and 1500 units per month for component 802B. Why not adopt this schedule?

While this schedule would be quite appealing to the production department, it may be undesirable from a total-cost point of view. In particular, this schedule ignores inventory costs. Consider the projected inventory levels that would result from this schedule calling for constant production (Figure 9.5). We see that this production schedule would lead to high inventory levels. When we consider the cost of tied-up capital and storage space, a schedule that provides lower inventory levels might be economically more desirable.

At the other extreme of the constant-rate production schedule is the produce-to-meet-demand approach. While this schedule eliminates the inventory-holding cost problem, the wide monthly fluctuations in production levels may cause some serious production

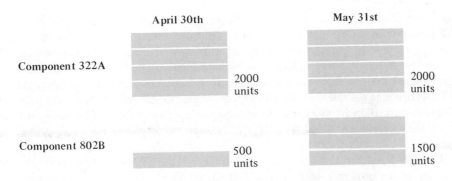

Figure 9.5
Projected Inventory Levels under a Constant-Rate Production Schedule

problems and costs. For example, production capacity would have to be available to meet the total 8000-unit peak demand in June. Also, unless other components could be scheduled on the same production equipment in April and May, there would be significant unused capacity and thus low machine utilization in those months. These large production variations might also require substantial labor adjustments, which in turn could lead to increased employee turnover and training problems. Thus it appears that the best production schedule will be one that is a compromise between the two alternatives.

The production manager will want to identify and consider the following costs:

1. Production costs
2. Storage costs
3. Change-in-production-level costs

In the remainder of this section we show how a linear programming model of the production and inventory process for Bollinger Electronics can be formulated to account for these costs in such a fashion that the total cost is minimized.

In order to develop the model, we will use a double-subscript notation for the decision variables in the problem. We let the first subscript indicate the product number and the second subscript the month. Thus, in general, we let x_{im} denote the production volume in units for product i in month m. Here $i = 1, 2$ and $m = 1, 2, 3$; $i = 1$ refers to component 322A, $i = 2$ refers to component 802B, $m = 1$ refers to April, $m = 2$ refers to May, and $m = 3$ refers to June. The purpose of the double subscript is to provide a more descriptive notation. We could simply use x_6 to represent the number of units of product 2 produced in month 3, but x_{23} is more descriptive in that we know directly the product and month the variable represents.

If component 322A costs $20 per unit produced and component 802B costs $10 per unit produced, the production cost part of the objective function becomes

$$\text{Production cost} = 20x_{11} + 20x_{12} + 20x_{13} + 10x_{21} + 10x_{22} + 10x_{23}$$

You should note that in this particular problem the production cost per unit is the same each month, and thus we need not include production costs in the objective function; that is, no matter what production schedule is selected, the total production costs will remain the same. These are not relevant costs for the production scheduling decision under consideration. In cases where the cost per unit is expected to change each month, the variable production costs per unit per month must be included in the objective function. For the Bollinger Electronics problem the solution will be the same whether or not these costs are included. We have elected to include them so that the value of the linear programming objective function will include all the costs associated with the problem.

To incorporate the relevant inventory costs into the model, we introduce the following double-subscripted decision variable to indicate the number of units of inventory for each product for each month. We let s_{im} be the inventory level for product i at the end of month m.

Bollinger has determined that on a monthly basis, inventory holding costs are 1.5% of the cost of the product—that is, $(0.015)(\$20) = \$0.30$ per unit for component 322A and $(0.015)(\$10) = \$0.15$ per unit for component 802B. A common assumption made in linear programming approaches to the production scheduling problem is now invoked. We assume that monthly ending inventories are an acceptable approximation to the average inventory levels throughout the month. Given this assumption, the inventory-holding cost portion of the objective function can be written as follows:

$$\text{Inventory holding cost} = 0.30s_{11} + 0.30s_{12} + 0.30s_{13} + 0.15s_{21} + 0.15s_{22} + 0.15s_{23}$$

In order to incorporate the costs due to fluctuations in production levels from month to month, we need to define the following additional decision variables:

I_m = increase in the total production level during month m compared with month $m - 1$

D_m = decrease in the total production level during month m compared with month $m - 1$

After estimating the effects of employee layoffs, turnovers, reassignment training costs, and other costs associated with fluctuating production levels, Bollinger estimates that the cost associated with increasing the production level for any given month is $0.50 per unit increase. A similar cost associated with decreasing the production level for any given month is $0.20 per unit. Thus the third portion of the objective function can be written as follows:

$$\text{Production fluctuation costs} = 0.50I_1 + 0.50I_2 + 0.50I_3 + 0.20D_1 + 0.20D_2 + 0.20D_3$$

You should note here that Bollinger has elected to measure the cost associated with production fluctuations as a function of the change in the total number of units produced in month m compared with the total number of units produced in month $m - 1$. In other production scheduling applications the production fluctuations might be measured in terms of machine hours or labor hours required rather than in terms of the total number of units produced.

Combining all three costs, the complete objective function becomes:

$$\begin{aligned}
\text{Objective function} = {} & 20x_{11} + 20x_{12} + 20x_{13} + 10x_{21} + 10x_{22} \\
& + 10x_{23} + 0.30s_{11} + 0.30s_{12} + 0.30s_{13} + 0.15s_{21} \\
& + 0.15s_{22} + 0.15s_{23} + 0.50I_1 + 0.50I_2 + 0.50I_3 \\
& + 0.20D_1 + 0.20D_2 + 0.20D_3
\end{aligned}$$

Now let us consider the constraints. First we must guarantee that the schedule meets customer demand. Since the units shipped can come from the current month's production or from inventory carried over from previous periods, we have the following basic requirements:

$$\left(\begin{array}{c} \text{Ending} \\ \text{inventory} \\ \text{from previous} \\ \text{month} \end{array}\right) + \left(\begin{array}{c} \text{current} \\ \text{production} \end{array}\right) \geq \left(\begin{array}{c} \text{this month's} \\ \text{demand} \end{array}\right)$$

The difference between the left-hand side and the right-hand side will be the amount of ending inventory at the end of this month. Thus the demand requirement takes the form

$$\left(\begin{array}{c} \text{Ending} \\ \text{inventory} \\ \text{from previous} \\ \text{month} \end{array}\right) + \left(\begin{array}{c} \text{current} \\ \text{production} \end{array}\right) - \left(\begin{array}{c} \text{ending} \\ \text{inventory} \\ \text{for this} \\ \text{month} \end{array}\right) = \left(\begin{array}{c} \text{this} \\ \text{month's} \\ \text{demand} \end{array}\right)$$

Suppose that the inventories at the beginning of the 3-month scheduling period were 500 units for component 322A and 200 units for component 802B. Recalling that the demand for both products in the first month (April) was 1000 units, the constraints for meeting demand in the first month become

$$500 + x_{11} - s_{11} = 1000$$
$$200 + x_{21} - s_{21} = 1000$$

Moving the constants to the right-hand side, we have

$$x_{11} - s_{11} = 500$$
$$x_{21} - s_{21} = 800$$

Similarly, we need demand constraints for both products in the second and third months. These can be written as follows:

Month 2: $s_{11} + x_{12} - s_{12} = 3000$
$s_{21} + x_{22} - s_{22} = 500$

Month 3: $s_{12} + x_{13} - s_{13} = 5000$
$s_{22} + x_{23} - s_{23} = 3000$

If the company specifies a minimum inventory level at the end of the 3-month period of at least 400 units of component 322A and at least 200 units of component 802B, we can add the constraints

$$s_{13} \geq 400$$
$$s_{23} \geq 200$$

Let us suppose that we have the additional information available on production, labor, and storage capacity given in Table 9.8. Machine, labor, and storage space requirements are given in Table 9.9. To reflect these limitations, the following constraints are necessary:

Table 9.8
Machine, Labor, and Storage Capacities for Bollinger Electronics

Month	Machine Capacity (hours)	Labor Capacity (hours)	Storage Capacity (square feet)
April	400	300	10,000
May	500	300	10,000
June	600	300	10,000

Table 9.9
Machine, Labor, and Storage Requirements for Components 322A and 802B

Component	Machine (hours/unit)	Labor (hours/unit)	Storage (sq. ft./unit)
322A	0.10	0.05	2
802B	0.08	0.07	3

Machine capacity:

$$0.10x_{11} + 0.08x_{21} \leq 400 \qquad \text{Month 1}$$
$$0.10x_{12} + 0.08x_{22} \leq 500 \qquad \text{Month 2}$$
$$0.10x_{13} + 0.08x_{23} \leq 600 \qquad \text{Month 3}$$

Labor capacity:

$$0.05x_{11} + 0.07x_{21} \leq 300 \qquad \text{Month 1}$$
$$0.05x_{12} + 0.07x_{22} \leq 300 \qquad \text{Month 2}$$
$$0.05x_{13} + 0.07x_{23} \leq 300 \qquad \text{Month 3}$$

Storage capacity:

$$2s_{11} + 3s_{21} \leq 10,000 \qquad \text{Month 1}$$
$$2s_{12} + 3s_{22} \leq 10,000 \qquad \text{Month 2}$$
$$2s_{13} + 3s_{23} \leq 10,000 \qquad \text{Month 3}$$

One final set of constraints must be added. These are necessary in order to guarantee that I_m and D_m will reflect the increase or decrease in the total production level for month m. Suppose that the production levels for March, the month before the start of the current production scheduling problem, had been 1500 units of component 322A and 1000 units of component 802B for a total production level of $1500 + 1000 = 2500$ units. We can find the amount of the change in production for April from the relationship

$$\text{April production} - \text{March production} = \text{change}$$

Using the April production decision variables, x_{11} and x_{21}, and the March production of 2500 units, the above relationship can be rewritten as

$$x_{11} + x_{21} - 2500 = \text{change}$$

Note that the change can be positive or negative. A positive change reflects an increase in the total production level, and a negative change reflects a decrease in the total production level. Using the above relationship, the increase in production variable for April, I_1, and the decrease in production variable for April, D_1, can be used to specify the following constraint for the change in total production for the month of April:

$$x_{11} + x_{21} - 2500 = I_1 - D_1$$

Of course, we cannot have an increase in production and a decrease in production during the same 1-month period; thus either I_1 or D_1 will be zero. If April requires 3000 units of production, we will have $I_1 = 500$ and $D_1 = 0$. If April requires 2200 units of production, we will have $I_1 = 0$ and $D_1 = 300$. This approach of denoting the change in production level as the difference between two nonnegative variables, I_1 and D_1, permits both positive and negative changes in the total production level. If a single variable, say c_m, had been used to represent the change in production level, then because of the nonnegativity requirement, only positive changes would be permitted.

Using the same approach in May and June (always subtracting the previous month's total production from the current month's total production), we have the following constraints for the second and third months of the production scheduling period:

$$(x_{12} + x_{22}) - (x_{11} + x_{21}) = I_2 - D_2$$
$$(x_{13} + x_{23}) - (x_{12} + x_{22}) = I_3 - D_3$$

Placing the variables on the left-hand side and the constants on the right-hand side, the complete set of what are commonly referred to as production-smoothing constraints can be written as

$$
\begin{aligned}
x_{11} + x_{21} \qquad\qquad\qquad\qquad - I_1 + D_1 &= 2500 \\
-x_{11} - x_{21} + x_{12} + x_{22} \qquad\qquad - I_2 + D_2 &= 0 \\
- x_{12} - x_{22} + x_{13} + x_{23} - I_3 + D_3 &= 0
\end{aligned}
$$

The initially rather small, two-product, 3-month scheduling problem has now developed into an 18-variable, 20-constraint linear programming problem. Note that in the problem we were concerned only with one type of machine process, one type of labor, and one type of storage area. In actual production scheduling problems you may encounter several machine types, several labor grades, and/or several storage areas. Thus you are probably beginning to realize how large-scale linear programs of production systems come about. A typical application might involve developing a production schedule for 100 products over a 12-month horizon. Such a problem could have over 1000 variables and constraints.

The computer solution to the Bollinger Electronics production scheduling problem is shown in Figure 9.6. A portion of the managerial report based on the computer solution is shown in Table 9.10.

Let us now consider the monthly variation in the production and inventory schedule shown in Table 9.10. Recall that the inventory cost for component 802B is one-half the inventory cost for component 322A. Therefore, as might be expected, component 802B

```
                    OBJECTIVE FUNCTION VALUE

        1)          225295.000

        VARIABLE          VALUE          REDUCED COST
          X11          500.000000          .000000
          X12         3200.000000          .000000
          X13         5200.000000          .000000
          X21         2500.000000          .000000
          X22         2000.000000          .000000
          X23            .000000           .060715
          S11            .000000           .192856
          S12          200.000000          .000000
          S13          400.000000          .000000
          S21         1700.000000          .000000
          S22         3200.000000          .000000
          S23          200.000000          .000000
          I1           500.000000          .000000
          I2          2200.000000          .000000
          I3             .000000           .000000
          D1             .000000           .700000
          D2             .000000           .700000
          D3             .000000           .700000


        ROW        SLACK OR SURPLUS        DUAL PRICES
          2)            .000000          -20.000000
          3)            .000000          -10.000000
          4)            .000000          -20.107140
          5)            .000000          -10.150000
          6)            .000000          -20.500000
          7)            .000000          -10.439290
          8)            .000000          -20.800000
          9)            .000000          -10.589280
         10)         150.000000            .000000
         11)          20.000000            .000000
         12)          79.999990            .000000
         13)         100.000000            .000000
         14)            .000000           2.142852
         15)          40.000000            .000000
         16)        4900.000000            .000000
         17)            .000000            .046429
         18)        8600.000000            .000000
         19)            .000000            .500000
         20)            .000000            .500000
         21)            .000000            .500000
```

Figure 9.6
Computer Solution of the Bollinger Electronics Production Scheduling Problem Using LINDO/PC

Table 9.10
Minimum-Cost Production Schedule Information for Bollinger
Electronics

Activity	April	May	June
Production			
Component 322A	500	3,200	5,200
Component 802B	2,500	2,000	0
Totals	3,000	5,200	5,200
Ending inventory			
Component 322A	0	200	400
Component 802B	1,700	3,200	200
Machine usage			
Scheduled hours	250	480	520
Slack capacity hours	150	20	80
Labor usage			
Scheduled hours	200	300	260
Slack capacity hours	100	0	40
Storage usage			
Scheduled storage	5,100	10,000	1,400
Slack capacity	4,900	0	8,600

Total schedule cost (including production, inventory, and
   production smoothing) = $225,295.00

is produced heavily in the first month (April) and then held in inventory for the demand that will occur in future months. Component 322A tends to be produced when needed, and only small amounts are carried in inventory.

The costs of increasing and decreasing the total production volume tend to smooth (make small) the monthly variations. In fact, the minimum cost schedule calls for a 500-unit increase in total production in April and a 2200-unit increase in total production in May. The May production level of 5200 units is then maintained during June.

The machine usage section of the report shows ample machine capacity available in all 3 months. However, labor and storage capacity both show full utilization (slack = 0 for row 14 and row 17 in Figure 9.6) in the month of May. The dual price of 2.142852 shows that an additional hour of labor capacity in May will improve the objective function (lower cost) by approximately $2.14. This information may help the production manager decide whether to add labor overtime during the month of May. A similar interpretation for the dual price of 0.046429 for row 17 shows that each additional square foot of storage space made available during May will improve the objective function by slightly less than 5 cents per square foot.

We have seen in this illustration that a linear programming model (18 variables and 20 constraints) of a relatively small two-product, 3-month production system has provided some valuable information in terms of identifying a minimum-cost production schedule. In larger production systems, where the number of variables and constraints are too large to track manually, linear programming models can provide a significant advantage in developing cost-saving production schedules.

Labor Planning

Labor planning or scheduling problems frequently occur when managers must make decisions involving departmental staffing requirements for a given period of time. This is particularly true when labor assignments have some flexibility and at least some labor effort can be assigned to more than one department or work center. This is often the case when employees have been cross-trained on two or more jobs. In the following example we show how linear programming can be used to determine not only an optimal product mix but also an optimal labor allocation for the various departments.

McCarthy's Everyday Glass Company is planning to produce two styles of drinking glasses during the next month. The glasses are processed in four separate departments. Excess equipment capacity is available and will not be a constraining factor. However, the company's labor resources are limited and will probably limit the production volume for the two products. The labor requirements per case produced (one dozen glasses) are shown in Table 9.11.

Table 9.11
Hours of Labor per Case of Product

Department	Product 1	Product 2
1	0.070	0.100
2	0.050	0.084
3	0.100	0.067
4	0.010	0.025

The company makes a profit of $1.00 per case of product 1 and $0.90 per case of product 2. If the number of hours available in each department is fixed, we can formulate McCarthy's problem as a standard product-mix linear program. We use the usual notation:

x_1 = cases of product 1 manufactured

x_2 = cases of product 2 manufactured

b_i = hours of labor available in department i, i = 1, 2, 3, 4

The linear program can be written as

$$\max \quad 1.00x_1 + 0.90x_2$$

s.t.

$$0.070x_1 + 0.100x_2 \leq b_1$$
$$0.050x_1 + 0.084x_2 \leq b_2$$
$$0.100x_1 + 0.067x_2 \leq b_3$$
$$0.010x_1 + 0.025x_2 \leq b_4$$
$$x_1, x_2 \geq 0$$

To solve the usual product-mix problem, we would ask the production manager to specify the hours available in each department (b_1, b_2, b_3, and b_4); then we could solve for the profit-maximizing product mix. However, in this case we assume that the manager has some flexibility in allocating labor resources, and we would like to make a recommendation for this allocation as well as determining the optimal product mix.

Suppose that after consideration of the training and experience qualifications of the workers, we find this additional information:

Possible Labor Assignments	Hours of Labor Available
Department 1 only	430
Department 2 only	400
Department 3 only	500
Department 4 only	135
Departments 1 or 2	570
Departments 3 or 4	300
Total available	2335

Of the 2335 hours available for the month's production, we see that 870 hours can be allocated with some management discretion. The constraints for the hours available per department are as follows:

$$b_1 \leq 430 + 570 = 1000$$
$$b_2 \leq 400 + 570 = 970$$
$$b_3 \leq 500 + 300 = 800$$
$$b_4 \leq 135 + 300 = 435$$

Since the 570 hours that have a flexible assignment between departments 1 and 2 cannot be assigned to both departments simultaneously, we need the following additional constraint:

$$b_1 + b_2 \leq 430 + 400 + 570 = 1400$$

Similarly, for the 300 hours that can be allocated between departments 3 and 4, we need the constraint

$$b_3 + b_4 \leq 500 + 135 + 300 = 935$$

In this formulation we are now treating the labor assignments to departments as variables. The objective function coefficients for these variables will be zero, since the b_i variables do not directly affect profit. Thus placing all variables on the left-hand side of the constraints, we have the following complete formulation:

$$\text{max} \quad 1.00x_1 + 0.90x_2 + 0b_1 + 0b_2 + 0b_3 + 0b_4$$

$$\text{s.t.}$$

$$0.070x_1 + 0.100x_2 - b_1 \qquad\qquad\qquad \leq \quad 0$$

$$0.050x_1 + 0.084x_2 \qquad - b_2 \qquad\qquad\quad \leq \quad 0$$

$$0.100x_1 + 0.067x_2 \qquad\qquad - b_3 \qquad\quad \leq \quad 0$$

$$0.010x_1 + 0.025x_2 \qquad\qquad\qquad - b_4 \leq \quad 0$$

$$b_1 \qquad\qquad\qquad\qquad \leq 1000$$

$$b_2 \qquad\qquad\qquad \leq \quad 970$$

$$b_3 \qquad\qquad \leq \quad 800$$

$$b_4 \leq \quad 435$$

$$b_1 + b_2 \qquad\qquad \leq 1400$$

$$b_3 + b_4 \leq \quad 935$$

$$x_1, x_2, b_1, b_2, b_3, b_4 \geq 0$$

This linear programming model will actually solve two problems: (1) it will find the optimal product mix for the planning period, and (2) it will allocate the total labor resource to the departments in such a fashion that profits will be maximized. The solution to this six-variable, 10-constraint model is shown in Table 9.12.

Note that the optimal labor plan utilizes all 2335 hours of labor by making the most profitable allocations. In this particular solution there is no idle time in any of the departments. This will not always be the case in problems of this type; however, if the manager does have the freedom to assign certain employees to different departments, the effect will probably be a reduction in the overall idle time. The linear programming model automatically assigns such employees to the departments in the most profitable manner. If the manager had used judgment to allocate the hours to the departments, and we had then solved the product-mix problem with fixed b_i, we would in all probability have found slack in some departments while other departments represented bottlenecks because of insufficient resources.

Variations in the basic formulation of this section might be used in situations such as allocating raw material resources to products, allocating machine time to products, and allocating sales force time to product lines or sales territories.

Table 9.12
Optimal Production Plan and Labor
Allocation for McCarthy's Everyday
Glass Company

Production plan:
   Product 1 = 4700 cases
   Product 2 = 4543 cases
Labor allocation:
   Department 1   783 hours
   Department 2   617 hours
   Department 3   774 hours
   Department 4   <u>161</u> hours
     Total   2335 hours

    Profit = $8789

9.4

BLENDING PROBLEMS

Blending problems arise whenever a manager must decide how to blend two or more resources in order to produce one or more products. In these situations the resources contain one or more essential ingredients that must be blended in such a manner that the final products will contain specific percentages of the essential ingredients. In most of these applications, then, management must decide how much of each resource to purchase in order to satisfy product specifications and product demands at minimum cost.

These types of problems occur frequently in the petroleum industry (such as blending crude oil to produce different-octane gasolines), chemical industry (such as blending chemicals to produce fertilizers, weed killers, and so on), and food industry (such as blending input ingredients to produce soft drinks, soups, and so on). Because of the widespread application of blending problems, the objective in this section is to illustrate how linear programming can be applied to solve these types of problems.

The Grand Strand Oil Company produces regular-grade and premium-grade gasoline products, which are sold to independent distributors in the southeastern United States. The Grand Strand refinery manufactures the gasoline products by blending three petroleum components. The gasolines are sold at different prices and the petroleum components have different costs. The firm would like to determine how to mix or blend the three components into the two gasoline products in such a way as to maximize profits.

Data available show that the regular-grade gasoline can be sold for $0.50 per gallon and the premium-grade gasoline for $0.54 per gallon. For the current production planning period, Grand Strand can obtain the three petroleum components at the cost per gallon and in the quantities shown in Table 9.13.

Table 9.13
Petroleum Cost and Supply for the Grand Strand Blending Problem

Component	Cost/Gallon	Maximum Available
1	$0.25	5,000 gallons
2	$0.30	10,000 gallons
3	$0.42	10,000 gallons

The product specifications for the regular and premium gasolines restrict the amounts of each component that can be used in each gasoline product. The product specifications are listed in Table 9.14. Current commitments to distributors require Grand Strand to produce at least 10,000 gallons of regular-grade gasoline.

The Grand Strand blending problem is to determine how many gallons of each component should be used in the regular-grade gasoline blend and how many gallons of each component should be used in the premium-grade gasoline blend. The optimal blending solution should maximize the firm's profit, subject to the constraints on the available petroleum supplies shown in Table 9.13, the product specifications shown in Table 9.14, and the required 10,000 gallons of regular-grade gasoline.

Table 9.14
Product Specifications for the Grand Strand Blending
Problem

Product	Specifications
Regular gasoline	At most 30% component 1 At least 40% component 2 At most 20% component 3
Premium gasoline	At least 25% component 1 At most 40% component 2 At least 30% component 3

We can use the following double-subscript notation to define the decision variables for the problem:

Let

$$x_{ij} = \text{gallons of component } i \text{ used in gasoline } j,$$
$$\text{where } i = 1, 2, \text{ or } 3 \text{ for components } 1, 2, \text{ or } 3,$$
$$\text{and } j = r \text{ if regular or } j = p \text{ if premium}$$

The six decision variables become

$$x_{1r} = \text{gallons of component 1 in regular gasoline}$$
$$x_{2r} = \text{gallons of component 2 in regular gasoline}$$
$$x_{3r} = \text{gallons of component 3 in regular gasoline}$$
$$x_{1p} = \text{gallons of component 1 in premium gasoline}$$
$$x_{2p} = \text{gallons of component 2 in premium gasoline}$$
$$x_{3p} = \text{gallons of component 3 in premium gasoline}$$

Note that previously we have always used numbers as the subscripts for decision variables. Continuing to use numerical subscripts, we could have let $j = 1$ for regular gasoline and $j = 2$ for premium gasoline. However, the use of the r and p subscripts is descriptive and will enable us easily to identify the gasoline product being referred to by the decision variable. As a general rule, the person developing a linear programming model is free to use the notation that is most descriptive of the problem under study. In the linear programming formulations presented in this text, we use x to denote a decision variable. Although this is the most common notation, other letters can be used for decision variables based on the preference of the person developing the formulation.

Using the notation for the six decision variables defined above, the total number of gallons of each type of gasoline produced can be expressed by summing the number of gallons in the components blended. That is,

Total Gallons Produced

$$\text{Regular gasoline} = x_{1r} + x_{2r} + x_{3r}$$
$$\text{Premium gasoline} = x_{1p} + x_{2p} + x_{3p}$$

Similarly, the total gallons of each component used can be expressed by the following sums:

Total Petroleum Component Usage

$$\text{Component 1} = x_{1r} + x_{1p}$$
$$\text{Component 2} = x_{2r} + x_{2p}$$
$$\text{Component 3} = x_{3r} + x_{3p}$$

The objective function of maximizing the profit contribution can be developed by identifying the difference between the total revenue from the two types of gasoline and the total cost of the three petroleum components. By multiplying the $0.50 per gallon price by the total gallons of regular gasoline, the $0.54 per gallon price by the total gallons of premium gasoline, and the component cost per gallon figures in Table 9.13 by the total gallons of each component used, the objective function can be written as follows:

$$\max \quad 0.50(x_{1r} + x_{2r} + x_{3r}) + 0.54(x_{1p} + x_{2p} + x_{3p})$$
$$-0.25(x_{1r} + x_{1p}) - 0.30(x_{2r} + x_{2p}) - 0.42(x_{3r} + x_{3p})$$

By combining terms the objective function can be written as

$$\max \quad 0.25x_{1r} + 0.20x_{2r} + 0.08x_{3r} + 0.29x_{1p} + 0.24x_{2p} + 0.12x_{3p}$$

The limitations on the availability of the three petroleum components can be expressed by the following three constraints:

$$x_{1r} + x_{1p} \leq 5{,}000 \qquad \text{Component 1}$$
$$x_{2r} + x_{2p} \leq 10{,}000 \qquad \text{Component 2}$$
$$x_{3r} + x_{3p} \leq 10{,}000 \qquad \text{Component 3}$$

Six constraints are now required to meet the product specifications stated in Table 9.14. The first specification states that component 1 can account for at most 30% of the total gallons of regular gasoline produced. That is,

$$\frac{x_{1r}}{x_{1r} + x_{2r} + x_{3r}} \leq 0.30$$

or

$$x_{1r} \leq 0.30(x_{1r} + x_{2r} + x_{3r})$$

Rewriting this constraint with the variables on the left-hand side and a constant on the right-hand side, the first product specification constraint becomes

$$0.70x_{1r} - 0.30x_{2r} - 0.30x_{3r} \leq 0$$

The second product specification listed in Table 9.14 can be written as

$$\frac{x_{2r}}{x_{1r} + x_{2r} + x_{3r}} \geq 0.40$$

or

$$x_{2r} \geq 0.40(x_{1r} + x_{2r} + x_{3r})$$

and thus

$$-0.40x_{1r} + 0.60x_{2r} - 0.40x_{3r} \geq 0$$

Similarly, the four additional blending specifications shown in Table 9.14 can be written as

$$-0.20x_{1r} - 0.20x_{2r} + 0.80x_{3r} \leq 0$$
$$0.75x_{1p} - 0.25x_{2p} - 0.25x_{3p} \geq 0$$
$$-0.40x_{1p} + 0.60x_{2p} - 0.40x_{3p} \leq 0$$
$$-0.30x_{1p} - 0.30x_{2p} + 0.70x_{3p} \geq 0$$

The constraint for at least 10,000 gallons of the regular-grade gasoline is written

$$x_{1r} + x_{2r} + x_{3r} \geq 10,000$$

Thus the complete linear programming model with six decision variables and 10 constraints can be written as follows:

max $0.25x_{1r} + 0.20x_{2r} + 0.08x_{3r} + 0.29x_{1p} + 0.24x_{2p} + 0.12x_{3p}$
s.t.

$$
\begin{aligned}
x_{1r} &+ x_{1p} &\leq 5,000 \\
x_{2r} &+ x_{2p} &\leq 10,000 \\
x_{3r} &+ x_{3p} &\leq 10,000 \\
0.70x_{1r} - 0.30x_{2r} - 0.30x_{3r} & &\leq 0 \\
-0.40x_{1r} + 0.60x_{2r} - 0.40x_{3r} & &\geq 0 \\
-0.20x_{1r} - 0.20x_{2r} + 0.80x_{3r} & &\leq 0 \\
0.75x_{1p} - 0.25x_{2p} - 0.25x_{3p} &\geq 0 \\
-0.40x_{1p} + 0.60x_{2p} - 0.40x_{3p} &\leq 0 \\
-0.30x_{1p} - 0.30x_{2p} + 0.70x_{3p} &\geq 0 \\
x_{1r} + x_{2r} + x_{3r} & &\geq 10,000 \\
x_{1r}, x_{2r}, x_{3r}, x_{1p}, x_{2p}, x_{3p} &\geq 0
\end{aligned}
$$

The computer solution to the Grand Strand blending problem is shown in Figure 9.7. The blending solution that provides a profit of $4650 is summarized in Table 9.15. The optimal blending strategy shows that 10,000 gallons of regular gasoline should be produced. Regular gasoline will consist of a blend of component 1 (12.5%) and component 2 (87.5%). The 15,000 gallons of premium gasoline are to be manufactured from a blend

```
                    OBJECTIVE FUNCTION VALUE

        1)     46500.00000

        VARIABLE          VALUE           REDUCED COST
              X1R       1250.000000          .000000
              X2R       8750.000000          .000000
              X3R          .000000           .000000
              X1P       3750.000000          .000000
              X2P       1250.000000          .000000
              X3P      10000.000000          .000000


        ROW      SLACK OR SURPLUS       DUAL PRICES
          2)          .000000            .290000
          3)          .000000            .240000
          4)          .000000            .120000
          5)        1750.000000          .000000
          6)        4750.000000          .000000
          7)        2000.000000          .000000
          8)          .000000            .000000
          9)        4750.000000          .000000
         10)        5500.000000          .000000
         11)          .000000           -.040000
```

Figure 9.7
Computer Solution of the Grand Strand Blending Problem Using LINDO/PC

Table 9.15
Grand Strand Gasoline Blending Strategy

Gasoline	Gallons of Component (percentage)			Total
	Component 1	Component 2	Component 3	
Regular	1250 (12.5%)	8750 (87.5%)	—	10,000
Premium	3750 (25.0%)	1250 (8.3%)	10,000 (66.7%)	15,000

of all three petroleum components: 25.0% component 1, 8.3% component 2, and 66.7% component 3.

The interpretation of the slack and surplus variables associated with the product specification constraints (rows 5 to 10) in Figure 9.7 needs some clarification. If the constraint is a $\leq$ constraint, the value of the slack can be interpreted as the gallons of component usage below the maximum amount of the component usage specified by the constraint. For example, the slack of 1750 for row 5 shows that component 1 usage is 1750 gallons below the maximum amount of component 1 that could have been used in the production of 10,000 gallons of regular gasoline. If the product specification constraint is a $\geq$ constraint, a surplus variable shows the gallons of component usage above the minimum amount of component usage specified by the blending constraint. For example, the surplus of 4750 for row 6 shows that component 2 usage is 4750 gallons above the minimum amount of component 2 that could have to be used in the production of 10,000 gallons of regular gasoline.

Summary

In this chapter we have presented a broad range of situations that illustrate how linear programming can be a useful decision-making aid. Using a variety of application situations, we have formulated and solved problems from the areas of marketing, finance, and production management. In addition, we have shown how linear programming can be applied to blending problems.

All the illustrations presented in this chapter were simplified versions of actual situations in which linear programming has been applied. In real-world applications the reader will find that the problem is not as concisely stated, the data are not as readily available, and the problem has a larger number of variables and constraints. However, a thorough study of the applications in this chapter is a good place for the reader who eventually hopes to apply linear programming to real-world problems to begin.

In conjunction with most of the applications we have included computer output provided by the LINDO/PC microcomputer software package. This provided us with an opportunity to discuss more fully the interpretation of computer output and to perform sensitivity analysis. In the chapter-ending problems, we present computer output for some of the other applications. The questions asked concerning this computer output are suggestive of the type of information that should be included in a managerial report following a linear programming analysis.

Problems

Note to Student.   The problems for this chapter have been designed to give you an understanding and appreciation of the broad range of problems that can be formulated as linear programs. You should be able to formulate the linear programming model for each of the problems. However, you will need access to a linear programming computer package in order to develop the solution and make the requested interpretations.

1. *Product mix.* Better Products, Inc. is a small manufacturer of three products. The products are produced on two machines. In a typical week, 40 hours of time are available on each machine. Profit contribution and production time in hours per unit are as follows:

	Product 1	Product 2	Product 3
Profit/unit	$30	$50	$20
Machine 1 time/unit	0.5	2.0	0.75
Machine 2 time/unit	1.0	1.0	0.5

Two operators are required for machine 1. Thus 2 hours of labor must be scheduled for each hour of machine 1 time. Only one operator is required for machine 2. A maximum of 100 labor hours is available for assignment to the machines during the coming week. Other production requirements are that product 1 cannot account for more than 50% of the units produced and that product 3 must account for at least 20% of the units produced.

a. How many units of each product should be produced in order to maximize the profit contribution? What is the projected weekly profit associated with your solution?

b. How many hours of production time will be scheduled on each machine?

c. What is the value of an additional hour of labor?

d. Assume that labor capacity can be increased to 120 hours. Would you be interested in this additional resource? Develop the optimal product mix assuming the extra hours are made available.

2. *Media selection.* The Westchester Chamber of Commerce periodically sponsors public service seminars and programs. Currently, promotional plans are under way for this year's program. Advertising alternatives include television, radio, and newspaper. Audience estimates, costs, and maximum media usage limitations are shown below:

	Television	Radio	Newspaper
Audience per advertisement	100,000	18,000	40,000
Cost per advertisement	$2,000	$300	$600
Maximum media usage limitation	10	20	10

To ensure a balanced usage of advertising media, radio advertisements are not to exceed 50% of the total number of advertisements authorized. In addition, it has been requested that television account for at least 10% of the total number of advertisements authorized.

a. If the promotional budget is limited to $18,200, how many commercial messages should be run on each medium in order to maximize total audience contact? What is the allocation of the budget among the three media, and what is the total audience reached?

b. What is the estimated audience contact that would result from an extra $100 allocated to the advertising budget?

3. *Diet problem.* Bluegrass Farms, Inc. in Lexington, Kentucky, is experimenting with a special diet for its racehorses. The feed components available for the diet are a standard horse-feed product, a vitamin-enriched oat product, and a new vitamin-and-mineral feed additive. The nutritional values in units per pound and costs for the three feed components are as follows:

	Standard	Enriched Oats	Additive
Ingredient A	0.8	0.2	0
Ingredient B	1.0	1.5	3.0
Ingredient C	0.1	0.6	2.0
Cost per pound	$0.25	$0.50	$3.00

a. Suppose that the horse trainer sets the minimum daily diet requirement at three units of ingredient A, six units of ingredient B, and four units of ingredient C. Also suppose that for weight control the trainer does not want the total daily feed for a horse to exceed 6 pounds. What is the optimal daily mix of the three feed components?

b. What is the cost per pound for the daily mix?

c. Using the shadow price, determine what would happen to the total cost if the total daily feed allowance were increased from 6 to 7 pounds? Explain why this occurs.

4. *Overtime planning.* Hartmann Company is trying to determine how much of each of two products should be produced over the coming planning period. The only serious constraints involve labor availability in three departments. Shown below is information concerning labor availability, labor utilization, and product profitability.

	Product 1	Product 2	Labor Available
Profit/unit	$30.00	$15.00	—
Dept. A hours/unit	1.00	0.35	100 hours
Dept. B hours/unit	0.30	0.20	36 hours
Dept. C hours/unit	0.20	0.50	50 hours

a. Develop a linear programming model of the Hartmann Company's problem. Solve it to determine the optimal production quantities of products 1 and 2.

b. In computing the per-unit profit Hartmann does not deduct labor costs because they are considered fixed for the upcoming planning period. However, suppose that overtime can be scheduled in some of the departments. Which departments would you recommend scheduling for overtime? How much would you be willing to pay per hour of overtime in each department?

c. Suppose that 10, 6, and 8 hours of overtime may be scheduled in departments A, B, and C, respectively. The cost per hour of overtime is $18 in department A, $22.50 in department B, and $12 in department C. Formulate a linear programming model that can be used to determine optimal production quantities if overtime is made available. What are the optimal production quantities, and what is the revised profit? How much overtime do you recommend using in each department? What is the increase in profit if overtime is used?

5. *Investment and loan planning.* The employee credit union at State University is planning the usage of funds for the coming year. The credit union makes four types of loans to its members. In addition, it invests in "risk-free" securities in order to stabilize income. The various revenue-producing investments together with annual rates of return are as follows:

Type of Loan/ Investment	Annual Rate of Return (%)	
Secured loans		
Automobile	8	Y_1
Furniture	10	Y_2
Other secured loans	11	Y_3
Signature loans	12	Y_4
"Risk-free" securities	9	Y_5

State laws and credit union policies impose the following restrictions on the composition of the credit union's loans and investments:

(1) "Risk-free" securities may not exceed 30% of total funds.
(2) Signature loans may not exceed 10% of total loans.
(3) Furniture loans plus "other secured loans" may not exceed 50% of the total of the three types of secured loans.
(4) Signature loans plus "other secured loans" may not exceed the amount invested in "risk-free" securities.

If the firm projects $2 million available for loans and investments during the coming year, how should the funds be allocated to each of the loan investment alternatives in order to maximize total annual return? What is the projected annual dollar return?

6. *Quality assurance.* Hilltop Coffee manufactures a coffee product by blending three types of coffee beans. The cost per pound and the available pounds of each bean are as follows:

Bean	Cost/ Pound	Available Pounds
1	$0.50	500
2	0.70	600
3	0.45	400

Consumer tests with coffee products were used to provide quality ratings on a 0-to-100 scale, with higher ratings indicating higher quality. Product quality standards for the blended coffee require a consumer rating for aroma to be at least 75 and a consumer rating for taste to be at least 80. The individual ratings of the aroma and taste for coffee made from 100% of each bean are as follows:

It can be assumed that the aroma and taste attributes of the coffee blend will be a weighted average of the attributes of the beans used in the blend.

a. What is the minimum cost blend of the three beans that will meet the quality standards and provide 1000 pounds of the blended coffee product?

Bean	Aroma Rating	Taste Rating
1	75	86
2	85	88
3	60	75

b. What is the bean cost per pound of the coffee blend?

c. Use the surplus variables to determine the aroma and taste ratings for the coffee blend.

d. If additional coffee were to be produced, what would be the expected cost per pound?

7. *Blending problem.* Ajax Fuels, Inc. is developing a new additive for airplane fuels. The additive is a mixture of three liquid ingredients: A, B, and C. For proper performance, the total amount of additive (amount of A + amount of B + amount of C) must be at least 10 ounces per gallon of fuel. However, because of safety reasons, the amount of additive must not exceed 15 ounces per gallon of fuel. The mix or blend of the three ingredients is critical. At least 1 ounce of ingredient A must be used for every ounce of ingredient B. The amount of ingredient C must be greater than one-half the amount of ingredient A. If the cost per ounce for ingredients A, B, and C is $0.10, $0.03, and $0.09, respectively, find the minimum cost mixture of A, B, and C for each gallon of airplane fuel.

8. *Labor planning.* G. Kunz and Sons, Inc. manufactures two products used in the heavy equipment industry. Both products require manufacturing operations in two departments. Production time in hours and profit figures for the two products are as follows:

	Product 1	Product 2
Profit/unit	$25	$20
Dept. A hours	6	8
Dept. B hours	12	10

For the coming production period, Kunz has a total of 900 hours of labor available, which can be allocated to either of the two departments. Let b_1 be the hours assigned to department A and b_2 be the hours assigned to department B. Find the production plan and labor allocation (hours assigned in each department) that will maximize profits.

9. *Portfolio selection.* National Insurance Associates carries an investment portfolio on a variety of stocks, bonds, and other investment alternatives. Currently $200,000 of funds has become available and must be considered for new investment opportunities. The four stock options National is considering and the relevant financial data are as follows:

	Investment Alternative			
	A	B	C	D
Price per share	$100	$50	$80	$40
Annual rate of return	0.12	0.08	0.06	0.10
Risk measure per dollar invested	0.10	0.07	0.05	0.08

The risk measure indicates the relative uncertainty associated with the stock in terms of its realizing the projected annual return. The risk measures are provided by the firm's top financial advisor.

National's top management has stipulated the following investment guidelines:

(1) Annual rate of return for the portfolio must be at least 9%   200,000 × .09 = 18000

(2) No one stock can account for more than 50% of the total dollar investment.

a. Use linear programming to develop an investment portfolio that minimizes risk.

b. If the firm ignores risk and uses a maximum return-on-investment strategy, what is the investment portfolio?

c. What is the dollar difference between the portfolio recommended in parts (a) and (b)? Why might the company prefer the model development in part (a)?

10. *Production routing*. Lurix Electronics manufactures two products that can be produced on two different production lines. Both products have their lowest production costs when produced on the more modern of the two production lines. However, the modern production line does not have the capacity to handle the total production. As a result, some production will have to be routed to an older production line. Shown below are the data for total production requirements, production line capacities, and production costs:

	Production Cost/Unit		Minimum Production Requirements
	Modern Line	Old Line	
Product 1	$3.00	$5.00	500 units
Product 2	$2.50	$4.00	700 units
Production line capacities	800	600	

Formulate a linear programming model that can be used to make the production routing decision. What are the recommended decision and the total cost? (Use notation of the form x_{11} = units of product 1 produced on line 1.)

11. *Purchasing*. Edwards Manufacturing Company purchases two component parts from three different suppliers. The suppliers have limited capacity, and no one supplier can meet all of Edwards' needs. In addition, the suppliers differ in the prices charged for the components. Component price data are as follows:

	Supplier		
Component	1	2	3
1	$12	$13	$14
2	$10	$11	$10

Each supplier has a limited capacity in terms of the total number of components it can supply. However, as long as Edwards provides sufficient advance orders, each supplier can devote its capacity to component 1, component 2, or any combination of the two components, as long as the total number of units ordered is within its capacity. Supplier capacities are as follows:

Supplier	**Total Component Capacity**
Supplier 1	600
Supplier 2	1000
Supplier 3	800

If the Edwards production plan for the next production period includes 1000 units of component 1 and 800 units of component 2, what purchases do you recommend? That is, how many units of each component should be ordered from each supplier? What is the total purchase cost for the components? (For practice in using double-subscripted decision variables, use notation of the form x_{ij} = number of units of component i purchased from supplier j.)

12. *Make or buy.* The Carson Stapler Manufacturing Company forecasts a 5000-unit demand for its Sure-Hold model during the next quarter. This stapler is assembled from three major components: base, staple cartridge, and handle. Until now Carson has manufactured all three components. However, the forecast of 5000 units is a new high in sales volume, and it is doubtful that the firm will have sufficient production capacity to make all the components. The company is considering contracting a local firm to produce at least some of the components. The production time requirements per unit are as follows:

	Production Time (hours)			**Total Department Time Available (hours)**
Department	Base	Cartridge	Handle	
A	0.03	0.02	0.05	400
B	0.04	0.02	0.04	400
C	0.02	0.03	0.01	400

After considering the firm's overhead, material, and labor costs, the accounting department has determined the unit manufacturing cost for each component. These data, along with the purchase price quotations by the contracting firm, are as follows:

Component	Manufacturing Cost	Purchase Cost
Base	$0.75	$0.95
Cartridge	$0.40	$0.55
Handle	$1.10	$1.40

a. Determine the make-or-buy decision for Carson that will meet the 5000-unit demand at a minimum total cost. How many units of each component should be made and how many purchased?

b. Which departments are limiting the manufacturing volume? If overtime could be considered at the additional cost of $3 per hour, which department(s) should be allocated the overtime? Explain.

c. Suppose that up to 80 hours of overtime can be scheduled in department A. What do you recommend?

13. *Blending problem.* Seastrand Oil Company produces two grades of gasoline: regular and high-octane. Both types of gasoline are produced by blending two types of crude oil. Although both types of crude oil contain the two important ingredients required to produce both gasolines, the percentage of important ingredients in each type of crude oil differs, as well as the cost per gallon. The percentage of ingredients A and B in each type of crude oil, and the cost per gallon, are shown below:

Type of Crude Oil	Cost	Ingredient A	Ingredient B	Other Ingredients	
1	$0.10	20%	60%	20%	Crude 1 is 60% ingredient B
2	$0.15	50%	30%	20%	

Each gallon of regular must contain at least 40% of A, whereas each gallon of high-octane can contain at most 50% of B. Daily demand for regular octane gasoline is 800,000 gallons, and daily demand for high-octane is 500,000 gallons. How many gallons of each type of crude oil should be used in regular and in high-octane gasoline in order to satisfy daily demand at a minimum cost? Define the four decision variables as follows:

$$x_{11} = \text{gallons of crude 1 used in regular gasoline}$$

$$x_{12} = \text{gallons of crude 1 used in high-octane gasoline}$$

$$x_{21} = \text{gallons of crude 2 used in regular gasoline}$$

$$x_{22} = \text{gallons of crude 2 used in high-octane gasoline}$$

14. *Cutting stock*. The Ferguson Paper Company produces rolls of paper for use in adding machines, desk calculators, and cash registers. The rolls, which are 200 feet long, are produced in widths of $1\frac{1}{2}$, $2\frac{1}{2}$, and $3\frac{1}{2}$ inches. The production process provides 200-foot rolls in 10-inch widths only. The firm must therefore cut the rolls to the desired final product sizes. The seven cutting alternatives and the amount of waste generated by each are as follows:

Cutting Alternative	Number of Rolls			Waste (inches)
	$1\frac{1}{2}$ in.	$2\frac{1}{2}$ in.	$3\frac{1}{2}$ in.	
1	6	0	0	1
2	0	4	0	0
3	2	0	2	0
4	0	1	2	$\frac{1}{2}$
5	1	3	0	1
6	1	2	1	0
7	4	0	1	$\frac{1}{2}$

The minimum production requirements for the three products are as follows:

Roll Width (inches)	Minimum Production Requirements
$1\frac{1}{2}$	1000 rolls
$2\frac{1}{2}$	2000 rolls
$3\frac{1}{2}$	4000 rolls

a. If the company wants to minimize the number of 10-inch rolls that must be manufactured, how many 10-inch rolls will be processed on each cutting alternative? How many rolls are required, and what is the total waste (inches)?

b. If the company wants to minimize the waste generated, how many 10-inch rolls will be processed on each cutting alternative? How many 10-inch rolls are required, and what is the total waste (inches)?

c. What are the differences in approaches (a) and (b) to this trim problem? In this case, which objective do you prefer? Explain. What are the types of situations that would make the other objective the more desirable?

15. *Inspection*. The Get-Well Pill Company inspects capsule medicine products by passing the capsules over a special lighting table where inspectors visually check for cracked or partially filled capsules. Currently any of three inspectors can be assigned to the visual inspection task. The inspectors, however, differ in accuracy and speed abilities and are paid at slightly different wage rates. The differences are as follows:

Inspector	Speed (units per hour)	Accuracy (%)	Hourly Wage
Davis	300	98	$5.90
Wilson	200	99	$5.20
Lawson	350	96	$5.50

Operating on a full 8-hour shift, the company needs at least 2000 capsules inspected with no more than 2% of these capsules having inspection errors. In addition, because of the fatigue factor of this inspection process, no one inspector can be assigned this task for more than 4 hours per day. How many hours should each inspector be assigned to the capsule inspection process during an 8-hour day if it is desired to minimize the cost of inspection? What volume will be inspected per day, and what is the daily capsule inspection cost?

16. *Equipment acquisition.* The Two-Rivers Oil Company near Pittsburgh transports gasoline to its distributors by trucks. The company has recently received a contract to begin supplying gasoline distributors in southern Ohio and has $600,000 available to spend on the necessary expansion of its fleet of gasoline tank trucks. Three models of gasoline tank truck are available:

Truck Model	Capacity (gallons)	Purchase Cost	Monthly Operating Costs, Including Depreciation
Super Tanker	5000	$67,000	$550
Regular Line	2500	$55,000	$425
Econo-Tanker	1000	$46,000	$350

The company estimates that the monthly demand for the region will be 550,000 gallons of gasoline. Due to the size and speed differences of the trucks, the different truck models will vary in terms of the number of deliveries or round trips possible per month. Trip capacities are estimated at 15 per month for the Super Tanker, 20 per month for the Regular Line, and 25 per month for the Econo-Tanker. Based on maintenance and driver availability, the firm does not want to add more than 15 new vehicles to its fleet. In addition, the company would like to make sure that it purchases at least three of the new Econo-Tankers to use on the short-run, low-demand routes. As a final constraint, the company does not want more than half of the new models to be Super Tankers.

a. If the company wishes to satisfy the gasoline demand with a minimum monthly operating expense, how many models of each truck should be purchased?

b. If the company did not require at least three Econo-Tankers and allows as many Super Tankers as needed, what would the company strategy be?

17. *Multiperiod planning.* The Silver Star Bicycle Company will be manufacturing both men's and women's models for their Easy-Pedal 10-speed bicycles during the next 2 months, and the company would like a production schedule indicating how many

bicycles of each model should be produced in each month. Current demand forecasts call for 150 men's and 125 women's models to be shipped during the first month and 200 men's and 150 women's models to be shipped during the second month. Additional data are shown below:

Model	Production Costs	Labor Required for Manufacturing (hours)	Labor Required for Assembly (hours)	Current Inventory
Men's	$40	10	3	20
Women's	$30	8	2	30

Last month the company used a total of 4000 hours of labor. The company's labor relations policy will not allow the combined total hours of labor (manufacturing plus assembly) to increase or decrease by more than 500 hours from month to month. In addition, the company charges monthly inventory at the rate of 2% of the production cost based on the inventory levels at the end of the month. The company would like to have at least 25 units of each model in inventory at the end of the 2 months.

a. Establish a production schedule that minimizes production and inventory costs and satisfies the labor-smoothing, demand, and inventory requirements. What inventories will be maintained, and what are the monthly labor requirements?

b. If the company changed the constraints so that monthly labor increases and decreases could not exceed 250 hours, what would happen to the production schedule? How much will the cost increase? What would you recommend?

18. *Labor balancing.* The Williams Calculator Company manufactures two kinds of calculators: the TW100 and the TW200. The assembly process requires three people. The assembly times are as follows:

	Assembler 1	Assembler 2	Assembler 3
TW100	4 min	2 min	3½ min
TW200	3 min	4 min	3 min
Maximum hours available per day	8	8	8

The company policy is to balance workloads on all assembly jobs. In fact, management wants to schedule work so that no assembler will have more than 30 minutes more work per day than other assemblers. This means that in a regular 8-hour shift, all assemblers will be assigned at least 7½ hours of work. If the firm makes a $2.50 profit for each TW100 and a $3.50 profit for each TW200, how many units of each calculator should be produced per day? How much time will each assembler be assigned per day?

19. *Staff scheduling.* Western Family Steakhouse offers a variety of low-cost meals and quick service. Other than management, the steakhouse operates with two full-time

employees who work 8 hours per day. All the rest of the employees are part-time employees who are scheduled for 4-hour shifts during meal times. On Saturdays the steakhouse is open from 11:00 A.M. to 10:00 P.M. Management would like a schedule for part-time employees that will minimize labor costs and still provide excellent customer service. The average wage rate for the part-time employees is $3.60 per hour. The total number of full-time and part-time employees needed varies with the time of the day as follows:

Time	Total Number of Employees
11:00 A.M.–Noon	9
Noon–1:00 P.M.	9
1:00 P.M.–2:00 P.M.	9
2:00 P.M.–3:00 P.M.	3
3:00 P.M.–4:00 P.M.	3
4:00 P.M.–5:00 P.M.	3
5:00 P.M.–6:00 P.M.	6
6:00 P.M.–7:00 P.M.	12
7:00 P.M.–8:00 P.M.	12
8:00 P.M.–9:00 P.M.	7
9:00 P.M.–10:00 P.M.	7

One of the full-time employees comes on duty at 11:00 A.M., works 4 hours, takes an hour off, and returns for another 4 hours. The other full-time employee comes to work at 1:00 P.M. and works the same 4-hour-on, 1-hour-off, 4-hour-on work pattern.

a. Develop a minimum-cost schedule for the part-time employees.

b. What is the total payroll for the part-time employees? How many part-time shifts are needed? Use the surplus variables to comment on the desirability of scheduling at least some of the part-time employees for 3-hour shifts.

c. Assume part-time employees can be assigned either a 4-hour shift or a 3-hour shift. Develop a minimum-cost schedule for the part-time employees. How many part-time shifts are needed and what is the cost savings compared with the previous schedule?

20. *Interpretation of computer output.* Shown below is a portion of the computer output from using LINDO/PC to solve the media selection problem for the Relax-and-Enjoy Lake Development Corporation (see Section 9.1).

a. How much would the expected exposure increase per dollar added to the budget? Given the current budget, what is the average exposure per advertising dollar? Does the marginal return from enlarging the budget seem to make enlarging the budget a good investment?

b. From an analysis of the dual prices, comment on whether or not the television commercials are a good idea.

```
              OBJECTIVE FUNCTION VALUE

   1)      2370.0000

      VARIABLE         VALUE          REDUCED COST
         X1         10.000000            .000000
         X2           .000000          64.999990
         X3         25.000000            .000000
         X4          2.000000            .000000
         X5         30.000000            .000000

      ROW      SLACK OR SURPLUS       DUAL PRICES
        2)        40.000000             .000000
        3)        10.000000             .000000
        4)          .000000           16.000000
        5)         2.000000             .000000
        6)          .000000           14.000000
        7)          .000000             .060000
        8)          .000000          -25.000000
        9)      3000.000000             .000000
       10)     11500.000000             .000000
```

Media Availability

Budget

T.V. Restriction

Audience Coverage

Case Problem
Environmental Protection

Skillings Industrial Chemicals, Inc. operates a refinery in southwestern Ohio near the Ohio River. The company's primary product is manufactured from a chemical process that requires the use of two raw materials denoted as material A and material B. The production of 1 pound of the finished product requires the use of 1 pound of material A and 2 pounds of material B. The output of the chemical process is 1 pound of finished product, 1 pound of liquid waste material, and 1 pound of solid waste by-product. The solid waste by-product is given to a local fertilizer plant as payment for picking it up and disposing of it. Since the liquid waste material has no market value, the refinery has been dumping it directly into the Ohio River. Skillings' manufacturing process is shown schematically in Figure 9.8.

Recently imposed governmental pollution guidelines established by the Environmental Protection Agency will not permit disposal of the liquid waste directly into the river. The refinery's research group has developed the following set of alternative uses for the liquid waste material:

1. Produce a secondary product K by adding 1 pound of raw material A to every pound of liquid waste.
2. Produce a secondary product M by adding 1 pound of raw material B to every pound of liquid waste.
3. Specially treat the liquid waste so that it meets pollution standards before dumping it directly into the river.

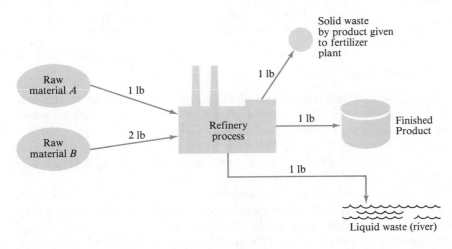

Figure 9.8
Manufacturing Process at Skillings Industrial Chemicals, Inc.

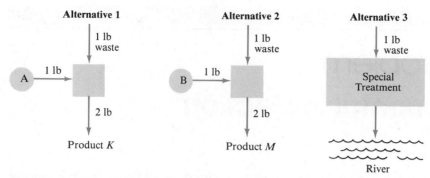

Figure 9.9
Alternatives for Handling the Refinery Liquid Waste

These three alternatives are depicted in Figure 9.9.

The company's management knows that the secondary products will be low in quality and may not be very profitable. However, management is also aware of the fact that the special treatment alternative will be a relatively expensive operation. The company's problem is to determine how to satisfy the pollution regulations and still maintain the highest possible profit. How should the liquid waste material be handled? Should Skillings produce product K, produce product M, use the special treatment, or employ some combination of the three alternatives?

Last month 10,000 pounds of the company's primary product were produced. The accounting department has prepared a cost report showing the breakdown of fixed and variable expenses that were incurred during the month.

Cost Analysis for 10,000 Pounds of Primary Product

Fixed cost allocation	Administrative expenses	$12,000
	Refinery overhead	4,000
Variable costs	Raw material A	15,000
	Raw material B	16,000
	Direct labor	5,000
	Total	$52,000

In the above cost analysis the fixed cost portion of the expenses is the same every month regardless of production level. Direct labor costs are expected to run $0.20 per pound for product K and $0.10 per pound for product M.

The company's primary product sells for $5.70 per pound. Secondary products K and M sell for $0.85 per pound and $0.65 per pound, respectively. The special treatment of the liquid waste will cost $0.25 per pound.

One of the company's accountants feels that product K is too expensive to manufacture and cannot be sold at a price that recovers its material and labor cost. The accountant's recommendation is to eliminate product K as an alternative.

For the upcoming production period, 5000 pounds of raw material A and 7000 pounds of raw material B will be available. Develop a production and waste disposal plan for the production period.

Managerial Report

Develop an approach to the problem that will allow the company to determine how much primary product to produce given the limitations on the amounts of the raw material available. Include recommendations as to how the company should dispose of the liquid waste to satisfy the environmental protection guidelines. How many pounds of product K should be produced? How many pounds of product M should be produced? How many pounds of liquid waste should be specially treated and dumped directly into the river? Include a discussion and analysis of the following in your report.

1. A cost analysis showing the profit contribution per pound for the primary product, product K, and product M.
2. The optimal production quantities and waste disposal plan, including the projected profit.
3. A discussion of the value of additional pounds of each raw material.
4. A discussion of the sensitivity analysis of the objective function coefficients.
5. Comments on the accountant's recommendation to eliminate product K as an alternative. Does the recommendation appear reasonable? What is your reaction to the recommendation? How would the optimal solution change if product K were eliminated?

Quantitative Methods in Practice
Marathon Oil Company*
Findlay, Ohio

Marathon Oil Company was founded in 1887 when 14 oilmen pooled their properties to organize an oil-producing company in the Trenton Rock oil fields of Ohio. In 1924 Marathon entered the refining and marketing phase of the petroleum industry. Today, Marathon is a fully integrated oil company with significant international operations. It employs over 18,000 people, and company activities extend to six continents. In the United States the company markets petroleum products in 21 states, primarily in the Midwest and Southeast.

Management Science at Marathon Oil Company

Most of the management science applications at Marathon Oil involve the firm's Operations Research Department. This department was formed in 1963 in order to aid problem solving and decision making in all areas of the company. Approximately 50% of the applications involve linear programming. Typical problems include refinery models, distribution models, gasoline and fuel oil blending models, and crude oil evaluation studies. Another 30% of the applications involve complex chemical engineering simulation models of process operations. The remainder of the management science applications involves solution techniques using nonlinear programming, network flow algorithms, and statistical techniques such as regression analysis.

A Marketing Planning Model

Marathon Oil Company has four refineries within the United States, operates 50 light products terminals, and has product demand at over 100 locations. The Marketing Operations Division is faced with the problem of determining which refinery should supply which terminal, and at the same time determining which products should be transported via which pipeline, barge, or tanker in order to achieve a minimum cost. Product demand must be satisfied, and the supply capability of each refinery must not be exceeded. To help solve this difficult problem, Marathon's Operations Research Department developed a marketing planning model for the Marketing Operations Division.

The marketing planning model is a large-scale linear programming model that takes into account sales not only at Marathon product terminals but also at all exchange locations.

*The authors are indebted to Jerry T. Ranney and Keith R. Weiss of Marathon Oil Company, Findlay, Ohio, for providing this application.

An exchange contract is an agreement with other oil product marketers that involves exchanging or trading Marathon's products for theirs at different locations. Thus some geographic imbalance between supply and demand can be reduced. Both sides of the exchanges are represented, since this not only affects the net requirements at a demand location but in addition has important financial implications. All pipelines, barges, and tankers within Marathon's marketing area are also represented in the linear programming model.

The optimization of gasoline blending for each refinery, based on blendstock availabilities and the gasoline demand structure, is accomplished in the model by the inclusion of gasoline blending submodels. Thus the linear programming model is a combination of a blending model and a transportation model.

The objective of the linear programming model is to minimize the cost of meeting a given demand structure, taking into account sales price, pipeline tariffs, exchange contract costs, product demand, terminal operating costs, refining costs, and product purchases. The current linear programming problem size is approximately 1800 rows by 6000 columns. The IBM MPSX/370 system solves the problem in less than 3 minutes using an IBM 3081 computer system.

The marketing planning model is used to solve a wide variety of planning problems. These vary from evaluating gasoline blending economics to analyzing the economics of a new terminal or pipeline. Although the types of problems that can be solved are almost unlimited, the model is most effective in handling the following:

1. Evaluating additional product demand locations, pipelines, refinery units, and exchange contracts
2. Determining profitability of shifting sales from one product demand location to another
3. Showing effects on refinery gasoline blending when octane requirements are increased, blendstock availabilities are decreased, or there is a major shift in the demand pattern
4. Determining the effects on supply and distribution when a pipeline increases its tariff
5. Optimizing production of the three grades of gasoline at the four refineries

The linear programming model not only solves these problems, but also gives the financial impact of each solution.

Benefits

With daily sales of about 10 million gallons of refined light product, a saving of even one-thousandth of a cent per gallon can result in significant long-term savings. At the same time, what may appear to be a savings in one area, such as refining or transportation, may actually add to overall costs when the effects are fully realized throughout the system. The marketing planning model allows a simultaneous examination of this total effect.

Questions

1. What is the primary objective of Marathon's marketing planning model?
2. Describe the types of problems the marketing planning model is most effective in handling.
3. If daily savings using the model are one-tenth of a cent per gallon sold, what is the projected daily savings?

10

Linear Programming: The Simplex Method

In Chapter 7 we showed how the graphical solution procedure can be used to solve linear programming problems involving two decision variables. However, most linear programming problems are too large to be solved graphically and thus an algebraic solution procedure must be employed. The most widely used algebraic procedure for solving linear programming problems is called the *simplex method*.[1] Computer programs based on this method can routinely solve linear programming problems having as many as several thousand variables and several thousand constraints.

10.1

AN ALGEBRAIC OVERVIEW OF THE SIMPLEX METHOD

Let us return to the RMC problem from Chapter 7. Given constraints on the availability of three materials, RMC's problem was to determine how many tons of fuel additive (x_1) and how many tons of solvent base (x_2) to produce in order to maximize profit. The RMC problem written in standard form is as follows:

[1]Recently N. Karmarkar, at Bell Labs, developed a new linear programming procedure that some say will eventually supersede the simplex method. At this time the simplex method is by far the most widely used.

$$\max 40x_1 + 30x_2 + 0s_1 + 0s_2 + 0s_3 \qquad (10.1)$$

s.t.

$$\tfrac{2}{5}x_1 + \tfrac{1}{2}x_2 + 1s_1 \qquad\qquad = 20 \qquad (10.2)$$

$$\tfrac{1}{5}x_2 \qquad + 1s_2 \qquad = 5 \qquad (10.3)$$

$$\tfrac{3}{5}x_1 + \tfrac{3}{10}x_2 \qquad\qquad + 1s_3 = 21 \qquad (10.4)$$

$$x_1, x_2, s_1, s_2, s_3 \geq 0 \qquad (10.5)$$

Algebraic Properties of the Simplex Method

Constraint equations (10.2) to (10.4) form a system of three simultaneous linear equations with five variables. When a set of simultaneous linear equations has more variables than constraints, one can expect an infinite number of solutions. The simplex method is an algebraic procedure that can be used to solve a system of simultaneous linear equations involving more variables than equations. In addition, the simplex method will identify a solution that provides the best possible value for the objective function.

We cannot expect that every solution to equations (10.2)–(10.4) will also satisfy the nonnegativity conditions $x_1, x_2, s_1, s_2, s_3 \geq 0$. Consequently not every solution to equations (10.2)–(10.4) will be a feasible solution. When solving a set of simultaneous linear equations, the simplex method eliminates from consideration those solutions that do not also satisfy the nonnegativity requirements.

Determining a Basic Solution

As noted, the RMC constraint equations (10.2)–(10.4) have more variables (five) than equations (three). The simplex method finds solutions for these equations by assigning zero values for two of the variables and then solving for the values of the remaining three variables. For example, suppose that we set $x_2 = 0$ and $s_1 = 0$. The system of constraint equations then becomes

$$\tfrac{2}{5}x_1 \qquad\qquad = 20 \qquad (10.6)$$

$$1s_2 \qquad = 5 \qquad (10.7)$$

$$\tfrac{3}{5}x_1 \qquad + 1s_3 = 21 \qquad (10.8)$$

By setting $x_2 = 0$ and $s_1 = 0$ we have reduced the system of three simultaneous linear equations with five variables to a system of three simultaneous equations with three variables (x_1, s_2, and s_3).

Using equation (10.6) to solve for x_1, we have

$$\tfrac{2}{5}x_1 = 20$$
$$x_1 = \tfrac{5}{2}(20) = 50$$

Equation (10.7) provides $s_2 = 5$. And substituting $x_1 = 50$ into equation (10.8) provides

$$\tfrac{3}{5}(50) + 1s_3 = 21$$

or

$$s_3 = 21 - \tfrac{3}{5}(50) = -9$$

Thus we have found the following solution to the three-equation, five-variable set of linear equations determined by the RMC constraints:

$$x_1 = 50$$
$$x_2 = 0$$
$$s_1 = 0$$
$$s_2 = 5$$
$$s_3 = -9$$

This solution is referred to as a *basic solution* for the RMC linear programming problem.

In order to provide a general procedure for determining a basic solution, consider a standard-form linear programming problem consisting of n variables (including decision variables, slack variables, and surplus variables) and m linear equations, where n is greater than m.

A Basic Solution   *To find a basic solution, set $n - m$ of the variables equal to zero and solve the m linear constraint equations for the remaining m variables.*[2]

In terms of the RMC problem, a basic solution can be obtained by setting any two variables equal to zero and then solving the system of three linear equations for the remaining three variables. We shall refer to the $n - m$ variables set equal to zero as the *nonbasic variables* and the remaining m variables (allowed to be nonzero) as the *basic variables*. Thus in the example above, x_2 and s_1 are the nonbasic variables and x_1, s_2, and s_3 are the basic variables.

Basic Feasible Solutions

A basic solution can be either feasible or infeasible. A *basic feasible solution* is a basic solution that also satisfies the nonnegativity conditions. The basic solution found by setting x_2 and s_1 equal to 0, and then solving for x_1, s_2, and s_3, is not a feasible solution because $s_3 = -9$. However, suppose that we had chosen to make x_1 and x_2 nonbasic variables (that is, $x_1 = 0$ and $x_2 = 0$). Solving for the corresponding basic solution is easy, because the three constraint equations reduce to

$$s_1 \quad = 20$$
$$s_2 \quad = 5$$
$$s_3 = 21$$

The complete solution (including the nonbasic variables) corresponding to $x_1 = 0$ and $x_2 = 0$ is

$$x_1 = 0$$
$$x_2 = 0$$
$$s_1 = 20$$
$$s_2 = 5$$
$$s_3 = 21$$

---

[2]There are cases where a unique solution cannot be found for the resulting system of m equations in m variables. However, these cases will never be encountered when using the simplex method.

This solution is a basic solution since it was obtained by setting two of the variables equal to zero and solving for the other three variables. Moreover, it is a basic *feasible* solution since all of the variables are greater than or equal to zero.

In Figure 10.1 we show a graph of the feasible region for the RMC problem. We see that the basic feasible solution obtained by setting $x_1 = 0$ and $x_2 = 0$ corresponds to extreme point ① of the feasible region. This is not just a coincidence: All basic feasible solutions correspond to extreme points of the feasible region. Thus for every extreme point of the feasible region of a linear programming problem there is a corresponding basic feasible solution.

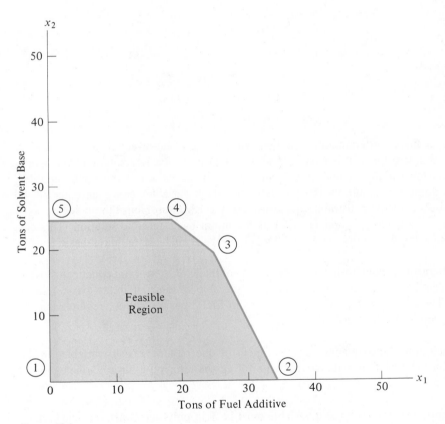

Figure 10.1
The Five Extreme Points of the Feasible Region for the RMC Problem

In Chapter 7 we showed that the optimal solution to a linear programming problem can be found at an extreme point. Since there is a corresponding basic feasible solution for every extreme point, we can now conclude that there is an optimal basic feasible solution.[3] The simplex method is an iterative procedure for moving from one basic feasible solution (extreme point) to another until the optimal solution is reached.

---

[3]We are only considering cases where there is an optimal solution. In the cases of infeasibility and unboundedness there is no optimal solution, so there cannot be an optimal basic feasible solution.

10.2

TABLEAU FORM

A basic feasible solution to the system of m linear constraint equations and n variables is required as a starting point for the simplex method. From this starting point the simplex method successively generates better basic feasible solutions to the system of linear equations. When the objective function can no longer be improved in this fashion, the optimal solution has been reached. The purpose of *tableau form* is to provide an initial basic feasible solution to get the simplex method started.

Recall that for the RMC problem the standard-form representation is

$$\max 40x_1 + 30x_2 + 0s_1 + 0s_2 + 0s_3$$

$$\text{s.t.}$$

$$\tfrac{2}{5}x_1 + \tfrac{1}{2}x_2 + 1s_1 \qquad\qquad = 20$$
$$\tfrac{1}{5}x_2 \qquad + 1s_2 \qquad = 5$$
$$\tfrac{3}{5}x_1 + \tfrac{3}{10}x_2 \qquad\qquad + 1s_3 = 21$$

$$x_1, x_2, s_1, s_2, s_3 \geq 0$$

When a linear programming problem with all less-than-or-equal-to constraints is written in standard form, it is easy to find an initial basic feasible solution. We simply set the decision variables equal to zero and solve for the values of the slack variables. Note that doing this results in the values of the slack variables being set equal to the right-hand-sides of the constraint equations. For the RMC problem this yields $x_1 = 0$, $x_2 = 0$, $s_1 = 20$, $s_2 = 5$, and $s_3 = 21$ as the initial basic feasible solution. This corresponds to using the origin, extreme point ① in Figure 10.1, as the initial basic feasible solution.

If we study the standard-form representation of the RMC constraint equations closely, we can identify two properties that make it possible to find an initial basic feasible solution. The *first property*, which enables us to find a basic solution, requires that the following conditions be satisfied:

a. For each constraint equation the coefficient of one of the m basic variables in that equation must be 1, and the coefficients for all the remaining basic variables in that equation must be 0.

b. The coefficient for each basic variable must be 1 in only one constraint equation.

When these conditions are satisfied, there is exactly one basic variable associated with each equation, and for each of the m equations it is a different basic variable. Thus if the $n - m$ nonbasic variables are set equal to zero, the values of the basic variables can be read from the right-hand side of the constraint equations.

The *second property* that enables us to find a basic feasible solution requires that the values on the right-hand sides of the constraint equations be nonnegative. This ensures that the basic solution obtained by setting the basic variables equal to the right-hand-side values is feasible.

If a linear programming problem satisfies the two properties above, it is said to be in tableau form. Thus we see that the standard-form representation of the RMC problem is already in tableau form. In fact, the standard form and tableau form for linear programs that have all less-than-or-equal-to constraints and nonnegative right-hand-side values are the same. Later in this chapter we will show how to set up tableau form for problems involving equality and greater-than-or-equal-to constraints; in these cases the standard-form representation of the problem and the tableau-form representation are not the same.

To summarize, the following three steps are necessary in order to prepare a linear programming problem for solution using the simplex method:

Step 1 Formulate the problem.

Step 2 Set up the standard-form representation of the problem by adding slack and/or subtracting surplus variables.

Step 3 Set up the tableau-form representation of the problem.

10.3

SETTING UP THE INITIAL SIMPLEX TABLEAU

After a linear programming problem has been converted to tableau form, we can identify an initial basic feasible solution that can be used to begin the simplex method. To provide a convenient means for performing the calculations required by the simplex method, we will first develop what is referred to as the *simplex tableau*.

Part of the initial simplex tableau is a table containing all the coefficients shown in the tableau-form representation of a linear program. If we adopt the general notation

$$c_j = \text{objective function coefficient for variable } j$$
$$b_i = \text{right-hand-side value for constraint } i$$
$$a_{ij} = \text{coefficient associated with variable } j \text{ in constraint } i$$

we can show this portion of the simplex tableau as follows:

$$
\begin{array}{cccc|c}
c_1 & c_2 & \cdots & c_n & \\
\hline
a_{11} & a_{12} & \cdots & a_{1n} & b_1 \\
a_{21} & a_{22} & \cdots & a_{2n} & b_2 \\
\cdot & \cdot & \cdots & \cdot & \cdot \\
\cdot & \cdot & \cdots & \cdot & \cdot \\
\cdot & \cdot & \cdots & \cdot & \cdot \\
a_{m1} & a_{m2} & \cdots & a_{mn} & b_m
\end{array}
$$

Thus for the RMC problem we obtain the following partial initial simplex tableau:

$$
\begin{array}{ccccc|c}
40 & 30 & 0 & 0 & 0 & \\
\hline
2/5 & 1/2 & 1 & 0 & 0 & 20 \\
0 & 1/5 & 0 & 1 & 0 & 5 \\
3/5 & 3/10 & 0 & 0 & 1 & 21
\end{array}
$$

Note that the row above the first horizontal line contains the coefficients of the objective function in the tableau-form representation of the problem. The elements appearing between the horizontal lines and to the left of the vertical line are the coefficients of the constraint equations, and the elements to the right of the vertical line are the corresponding right-hand-side values.

Later we may want to refer to the objective function coefficients, all the right-hand-side values, or all the coefficients in the constraints as a group. To do this we will find the following general notation helpful:

c row = row of objective function coefficients
b column = column of right-hand-side values of the constraint equations
A matrix = m rows and n columns of coefficients of the variables in the constraint equations

Using this notation we can show the above portion of the initial simplex tableau as follows:

c row	
A matrix	b column

To help us recall that each of the columns contains the coefficients of one variable, we will write the variable associated with each column directly above the column. Doing this for the RMC problem, we obtain

x_1	x_2	s_1	s_2	s_3	
40	30	0	0	0	
$2/5$	$1/2$	1	0	0	20
0	$1/5$	0	1	0	5
$3/5$	$3/10$	0	0	1	21

The initial simplex tableau contains the tableau form of the problem; thus it is easy to identify the initial basic feasible solution. First, we note that for each basic variable there is a corresponding column that has a 1 in the only nonzero position. Such columns are known as *unit columns* or *unit vectors*. Second, there is a row of the tableau associated with each basic variable. This row has a 1 in the unit column corresponding to the basic variable. The value of each basic variable is then given by the b_i value in the row associated with the basic variable. For example, in the RMC problem, row 3 of the simplex tableau is associated with basic variable s_3 since this row has a 1 in the unit column corresponding to s_3; therefore the value of this basic variable is given by $s_3 = b_3 = 21$. Table 10.1 shows the column corresponding to basic variable s_2, the row associated with s_2, and its value, $s_2 = 5$.

Table 10.1
Illustration of Procedure for Identifying Values of Basic Variables from the Simplex Tableau

	x_1	x_2	s_1	s_2	s_3	
	40	30	0	0	0	
	$\frac{2}{5}$	$\frac{1}{2}$	1	0	0	20
Row associated with s_2 $\longrightarrow$	0	$\frac{1}{5}$	0	1	0	5
	$\frac{3}{5}$	$\frac{3}{10}$	0	0	1	21

Column associated
with s_2

Value of s_2

10.4

IMPROVING THE SOLUTION

In order to improve the initial basic feasible solution, the simplex method must generate a new basic feasible solution (extreme point) that yields a better value for the objective function. To do so requires changing the set of basic variables; this is accomplished by selecting one of the current nonbasic variables to make basic and one of the current basic variables to make nonbasic in such a fashion that the new basic feasible solution yields an improved value for the objective function. The simplex method provides an easy way to carry out this change of variables in the basic feasible solution.

For computational convenience we will add two new columns to the present form of the simplex tableau. One column is labeled "Basis" and the other column is labeled "c_B." In the *Basis* column we list the current basic variables, and in the column labeled c_B we list the corresponding objective function coefficient for each of these basic variables. For the RMC problem this results in the following initial simplex tableau:

Basis	c_B	x_1	x_2	s_1	s_2	s_3	
		40	30	0	0	0	
s_1	0	$\frac{2}{5}$	$\frac{1}{2}$	1	0	0	20
s_2	0	0	$\frac{1}{5}$	0	1	0	5
s_3	0	$\frac{3}{5}$	$\frac{3}{10}$	0	0	1	21

Note that in the column labeled *Basis*, s_1 is listed as the first basic variable since its value is given by the right-hand-side value for the first equation (that is, $s_1 = b_1 = 20$); s_2 is listed second, since its value is given by $s_2 = b_2 = 5$; and $s_3 = b_3 = 21$ is listed last.

Can we improve the value of the objective function by moving to a new basic feasible solution? To help find out if this is possible, we add two rows to the bottom of the tableau. The first row, labeled z_j, represents the decrease in the value of the objective function that will result if one unit of the variable corresponding to the *j*th column of the *A* matrix is brought into the basis; that is, if this variable is made a basic variable with a value of 1. The term basis is used here to refer to the set of basic variables. The second row, labeled $c_j - z_j$, represents the net change in the value of the objective function if one unit of the variable corresponding to the jth column of the A matrix is brought into solution. We refer to $c_j - z_j$ as the *net evaluation row*.

Let us first see how the entries in the z_j row are computed. Suppose that we consider increasing the value of the nonbasic variable x_1 by one unit; that is, from $x_1 = 0$ to $x_1 = 1$. In order to make this change and at the same time continue to satisfy the constraint equations, the values of some of the other variables will have to be changed. As we will show, the simplex method requires that the necessary changes be made to basic variables only. For example, in the first constraint we have

$$\tfrac{2}{5}x_1 + \tfrac{1}{2}x_2 + 1s_1 = 20$$

The current basic variable in this constraint equation is s_1. Assuming that x_2 remains a nonbasic variable with a value of 0, if x_1 is increased in value by 1, then s_1 must be decreased by $\tfrac{2}{5}$ for the constraint to be satisfied. Similarly, if we were to increase the value of x_1 by 1 (and keep $x_2 = 0$), we can see from the second and third equations that although s_2 would not decrease, s_3 would decrease by $\tfrac{3}{5}$.

From analyzing all the constraint equations, we see that making x_1 a basic variable with a value of 1 will result in a decrease of $\tfrac{2}{5}$ units in s_1, a decrease of 0 units in s_2, and a decrease of $\tfrac{3}{5}$ units in s_3. Thus we see that the coefficients in the x_1 column indicate the amount of decrease in the current basic variables when the nonbasic variable x_1 is increased from 0 to 1. In general, all the column coefficients can be interpreted this way. For instance, if we make x_2 a basic variable at a value of 1 (while keeping x_1 a nonbasic variable at a value of 0), s_1 will decrease by $\tfrac{1}{2}$, s_2 will decrease by $\tfrac{1}{5}$, and s_3 will decrease by $\tfrac{3}{10}$.

Recall that the values in the c_B column of the simplex tableau are the objective function coefficients for the current basic variables. Hence, to compute the values in the z_j row (the decrease in value of the objective function resulting from bringing one unit of x_j into the basis), we form the sum of the products obtained by multiplying the elements in the c_B column by the corresponding elements in the jth column of the A matrix. Doing this we obtain

$$z_1 = 0(\tfrac{2}{5}) + 0(0) + 0(\tfrac{3}{5}) = 0$$
$$z_2 = 0(\tfrac{1}{2}) + 0(\tfrac{1}{5}) + 0(\tfrac{3}{10}) = 0$$
$$z_3 = 0(1) + 0(0) + 0(0) = 0$$
$$z_4 = 0(0) + 0(1) + 0(0) = 0$$
$$z_5 = 0(0) + 0(0) + 0(1) = 0$$

Since the objective function coefficient of x_1 is 40, the value of $c_1 - z_1$ is $40 - 0 = 40$. This indicates that the net result of bringing one unit of x_1 into the current basis will be an increase in profit of \$40. Hence in the net evaluation row corresponding to x_1 we enter 40. In the same manner we can calculate the $c_j - z_j$ values for the remaining variables. The result is the following initial simplex tableau:

Basis	c_B	x_1	x_2	s_1	s_2	s_3	
		40	30	0	0	0	
s_1	0	$\frac{2}{5}$	$\frac{1}{2}$	1	0	0	20
s_2	0	0	$\frac{1}{5}$	0	1	0	5
s_3	0	$\frac{3}{5}$	$\frac{3}{10}$	0	0	1	21
	z_j	0	0	0	0	0	0
	$c_j - z_j$	40	30	0	0	0	↑

Profit

In this tableau we also see a 0 in the z_j row in the last column. This zero represents the profit associated with the current basic feasible solution. It was computed by multiplying the values of the basic variables, which are given in the last column of the simplex tableau, by their corresponding contribution to profit as given in the c_B column. Profit $= 0(20) + 0(5) + 0(21) = 0$.

From the net evaluation row we see that each ton of fuel additive (x_1) increases the value of the objective function by 40 and each ton of solvent base (x_2) increases the value of the objective function by 30. Since x_1 causes the largest per-unit increase, we choose it as the variable to bring into the basis. We must next determine which of the current basic variables to make nonbasic. In doing so we first note that since each unit of x_1 that is brought into the solution increases the objective function by \$40, we would like to make x_1 as large as possible.

In discussing how to compute the z_j values, we noted that each of the coefficients in the x_1 column indicates the amount of decrease in the corresponding basic variable that would result from increasing x_1 by one unit. Hence only the positive coefficients need to be considered in determining the current basic variable that will become nonbasic at a value of zero. Considering the first row, we see that every ton of fuel additive produced will cause us to use $\frac{2}{5}$ tons of material 1 (i.e., reduce s_1 by $\frac{2}{5}$). In the *current solution*, $s_1 = 20$ and $x_1 = 0$. Thus—considering this row only—the maximum possible value of x_1 can be calculated by solving

$$\tfrac{2}{5}x_1 = 20$$

which provides

$$x_1 = \tfrac{5}{2}(20) = 50$$

If x_1 is increased to 50 (and x_2 remains a nonbasic variable with a value of 0), s_1 will have to be reduced to zero in order to satisfy the first constraint:

$$\tfrac{2}{5}x_1 + \tfrac{1}{2}x_2 + 1s_1 = 20$$

Considering the second row, $0x_1 + \frac{1}{5}x_2 + 1s_2 = 5$, we see that the coefficient of x_1 is 0. Thus increasing x_1 will not have any effect on s_2; that is, increasing x_1 cannot drive the basic variable in the second row (s_2) to zero. Indeed, increases in x_1 will leave s_2 unchanged.

Finally, since the coefficient of x_1 is $\frac{3}{5}$ in the third row, every unit that we increase x_1 will cause a decrease of $\frac{3}{5}$ units in s_3. Since the value of s_3 is currently $s_3 = 21$, we can solve

$$\tfrac{3}{5}x_1 = 21$$

to find the maximum possible increase in x_1 before s_3 will become nonbasic at a value of 0. Solving, we see that x_1 cannot be any larger than $\tfrac{5}{3}(21) = 35$.

Considering the three rows (constraints) simultaneously, we see that row 3 is the most restrictive. That is, producing 35 tons of fuel additive will use all of the material 3 available and force the corresponding slack variable to become nonbasic at a value of $s_3 = 0$.

In making the decision to produce as many tons of fuel additive as possible, we must change the set of variables in the basic feasible solution (i.e., obtain a new *basis*). The nonbasic variable x_1 will now become a basic variable while the previous basic variable, s_3, will become a nonbasic variable with $s_3 = 0$. This interchange of roles between two variables is the essence of the simplex method. The way the simplex method moves from one basic feasible solution to another is by selecting a nonbasic variable to replace one of the current basic variables. This process of moving from one basic feasible solution to another is called an *iteration*. We now summarize the rules for selecting a nonbasic variable to make basic and selecting a current basic variable to make nonbasic.

Criterion for Entering a New Variable into the Basis

Look at the net evaluation row ($c_j - z_j$) and select the variable to enter the basis that will cause the largest per-unit improvement in the value of the objective function. In the case of a tie, we follow the convention of selecting the variable to enter the basis that corresponds to the leftmost of the columns.

Criterion for Removing a Variable from the Current Basis

Suppose that the incoming basic variable corresponds to column j in the A portion of the simplex tableau. For each row i compute the ratio b_i/a_{ij}, for each a_{ij} greater than 0. The basic variable to remove from the basis corresponds to the minimum of these ratios. In case of a tie, we follow the convention of selecting the variable to leave the basis that corresponds to the uppermost of the tied rows.

Let us illustrate the iterative procedure by applying it to the RMC problem. To illustrate the computations involved, we add an extra column to the right of the tableau showing the b_i/a_{ij} ratios.

		x_1	x_2	s_1	s_2	s_3		$\dfrac{b_i}{a_{i1}}$
Basis	c_B	40	30	0	0	0		
s_1	0	$\tfrac{2}{5}$	$\tfrac{1}{2}$	1	0	0	20	$\dfrac{20}{\tfrac{2}{5}} = 50$
s_2	0	0	$\tfrac{1}{5}$	0	1	0	5	—
s_3	0	$\left(\tfrac{3}{5}\right)$	$\tfrac{3}{10}$	0	0	1	21	$\dfrac{21}{\tfrac{3}{5}} = 35$
	z_j	0	0	0	0	0	0	
	$c_j - z_j$	40	30	0	0	0		

We see that $c_1 - z_1 = 40$ is the largest positive value in the $c_j - z_j$ row. Hence x_1 is selected to become the new basic variable. Checking the ratios b_i/a_{i1} for values of a_{i1} greater than 0, we see that $b_3/a_{31} = 35$ is the minimum of these ratios. Thus, the current basic variable associated with row 3 (s_3) is the variable selected to leave the basis. In the tableau we have circled $a_{31} = \frac{3}{5}$ to indicate that the variable corresponding to the first column is to enter the basis and that the basic variable corresponding to the third row is to leave the basis. Adopting the usual linear programming terminology, we refer to this circled element as the *pivot element*. The column and the row containing the pivot element are called the *pivot column* and the *pivot row*, respectively.

To improve the current solution of $x_1 = 0$, $x_2 = 0$, $s_1 = 20$, $s_2 = 5$, and $s_3 = 21$, we should increase x_1 to 35. The production of 35 tons of fuel additive results in a profit of $40(35) = 1400$. In producing 35 tons of fuel additive, we will use all the available material 3 and thus s_3 will be reduced to zero. Hence x_1 will become the new basic variable, replacing s_3 in the old basis.

10.5

CALCULATING THE NEXT TABLEAU

In the previous section we concluded that the initial basic feasible solution obtained by setting $x_1 = 0$ and $x_2 = 0$ could be improved by introducing x_1 into the basis to replace s_3. To determine the new basic feasible solution corresponding to making x_1 a basic variable, it will be necessary to update the simplex tableau.

Recall that the initial simplex tableau contains the coefficients of the tableau-form representation of the linear program. Because of the special properties of the tableau form, the initial simplex tableau contains a unit column corresponding to each basic variable.

We now want to update the simplex tableau in such a fashion that the column associated with the new basic variable is a unit column; in this way its value will be given by the right-hand-side value of the corresponding row. Thus we would like the column in the new tableau corresponding to x_1 to look just like the column corresponding to s_3 in the original tableau. Hence our goal is to make the column in the A matrix corresponding to x_1 appear as

$$0$$
$$0$$
$$1$$

The way in which we transform the simplex tableau so that it still represents an equivalent system of constraint equations with the above properties is to use the following *elementary row operations*.

Elementary Row Operations

1. Multiply any row (equation) by a nonzero number.
2. Replace any row (equation) by the result of adding or subtracting a multiple of another row (equation) to it.

The application of these elementary row operations to a system of simultaneous linear equations will not change the solution to the system of equations; however, the elementary row operations will change the coefficients of the variables and the values of the right-hand sides.

The objective in performing elementary row operations is to transform the system of constraint equations into a form that makes it easy to identify the new basic feasible solution. Consequently we must perform the elementary row operations in such a manner that we transform the column for the variable entering the basis into a unit column. We emphasize that the feasible solutions to the original constraint equations are the same as the feasible solutions to the modified constraint equations obtained by performing elementary row operations. However, many of the numerical values in the simplex tableau will change as the result of performing these row operations. Thus the present method of referring to elements in the simplex tableau may lead to confusion.

Up to now we have made no distinction between the A matrix and b column coefficients in the tableau-form representation of the problem and the corresponding coefficients in the simplex tableau. Indeed, we showed that the initial simplex tableau is formed by properly placing the a_{ij}, c_j, and b_i elements as given in the tableau-form representation of the problem into the simplex tableau. We will refer to the portion of the simplex tableau that initially contained the a_{ij} values with the symbol $\overline{A}$, and the portion of the tableau that initially contained the b_i values with the symbol $\overline{b}$. In terms of the simplex tableau, elements in $\overline{A}$ will be denoted by $\overline{a}_{ij}$ and elements in $\overline{b}$ will be denoted by $\overline{b}_i$. We recognize that $\overline{A} = A$ and $\overline{b} = b$ in the initial simplex tableau. However, in subsequent simplex tableaus this relationship will not hold. The overbar notation should avoid any confusion when we wish to distinguish between the original constraint coefficient values a_{ij} and right-hand-side values b_i of the tableau form, and the simplex tableau elements $\overline{a}_{ij}$ and $\overline{b}_i$.

Now let us see how elementary row operations are used to create the next simplex tableau for the RMC problem. Recall that the goal is to transform the column in the $\overline{A}$ portion of the simplex tableau corresponding to x_1 to a unit column; that is,

$$\overline{a}_{11} = 0$$
$$\overline{a}_{21} = 0$$
$$\overline{a}_{31} = 1$$

In order to set $\overline{a}_{31} = 1$, we perform the first elementary row operation by multiplying the pivot row (row 3) by $\frac{5}{3}$ to obtain the equivalent equation

$$\tfrac{5}{3}(\tfrac{3}{5}x_1 + \tfrac{3}{10}x_2 + 0s_1 + 0s_2 + 1s_3) = \tfrac{5}{3}(21)$$

or

$$1x_1 + \tfrac{1}{2}x_2 + 0s_1 + 0s_2 + \tfrac{5}{3}s_3 = 35 \tag{10.9}$$

We refer to (10.9) in the updated simplex tableau as the *new pivot row*.

Making this substitution results in the following tableau:

Basis	c_B	x_1	x_2	s_1	s_2	s_3	
		40	30	0	0	0	
		$\frac{2}{5}$	$\frac{1}{2}$	1	0	0	20
		0	$\frac{1}{5}$	0	1	0	5
		1	$\frac{1}{2}$	0	0	$\frac{5}{3}$	35
	z_j						
	$c_j - z_j$						

Since $\bar{a}_{21} = 0$, no row operations need be performed on the second row of the tableau. To obtain $\bar{a}_{11} = 0$, we multiply the new pivot row by $-\frac{2}{5}$ to obtain the equivalent equation

$$-\frac{2}{5}x_1 - \frac{1}{5}x_2 + 0s_1 + 0s_2 - \frac{2}{3}s_3 = -14 \qquad (10.10)$$

Adding equation (10.10) to the material 1 equation (row 1), we have

$$(-\frac{2}{5}x_1 - \frac{1}{5}x_2 - \frac{2}{3}s_3) + (\frac{2}{5}x_1 + \frac{1}{2}x_2 + 1s_1) = 20 - 14$$

or

$$0x_1 + \frac{3}{10}x_2 + 1s_1 - \frac{2}{3}s_3 = 6 \qquad (10.11)$$

Replacing row 1 with this equation in the new tableau gives the following simplex tableau:

Basis	c_B	x_1	x_2	s_1	s_2	s_3	
		40	30	0	0	0	
s_1	0	0	$\frac{3}{10}$	1	0	$-\frac{2}{3}$	6
s_2	0	0	$\frac{1}{5}$	0	1	0	5
x_1	40	1	$\frac{1}{2}$	0	0	$\frac{5}{3}$	35
	z_j						1400
	$c_j - z_j$						

The corresponding system of equations is (terms having zero coefficients are dropped)

$$\frac{3}{10}x_2 + 1s_1 \qquad - \frac{2}{3}s_3 = 6$$
$$\frac{1}{5}x_2 \qquad + 1s_2 \qquad = 5$$
$$1x_1 + \frac{1}{2}x_2 \qquad + \frac{5}{3}s_3 = 35$$

Assigning zero values to the nonbasic variables x_2 and s_3 permits us to identify the following new basic feasible solution:

$$s_1 = 6$$
$$s_2 = 5$$
$$x_1 = 35$$

This solution is also provided by the last column in the new simplex tableau. The profit associated with this solution is obtained by multiplying the solution values for the basic variables as given in the $\bar{b}$ column by their corresponding objective function coefficients as given in the c_B column; that is,

$$0(6) + 0(5) + 40(35) = 1400$$

Interpreting the Results of an Iteration

Starting with the initial simplex tableau, elementary row operations are used to change the elements in the simplex tableau in such a manner that we are able to identify a new basic feasible solution that improves the value of the objective function. Carrying out the process of creating a new simplex tableau is referred to as an iteration of the simplex method. In our example the initial basic feasible solution was

$$
\begin{aligned}
x_1 &= 0 \\
x_2 &= 0 \\
s_1 &= 20 \\
s_2 &= 5 \\
s_3 &= 21
\end{aligned}
$$

with a corresponding profit of \$0. One iteration of the simplex method moved us to another basic feasible solution with an objective function value of \$1400. This new basic feasible solution is

$$
\begin{aligned}
x_1 &= 35 \\
x_2 &= 0 \\
s_1 &= 6 \\
s_2 &= 5 \\
s_3 &= 0
\end{aligned}
$$

In Figure 10.2 we see that the initial basic feasible solution corresponds to extreme point ①. The first iteration moved us in the direction of the greatest increase per unit in profit, that is, along the x_1 axis. We moved away from extreme point ① in the x_1 direction until we could not move further without violating one of the constraints. The tableau we calculated after one iteration is the basic feasible solution corresponding to extreme point ②.

We note from Figure 10.2 that at extreme point ② the material 3 constraint is binding and that there is slack in the other two constraints. From the simplex tableau we see that the amount of slack for these two constraints is given by $s_1 = 6$ and $s_2 = 5$.

Moving toward a Better Solution

To again see if a better basic feasible solution can be found, we need to calculate the z_j and $c_j - z_j$ rows for the new simplex tableau. Recall that the elements in the z_j row are the sum of the products obtained by multiplying the elements in the c_B column of the simplex tableau by the corresponding elements in the columns of the $\overline{A}$ matrix. Thus we obtain

$$
\begin{aligned}
z_1 &= 0(0) & + \; 0(0) \; + 40(1) &= 40 \\
z_2 &= 0(\tfrac{3}{10}) & + \; 0(\tfrac{1}{5}) + 40(\tfrac{1}{2}) &= 20 \\
z_3 &= 0(1) & + \; 0(0) \; + 40(0) &= 0 \\
z_4 &= 0(0) & + \; 0(1) \; + 40(0) &= 0 \\
z_5 &= 0(-\tfrac{2}{3}) & + \; 0(0) \; + 40(\tfrac{5}{3}) &= \tfrac{200}{3}
\end{aligned}
$$

Subtracting z_j from c_j to obtain the net evaluation row, we get the complete new simplex tableau:

Basis	c_B	x_1	x_2	s_1	s_2	s_3	
		40	30	0	0	0	
s_1	0	0	$3/10$	1	0	$-2/3$	6
s_2	0	0	$1/5$	0	1	0	5
x_1	40	1	$1/2$	0	0	$5/3$	35
z_j		40	20	0	0	$200/3$	1400
$c_j - z_j$		0	10	0	0	$-200/3$	

Let us now analyze the $c_j - z_j$ row to see if we can introduce a new variable into the basis and continue to improve the objective function. Using the rule for determining

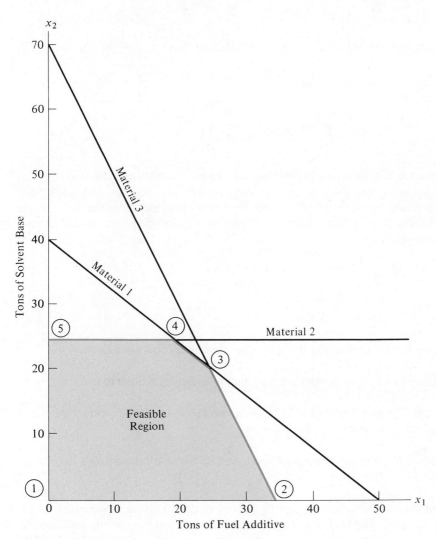

Figure 10.2
Feasible Solution Region
for the RMC Problem

which variable should enter the basis next, we select x_2, since it has the highest positive coefficient in the $c_j - z_j$ row.

To determine which variable will be removed from the basis when x_2 enters, we must compute for each row i the ratio $\bar{b}_i/\bar{a}_{i2}$ (remember, though, that we should compute this ratio only if $\bar{a}_{i2}$ is greater than zero); then we select the variable to leave the basis that corresponds to the minimum ratio. As before, we will show these ratios in an extra column of the simplex tableau:

Basis	c_B	x_1 40	x_2 30	s_1 0	s_2 0	s_3 0		$\dfrac{\bar{b}_i}{\bar{a}_{i2}}$
s_1	0	0	③⁄₁₀	1	0	$-\frac{2}{3}$	6	$\dfrac{6}{3/10} = 20$
s_2	0	0	$\frac{1}{5}$	0	1	0	5	$\dfrac{5}{1/5} = 25$
x_1	40	1	$\frac{1}{2}$	0	0	$\frac{5}{3}$	35	$\dfrac{35}{1/2} = 70$
z_j		40	20	0	0	$\frac{200}{3}$	1400	
$c_j - z_j$		0	10	0	0	$-\frac{200}{3}$		

Since 20 is the minimum ratio, s_1 will leave the basis. The pivot element is $\bar{a}_{12} = \frac{3}{10}$, which is circled in the above tableau. The nonbasic variable x_2 must now be made a basic variable. This means that we must perform the elementary row operations that will convert the x_2 column into a unit column; that is, we will have to transform the second column in the tableau to the form

$$
\begin{matrix}
1 \\
0 \\
0
\end{matrix}
$$

We can do this by performing the following elementary row operations:

Step 1 Multiply every element in row 1 (the pivot row) by $\frac{10}{3}$ in order to make $\bar{a}_{12} = 1$.

Step 2 Multiply the new row 1 (that is, the new pivot row) by $\frac{1}{5}$ and subtract the result from row 2 in order to make $\bar{a}_{22} = 0$.

Step 3 Multiply the new pivot row by $\frac{1}{2}$ and subtract the result from row 3 in order to make $\bar{a}_{32} = 0$.

Although the above elementary row operations again change the appearance of the simplex tableau, they do not alter the solutions to the system of equations contained in the tableau. The only difference is that now we have x_2, s_2, and x_1 as the basic variables, and s_1 and s_3 as the nonbasic variables. The new tableau resulting from these row operations is as follows:

Basis	c_B	x_1 40	x_2 30	s_1 0	s_2 0	s_3 0	
x_2	30	0	1	$10/3$	0	$-20/9$	20
s_2	0	0	0	$-2/3$	1	$4/9$	1
x_1	40	1	0	$-5/3$	0	$25/9$	25
z_j		40	30	$100/3$	0	$400/9$	1600
$c_j - z_j$		0	0	$-100/3$	0	$-400/9$	

Note that the values of the basic variables are $x_2 = 20$, $s_2 = 1$, and $x_1 = 25$, and the corresponding profit is $30(20) + 0(1) + 40(25) = 1600$.

We must now determine whether or not to bring any other variable into the basis and thereby move to another basic feasible solution. Looking at the net evaluation row, we see that every element is zero or negative. Since $c_j - z_j$ is less than or equal to zero for both of the nonbasic variables s_1 and s_3, any attempt to bring a nonbasic variable into the basis at this point will result in lowering the current value of the objective function. Hence the above tableau represents the optimal solution. In general, the simplex method uses the following criterion to determine if the optimal solution has been obtained.

Stopping Criterion   The optimal solution to a maximization linear programming problem has been reached when all of the entries in the net evaluation row ($c_j - z_j$) are zero or negative. In such cases the optimal solution is the current basic feasible solution.

Interpreting the Optimal Solution

We see that in the final solution to the RMC problem the basic variables are x_2, s_2, and x_1. The complete optimal solution to the RMC problem is thus $x_1 = 25$, $x_2 = 20$, $s_1 = 0$, $s_2 = 1$, and $s_3 = 0$, with a corresponding value of the objective function of $1600. Thus if the management of RMC wants to maximize profit, they should produce 25 tons of fuel additive and 20 tons of solvent base. In addition, management should note that there will be 1 ton of material 2 remaining. If it is possible to make alternate use of this additional resource, management should plan to do so.

We can also see that with $s_1 = 0$ and $s_3 = 0$, there is no slack associated with the material 1 and material 3 constraints. The constraints for these materials are both binding in the optimal solution. If it is possible to obtain additional amounts of these two materials, management should consider doing so.

Referring to Figure 10.2, we can see graphically the process we followed using the simplex method to find an optimal solution. The initial basic feasible solution corresponded to the origin ($x_1 = 0$, $x_2 = 0$, $s_1 = 20$, $s_2 = 5$, $s_3 = 21$). The first iteration caused x_1 to enter the basis and s_3 to leave. The new basic feasible solution corresponded to extreme point ② ($x_1 = 35$, $x_2 = 0$, $s_1 = 6$, $s_2 = 5$, $s_3 = 0$). At the next iteration x_2 entered the basis and s_1 left. This brought us to extreme point ③, the optimal solution ($x_1 = 25$, $x_2 = 20$, $s_1 = 0$, $s_2 = 1$, $s_3 = 0$).

Recalling the graphical solution procedure, we see that the simplex method has led us to the same solution. For the RMC problem, with only two variables, we had a choice of using the graphical or simplex method. For problems with more than two variables we will always use the simplex method.

10.6

SOLUTION OF A SAMPLE PROBLEM

In this section we illustrate the use of the simplex method for a linear programming problem involving four decision variables. To check your understanding of the previous sections, you should attempt to solve the problem before studying the solution presented.

Solve the following linear program using the simplex method:

$$\max \ 4x_1 + 6x_2 + 3x_3 + 1x_4$$

s.t.

$$\tfrac{3}{2}x_1 + 2x_2 + 4x_3 + 3x_4 \le 550$$
$$4x_1 + 1x_2 + 2x_3 + 1x_4 \le 700$$
$$2x_1 + 3x_2 + 1x_3 + 2x_4 \le 200$$
$$x_1, x_2, x_3, x_4 \ge 0$$

First we add slack variables to convert the problem to standard form:

$$\max \ 4x_1 + 6x_2 + 3x_3 + 1x_4 + 0s_1 + 0s_2 + 0s_3$$

s.t.

$$\tfrac{3}{2}x_1 + 2x_2 + 4x_3 + 3x_4 + 1s_1 \qquad\qquad = 550$$
$$4x_1 + 1x_2 + 2x_3 + 1x_4 \qquad + 1s_2 \qquad = 700$$
$$2x_1 + 3x_2 + 1x_3 + 2x_4 \qquad\qquad + 1s_3 = 200$$
$$x_1, x_2, x_3, x_4, s_1, s_2, s_3 \ge 0$$

The next step is to write the problem in tableau form. Since all the constraints are less-than-or-equal-to constraints, and since the right-hand-side values for the constraints are all nonnegative, the standard form and tableau form are the same. Thus we can set up the initial simplex tableau and begin the simplex method.

Basis	c_B	x_1	x_2	x_3	x_4	s_1	s_2	s_3		$\dfrac{\bar{b}_i}{\bar{a}_{i2}}$
		4	6	3	1	0	0	0		
s_1	0	$\tfrac{3}{2}$	2	4	3	1	0	0	550	$^{550}/_2 = 225$
s_2	0	4	1	2	1	0	1	0	700	$^{700}/_1 = 700$
s_3	0	2	③	1	2	0	0	1	200	$^{200}/_3 = 66\tfrac{2}{3}$
z_j		0	0	0	0	0	0	0	0	
$c_j - z_j$		4	6	3	1	0	0	0		

Two iterations of the simplex method are required to reach the optimal solution. Result of iteration 1:

Basis	c_B	x_1 4	x_2 6	x_3 3	x_4 1	s_1 0	s_2 0	s_3 0		b_i / a_{i3}
s_1	0	$1/6$	0	$\boxed{10/3}$	$5/3$	1	0	$-2/3$	$416 2/3$	125
s_2	0	$10/3$	0	$5/3$	$1/3$	0	1	$-1/3$	$633 1/3$	380
x_2	6	$2/3$	1	$1/3$	$2/3$	0	0	$1/3$	$66 2/3$	200
z_j		4	6	2	4	0	0	2	400	
$c_j - z_j$		0	0	1	-3	0	0	-2		

Result of iteration 2:

Basis	c_B	x_1 4	x_2 6	x_3 3	x_4 1	s_1 0	s_2 0	s_3 0	
x_3	3	$3/60$	0	1	$15/30$	$3/10$	0	$-6/30$	125
s_2	0	$195/60$	0	0	$-15/30$	$-5/10$	1	0	425
x_2	6	$39/60$	1	0	$15/30$	$-1/10$	0	$12/30$	25
z_j		$81/20$	6	3	$9/2$	$3/10$	0	$54/30$	525
$c_j - z_j$		$-1/20$	0	0	$-7/2$	$-3/10$	0	$-54/30$	

Since the $c_j - z_j$ elements are all less than or equal to zero, there is no nonbasic variable that we can introduce into solution and obtain an increase in the value of the objective function. Therefore the current solution is optimal. The complete optimal solution is given by

$$x_1 = 0$$
$$x_2 = 25$$
$$x_3 = 125$$
$$x_4 = 0$$
$$s_1 = 0$$
$$s_2 = 425$$
$$s_3 = 0$$

The value of the objective function is 525.

10.7

TABLEAU FORM: THE GENERAL CASE

When a linear program contains all less-than-or-equal-to constraints with nonnegative right-hand-side values, it is easy to set up a tableau form. In this case, we simply add a slack variable to each constraint. However, obtaining tableau form is somewhat more complex if the linear program contains greater-than-or-equal-to constraints, equality constraints, and/or negative right-hand-side values. In this section we describe how to develop tableau form for each of these situations.

Greater-than-or-Equal-to Constraints

Suppose that in the RMC problem, management wanted to ensure that at least 10 tons of each product were produced. We could incorporate these new restrictions by adding a constraint that ensures that x_1 will be greater than or equal to 10 tons and adding another constraint that ensures that x_2 will be greater than or equal to 10 tons; that is, we can add the constraints

$$1x_1 \geq 10 \tag{10.12}$$

$$1x_2 \geq 10 \tag{10.13}$$

With these two additions our modified problem can now be written

$$\max 40x_1 + 30x_2$$
$$\text{s.t.}$$
$$\tfrac{2}{5}x_1 + \tfrac{1}{2}x_2 \leq 20$$
$$\tfrac{1}{5}x_2 \leq 5$$
$$\tfrac{3}{5}x_1 + \tfrac{3}{10}x_2 \leq 21$$
$$1x_1 \geq 10$$
$$1x_2 \geq 10$$
$$x_1, x_2 \geq 0$$

The graphical solution to this problem is shown in Figure 10.3 and is the same as the solution to the original RMC problem, that is, $x_1 = 25$, $x_2 = 20$. However, if we are going to use the simplex method for solving this problem, we need to know how to put the greater-than-or-equal-to constraints into the tableau form.

We can first use slack and surplus variables to write this RMC problem in the following standard form:

$$\max 40x_1 + 30x_2 + 0s_1 + 0s_2 + 0s_3 + 0s_4 + 0s_5$$
$$\text{s.t.}$$
$$\tfrac{2}{5}x_1 + \tfrac{1}{2}x_2 + 1s_1 = 20 \tag{10.14}$$
$$\tfrac{1}{5}x_2 + 1s_2 = 5 \tag{10.15}$$
$$\tfrac{3}{5}x_1 + \tfrac{3}{10}x_2 + 1s_3 = 21 \tag{10.16}$$
$$1x_1 - 1s_4 = 10 \tag{10.17}$$
$$1x_2 - 1s_5 = 10 \tag{10.18}$$
$$x_1, x_2\ s_1, s_2, s_3, s_4, s_5 \geq 0$$

Now let us reconsider the way we generated an initial basic feasible solution to get the simplex method started for the RMC problem. We set $x_1 = 0$, $x_2 = 0$ and selected the slack variables as our initial basic variables. Extension of this notion to the modified RMC problem would suggest setting $x_1 = 0$, $x_2 = 0$, and selecting as initial basic

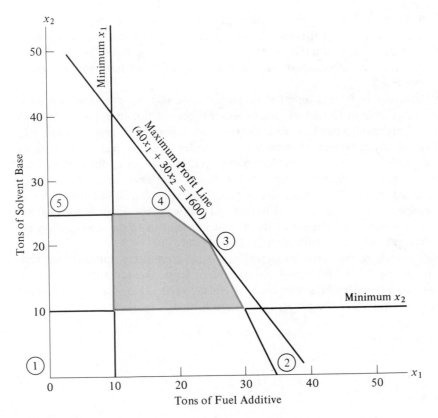

Figure 10.3
Graphical Solution to the Modified RMC Problem

variables the slack and surplus variables. However, looking at the graphical representation of this problem (Figure 10.3), we see that the solution corresponding to the origin is no longer feasible. The inclusion of the two greater-than-or-equal-to constraints ($x_1 \geq 10$ and $x_2 \geq 10$) has made the basic solution with $x_1 = x_2 = 0$ infeasible.

To see this another way, look at equations (10.17) and (10.18) in the standard-form representation of the problem. When x_1 and x_2 are set equal to zero, equations (10.17) and (10.18) reduce to

$$-1s_4 = 10$$

and

$$-1s_5 = 10$$

Thus setting x_1 and x_2 equal to zero gives us the basic solution

$$
\begin{aligned}
s_1 &= & 20 \\
s_2 &= & 5 \\
s_3 &= & 21 \\
s_4 &= & -10 \\
s_5 &= & -10
\end{aligned}
$$

Clearly this is not a basic feasible solution, since s_4 and s_5 violate the nonnegativity requirements. Thus our former method of creating an initial basic feasible solution by setting each of the decision variables to zero will not work. The difficulty here is that the standard form and the tableau form are equivalent only for problems with less-than-or-equal-to constraints.

In order to set up the tableau form for this problem, we shall resort to a mathematical "trick" that will enable us to find an initial basic feasible solution in terms of the slack variables s_1, s_2, and s_3 and two new variables we shall denote by a_4 and a_5. These two new variables constitute the mathematical trick. Variables a_4 and a_5 really have nothing to do with the RMC problem; they merely serve to enable us to set up the tableau form and thus obtain an initial basic feasible solution. Since these new variables have been artificially created in order just to get things going, we will refer to such variables as *artificial variables*. We caution the student to avoid confusing the notation for artificial variables with that used for elements of the A matrix. Elements of the A matrix always have two subscripts, whereas artificial variables have only one.

With the addition of two artificial variables, we can convert the standard-form representation of the modified RMC problem into tableau form. We add artificial variable a_4 to equation (10.17) and artificial variable a_5 to equation (10.18) to obtain the following representation of the system of equations in tableau form:

$$
\begin{array}{rcl}
\tfrac{2}{5}x_1 + \tfrac{1}{2}x_2 + 1s_1 & = & 20 \\
\tfrac{1}{5}x_2 + 1s_2 & = & 5 \\
\tfrac{3}{5}x_1 + \tfrac{3}{10}x_2 + 1s_3 & = & 21 \\
1x_1 - 1s_4 + 1a_4 & = & 10 \\
1x_2 - 1s_5 + 1a_5 & = & 10 \\
\end{array}
$$
$$x_1, x_2, s_1, s_2, s_3, s_4, s_5, a_4, a_5 \geq 0$$

Note that the subscripts on the artificial variables identify the constraints with which they are associated. This is also the convention we are using for slack and surplus variables; s_1 is associated with the first constraint, s_2 is associated with the second constraint, and so on. In this text we will always follow the convention of having the subscript associated with a slack, surplus, or artificial variable refer to the number of the constraint in the formulation.

Since the variables s_1, s_2, s_3, a_4, and a_5 each appear only once with a coefficient of 1, and since the right-hand sides are nonnegative, both requirements of the tableau form have been satisfied.

We can now obtain an initial basic feasible solution to the system of equations in tableau form by setting $x_1 = x_2 = s_4 = s_5 = 0$. This complete solution is

$$
\begin{array}{rcl}
x_1 & = & 0 \\
x_2 & = & 0 \\
s_1 & = & 20 \\
s_2 & = & 5 \\
s_3 & = & 21 \\
s_4 & = & 0 \\
\end{array}
$$

$$s_5 = 0$$
$$a_4 = 10$$
$$a_5 = 10$$

Is this solution feasible in terms of our real-world problem? No. It does not satisfy the requirements that we produce at least 10 tons of each of the products. Thus we must make an important distinction between a basic feasible solution for the tableau form of our problem and a basic feasible solution for the real-world problem. A basic feasible solution for the tableau form of a linear programming problem is not always a basic feasible solution to the real-world problem. This is because of the appearance of the artificial variables in the tableau form of the problem. However, since the standard-form representation of the problem does not include any of these artificial variables, a basic feasible solution for the standard-form representation will be feasible for the real-world problem. We see, then, that the standard-form representation is equivalent to the original problem, whereas whenever we have to add artificial variables the tableau-form representation is not.

The reason for creating tableau form is to obtain an initial basic feasible solution to start the simplex method. Thus we see that whenever it is necessary to introduce artificial variables, the initial simplex solution will not in general be feasible for the real-world problem. This situation is not as difficult as it might seem, however, since the only time we *must* have a feasible solution for the real-world problem is at the *last* iteration of the simplex method (that is, the optimal solution must be feasible). Thus if we could devise some means to guarantee that the artificial variables would be driven out of the basis before the optimal solution was reached, there would be no difficulty.

The way in which we guarantee that these artificial variables will be driven out before the optimal solution for the real-world problem is reached is to assign a very large cost to each of these variables in the objective function. For example, in the problem we are currently considering, we assign a very large negative number as the profit coefficient of each artificial variable in the objective function of the tableau form. Hence if these variables assume positive values, they will substantially reduce profits. As a result, these variables will be eliminated from the basis as soon as possible, and this is precisely what we want to happen.

As an alternative to picking a large negative number like $-100,000$ for the profit coefficient, we will denote the profit coefficient of each artificial variable by $-M$. Here it is assumed that $-M$ represents some very large negative number. This notation will make it easier to keep track of the elements of the simplex tableau that depend on the profit coefficients of the artificial variables. Using $-M$ as the profit coefficient for the artificial variables, we can now write the objective function for the tableau form of the problem:

$$\max z = 40x_1 + 30x_2 + 0s_1 + 0s_2 + 0s_3 + 0s_4 + 0s_5 - Ma_4 - Ma_5$$

Using the artificial variables a_4 and a_5, we now write the following initial simplex tableau:

Basis	c_B	x_1 40	x_2 30	s_1 0	s_2 0	s_3 0	s_4 0	s_5 0	a_4 $-M$	a_5 $-M$	
s_1	0	$\frac{2}{5}$	$\frac{1}{2}$	1	0	0	0	0	0	0	20
s_2	0	0	$\frac{1}{5}$	0	1	0	0	0	0	0	5
s_3	0	$\frac{3}{5}$	$\frac{3}{10}$	0	0	1	0	0	0	0	21
a_4	$-M$	①	0	0	0	0	-1	0	1	0	10
a_5	$-M$	0	1	0	0	0	0	-1	0	1	10
	z_j	$-M$	$-M$	0	0	0	M	M	$-M$	$-M$	$-20M$
	$c_j - z_j$	$40+M$	$30+M$	0	0	0	$-M$	$-M$	0	0	

The above tableau corresponds to the solution $s_1 = 20$, $s_2 = 5$, $s_3 = 21$, $a_4 = 10$, $a_5 = 10$, and $x_1 = x_2 = s_4 = s_5 = 0$. In terms of our simplex tableau, this is a basic feasible solution, since all the variables are greater than or equal to zero and $n - m$ of the variables are equal to zero. However, in terms of our modified RMC problem, $x_1 = x_2 = 0$ is clearly not feasible. This difficulty is caused by the fact that the artificial variables are in our current basic solution at positive values. Let us complete the simplex solution to this problem and see if the artificial variables are driven out of solution as we hope they will be.

We see that, at the first iteration, x_1 will be brought into the basis and a_4 will be driven out. The simplex tableau after this iteration is presented below.

Result of iteration 1:

Basis	c_B	x_1 40	x_2 30	s_1 0	s_2 0	s_3 0	s_4 0	s_5 0	a_4 $-M$	a_5 $-M$	
s_1	0	0	$\frac{1}{2}$	1	0	0	$\frac{2}{5}$	0	$-\frac{2}{5}$	0	16
s_2	0	0	$\frac{1}{5}$	0	1	0	0	0	0	0	5
s_3	0	0	$\frac{3}{10}$	0	0	1	$\frac{3}{5}$	0	$-\frac{3}{5}$	0	15
x_1	40	1	0	0	0	0	-1	0	1	0	10
a_5	$-M$	0	1	0	0	0	0	-1	0	1	10
	z_j	40	$-M$	0	0	0	-40	M	40	$-M$	$400-10M$
	$c_j - z_j$	0	$30+M$	0	0	0	40	$-M$	$-M-40$	0	

The current solution is still not feasible, since artificial variable a_5 is in the basis at a positive value. The solution does not satisfy the $x_2 \geq 10$ requirement. Graphically we see, in Figure 10.4, that this iteration has moved us from the origin (labeled Ⓐ) to point Ⓑ, which is still not in the feasible region.

Since a_4 is an artificial variable that was added simply to obtain an initial basic feasible solution, once a_4 is eliminated from the basis we can drop its associated column from the simplex tableau. Thus we obtain the following revised tableau:

Basis	c_B	x_1 40	x_2 30	s_1 0	s_2 0	s_3 0	s_4 0	s_5 0	a_5 $-M$	
s_1	0	0	½	1	0	0	⅖	0	0	16
s_2	0	0	⅕	0	1	0	0	0	0	5
s_3	0	0	³⁄₁₀	0	0	1	⅗	0	0	15
x_1	40	1	0	0	0	0	-1	0	0	10
a_5	$-M$	0	①	0	0	0	0	-1	1	10
z_j		40	$-M$	0	0	0	-40	M	$-M$	$400 - 10M$
$c_j - z_j$		0	$30 + M$	0	0	0	40	$-M$	0	

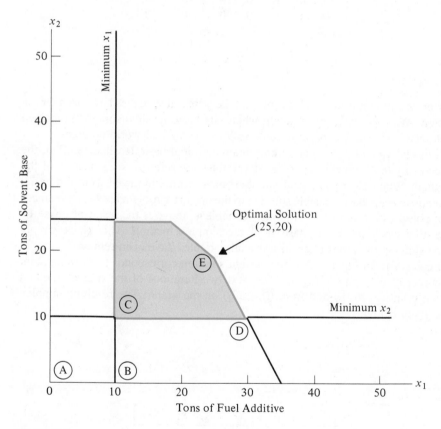

Figure 10.4
Sequence of Simplex Solutions
to the Modified RMC Problem

At the next iteration x_2 will be brought into solution and a_5 will be driven out. The simplex tableau after this iteration is presented below. Note that the a_5 column has been dropped, since it is no longer necessary.

Result of iteration 2:

Basis	c_B	x_1 40	x_2 30	s_1 0	s_2 0	s_3 0	s_4 0	s_5 0	
s_1	0	0	0	1	0	0	$\frac{2}{5}$	$\frac{1}{2}$	11
s_2	0	0	0	0	1	0	0	$\frac{1}{5}$	3
s_3	0	0	0	0	0	1	$\left(\frac{3}{5}\right)$	$\frac{3}{10}$	12
x_1	40	1	0	0	0	0	-1	0	10
x_2	30	0	1	0	0	0	0	-1	10
z_j		40	30	0	0	0	-40	-30	700
$c_j - z_j$		0	0	0	0	0	40	30	

The current solution is now feasible, since all the artificial variables have been driven out of solution. We now have the situation where the basic feasible solution contained in the simplex tableau is also a basic feasible solution to the real-world problem.

When artificial variables are required to obtain an initial basic feasible solution, the iterations necessary to eliminate the artificial variables are referred to as phase I of the simplex method. When all the artificial variables have been eliminated from the basis, phase I is complete and a basic feasible solution to the original problem has been obtained. In this case, phase I involved two iterations; the tableau above is the result of phase I.

We are now ready to begin phase II of the simplex method. This phase simply continues the simplex iterations after all artificial variables have been removed.

As you can see from Figure 10.4, the current solution corresponds to extreme point Ⓒ on the corner of the feasible region. The next two iterations of the simplex method move us from point Ⓒ to Ⓓ and from Ⓓ to Ⓔ on the graph. The resulting simplex tableaus are given below:

Result of iteration 3:

Basis	c_B	x_1 40	x_2 30	s_1 0	s_2 0	s_3 0	s_4 0	s_5 0	
s_1	0	0	0	1	0	$-\frac{2}{3}$	0	$\left(\frac{3}{10}\right)$	3
s_2	0	0	0	0	1	0	0	$\frac{1}{5}$	3
s_4	0	0	0	0	0	$\frac{5}{3}$	1	$\frac{1}{2}$	20
x_1	40	1	0	0	0	$\frac{5}{3}$	0	$\frac{1}{2}$	30
x_2	30	0	1	0	0	0	0	-1	10
z_j		40	30	0	0	$\frac{200}{3}$	0	-10	1500
$c_j - z_j$		0	0	0	0	$-\frac{200}{3}$	0	10	

Result of iteration 4:

Basis	c_B	x_1	x_2	s_1	s_2	s_3	s_4	s_5	
		40	30	0	0	0	0	0	
s_5	0	0	0	$10/3$	0	$-20/9$	0	1	10
s_2	0	0	0	$-2/3$	1	$4/9$	0	0	1
s_4	0	0	0	$-5/3$	0	$25/9$	1	0	15
x_1	40	1	0	$-5/3$	0	$25/9$	0	0	25
x_2	30	0	1	$10/3$	0	$-20/9$	0	0	20
z_j		40	30	$100/3$	0	$400/9$	0	0	1600
$c_j - z_j$		0	0	$-100/3$	0	$-400/9$	0	0	

Just as with the graphical approach, we see that the addition of the two greater-than-or-equal-to constraints has not changed the optimal solution. However, it has taken more iterations to get to this point. This is because it took two iterations to eliminate the artificial variables (phase I) and hence obtain a basic feasible solution for the real-world problem.

Fortunately, once we obtain the initial simplex tableau using artificial variables, we need not concern ourselves with worrying about whether the basic solution at a particular iteration is feasible for the real-world problem. We need only follow all the rules for the simplex method. If we reach the stopping criterion (that is, all $c_j - z_j \leq 0$) and all the artificial variables have been eliminated from the solution, then we have found the optimal solution to our linear program. On the other hand, if we reach the stopping criterion and one or more of the artificial variables remains in solution at a positive value, then there is no feasible solution to the real-world problem. This special case will be discussed in more detail in Section 10.9.

Equality Constraints

When an equality constraint occurs in a linear programming problem, we need only add an artificial variable to get an initial basic feasible solution for the simplex tableau. For example, if we had the equality constraint

$$6x_1 + 4x_2 - 5x_3 = 30$$

we would simply add an artificial variable, say a_1, to enable us to create an initial basic feasible solution in the tableau. The above equation would then become

$$6x_1 + 4x_2 - 5x_3 + 1a_1 = 30$$

Once we have created the tableau form by adding artificial variables to all the equality constraints, the simplex method proceeds exactly as in the case for the greater-than-or-equal-to constraint situation.

Eliminating Negative Right-Hand-Side Values

One of the properties of tableau form of a linear program is that the values on the right-hand sides of the constraints have to be nonnegative. In formulating a linear programming problem we may find that one or more of the constraints have negative right-hand-side values. For example, suppose that management of RMC had specified that the number of tons of fuel additive produced had to be less than or equal to the number of tons of solvent base after 5 tons of solvent base had been saved for use by RMC in the development of a fiberglass cleaner. We could formulate this constraint as

$$1x_1 \leq 1x_2 - 5 \tag{10.19}$$

Subtracting x_2 from both sides of the inequality allows us to place all the variables on the left-hand side of the constraint and the constant on the right-hand side. Thus we have

$$1x_1 - 1x_2 \leq -5 \tag{10.20}$$

Since this is a constraint with a negative right-hand side, we can develop an equivalent constraint with a nonnegative right-hand side by multiplying both sides of the constraint by -1. In doing so we recognize that multiplying an inequality constraint by -1 changes the direction of the inequality.

Thus to convert equation (10.20) to an equivalent constraint with a nonnegative right-hand-side value, we multiply by -1 to obtain

$$-x_1 + x_2 \geq 5 \tag{10.21}$$

We now have an acceptable nonnegative right-hand-side value. Tableau form for this constraint can now be obtained by subtracting a surplus variable and adding an artificial variable.

For a greater-than-or-equal-to constraint, multiplying by -1 creates an equivalent less-than-or-equal-to constraint. For example, suppose that we had the following greater-than-or-equal-to constraint:

$$6x_1 + 3x_2 - 4x_3 \geq -20$$

Multiplying by -1 to obtain an equivalent constraint with a nonnegative right-hand-side value leads to the following less-than-or-equal-to constraint:

$$-6x_1 - 3x_2 + 4x_3 \leq 20$$

Tableau form can be created for this constraint by adding a slack variable.

For an equality constraint with a negative right-hand-side value, we simply multiply by -1 to obtain an equivalent constraint with a nonnegative right-hand-side value. An artificial variable can then be added to create the tableau form.

Summary of the Steps to Create Tableau Form

Step 1 If the original formulation of the linear programming problem contains one or more constraints with negative right-hand sides, multiply each of these constraints by -1. Doing this will change the direction of the inequalities. This step will provide an equivalent linear program with nonnegative right-hand sides.

Step 2 For $\leq$ constraints, add a slack variable to obtain an equality constraint. The coefficient of the slack variable in the objective function is assigned a value of zero. This provides the tableau form for the constraint and the slack variable becomes one of the basic variables in the initial basic feasible solution.

Step 3 For $\geq$ constraints, subtract a surplus variable to obtain an equality constraint, and then add an artificial variable to obtain the tableau form. The coefficient of the surplus variable in the objective function is assigned a value of zero. The coefficient of the artificial variable in the objective function is assigned a value of $-M$. The artificial variable becomes one of the basic variables in the initial basic feasible solution.

Step 4 For equality constraints, add an artificial variable to obtain the tableau form. The coefficient of the artificial variable in the objective function is assigned a value of $-M$. The artificial variable becomes one of the basic variables in the initial basic feasible solution.

To obtain some practice in applying the above steps, convert the following example problem into tableau form and then set up the initial simplex tableau:

$$\max \quad 6x_1 + 3x_2 + 4x_3 + 1x_4$$
$$\text{s.t.}$$
$$-2x_1 - \tfrac{1}{2}x_2 + 1x_3 - 6x_4 = -60$$
$$1x_1 \qquad + 1x_3 + \tfrac{2}{3}x_4 \leq 20$$
$$-1x_2 - 5x_3 \qquad \leq -50$$
$$x_1, x_2, x_3, x_4 \geq 0$$

To eliminate the negative right-hand-side values in constraints 1 and 3, we apply step 1. Multiplying both constraints by -1, we obtain the following equivalent linear program:

$$\max \quad 6x_1 + 3x_2 + 4x_3 + 1x_4$$
$$\text{s.t.}$$
$$2x_1 + \tfrac{1}{2}x_2 - 1x_3 + 6x_4 = 60$$
$$1x_1 \qquad + 1x_3 + \tfrac{2}{3}x_4 \leq 20$$
$$1x_2 + 5x_3 \qquad \geq 50$$
$$x_1, x_2, x_3, x_4 \geq 0$$

Note that the direction of the inequality in constraint 3 has been reversed as a result of multiplying the constraint by -1. By applying step 4 for constraint 1, step 2 for constraint 2, and step 3 for constraint 3, we obtain the following tableau form:

$$\max \; 6x_1 + 3x_2 + 4x_3 + 1x_4 + 0s_2 + 0s_3 - Ma_1 - Ma_3$$
$$\text{s.t.}$$
$$2x_1 + \tfrac{1}{2}x_2 - 1x_3 + 6x_4 \qquad\qquad + 1a_1 \qquad = 60$$
$$1x_1 \qquad + 1x_3 + \tfrac{2}{3}x_4 + 1s_2 \qquad = 20$$
$$1x_2 + 5x_3 \qquad\qquad - 1s_3 \qquad + 1a_3 = 50$$
$$x_1, x_2, x_3, x_4, s_2, s_3, a_1, a_3 \geq 0$$

The initial simplex tableau corresponding to this tableau form is

		x_1	x_2	x_3	x_4	s_2	s_3	a_1	a_3	
Basis	c_B	6	3	4	1	0	0	$-M$	$-M$	
a_1	$-M$	2	1/2	-1	6	0	0	1	0	60
s_2	0	1	0	1	2/3	1	0	0	0	20
a_3	$-M$	0	1	5	0	0	-1	0	1	50
	z_j	$-2M$	$-\frac{3}{2}M$	$-4M$	$-6M$	0	M	$-M$	$-M$	$-110M$
	$c_j - z_j$	$6+2M$	$3+\frac{3}{2}M$	$4+4M$	$1+6M$	0	$-M$	0	0	

10.8

SOLVING A MINIMIZATION PROBLEM USING THE SIMPLEX METHOD

There are two ways in which we can use the simplex method to solve a minimization problem. The first approach requires that we change the rule used to introduce a variable into the basis. Recall that in the maximization case we select the variable with the largest positive $c_j - z_j$ as the variable to introduce next into the basis. This is because the value of $c_j - z_j$ tells us the amount the objective function will increase if one unit of the variable in column j is brought into solution. To solve the minimization problem, we can simply reverse this rule. That is, we can select the variable with the most negative $c_j - z_j$ as the one to introduce next. Of course, this approach means that the stopping rule for the optimal solution will also have to be changed. Using this approach to solve a minimization problem, we would stop when every value in the net evaluation row is zero or positive.

The second approach to solving the minimization problem is the one we will employ in this book. It is based on the fact that any minimization problem can be converted to an equivalent maximization problem by multiplying the objective function by -1. Solving the resulting maximization problem will provide the optimal solution to the minimization problem.

Let us illustrate this second approach by using the simplex method to solve the Innis Investments problem introduced in Chapter 7. Recall that in this problem management wanted to minimize the total risk of the portfolio subject to constraints involving funds available, annual income, and the amount to be invested in the money market fund. The linear programming model for this problem is restated below, with x_1 = units purchased in the stock fund and x_2 = units purchased in the money market fund.

$$\min \quad 8x_1 + 3x_2$$

s.t.

$$50x_1 + 100x_2 \leq 1,200,000 \qquad \text{Funds available}$$
$$5x_1 + 4x_2 \geq 60,000 \qquad \text{Annual income}$$
$$1x_2 \geq 3,000 \qquad \text{Minimum units in money market}$$
$$x_1, x_2 \geq 0$$

To solve this problem using the simplex method, we first multiply the objective function by -1 to convert the minimization problem into the following equivalent maximization problem:

$$\text{max} -8x_1 - 3x_2$$

s.t.

$$50x_1 + 100x_2 \leq 1,200,000 \quad \text{Funds available}$$
$$5x_1 + 4x_2 \geq 60,000 \quad \text{Minimum return}$$
$$1x_2 \geq 3,000 \quad \text{Minimum units in money market}$$
$$x_1, x_2 \geq 0$$

The tableau form for this problem is

$$\text{max} -8x_1 - 3x_2 + 0s_1 + 0s_2 + 0s_3 - Ma_2 - Ma_3$$

s.t.

$$50x_1 + 100x_2 + 1s_1 = 1,200,000$$
$$5x_1 + 4x_2 - 1s_2 + 1a_2 = 60,000$$
$$1x_2 - 1s_3 + 1a_3 = 3,000$$
$$x_1, x_2, s_1, s_2, s_3, a_1, a_2 \geq 0$$

The initial simplex tableau is shown below:

Basis	c_B	x_1 -8	x_2 -3	s_1 0	s_2 0	s_3 0	a_2 $-M$	a_3 $-M$	
s_1	0	50	100	1	0	0	0	0	$1,200,000$
a_2	$-M$	5	4	0	-1	0	1	0	$60,000$
a_3	$-M$	0	①	0	0	-1	0	1	$3,000$
	z_j	$-5M$	$-5M$	0	M	M	$-M$	$-M$	$-63,000M$
	$c_j - z_j$	$-8 + 5M$	$-3 + 5M$	0	$-M$	$-M$	0	0	

At the first iteration x_2 is brought into the basis and a_3 is eliminated. After dropping the a_3 column from the tableau, the result of the first iteration is shown below.

Basis	c_B	x_1 -8	x_2 -3	s_1 0	s_2 0	s_3 0	a_2 $-M$	
s_1	0	50	0	1	0	100	0	$900,000$
a_2	$-M$	⑤	0	0	-1	4	1	$48,000$
x_2	-3	0	1	0	0	-1	0	$3,000$
	z_j	$-5M$	-3	0	M	$-4m + 3$	$-M$	$-9,000-48,000M$
	$c_j - z_j$	$-8 + 5M$	0	0	$-M$	$4M - 3$	0	

Continuing with the simplex method, two more iterations provide the final simplex tableau:

		x_1	x_2	s_1	s_2	s_3	
Basis	c_B	-8	-3	0	0	0	
s_3	0	0	0	$1/60$	$1/6$	1	$7{,}000$
x_1	-8	1	0	$-1/75$	$-1/3$	0	$4{,}000$
x_2	-3	0	1	$1/60$	$1/6$	0	$10{,}000$
	z_j	-8	-3	$17/300$	$13/6$	0	$-62{,}000$
	$c_j - z_j$	0	0	$-17/300$	$-13/6$	0	

In Chapter 7 we used the graphical solution procedure to determine the optimal solution. The feasible region and solution are shown again in Figure 10.5. The simplex method has provided the same solution, with $x_1 = 4000$, $x_2 = 10{,}000$, $s_1 = 0$, $s_2 = 0$, and $s_3 = 7000$. Note, however that, as shown in the final simplex tableau, the value of the objective function is $-62{,}000$. We must now multiply this value by -1 to obtain the value of the objective function to the original minimization problem (minimum portfolio risk $= 62{,}000$).

In the next section we concentrate on discussing some important special cases that may occur when trying to solve any linear programming problem. We will only consider the case for maximization problems, recognizing that all minimization problems may be placed into this form by multiplying the objective function by -1.

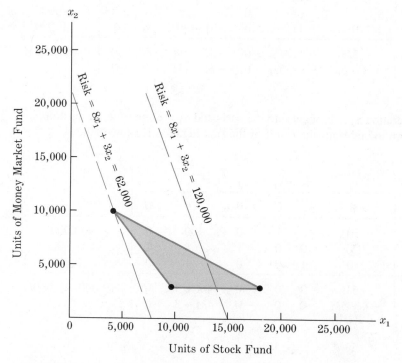

Figure 10.5
Graphical Solution for Innis Investments Problem

10.9

SPECIAL CASES

In Chapter 7 we discussed how infeasibility, unboundedness, and alternate optima could occur when solving linear programming problems using the graphical solution procedure. These special cases can also arise when using the simplex method. In addition, a special case referred to as *degeneracy* can theoretically cause difficulties for the simplex method. In this section we show how these special cases can be recognized and handled when the simplex method is used.

Infeasibility

Infeasibility occurs whenever there is no solution to the linear program that satisfies all the constraints, including the nonnegativity conditions. From the perspective of the graphical solution procedure, this means that there is no feasible region. Let us now see how infeasibility is recognized when the simplex method is used.

We mentioned in Section 10.7, when discussing artificial variables, that infeasibility could be recognized when the stopping criterion indicated an optimal solution and one or more of the artificial variables remained in the solution at a positive value. As an illustration of this phenomenon, let us consider the modification of the RMC problem that called for producing at least 30 tons of fuel additive and 15 tons of solvent base. (We saw in Section 7.8 that there was no feasible solution to this problem.) The formulation of the RMC problem that incorporates these changes is restated below:

$$\max 40x_1 + 30x_2$$

s.t.

$$\tfrac{2}{5}x_1 + \tfrac{1}{2}x_2 \le 20$$
$$\tfrac{1}{5}x_2 \le 5$$
$$\tfrac{3}{5}x_1 + \tfrac{3}{10}x_2 \le 21$$
$$x_1 \ge 30$$
$$x_2 \ge 15$$
$$x_1, x_2 \ge 0$$

The simplex solution to this problem is presented below (note that two artificial variables were added to the last two rows in order to obtain a basic feasible solution in the initial simplex tableau).

Initial tableau:

Basis	c_B	x_1 40	x_2 30	s_1 0	s_2 0	s_3 0	s_4 0	s_5 0	a_4 $-M$	a_5 $-M$	
s_1	0	$\tfrac{2}{5}$	$\tfrac{1}{2}$	1	0	0	0	0	0	0	20
s_2	0	0	$\tfrac{1}{5}$	0	1	0	0	0	0	0	5
s_3	0	$\tfrac{3}{5}$	$\tfrac{3}{10}$	0	0	1	0	0	0	0	21
a_4	$-M$	①	0	0	0	0	-1	0	1	0	30
a_5	$-M$	0	1	0	0	0	0	-1	0	1	15
z_j		$-M$	$-M$	0	0	0	M	M	$-M$	$-M$	$-45M$
$c_j - z_j$		$40+M$	$30+M$	0	0	0	$-M$	$-M$	0	0	

Second tableau:

Basis	c_B	x_1 40	x_2 30	s_1 0	s_2 0	s_3 0	s_4 0	s_5 0	a_5 $-M$	
s_1	0	0	$\frac{1}{2}$	1	0	0	$\frac{2}{5}$	0	0	8
s_2	0	0	$\frac{1}{5}$	0	1	0	0	0	0	5
s_3	0	0	$\textcircled{\frac{3}{10}}$	0	0	1	$\frac{3}{5}$	0	0	3
x_1	40	1	0	0	0	0	-1	0	0	30
a_5	$-M$	0	1	0	0	0	0	-1	1	15
z_j		40	$-M$	0	0	0	-40	M	$-M$	$1200-15M$
c_j-z_j		0	$30+M$	0	0	0	40	$-M$	0	

Final tableau:

Basis	c_B	x_1 40	x_2 30	s_1 0	s_2 0	s_3 0	s_4 0	s_5 0	a_5 $-M$	
s_1	0	0	0	1	0	$-\frac{5}{3}$	$-\frac{3}{5}$	0	0	3
s_2	0	0	0	0	1	$-\frac{2}{3}$	$-\frac{2}{5}$	0	0	3
x_2	30	0	1	0	0	$\frac{10}{3}$	2	0	0	10
x_1	40	1	0	0	0	0	-1	0	0	30
a_5	$-M$	0	0	0	0	$-\frac{10}{3}$	-2	-1	1	5
z_j		40	30	0	0	$100+\frac{10}{3}M$	$20+2M$	M	$-M$	$1500-5M$
c_j-z_j		0	0	0	0	$-100-\frac{10}{3}M$	$-20-2M$	$-M$	0	

Just as you might have expected, one of the artificial variables, a_5, is in the final solution. Note that $c_j - z_j \leq 0$ for all the variables; therefore, according to the rules we established earlier, this should be the optimal solution. But this solution is not feasible for our real-world problem, since it has $x_1 = 30$ and $x_2 = 10$. (Recall that we had to make at least 15 tons of solvent base.) The fact that artificial variable a_5 is in the solution at a value of 5 tells us that the final solution violates the fifth constraint ($x_2 \geq 15$) by 5 units.

In summary, a linear program is infeasible if there is no solution that satisfies all the constraints and nonnegativity conditions simultaneously. Graphically, we recognize this situation as the case where there is no feasible region. In terms of the simplex solution procedure, we know that if one or more of the artificial variables remain in the final solution at a positive value, there is no feasible solution to the real-world problem.

In closing, we note that for linear programming problems with only $\leq$ constraints and nonnegative right-hand sides there will always be a feasible solution. Since it is not necessary to introduce artificial variables to set up the initial simplex tableau, there could not possibly be an artificial variable in the final solution.

Unboundedness

For maximization problems we say that a linear program is unbounded if the value of the solution may be made infinitely large without violating any constraints. We mentioned, while discussing unboundedness from a graphical point of view in Section 7.8, that unbounded profit maximization problems do not occur in practice. Thus, when this case occurs we can generally look for an error in our formulation.

The simplex method will automatically uncover any unboundedness that exists before the final tableau is reached. What will happen is that the rule for determining the variable to be removed from the solution will not work. Recall that we calculated the ratio $\bar{b}_i/\bar{a}_{ij}$ for each of the elements of column j which were *positive*. Then we picked the smallest ratio to tell us which variable to remove from the current basic feasible solution.

The coefficients in a particular column of $\bar{A}$ indicate how much each of the current basic variables will decrease if one unit of the variable associated with that particular column is brought into solution. Suppose, then, that for a particular linear program we found that $c_2 - z_2 = 5 > 0$, and that all the $\bar{a}_{i2}$ in column 2 were ≤ 0. This would mean that each unit of x_2 brought into solution would increase the objective function by five units. Furthermore, since $\bar{a}_{i2} \leq 0$ for all i, this would mean that none of the current basic variables would be driven to zero, no matter how many units of x_2 we introduced. Thus we could introduce an infinite amount of x_2 into solution and still maintain feasibility. Since each unit of x_2 increases the objective function by 5, you can see that we would have an unbounded solution in this case. Hence *the way we recognize the unbounded situation is that all the $\bar{a}_{ij}$ are ≤ 0 in column j, and the simplex method indicates that variable x_j is to be introduced into solution.*

To illustrate this concept let us consider the example of an unbounded problem that we introduced in Section 7.8:

$$\max 2x_1 + 1x_2$$

$$\text{s.t.}$$

$$1x_1 \qquad \geq 2$$

$$1x_2 \leq 5$$

$$x_1, x_2 \geq 0$$

We first subtract a surplus variable, s_1, from the first constraint equation and add a slack variable, s_2, to the second constraint equation to obtain the standard form. We then add an artificial variable, a_1, to the first constraint equation in order to obtain the tableau form and set up the initial simplex tableau in terms of the basic variables a_1 and s_2. After bringing in x_1 at the first iteration and dropping the a_1 column, our simplex tableau is as follows:

Basis	c_B	x_1	x_2	s_1	s_2	
		2	1	0	0	
x_1	2	1	0	-1	0	2
s_2	0	0	1	0	1	5
z_j		2	0	-2	0	4
$c_j - z_j$		0	1	2	0	

Since the s_1 column has the largest positive $c_j - z_j$, we know we can increase the value of the objective function most rapidly by bringing s_1 into the basis. But $\bar{a}_{13} = -1$ and $\bar{a}_{23} = 0$; hence we cannot form the ratio $\bar{b}_i/\bar{a}_{i3}$ for positive $\bar{a}_{i3}$, since there are none. This is our indication that the solution to the linear program is unbounded. We interpret this condition below.

Each unit of s_1 that we bring into the basis drives zero units of s_2 out of solution and gives us an extra unit of x_1, since $\bar{a}_{13} = -1$. This is because s_1 is a surplus variable and can be interpreted as the amount of product 1 we produce over the minimum amount required; that is, $x_1 \geq 2$. Our simplex tableau has indicated that we can introduce as much of s_1 as desired without violating any constraints; thus, we can make as much as we want above the minimum amount of x_1 required. Since the objective function coefficient associated with x_1 is positive, there will be no upper bound on the value of the objective function.

In summary, a maximization linear program is unbounded if it is possible to make the value of the optimal solution as large as desired without violating any of the constraints. We can recognize this condition graphically as the case where the feasible region extends to infinity in a direction in which the objective function increases. When employing the simplex solution procedure, an unbounded linear program is easy to recognize. If at some iteration the simplex method tells us to introduce x_j into solution and all the $\bar{a}_{ij}$ are less than or equal to zero in the jth column, we recognize that we have a linear program with an unbounded solution.

We emphasize that the case of an unbounded solution will never occur in real-world cost-minimization or profit-maximization problems because it is not possible to reduce costs to minus infinity or to increase profits to plus infinity. Thus, if we encounter this situation when solving a linear programming model in practice, we should go back and examine carefully our formulation of the problem to determine if we have made an error, or if the linear programming model is inappropriate.

Alternate Optimal Solutions

A linear program with two or more optimal solutions is said to have alternate optima. In Section 7.6 we saw that alternate optima could be recognized whenever the objective function line was parallel to one of the binding constraints. When using the simplex method of solution, one will not recognize that a linear program has alternate optima until the final simplex tableau. Then if the program has alternate optima, $c_j - z_j$ will equal zero for one or more of the variables not in solution.

To illustrate the occurrence of alternate optima when the simplex method is being used, consider the following modification of the RMC problem (the objective function has been changed from $40x_1 + 30x_2$ to $40x_1 + 50x_2$):

$$\max 40x_1 + 50x_2$$

s.t.

$$\tfrac{2}{5}x_1 + \tfrac{1}{2}x_2 \leq 20$$
$$\tfrac{1}{5}x_2 \leq 5$$
$$\tfrac{3}{5}x_1 + \tfrac{3}{10}x_2 \leq 21$$
$$x_1, x_2 \geq 0$$

The graphical solution to this problem is shown in Figure 10.6

The final simplex tableau for this problem is shown below:

		x_1	x_2	s_1	s_2	s_3	
Basis	c_B	40	50	0	0	0	
x_1	40	1	0	$\tfrac{5}{2}$	$-\tfrac{25}{4}$	0	$\tfrac{75}{4}$
x_2	50	0	1	0	5	0	25
s_3	0	0	0	$-\tfrac{3}{2}$	$\tfrac{9}{4}$	1	$\tfrac{9}{4}$
	z_j	40	50	100	0	0	2000
	$c_j - z_j$	0	0	-100	0	0	

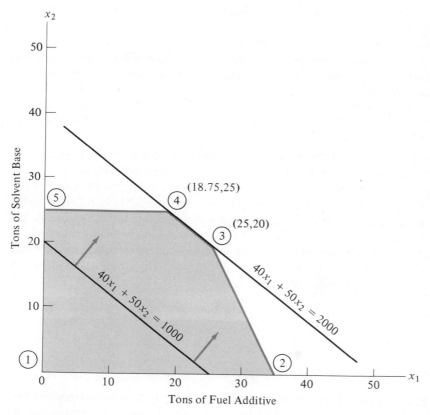

Figure 10.6
Modified RMC Problem
With Alternate Optima

All values in the net evaluation row are less than or equal to zero, indicating that we have reached the optimal solution. This solution yields $x_1 = 75/4 = 18.75$, $x_2 = 25$, and $s_3 = 9/4$. Note, however, that the entry in the net evaluation row for the nonbasic variable s_2 is equal to zero. This indicates that the linear program has alternate optima. That is, since the $c_j - z_j$ value corresponding to s_2 is equal to zero, we could introduce s_2 into the solution without changing the value of the optimal solution. The tableau, after introducing s_2, is

Basis	c_B	x_1 40	x_2 50	s_1 0	s_2 0	s_3 0	
x_1	40	1	0	$-5/3$	0	$25/9$	25
x_2	50	0	1	$10/3$	0	$-20/9$	20
s_2	0	0	0	$-2/3$	1	$4/9$	1
z_j		40	50	100	0	0	2000
$c_j - z_j$		0	0	-100	0	0	

After introducing s_2 we have a different solution: $x_1 = 25$, $x_2 = 20$, and $s_2 = 1$. However, this solution is still optimal ($c_j - z_j \leq 0$ for all j). Another way to confirm that this solution is still optimal is to note that the value of the objective function has remained at 2000.

In summary, we can recognize that a linear program has alternate optima by observing graphically that the objective function is parallel to one of the binding constraints. When using the simplex method, we can recognize alternate optima if $c_j - z_j$ equals zero for one of the variables not in solution.

Degeneracy

A linear program is said to be *degenerate* if one or more of the variables in the basic solution has a value of zero. *Degeneracy* does not cause any particular difficulties for the graphical solution procedure; however, degeneracy can cause some difficulties when the simplex method is used to solve a linear program. It is theoretically possible for the simplex algorithm to cycle when there are a number of degenerate solutions. That is, the algorithm could alternate among a set of nonoptimal solutions without increasing the objective function. If this happened, the optimal solution would never be reached. Cycling has not proved to cause significant difficulty in practice. Therefore we leave further discussion of degeneracy to more advanced texts.

10.10
SENSITIVITY ANALYSIS WITH THE SIMPLEX TABLEAU

In Chapter 8 we introduced sensitivity analysis as the study of how the optimal solution and the value of the optimal solution to a linear program change, given changes in the various coefficients of the problem. First, we showed how graphical sensitivity analysis can be performed for linear programs involving two decision variables; then, as part of the discussion of the computer solution of linear programs, we showed how sensitivity analysis can be performed with the help of computer output. The information contained in the final simplex tableau is what is used by the computer to compute the shadow and/ or dual prices, as well as ranges for the objective function coefficients and ranges for the right-hand-side values.

Objective Function Coefficients

Sensitivity analysis for an objective function coefficient involves placing a range on the coefficient's value. We call this range the *range of optimality*. As long as the actual value of the objective function coefficient is within the range of optimality, the current basic feasible solution will remain optimal. Thus, for a nonbasic variable, the range of optimality defines the possible objective function coefficient values for which that variable will remain nonbasic. In contrast, the range of optimality for a basic variable defines the objective function coefficient values for which that variable will remain basic, and hence part of the current optimal basic feasible solution.

In computing the range of optimality for an objective function coefficient, all other coefficients in the problem are assumed to remain at their original values; in other words, *only one coefficient is allowed to change at a time*. To illustrate the process of computing ranges for objective function coefficients, recall the RMC problem. The final simplex tableau is restated below.

		x_1	x_2	s_1	s_2	s_3	
Basis	c_B	40	30	0	0	0	
x_2	30	0	1	$10/3$	0	$-20/9$	20
s_2	0	0	0	$-2/3$	1	$4/9$	1
x_1	40	1	0	$-5/3$	0	$25/9$	25
	z_j	40	30	$100/3$	0	$400/9$	1600
	$c_j - z_j$	0	0	$-100/3$	0	$-400/9$	

When the simplex method is used to solve a linear programming problem, an optimal solution is recognized when all entries in the net evaluation row ($c_j - z_j$'s) are ≤ 0. Clearly the above tableau is optimal. However, if a change in one of the objective function coefficients were to cause one or more of the $c_j - z_j$ values for a nonbasic variable to become positive, then the solution would no longer be optimal; in this case one or more additional simplex iterations would be necessary to find the new optimal solution. The range of optimality for an objective function coefficient, then, is determined by those values that maintain

$$c_j - z_j \leq 0 \tag{10.22}$$

for all nonbasic variables.

Thus, to determine the range of optimality for an objective function coefficient (say c_k), we compute the value of the left-hand side of inequality (10.22) using c_k as the objective function coefficient for x_k and the appropriate numerical values in the final simplex tableau for everything else.

Let us illustrate the approach by computing the range of optimality for c_1 (the profit per ton of fuel additive) from the final simplex tableau of the RMC problem. Using c_1 (not 40) as the coefficient of x_1, the final simplex tableau is as follows:

		x_1	x_2	s_1	s_2	s_3	
Basis	c_B	c_1	30	0	0	0	
x_2	30	0	1	$10/3$	0	$-20/9$	20
s_2	0	0	0	$-2/3$	1	$4/9$	1
x_1	c_1	1	0	$-5/3$	0	$25/9$	25
	z_j	c_1	30	$100 - 5/3c_1$	0	$-200/9 + 25/9c_1$	$600 + 25c_1$
	$c_j - z_j$	0	0	$5/3c_1 - 100$	0	$200/9 - 25/9c_1$	

Note that this tableau is the same as the previous optimal tableau except for c_1 replacing 40. Thus we have a c_1 in the objective function row and the c_B column, and the z_j and $c_j - z_j$ rows have been recomputed using c_1 instead of 40. The $c_j - z_j$ entries for the basic variables are all still zero; thus the current solution will remain optimal as long as the value of c_1 is such that $c_j - z_j \leq 0$ for the two nonbasic variables s_1 and s_3. Hence

$$5/3c_1 - 100 \leq 0$$

and

$$200/3 - 25/9\,c_1 \leq 0$$

Using the first inequality we obtain

$$5/3\,c_1 \leq 100 \quad \text{or} \quad c_1 \leq 60$$

Using the second inequality we obtain

$$25/9\,c_1 \geq 200/3$$
$$c_1 \geq (9/25)(200/3)$$
$$c_1 \geq 24$$

Therefore, the range of optimality for c_1 is given by

$$24 \leq c_1 \leq 60$$

This is the same range we computed in Chapter 8 using the graphical approach. However, it was a little easier to compute the range of optimality here because of the information contained in the final simplex tableau.

To see how the management of RMC can make use of the above sensitivity analysis information, suppose that because of an increase in production costs the profit per ton on the fuel additive is reduced to \$30 per ton. The range of optimality indicates that the current solution $x_1 = 25$, $x_2 = 20$, $s_1 = 0$, $s_2 = 1$, and $s_3 = 0$ is still optimal. To verify this, let us recalculate the final simplex tableau for RMC after c_1 has been reduced to \$30. The result is shown below:

		x_1	x_2	s_1	s_2	s_3	
Basis	c_B	30	30	0	0	0	
x_2	30	0	1	$10/3$	0	$-20/9$	20
s_2	0	0	0	$-2/3$	1	$4/9$	1
x_1	30	1	0	$-5/3$	0	$25/9$	25
	z_j	30	30	50	0	$50/3$	1350
	$c_j - z_j$	0	0	-50	0	$-50/3$	

Since all the $c_j - z_j$ values are less than or equal to zero, the solution is optimal. As you can see, this solution is the same as our previous optimal solution. Note, however, that because of the decrease in profit for the fuel additive, the total profit has been reduced to $30(25) + $30(20) = $1350.

What would happen if the profit per ton were reduced even further—for instance, to \$20? Again we refer to the range of optimality for c_1. Since $c_1 = 20$ is outside the range, we know that a change this large will cause a new solution to be optimal. Consider the following simplex tableau, which was obtained by setting $c_1 = 20$:

		x_1	x_2	s_1	s_2	s_3	
Basis	c_B	20	30	0	0	0	
x_2	30	0	1	$10/3$	0	$-20/9$	20
s_2	0	0	0	$-2/3$	1	$4/9$	1
x_1	20	1	0	$-5/3$	0	$25/9$	25
	z_j	20	30	$200/3$	0	$-100/9$	1100
	$c_j - z_j$	0	0	$-200/3$	0	$100/9$	

As expected, the solution $x_1 = 25$, $x_2 = 20$, $s_1 = 0$, $s_2 = 1$, $s_3 = 0$ is no longer optimal. The entry corresponding to column s_3 in the net evaluation row is now greater than zero. This implies that at least one more simplex iteration must be performed to reach the optimal solution. Check for yourself by continuing the simplex iterations on the above tableau to see that the new optimal solution will require the production of $18\frac{3}{4}$ tons of fuel additive and 25 tons of solvent base.

We now see how the range of optimality can be used to determine whether or not a change in the objective function coefficient of a variable will cause a change in the optimal solution. By using the range of optimality to determine whether or not the change in a coefficient is large enough to cause a change in the optimal solution, we can often avoid formulating and solving a modified linear programming problem.

Let us now compute the range of optimality for c_2 (the profit per ton of solvent base). The final simplex tableau obtained with c_2 (not 30) as the objective function coefficient of x_2 is shown below:

		x_1	x_2	s_1	s_2	s_3	
Basis	c_B	40	c_2	0	0	0	
x_2	c_2	0	1	$10/3$	0	$-20/9$	20
s_2	0	0	0	$-2/3$	1	$4/9$	1
x_1	40	1	0	$-5/3$	0	$25/9$	25
	z_j	40	c_2	$-200/3 + 10/3 c_2$	0	$1000/9 - 20/9 c_2$	$1000 + 20c_2$
	$c_j - z_j$	0	0	$200/3 - 10/3 c_2$	0	$-1000/9 + 20/9 c_2$	

As before, this revised tableau is easy to compute. The changes required involve the coefficients in the x_2 column, the z_j entries for x_2 and the nonbasic variables, and the $c_j - z_j$ values for the nonbasic variables. In computing the range of optimality we are concerned only with the $c_j - z_j$ values for the nonbasic variables. Given these revised $c_j - z_j$ values, we can form the following inequalities [see expression (10.22)]:

$$200/3 - 10/3 c_2 \leq 0$$
$$-1000/9 + 20/9 c_2 \leq 0$$

Using the first inequality we obtain

$$10/3 c_2 \geq 200/3$$
$$c_2 \geq (3/10)(200/3)$$
$$c_2 \geq 20$$

With the second inequality we obtain

$$20/9 \, c_2 \leq 1000/9$$
$$c_2 \leq (9/20)(1000/9)$$
$$c_2 \leq 50$$

Therefore, the range of optimality for c_2 is given by

$$20 \leq c_2 \leq 50$$

We see that as long as the profit per ton of solvent base is between \$20 and \$50, the production quantities of 25 tons of fuel additive and 20 tons of solvent base will be optimal.

Both c_1 and c_2 were objective function coefficients of basic variables. The range of optimality for nonbasic variables is even easier to compute, since a change in the objective function coefficient for a nonbasic variable causes only two elements to change in the simplex tableau. To illustrate the approach we show below the final simplex tableau for the RMC problem that was obtained using c_{s_1} (not 0) as the objective function coefficient of s_1:

		x_1	x_2	s_1	s_2	s_3	
Basis	c_B	40	30	c_{s_1}	0	0	
x_2	30	0	1	$10/3$	0	$-20/9$	20
s_2	0	0	0	$-2/3$	1	$4/9$	1
x_1	40	1	0	$-5/3$	0	$25/9$	25
z_j		40	30	$100/3$	0	$400/9$	1600
$c_j - z_j$		0	0	$c_{s_1} - 100/3$	0	$-400/9$	

Note that the only changes in the tableau are in the s_1 column. Applying inequality (10.22) to compute the range of optimality, we get

$$c_{s_1} - 100/3 \leq 0$$
$$c_{s_1} \leq 100/3$$

Therefore, the range of optimality for c_{s_1} is given by

$$-\infty < c_{s_1} \leq 100/3.$$

As long as the objective function coefficient for s_1 is $\leq 100/3$, the current solution will be optimal. In addition, there is no lower bound on how much the coefficient may be decreased.

The same analysis holds for all nonbasic variables. Specifically, it can be shown that there is no lower limit on how much the coefficient of a nonbasic variable can be decreased; in addition, the upper limit on how much it can be increased before it is profitable to bring the nonbasic variable into solution is given by z_j. Thus the range of optimality for the objective function coefficient of each nonbasic variable is given by

$$-\infty < c_j \le z_j$$

Since s_1 is a slack variable in the RMC problem, it is clear that its objective function coefficient is not subject to variability. It will remain 0, and hence s_1 would never be brought into the solution. We will see in the next subsection that the upper limit on the range for a slack variable is the shadow price for the corresponding constraint.

We now present a summary of the steps to compute the range of optimality for objective function coefficients. In stating the steps we assume that it is desired to compute the range for c_k.

1. Replace the numerical value for the objective function coefficient of x_k with c_k everywhere it appears in the final simplex tableau.
2. Recompute the $c_j - z_j$ entries for each nonbasic variable. (If variable x_k is itself nonbasic, it is only necessary to recompute $c_k - z_k$.)
3. Apply inequality (10.22) to each recomputed $c_j - z_j$.
4. Solve the resulting inequalities for the upper and lower bounds on the range of optimality. If there are two or more upper bounds on c_k, the smaller of these is the upper bound on the range. Similarly, if there are two or more lower bounds, the largest of these is the lower bound on the range.

The ranges we have developed are for the objective function coefficients of the problem solved by the simplex method. If the original problem involved minimization, its objective function would have been multiplied by (-1) prior to solving. To find the range for the original coefficients multiply the upper and lower limits by (-1) and change the direction of the inequalities.

Right-Hand Sides and Shadow Prices

In many linear programming problems we can interpret the right-hand sides (b_i's) as the resources available. For example, in the RMC problem the right-hand-side values represent the number of tons of each of three raw materials available. Valuable management information can be provided if we know how much it would be worth to the company to have more of each type of raw material. Sensitivity analysis of the right-hand sides can help provide this information.

Shadow Prices[4]

In Chapter 8 we stated that the change in value of the objective function per unit increase in the value of the right-hand side was called the shadow price. Using the graphical approach, we saw how the value of the shadow price could be computed by increasing the value of the right-hand side, resolving the problem, and then computing the increase in value per unit increase in the right-hand side.

When the simplex method is used to solve a linear programming problem, the values of the shadow prices are much easier to obtain. They are obtained from the z_j values for the slack and surplus variables in the final simplex tableau. To illustrate this point, the final simplex tableau for the RMC problem is reproduced below:

---

[4]We assume in the development of this subsection that the objective function involves maximization. For a minimization problem, recall that we multiply the objective function by -1 before solving using the simplex method.

		x_1	x_2	s_1	s_2	s_3	
Basis	c_B	40	30	0	0	0	
x_2	30	0	1	$10/3$	0	$-20/9$	20
s_2	0	0	0	$-2/3$	1	$4/9$	1
x_1	40	1	0	$-5/3$	0	$25/9$	25
z_j		40	30	$100/3$	0	$400/9$	1600
$c_j - z_j$		0	0	$-100/3$	0	$-400/9$	

The shadow price for the material 1 constraint is $100/3 = \$33.33$; for the material 2 constraint it is $.00$; and for the material 3 constraint it is $400/9 = \$44.44$. Thus an additional ton of material 1 is worth $\$33.33$ to RMC and an additional ton of material 3 is worth $\$44.44$ (recall that this is the value we obtained in Chapter 8). If RMC has an opportunity to purchase additional materials, we know that material 3 is the most valuable and that the company should be willing to pay up to $\$44.44$ per ton for it.

In order to explain why the z_j values for the slack variables in the final simplex tableau are the shadow prices, let us consider first any slack variables that are part of the optimal basic feasible solution. Each of these variables will have a z_j value of zero, implying a shadow price of zero for the corresponding constraint. Referring to the RMC problem, we see that s_2 is a basic variable. How much would you be willing to pay for an additional ton of material 2? Since RMC is not using all of material 2 ($s_2 = 1$), we already have an excess supply of this resource. Thus, any additional amount of material 2 is of no value to the company. In general, if a slack variable is a basic variable in the optimal solution, the shadow price of the corresponding resource is zero. This is, of course, the value of z_j for any slack variable in the basis.

Consider now the nonbasic slack variables. Let us take s_1 as an example. In the previous subsection we found that the current solution would remain optimal as long as the objective function coefficient for s_1 (here denoted c_{s_1}) stayed in the following range:

$$-\infty < c_{s_1} \le 100/3$$

This implies that the variable s_1 should not be increased from its current value of zero unless it was worth more than $\$100/3 = \$33.33$ to do so. In other words, RMC should use all of material 1 unless it is paid more than $\$100/3$ not to use it. We can conclude then that $\$100/3$ is the value to RMC of 1 ton of material 1 in the production of fuel additive and solvent base. Thus, if additional amounts of this material could be purchased, RMC should be willing to pay up to $\$100/3 = \$33.33$ per ton for it. A similar interpretation can be given to the z_j value for each of the nonbasic slack variables. That is, z_j is the value of one additional unit of the resource in the row corresponding to that slack variable. In summary, when the simplex method is used to solve a linear program, the shadow price for resource availability in a less-than-or-equal-to constraint is given by the z_j value for the corresponding slack variable.

With a greater-than-or-equal-to constraint, the value of the shadow price will be less than or equal to zero because an increase in the value of the right-hand side is no longer helpful; it makes it more difficult to satisfy the constraint. As a result (since we always work with a maximization objective function in the simplex tableau), the optimal value of the objective function can be expected to decrease. The shadow price gives the amount of the expected change—a negative number, since we expect a decrease. As you might expect, the shadow price for a greater-than-or-equal-to constraint is given by the negative of the z_j entry for the corresponding surplus variable in the optimal simplex tableau.

Finally, it is possible to compute shadow prices for equality constraints. We will not discuss this case in detail here, since we have recommended dropping each artificial-variable column from the simplex tableau as soon as the corresponding artificial variable is selected to leave the basis. However, if we had not dropped those columns from the simplex tableau, the shadow prices would have been given by the z_j values for the artificial variables.

In conclusion, when the simplex method is used to solve a linear programming problem, the shadow prices for the constraints are contained in the final simplex tableau. The following table summarizes the method for determining the shadow prices for $\leq$ and $\geq$ constraints:

Constraint Type	Shadow Price Given by
$\leq$	z_j value for slack variable associated with constraint
$\geq$	Negative of z_j value for surplus variable associated with constraint

As previously indicated, we are assuming that the problem involves a maximization objective function. Recall that we can convert a minimization problem to a maximization problem by multiplying the objective function by -1 before using the simplex method. Therefore, for minimization problems we need to multiply the shadow prices as computed above by -1 in order to determine the effect of a right-hand-side change on the original minimization problem.

Range of Feasibility

As we have just seen, the z_j row in the final simplex tableau can be used to predict the change in the value of the objective function per unit change in one of the b_i. But here is the catch: This interpretation can be used only as long as the change in the b_i is not large enough to make the current basis infeasible. Thus, we will be interested in determining how much a particular b_i can be changed without causing a change in the current optimal basis. In effect, we will do this by calculating a range of values over which a particular b_i can vary without any of the current basic variables becoming infeasible (i.e., less than zero). This range of values will be referred to as the *range of feasibility*.

To demonstrate the effect of increasing a resource by several units, consider increasing the amount of material 3 by 9 tons. Will the new basic solution be feasible? If so, we can expect an increase in the objective function of 9($400/9) = $400. Shown below is the final simplex tableau we would obtain if RMC had 30 tons (not 21) of material 3:

		x_1	x_2	s_1	s_2	s_3	
Basis	c_B	40	30	0	0	0	
x_2	30	0	1	$10/3$	0	$-20/9$	0
s_2	0	0	0	$-2/3$	1	$4/9$	5
x_1	40	1	0	$-5/3$	0	$25/9$	50
z_j		40	30	$100/3$	0	$400/9$	2000
$c_j - z_j$		0	0	$-100/3$	0	$-400/9$	

Clearly this new optimal solution is feasible, since all the basic variables are non-negative. Note also that, just as predicted, the value of the optimal solution has increased by $9(400/9) = 400$. You may wonder whether we had to completely re-solve the problem to find this solution. The answer is no! The only changes in this final simplex tableau (from the one with $b_3 = 21$) are the differences in the values of the basic variables and the value of the objective function. That is, only the last column has changed. The entries in this new last column of the simplex tableau have been obtained by merely adding 9 times the first four entries in the s_3 column to the last column in the previous optimal tableau:

$$\begin{bmatrix} \text{New} \\ \text{solution} \end{bmatrix} = \begin{bmatrix} 20 \\ 1 \\ 25 \\ 1600 \end{bmatrix} + 9 \begin{bmatrix} -20/9 \\ 4/9 \\ 25/9 \\ 400/9 \end{bmatrix} = \begin{bmatrix} 0 \\ 5 \\ 50 \\ 2000 \end{bmatrix}$$

The reason that we could do this is as follows: The entries in the s_3 column indicate how many units of the current basic variables will be driven out of solution if one unit of variable s_3 is introduced into our solution. Forcing one unit of s_3 into solution is the same as reducing the availability of material 3 by one unit. Increasing b_3 by one unit (the availability of material 3) has just the reverse effect. Therefore, the entries in the s_3 column indicate the change in the value of the current basic variables corresponding to a one-unit increase in b_3. Similarly, the change in the value of the objective function per unit increase in b_3 is given by the value of z_j in the s_3 column (the shadow price). In our case the availability of material 3 increased by 9 units; thus we multiplied the first four entries in the s_3 column by 9 to obtain the change in the value of the solution.

How do we know when a change in b_3 is so large that the current basis will become infeasible? We will first answer this question specifically for the RMC problem and then state the general procedure for less-than-or-equal-to constraints. The approach taken with greater-than-or-equal-to constraints will then be discussed.

We begin by showing how to compute upper and lower bounds for the maximum amount that b_3 can be changed before the current optimal basis becomes infeasible. We have seen how to find the new basic feasible solution values given a 9-unit increase in b_3. In general, given a change in b_3 of Δb_3, the new values for the basic variables are given by

$$\begin{bmatrix} x_2 \\ s_2 \\ x_1 \end{bmatrix} = \begin{bmatrix} 20 \\ 1 \\ 25 \end{bmatrix} + \Delta b_3 \begin{bmatrix} -20/9 \\ 4/9 \\ 25/9 \end{bmatrix} = \begin{bmatrix} 20 - 20/9\,\Delta b_3 \\ 1 + 4/9\,\Delta b_3 \\ 25 + 25/9\,\Delta b_3 \end{bmatrix} \qquad (10.23)$$

As long as the value of each variable in the new basic solution remains nonnegative, the new basic solution will remain feasible and therefore optimal. We can keep the variables nonnegative by limiting the change in b_3 (that is, Δb_3) so that we satisfy each of the following conditions:

$$20 - {}^{20}\!/\!_9 \Delta b_3 \geq 0 \tag{10.24}$$

$$1 + {}^{4}\!/\!_9 \Delta b_3 \geq 0 \tag{10.25}$$

$$25 + {}^{25}\!/\!_9 \Delta b_3 \geq 0 \tag{10.26}$$

The left-hand sides of the above inequalities represent the values of the basic variables after b_3 has been changed by Δb_3.

Working algebraically with inequalities (10.24), (10.25), and (10.26), we get

$$\Delta b_3 \leq ({}^{9}\!/\!_{20}) 20 \quad \text{or} \quad \Delta b_3 \leq 9$$
$$\Delta b_3 \geq ({}^{9}\!/\!_4)(-1) \quad \text{or} \quad \Delta b_3 \geq -{}^{9}\!/\!_4$$
$$\Delta b_3 \geq ({}^{9}\!/\!_{25})(-25) \quad \text{or} \quad \Delta b_3 \geq -9$$

Since we must satisfy all three inequalities, the most restrictive limits on Δb_3 determine the maximum permissable changes. Therefore, we have

$$-{}^{9}\!/\!_4 \leq \Delta b_3 \leq 9 \tag{10.27}$$

The initial amount of material 3 available was 21 tons. Using $b_3 = 21 + \Delta b_3$, where b_3 is the number of tons of material 3 available, we add 21 to each term in expression (10.27) and obtain

$$21 - {}^{9}\!/\!_4 \leq 21 + \Delta b_3 \leq 21 + 9$$
$$18{}^{3}\!/\!_4 \leq b_3 \leq 30$$

The above range of values for b_3 indicates that as long as the amount of material 3 available is between $18{}^{3}\!/\!_4$ and 30 tons, the current basis will remain feasible and optimal. Thus we have found the range of feasibility for the right-hand-side of the material 3 constraint.

Since the shadow price is $400/9, we know that we can improve the profit by $44.44 for each additional ton of material 3. We now know that this shadow price will accurately predict the change in value of the objective function for increases of up to 9 tons of material 3. Furthermore, the range of feasibility also tells us that the shadow price will accurately predict a reduction of $44.44 for each unit of reduction in the material 3 availability up to a $2{}^{1}\!/\!_4$-ton reduction.

Our computation of the range of feasibility has involved only the material 3 constraint. The procedure for calculating the range of feasibility for the right-hand-side value of any less-than-or-equal-to constraint is the same. The first step, [paralleling equation (10.23)] for a general constraint i, is to calculate the range of values for Δb_i that satisfy the conditions shown below:

$$\begin{bmatrix} \overline{b}_1 \\ \overline{b}_2 \\ \vdots \\ \overline{b}_m \end{bmatrix} + \Delta b_i \begin{bmatrix} \overline{a}_{1j} \\ \overline{a}_{2j} \\ \vdots \\ \overline{a}_{mj} \end{bmatrix} \geq \begin{bmatrix} 0 \\ 0 \\ \vdots \\ 0 \end{bmatrix} \qquad (10.28)$$

Current solution (last column of the final simplex tableau)

Column of the final simplex tableau corresponding to the *slack* variable associated with constraint i

These conditions establish a lower and an upper limit on Δb_i. Given these limits, the range of feasibility can be established.

Similar arguments can be used to develop a procedure for determining the range of feasibility for the right-hand-side value of a greater-than-or-equal-to constraint. Essentially the procedure is the same, with the column corresponding to the surplus variable associated with the constraint playing the central role. For a general greater-than-or-equal-to constraint i, we first calculate the range of values for Δb_i that satisfy the conditions shown in equation (10.29):

$$\begin{bmatrix} \overline{b}_1 \\ \overline{b}_2 \\ \vdots \\ \overline{b}_m \end{bmatrix} - \Delta b_i \begin{bmatrix} \overline{a}_{1j} \\ \overline{a}_{2j} \\ \vdots \\ \overline{a}_{mj} \end{bmatrix} \geq \begin{bmatrix} 0 \\ 0 \\ \vdots \\ 0 \end{bmatrix} \qquad (10.29)$$

Current solution

Column of the final simplex tableau corresponding to the *surplus* variable associated with constraint i

Once again, these conditions establish a lower and an upper limit on Δb_i. Given these limits, the range of feasibility is easily determined.

A range of feasibility for the right-hand-side value of an equality constraint can also be computed. To do so for equality constraint i, one could use the column of the final simplex tableau corresponding to the artificial variable associated with constraint i in equation (10.28). Since we have suggested dropping the artificial variable columns from the simplex tableau as soon as the artificial variable becomes nonbasic, these columns will not be available in the final tableau. Thus more involved calculations are required to compute a range of feasibility for equality constraints. Details may be found in more advanced texts.

As long as the change in a right-hand-side value is such that b_i stays within its range of feasibility, the same basis will remain feasible and optimal. Changes that force b_i outside its range of feasibility require performing additional simplex iterations to find the new optimal basic feasible solution. More advanced linear programming texts show how this can be done without completely resolving the problem.

Simultaneous Changes

By reviewing the procedures for developing the range of optimality and the range of feasibility, we note that only one coefficient at a time was permitted to vary. That is why our statements concerning changes within these ranges were made with the understanding that no other coefficients are permitted to change. However, sometimes we can make the same statements when either two or more objective function coefficients or two or more right-hand sides are varied simultaneously. When the simultaneous changes satisfy the 100% rule, the same statements are applicable. The 100% rule was explained in Chapter 8, but we will briefly review it here.

Let us call the amount a coefficient can be increased before reaching the upper limit of its range the allowable increase, and the amount a coefficient can be decreased before reaching the lower limit of its range the allowable decrease. Now suppose that simultaneous changes are made in two, or more, objective function coefficients. For each coefficient changed, we compute the percentage of the allowable increase, or decrease, represented by the change. If the sum of the percentages for all changes does not exceed 100%, we say that the 100% rule is satisfied and that the simultaneous changes will not cause a change in the optimal solution. However, just as with a single objective function coefficient change, the value of the solution will change because of the change in the coefficients.

Similarly, if two or more changes in constraint right-hand-side values are made, we again compute the percentage of allowable increase or allowable decrease represented by each change. If the sum of the percentages for all changes does not exceed 100%, we say that the 100% rule is satisfied. The shadow prices are then valid for determining the change in value of the objective function associated with the right-hand-side changes.

Summary

In Chapter 7 we showed how linear programming problems with two decision variables can be solved using the graphical method. In this chapter the simplex method was introduced as an algebraic procedure for solving linear programming problems. Although the simplex method can be used to solve small linear programs by hand calculations, as problems get larger, even the simplex method becomes too cumbersome for efficient hand computation. As a result we must utilize a computer if we want to solve large linear programs in any reasonable length of time. In Chapter 8 we showed how computer software packages can be used to solve linear programs. The computational procedures of these software packages are based on the simplex method.

We described how developing the tableau form of a linear program is a necessary step in the simplex solution procedure. This required learning how to convert greater-than-or-equal-to constraints, equality constraints, and constraints with negative right-hand-side values into the form necessary to write a linear program in tableau form.

For linear programs with greater-than-or-equal-to constraints and/or equality constraints, artificial variables are used in order to obtain tableau form. An objective function coefficient of $-M$, where M is a very large number, is assigned to each artificial variable. If there is a feasible solution to the real-world problem, all artificial variables will be driven out of solution before the simplex method reaches its stopping criterion. The iterations required to remove the artificial variables from solution constitute what is called phase I of the simplex method.

Two techniques were mentioned for solving minimization problems. The first approach involved changing the rule for introducing a variable into solution and changing the stopping criterion. The second approach involved multiplying the objective function by -1 to obtain an equivalent maximization problem. With this change any minimization problem can be solved using the steps required for a maximization problem.

As a review of the material in this chapter, we now present a detailed step-by-step procedure for solving linear programs using the simplex method.

Step 1   Formulate a linear programming model of the problem.

Step 2   Define an equivalent linear program by performing the following operations.
    a. Multiply each constraint with a negative right-hand-side value by -1 and change the direction of the constraint inequality;
    b. For a minimization problem convert the problem to an equivalent maximization problem by multiplying the objective function by -1.

Step 3   Set up the standard-form representation of the linear program by adding slack and subtracting surplus variables.

Step 4   Set up the tableau-form representation of the linear program in order to obtain an initial basic feasible solution. All linear programs must be put in this form before the initial simplex tableau can be obtained.

Step 5   Set up the initial simplex tableau to keep track of the calculations required by the simplex method.

Step 6   Choose the nonbasic variable with the largest $c_j - z_j$ to bring into the basis.

Step 7   Choose as the pivot row that row with the smallest ratio of $\bar{b}_i/\bar{a}_{ij}$ for $\bar{a}_{ij} > 0$. This ratio is used to determine which variable will leave the basis when variable j enters the basis. This ratio also indicates how many units of variable j can be introduced into solution before the basic variable in the ith row equals zero.

Step 8   Perform the necessary elementary row operations to convert the column for the incoming variable to a unit column. Once these row operations have been performed, read the values of the basic variables from the $\bar{b}$ column of the tableau.

Step 9   Test for optimality. If $c_j - z_j \leq 0$ for all columns, we have the optimal solution. If not, return to step 6.

In Section 10.9 we discussed how the special cases of infeasibility, unboundedness, alternate optima, and degeneracy can occur when solving linear programming problems with the simplex method. In Section 10.10 we showed how sensitivity analysis can be performed using the information in the final simplex tableau. This included computing the range of optimality for objective function coefficients, shadow prices, and the range of feasibility for the right-hand sides. This sensitivity information is routinely made available as part of the solution provided by most linear programming computer packages.

In discussing sensitivity analysis, we stressed that the computations of ranges and shadow prices were based on the assumption that only one coefficient was permitted to change. It is possible to do some limited sensitivity analysis on the effect of changing more than one coefficient at a time; the 100% rule was mentioned as being useful in this context.

Glossary

Simplex method   An algebraic procedure for solving linear programming problems. The simplex method uses elementary row operations to iterate from one basic feasible solution (extreme point) to another, until the optimal solution is reached.

Basic solution   Given a linear program in standard form, with n variables and m constraints, a basic solution is obtained by setting $n - m$ of the variables equal to zero and solving the constraint equations for the values of the other m variables. If a unique solution exists, it is a basic solution.

Basic feasible solution   A basic solution that is also feasible; that is, it satisfies the nonnegativity conditions. A basic feasible solution corresponds to an extreme point.

Tableau form   The form in which a linear program must be written before setting up the initial simplex tableau. When a linear program is written in this form, its A matrix contains m unit columns corresponding to the basic variables, and the values of these basic variables are given by the values in the b column. A further requirement is that the entries in the b column be greater than or equal to zero.

Simplex tableau   A table used to keep track of the calculations made when using the simplex method.

Unit vector or unit column   A vector, or column of a matrix, which has a zero in every position except one. In the nonzero position there is a 1. There is a unit column in the simplex tableau for each basic variable.

Net evaluation row   The row in the simplex tableau that contains the value of $c_j - z_j$ for every variable (column).

Current solution   When carrying out the simplex method, the current solution refers to the current basic feasible solution (extreme point).

Basis   The set of variables that are not restricted to equal zero in the current basic solution. The variables that make up the basis are termed basic variables, and the remaining variables are called nonbasic variables.

Iteration   An iteration of the simplex method consists of the sequence of steps (row operations) performed in moving from one basic feasible solution to another.

Pivot element   The element of the simplex tableau that is in both the pivot row and the pivot column.

Pivot column   The column in the simplex tableau corresponding to the nonbasic variable that is about to be introduced into solution.

Pivot row   The row in the simplex tableau corresponding to the basic variable that will leave the solution.

Elementary row operations   Operations that may be performed on a system of simultaneous equations without changing the solution to the system of equations.

Artificial variable   A variable that has no physical meaning in terms of the original linear programming problem, but serves merely to enable a basic feasible solution to be created for starting the simplex method. Artificial variables are assigned an objective function coefficient of $-M$, where M is a very large number.

Phase I   When artificial variables are present in the initial simplex tableau, phase I refers to the iterations of the simplex method that are used to drive the artificial variables out of solution. At the end of phase I, the basic feasible solution in the simplex tableau is also feasible for the real-world problem.

Degeneracy   A situation that exists when one or more of the basic variables has a value of zero.

Range of optimality   The range of values over which an objective function coefficient may vary without causing a change in the optimal solution (the values of the variables will remain unchanged, but the value of the objective function may change).

Shadow price   The change in value of the objective function per unit increase in the value of the right-hand side associated with a linear programming constraint.

Range of feasibility   The range of values over which a b_i may vary without causing the current basic solution to become infeasible. The value of the variables in the solution will change, but the same variables will remain basic.

Problems

1. Solve the following system of linear equations (find the values of x_1 and x_2 that satisfy both equations):

$$6x_1 + 3x_2 = 33$$
$$10x_1 - 2x_2 = 6$$

2. Solve the following system of linear equations:

$$1x_1 + 3x_2 - 1x_3 = 4$$
$$2x_1 + 4x_2 + 2x_3 = 22$$
$$5x_1 - 2x_2 + 1x_3 = 27$$

3. Consider the following linear program:

$$\max \quad 5x_1 + 9x_2$$
$$\text{s.t.}$$
$$\tfrac{1}{2}x_1 + 1x_2 \leq 8$$
$$1x_1 + 1x_2 \geq 10$$
$$\tfrac{1}{4}x_1 + \tfrac{3}{2}x_2 \geq 6$$
$$x_1, x_2 \geq 0$$

a. Write the problem in standard form.
b. How many variables will be set equal to zero in a basic solution for this problem? Explain.
c. Find the basic solution that corresponds to s_1 and s_2 equal to zero.
d. Find the basic solution that corresponds to x_1 and s_3 equal to zero.
e. Are your solutions for part (c) and/or (d) basic feasible solutions? Extreme-point solutions? Explain.
f. Use the graphical approach to determine the solutions found in parts (c) and (d). Do the graphical results agree with your answer to part (e)? Explain.

4. The following partial initial simplex tableau is given:

Basis	c_B	x_1	x_2	x_3	s_1	s_2	s_3	
		5	20	25	0	0	0	
		2	1	0	1	0	0	40
		0	2	1	0	1	0	30
		3	0	$-\frac{1}{2}$	0	0	1	15
z_j								
$c_j - z_j$								

a. Complete the initial tableau.
b. Write the problem in its tableau form.
c. What is the initial basis? Does this correspond to the origin? Explain.
d. What is the value of the objective function at this initial solution?
e. For the next iteration, what variable should enter the basis and what variable should leave the basis?
f. How many units of the entering variable will be in the next solution? Before making this first iteration, what should be the value of the objective function after the first iteration?
g. Find the optimal solution using the simplex method.

5. Solve the following linear program using the graphical approach:

$$\max \quad 4x_1 + 5x_2$$

s.t.

$$2x_1 + 2x_2 \leq 20$$
$$3x_1 + 7x_2 \leq 42$$
$$x_1, x_2 \geq 0$$

Put the linear program in tableau form and solve using the simplex method. Show the sequence of extreme points generated by the simplex method.

6. Explain in your own words why the tableau form and the standard form are the same for problems with less-than-or-equal-to constraints and nonnegative b_i's.

7. Solve the Ryland Farm problem (7.32) using the simplex method. Locate the solution found at each iteration on the graph of the feasible region.

8. Recall the Par, Inc. problem (see 7.13). The mathematical model for this problem is restated below:

$$\max \quad 10x_1 + 9x_2$$

s.t.

$\frac{7}{10}x_1 + 1x_2 \leq 630$		Cutting and dyeing
$\frac{1}{2}x_1 + \frac{5}{6}x_2 \leq 600$		Sewing
$1x_1 + \frac{2}{3}x_2 \leq 708$		Finishing
$\frac{1}{10}x_1 + \frac{1}{4}x_2 \leq 135$		Inspection and packaging
$x_1, x_2 \geq 0$		

where

$$x_1 = \text{number of standard bags produced}$$
$$x_2 = \text{number of deluxe bags produced}$$

a. Use the simplex method to determine how many bags of each model Par should manufacture.

b. What is the profit Par can earn with the above production quantities?

c. How many hours of production time will be scheduled for each operation?

d. What is the slack time in each operation?

9. Solve the following linear program:

$$\max \quad 2.5x_1 + 5x_2 + 1x_3 + 1x_4$$
$$\text{s.t.}$$
$$1x_1 + 1.4x_2 + 0.2x_3 + 0.8x_4 \leq 1600$$
$$2x_1 + 2x_2 + 1.6x_3 + 1x_4 \leq 1300$$
$$1.2x_1 + 1x_2 + 1x_3 + 1.2x_4 \leq 960$$
$$x_1, x_2, x_3, x_4 \geq 0$$

10. Solve the following linear program using both the graphical and the simplex methods:

$$\max \quad 2x_1 + 8x_2$$
$$\text{s.t.}$$
$$3x_1 + 9x_2 \leq 45$$
$$2x_1 + 1x_2 \geq 12$$
$$x_1, x_2 \geq 0$$

Show graphically how the simplex method moves from one basic feasible solution to another. Find the coordinates of all extreme points of the feasible region.

11. How many basic solutions are there to a linear program that has seven variables and four constraints when written in standard form?

12. Explain in your own words why, when we are trying to determine which basic variable to eliminate at a particular iteration, we consider only the $\bar{a}_{ij}$ that are strictly greater than zero.

13. Referring to problem 8, suppose that instead of introducing x_1 into the solution at the first iteration of the simplex method for the Par, Inc. problem, you had mistakenly introduced x_2.

a. Conduct the simplex calculations for the Par, Inc. problem and introduce x_2 into the basis at the first iteration. Then continue with the simplex method until an optimal solution has been reached.

b. Do we always have to introduce the variable into the solution that has the largest $c_j - z_j$ value?

c. Why does the criterion for introducing the variable into the solution use the largest $c_j - z_j$ value?

14. Suppose that we did not remove the basic variable with the smallest ratio of $\bar{b}_i / \bar{a}_{ij}$ at a particular iteration. What effect would this have on the simplex tableau for our next solution?

15. Suppose that a company manufactures three products from two raw materials, where the amount of raw material in each unit of each product is given.

	Product *A*	Product *B*	Product *C*
Raw material I	7 lb	6 lb	3 lb
Raw material II	5 lb	4 lb	2 lb

If the company has available 100 pounds of material I and 200 pounds of material II, and if the profits for the three products are $20, $20, and $15, how much of each product should be produced in order to maximize profits?

16. HighTech Industries imports electronic components that are used to assemble two personal computer models; one is the HT Portable, the other is the HT Deskpro. The Deskpro generates a profit contribution of $50 per unit, and the Portable generates a profit contribution of $40 per unit. The Deskpro requires 3 hours of assembly time, and the Portable requires 5 hours; only 150 hours of assembly time are available next week. Also, HighTech currently has only 20 of the display units used in the Portable; thus no more than 20 units of the Portable may be assembled. Each unit of the Deskpro requires 8 square feet and each unit of the Portable requires 5 square feet of warehouse space. Only 300 square feet are currently available in the warehouse. Determine how many units of each model should be produced next week if it is desired to maximize profit contribution.

17. Liva's Lumber, Inc. manufactures three types of plywood. The data below summarize the production hours per unit in each of three production operations and other data for the problem:

Plywood	Operations (hours)			Profit/ Unit
	I	II	III	
Grade *A*	2	2	4	$40
Grade *B*	5	5	2	$30
Grade *X*	10	3	2	$20
Maximum time available	900	400	600	

How many units of each grade of lumber should be produced?

18. Ye Olde Cording Winery in Peoria, Illinois, makes three kinds of authentic German wine: Heidelberg Sweet, Heidelberg Regular, and Deutschland Extra Dry. The raw materials, labor, and profit for a gallon of each of these wines are summarized below:

Wine	Grapes Grade A (bushels)	Grapes Grade B (bushels)	Sugar (pounds)	Labor (hours)	Profit/ Gallon
Heidelberg Sweet	1	1	2	2	$1.00
Heidelberg Regular	2	0	1	3	$1.20
Deutschland Extra Dry	0	2	0	1	$2.00

If the Winery has 150 bushels of grade A grapes, 150 bushels of grade B grapes, 80 pounds of sugar, and 225 labor-hours available during the next week, what product mix of wines will maximize the company's profit?
a. Solve using the simplex method.
b. Interpret all slack variables.
c. An increase in what resources could improve the company's profit?

19. Set up the tableau form for the following linear program (do not attempt to solve):

$$\max \quad 4x_1 + 2x_2 - 3x_3 + 5x_4$$
$$\text{s.t.}$$
$$2x_1 - 1x_2 + 1x_3 + 2x_4 \geq 50$$
$$3x_1 \qquad - 1x_3 + 2x_4 \leq 80$$
$$1x_1 + 1x_2 \qquad + 1x_4 = 60$$
$$x_1, x_2, x_3, x_4 \geq 0$$

20. Set up the tableau form for the following linear program (do not attempt to solve):

$$\min \quad 4x_1 + 5x_2 + 3x_3$$
$$\text{s.t.}$$
$$4x_1 \qquad + 2x_3 \geq \quad 20$$
$$1x_2 - 1x_3 \leq \quad -8$$
$$1x_1 - 2x_2 \qquad = \quad -5$$
$$2x_1 + 1x_2 + 1x_3 \leq \quad 12$$
$$x_1, x_2, x_3 \geq 0$$

21. Solve the following linear program:

$$\min \quad 3x_1 + 4x_2 + 8x_3$$
$$\text{s.t.}$$
$$4x_1 + 2x_2 \qquad \geq 12$$
$$4x_2 + 8x_3 \geq 16$$
$$x_1, x_2, x_3 \geq 0$$

22. Solve the following linear program:

$$\min \quad 4x_1 + 2x_2 + 3x_3$$

s.t.

$$1x_1 + 3x_2 \qquad \geq 15$$
$$1x_1 \qquad + 2x_3 \geq 10$$
$$2x_1 + 1x_2 \qquad \geq 20$$
$$x_1, x_2, x_3 \geq 0$$

23. Recall the Photo Chemicals problem (Chapter 7, problem 29). The mathematical model for this problem is shown below.

$$\min \quad 1x_1 + 1x_2$$

s.t.

$$1x_1 + 2x_2 \geq 80 \qquad \text{Raw material}$$
$$1x_1 \qquad \geq 30 \qquad \text{Product 1}$$
$$1x_2 \geq 20 \qquad \text{Product 2}$$
$$x_1, x_2 \geq 0$$

where

$$x_1 = \text{gallons of product 1 produced}$$
$$x_2 = \text{gallons of product 2 produced}$$

a. Solve this problem using the simplex method.
b. Show on a graph the sequence of solutions generated.
c. How many iterations are required for phase I?
d. How many iterations are required for phase II?

24. Recall the M&D Chemicals problem (Chapter 7, problem 22). The mathematical model for this problem is shown below.

$$\min \quad 2x_1 + 3x_2$$

s.t.

$$1x_1 \qquad \geq 125 \qquad \text{Demand for product 1}$$
$$1x_1 + 1x_2 \geq 350 \qquad \text{Total production requirement}$$
$$2x_1 + 1x_2 \leq 600 \qquad \text{Processing time limitation}$$
$$x_1, x_2 \geq 0$$

where

$$x_1 = \text{gallons of product 1}$$
$$x_2 = \text{gallons of product 2}$$

a. Solve this problem using the simplex method.
b. Show on a graph the sequence of extreme-point solutions generated.

c. How many iterations are required for phase I?

d. How many iterations are required for phase II?

25. Kirkman Brothers ice cream parlors sell three different flavors of Dairy Sweet ice milk: chocolate, vanilla, and banana. Due to extremely hot weather and a high demand for its products, Kirkman has run short of its supply of ingredients: milk, sugar, and cream. Hence Kirkman will not be able to fill all the orders received from its retail outlets, the ice cream parlors. Due to these circumstances, Kirkman has decided to make the best amounts of the three flavors given the constraints on supply of the basic ingredients. The company will then ration the ice milk to the retail outlets.

   Kirkman has collected the following data on profitability of the various flavors, availability of supplies, and amounts required for each flavor.

| | | Usage/Gallon | | |
| | Profit/ | Milk | Sugar | Cream |
Flavor	Gallon	(gallons)	(pounds)	(gallons)
Chocolate	$1.00	0.45	0.50	0.10
Vanilla	$0.90	0.50	0.40	0.15
Banana	$0.95	0.40	0.40	0.20
Maximum available		200	150	60

   Determine the optimal product mix for Kirkman Brothers. What additional resources should be used?

26. Uforia Corporation sells two different brands of perfume: Incentive and Temptation No. 1. Uforia sells exclusively through department stores and employs a three-person sales staff to call on its customers. The amount of sales time necessary for each sales representative to sell one case of each product varies with experience and ability. Data on the average time for each of Uforia's three sales representatives is presented below.

| | Average Sales Time per Case (minutes) | |
Salesperson	Incentive	Temptation No. 1
John	10	15
Brenda	15	10
Red	12	6

   Each sales representative spends approximately 80 hours per month in the actual selling of these two products. Cases of Incentive and Temptation No. 1 sell at profits of $30 and $25, respectively. How many cases of each perfume should each person sell during the next month in order to maximize the firm's profits? (*Hint:* Let $x_1 = $ number of cases of Incentive sold by John, $x_2 = $ number of cases of Temptation No. 1 sold by John, $x_3 = $ number of cases of Incentive sold by Brenda, and so on.)

Note: In problems 27 to 32, we provide examples of linear programs that result in one or more of the following situations:

1. Optimal solution
2. Infeasible solution
3. Unbounded solution
4. Alternate optimal solution
5. Degenerate solution

For each linear program, determine the solution situation that exists and indicate how you identified each situation using the simplex method. For the problems with alternate optimal solutions, calculate at least two optimal solutions.

27. max $4x_1 + 8x_2$

    s.t.

$$2x_1 + 2x_2 \leq 10$$
$$-1x_1 + 1x_2 \geq 8$$
$$x_1, x_2 \geq 0$$

28. min $3x_1 + 3x_2$

    s.t.

$$2x_1 + 0.5x_2 \geq 10$$
$$2x_1 \qquad\quad \geq 4$$
$$4x_1 + 4x_2 \geq 32$$
$$x_1, x_2 \geq 0$$

29. max $1x_1 + 1x_2$

    s.t.

$$8x_1 + 6x_2 \geq 24$$
$$4x_1 + 6x_2 \geq -12$$
$$2x_2 \geq 4$$
$$x_1, x_2 \geq 0$$

30. max $2x_1 + 1x_2 + 1x_3$

    s.t.

$$4x_1 + 2x_2 + 2x_3 \geq 4$$
$$2x_1 + 4x_2 \qquad\quad \leq 20$$
$$4x_1 + 8x_2 + 2x_3 \leq 16$$
$$x_1, x_2, x_3 \geq 0$$

31. max $2x_1 + 4x_2$

    s.t.

$$1x_1 + \tfrac{1}{2}x_2 \leq 10$$
$$1x_1 + 1x_2 = 12$$
$$1x_1 + \tfrac{3}{2}x_2 \leq 18$$
$$x_1, x_2 \geq 0$$

32. min $\quad -4x_1 + 5x_2 + 5x_3$

s.t.

$$-1x_2 + 1x_3 \geq 2$$
$$-1x_1 + 1x_2 + 1x_3 \geq 1$$
$$-1x_3 \geq 1$$
$$x_1, x_2, x_3 \geq 0$$

33. Supersport Footballs, Inc. manufactures three kinds of football: an All-Pro model, a College model, and a High School model. All three footballs require operations in the following departments: cutting and dyeing, sewing, and inspection and packaging. The production times and maximum production availabilities are shown below:

	Production Time (minutes)		
Model	Cutting and Dyeing	Sewing	Inspection and Packaging
All-Pro	12	15	3
College	10	15	4
High school	8	12	2
Time available	300 hours	200 hours	100 hours

Current orders indicate that at least 1000 All-Pro footballs must be manufactured.
  a. If Supersport realizes a profit of $3 for each All-Pro model, $5 for each College model, and $4 for each High School model, how many footballs of each type should be produced? What occurs in the solution of this problem? Why?
  b. If Supersport can increase sewing time to 300 hours and inspection and packaging time to 150 hours by using overtime, what is your recommendation?

34. Refer to problem 8. Suppose the management at Par, Inc. learned that the accounting department made a mistake and that the profit contribution on the deluxe bag was really $18 per bag. Shown below is a partial simplex tableau corresponding to the optimal basic feasible solution with $c_1 = 10$ and $c_2 = 9$ (the only difference is that we have changed c_2 to 18):

Basis	c_B	x_1 10	x_2 18	s_1 0	s_2 0	s_3 0	s_4 0	
x_2	18	0	1	$^{30}/_{16}$	0	$-^{21}/_{16}$	0	252
s_2	0	0	0	$-^{15}/_{16}$	1	$^{25}/_{160}$	0	120
x_1	10	1	0	$-^{20}/_{16}$	0	$^{300}/_{160}$	0	540
s_4	0	0	0	$-^{11}/_{32}$	0	$^{45}/_{320}$	1	18
	z_j							
	$c_j - z_j$							

  a. Calculate the remainder of the simplex tableau and show that the simplex method indicates that the current solution is not optimal.

b. Find the optimal solution with $c_2 = 18$. What new variable enters the basis? What variable leaves?

c. Refer to the original graphical solution of the Par, Inc. problem (see Chapter 7, problem 13). What extreme point is now optimal? What constraints are now binding?

35. Refer again to the HighTech Industries situation (problem 16). Suppose that management wanted to guarantee a combined total production for both models of at least 25 units.
    a. Formulate and solve using the simplex method.
    b. Show on a graph the sequence of extreme points generated.

36. Reconsider problem 35. Suppose that management had required a total production (both models together) of at least 50 units. Solve using the simplex method and comment on the result.

37. Consider the linear program

$$\max \quad 7.5x_1 + 15x_2 + 10x_3$$

s.t.

$$2x_1 \qquad\quad + \quad 2x_3 \le 8$$
$$\tfrac{1}{2}x_1 + \quad 2x_2 + \quad 1x_3 \le 3$$
$$1x_1 + \quad 1x_2 + \quad 2x_3 \le 6$$
$$x_1, x_2, x_3 \ge 0$$

    a. Find the optimal solution.
    b. Calculate the range of optimality for c_1.
    c. What would be the effect of a 2.5-unit increase in c_1 (from 7.5 to 10) on the optimal solution and the value of that solution?
    d. Calculate the range of optimality for c_3.
    e. What would be the effect of a 5-unit increase in c_3 (from 10 to 15) on the optimal solution and the value of that solution?

38. Consider again the linear programming problem presented in problem 37.
    a. Compute the ranges of feasibility for b_1, b_2, and b_3.
    b. How much will the value of the objective function change if b_1 is increased from 8 to 9?
    c. How much will the value of the objective function change if b_2 is increased from 3 to 4?
    d. How much will the value of the objective function change if b_3 is increased from 6 to 7?

39. Recall the Par, Inc. problem (problem 8). The final simplex tableau is

Basis	c_B	x_1 10	x_2 9	s_1 0	s_2 0	s_3 0	s_4 0	
x_2	9	0	1	$30/16$	0	$-21/16$	0	252
s_2	0	0	0	$-15/16$	1	$5/32$	0	120
x_1	10	1	0	$-20/16$	0	$30/16$	0	540
s_4	0	0	0	$-11/32$	0	$9/64$	1	18
z_j		10	9	$70/16$	0	$111/16$	0	7668
$c_j - z_j$		0	0	$-70/16$	0	$-111/16$	0	

a. Calculate the range of optimality for the profit contribution, c_1, of the standard bag.

b. Calculate the range of optimality for the profit contribution, c_2, of the deluxe bag.

c. If the profit contribution per deluxe bag drops to $7 per unit, how will the optimal solution be affected?

d. What unit profit contribution would be necessary for the deluxe bag before Par, Inc. would consider changing its current production plan?

e. If the profit contribution of the deluxe bags can be increased to $15 per unit, what is the optimal production plan? State what you think will happen before you compute the new optimal solution.

40. For the Par, Inc. problem (problem 39):

a. Calculate the range of feasibility for b_1 (cutting and dyeing time capacity).

b. Calculate the range of feasibility for b_2 (sewing capacity).

c. Calculate the range of feasibility for b_3 (finishing capacity).

d. Calculate the range of feasibility for b_4 (inspection and packaging capacity).

e. Which of these four departments are you interested in scheduling for overtime? Explain.

41. a. Calculate the final simplex tableau for the Par, Inc. problem (problem 39) after increasing b_1 from 630 to $682\frac{4}{11}$.

b. Would the current basis be optimal if b_1 were increased further? If not, what would be the new optimal basis?

42. For the Par, Inc. problem (problem 39):

a. How much would profit increase if an additional 30 hours became available in the cutting and dyeing department (that is, b_1 were increased from 630 to 660)?

b. How much would profit decrease if 40 hours were removed from the sewing department?

c. How much would profit decrease if because of an employee accident there were only 570 hours instead of 630 available in the cutting and dyeing department?

43. Below are additional conditions encountered by Par, Inc. (problem 39).

a. Suppose that because of some new machinery Par, Inc. was able to make a small reduction in the amount of time it took to do the cutting and dyeing (constraint 1) for a standard bag. What effect would this have on the objective function?

b. Management believes that by buying a new sewing machine the sewing time for standard bags can be reduced from $\frac{1}{2}$ hour to $\frac{1}{3}$ hour. Do you think this machine would be a good investment? Why?

44. Consider the following linear program:

$$\max \quad 3x_1 + 1x_2 + 5x_3 + 3x_4$$
$$\text{s.t.}$$
$$3x_1 + 1x_2 + 2x_3 \qquad\qquad = 30$$
$$2x_1 + 1x_2 + 3x_3 + 1x_4 \geq 15$$
$$2x_2 \qquad\quad + 3x_4 \leq 25$$
$$x_1, x_2, x_3, x_4 \geq 0$$

a. Find the optimal solution.

b. Calculate the range of optimality for c_3.

c. What would be the effect of a 4-unit decrease in c_3 (from 5 to 1) on the optimal solution and the value of that solution?

d. Calculate the range of optimality for c_2.

e. What would be the effect of a 3-unit increase in c_2 (from 1 to 4) on the optimal solution and the value of that solution?

45. Consider the final simplex tableau shown below.

Basis	c_B	x_1	x_2	x_3	x_4	s_1	s_2	s_3	
		4	6	3	1	0	0	0	
x_3	3	$3/60$	0	1	$1/2$	$3/10$	0	$-6/30$	125
s_2	0	$195/60$	0	0	$-1/2$	$-5/10$	1	-1	425
x_2	6	$39/60$	1	0	$1/2$	$-1/10$	0	$12/30$	25
z_j		$81/20$	6	3	$9/2$	$3/10$	0	$54/30$	525
$c_j - z_j$		$-1/20$	0	0	$-7/2$	$-3/10$	0	$-54/30$	

The original right-hand-side values were $b_1 = 550$, $b_2 = 700$, and $b_3 = 200$.

a. Calculate the range of feasibility for b_1.

b. Calculate the range of feasibility for b_2.

c. Calculate the range of feasibility for b_3.

46. Refer again to problem 16, involving HighTech Industries.

a. Calculate the range of optimality for the profit contribution of the Deskpro.

b. Calculate the range of optimality for the profit contribution of the Portable.

c. Suppose that a change in material costs reduces the profit contribution per unit for the Deskpro to $30. How will the optimal solution be affected?

d. Suppose that the profit contribution for the Deskpro drops to $20. How will the optimal solution be affected?

47. Refer again to problem 16, involving HighTech Industries.

a. Calculate the range of feasibility for assembly time availability.

b. Calculate the range of feasibility for warehouse space availability.

c. What are the dual prices for assembly time and warehouse availability?

d. Over what range is the dual price for assembly time availability applicable?

Quantitative Methods in Practice
Performance Analysis Corporation*
Chapel Hill, North Carolina

Performance Analysis Corporation, founded in 1979, is a management consulting company that specializes in the use of quantitative methods to design more efficient and effective operations for a wide variety of chain stores. Performance Analysis Corporation has evaluated the operation of banks, savings and loans, grocery chains, etc. Recently the company has become involved in evaluating the efficiency of fast-food outlets. In the following application we describe how linear programming methodology has been used to provide an evaluation model for a chain of fast-food restaurants.

Fast-Food Business

The fast-food business for a chain such as McDonalds, Kentucky Fried Chicken, etc., is characterized by hundreds, or even thousands, of individual restaurants, some of which are company owned and some of which are franchised. A typical restaurant may gross close to a million dollars annually; thus the impact of relatively minor improvements at a large proportion of the restaurants can have a substantial effect on a chain's profitability and market share.

Although each individual restaurant in a given chain usually offers the same type of menu (with some minor geographical variations), they often must deal with vastly different environments and competition. In addition, the age of the restaurant, facade used, ease of access and egress, hours of operation, scale of operation, etc., can vary substantially from restaurant to restaurant.

A major objective of company management in the fast-food industry involves the performance evaluations of managers of individual restaurants in the chain. These evaluations are the basis for awarding year-end bonuses and for personal advancement purposes. Unfortunately there is not a single measure of performance such as profit that can be used as the basis for the evaluation, since other measures such as market share and rate of growth are also important.

---

*The authors are indebted to Richard C. Morey of Performance Analysis Corp., Chapel Hill, N.C., for providing this application.

A Linear Programming Evaluation Model

One approach to the store evaluation problem utilizes the concept of Pareto optimality. According to this concept, a restaurant in a given chain is *relatively* inefficient if there are other restaurants in the same chain that have the following characteristics:

1. Have the same or worse environment
2. Produce at least the same levels of *all* outputs
3. Utilize no more of *any* resource and *less* of at least one of the resources

The mechanism for discovering which of the restaurants are Pareto inefficient involves the development and solution of a linear programming model. Constraints on the problem involve requirements concerning the minimum acceptable levels of output (e.g., profit, market share, etc.) and conditions imposed by uncontrollable elements in the environment. The objective function calls for the minimization of the resources necessary to produce the output. Solution of the model produces the following output for each restaurant:

1. A score that assesses the level of so-called relative technical efficiency achieved by the particular restaurant over the time period in question.
2. The reduction in controllable resources and/or the augmentation of outputs over the time period in question for an inefficient restaurant to have been rated as efficient.
3. A peer group of other restaurants with which each restaurant can be compared in the future.

Sensitivity analysis, especially that concerning the shadow prices, provides important managerial information. For each constraint concerning a minimum acceptable output level, the shadow price tells the manager how much one more unit of output would increase his/her efficiency measure. Analysis of the ranges for each of the constraint coefficients (the a_{ij}'s) provides information concerning how much outputs could be reduced or inputs increased before the restaurant would become inefficient.

Types of Factors Utilized

The approach is capable of handling three types of factors: quantitative controllable factors such as salaries paid, local advertising expenditures, etc.; uncontrollable quantitative factors such as the median income in the geographic area served by the restaurant, the unemployment rate, etc.; and qualitative factors such as the degree of competition, appearance of restaurant, etc. The outputs include total sales of various types (e.g., by time of day), profits, market share, rate of growth of sales, etc.

Benefits

The analysis typically identifies 40–50% of the restaurants as underperforming given the previously stated conditions concerning the inputs available and outputs produced. We have found that if all of the relative inefficiencies identified are eliminated simultaneously, the resulting increase in corporate profits is typically in the neighborhood of 5–10%. This is truly a substantial increase given the large scale of operations involved.

The district manager has an objective score card for each restaurant manager that indicates areas (e.g., overtime salary) where improvements may be in order. The efficient restaurants can be used to generate a set of best practices that can be models for other restaurants. Of primary benefit are the reactions of restaurant managers who appreciate that the evaluation process that they are subject to recognizes the environment they are forced to operate within, deals with noncommensurability of outputs involved, is theory based and nonpolitical, and is defensible, understandable, and equitable.

Questions

1. State in your own words what it means for one restaurant in a chain to be relatively inefficient relative to another restaurant in the same chain.
2. Suppose the evaluation model showed that for a particular restaurant the resource mix necessary to produce a given output mix was 90% of what another restaurant was using to produce that same mix of output. Would you conclude that the restaurant was relatively efficient or inefficient? Why?

CHAPTER

11

Transportation, Assignment, and Transshipment Problems

The transportation, assignment, and transshipment problems are special cases of the general linear programming model presented in Chapters 7–10; thus these problems can be formulated and solved as linear programs. A separate chapter is devoted to these problems for two reasons. First, because of the wide variety of applications that can be solved as transportation, assignment, or transshipment problems, they are of practical importance. Second, these problems have a mathematical structure that has enabled quantitative analysts to develop very efficient specialized solution procedures for solving them.

We will see that a transportation problem involving 12 variables and seven constraints can be solved fairly easily manually if a special-purpose solution procedure is used. However, in order to solve a problem of this size using a standard linear programming approach, a computer code is required if the solution is to be developed in a reasonable amount of time. For very large problems, computer programs are also used to carry out the computations for the specialized solution procedures; in such cases the advantage of these specialized solution procedures—as compared with a general linear programming approach—lies primarily in the speed with which the problems can be solved.

The approach we take in this chapter is to introduce each problem with an illustrative application. We then show how a linear programming model can be formulated and solved using LINDO/PC. Next we show how a general linear programming model can be developed to handle problems of any size. Finally, for the transportation and assignment problems, specialized solution procedures are presented.

11.1

THE TRANSPORTATION PROBLEM

The *transportation problem* arises frequently in planning for the distribution of goods and services from several supply locations to several demand locations. Usually the quantity of goods available at each supply location (*origin*) is fixed or limited, and there is a specified amount needed (demand) at each user location (*destination*). With a variety of shipping routes and differing transportation costs for the routes, the objective is to determine how many units should be shipped from each origin to each destination so that all destination demands are satisfied and the total transportation cost is minimized.

Let us illustrate the transportation problem by considering the problem faced by Foster Generators, Inc. This problem involves the transportation of a product from three plants to four distribution centers. Foster Generators, Inc. has production operations in Cleveland, Ohio; Bedford, Indiana; and York, Pennsylvania. Production capacities for these plants over the next 3-month planning period for one particular type of generator are as follows:

Origin	Plant		Three-Month Production Capacity (units)
1	Cleveland		5,000
2	Bedford		6,000
3	York		2,500
		Total	13,500

Suppose that the firm distributes its generators through four regional distribution centers located in Boston, Chicago, St. Louis, and Lexington, Kentucky; the 3-month forecast of demand for the distribution centers is as follows:

Destination	Distribution Center		Three-Month Demand Forecast (units)
1	Boston		6,000
2	Chicago		4,000
3	St. Louis		2,000
4	Lexington		1,500
		Total	13,500

Management would like to determine how much of its production should be shipped from each plant to each distribution center. Figure 11.1 shows graphically the 12 distribution routes that Foster can use.

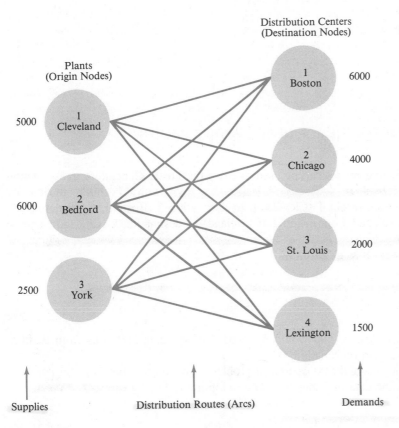

Figure 11.1
The Network Representation of the Foster Generators Transportation Problem

In Figure 11.1 we refer to the circles as *nodes* and the lines connecting the circles as *arcs*. The corresponding graph of interconnected nodes and arcs is called a *network*. Thus we see that the transportation problem can be represented graphically as a network; for this reason the problem is often referred to as a *network flow problem*. The goods shipped from the origins to the destinations represent the flow in the network.

With identical production costs at the three plants, the only variable costs involved are transportation costs. Thus the problem becomes one of determining the distribution routes to be used and the quantity to be shipped via each route so that all distribution center demands can be met with a minimum total transportation cost. The transportation costs for each unit shipped on each route are given in Table 11.1.

Table 11.1
Transportation Costs per Unit for the Foster Generators
Transportation Problem

	Destination			
Origin	Boston	Chicago	St. Louis	Lexington
Cleveland	3	2	7	6
Bedford	7	5	2	3
York	2	5	4	5

11.2

THE TRANSPORTATION PROBLEM: A LINEAR PROGRAMMING FORMULATION

A linear programming model can be used to solve the Foster Generators transportation problem. We will use double-subscripted decision variables, with x_{11} denoting the number of units shipped from origin 1 (Cleveland) to destination 1 (Boston), x_{12} denoting the number of units shipped from origin 1 (Cleveland) to destination 2 (Chicago), and so on. In general, the decision variables for a transportation problem having m origins and n destinations are written as follows:

$$x_{ij} = \text{number of units shipped from origin } i \text{ to destination } j,$$
$$\text{where i } = 1, 2, \ldots, m \text{ and } j = 1, 2, \ldots, n$$

Using this notation, $x_{24} = 500$ would correspond to shipping 500 units from Bedford (origin 2) to Lexington (destination 4).

Since the objective of the transportation problem is to minimize the total transportation cost, we can use the data in Table 11.1 to develop the following cost expressions:

Transportation cost for the
units shipped from Cleveland $= 3x_{11} + 2x_{12} + 7x_{13} + 6x_{14}$

Transportation cost for the
units shipped from Bedford $= 7x_{21} + 5x_{22} + 2x_{23} + 3x_{24}$

Transportation cost for the
units shipped from York $= 2x_{31} + 5x_{32} + 4x_{33} + 5x_{34}$

The sum of the above expressions provides the objective function showing the total transportation cost for Foster Generators, Inc.

Constraints are needed for a transportation problem because each origin has a limited supply and each destination has a specific demand. Consider the supply constraints first; note that the capacity at the Cleveland plant is 5000 units. With the total number of units shipped from the Cleveland plant expressed as $x_{11} + x_{12} + x_{13} + x_{14}$, the supply constraint for the Cleveland plant can be written as

$$x_{11} + x_{12} + x_{13} + x_{14} \leq 5000 \qquad \text{Cleveland supply}$$

With three origins (plants), the Foster Generators transportation problem has three supply constraints. Given the capacity of 6000 units at the Bedford plant and 2500 units at the York plant, the two additional supply constraints are as follows:

$$x_{21} + x_{22} + x_{23} + x_{24} \leq 6000 \qquad \text{Bedford supply}$$
$$x_{31} + x_{32} + x_{33} + x_{34} \leq 2500 \qquad \text{York supply}$$

With the four distribution centers as the destinations, the following four demand constraints are needed to ensure that destination demands will be satisfied:

$$x_{11} + x_{21} + x_{31} = 6000 \qquad \text{Boston demand}$$
$$x_{12} + x_{22} + x_{32} = 4000 \qquad \text{Chicago demand}$$
$$x_{13} + x_{23} + x_{33} = 2000 \qquad \text{St. Louis demand}$$
$$x_{14} + x_{24} + x_{34} = 1500 \qquad \text{Lexington demand}$$

Combining the objective function and constraints into one model provides the following 12-variable, seven-constraint linear programming formulation of the Foster Generators transportation problem:

$$\min \quad 3x_{11} + 2x_{12} + 7x_{13} + 6x_{14} + 7x_{21} + 5x_{22} + 2x_{23} + 3x_{24} + 2x_{31} + 5x_{32} + 4x_{33} + 5x_{34}$$

s.t

$$
\begin{array}{lll}
x_{11} + x_{12} + x_{13} + x_{14} & & \leq 5000 \\
\quad x_{21} + x_{22} + x_{23} + x_{24} & & \leq 6000 \\
\quad\quad x_{31} + x_{32} + x_{33} + x_{34} & \leq 2500 \\
x_{11} \quad\quad + x_{21} \quad\quad + x_{31} & & = 6000 \\
\quad x_{12} \quad\quad + x_{22} \quad\quad + x_{32} & & = 4000 \\
\quad x_{13} \quad\quad + x_{23} \quad\quad + x_{33} & = 2000 \\
\quad x_{14} \quad\quad + x_{24} \quad\quad + x_{34} & = 1500
\end{array}
$$

$$x_{ij} \geq 0 \qquad \text{for } i = 1, 2, 3 \text{ and } j = 1, 2, 3, 4$$

The LINDO/PC solution to the Foster Generators problem (see Figure 11.2) shows that the minimum total transportation cost is $39,500. The values for the decision variables are the optimal amounts to ship over each route. For example, with $x_{11} = 3500$, we see that 3500 units should be shipped from Cleveland to Boston and with $x_{12} = 1500$, 1500 units should be shipped from Cleveland to Chicago. Other values of the decision variables indicate the remaining shipping quantities and routes. The minimum-cost transportation schedule is shown in Table 11.2. Figure 11.3 provides a graphical summary of the optimal solution.

Note that the optimal values for the decision variables in the Foster Generators problem are all integers ($x_{11} = 3500$, $x_{12} = 1500$, and so on). This result is a property that will hold true under very general conditions when solving any transportation, assignment, or transshipment problem. That is, because of the special structure of the

```
                    OBJECTIVE FUNCTION VALUE

        1)            39500.0000

        VARIABLE           VALUE          REDUCED COST
             X11       3500.000000           .000000
             X12       1500.000000           .000000
             X13           .000000          8.000000
             X14           .000000          6.000000
             X21           .000000          1.000000
             X22       2500.000000           .000000
             X23       2000.000000           .000000
             X24       1500.000000           .000000
             X31       2500.000000           .000000
             X32           .000000          4.000000
             X33           .000000          6.000000
             X34           .000000          6.000000


        ROW      SLACK OR SURPLUS       DUAL PRICES
             2)           .000000          3.000000
             3)           .000000           .000000
             4)           .000000          4.000000
             5)           .000000         -6.000000
             6)           .000000         -5.000000
             7)           .000000         -2.000000
             8)           .000000         -3.000000
```

Figure 11.2
Computer Solution of the Foster Generators Problem Using LINDO/PC

constraints for these problems, it can be shown that the solution values for a transportation, assignment, or transshipment problem will always be integer if the supplies at the origin nodes and the demands at the destination nodes are all integer. Since this will always be the case for the problems we consider in this chapter, the optimal solutions we obtain will always be integer. In the next chapter we present an approach for solving other types of linear programming problems in which the nature of the problem requires some or all of the decision variables to be integer.

Table 11.2
Optimal Solution to the Foster Generators Transportation Problem

Route		Units Shipped	Per-Unit Cost	Total Cost
From	To			
Cleveland	Boston	3500	$3	$10,500
Cleveland	Chicago	1500	$2	3,000
Bedford	Chicago	2500	$5	12,500
Bedford	St. Louis	2000	$2	4,000
Bedford	Lexington	1500	$3	4,500
York	Boston	2500	$2	5,000
				$39,500

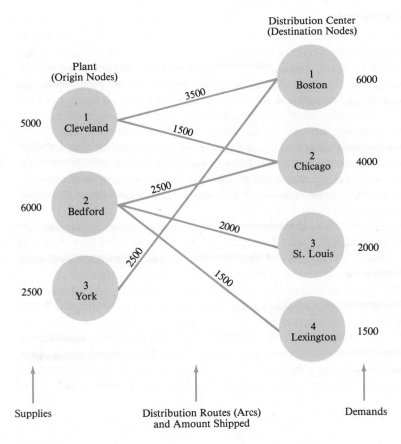

Figure 11.3
Optimal Solution to the Foster Generators Transportation Problem

Special Considerations

Variations of the basic transportation problem may involve one or more of the following situations:

1. Total supply not equal to total demand
2. Maximization objective function rather than minimization
3. Constraints on specific routes, such as route capacities or route minimums
4. Unacceptable routes

With slight modifications in the linear programming model, these situations can be taken into consideration in arriving at the optimal transportation solution.

A situation that often occurs is the case where the *total supply is not equal to the total demand*. If total supply exceeds total demand, no modification in the linear programming formulation is necessary. Excess supply will appear as slack in the linear programming solution. Slack for any particular origin can be interpreted as the unused supply or amount not shipped from the origin. If total supply is less than total demand, the linear programming model will not have a feasible solution because the demand constraints cannot be satisfied. In this case a modification in the linear programming formulation is necessary to develop the desired transportation problem solution. Specifically, we introduce a dummy origin (plant) with supply capacity exactly equal to the excess of total demand over total supply. We assign a zero cost per unit to every route out of the dummy origin so that the value of the optimal solution will still represent the total transportation cost for the problem (no shipments will actually be made from the dummy origin). With the inclusion of the dummy plant, total supply is made equal to total demand and a linear programming model can be used to generate a solution. At the optimal solution, destinations showing shipments being received from the dummy plant will be the destinations experiencing a shortfall or unsatisfied demand. Thus, with the inclusion of the dummy plant the transportation problem will provide a minimum-cost shipping schedule for the available supply and will also indicate which destinations will have unsatisfied demand.

In some problem formulations *it may be desirable to consider profit or revenue per unit shipped rather than cost per unit*. Using the profit or revenue per unit values as coefficients in the objective function, we simply solve a maximization rather than a minimization linear program. The constraints are not affected by this change.

The transportation problem formulation can be further modified to take into account *capacities on one or more of the shipping routes*. For example, suppose that the York-to-Boston route (origin 3 to destination 1) was found to have a capacity of 1000 units because of limited space availability on its normal mode of transportation. This limited route capacity can be taken into consideration by adding a constraint specifying an upper limit on the corresponding decision variable. With x_{31} denoting the amount shipped from York to Boston, the route capacity constraint for the York-to-Boston route would appear as

$$x_{31} \leq 1000$$

Similarly, route minimums can be specified. For example,

$$x_{22} \geq 2000$$

would guarantee that a previously committed order for a Bedford to Chicago delivery of 2000 units would be maintained in the optimal solution.

As a final special situation, we note that in transportation problems it may not be possible to establish a route from every origin to every destination. That is, *some routes may be unacceptable*. To handle this situation we simply remove the corresponding decision variable from the linear programming formulation of the problem. For example, if the Cleveland-to-St. Louis route were determined to be unacceptable or unusable, x_{13} could be removed from the linear programming formulation. Solving the resulting 11-variable, seven-constraint model would provide the optimal solution while guaranteeing that the Cleveland-to-St. Louis route is not used. Alternatively, if the problem has already been formulated, a constraint such as $x_{13} = 0$ can be added to the formulation to guarantee that the unacceptable route will not be used.

A General Linear Programming Formulation of the Transportation Problem

In order to show the general linear programming formulation of the transportation problem, we use the following notation:

i = index for origins, $i = 1, 2, \ldots, m$

j = index for destinations, $j = 1, 2, \ldots, n$

x_{ij} = number of units shipped from origin i to destination j

c_{ij} = cost per unit of shipping from origin i to destination j

s_i = supply or capacity in units at origin i

d_j = demand in units at destination j

The general formulation of the m-origin, n-destination transportation problem is

$$\min \ \sum_{i=1}^{m} \sum_{j=1}^{n} c_{ij} x_{ij}$$

s.t.

$$\sum_{j=1}^{n} x_{ij} \leq s_i \qquad i = 1, 2, \ldots, m \qquad \text{Supply}$$

$$\sum_{i=1}^{m} x_{ij} = d_j \qquad j = 1, 2, \ldots, n \qquad \text{Demand}$$

$$x_{ij} \geq 0 \qquad \text{for all } i \text{ and } j$$

If the transportation problem has a total supply (Σs_i) less than total demand (Σd_j), a dummy origin with a supply exactly equal to the difference between the total demand and the total supply must be added. If we let s_{m+1} indicate the fictitious supply, then

$$s_{m+1} = \sum_{j=1}^{n} d_j - \sum_{i=1}^{m} s_i$$

As we indicated previously, to ensure that the value of the optimal solution will still represent the total transportation cost for goods actually shipped, all objective function coefficients for the dummy origin will be set equal to zero (no shipments will actually be made from the dummy origin).

In cases where specific routes have capacities, we add constraints of the form $x_{ij} \leq L_{ij}$, where L_{ij} corresponds to an upper limit or capacity for the route from origin i to destination j. Similarly, if specific routes have minimum shipment levels that must be maintained, we add constraints of the form $x_{ij} \geq L_{ij}$. In this case L_{ij} corresponds to the minimum acceptable level for shipments from origin i to destination j.

11.3

THE TRANSPORTATION PROBLEM: A SPECIAL-PURPOSE SOLUTION PROCEDURE

Solving transportation problems using a general-purpose linear programming code, such as LINDO/PC, is fine for small- to medium-sized problems. However, often transportation problems are very large (a problem with 100 origins and 1000 destinations would have 100,000 variables), and thus more efficient solution procedures are needed. The special mathematical structure of the transportation problem has enabled quantitative analysts to develop special-purpose solution procedures that greatly simplify the computations.

In the previous section we introduced the Foster Generators, Inc. transportation problem and showed how it could be formulated and solved as a linear program. The linear programming formulation involved 12 variables and seven constraints. In this section we show a special-purpose solution procedure that takes advantage of the special network structure of the transportation problem and makes it possible to solve small transportation problems by hand.

Let us see how the special-purpose solution procedure works by applying it to the Foster Generators problem. The special-purpose solution procedure for the transportation problem involves first finding an initial feasible solution and then proceeding iteratively to make improvements in the solution until an optimal solution is reached. In order to summarize the data conveniently and to keep track of the calculations, a *transportation tableau* is employed. The transportation tableau for the Foster Generators problem is presented in Table 11.3.

Table 11.3
Transportation Tableau for the Foster Generators Transportation Problem

| | | Destination | | | | Origin Supply |
		Boston	Chicago	St. Louis	Lexington	
	Cleveland	3	2	7	6	5,000
Origin	Bedford	7	5	2	3	6,000
	York	2	5	4	5	2,500
	Destination Demand	6,000	4,000	2,000	1,500	13,500

Cell corresponding to shipments from Bedford to Boston

Total supply and total demand

Note that the 12 *cells* in the tableau correspond to the 12 shipping routes (arcs) shown in Figure 11.1; that is, each cell corresponds to the route from one plant to one distribution center. The entries in the right-hand border of the tableau represent the supply available at each plant, and the entries in the bottom border represent the demand at each distribution center; note also that total supply equals total demand. The entries in the upper right-hand corner of each cell represent the per-unit cost of shipping over the corresponding route.

Once the transportation tableau is complete, we can proceed with the calculations necessary to determine the minimum-cost solution. To begin, let us see how we can obtain an initial feasible solution.

Finding an Initial Feasible Solution: The Minimum-Cost Method

The *minimum-cost method* for identifying an initial feasible solution requires that we begin by allocating as many units as possible to the minimum-cost route. In Table 11.3 we see that the Cleveland–Chicago, Bedford–St. Louis, and the York–Boston routes each qualify as the minimum-cost route, since they each have a per-unit transportation cost of 2. When ties such as this occur, we will follow the practice of selecting the route over which we can ship the most units. Since this corresponds to shipping 4000 units from Cleveland to Chicago, we write 4000 in the Cleveland–Chicago cell of our transportation tableau. This reduces the supply at Cleveland from 5000 to 1000; hence we cross out the 5000 supply value and replace it with the revised value of 1000. In addition, since shipping 4000 units on this route satisfies the demand at Chicago, we cross out the 4000 Chicago value and replace it with 0. The Chicago demand is now zero. Thus, we eliminate this column from further consideration by drawing a line through the column. Our transportation tableau now appears as shown in tableau A.

Tableau A

	Boston	Chicago	St. Louis	Lexington	Supply
Cleveland	3	2 4000	7	6	1000 ~~5000~~
Bedford	7	5	2	3	6000
York	2	5	4	5	2500
Demand	6000	~~4000~~ 0	2000	1500	

Now we look at all unlined cells in order to identify the new minimum-cost route. There is a tie between the Bedford–St. Louis and York–Boston routes. But since more units can be shipped over the York–Boston route, we choose it for the next allocation. This results in an allocation of 2500 units over the York–Boston route. Thus the York supply is reduced to zero, and we eliminate this row from further consideration by lining through it. Continuing this process results in an allocation of 2000 units over the Bedford–St. Louis route and results in the elimination of the St. Louis column since its demand goes to zero. The transportation tableau we obtain after carrying out the second and third allocations is shown in tableau B.

Tableau B

	Boston	Chicago	St. Louis	Lexington	Supply
Cleveland	3	2	7	6	1000 ~~5000~~
		4000			
Bedford	7	5	2	3	4000 ~~6000~~
			2000		
~~York~~	2	5	4	5	0 ~~2500~~
	2500				
Demand	~~6000~~ 3500	~~4000~~ 0	~~2000~~ 0	1500	

We now have two routes that qualify for the minimum-cost route with a value of 3: Cleveland–Boston and Bedford–Lexington. Since a maximum of 1000 units can be shipped over the Cleveland–Boston route as compared with 1500 over the Bedford–Lexington route, we will next allocate 1500 units to the Bedford–Lexington route. Doing so results in a demand of zero at Lexington, and hence this column is eliminated. The next minimum-cost allocation then becomes 1000 over the Cleveland–Boston route. The transportation tableau now appears as shown in tableau C.

The only remaining unlined cell is now Bedford–Boston. Allocating 2500 units over this route uses up the remaining supply at Bedford and satisfies all the demand at Boston. The resulting tableau is shown in tableau D.

This solution is feasible, since all the demand is satisfied and all the supply is used. The total transportation cost resulting from this solution is calculated in Table 11.4.

The method that we discuss in the next subsection provides an iterative procedure for moving from the initial feasible solution provided by the minimum-cost method to an optimal solution. This method can be implemented only if the initial feasible solution of an m-origin, n-destination transportation problem utilizes exactly $m + n - 1$ transportation routes. Hence the Foster Generators transportation problem must have $3 + 4 - 1 = 6$ transportation routes in the initial solution. For the Foster Generators problem, the initial feasible solution just found satisfies this condition. However, *to guarantee that the minimum-cost method will always generate initial feasible solutions with $m + n - 1$ routes being assigned shipments, we must modify the method somewhat.*

Tableau C

	Boston	Chicago	St. Louis	Lexington	Supply
Cleveland	3 1000	2 4000	7	6	0 ~~1000~~ ~~5000~~
Bedford	7	5	2 2000	3 1500	2500 ~~4000~~ ~~6000~~
York	2 2500	5	4	5	0 ~~2500~~
Demand	~~6000~~ ~~3500~~ 2500	~~4000~~ 0	~~2000~~ 0	~~1500~~ 0	

Tableau D

	Boston	Chicago	St. Louis	Lexington	Supply
Cleveland	3 1000	2 4000	7	6	0 ~~1000~~ ~~5000~~
Bedford	7 2500	5	2 2000	3 1500	0 ~~2500~~ ~~4000~~ ~~6000~~
York	2 2500	5	4	5	0 ~~2500~~
Demand	~~6000~~ ~~3500~~ ~~2500~~ 0	~~4000~~ 0	~~2000~~ 0	~~1500~~ 0	

Table 11.4
Total Cost of Initial Feasible Solution Using the Minimum-Cost Method

| Route | | Units | Per-Unit | Total |
From	To	Shipped	Cost	Cost
Cleveland	Boston	1000	$3	$ 3,000
Cleveland	Chicago	4000	$2	8,000
Bedford	Boston	2500	$7	17,500
Bedford	St. Louis	2000	$2	4,000
Bedford	Lexington	1500	$3	4,500
York	Boston	2500	$2	5,000
				$42,000

Note that when we made our last allocation of 2500 units over the Bedford–Boston route, we simultaneously exhausted all the supply at Bedford and the demand at Boston. In developing an initial feasible solution, the last allocation will always reduce both the remaining row supply and column demand to zero. If this situation were to occur at *any prior iteration*, however, we would obtain an initial feasible solution with less than $m + n - 1$ transportation routes in use. To prevent this situation from occurring, whenever we reach an iteration that results in the supply at an origin and the demand at a destination being both reduced to zero simultaneously, we must proceed as follows:

1. Eliminate the row and column in question by drawing a line through each.
2. In addition to the assignment to the cell at the intersection of the lined-out row and column, we assign a shipment of zero units to any unoccupied cell in either the lined-out row or column. We treat this cell the same as all other cells to which shipments are assigned.

To see how the above procedure is applied, consider the following transportation problem consisting of three origins and four destinations; the initial transportation tableau is shown in tableau E. Carrying out the steps of the minimum-cost method we would first allocate 10 units to the O_2-D_1 route followed by an allocation of 10 units to the O_1-D_3 route. The resulting transportation tableau is shown in tableau F.

According to the minimum-cost method our next allocation will be 15 units to the O_3-D_4 route. However, we see that making this allocation will simultaneously reduce the O_3 supply and the D_4 demand to zero. When we make this allocation, in order to guarantee that there will be two cell assignments whenever both a row and column are lined out (except when the last cell is assigned), we must also assign a shipment of 0 units to one of the unoccupied cells in the O_3 row or the D_4 column. Assigning 0 units to the O_3-D_1 cell results in transportation tableau G on page 434.

We leave it as an exercise to the reader to demonstrate that continued application of the minimum-cost method will result in an initial feasible solution consisting of $m + n - 1 = 3 + 4 - 1 = 6$ transportation routes, one of which has a shipment of 0.

There are many other methods available for finding initial feasible solutions for the transportation problem. Two of the most commonly used approaches are the northwest corner rule and Vogel's approximation method. These two approaches differ in that

Tableau E

Origin	D_1	D_2	D_3	D_4	Supply
O_1	6	8	3	10	30
O_2	2	9	5	7	15
O_3	7	8	6	4	15
Demand	10	25	10	15	

Destination

Tableau F

	D_1	D_2	D_3	D_4	Supply
O_1	6	8	3 ~10~	10	20 ~30~
O_2	2 ~10~	9	5	7	5 ~15~
O_3	7	8	6	4	15
Demand	~10~ 0	25	~10~ 0	15	

allocations made using Vogel's approximation method take into consideration the cost of allocations (as does the minimum-cost method we use), whereas the northwest corner rule ignores costs to obtain an initial feasible solution. None of these approaches provides the optimal solution unless a lot of good luck is involved. The minimum-cost rule

Tableau G

	D_1	D_2	D_3	D_4	Supply
O_1	6	8	3 10	10	20 ~~30~~
O_2	2 10	9	5	7	5 ~~15~~
O_3	7 0	8	6	4 15	0 ~~15~~
Demand	~~10~~ 0	25	~~10~~ 0	~~15~~ 0	

Flow of 0 created

both reduced to 0

introduced here is easy to apply and takes cost into account to provide a good initial feasible solution. Thus this is the approach we will use for finding initial feasible solutions.

Summary of the Minimum-Cost Method

Before moving on to the second phase of the solution procedure and attempting to improve the initial feasible solution, let us restate the steps of the minimum-cost method for obtaining an initial feasible transportation solution.

Step 1   Identify the cell in the transportation tableau with the lowest cost and assign as many units as possible to this transportation route or cell. In case of a tie, choose the cell over which the most units can be shipped. If ties still exist, choose any of the tied cells.

Step 2   Reduce the row supply and the column demand by the amount assigned to the cell identified in step 1.

Step 3   If *all* row supplies and column demands have been exhausted, then stop; the allocations made will provide an initial feasible solution. Otherwise continue with step 4.

Step 4 If the row supply is now zero, eliminate the row from further consideration by drawing a line through it. If the column demand is now zero, eliminate the column by drawing a line through it. If both a row and column are lined out, make another allocation of 0 units to any unoccupied cell in the lined-out row or column.

Step 5 Continue with step 1 for all unlined rows and columns.

Moving to an Optimal Solution: The Stepping-Stone Method

The *stepping-stone method* provides an iterative procedure for moving from an initial feasible solution to an optimal solution. We will use the stepping-stone method to evaluate the economics of shipping via transportation routes that are not currently part of the transportation solution. If we can find cost-reducing routes, the current solution will be revised by making shipments via these new routes. By continuing to evaluate the costs associated with routes that are not in the current solution, we will know that we have reached the optimal solution when all routes not in the current solution would increase costs if they were brought into the solution.

To see how the stepping-stone method works, let us return to the initial feasible solution for the Foster Generators problem found by the minimum-cost method (tableau H):

Tableau H

	Boston	Chicago	St. Louis	Lexington	Supply
Cleveland	3 1000	2 4000	7	6	5000
Bedford	7 2500	5	2 2000	3 1500	6000
York	2 2500	5	4	5	2500
Demand	6000	4000	2000	1500	

Suppose that we were to allocate 1 unit to the route or cell in row 2 and column 2; that is, ship one unit on the currently unused route from Bedford to Chicago. In order to satisfy the Chicago demand exactly, we would have to reduce the number of units in the Cleveland–Chicago cell to 3999. But then we would have to increase the amount in the Cleveland–Boston cell to 1001 so that the total Cleveland supply of 5000 units could be shipped. Finally, we would reduce the Bedford–Boston cell by 1 in order to exactly satisfy the Boston demand. Tableau I summarizes the series of adjustments just described.

Tableau I

	Boston	Chicago	St. Louis	Lexington	Supply
Cleveland	3 1001 ~~1000~~	2 3999 ~~4000~~	7	6	5000
Bedford	7 2499 ~~2500~~	5 1	2 2000	3 1500	6000
York	2 2500	5	4	5	2500
Demand	6000	4000	2000	1500	

What is the added or reduced cost that will result from allocating one unit to the Bedford–Chicago route? Let us calculate the net effect of this change. The cost adjustments are as follows:

Changes		Effect on Cost
Add 1 unit to the Bedford–Chicago Route		+5
Reduce the Cleveland–Chicago Route by 1 unit		−2
Add 1 unit to the Cleveland–Boston Route		+3
Reduce the Bedford–Boston Route by 1 unit		−7
	Net effect	−1

This analysis shows that the total transportation cost can be reduced by \$1 for every unit shipped over the Bedford–Chicago route if corresponding changes are made in other routes as shown.

Before making additions to this new route, let us consider the general procedure for evaluating the costs associated with a new cell or route and then check all currently unused routes to find the best route to add to the current transportation solution.

The method we have just demonstrated for evaluating the Bedford–Chicago route is known as the *stepping-stone method*. Note that in considering the addition of this new route, we evaluated its effect on other routes *currently in the transportation solution*, referred to as *occupied* cells. In total we considered changes in four cells, the new cell and three *current solution* or *occupied* cells. In effect, we can view these four cells as forming a path, or *stepping-stone path*, in the tableau, where the corners of the path are current solution cells. The idea is to view the tableau as a pond with the current solution cells as stones sticking up in the pond. To identify the stepping-stone path for a new cell, we move in horizontal and vertical directions using current solution cells as the stones at the corners of the path by which we can step from stone to stone and return to the new cell we initially started with. To help focus our attention on which occupied cells are part of the current stepping-stone path, we draw each occupied cell in the stepping-stone path as a cylinder; this should help to reinforce the image of these cells as stones sticking up in the pond. Hence, when evaluating the Bedford–Chicago route using the stepping-stone method, we would depict the solution as in tableau J.

Tableau J

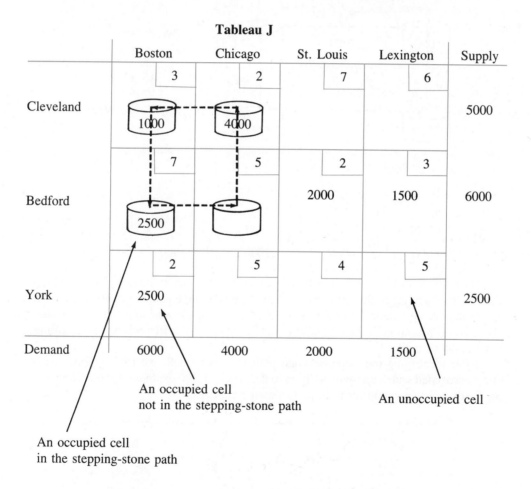

An occupied cell
not in the stepping-stone path

An unoccupied cell

An occupied cell
in the stepping-stone path

In the above stepping-stone path we depicted the sequence of adjustments as proceeding from the Bedford–Chicago cell to the Cleveland–Chicago cell to the Cleveland–Boston cell to the Bedford–Boston cell and then back to the Bedford–Chicago cell; that is, the adjustments were made moving in a counterclockwise fashion. You should convince yourself that exactly the same adjustments appear if we had proceeded in a clockwise direction.

For example, let us consider how to compute the stepping-stone path if we were to use the Cleveland–St. Louis route. The dotted line in tableau K represents the stepping-stone path for the Cleveland–St. Louis route or cell. In terms of a transportation tableau, the stepping-stone path represents the sequence of adjustments that are necessary to maintain a feasible solution, given that one unit is to be shipped through a new or currently unoccupied cell.

Tableau K

	Boston	Chicago	St. Louis	Lexington	Supply
Cleveland	3 1000	2 4000	7	6	5000
Bedford	7 2500	5	2 2000	3 1500	6000
York	2 2500	5	4	5	2500
Demand	6000	4000	2000	1500	

Note that in order to carry out the adjustments necessary to increase the flow on the Cleveland–St. Louis route, the corners of the stepping-stone path are established in such a way that as we "jump" from stone to stone on this path we jump over the occupied Cleveland–Chicago cell. This type of situation frequently arises when we determine a stepping-stone path.

After identifying the stepping-stone path for a new cell, we can evaluate the net effect associated with a one-unit addition to the new cell. For example, for the Cleveland–St. Louis cell this would result in the following changes:

Changes	Effect on Cost
Add 1 unit to the Cleveland–St. Louis Route	+7
Reduce the Bedford–St. Louis Route by 1 unit	−2
Add 1 unit to the Bedford–Boston Route	+7
Reduce the Cleveland–Boston Route by 1 unit	−3
Net effect	+9

Thus we see that the Cleveland–St. Louis route is unattractive; shipping one additional unit over this route will result in a \$9 increase in the total transportation cost.

Finding the stepping-stone path for each possible new cell enables us to identify the cost effect for each new cell or route. Evaluating this cost effect for all possible new cells leads to transportation tableau L. The per-unit cost effect for each possible new cell is circled in the cell.

On the basis of the calculated per-unit changes, we see that the best cell in terms of cost reduction is the Bedford–Chicago cell, with a \$1 decrease in cost for every unit shipped on this route. The question now is: How much should we ship over this new route? Since the total cost decreases by \$1 per unit shipped, we would like to ship the

Tableau L

	Boston	Chicago	St. Louis	Lexington	Supply
Cleveland	3 1000	2 4000	(+9) 7	(+7) 6	5000
Bedford	7 2500	(−1) 5	2 2000	3 1500	6000
York	2 2500	(+4) 5	(+7) 4	(+7) 5	2500
Demand	6000	4000	2000	1500	

maximum possible number of units. We know from our previous stepping-stone calculation that each unit shipped over the Bedford–Chicago route results in an increase of one unit shipped from Cleveland to Boston and a decrease of one unit in both the amount shipped from Bedford to Boston (currently 2500) and the amount shipped from Cleveland to Chicago (currently 4000). Because of this the maximum we can ship over the Bedford–Chicago route is 2500. This results in a reduction of 2500 units on the Cleveland–Chicago route, an increase of 2500 units on the Cleveland–Boston route, and a decrease of 2500 units on the Bedford–Boston route. Tableau M shows this new solution.

Note that the only changes from the previous tableau are located on the stepping-stone path originating in the Bedford–Chicago cell. We can now use the stepping-stone method to recalculate the per-unit changes resulting from attempting to add new cells or routes to this new solution. Doing so we get tableau N. Note that the stepping-stone path used to evaluate the York–St. Louis cell is indicated by the dashed line in the tableau.

The per-unit change for every possible new cell is now greater than or equal to zero. Thus since there is no new route that will decrease the total cost, we have reached the

Tableau M

	Boston	Chicago	St. Louis	Lexington	Supply
Cleveland	3 3500	2 1500	7	6	5000
Bedford	7	5 2500	2 2000	3 1500	6000
York	2 2500	5	4	5	2500
Demand	6000	4000	2000	1500	

Tableau N

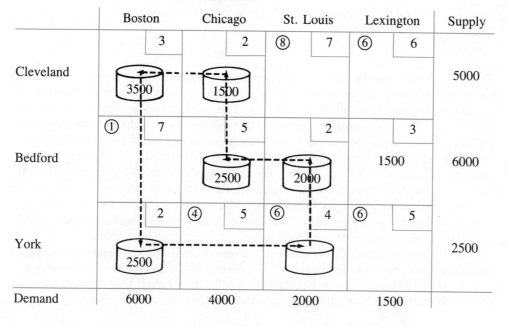

	Boston	Chicago	St. Louis	Lexington	Supply
Cleveland	3 3500	2 1500	⑧ 7	⑥ 6	5000
Bedford	① 7	5 2500	2 2000	3 1500	6000
York	2 2500	④ 5	⑥ 4	⑥ 5	2500
Demand	6000	4000	2000	1500	

optimal solution. The optimal solution, together with its total cost, is summarized in Table 11.5. As expected, this is exactly the same solution as obtained when we solved the problem using a linear programming model (Table 11.2).

Table 11.5
Optimal Solution to the Foster Generators Transportation Problem

Route		Units	Per-Unit	Total
From	To	Shipped	Cost	Cost
Cleveland	Boston	3500	$3	$10,500
Cleveland	Chicago	1500	$2	3,000
Bedford	Chicago	2500	$5	12,500
Bedford	St. Louis	2000	$2	4,000
Bedford	Lexington	1500	$3	4,500
York	Boston	2500	$2	5,000
				$39,500

Maintaining $m + n - 1$ Transportation Routes Using the Stepping-Stone Method

In the discussion of the minimum-cost method we stated that a requirement of the iterative procedure for finding an optimal solution is that the initial feasible solution must utilize $m + n - 1$ transportation routes. This requirement must also be maintained at each iteration of our stepping-stone solution procedure. Although we had no difficulty with the Foster Generators problem, situations can arise where as a result of making an allocation to a new cell the allocation to more than one of the unoccupied cells is reduced to zero. This would cause us to have fewer than $m + n - 1$ transportation routes in the current solution. To provide an illustration of such a situation let us consider the following modification of the Foster Generators transportation problem.

Suppose that the original supply at Cleveland were 3500 (instead of 5000) and that the demand at Chicago were 2500 (instead of 4000). The initial feasible solution we would obtain using the minimum-cost method is shown in tableau O:

Now if we were to consider shipping 2500 units over the Bedford–Chicago route as we did previously, the number of units shipped over the Cleveland–Chicago route would be reduced to zero, the number shipped over the Cleveland–Boston route would be increased to 3500, and the number shipped over the Bedford–Boston route would be reduced to zero. Thus two cells would be simultaneously reduced to zero, and hence in our new solution we would have only five transportation routes being utilized instead of the required six. To maintain a solution with six transportation routes, then, we arbitrarily select either the Cleveland–Chicago route or the Bedford–Boston route to receive a shipment of zero units. Selecting the Bedford–Boston route results in transportation tableau P.

In further computations the Bedford–Boston cell is treated like any other occupied cell. The assignment of a shipment of zero units in cases such as this guarantees that we will always utilize $m + n - 1$ transportation routes at any iteration of the solution procedure.

Tableau O

	Boston	Chicago	St. Louis	Lexington	Supply
Cleveland	3 1000	2 2500	7	6	3500
Bedford	7 2500	5	2 2000	3 1500	6000
York	2 2500	5	4	5	2500
Demand	6000	2500	2000	1500	

Tableau P

	Boston	Chicago	St. Louis	Lexington	Supply
Cleveland	3 3500	2	7	6	3500
Bedford	7 0	5 2500	2 2000	3 1500	6000
York	2 2500	5	4	5	2500
Demand	6000	2500	2000	1500	

The most difficult part of the solution procedure we have outlined is the identification of every stepping-stone path so that we can calculate the cost-per-unit change in each new cell. There is an easier way to make these cost-per-unit calculations; it is called the *modified distribution (MODI) method*. Let us demonstrate how this method can be used to calculate the per-unit changes for the new or unoccupied cells.

Modified Distribution (MODI) Method

The MODI method provides a simple approach for determining the best unoccupied cell to bring into solution. This method requires that we define an index u_i for each row of the tableau and an index v_j for each column of the tableau. The values of these indices are found by requiring that the cost coefficient for each occupied cell equal $u_i + v_j$. If we define c_{ij} to be the per-unit cost of shipping from origin i to destination j, then we require that $u_i + v_j = c_{ij}$ for each occupied cell.

Requiring that $u_i + v_j = c_{ij}$ for all the occupied cells in the final tableau of the Foster Generators problem leads to a system of six equations and seven variables:

Cleveland–Boston	$u_1 + v_1 = 3$
Cleveland–Chicago	$u_1 + v_2 = 2$
Bedford–Chicago	$u_2 + v_2 = 5$
Bedford–St. Louis	$u_2 + v_3 = 2$
Bedford–Lexington	$u_2 + v_4 = 3$
York–Boston	$u_3 + v_1 = 2$

Since there is one more variable than equation in the above system, we can set any one of the variables equal to an arbitrary value and then solve for the values of the other variables. We will always set $u_1 = 0$ and then solve for the values of the other variables. Setting $u_1 = 0$, we get the following system of equations:

$$0 + v_1 = 3$$
$$0 + v_2 = 2$$
$$u_2 + v_2 = 5$$
$$u_2 + v_3 = 2$$
$$u_2 + v_4 = 3$$
$$u_3 + v_1 = 2$$

Solving these equations leads to the following values for $u_1, u_2, u_3, v_1, v_2, v_3$, and v_4:

$$
\begin{array}{ll}
u_1 = \ \ \ 0 & v_1 = \ \ \ 3 \\
u_2 = \ \ \ 3 & v_2 = \ \ \ 2 \\
u_3 = -1 & v_3 = -1 \\
& v_4 = \ \ \ 0
\end{array}
$$

It can be shown that $e_{ij} = c_{ij} - u_i - v_j$ represents the per-unit change in total cost resulting from allocating one unit to the unoccupied cell in row i and column j. Rewriting the final tableau for the Foster Generators problem and replacing the previous marginal information with the values of u_i and v_j, we obtain tableau Q, see page 444. Once again the per-unit cost effect for each new cell (e_{ij}) has been circled.

Note how much easier it is to compute the net changes using the MODI method. For example, $e_{13} = c_{13} - u_1 - v_3 = 7 - 0 - (-1) = 8$ represents the net change in the total cost that would result from allocating one unit to the cell in row 1 and column

Tableau Q

u_i \ v_j	3	2	-1	0
0	3 / 3500	2 / 1500	⑧ 7	⑥ 6
3	① 7	5 / 2500	2 / 2000	3 / 1500
-1	2 / 2500	④ 5	⑥ 4	⑥ 5

3. We also observe that the e_{ij} calculated by the MODI method are exactly the same as the net changes calculated by the stepping-stone method. It is still necessary to search for a stepping-stone path to determine which route to remove from the solution once the best route to bring into the solution has been identified. However, it is not necessary to generate a stepping-stone path for any of the other unoccupied cells. Thus, considerable savings in the work required at each iteration can be obtained by employing the MODI method in the calculation of the e_{ij} for each unoccupied cell.

Summary of the Special-Purpose Solution Procedure for the Transportation Problem

In the preceding discussion we showed how the minimum-cost method can be used to obtain an initial feasible solution to the transportation problem. We then illustrated how the stepping-stone method can be used to determine which route (if any) to bring into the solution, which route to remove from the solution, and the number of units to ship over the new route. Finally, we showed that the MODI method—as compared with the stepping-stone method—provides an easier way to determine which route to bring into the solution.

This discussion suggests that we employ the following approach to solve the transportation problem: (1) use the minimum-cost method to determine an initial feasible solution; (2) use the MODI method to determine which new route (if any) to bring into the solution; and (3) use the stepping-stone method to determine which route to remove from the solution and how many units to ship over the new route. Since we have already provided a summary of the steps needed to carry out the minimum-cost method, we will not repeat the details of this method in summarizing the following special-purpose solution procedure for the transportation problem.

Step 1   Use the minimum-cost method to identify an initial feasible solution consisting of $m + n - 1$ occupied cells.

Step 2   Letting $u_1 = 0$, use the occupied cells of the transportation tableau to compute row indices $u_2, u_3, \ldots$ and column indices $v_1, v_2, v_3, \ldots$ such that

$$u_i + v_j = c_{ij}$$

for all occupied cells.

Step 3   Compute the cost e_{ij} of adding one unit to each unoccupied cell using the equation

$$e_{ij} = c_{ij} - u_i - v_j$$

Step 4   In a minimization problem, if the per-unit changes (e_{ij}'s) for all unoccupied cells are nonnegative, the solution is optimal. However, if negative per-unit changes exist, identify the best cell (most negative per-unit change) and continue.

Step 5   For the best cell, find the stepping-stone path through the transportation tableau. Label the best cell as cell 1 and number sequentially 2, 3, 4, . . ., the occupied cells on the corners of the stepping-stone path. Determine the even-numbered stepping-stone cell over which the smallest quantity is being shipped. Add this quantity to the new cell and all other odd-numbered cells. Subtract this quantity from all even-numbered cells. If more than one of the currently occupied cells on the stepping-stone path is forced to zero, maintain the requirement of $m + n - 1$ occupied cells by entering a shipment of zero units on one or more of the cells that were forced to zero. Return to step 2.

Handling Special Situations

Let us see how the following special situations are handled with the special-purpose solution procedure:

1. Total supply not equal to total demand
2. Maximization objective
3. Unacceptable transportation routes

The case where the total supply is not equal to the total demand can be handled easily by the special-purpose solution procedure if we first introduce a dummy origin or dummy destination. If total supply is greater than total demand, introduce a *dummy destination* with demand exactly equal to the excess of supply over demand. Similarly, if total demand is greater than total supply, introduce a *dummy origin* with supply exactly equal to the excess of demand over supply. In either case, assign cost coefficients of zero to every route into a dummy destination and every route out of a dummy origin. This is because no shipments will actually be made from a dummy origin or to a dummy destination when the solution is implemented.

The special-purpose solution procedure can also be used to solve maximization problems. The only modification necessary involves the selection of an unoccupied cell to allocate units to. Instead of picking the cell with the most negative e_{ij} value, we pick that cell for which e_{ij} is largest. That is, we pick the cell that will cause the largest per-unit increase in the objective function.

To handle unacceptable transportation routes, we require that unacceptable assignments carry an extremely high cost, denoted M, in order to keep them out of solution. Thus if we have a transportation route from an origin to a destination that for some reason cannot be used, we simply assign this route a per-unit cost of M, and thus this route will not enter the solution. Unacceptable routes would be assigned a per-unit value of $-M$ in a maximization problem.

Let us now consider another example to show how special situations can be handled. In the process we will also show how production costs can be taken into account in a transportation problem. Suppose that we have three plants (origins) with production capacities as follows:

Plants	Production Capacity
P_1	50
P_2	40
P_3	30
Total	120

We also have demand for the product at three retail outlets (destinations). The demand forecasts for the current planning period are presented below:

Retail Outlets	Forecasted Demand
R_1	45
R_2	15
R_3	30
Total	90

The production cost at each plant is different, and the sales prices at the retail outlets vary. Taking prices, production costs, and shipping costs into consideration, the profits for producing one unit at plant i, shipping it to retail outlet j, and selling it at retail outlet j are presented in Table 11.6.

Table 11.6
Profit per Unit for Producing at Plant i and Selling
at Retail Outlet j

		Retail Outlets		
		R_1	R_2	R_3
	P_1	2	8	10
Plants	P_2	6	11	6
	P_3	12	7	9

We note first that the total production capacity exceeds the total demand at the retail outlets. Thus we must introduce a dummy retail outlet with demand exactly equal to the excess production capacity. We therefore add retail outlet R_4 with a demand of 30 units. The per-unit profit for shipping from each plant to retail outlet R_4 is set to zero, since these units will not actually be shipped. To obtain an initial feasible solution, we use the minimum-cost method. However, since this is a maximization problem, the minimum-cost method must be changed to a corresponding maximum-profit method. That is, in general we select the shipping route that will maximize profit instead of minimizing cost. The initial feasible solution obtained using this approach is shown in tableau R.

Tableau R

	R_1	R_2	R_3	R_4	Supply
P_1	2	8	10	0	50
			30	20	
P_2	6	11	6	0	40
	15	15		10	
P_3	12	7	9	0	30
	30				
Demand	45	15	30	30	

Now let us compute the value of $e_{ij} = c_{ij} - u_i - v_j$, where the value of e_{ij} represents the per-unit change in total profit resulting from allocating one unit to the unoccupied cell in row i and column j; tableau S shows the values of u_i, v_j, and e_{ij} that we obtained.

Since this is a maximization problem, we look for the cell with the largest positive e_{ij}. However, since each e_{ij} value is negative, introducing any new allocation will only reduce the profit. Thus, the initial solution is optimal. When implementing this solution, we would ship 30 units from plant P_1 to retail outlet R_3, 15 units from P_2 to R_1, 15 units from P_2 to R_2, and 30 units from P_3 to R_1. Thus we are left with an excess supply of 20 units at P_1 and 10 units at P_2.

Computer Solution

Although the specialized solution procedures presented in this section make it possible to solve small transportation problems by hand, the amount of computation can become prohibitive for modest-sized problems. Consequently, microcomputer software packages

Tableau S

v_j : 6		11		10		0		Supply
u_i								
⊝4	2	⊝3	8		10		0	
0				30		20		50
	6		11	⊝4	6		0	
0	15		15			10		40
	12	⊝10	7	⊝7	9	⊝6	0	
6	30							30
Demand	45		15		30		30	

such as *The Management Scientist* have been developed to take advantage of the special network structure of the transportation problem.

To solve a transportation problem such as the Foster Generators problem using the transportation module of *The Management Scientist*, the user must enter the following data:

1. The number of origins
2. The number of destinations
3. The amount of supply at each origin
4. The amount of demand at each destination
5. The per-unit cost of shipping from each origin to each destination

A portion of the output for the Foster Generators problem is shown in Figure 11.4; note that origin 1 corresponds to Cleveland, origin 2 to Bedford, and origin 3 to York. Similarly, destination 1 corresponds to Boston, destination 2 to Chicago, and so on. The ease of use of such a package makes it an attractive alternative when solving transportation problems.

11.4

THE ASSIGNMENT PROBLEM

The *assignment problem* arises in a variety of decision-making situations. For example, typical assignment problems involve assigning jobs to machines, assigning workers to tasks or projects, assigning sales personnel to sales territories, assigning contracts to bidders, and so on. A distinguishing feature of the assignment problem is that *one* job,

```
OPTIMAL SHIPMENT SCHEDULE
*************************

SHIP
FROM                TO DESTINATION
ORIGIN      1       2       3       4
******     ****    ****    ****    ****

  1        3500    1500      0       0

  2           0    2500    2000    1500

  3        2500       0       0       0


TOTAL TRANSPORTATION COST OR REVENUE        39,500
```

Figure 11.4
Optimal Solution to the Foster Generators Problem Using *The Management Scientist* Software
Package

worker, etc., is assigned to *one and only one* machine, project, etc. Specifically, we
look for the set of assignments that will optimize a stated objective, such as minimize
cost, minimize time, or maximize profit.

As an illustration of the assignment problem, let us consider the case of Fowle
Marketing Research, Inc., which has just received requests for market research studies
from three new clients. The company is faced with the task of assigning project leaders
to each of these three new research studies. Currently three individuals are relatively free
from other major commitments and are available for the project leader assignments.
Fowle's management realizes, however, that the time required to complete each study
will depend on the experience and ability of the project leader assigned to the study.
Since the three projects have been judged to have approximately the same priority, the
company would like to assign project leaders such that the total number of days required
to complete all three projects is minimized. If a project leader is to be assigned to one
and only one client, what assignments should be made?

In order to answer the assignment question, Fowle's management must first consider
all possible project leader–client assignments and then estimate the corresponding project
completion times. With three project leaders and three clients, there is a total of nine
possible assignment alternatives. The alternatives and the estimated project completion
times in days are summarized in Table 11.7. Using these data, we see that Terry would
require 10 days to complete client 1's project, while Carle would require 9 days for the

Table 11.7
Estimated Project Completion Times (days) for the
Fowle, Inc. Assignment Problem

Project Leader	Client		
	1	2	3
1. Terry	10	15	9
2. Carle	9	18	5
3. McClymonds	6	14	3

same project. Similar completion time statements can be made about any of the other possible assignments.

11.5

THE ASSIGNMENT PROBLEM: A LINEAR PROGRAMMING FORMULATION

Let us develop the linear programming model that can be used to solve Fowle's assignment problem. As in the transportation problem, we will find it helpful to use double-subscripted decision variables, with x_{11} denoting the assignment of project leader 1 (Terry) to client 1, x_{12} denoting the assignment of project leader 1 (Terry) to client 2, and so on. We will let the decision variable equal 1 if the assignment is made and 0 if the assignment is not made. Thus the decision variables for the Fowle, Inc. assignment problem will be defined as follows:

$$x_{ij} = \begin{cases} 1 \text{ if project leader } i \text{ is assigned to client } j \\ 0 \text{ otherwise} \end{cases} \qquad \text{where } i = 1, 2, 3 \text{ and } j = 1, 2, 3$$

Using this notation, $x_{21} = 1$ and $x_{31} = 0$ would tell us that project leader 2 (Carle) is assigned to client 1 and project leader 3 (McClymonds) is not assigned to client 1.

Since we are interested in the total number of days required to complete the three client projects, we can use the completion time data in Table 11.7 to develop the following completion time expressions:

Days required for Terry's assignment $= 10x_{11} + 15x_{12} + 9x_{13}$

Days required for Carle's assignment $= 9x_{21} + 18x_{22} + 5x_{23}$

Days required for McClymonds' assignment $= 6x_{31} + 14x_{32} + 3x_{33}$

The sum of the days required for the three project leaders will provide the total days required to complete the three assignments.

The constraints for the assignment problem reflect the conditions that each project leader can be assigned to at most one client and that each client must have one assigned project leader. These constraints are written as follows:

$$
\begin{array}{ll}
x_{11} + x_{12} + x_{13} \leq 1 & \text{Terry's assignment} \\
x_{21} + x_{22} + x_{23} \leq 1 & \text{Carle's assignment} \\
x_{31} + x_{32} + x_{33} \leq 1 & \text{McClymonds' assignment} \\
x_{11} + x_{21} + x_{31} = 1 & \text{Client 1} \\
x_{12} + x_{22} + x_{32} = 1 & \text{Client 2} \\
x_{13} + x_{23} + x_{33} = 1 & \text{Client 3}
\end{array}
$$

Combining the objective function and constraints into one model provides the following nine-variable, six-constraint linear programming formulation of the Fowle, Inc. assignment problem:

$$\min \quad 10x_{11} + 15x_{12} + 9x_{13} + 9x_{21} + 18x_{22} + 5x_{23} + 6x_{31} + 14x_{32} + 3x_{33}$$
$$\text{s.t.}$$

$$
\begin{array}{llllllll}
x_{11} + & x_{12} + & x_{13} & & & & & \leq 1 \\
& & & x_{21} + & x_{22} + & x_{23} & & \leq 1 \\
& & & & & & x_{31} + x_{32} + x_{33} \leq 1 \\
x_{11} & & & + x_{21} & & & + x_{31} & = 1 \\
& x_{12} & & & + x_{22} & & + x_{32} & = 1 \\
& & x_{13} & & & + x_{23} & + x_{33} = 1
\end{array}
$$

$$x_{ij} \geq 0 \quad \text{for } i = 1, 2, 3 \text{ and } j = 1, 2, 3$$

At this point have you noticed any similarities between the assignment problem and the transportation problem? Viewing the project leaders as origins, each with a supply of 1, and the clients as destinations, each with a demand of 1, we see that the assignment problem is a special case of the transportation problem. Indeed, the assignment problem can be viewed as a transportation problem where all the supplies and all the demands are equal to 1.

In Figure 11.5 we show the network representation of the assignment problem. In this figure the nodes correspond to project leaders or clients and the arcs represent possible assignments. Note the similarity between the network representation of the assignment problem (Figure 11.5) and the network representation of the transportation problem (Figure 11.1).

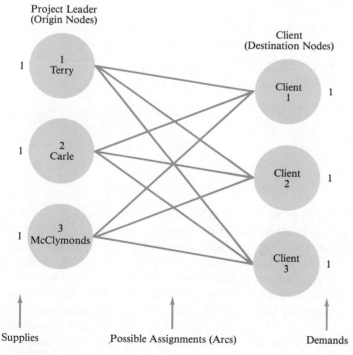

Figure 11.5
The Assignment Problem Viewed as a Special Case of the Transportation **Problem**

Figure 11.6 shows the LINDO/PC computer solution of the Fowle, Inc. assignment problem. Terry is assigned to client 2 ($x_{12} = 1$), Carle is assigned to client 3 ($x_{23} = 1$), and McClymonds is assigned to client 1 ($x_{31} = 1$). The total completion time required is 26 days. This solution is summarized in Table 11.8.

```
                    OBJECTIVE FUNCTION VALUE

        1)         26.0000000

        VARIABLE          VALUE          REDUCED COST
            X11          .000000           2.000000
            X12         1.000000            .000000
            X13          .000000           4.000000
            X21          .000000           1.000000
            X22          .000000           3.000000
            X23         1.000000            .000000
            X31         1.000000            .000000
            X32          .000000           1.000000
            X33          .000000            .000000
```

Figure 11.6
Computer Solution of Fowle, Inc. Assignment Problem Using LINDO/PC

Table 11.8
Optimal Project Leader Assignments for the Fowle, Inc. Problem

Project Leader	Assigned Client	Days
Terry	2	15
Carle	3	5
McClymonds	1	6
	Total	26

Handling Special Situations

Since the assignment problem can be viewed as a transportation problem, the special considerations that may arise in an assignment problem parallel those for the transportation problem discussed in Section 11.2. For example, consider the case where total supply does not equal total demand. Using the terminology of the Fowle Marketing Research, Inc. assignment problem, supply not equal to demand occurs whenever the total number of project leaders is not equal to the total number of clients. With more project leaders than clients (that is, supply greater than demand), the linear programming model will still provide the optimal solution. Any extra project leaders will simply remain unassigned. However, if total supply is less than total demand, the linear programming model will not generate a feasible solution because the demand constraints cannot be satisfied. Perhaps the easiest way to modify the linear program when demand exceeds supply is to add a dummy origin (project leader) with a fictitious supply equal to the difference between the total demand and the total supply. For example, if the firm had three project leaders and five clients, a dummy origin (project leader) would be added with a capacity for handling two clients. The objective function coefficients for any assignments from the dummy origin would be zero to ensure that the value of the optimal solution will still provide the total number of days required to complete the three assignments (no assignments will actually be made from the dummy origin). In this case the optimal solution provides the best assignment for the available supply of project leaders and also indicates which clients must remain unassigned.

If the assignment alternatives are evaluated in terms of revenue or profit rather than time or cost, the linear programming formulation can be solved as a maximization rather than a minimization problem. In addition, if one or more assignments are unacceptable, the corresponding decision variable can be removed from the linear programming formulation. This situation would exist, for example, if a project leader did not have the experience necessary for one or more of the client assignments. Finally, note that for problems that have already been formulated, unacceptable assignments can be handled by adding constraints that set the unacceptable decision variables equal to 0.

A General Linear Programming Formulation of the Assignment Problem

The general assignment problem is one that involves m agents and n tasks. If we let $x_{ij} = 1$ or 0 according to whether agent i is assigned to task j or not, and if c_{ij} denotes the cost of assigning agent i to task j, then we can write the general assignment model as follows:

$$\min \; \sum_{i=1}^{m} \sum_{j=1}^{n} c_{ij}x_{ij}$$

s.t.

$$\sum_{j=1}^{n} x_{ij} \leq 1 \qquad i = 1, 2, \ldots, m \qquad \text{Agents}$$

$$\sum_{i=1}^{m} x_{ij} = 1 \qquad j = 1, 2, \ldots, n \qquad \text{Tasks}$$

$$x_{ij} \geq 0 \qquad \text{for all } i \text{ and } j$$

If the number of tasks, n, exceeds the number of agents, m, a dummy agent with a capacity of $n - m$ must be included in order to obtain a feasible solution.

Handling Multiple Assignments

At the beginning of this section we indicated that a distinguishing feature of the assignment problem is that *one* agent is assigned to *one and only one* task. In situations where one agent can be assigned to two or more tasks, the linear programming formulation of the problem can be easily modified to account for such cases. For example, let us assume that in the Fowle Marketing Research problem Terry was permitted to be assigned to up to two clients; in this case the constraint representing Terry's assignment would be rewritten as $x_{11} + x_{12} + x_{13} \leq 2$. In general, if a_i denotes the upper limit for the number of tasks to which agent i can be assigned, we can write the agent constraints as

$$\sum_{j=1}^{n} x_{ij} \leq a_i \qquad i = 1, 2, \ldots, m$$

Thus we see that one advantage of formulating and solving assignment problems as linear programs is that special cases such as the situation involving multiple assignments can be easily handled.

11.6

THE ASSIGNMENT PROBLEM: A SPECIAL-PURPOSE SOLUTION PROCEDURE

As mentioned in the previous section, the assignment problem is a special case of the transportation problem. Thus the special-purpose solution procedure presented for the transportation problem could be used to solve the assignment problem. However, the assignment problem has an even more special structure. Because of this additional special structure, special-purpose solution procedures have been designed specifically to solve the assignment problem; one such procedure is called the *Hungarian method*. In this section we will show how the Hungarian method can be used to solve the Fowle Marketing Research problem.

Recall that the Fowle Marketing Research problem involved assigning project leaders to research projects; there were three project leaders available and three research projects to be completed. Fowle's assignment alternatives and estimated project completion times in days are restated in Table 11.9. We refer to this table as the *initial matrix* for the Hungarian method.

Table 11.9
Estimated Project Completion Times (days) for the
Fowle, Inc. Assignment Problem

Project Leader	Client		
	1	2	3
Terry	10	15	9
Carle	9	18	5
McClymonds	6	14	3

The Hungarian method involves what is called matrix reduction. By subtracting and adding appropriate values in the matrix, the method determines an optimal solution to the assignment problem. There are three major steps associated with the procedure. Step 1 provides the initial matrix reduction.

Step 1 Reduce the initial matrix by subtracting the smallest element in each row from every element in that row. Then, using the row-reduced matrix, subtract the smallest element in each column from every element in that column.

Thus we first reduce the matrix in Table 11.9 by subtracting the minimum value in each row from each element in the row. With the minimum values of 9 for row 1, 5 for row 2, and 3 for row 3, the row-reduced matrix is

	1	2	3
Terry	1	6	0
Carle	4	13	0
McClymonds	3	11	0

The assignment problem represented by this reduced matrix is equivalent to the original assignment problem in the sense that the same solution will be optimal. To understand why, first note that the row 1 minimum element, 9, has been subtracted from every element in the first row. Since Terry must still be assigned to one of the clients, the only change is that in this revised problem the time for any assignment will be nine days less. Similarly, Carle and McClymonds are shown with completion times requiring five and three fewer days, respectively.

Continuing with step 1 in the matrix reduction process, we now subtract the minimum element in each column of the row-reduced matrix from every element in the column. This also leads to an equivalent assignment problem; that is, the same solution will still be optimal but the times required to complete each project are reduced. With the minimum values of 1 for column 1, 6 for column 2, and 0 for column 3, the column reduced matrix is

	1	2	3
Terry	0	0	0
Carle	3	7	0
McClymonds	2	5	0

The goal of the Hungarian method is to continue reducing the matrix until the value of one of the solutions is zero; that is, until an assignment of project leaders to clients can be made that, in terms of the reduced matrix, requires a total time expenditure of zero days. Then, as long as there are no negative elements in the matrix, the zero-valued solution will be optimal. The way in which we perform this further reduction and recognize when we have reached an optimal solution is described in the following two steps.

Step 2 Find the minimum number of lines that must be drawn through the rows and the columns of the current matrix so that all the zeros in the matrix will be covered. If the minimum number of lines is the same as the number of rows (or equivalently, columns) in the matrix, an optimal assignment with value zero can be made. If the minimum number of lines is less than the number of rows, go to step 3.

Applying step 2 as shown below, we see that the minimum number of lines required to cover all the zeros is 2. Thus we must continue to step 3:

	1	**2**	**3**	
Terry	0̶	0̶	0̸	Two lines will cover
Carle	3	7	0̸	all the zeros (step 2)
McClymonds	②	5	0̸	

Step 3 Subtract the value of the smallest unlined element from every unlined element and add this same value to every element at the intersection of two lines. All other elements remain unchanged. Return to step 2 and continue until the minimum number of lines necessary to cover all the zeros in the matrix is equal to the number of rows.

The minimum unlined element is 2. In the matrix above we have circled this element. Subtracting 2 from all unlined elements and adding 2 to the intersection element for Terry and client 3 produces the new matrix shown below:

	1	2	3
Terry	0	0	2
Carle	1	5	0
McClymonds	0	3	0

Returning to step 2, we find that the minimum number of straight lines required to cover all the zeros in the current matrix is 3. The following matrix illustrates the results we obtained.

	1	2	3	
Terry	~~0~~	~~0~~	~~2~~	Three lines must be drawn to
Carle	1	5	0̸	cover all zeros; therefore the opti-
McClymonds	~~0~~	~~3~~	~~0~~	mal solution has been reached

According to step 2, then, it must be possible to find an assignment with a value of zero. Such an assignment can be found by first locating any row or column that contains only one zero. We draw a square around the zero, indicating an assignment, and eliminate that row and column from further consideration. Since row 2 has only one zero in the Fowle, Inc. problem, we assign Carle to 3 and eliminate row 2 and column 3 from further consideration. McClymonds must then be assigned to 1 (the only remaining zero in row 3), and finally Terry to 2. The solution to the Fowle, Inc. problem is shown below; in terms of the reduced matrix it requires a time expenditure of zero days.

	1	2	3
Terry	0	[0]	2
Carle	1	5	[0]
McClymonds	[0]	3	0

The value of the optimal assignment can be found by referring to the original assignment problem and summing the solution times associated with the optimal assignment;

in this case Terry to 2, Carle to 3, and McClymonds to 1. Thus we obtain the solution time of $15 + 5 + 6 = 26$ days.

Finding the Minimum Number of Lines

Sometimes it is not obvious how the lines should be drawn through the rows and columns of the matrix in order to cover all the zeros with the smallest number of lines. In these cases the following heuristic works well. Choose any row or column with a single zero. If it is a row, draw a line through the column the zero is in; if it is a column, draw a line through the row the zero is in. Continue in this fashion until all the zeros are covered.

If you make the mistake of drawing too many lines to cover the zeros in the reduced matrix, and thus conclude an optimal solution has been reached when it has not, you will find that you cannot identify a zero-value assignment. Thus if you think you have reached the optimal solution but the zero-value assignments cannot be found, go back to the previous step and check to see if you have actually determined the minimum number of lines necessary to cover the zero elements.

Handling Special Situations

We now discuss how to handle the following special situations when using the Hungarian method:

1. Number of agents not the same as the number of tasks
2. Maximization objective
3. Unacceptable assignments

The special-purpose solution procedure for the assignment problem requires that the number of rows (agents, people, objects, and so on) equal the number of columns (tasks, clients, and so on). Suppose that in the Fowle, Inc. example four project leaders had been available for assignment to the three new clients. Fowle still faces the same basic problem—namely, which project leaders should be assigned to which clients in order to minimize the total days required. The project completion time estimates with a fourth project leader are shown in Table 11.10.

Table 11.10
Estimated Project Completion Time (days) for the Fowle, Inc. Assignment Problem with Four Project Leaders

Project Leader	Client		
	1	2	3
Terry	10	15	9
Carle	9	18	5
McClymonds	6	14	3
Higley	8	16	6

We have seen how to apply the Hungarian method when the number of rows and columns are equal. Therefore, we can apply the same procedure if we can add a new client. Since we do not have another client, we simply add a *dummy column*, or a dummy client. Since this dummy client is nonexistent, the project leader assigned to the dummy client in the optimal assignment solution will in effect be the unassigned project leader.

What project completion time estimates should we show in this new dummy column? Actually any arbitrary value is acceptable as long as all project leaders are given the same completion time. However, since the dummy client assignment will not take place, a zero project completion time for all project leaders seems logical. The Fowle, Inc. assignment problem with a dummy client, labeled D, is shown in Table 11.11. Problem 15 at the end of the chapter asks you to use the Hungarian method to determine the optimal solution to this problem.

Table 11.11
Estimated Project Completion Time (days) for the Fowle, Inc. Assignment Problem with a Dummy Client

Project Leader	Client 1	2	3	D ←Dummy client
Terry	10	15	9	0
Carle	9	18	5	0
McClymonds	6	14	3	0
Higley	8	16	6	0

Note that if we had considered the case of four new clients and only three project leaders, we would have had to add a *dummy row* (dummy project leader) in order to apply the Hungarian method. The client receiving the dummy leader would not actually be assigned an immediate project leader and would have to wait until one becomes available. In general, in order to solve an assignment problem using the Hungarian method, it may be necessary to add several dummy rows or dummy columns, but never both.

To illustrate how maximization assignment problems can be handled, let us consider the problem facing management of Salsbury Discounts, Inc. Suppose that Salsbury Discounts, Inc. has just leased a new store and is attempting to determine where various departments should be located within the store. The store manager has four locations that have not yet been assigned a department and is considering five departments that might occupy the four locations. The departments under consideration are a shoe, a toy, an auto parts, a housewares, and a record department. The store manager would like to determine the optimal assignment of departments to locations in order to maximize profits. After a careful study of the layout of the remainder of the store, and based on his experience with similar stores, the store manager has estimated the expected annual profit for each department in each location. These data are presented in Table 11.12.

We now have an assignment problem that requires a maximization objective. However, we have a problem involving more rows than columns. Thus we must first add a dummy column, corresponding to a dummy or fictitious location, in order to apply the Hungarian method. After adding a dummy column, we obtain the 5 × 5 Salsbury Discounts, Inc. assignment problem shown in Table 11.13.

We can obtain an equivalent minimization assignment problem by converting all the elements in the matrix to opportunity losses. This conversion is accomplished by subtracting every element in each column from the largest element in the column.

The assignment that minimizes *opportunity loss* leads to the same solution that maximizes the value of the assignment in the original problem. Thus any maximization

Table 11.12
Estimated Annual Profit (thousands of dollars) for Each
Department-Location Combination

Department	Location			
	1	2	3	4
Shoe	10	6	12	8
Toy	15	18	5	11
Auto parts	17	10	13	16
Housewares	14	12	13	10
Record	14	16	6	12

Table 11.13
Estimated Annual Profit (thousands of dollars) for Each Department-Location
Combination, Including a Dummy Location

Department	Location				
	1	2	3	4	5 ←——— Dummy location
Shoe	10	6	12	8	0
Toy	15	18	5	11	0
Auto parts	17	10	13	16	0
Housewares	14	12	13	10	0
Record	14	16	6	12	0

assignment problem can be converted to a minimization problem by converting the assignment matrix to one in which the elements represent opportunity losses. Hence we begin our solution to this maximization assignment problem by developing an assignment matrix where each element represents the opportunity loss from not making the "best" assignment. The opportunity losses are presented in Table 11.14.

Table 11.14
Opportunity Loss (thousands of dollars) for Each Department-Location
Combination

Department	Location				
	1	2	3	4	5 ←——— Dummy location
Shoe	7	12	1	8	0
Toy	2	0	8	5	0
Auto parts	0	8	0	0	0
Housewares	3	6	0	6	0
Record	3	2	7	4	0

The opportunity loss from putting the shoe department in location 1 is $7000. That is, if we put the shoe department, instead of the best department (auto parts), in that location, we forgo the opportunity to make an additional $7000 in profit. The opportunity loss associated with putting the toy department in location 2 is zero, since it yields the highest profit in that location. What about the opportunity losses associated with the dummy column? Well, the assignment of a department to this ''dummy'' location means that the department will not be assigned a store location in the optimal solution. Since all departments earn the same amount from this dummy location, zero, the opportunity loss for each department is zero.

Following steps 1, 2, and 3 of the Hungarian method, we can proceed to determine the maximum profit assignment. Problem 16(b) at the end of this chapter asks you to use the Hungarian method to determine the optimal solution to this problem.

As an illustration of how we can handle unacceptable assignments, suppose that in the Salsbury Discounts, Inc. assignment problem the store manager believed that the toy department should not be considered for location 2 and the auto parts department should not be considered for location 4. Essentially the store manager is saying that, based on other considerations, such as size of area, adjacent departments, and so on, these two assignments are unacceptable.

Using the same approach for the assignment problem that we did for the transportation problem, we assign a value of M for unacceptable minimization assignments and a value of $-M$ for unacceptable maximization assignments, where M is an arbitrarily large value. In fact, M is assumed so large that M plus or minus any value is still extremely large. Thus an M-valued element in an assignment matrix retains its M value throughout the matrix reduction calculations. An M-valued element can never be zero; so it can never be an assignment in the final solution. The Salsbury Discounts, Inc. assignment problem with the two unacceptable assignments is shown in Table 11.15. When this assignment matrix is converted to an opportunity loss matrix, the $-M$ profit value will be changed to M. Problem 17(b) at the end of this chapter asks you to solve this assignment problem.

Table 11.15
Estimated Profit for the Salsbury Department-Location Combinations

Department	Location 1	2	3	4	5
Shoe	10	6	12	8	0
Toy	15	$-M$	5	11	0
Auto parts	17	10	13	$-M$	0
Housewares	14	12	13	10	0
Record	14	16	6	12	0

11.7

THE TRANSSHIPMENT PROBLEM

In the transportation problem shipments were permitted only from origin nodes directly to destination nodes. In the *transshipment problem* intermediate nodes, referred to as transshipment nodes, are added to account for locations such as warehouses, where goods from the origin nodes can be stored temporarily prior to being shipped to the destination nodes. In this more general type of distribution problem, shipments are permitted to occur between any pair of the three general types of nodes: origin nodes, transshipment nodes, and destination nodes. For example, the transshipment problem permits shipments of goods from one supply location (origin) to another supply location, from one transshipment location to another, and from one destination location to another.

As was true for the transportation problem, the quantity of goods available at each origin is fixed or limited. In addition, the destination demands are known and fixed. Thus the objective in the transshipment problem is to determine how many units should be shipped from one location to another so that all destination demands are satisfied with the minimum possible total transportation cost.

In order to illustrate the transshipment problem, let us consider the problem faced by Ryan Electronics. Ryan is an electronics company with production facilities located in Denver and Atlanta. Components produced at either facility may be shipped to either of the firm's regional warehouses, which are located in Kansas City and Louisville. From the regional warehouses the firm supplies retail outlets located in Detroit, Miami, Dallas, and New Orleans. The key features of the problem are shown in the transshipment network depicted in Figure 11.7. Note that the supply at each production facility or plant and the demand at each retail outlet are shown in the left and right margins, respectively. Note also that we have numbered the nodes in the network with nodes 1 and 2 the origin nodes, nodes 3 and 4 the transshipment nodes, and nodes 5, 6, 7, and 8 the destination nodes. Table 11.16 shows the transportation cost per unit for each distribution route in the network.

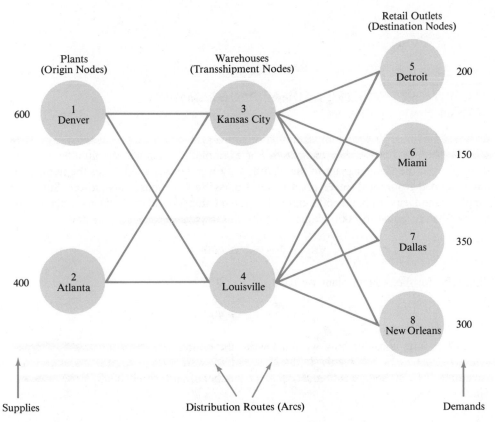

Figure 11.7
Network Representation of the Ryan Electronics Transshipment Problem

Table 11.16
Unit Transportation Costs for the Ryan Electronics Transshipment Problem

Warehouse

		Kansas City	Louisville
	Denver	2	3
Plant			
	Atlanta	3	1

Retail Outlet

		Detroit	Miami	Dallas	New Orleans
	Kansas City	2	6	3	6
Warehouse					
	Louisville	4	4	6	5

11.8

THE TRANSSHIPMENT PROBLEM: A LINEAR PROGRAMMING FORMULATION

To begin the linear programming formulation of the problem, we let x_{ij} denote the number of units shipped from node i to node j. For example, x_{13} denotes the number of units shipped from the Denver plant to the Kansas City warehouse, x_{14} denotes the number of units shipped from the Denver plant to the Louisville warehouse, and so on. Since the supply at the Denver plant is 600 units, the amount shipped out of the Denver plant must be less than or equal to 600. Mathematically this supply constraint is written

$$x_{13} + x_{14} \leq 600$$

Similarly, for the Atlanta plant we have

$$x_{23} + x_{24} \leq 400$$

Let us now consider how we must write the constraints corresponding to the two transshipment nodes. For node 3 (the Kansas City warehouse) we must guarantee that the number of units shipped out must equal the number of units shipped into the warehouse. Since

Number of units
shipped out of node 3 $= x_{35} + x_{36} + x_{37} + x_{38}$

and

Number of units
shipped into node 3 $= x_{13} + x_{23}$

then

$$x_{35} + x_{36} + x_{37} + x_{38} = x_{13} + x_{23}$$

Placing all the variables on the left-hand side of the expression enables us to write the constraint corresponding to node 3 as

$$- x_{13} - x_{23} + x_{35} + x_{36} + x_{37} + x_{38} = 0$$

In a similar manner, the constraint corresponding to node 4 is

$$- x_{14} - x_{24} + x_{45} + x_{46} + x_{47} + x_{48} = 0$$

In order to develop the constraints associated with the destination nodes, we recognize that for each node the amount shipped to the destination must equal the demand. For example, to satisfy the demand for 200 units at node 5 (the Detroit retail outlet), we can write

$$x_{35} + x_{45} = 200$$

Similarly, for nodes 6, 7, and 8, we have the following constraints:

$$x_{36} + x_{46} = 150$$
$$x_{37} + x_{47} = 350$$
$$x_{38} + x_{48} = 300$$

As usual, the objective function reflects the total shipping cost over the 12 shipping routes. Combining the objective function and constraints leads to a 12-variable, eight-constraint linear programming model of the Ryan Electronics transshipment problem (see Figure 11.8).

min $2x_{13} + 3x_{14} + 3x_{23} + 1x_{24} + 2x_{35} + 6x_{36} + 3x_{37} + 6x_{38} + 4x_{45} + 4x_{46} + 6x_{47} + 5x_{48}$

s.t.

$$
\begin{array}{llll}
x_{13} + x_{14} & & \leq 600 & \left.\right\} \text{Origin node} \\
x_{23} + x_{24} & & \leq 400 & \left.\right\} \text{constraints} \\
-x_{13} \quad - x_{23} \quad + x_{35} + x_{36} + x_{37} + x_{38} & & = 0 & \left.\right\} \text{Transshipment node} \\
- x_{14} \quad - x_{24} \qquad\qquad + x_{45} + x_{46} + x_{47} + x_{48} & = 0 & & \left.\right\} \text{constraints} \\
x_{35} \qquad\qquad\qquad + x_{45} & & = 200 \\
x_{36} \qquad\qquad\qquad + x_{46} & & = 150 & \left.\right\} \\
x_{37} \qquad\qquad\qquad\qquad + x_{47} & & = 350 & \left.\right\} \text{Destination node constraints} \\
x_{38} \qquad\qquad\qquad\qquad\qquad + x_{48} & = 300 & & \left.\right\}
\end{array}
$$

$$x_{ij} \geq 0 \text{ for all } i \text{ and } j$$

Figure 11.8
Linear Programming Formulation of the Ryan Electronics Transshipment Problem

Note that in the linear programming formulation of the transshipment problem we have one variable for each possible shipping route and one constraint for each node.

The optimal solution was obtained using LINDO/PC. Figure 11.9 shows the computer output and Table 11.17 summarizes the optimal solution.

```
              OBJECTIVE FUNCTION VALUE

    1)          5200.00000

    VARIABLE          VALUE           REDUCED COST
      X13          600.000000           .000000
      X14             .000000           .000000
      X23             .000000          3.000000
      X24          400.000000           .000000
      X35          200.000000           .000000
      X36             .000000          1.000000
      X37          350.000000           .000000
      X38           50.000000           .000000
      X45             .000000          3.000000
      X46          150.000000           .000000
      X47             .000000          4.000000
      X48          250.000000           .000000
```

Figure 11.9
Computer Solution to Ryan Electronics Transshipment Problem Using LINDO/PC

Table 11.17
Optimal Solution to the Ryan Electronics Transshipment Problem

| Route | | Units | Per-Unit | Total |
From	To	Shipped	Cost	Cost
Denver	Kansas City	600	$2	$1200
Atlanta	Louisville	400	$1	400
Kansas City	Detroit	200	$2	400
Kansas City	Dallas	350	$3	1050
Kansas City	New Orleans	50	$6	300
Louisville	Miami	150	$4	600
Louisville	New Orleans	250	$5	1250
				$5200

As we mentioned at the beginning of this section, in some transshipment problems it is possible to have shipments between plants, between warehouses, and/or between destinations. All such shipping patterns are possible in a transshipment problem. We still only require one constraint per node, but the constraints may involve more variables. For origin nodes we require that the sum of the shipments out minus the shipments in must be less than or equal to the origin supply. For destination nodes the sum of the shipments in minus the sum of the shipments out must equal demand. For transshipment nodes we require that the sum of the shipments out must equal the sum of the shipments in, just as before.

One final case deserves mention. Sometimes there are shipping capacities on routes. In this case we simply add an upper bound constraint on the variable representing the amount shipped over the capacitated route. This is the same way route capacities are handled for the transportation problem. We refer to this more general type of transshipment problem as the *capacitated transshipment problem*.

Special-purpose solution procedures have also been developed for the transshipment problem. One approach makes use of the fact that any transshipment problem can be converted into an equivalent transportation problem; then a special-purpose solution procedure for the transportation problem (such as we introduced in Section 11.3) is used to solve the modified transshipment problem. Details regarding the use of this type of approach, as well as even more efficient procedures, can be found in more advanced books on network models.

Summary

In this chapter we showed how the transportation, assignment, and transshipment problems can be modeled and solved as linear programs. In addition, we also showed how special-purpose solution procedures can be used to solve the transportation and assignment problems. These special-purpose solution procedures are the only practical way to solve small problems by hand, moderate-sized problems on a microcomputer, and very large problems on a mainframe computer.

An important feature to note regarding each of these problems is that under very general conditions, their optimal solutions are integral. That is, when solving any transportation, assignment, or transshipment problem for which the supplies at the origin nodes and the demands at the destination nodes are all integers, the solution will always consist of integer values.

Glossary

Transportation problem A problem that involves shipping goods from a set of origins to a set of destinations. Often, the objective is to determine how many units should be shipped from each origin to each destination so that all destination demands are satisfied and the total transportation cost is minimized.

Network A graphical description of a problem consisting of numbered circles (nodes) interconnected by a series of lines (arcs). The transportation, assignment, and transshipment problems can be represented as networks.

Minimum-cost method A procedure used to find an initial feasible solution to a transportation problem.

Stepping-stone method A procedure for identifying which routes will receive flow adjustments when a shipment is made over an unused route in the special-purpose solution procedure for the transportation problem.

Modified distribution (MODI) method A procedure for determining the per-unit cost change associated with shipping over an unused route in the special-purpose solution procedure for a transportation problem.

Dummy destination A destination added to make total supply equal to total demand in a transportation problem. The demand assigned to the dummy destination is the excess of the actual supply over the actual demand.

Dummy origin An origin added to make total supply equal to total demand in a transportation problem. The supply assigned to the dummy origin is the excess of the actual demand over the actual supply.

Assignment problem A problem that often involves the assignment of agents to tasks. The objective is to find the set of assignments that will optimize a stated objective, such as minimize cost, minimize time, or maximize profit.

Hungarian method   A special-purpose solution procedure for solving the assignment problem.

Dummy column(s)   Extra column(s) added to an assignment problem to provide the equal number of rows and columns required by the Hungarian method.

Dummy row(s)   Extra row(s) added to an assignment problem to provide the equal number of rows and columns required by the Hungarian solution procedure.

Opportunity loss   For each cell in an assignment matrix the opportunity loss is the difference between the largest value in the column and the value in the cell. The entries in the cells of an assignment matrix must be converted to opportunity losses to solve maximization problems using the Hungarian method.

Transshipment problem   An extension of the transportation problem to distribution problems involving intermediate nodes, referred to as transshipment nodes, which are added to account for locations such as warehouses, where goods from the origin nodes can be stored temporarily prior to being shipped to the destination nodes.

Problems

1. Consider the following transportation problem:

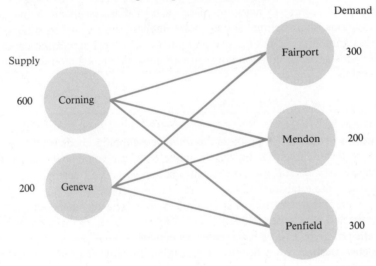

The transportation costs per unit are as follows:

	Fairport	**Mendon**	**Penfield**
Corning	16	10	14
Geneva	12	12	20

   a. Develop a linear programming model for this problem. Be sure to define all decision variables. What is the minimum cost solution?
   b. Set up the transportation tableau for this problem.
   c. Use the minimum-cost method to find an initial feasible solution.
   d. Use the special-purpose solution procedure to find an optimal solution.

2. A product is produced at three plants and shipped to three warehouses; the transportation costs per unit are shown in the following table:

		Warehouse			**Plant**
		W_1	W_2	W_3	**Capacity**
Plant	P_1	20	16	24	300
	P_2	10	10	8	500
	P_3	12	18	10	100
Warehouse demands		200	400	300	

a. Develop a linear programming model for minimizing the transportation cost; solve this model to determine the minimum-cost solution.

b. Suppose that the entries in the table above represent profit per unit from producing at plant i and shipping to warehouse j. How does the model formulation change from that in part (a)?

c. Use the special-purpose solution procedure to solve the original problem involving transportation costs.

3. Arnoff Enterprises manufactures the central processing unit (CPU) for a line of personal computers. The CPUs are manufactured in Seattle, Columbus, and New York and shipped to warehouses in Pittsburgh, Mobile, Denver, Los Angeles, and Washington, D.C., for further distribution. The transportation tableau below shows the number of CPUs available at each plant and the number of CPUs required by each warehouse. The shipping costs (dollars per unit) are also shown.

a. Determine the amount that should be shipped from each plant to each warehouse in order to minimize the total transportation cost.

b. The Pittsburgh warehouse has just increased its order by 1000 units and Arnoff has authorized the Columbus plant to increase its production by 1000 units. Do you expect this development to lead to an increase or a decrease in the total transportation cost? Solve for the new optimal solution.

			Warehouse				**Units**
		Pittsburgh	Mobile	Denver	Los Angeles	Washington	Available
Plant	Seattle	10	20	5	9	10	9 000
	Columbus	2	10	8	30	6	4 000
	New York	1	20	7	10	4	8 000
	Units Required	3000	5000	4000	6000	3000	21,000

4. Consider the following minimum-cost transportation problem:

		Destination			
		Boston	Atlanta	Houston	**Supply**
Origin	Detroit	5	2	3	100
	St. Louis	8	4	3	300
	Denver	9	7	5	300
	Demand	300	200	200	

a. Develop a linear programming model for this transportation problem.
b. The computer solution to this problem is shown below. What is the minimum-cost solution? How many units are shipped over each transportation route?

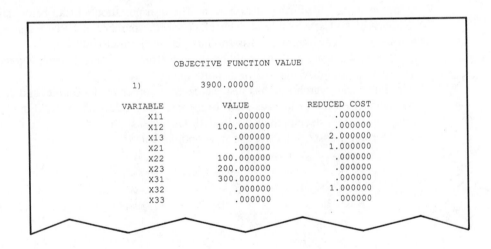

```
                    OBJECTIVE FUNCTION VALUE

        1)            3900.00000

        VARIABLE         VALUE           REDUCED COST
          X11          .000000             .000000
          X12       100.000000             .000000
          X13          .000000            2.000000
          X21          .000000            1.000000
          X22       100.000000             .000000
          X23       200.000000             .000000
          X31       300.000000             .000000
          X32          .000000            1.000000
          X33          .000000             .000000
```

c. Assume that a requirement is that 100 units must be shipped over the Detroit–Boston route. How would the linear programming model have to be modified to reflect this change?
d. Suppose that a labor dispute temporarily eliminates the Denver–Boston and the St. Louis–Atlanta routes. How would the linear programming model have to be revised to reflect these changes?
e. Solve the transportation problem first with the modification in part (c) and then resolve with the modification in part (d). What effect will each of these changes have on the total transportation cost and the specific transportation schedule?

5. Consider the following minimum cost transportation problem:

		Destination			
		Los Angeles	San Francisco	San Diego	Supply
Origin	San Jose	4	10	6	100
	Las Vegas	8	16	6	300
	Tucson	14	18	10	300
	Demand	200	300	200	700

   a. Find an initial feasible solution.
   b. Use the special-purpose solution procedure to find an optimal solution.
   c. How would the optimal solution change if we must ship 100 units on the Tucson–San Diego route?
   d. Because of road construction, the Las Vegas–San Diego route is now unacceptable. Resolve the initial problem with this change.

6. Consider the minimum-cost transportation problem show below:

	D_1	D_2	D_3	Supply
O_1	6	8	8	250
O_2	18	12	14	150
O_3	8	12	10	100
Demand	150	200	150	

a. Find an initial feasible solution.
b. Use the special-purpose solution procedure to find an optimal solution.
c. Using your solution to part (b), identify an alternate optimal solution.

7. Solve the following minimum-cost transportation problem:

	D_1	D_2	D_3	Supply
	Destination			
O_1	1	3	4	200
Origin O_2	2	6	8	500
O_3	2	5	7	300
Demand	200	100	400	

Since total supply (1000 units) exceeds total demand (700 units), which origins may consider alternate uses for their excess supply and still maintain a minimum total transportation cost solution?

8. Klein Chemicals, Inc. produces a special oil-base material that is currently in short supply. Four of Klein's customers have already placed orders that in total exceed the combined capacity of Klein's two plants. Klein's management faces the problem of deciding how many units it should supply to each customer. Since the four customers are in different industries, the pricing structure allows different prices to be charged to different customers. However, slightly different production costs at the two plants and varying transportation costs between the plants and customers make a "sell to the highest bidder" strategy unacceptable. After considering price, production costs, and transportation costs, Klein has established the following profit per unit for each plant-customer alternative.

		Customer			
		D_1	D_2	D_3	D_4
Plant	Clifton Springs	$32	$34	$32	$40
	Danville	$34	$30	$28	$38

The plant capacities and customer orders are as follows:

Plant	Capacity (units)	Customer	Orders (units)
Clifton Springs	5000	D_1	2000
		D_2	5000
Danville	3000	D_3	3000
		D_4	2000

How many units should each plant produce for each customer in order to *maximize* the total profit? Which customer demands will not be met?

9. Sound Electronics, Inc. produces a battery-operated tape recorder at plants located in Martinsville, North Carolina; Plymouth, New York; and Franklin, Missouri. The unit transportation costs for shipments from the three plants to distribution centers in Chicago, Dallas, and New York are as follows:

	To		
From	Chicago	Dallas	New York
Martinsville	1.45	1.60	1.40
Plymouth	1.10	2.25	0.60
Franklin	1.20	1.20	1.80

After considering transportation costs, management has decided not to use the Plymouth–Dallas route. The plant capacities and distributor orders for the next month are as follows:

Plant	Capacity (units)	Distributor	Order (units)
Martinsville	400	Chicago	400
Plymouth	600	Dallas	400
Franklin	300	New York	400

Because of different wage scales at the three plants, the unit production cost varies from plant to plant. Assuming that the costs are $29.50 per unit at Martinsville, $31.20 per unit at Plymouth, and $30.35 per unit at Franklin, find the production and distribution plan that minimizes the total production and transportation cost.

10. The Ace Manufacturing Company has orders for three similar products:

Product	Orders (units)
A	2000
B	500
C	1200

Three machines are available for the manufacturing operations. All three machines can produce all the products at the same production rate. However, due to varying defect percentages of each product on each machine, the unit costs of the products vary depending on the machine used. Machine capacities for the next week, and the unit costs, are as follows:

Machine	Capacity (units)
I	1500
II	1500
III	1000

Machine		Product A	Product B	Product C
	I	$1.00	$1.20	$0.90
Machine	II	$1.30	$1.40	$1.20
	III	$1.10	$1.00	$1.20

a. Use the transportation model to develop the minimum-cost production schedule for the products and machines.

b. Find an alternate optimal production schedule.

11. Forbelt Corporation has a 1-year contract to supply motors for all refrigerators produced by the Ice Age Corporation. Ice Age manufactures the refrigerators at four locations around the country: Boston, Dallas, Los Angeles, and St. Paul. Plans call for the following number (in thousands) of refrigerators to be produced at each location:

Boston	50
Dallas	70
Los Angeles	60
St. Paul	80

Forbelt has three plants that are capable of producing the motors. The plants and production capacities (in thousands) are as follows:

Denver	100
Atlanta	100
Chicago	150

Because of varying production and transportation costs, the profit Forbelt earns on each lot of 1000 units depends on which plant it was produced at and which destination it was shipped to. The following table gives the accounting department estimates of the profit per unit (shipments will be made in lots of 1000 units):

| | **Shipped to** | | | |
| | | | Los | |
Produced at	Boston	Dallas	Angeles	St. Paul
Denver	7	11	8	13
Atlanta	20	17	12	10
Chicago	8	18	13	16

Given profit maximization as a criterion, Forbelt would like to determine how many motors should be produced at each plant and how many motors should be shipped from each plant to each destination.

12. Scott and Associates, Inc. is an accounting firm that has three new clients. Three project leaders will be assigned to the three clients. Based on the different backgrounds and experiences of the leaders, the various leader–client assignments differ in terms of projected completion times. The possible assignments and the estimated completion times in days are shown below.

| **Project** | **Client** | | |
Leader	1	2	3
Jackson	10	16	32
Ellis	14	22	40
Smith	22	24	34

a. Formulate the problem as a linear program and solve. What is the total time required?
b. Use the Hungarian method to obtain the optimal solution.

13. In problem 12, assume that one additional employee is available for possible assignment. The following table shows the assignment alternatives and the estimated completion times:

Project	Client		
Leader	1	2	3
Jackson	10	16	32
Ellis	14	22	40
Smith	22	24	34
Burton	14	18	36

a. What is the optimal assignment?

b. How did the assignment change compared to the best assignment possible in problem 12? Was there any savings associated with considering Burton as one of the possible project leaders?

c. Which project leader remains unassigned?

14. Wilson Distributors, Inc. is opening two new sales territories in the Western states. Three individuals currently selling in the Midwest and the East are being considered for promotion to regional sales manager positions in the two new sales territories. Management has estimated total annual sales (in thousands of dollars) for the assignment of each individual to each sales territory. The sales projections are as follows:

	Sales Region	
Regional Manager	Northwest	Southwest
Bostock	$100	$95
McMahon	$85	$80
Miller	$90	$75

a. Formulate and solve a linear programming model to obtain the optimal solution.

b. Use the Hungarian method to obtain the optimal solution.

15. Solve the Fowle Marketing Research, Inc. assignment problem (Section 11.6) with four project leaders available for assignment to the three clients. The estimated project completion times in days are as follows:

Project	Client		
Leader	1	2	3
Terry	10	15	9
Carle	9	18	5
McClymonds	6	14	3
Higley	8	16	6

16. **a.** Formulate a linear programming model of the Salsbury Discounts, Inc. department-location assignment problem using the estimated annual profit data provided in Table 11.12; solve for the department-location assignment that maximizes profit.
    b. Use the Hungarian method to solve the Salsbury Discounts, Inc. problem.

17. Consider the Salsbury Discounts, Inc. assignment problem with two unacceptable assignments (see Table 11.15).
    a. Formulate and solve a linear programming model for this problem.
    b. Use the Hungarian method to solve this problem.

18. In a job shop operation, four jobs may be performed on any of four machines. The number of hours required for each job on each machine are summarized below. What is the minimum total time job-machine assignment?

		Machine		
Job	*A*	*B*	*C*	*D*
1	32	18	32	26
2	22	24	12	16
3	24	30	26	24
4	26	30	28	20

19. Mayfax Distributors, Inc. have four sales territories, each of which must be assigned a sales representative. From past experience the firm's sales manager has estimated the sales volume for each sales representative in each sales territory. Find the sales representative-territory assignments that will maximize sales (data given in thousands).

Sales		Sales Territory		
Representative	*A*	*B*	*C*	*D*
Washington	44	80	52	60
Benson	60	56	40	72
Fredricks	36	60	48	48
Hodson	52	76	36	40

20. Each Monday the drivers of the Metor Bus System indicate their preferences for the various bus routes open during the coming week. With 1 indicating a first choice and 5 indicating a last choice, what is the driver-route assignment that minimizes the sum of the choice values?

Driver	Route				
	A	*B*	*C*	*D*	*E*
1	3	4	2	1	5
2	3	5	2	1	4
3	5	3	2	1	4
4	4	3	2	1	5
5	5	4	1	2	3

21. Four secretaries are available to type any of three company reports. Given the typing times in hours, what is the minimum total time secretary-report assignment?

Secretary	Report		
	A	*B*	*C*
Phyllis	24	12	10
Linda	19	11	11
Dave	25	16	16
Marlene	25	14	13

22. Four trucks must be dispatched to each of four customer locations. The assignments and the distances traveled by each truck in making the trips are shown below. What truck-customer assignments minimize the total distance traveled by the four trucks? Note that two unacceptable assignments are indicated because the specific truck involved is not equipped to carry the type of shipment involved. The unacceptable assignments show *M* as the distance traveled.

Truck	Customer			
	A	*B*	*C*	*D*
1	130	125	120	135
2	120	110	100	120
3	125	120	*M*	140
4	150	150	140	*M*

23. A market research firm has three clients who have each requested that the firm conduct a sample survey. Four statisticians are available to assign to these three projects; however, all four statisticians are busy, and therefore each can handle at most one of the clients. The following data show the number of hours it would take for each statistician to complete each job; the differences in time are due to differences in experience and ability among the statisticians.

	Client		
Statistician	*A*	*B*	*C*
1	150	210	270
2	170	230	220
3	180	230	225
4	160	240	230

a. Formulate and solve a linear programming model for this problem.
b. Suppose that the time it takes statistician 4 to complete the job for client *A* is increased from 160 to 165 hours. What effect will this have on the solution?
c. Suppose that the time it takes statistician 4 to complete the job for client *A* is decreased to 140 hours. What effect will this have on the solution?
d. Suppose that the time it takes statistician 3 to complete the job for client *B* increases to 250 hours. What effect will this have on the solution?

24. A company has two plants (P_1 and P_2), one regional warehouse (*W*), and two retail outlets (R_1 and R_2). The plant capacities, retail outlet demands, and the per-unit shipping costs are shown in the following network:

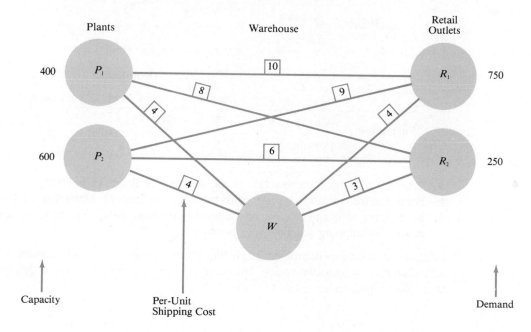

a. Formulate a linear programming model to minimize shipping costs for this problem.
b. If you have access to a linear programming computer code, determine the optimal solution for the model formulated in part (a).
c. What change would have to be made in the linear programming model if the maximum amount of goods that can be shipped from *W* to R_1 is 500? How would this change the optimal solution?

25. Adirondack Paper Mills, Inc. has paper plants located in Augusta, Maine, and Tupper Lake, New York. Warehouse facilities are located in Albany, New York, and Portsmouth, New Hampshire. Distributors are located in Boston, New York, and Philadelphia. The plant capacities and distributor demands for the next month are as follows:

Plant	Capacity (units)	Distributor	Demand (units)
Augusta	300	Boston	150
Tupper Lake	100	New York	100
		Philadelphia	150

The unit transportation costs for shipments from the two plants to the two warehouses and from the two warehouses to the three distributors are shown below.

		Warehouse	
		Albany	Portsmouth
Plant	Augusta	7	5
	Tupper Lake	3	4

		Distributor		
		Boston	New York	Philadelphia
Warehouse	Albany	8	5	7
	Portsmouth	5	6	10

a. Draw the network representation of the Adirondack Paper Mills problem.
b. Formulate the Adirondack Paper Mills problem as a linear programming problem.
c. If you have access to a linear programming computer code, determine the minimum-cost shipping schedule for the problem.

26. Consider a transshipment problem consisting of three origin nodes, two transshipment nodes, and four destination nodes. The supplies at the origin nodes and the demands at the destination nodes are as follows:

Origin	Supply	Destination	Demand
1	400	1	200
2	450	2	500
3	350	3	300
		4	200

The per-unit shipping costs are provided in the following table.

			To					
			Transshipment		Destination			
			1	2	1	2	3	4
	Origin	1	6	8	—	—	—	—
		2	8	12	—	—	—	—
From		3	10	5	—	—	—	—
	Transshipment	1	—	—	9	7	6	10
		2	—	—	7	9	6	8

a. Draw the network representation of this problem.
b. Formulate this transshipment problem as a linear program.
c. Solve for the optimal solution.

27. Moore and Harman Company is in the business of buying and selling grain. An important aspect of the company's business is arranging for the purchased grain to be shipped to customers. If the company can keep freight costs low, profitability will be improved.

Currently the company has purchased three rail cars of corn at Muncie, Indiana; six rail cars at Brazil, Indiana; and five rail cars at Xenia, Ohio. Twelve carloads of grain have been sold. The locations and the amount sold at each location are as follows:

Location	Number of Rail Car Loads
Macon, Ga.	2
Greenwood, S.C.	4
Concord, S.C.	3
Chatham, N.C.	3

All shipments must be routed through either Louisville or Cincinnati. Given below are the shipping costs per bushel (in cents) from the origins to Louisville and Cincinnati as well as the costs per bushel to ship from Louisville and Cincinnati to the destinations.

		To	
		Louisville	Cincinnati
From	Muncie	8	6
	Brazil	3	8
	Xenia	9	3

		To			
		Macon	Greenwood	Concord	Chatham
From	Louisville	44	34	34	32
	Cincinnati	57	35	28	24

Determine a shipping schedule that will minimize the freight costs necessary to satisfy demand. Which (if any) rail cars of grain must be held at the origin until buyers can be found?

Case Problem
Assigning Umpire Crews*

The American Baseball League consists of 14 professional baseball teams organized into two divisions: the Western Division, with Seattle, Oakland, California, Texas, Kansas City, Minnesota, and Chicago; and the Eastern Division, with Milwaukee, Detroit, Cleveland, Toronto, Baltimore, New York, and Boston.

In addition to the schedules for each team, the American League must determine the best way to assign the umpire crews to the various games played throughout the league. Umpire crews are assigned to specific home-team cities for the two-, three-, or four-game series in that city but are not assigned on an individual-game basis. Since there are 14 American League teams, there can be as many as seven "games" (doubleheaders count as one "game" in assigning crews); hence seven umpire crews must be assigned.

Several considerations are important in making the umpire crew assignments. Because of the amount of travel required, airline costs can be substantial. Thus from a cost point of view umpire crew assignments with minimum travel distances are desired. However, a second consideration in the assignment of the umpire crews is that there should be a balance such that each crew works approximately the same number of games with each team and in each city. The considerations of minimizing travel distances and at the same time balancing the crew assignments among the teams and cities are in conflict.

In addition to the above considerations, a number of requirements must be satisfied. The most important of these are:

1. A crew cannot travel from city A to city B if the last game in city A is a night game and the first game in city B is an afternoon game on the next day.
2. A crew cannot travel from a West Coast location (Seattle, Oakland, or California) to Chicago or any Eastern Division city without a day off.
3. Because of flight scheduling difficulties, a crew traveling into or out of Toronto must have a day off unless coming from or going to New York, Boston, Detroit, or Cleveland.
4. Any crew traveling from a night game in Seattle, Oakland, or California cannot be assigned to Kansas City or Texas for a game on the next day.
5. No crew should be assigned to the same team for more than two series in a row.

The umpire crews have already been scheduled for the first four series of the five-series schedule shown in Table 11.18. Table 11.19 summarizes the crew assignments for the first four series in the schedule and shows the pairings for the fifth series. The number next to each team identification indicates the umpire crew assigned for that pairing. For

*The authors are indebted to James R. Evans, consultant to the American League, New York, N.Y., for providing this case problem.

Table 11.18
Segment of the American League Schedule Showing Five Series

Series	Date	SEA	OAK	CAL	TEX	KC	MIN	CHI	MKE	DET	CLE	TOR	BAL	NY	BOS
1	Mon.		CAL*		BOS*		SEA		TOR*	NY*	KC*		CHI*		
	Tues.		CAL*		BOS*		SEA		TOR*	NY*	KC*		CHI*		
	Wed.		CAL		BOS*		SEA		TOR*	NY	KC*		CHI*		
2	Thurs.	DET*		MKE*	KC*			CHI*				TOR*			MIN*
	Fri.	DET*	NY*	MKE*	KC*			CHI*				TOR*			MIN*
	Sat.	DET*	NY	MKE*	KC*			CHI				TOR*			MIN*
	Sun.	DET	NY(2)	MKE	KC*			CHI				TOR			MIN*
3	Mon.	MKE*		NY*		BOS*							MIN*		
	Tues.	MKE*	DET*	NY*	CHI*	BOS*						CLE*	MIN*		
	Wed.	MKE*	DET*	NY*	CHI*	BOS*						CLE*	MIN*		
	Thurs.	MKE*	DET	NY*	CHI*							CLE*			
4	Fri.	NY*	MKE*	DET*	BAL*		CLE*	KC*				BOS*			
	Sat.	NY*	MKE	DET*	BAL*		CLE*	KC*				BOS			
	Sun.	NY*	MKE	DET	BAL*		CLE	KC				BOS			
5	Mon.					TEX*						BOS*			
	Tues.					TEX*	BOS*	CLE*	CAL*	SEA*		BAL*		OAK*	
	Wed.					TEX*	BOS*	CLE*	CAL*	SEA*		BAL*		OAK*	
	Thurs.					TEX*	BOS	CLE*	CAL	SEA*		BAL*		OAK*	

*Denotes night game or early-evening start.
(2)Denotes doubleheader (two games in one day).

Table 11.19
Umpire Crew Assignment for the First Four Series

Series	SEA	OAK	CAL	TEX	KC	MIN	CHI	MKE	DET	CLE	TOR	BAL	NY	BOS
1	DET[3]	CAL[5]		BOS[3]		SEA[7]		TOR[4]	NY[1]	KC[6]		CHI[2]		
2	MKE[2]	NY[2]	MKE[7]	KC[5]	BOS[5]					CHI[6]		TOR[4]		MIN[1]
3	NY[7]	DET[7]	NY[3]	CHI[6]		CLE[5]	KC[4]				CLE[1]	MIN[4]		
4		MKE[3]	DET[2]	BAL[6]		BOS	CLE	CAL	SEA		BOS[1]			
5					TEX						BAL		OAK	

Example: For the fourth series, umpire crew 1 is assigned to the Boston-at-Toronto series example, for the fourth series, crew 1 is assigned to the Boston–Toronto games, crew 2 is assigned to the Detroit–California games, and so on.

Table 11.20 shows the distances from the cities where the fourth series is being played to the cities where the fifth series is being played. There are some other issues that league management would like considered in assigning crews to the next series. Over the past nine series, crew 4 has umpired three series with Kansas City and three series with Milwaukee. Also, crew 5 has not been assigned to any games with New York, Toronto, or Detroit over the past month.

Table 11.20
A Matrix for Umpire Crew Assignment (Series 5)

From	To						
	KC	MIN	CHI	MKE	DET	TOR	NY
SEA(7)	1825	1399	2007	1694	1939	2124	2421
OAK(3)	1498	1589	2125	1845	2079	2286	2586
CAL(2)	1363	1536	2035	1756	1979	2175	2475
TEX(6)	506	853	798	843	982	1186	1383
MIN(5)	394	0	334	297	528	780	1028
CHI(4)	403	334	0	74	235	430	740
TOR(1)	968	897	497	583	206	0	366

Required

Prepare a written recommendation to league management concerning the assignment of umpire crews to the fifth series. Issues you may want to consider include:

1. What assignment will minimize distance traveled?
2. Where should crew 4 be assigned?
3. Where should crew 5 be assigned?

Quantitative Methods in Practice

Optimal Decision Systems, Inc.*
Cincinnati, Ohio

Optimal Decision Systems, Inc. (ODS) is a management consulting firm that specializes in the development and implementation of decision support systems for manufacturing, transportation, and distribution applications. ODS was formed in 1978 and has a clientele that includes many Fortune 500 companies.

Systems developed by ODS use computerized models to provide managers with a menu of "good" alternatives from which the "best" alternative can be selected. Several examples of the types of problems for which ODS has developed decision support systems are listed below:

1. Locating manufacturing and distribution facilities
2. Designing sales territories, including how various distribution centers should supply the territories
3. Routing and scheduling of truck fleets
4. Scheduling production systems to minimize inventory costs while maintaining desired service levels
5. Allocating capital to various investment opportunities

The majority of these applications (80%) have involved the development and implementation of large-scale mathematical programming models (linear programming, network, or mixed-integer linear programming models). Probability models and simulation have been the primary quantitative methodologies employed in the remaining applications. In addition, in almost every application, statistical analysis has played a heavy support role, particularly in the estimation of the parameters of the models.

Truck Fleet Management

The Fleet Management System (FMS) was developed by ODS for the management of private truck fleets. The heart of this system is a transshipment model that schedules and

*The authors are indebted to Richard A. Murphy and Thomas E. Thompson, Optimal Decision Systems, Inc., for providing this application.

routes the company fleet over a user-specified time horizon (usually 1 to 7 days) in a way that optimizes one of the following measures of performance:

1. Savings over the use of common-carrier truck fleets
2. Minimum total cost
3. Maximum total net revenue
4. Maximum load ratio (ratio of loaded miles to total miles driven by the fleet)
5. Some weighted combination of the above

   In determining the optimal solution, all user-specified constraints on the operation of the truck fleet are simultaneously satisfied. Examples of such constraints are:

1. Specified load movement, pickup and delivery times
2. Minimum or maximum levels of utilization of the fleet
3. Operating hours at pickup points and delivery points
4. Restrictions on driver work hours

   The Fleet Management System (FMS) accurately models the operation of a fleet, and thus the results of the optimization are extremely useful input to strategic (long-term), tactical (intermediate-term), and operational (short-term) planning. Some of the strategic issues that can be addressed by FMS are fleet sizing, the location of driver domiciles, equipment selection and mix, alternative operating practices (one-shift versus two-shift operation, use of double teams and/or trailer pools), and location of maintenance and refueling facilities. Tactical issues might include the timing and level of seasonal capacity such as leased drivers and equipment, the determination of which freight should be handled by common carrier and which should be handled by the private fleet, determination of appropriate internal pricing mechanisms, timing the increase or decrease of capacity by driver domicile and/or the determination of scheduling rules and procedures that yield efficient driver tours. The primary issue of operational planning is the determination of an efficient work tour for each driver.

A Transshipment Model for Truck Fleet Management

The primary function of the Fleet Management System is to determine an optimal schedule and route for each driver over the appropriate time horizon. For illustrative purposes, assume that all drivers (each with tractor and trailer) are located at a single domicile and that the objective is to maximize the savings that can be obtained over using common carriers for the same shipments. The system assumes the structure of a transshipment model. Capacity nodes represent the location of a driver at a particular point in time. Demand nodes represent the origin of a load movement which requires a truck to be made available for a load pickup. A driver at a capacity node is assigned to an arc connecting to a demand node. For each unit of flow on this arc (each driver assigned) cost is incurred that is the sum of the cost to travel to the location of the load movement plus any holding or delay costs that will be incurred if the driver experiences idle time. Arcs in the transshipment network are then used to assign the picked-up load to delivery locations. The net contribution on these delivery arcs is a savings the company realizes by using its own fleet of trucks rather than employing common carriers. This savings is the common-carrier cost less the fuel, labor, idle time, and any other costs incurred by the company in making its own deliveries. Note that on completion of the delivery, the driver's location is defined as a capacity node and thus the driver becomes available for reassignment at another point in time. Through the use of this transshipment model, the flow of the company's fleet of trucks can be scheduled over the time period of interest.

An Application and Results

The Fleet Management System was used to develop schedules for a Fortune 500 manufacturing company that operates a private fleet of over 100 drivers and tractors. The fleet is used primarily to move raw materials into and out of the company's manufacturing facilities located in over 40 locations throughout the United States and Canada. The fleet is also used to deliver finished goods to high-priority customer accounts where service levels are critical for continued business with the customer. Prior to implementation of the Fleet Management System, the fleet had been dispatched and managed on a purely manual basis, and the company was concerned about the high cost of the truck fleet operation.

The company's objective was to use the Fleet Management System to identify a set of short-range and long-range changes in the operation that could yield significant improvements in cost and efficiency. In this case, an annual saving of $1.9 million was possible through better freight selection and by scheduling the trucks more efficiently (with fewer empty miles). In addition specific recommendations were made to alter the size, location, and equipment mix of the truck fleet.

Questions

1. Draw a network that shows the transshipment model for truck fleet management.
2. What are the units of supply and demand at the nodes in your network? What are the units of flow over the shipping routes?

CHAPTER

12

Integer Linear Programming

In this chapter we turn our attention to a class of problems that are modeled as linear programs with the additional requirement that some or all of the decision variables must be integer. Such problems are called *integer linear programming* problems. The use of integer variables provides additional modeling flexibility. As a result, the number of practical applications that can be addressed with linear programming methodology is enlarged. The cost of the added flexibility is that problems involving integer variables are usually much more difficult to solve. In fact, although linear programming problems involving several thousand continuous variables can be routinely solved with commercial linear programming codes, the solution of integer linear programming problems involving less than 100 variables can cause difficulty. However, experienced quantitative analysts can usually identify the types of integer linear programs that are easiest to solve; in such cases, problems with hundreds (and sometimes thousands) of integer variables can be solved with available computer codes such as IBM's MPSX/370-MIP/370 and LINDO.

The plan of this chapter is to provide an applications-oriented introduction to integer linear programming. After a short section describing the different types of integer linear programming models, we show how a graphical procedure can be used to solve problems involving two decision variables. We then discuss, in some detail, two common integer linear programming applications: capital budgeting and distribution system design. The concluding section concerns the computer solution of integer linear programs. A new application involving bank location is introduced, formulated, and solved using LINDO/PC.

12.1

TYPES OF INTEGER LINEAR PROGRAMMING MODELS

The only difference between the problems studied in this chapter and the ones studied in the earlier chapters on linear programming is that some of the variables are required to be integer. If all of the variables are required to be integer, we say we have an *all-integer linear program*. Stated below is a two-variable, all-integer linear programming model:

$$\max \quad 2x_1 + 3x_2$$
$$\text{s.t.}$$
$$3x_1 + 3x_2 \leq 12$$
$$\tfrac{2}{3}x_1 + 1x_2 \leq 4$$
$$1x_1 + 2x_2 \leq 6$$
$$x_1, x_2 \geq 0 \text{ and integer}$$

You will note that if the phrase "and integer" is dropped from the above model, we are left with the familiar two-variable linear program. The linear program that results from dropping the integer requirements for the decision variables is referred to as the *LP* (linear programming) *Relaxation* of the integer linear program.

If some, but not all, of the decision variables in a problem are required to be integer, we say we have a *mixed-integer linear program*. The following is a two-variable, mixed-integer linear program:

$$\max \quad 3x_1 + 4x_2$$
$$\text{s.t.}$$
$$-1x_1 + 2x_2 \leq 8$$
$$1x_1 + 2x_2 \leq 12$$
$$2x_1 + 1x_2 \leq 16$$
$$x_1, x_2 \geq 0 \text{ and } x_2 \text{ integer}$$

The LP Relaxation of the above mixed-integer linear program is obtained by dropping the requirement that x_2 be integer.

In most practical applications the integer variables are only permitted to assume the values zero or one. In such cases we say we have a *binary* or a *0–1 integer linear program*. Zero–one problems may be either of the all-integer or mixed-integer type. The capital budgeting, distribution system design, and bank location problems discussed in later sections of this chapter all make use of *0–1* variables.

12.2

GRAPHICAL SOLUTION

Security Realty Investors currently has $1,365,000 that is available for new rental property investments. After an initial screening, Security has reduced the investment alternatives to a series of townhouses and a group of apartment buildings in a large apartment complex.

The townhouses can be purchased in blocks of three for the price of \$195,000 per block, but there are only four blocks of townhouses available for purchase at this time. Each building in the apartment complex contains 12 dwelling units and sells for \$273,000. The individual apartment buildings can be purchased separately, and the complex developer has agreed to build as many 12-unit buildings as Security would like to purchase.

Security's property manager is free to devote 140 hours per month to these investments. Each block of townhouses will require 4 hours of the property manager's time each month, while each apartment building will require 40 hours per month. The yearly cash flow (after deducting mortgage payments and operating expenses) is estimated to be \$2000 per block of townhouses and \$3000 per apartment building. Security would like to allocate its investment funds to apartment buildings and townhouses in order to maximize the yearly cash flow.

In order to develop an appropriate mathematical model for this problem, let

$$x_1 = \text{number of blocks of townhouses purchased}$$
$$x_2 = \text{number of apartment buildings purchased}$$

The objective function, measuring cash flow in thousands of dollars, can be written as

$$\max \quad 2x_1 + 3x_2$$

There are three constraints that must be satisfied:

$195x_1 + 273x_2 \leq 1365$	Funds available in thousands of dollars
$4x_1 + 40x_2 \leq 140$	Manager's time in hours
$x_1 \leq 4$	Townhouse availability in blocks

In addition, the variables must be restricted to nonnegative values. Also, since fractional values for the blocks of townhouses and/or number of apartment buildings are unacceptable, the decision variables x_1 and x_2 must be integer. Thus the complete model for the Security Realty problem is the following all-integer linear program:

$$\max \quad 2x_1 + 3x_2$$
$$\text{s.t.}$$
$$195x_1 + 273x_2 \leq 1365$$
$$4x_1 + 40x_2 \leq 140$$
$$x_1 \leq 4$$
$$x_1, x_2 \geq 0 \text{ and integer}$$

A first approach to solving such a problem might be to drop the integer requirements and solve the resulting LP Relaxation. You might then round the decision variables in an attempt to find the optimal solution to the integer linear program. However, as we shall see, such an approach may not yield the optimal solution. In fact, rounding the values of the decision variables can sometimes result in an infeasible solution.

The linear program resulting from dropping the integer requirements for the decision variables (the LP Relaxation) is written as follows:

$$\max \quad 2x_1 + 3x_2$$

$$\text{s.t.}$$

$$195x_1 + 273x_2 \leq 1365$$

$$4x_1 + 40x_2 \leq 140$$

$$x_1 \qquad\qquad \leq \quad 4$$

$$x_1, x_2 \geq 0$$

The optimal solution to the LP Relaxation (see Figure 12.1) is given by $x_1 = 2.44$ and $x_2 = 3.26$. The objective function value for this solution is 14.66, corresponding to a cash flow of \$14,660. However, this solution is not feasible for the integer linear programming problem, since the decision variables assume fractional values.

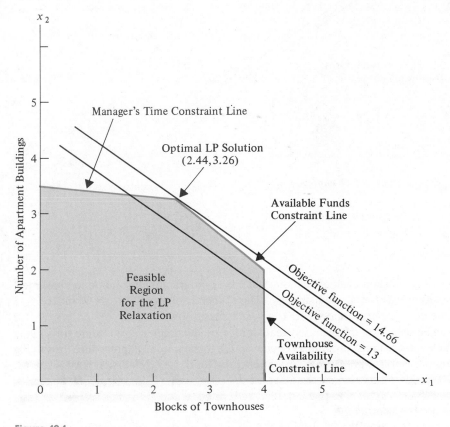

Figure 12.1
Graphical Solution to the LP Relaxation of the Security Realty Problem

Rounding the decision variables to the nearest integer value yields a solution of $x_1 = 2$ and $x_2 = 3$, with an objective function value of 13, or a \$13,000 annual cash flow. In Figure 12.2 we show the feasible solution points that provide integer values for x_1 and x_2. Is the rounded solution of $x_1 = 2$ and $x_2 = 3$ the optimal integer solution? The answer is no! As can be seen in Figure 12.2, the optimal integer solution is $x_1 = 4$ and $x_2 = 2$, with an objective function value of 14.00, or a \$14,000 annual cash flow. For

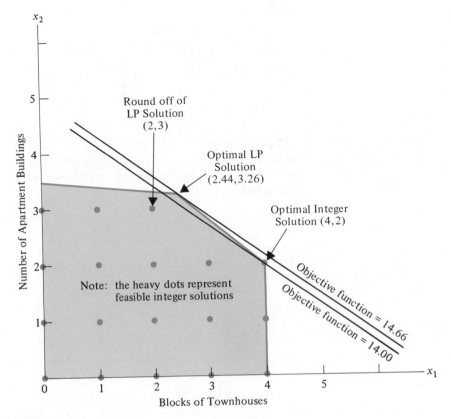

Figure 12.2
The Integer Solution to the Security Realty Problem

Security Realty, the approach of rounding the linear programming solution to the nearest integer solution was not a good strategy. The rounded solution of $x_1 = 2$ and $x_2 = 3$ would have cost Security Realty $1000 a year in cash flow.

As can be seen from the Security Realty problem, the graphical procedure for solving two-variable integer linear programs is quite similar to the graphical procedure for solving linear programs. First a graph of the feasible region for the LP Relaxation is constructed. Then the feasible integer points are denoted by heavy dots. The integer solution point on the best objective function line can then be located; this point is the optimal solution to the integer linear program.

From the analysis of the Security Realty Investors problem, an important observation can be made about the relationship between the value of the optimal integer solution and the value of the optimal LP Relaxation solution. This observation is stated for *maximization problems*[1] as property 1.

---

[1]For minimization problems, property 1 would be stated with *greater than* or *equal to* substituted for *less than* or *equal to*.

Property 1.

The value of the optimal solution to any integer or mixed-integer linear program involving maximization yields a value *less than* or *equal to* the value of the optimal solution to its LP Relaxation.

The above property means that an *upper bound* on the value of any maximization integer or mixed-integer linear program can be found by solving its associated LP Relaxation. This property can be seen in Figure 12.2. The optimal LP solution is on the highest objective function line and has a value of $14.66. The optimal integer solution is on a lower objective function line and has a smaller value, $14.00.

We note in closing this section that mixed-integer linear programs with two decision variables can be solved by a simple modification of the graphical procedure outlined above. Problem 5 at the end of the chapter requires the graphical solution of a mixed-integer linear program.

12.3

APPLICATIONS OF INTEGER LINEAR PROGRAMMING

In this section we discuss two applications involving *0–1* or binary integer variables: the capital budgeting and distribution system design problems. We have chosen these applications because they represent two areas in which integer linear programming has been used widely in practice. Through these applications you should begin to develop an appreciation of the flexibility in model development provided by *0–1* variables.

Capital Budgeting

Capital budgeting is an area where quantitative analysis has often led to considerable savings and/or increased profits. To provide an idea of what is involved in capital budgeting, let us consider the Ice-Cold Refrigerator problem and develop its linear programming formulation.

The Ice-Cold Refrigerator Company can invest funds in a variety of company projects that have varying capital requirements over the next 4 years. Faced with limited capital resources, the company must select the most profitable projects and budgets for the capital expenditures. The estimated present values of the projects, the capital requirements, and the available capital projections[2] are shown in Table 12.1.

The following definitions are chosen for the decision variables:

$x_1 = 1$ if the plant expansion project is accepted; 0 if rejected

$x_2 = 1$ if the warehouse expansion project is accepted; 0 if rejected

$x_3 = 1$ if the new machinery project is accepted; 0 if rejected

$x_4 = 1$ if the new product research project is accepted; 0 if rejected

[2]The estimated present value is the net return for the project discounted back to the beginning of year 1.

Table 12.1
Project Present Values, Capital Requirements, and Available Capital Projections for the Ice-Cold Refrigerator Company

Project	Estimated Present Value ($)	Capital Requirements ($)			
		Year 1	Year 2	Year 3	Year 4
Plant expansion	90,000	15,000	20,000	20,000	15,000
Warehouse ex-pansion	40,000	10,000	15,000	20,000	5,000
New machinery	10,000	10,000	0	0	4,000
New product re-search	37,000	15,000	10,000	10,000	10,000
Available funds		40,000	50,000	40,000	35,000

The linear programming formulation of this capital budgeting problem has a separate constraint for each year's available funds and a separate constraint requiring each variable to be less than or equal to 1. The linear programming formulation is given below (monetary units are expressed in thousands of dollars).

$$\max \quad 90x_1 + 40x_2 + 10x_3 + 37x_4$$

s.t.

$$
\begin{aligned}
15x_1 + 10x_2 + 10x_3 + 15x_4 &\le 40 \\
20x_1 + 15x_2 \phantom{{}+ 10x_3} + 10x_4 &\le 50 \\
20x_1 + 20x_2 \phantom{{}+ 10x_3} + 10x_4 &\le 40 \\
15x_1 + 5x_2 + 4x_3 + 10x_4 &\le 35 \\
x_1 \phantom{{}+ 5x_2 + 4x_3 + 10x_4} &\le 1 \\
x_2 \phantom{{}+ 4x_3 + 10x_4} &\le 1 \\
x_3 \phantom{{}+ 10x_4} &\le 1 \\
x_4 &\le 1 \\
x_1, x_2, x_3, x_4 &\ge 0
\end{aligned}
$$

The optimal solution to this linear program is $x_1 = 1$, $x_2 = 0.5$, $x_3 = 0.5$, and $x_4 = 1$, with a total estimated present value of $152,000. The difficulty with a linear programming approach to the capital budgeting problem is now readily apparent. Unless it is possible to implement the warehouse expansion and new machinery projects in 50% increments, the current solution is not feasible. Thus some adjustment in the linear programming solution, such as rounding x_2 and x_3 (possibly leading to a nonoptimal solution), must be made prior to implementation.

A preferable approach is to reformulate the Ice-Cold Refrigerator Company problem as a *0–1* integer linear program. The *0–1* integer linear programming formulation is shown below:

$$\max \quad 90x_1 + 40x_2 + 10x_3 + 37x_4$$

s.t.

$$15x_1 + 10x_2 + 10x_3 + 15x_4 \leq 40$$
$$20x_1 + 15x_2 \qquad\quad + 10x_4 \leq 50$$
$$20x_1 + 20x_2 \qquad\quad + 10x_4 \leq 40$$
$$15x_1 + 5x_2 + 4x_3 + 10x_4 \leq 35$$
$$x_1, x_2, x_3, x_4 = 0, 1$$

The LP Relaxation of this *0–1* integer program is given by the linear programming formulation shown previously.

The optimal integer solution[3] is $x_1 = 1$, $x_2 = 1$, $x_3 = 1$, and $x_4 = 0$ with a total estimated present value of \$140,000. We note that this optimal solution could not have been discovered by simply rounding the solution to the LP Relaxation. In fact, the best feasible solution that can be found by considering all possible roundings of the fractional variables in the solution to the LP Relaxation is $x_1 = 1$, $x_2 = 0$, $x_3 = 0$, $x_4 = 1$, with a total estimated present value of \$127,000. This is substantially less than the value of the optimal integer solution.

The ability to avoid fractional values is one of two main reasons that an integer programming formulation is usually preferred for capital budgeting problems. The second reason most quantitative analysts prefer a *0–1* integer programming model for the capital budgeting problem is the flexibility provided in developing certain nonbudgetary constraints. These constraints are often important in capital budgeting problems and can be formulated only through the use of *0–1*—sometimes called logical—variables.

Multiple-Choice and Mutually Exclusive Constraints

Suppose that instead of one warehouse expansion project, the Ice-Cold Refrigerator Company actually has three warehouse expansion projects under consideration. One of the warehouses *must* be expanded because of increasing product demand, but there is not sufficient new demand to make the expansion of more than one warehouse profitable. The following variable definitions and *multiple-choice constraint* could be incorporated into the previous *0–1* integer linear programming model to reflect this situation. Let

$x_2 = 1$ if the original warehouse expansion project is accepted; 0 if rejected

$x_5 = 1$ if the second warehouse expansion project is accepted; 0 if rejected

$x_6 = 1$ if the third warehouse expansion project is accepted; 0 if rejected

The multiple-choice constraint reflecting the requirement that one and only one of these projects must be selected is written as

$$x_2 + x_5 + x_6 = 1$$

It is easy to see why this is called a multiple-choice constraint. Since x_2, x_5, and x_6 are allowed to assume only the values 0 or 1, one and only one of these projects must be

---

[3]This solution was found using a computer solution procedure. Problem 7 asks you to develop the solution of this problem.

selected from among the three choices. Note that if fractional values (as in linear programming) were allowed for the decision variables, we could not enforce the requirement of selecting one and only one project (for example, $x_2 = \frac{1}{3}$, $x_5 = \frac{1}{3}$, $x_6 = \frac{1}{3}$ would satisfy the constraint).

If it had not been required that one warehouse be expanded, then the multiple-choice constraint could be written as

$$x_2 + x_5 + x_6 \leq 1$$

This modification allows for the case of no warehouse expansion ($x_2 = x_5 = x_6 = 0$), but does not permit more than one warehouse to be expanded. This type of constraint is often called a *mutually exclusive constraint*.

k Out of n Alternatives Constraint

An extension of the concept of a multiple-choice constraint can be used to model situations in which k out of a set of n projects must be selected. Suppose that x_2, x_5, x_6, x_7, and x_8 represent five potential warehouse expansion projects and it is considered necessary to accept *exactly* two of the five projects. The following constraint ensures that this new requirement is satisfied:

$$x_2 + x_5 + x_6 + x_7 + x_8 = 2$$

If it is required that no more than two of the projects be selected, we would use the following less-than-or-equal-to constraint:

$$x_2 + x_5 + x_6 + x_7 + x_8 \leq 2$$

Once again, each of the above variables must be restricted to *0–1* values.

Conditional and Corequisite Constraints

Sometimes the acceptance of one project is *conditional* upon the acceptance of another. For example, suppose for the Ice-Cold Refrigerator Company that the warehouse expansion project was conditional on the plant expansion project. That is, the company will not consider expanding the warehouse unless the plant is expanded. With x_1 representing plant expansion and x_2 representing warehouse expansion, the following conditional constraint could be introduced to enforce this requirement:

$$x_2 \leq x_1$$

or

$$x_2 - x_1 \leq 0$$

Since both x_1 and x_2 are required to be 0 or 1, we see that whenever x_1 is 0, x_2 will be forced to 0. When x_1 is 1, x_2 is also allowed to be 1; thus, both the plant and the warehouse can be expanded. However, we note that the above constraint does not force the warehouse expansion project (x_2) to be accepted if the plant expansion project (x_1) is.

If it were required that the warehouse expansion project be accepted whenever the plant expansion project was, and vice versa, then we would say that x_1 and x_2 represented *corequisite* projects. To model such a situation we simply write the above constraint as

$$x_2 = x_1$$

or

$$x_2 - x_1 = 0$$

This constraint forces x_1 and x_2 to take on the same value.

Cautionary Note on Sensitivity Analysis

Sensitivity analysis is often more critical for integer linear programming problems than for linear programming problems. A very small change in one of the coefficients in the constraints can cause a relatively large change in the value of the optimal solution. To see why this is so, consider the following integer programming model of a simple capital budgeting problem involving four projects and a budgetary constraint for a single time period:

$$\max \quad 40x_1 + 60x_2 + 70x_3 + 160x_4$$
$$\text{s.t.}$$
$$16x_1 + 35x_2 + 45x_3 + 85x_4 \leq 100$$
$$x_1, x_2, x_3, x_4 = 0, 1$$

The optimal solution to this problem can be quickly found by enumerating the alternatives; it is $x_1 = 1$, $x_2 = 1$, $x_3 = 1$, and $x_4 = 0$, with an objective function value of \$170. However, note that if the budget is increased by \$1 (from 100 to 101), the optimal solution changes to $x_1 = 1$, $x_2 = 0$, $x_3 = 0$, and $x_4 = 1$, with an objective function value of \$200. That is, one additional dollar in the budget would lead to a \$30 increase in the return. Surely management, when faced with such a situation, would increase the budget by \$1. Because of the extreme sensitivity of the value of the optimal solution to the constraint coefficients, practitioners usually recommend resolving the integer linear program several times with slight variations in the coefficients before attempting to choose a solution for implementation.

Distribution System Design

In Chapter 11 the following linear programming formulation for the transportation problem was developed:

$$\min \quad \sum_{i=1}^{m} \sum_{j=1}^{n} c_{ij} x_{ij}$$
$$\text{s.t.}$$
$$\sum_{j=1}^{n} x_{ij} \leq s_i \quad i = 1, 2, \ldots, m \quad \text{Supply}$$

$$\sum_{i=1}^{m} x_{ij} = d_j \quad j = 1, 2, \ldots, n \quad \text{Demand}$$

$$x_{ij} \geq 0 \qquad \text{for all } i \text{ and } j$$

where

$i =$ index for origins; $i = 1, 2, \ldots, m$

$j =$ index for destinations; $j = 1, 2, \ldots, n$

$x_{ij} =$ number of units shipped from origin i to destination j

$c_{ij} =$ cost per unit of shipping from origin i to destination j

$s_i =$ supply in units at origin i

$d_j =$ demand in units at destination j

In the transportation problem it is assumed that the origins and destinations are fixed. Consequently the problem is to determine how much of the product to ship from each origin to each destination in order to minimize the total transportation cost. However, in more general distribution system design problems, it is necessary to select the best locations for the origins as well as the amounts to ship from each origin to each destination.

Suppose that the origins represent m potential locations for plants with capacities s_i and the destinations represent n retail outlets with demand d_j. A more complex distribution system design problem must now be solved. If site i is selected for a plant location, there will be a fixed cost associated with plant construction and then a variable cost associated with the number of units shipped from plant i to the various retail outlets. On the other hand, if site i is not selected, then there is no fixed cost and no units can be shipped from site i. The introduction of one integer $0-1$ variable for each potential plant location allows us to develop a mixed-integer linear programming model for this distribution system design problem. Let

$y_i = 1$ if a plant is constructed at site i; 0 if not

$f_i =$ fixed cost of constructing a plant at site i with capacity s_i

To represent the constraint that nothing can be shipped from site i if a plant is not constructed, the supply constraints in the transportation model are modified as follows:

$$\sum_{j=1}^{n} x_{ij} \leq s_i y_i \qquad i = 1, 2, \ldots, m$$

or

$$\sum_{j=1}^{n} x_{ij} - s_i y_i \leq 0 \qquad i = 1, 2, \ldots, m$$

Also, another term must be added to the objective function to represent the fixed cost of plant construction at each site selected:

$$\text{Fixed cost of plant construction} = \sum_{i=1}^{m} f_i y_i$$

The complete model for our distribution system design problem can now be written:

$$\min \sum_{i=1}^{m} \sum_{j=1}^{n} c_{ij} x_{ij} + \sum_{i=1}^{m} f_i y_i$$

s.t.

$$\sum_{j=1}^{n} x_{ij} - s_i y_i \leq 0 \quad i = 1, 2, \ldots, m \qquad \text{Plant capacities}$$

$$\sum_{i=1}^{m} x_{ij} = d_j \quad j = 1, 2, \ldots, n \qquad \text{Demand at retail outlets}$$

$$x_{ij} \geq 0 \quad \text{for all } i \text{ and } j$$

$$y_i = 0, \ 1 \text{ for } i = 1, 2, \ldots, m$$

This basic model[4] can be expanded to accommodate distribution systems involving shipments from plants to warehouses to retail outlets, and multiple products.[5] Using the special properties of *0–1* variables, it can also be expanded to accommodate a variety of configuration constraints on the plant locations. For example, suppose that site 1 were in Dallas and site 2 in Fort Worth. A company might not want to locate plants in both Dallas and Fort Worth because the cities are so close together. To prevent this, the following constraint can be added to the model:

$$y_1 + y_2 \leq 1$$

This constraint was called a mutually exclusive constraint in the previous subsection. It allows either y_1 or y_2 to equal 1 but not both. If we had written the constraint as an equality, it would be the same as the multiple-choice constraint we encountered in the capital budgeting problem. Other constraints such as the conditional or corequisite constraint can be introduced to satisfy managerially specified requirements on the configuration of plant locations.

12.4

COMPUTER SOLUTION

As mentioned in the chapter introduction, computer programs for solving integer and mixed-integer linear programs are now widely available. Such codes are generally reliable for problems involving up to 100 or more integer variables and have often been used to solve specially structured problems with a few thousand variables.

Most of the general-purpose codes use a linear-programming-based *branch-and-bound solution procedure*. The branch-and-bound procedure divides the set of all feasible

---

[4]For computational reasons it is usually preferable to replace the m plant capacity constraints with mn shipping route capacity constraints of the form $x_{ij} \leq \min \{s_i, d_j\} y_i$ for $i = 1, \ldots, m$ and $j = 1, \ldots, n$. The coefficient for y_i in each of these constraints is the smaller of the origin capacity or the destination demand. These additional constraints often cause the solution of the LP Relaxation to be integer.

[5]A model of this type was used by a large food chain and resulted in substantial savings in distribution system costs. See Geoffrion and Graves, "Distribution System Design by Benders Decomposition," *Management Science*, January 1974.

integer solutions into smaller subsets (branching). Then various rules are used to (1) identify the subsets that are most likely to contain the optimal solution and (2) identify the subsets that need not be explored further because they could not possibly contain the optimal solution.

An upper bound on the value of the best solution in each subset is obtained by solving an LP Relaxation. Any time the solution to the LP Relaxation results in an integer solution, the best solution in the subset has been found and a lower bound for the subset is obtained. The best of the integer feasible solutions (considering all the subsets) is the optimal solution.

Whereas the branch-and-bound solution procedure can be used to solve small problems by hand it is very tedious; in practice a computer code is needed to solve integer linear programs. In this section we will show how another application of integer linear programming can be formulated and solved using LINDO/PC.

A Bank-Location Application

The long-range planning department for the Ohio Trust Company is considering expanding its operation into a 20-county region in northeastern Ohio (see Figure 12.3). Currently, Ohio Trust does not have a principal place of business in any of the 20 counties under consideration. According to the banking laws in Ohio, if a banking firm establishes a principal place of business (PPB) in any county, then branch banks can be established in that county and in any adjacent county. However, in order to establish a new principal place of business, Ohio Trust must either obtain approval for a new bank from the state's superintendent of banks or purchase an existing bank.

Table 12.2 provides a listing of the 20 counties in the region together with the adjacent counties. From the table we see that Ashtabula County is adjacent to Lake, Geauga, and Trumbull counties; Lake County is adjacent to Ashtabula, Cuyahoga, and Geauga counties; and so on.

As an initial step in its planning, Ohio Trust would like to determine the minimum number of PPBs necessary to do business throughout the 20-county region. A $0-1$ integer programming model can be used to solve this problem for Ohio Trust. Let us define the following decision variables:

$$x_i = 1 \text{ if a PPB is established in county } i; 0 \text{ otherwise}$$

With the goal of minimizing the number of PPBs needed, the objective function can be written as

$$\min \quad x_1 + x_2 + \cdots + x_{20}$$

In order to place branch banks in a county, the county must either contain a PPB or be adjacent to another county with a PPB. Thus there will be one constraint for each county. For example, the constraint for Ashtabula County would be written as follows:

$$x_1 + x_2 + x_{12} + x_{16} \geq 1 \qquad \text{Ashtabula}$$

Note that satisfaction of this constraint ensures that a PPB will be placed in Ashtabula County *or* in one or more of the adjacent counties. Thus this constraint guarantees that Ohio Trust will be able to place branch banks in Ashtabula County.

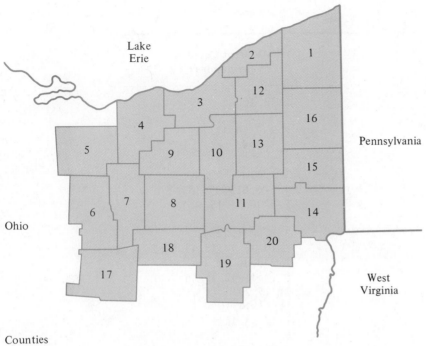

Lake
Erie

Pennsylvania

Ohio

West
Virginia

Counties

1. Ashtabula
2. Lake
3. Cuyahoga
4. Lorain
5. Huron
6. Richland
7. Ashland
8. Wayne
9. Medina
10. Summit

11. Stark
12. Geauga
13. Portage
14. Columbiana
15. Mahoning
16. Trumbull
17. Knox
18. Holmes
19. Tuscarawas
20. Carroll

Figure 12.3
Map of 20-County Area in Northeastern Ohio

The complete statement of the bank location problem is shown below:

$$\min \quad x_1 + x_2 + \quad \cdots \quad + x_{20}$$

s.t.

$$
\begin{array}{llll}
x_1 + x_2 \quad\ \ + x_{12} + x_{16} & \geq 1 & \text{Ashtabula} \\
x_1 + x_2 + x_3 + x_{12} & \geq 1 & \text{Lake} \\
\quad\quad \vdots & & \vdots \\
x_{11} + x_{14} + x_{19} + x_{20} \geq 1 & & \text{Carroll} \\
x_i = 0, 1 \quad i = 1, 2, \ldots, 20
\end{array}
$$

Given this 20-variable, 20-constraint problem formulation, we can now solve it using LINDO/PC. The input data are entered in the same manner as for a linear program. Then

Table 12.2
Counties in Region of Expansion for Ohio Trust

Counties under Consideration	Adjacent Counties (by number)
1. Ashtabula	2, 12, 16
2. Lake	1, 3, 12
3. Cuyahoga	2, 4, 9, 10, 12, 13
4. Lorain	3, 5, 7, 9
5. Huron	4, 6, 7
6. Richland	5, 7, 17
7. Ashland	4, 5, 6, 8, 9, 17, 18
8. Wayne	7, 9, 10, 11, 18
9. Medina	3, 4, 7, 8, 10
10. Summit	3, 8, 9, 11, 12, 13
11. Stark	8, 10, 13, 14, 15, 18, 19, 20
12. Geauga	1, 2, 3, 10, 13, 16
13. Portage	3, 10, 11, 12, 15, 16
14. Columbiana	11, 15, 20
15. Mahoning	11, 13, 14, 16
16. Trumbull	1, 12, 13, 15
17. Knox	6, 7, 18
18. Holmes	7, 8, 11, 17, 19
19. Tuscarawas	11, 18, 20
20. Carroll	11, 14, 19

to make LINDO/PC treat each of the 20 decision variables as *0–1* integer variables, we enter the LINDO/PC command "INTEGER 20." When the "GO" command is given, the LINDO/PC program will determine the optimal integer solution.

In Figure 12.4 we show a portion of the computer output. Note that the variable names used correspond to the first four letters in the name of each county. Using the output, we see that the optimal solution calls for principal places of business in Ashland, Stark, and Geauga counties. With PPBs in these three counties, Ohio Trust can place branch banks in all 20 counties (see Figure 12.5). All other decision variables have an optimal value of zero, indicating that a PPB should not be placed in these counties. Clearly the integer programming model could be enlarged to allow for expansion into a larger area or throughout the entire state.[6]

In closing this section, we comment briefly on the value of general-purpose mixed-integer linear programming codes. Such codes can be used for linear programming problems (including the special cases of the transportation, transshipment, and assignment problems), all-integer problems (like the Ohio Trust problem), and problems involving some continuous and some integer variables (mixed-integer linear programs). General-purpose codes are seldom the fastest for solving problems with special structures (such as the transportation, transshipment, and assignment problems); however, unless the

---

[6]A model of this type allowing for expansion throughout the state and some other variations is presented in Sweeney, D.J., L. Mairose, and R. Martin. "Strategic Planning in Bank Location," *AIDS Proceedings*, November 1979.

```
                OBJECTIVE FUNCTION VALUE

  1)      3.00000000

        VARIABLE          VALUE          REDUCED COST
            ASHT         .000000            .000000
            LAKE         .000000            .000000
            CUYA         .000000            .000000
            LORA         .000000            .000000
            HURO         .000000            .000000
            RICH         .000000           1.000000
            ASHL        1.000000            .000000
            WAYN         .000000            .000000
            MEDI         .000000            .000000
            SUMM         .000000            .000000
            STAR        1.000000            .000000
            GEAU        1.000000            .000000
            PORT         .000000            .000000
            COLU         .000000            .000000
            MAHO         .000000            .000000
            TRUM         .000000            .000000
            KNOX         .000000           1.000000
            HOLM         .000000            .000000
            TUSC         .000000            .000000
            CARR         .000000            .000000
```

Figure 12.4
Microcomputer Solution of Bank-Location Problem Using LINDO/PC

problems are very large, speed is usually not a critical issue. As long as a solution can be found in a reasonable amount of time, the practitioner is satisfied. Thus, it is probably better for most practitioners to become familiar with one general-purpose computer package that can be used on a variety of problems than to maintain a variety of computer codes that are designed for special problems. If special-purpose codes are needed for particular applications, experts can be consulted.

Summary

We have introduced an important extension of the linear programming model: the integer linear program. The only difference between an integer linear programming problem and a linear programming problem is the added integer restriction on some of the variables. If all of the variables are required to be integer, we have an all-integer linear program; if some, but not necessarily all, of the variables are required to be integer, we have a mixed-integer linear program. Finally, in cases where the integer variables are only permitted to assume the values 0 or 1, we have a *0–1* (binary) integer linear program. Binary integer linear programs may be either all integer or mixed integer.

There are two primary reasons for studying integer linear programming. First, in many applications fractional values of the decision variables are not permitted. Since we have seen that rounding the linear programming solution can provide poor results, methods for finding the optimal integer solution are needed. For any two-variable problem a simple extension of the graphical procedure for linear programs can be used to find the optimal

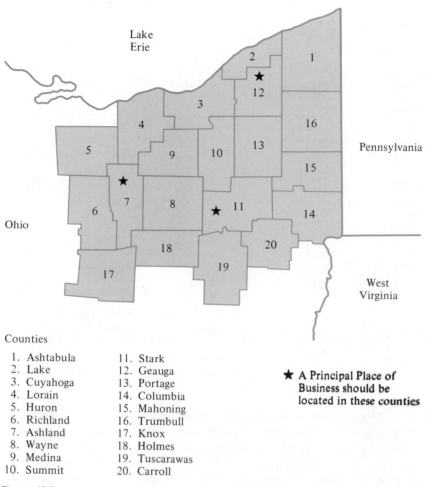

Lake
Erie

Pennsylvania

Ohio

West
Virginia

Counties

1. Ashtabula
2. Lake
3. Cuyahoga
4. Lorain
5. Huron
6. Richland
7. Ashland
8. Wayne
9. Medina
10. Summit

11. Stark
12. Geauga
13. Portage
14. Columbia
15. Mahoning
16. Trumbull
17. Knox
18. Holmes
19. Tuscarawas
20. Carroll

★ A Principal Place of
Business should be
located in these counties

Figure 12.5
Principal Place of Business Counties for Ohio Trust

integer solution. The branch-and-bound solution procedure is the most common procedure for solving larger integer linear programs. A major advantage of the branch-and-bound solution procedure is its flexibility; it can be used for both the all-integer and the mixed-integer linear programs. Almost all existing commercial computer codes (including LINDO/PC) employ the branch-and-bound approach. The software package available with this text, *The Management Scientist*, also employs the branch-and-bound approach.

A second reason for studying integer linear programming is that it provides increased modeling flexibility through the use of *0–1* variables. In the discussion of the capital budgeting and distribution system design problems, we saw how a number of important managerial considerations can be incorporated through the use of multiple-choice constraints, conditional constraints, and so on. In addition, the Ohio Trust problem presented in the previous section provided another example of the modeling flexibility available using integer variables.

In recent years, with the availability of commercial integer linear programming computer codes, we have seen a rapid growth in the use of integer linear programming.

As researchers develop solution procedures capable of solving integer linear programs with larger numbers of variables, we can expect to see a continuation of this growth and the development of new applications.

Glossary

Integer linear program A linear program with the additional requirement that some or all of the decision variables must be integer.

All-integer linear program An integer linear program in which all the decision variables are required to be integer.

LP Relaxation The linear program that results from dropping the integer requirements for the decision variables.

Mixed-integer linear program An integer linear program in which some, but not all, of the decision variables are required to be integer.

0–1 integer linear program An all-integer or mixed-integer linear program in which the integer variables are only permitted to assume the values 0 or 1.

Upper bound A value that is known to be greater than or equal to the value of any feasible solution. The solution to the LP Relaxation of an integer linear program provides an upper bound for a maximization problem.

Multiple-choice constraint A constraint requiring that the sum of two or more *0–1* variables equal 1. Thus any feasible solution makes a choice of one of these variables to set equal to 1.

Mutually exclusive constraint A constraint requiring that the sum of two or more *0–1* variables be less than or equal to 1. Thus if one of the variables equals 1, the others must equal 0. However, all variables could equal 0.

k out of n alternatives constraint An extension of the multiple-choice constraint. This constraint requires that the sum of *n 0–1* variables equal *k*.

Conditional constraints Constraints involving *0–1* variables that do not allow certain variables to equal 1 unless certain other variables are equal to 1.

Corequisite constraint A constraint requiring that two *0–1* variables be equal. Thus they are both in or out of solution together.

Branch-and-bound A solution procedure for integer linear programs that sequentially partitions the set of feasible solutions into smaller and smaller subsets until the optimal solution is found.

Problems

1. Indicate which of the following are all-integer linear programs, which are mixed-integer linear programs, and which are ordinary linear programs. For each of the all-integer and mixed-integer linear programs write the LP Relaxation. (Do not attempt to solve.)

   a. max $30x_1 + 25x_2$

   s.t.

   $$3x_1 + 1.5x_2 \leq 400$$
   $$1.5x_1 + 2x_2 \leq 250$$

$$1x_1 + 1x_2 \leq 150$$
$$x_1, x_2 \geq 0 \text{ and } x_2 \text{ integer}$$

b. min $3x_1 + 4x_2$
   s.t.

$$2x_1 + 4x_2 \geq 8$$
$$2x_1 + 6x_2 \geq 12$$
$$x_1, x_2 \geq 0 \text{ and integer}$$

c. min $30x_1 + 4x_2$
   s.t.

$$3x_1 + 2x_2 \geq 50$$
$$0.1x_1 + 0.2x_2 \geq 2$$
$$x_1, x_2 \geq 0 \text{ and } x_1 \text{ integer}$$

d. max $3x_1 + 4x_2$
   s.t.

$$-1x_1 + 2x_2 \leq 8$$
$$1x_1 + 2x_2 \leq 12$$
$$2x_1 + 1x_2 \leq 16$$
$$x_1, x_2 \geq 0 \text{ and integer}$$

e. max $20x_1 + 5x_2$
   s.t.

$$5x_1 + 1x_2 \leq 15$$
$$6x_1 + 4x_2 \leq 24$$
$$1x_1 + 1x_2 \leq 5$$
$$x_1, x_2 \geq 0$$

2. Consider the all-integer linear program given below:

$$\max \quad 5x_1 + 8x_2$$
$$\text{s.t.}$$
$$6x_1 + 5x_2 \leq 30$$
$$9x_1 + 4x_2 \leq 36$$
$$1x_1 + 2x_2 \leq 10$$
$$x_1, x_2 \geq 0 \text{ and integer}$$

a. Graph the constraints for this problem. Indicate with heavy dots all the feasible integer solutions.
b. Find the optimal solution to the LP Relaxation. Round down to find a feasible integer solution.
c. Find the optimal integer solution. Is it the same as the solution found in part (b) above by rounding down?

3. Consider the all-integer linear program given below:

$$\max \quad 1x_1 + 1x_2$$

s.t.

$$4x_1 + 6x_2 \leq 22$$
$$1x_1 + 5x_2 \leq 15$$
$$2x_1 + 1x_2 \leq 9$$
$$x_1, x_2 \geq 0 \text{ and integer}$$

a. Graph the constraints for this problem. Indicate with heavy dots all the feasible integer solutions.
b. Solve the LP Relaxation of this problem.
c. Find the optimal integer solution.

4. Consider the integer linear program given below:

$$\max \quad 10x_1 + 3x_2$$

s.t.

$$6x_1 + 7x_2 \leq 40$$
$$3x_1 + 1x_2 \leq 11$$
$$x_1, x_2 \geq 0 \text{ and integer}$$

a. Formulate and solve the LP Relaxation of the problem. Solve it graphically. Round down to find a feasible solution. State upper and lower bounds on the value of the optimal solution.
b. Solve the integer linear program graphically. Compare the value of this solution with the solution found in part (a).
c. Suppose the objective function changes to max $3x_1 + 6x_2$. Repeat parts (a) and (b) above.

5. Consider the mixed-integer linear program given below:

$$\max \quad 2x_1 + 3x_2$$

s.t.

$$4x_1 + 9x_2 \leq 36$$
$$7x_1 + 5x_2 \leq 35$$
$$x_1, x_2 \geq 0 \text{ and } x_1 \text{ integer}$$

a. Graph the constraints for this problem. Indicate on your graph all feasible mixed-integer solutions.
b. Find the optimal solution to the LP Relaxation. Round the value of x_1 down to find a feasible mixed-integer solution. Is this solution optimal? Why or why not?
c. Find the optimal solution for the mixed-integer linear program.

6. Consider the mixed-integer linear program given below.

$$\max \quad 1x_1 + 1x_2$$

s.t.

$$7x_1 + 9x_2 \leq 63$$

$$9x_1 + 5x_2 \le 45$$
$$3x_1 + 1x_2 \le 12$$
$$x_1, x_2 \ge 0 \text{ and } x_2 \text{ integer}$$

a. Graph the constraints for this problem. Indicate on your graph all feasible mixed-integer solutions.

b. Find the optimal solution to the LP Relaxation. Round the value of x_2 down to find a feasible mixed-integer solution. Specify upper and lower bounds on the value of the optimal solution to the mixed-integer linear program.

c. Find the optimal solution to the mixed-integer linear program.

7. The integer programming formulation of the Ice-Cold Refrigerator Company capital budgeting problem is presented below.

$$\max \quad 90x_1 + 40x_2 + 10x_3 + 37x_4$$

s.t.

$$15x_1 + 10x_2 + 10x_3 + 15x_4 \le 40$$
$$20x_1 + 15x_2 \qquad\quad + 10x_4 \le 50$$
$$20x_1 + 20x_2 \qquad\quad + 10x_4 \le 40$$
$$15x_1 + 5x_2 + 4x_3 + 10x_4 \le 35$$
$$x_1, x_2, x_3, x_4 = 0, 1$$

a. Solve using trial and error.

b. If you have a computer code for solving integer programs, use it to solve the problem.

8. Refer to the Ohio Trust bank-location problem introduced in Section 12.4. Table 12.2 shows the counties under consideration and the adjacent counties.

a. Write the complete integer programming model if Ohio Trust is considering expansion only into the following counties: Lorain, Huron, Richland, Ashland, Wayne, Medina, and Knox.

b. Solve the problem in part (a) using trial and error.

c. If you have a computer code for integer programs, use it to solve the problem.

9. Grave City is considering the relocation of a number of police substations in order to obtain better enforcement in high-crime areas. The locations being considered together with the areas that can be covered from these locations are given below.

Potential Locations for Substations	Areas Covered
A	1, 5, 7
B	1, 2, 5, 7
C	1, 3, 5
D	2, 4, 5
E	3, 4, 6
F	4, 5, 6
G	1, 5, 6, 7

    a. Formulate an integer programming model that could be solved to find the minimum number of locations necessary to provide coverage to all areas.

    b. Solve the problem in part (a) using any means at your disposal.

10. The Martin-Beck Company is in the process of planning for new production facilities and developing a more efficient distribution system design. At present they have one plant at St. Louis with a capacity of 30,000 units. But because of increased demand, management is considering four potential new plant sites: Detroit, Toledo, Denver, and Kansas City. The transportation tableau below summarizes the projected plant capacities, the cost per unit of shipping from each plant to each destination (upper right-hand corner of each cell), and the demand forecasts over a 1-year planning horizon.

	Boston	Atlanta	Houston	Capacities
Detroit	5	2	3	10,000
Toledo	4	3	4	20,000
Denver	9	7	5	30,000
Kansas City	10	4	2	40,000
St. Louis	8	4	3	30,000
Demand	30,000	20,000	20,000	

Suppose that the fixed costs of constructing the new plants are

Detroit	$175,000
Toledo	$300,000
Denver	$375,000
Kansas City	$500,000

The Martin-Beck Company would like to minimize the total cost of plant construction and distribution of goods.

    a. Develop a *0–1* mixed-integer linear programming model of this problem. (Do not attempt to solve.)

    b. Modify your formulation in part (a) to account for the policy restriction that one plant must be located in Detroit or in Toledo but not both. (Do not attempt to solve.)

    c. Modify your formulation in part (a) to account for the policy restriction that at most two plants can be located in Denver, Kansas City, and St. Louis. (Do not attempt to solve.)

    d. Suppose that there are two possible sizes for the Denver plant, the one mentioned earlier with a capacity of 30,000 units and a cost of $375,000, and another with a capacity of 60,000 units and a cost of $550,000. Modify your formulation in part (a) to account for this consideration. (Do not attempt to solve.)

11. Spencer Enterprises is attempting to choose among a series of new investment alternatives. The potential investment alternatives, the net present value of the future stream of returns, the capital requirements, and the available capital funds over the next 3 years are summarized below:

Alternative	Net Present Value ($)	Capital Requirements ($)		
		Year 1	Year 2	Year 3
Limited warehouse expansion	4,000	3,000	1,000	4,000
Extensive warehouse expansion	6,000	2,500	3,500	3,500
Test market new product	10,500	6,000	4,000	5,000
Advertising campaign	4,000	2,000	1,500	1,800
Basic research	8,000	5,000	1,000	4,000
Purchase new equipment	3,000	1,000	500	900
Capital funds available		10,500	7,000	8,750

a. Develop an integer programming model for maximizing the net present value. (Do not solve.)

b. Assume that only one of the warehouse expansion projects can be implemented. Modify your model of part (a).

c. Suppose that if the test marketing of the new product is carried out, then the advertising campaign must also be conducted. Modify your formulation of part (b) to reflect this new situation.

12. The following questions refer to a capital budgeting problem with six projects represented by 0–1 variables $x_1, x_2, x_3, x_4, x_5, x_6$.

a. Write a constraint modeling a situation in which two and only two of the projects 1, 3, 5, and 6 must be undertaken.

b. Write a constraint modeling a situation in which projects 3 and 5 must be undertaken simultaneously, if at all.

c. Write a constraint modeling a situation in which project 1 or 4 must be undertaken but not both.

d. Write constraints modeling a situation where project 4 cannot be undertaken unless projects 1 and 3 are also undertaken.

e. Revise the requirement in part (d) to accommodate the case in which, when projects 1 and 3 are undertaken, project 4 must also be undertaken.

13. The Northshore Bank is working to develop an efficient work schedule for full-time and part-time tellers. The schedule must provide for efficient operation of the bank including adequate customer service, employee breaks, and so on. On Fridays the bank is open from 9:00 A.M. to 7:00 P.M. The number of tellers necessary to provide adequate customer service during each hour of operation is summarized below.

Time	9–10	10–11	11–12	12–1	1–2	2–3	3–4	4–5	5–6	6–7
Number of Tellers	6	4	8	10	9	6	4	7	6	6

Each full-time employee starts on the hour and works a 4-hour shift, followed by 1 hour for lunch and then a 3-hour shift. Part-time employees work one 4-hour shift beginning on the hour and extending for 4 consecutive hours. Considering salary and fringe benefits, full-time employees cost the bank $7.50 per hour ($52.50 per day), and part-time employees cost the bank $4 per hour ($16 per day).

a. Formulate an integer programming model that can be used to develop a schedule that will satisfy customer service needs at a minimum employee cost. (*Hint*: Let x_i = number of full-time employees coming on duty at the beginning of hour i and y_i = number of part-time employees coming on duty at the beginning of hour i.)

b. Solve the linear programming relaxation of your model in part (a).

c. Solve for the optimal schedule of tellers. Comment on the solution.

d. After reviewing the solution to part (c), the bank manager has realized that some additional requirements must be specified. Specifically, she wants to ensure that one full-time employee is on duty at all times and that there is a staff of at least five full-time employees. Revise your model to incorporate these additional requirements and solve for the optimal solution.

14. CHB, Inc. is a bank holding company that is evaluating the potential for expanding into a 13-county region in the southwestern part of the state. State law permits establishing branches in any county that is adjacent to a county in which a PPB (principal place of business) is located. Below is a map of the 13-county region; the population of each county also is indicated on the map.

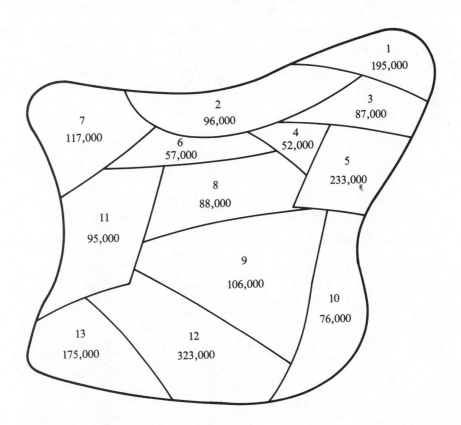

a. Assume that only one PPB can be established in the region. Where should it be located in order to maximize the population served? *Hint*: Review the Ohio Trust formulation in Section 12.4. Consider minimizing the population not served and introduce variable $y_i = 1$ if it is not possible to establish a branch in county i and $y_i = 0$ otherwise.

b. Suppose that two PPBs can be established in the region. Where should they be located to maximize the population served?

c. Management has learned that a bank located in county 5 is considering selling. If CHB, Inc. purchases this bank, it will establish for CHB a PPB in county 5 and provide a base for beginning expansion in the region. What advice would you give the management of CHB?

Case Problem
Textbook Publishing

ASW Publishing, Inc., a small publisher of college textbooks, must reach a decision regarding which books to publish next year. The books that the company is considering are listed in the following table, along with the projected sales that are expected from each book over the next 3 years if the book is published.

Book Subject	Type of Book	Projected Sales (units)
Business calculus	New	20,000
Finite mathematics	Revision	30,000
General statistics	New	15,000
Mathematical statistics	New	10,000
Business statistics	Revision	25,000
Finance	New	18,000
Financial accounting	New	25,000
Managerial accounting	Revision	50,000
English literature	New	20,000
German	New	30,000

The books that are listed as revisions are texts that ASW already has under contract; these texts are being considered for publication as new editions. The books that are listed as new have been reviewed by the company but contracts as yet have not been signed.

The company has three individuals who can be assigned to these projects, all of whom have varying amounts of time available; John has 60 days available, Susan has 40 days available, and Monica has 40 days available. The number of days required by each person to complete each project are shown on page 514; in this table an "X" indicates that the person will not be used for the project because of a lack of expertise in the area, a personality conflict with the author(s), or some other reason. At least two staff members are capable of being assigned to each project except the finance book.

ASW will not publish more than two statistics books or more than one accounting text in a single year. In addition, management has decided that one of the mathematics books (business calculus or finite math) must be published, but not both.

Managerial Report

Prepare a report for the general manager of ASW that describes your findings and recommendations regarding the best publication strategy for ASW to follow next year. In carrying out your analysis, assume that the fixed costs and the per-unit sales revenues

Book Subject	John	Susan	Monica
Business calculus	30	40	X
Finite mathematics	16	24	X
General statistics	24	X	30
Mathematical statistics	20	X	24
Business statistics	10	X	16
Finance	X	X	14
Financial accounting	X	24	26
Managerial accounting	X	28	30
English literature	40	34	30
German	X	50	36

are approximately equal for all books; thus management is interested primarily in maximizing the total sales volume.

The general manager has also asked that you include recommendations regarding the following possible changes:

1. If it would be advantageous to do so, Susan can be moved off another project in order to allow her to work 12 more days.
2. If it would be advantageous to do so, Monica can also be made available for another 10 days.
3. If one or more of the revisions could be postponed for another year, should they be? Clearly the company will risk losing market share by postponing a revision.

Include details of your analysis in an appendix to your report.

Quantitative Methods
in Practice

Ketron*
Arlington, Virginia

Ketron, Inc. is a consulting firm with several branch offices located throughout the United States. An important part of Ketron's business involves national defense and other government applications.

The Management Science Systems division of Ketron is responsible for the maintenance, development, enhancement, and marketing of MPSIII, a proprietary mathematical programming system for use on IBM computers. Members of the Management Science Systems division consult with users of MPSIII and assist them in developing and implementing solutions to their problems. One such mixed-integer programming (MIP) application developed for a major sporting equipment company is outlined below.

A Customer Order Allocation Model

A major sporting equipment company satisfies demand for its products by making shipments from its factories and other locations around the country where inventories are maintained. The company markets approximately 300 products and has about 30 sources of supply (factory and warehouse locations). The problem of interest is to determine how best to allocate customer orders to the various sources of supply such that the total manufacturing cost is minimized. Although transportation cost is not directly considered, it can be accounted for indirectly by not including variables corresponding to shipments from distant locations. Figure A12.1 provides a graphical representation of this problem. Note in the figure that each customer can receive shipments from only a few of the various sources of supply. For example, we see that customer 1 may be supplied by sources *A* or *B*, customer 2 may be supplied only by source *A*, and so on.

The customer order allocation problem is solved periodically. In a typical period there are between 30 and 40 customers to be supplied. Since most customers require several products, there are usually between 600 and 800 orders that must be assigned to the sources of supply.

The sporting equipment company classifies each customer order as either a "guaranteed" or a "secondary" order. Guaranteed orders are single-source orders in that they must be filled by a single supplier to ensure that the complete order will be delivered to the customer at one time. It is this "single source" requirement that necessitates the use

---

*The authors are indebted to J. A. Tomlin, Ketron, Inc., San Bruno, Calif., for providing this application.

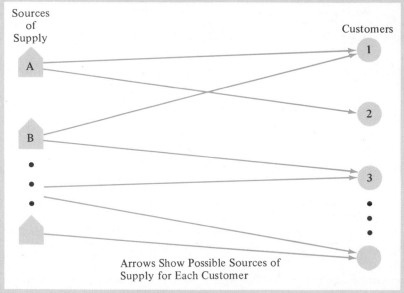

Sources
of
Supply

Customers

Arrows Show Possible Sources of
Supply for Each Customer

Figure A12.1
Graphical Representation of the Customer Order-Allocation Problem

of integer variables in the model. Approximately 80% of the company's orders are guaranteed orders.

Secondary orders can be split among the various sources of supply. These orders are made by customers restocking inventory, and there is no problem in receiving partial shipments from different sources at different times. The total of all secondary orders for a given product is treated as a goal or target in the model formulation. Deviations below the goal are permitted, but a penalty cost is associated with these deviations in the objective function. When deviations occur in the optimal solution, the secondary orders will not be completely satisfied; the ''shortfall'' is spread among customers in specified proportions.

Manufacturing considerations are such that raw material availability and the type of process used constrain the amount of production. In addition, groups of items that are similar may belong to a ''model group'' that must be jointly constrained at some factories. There are also several restrictions on international shipping. For various policy reasons, shipments between sources and customers in certain countries may not be made. This reduces the number of variables in the model but necessitates extensive data checking to ensure that all ''guaranteed'' orders have a permissible source. If they do not, some means must be found to make the problem feasible before even beginning to solve the mixed-integer programming model.

The primary objective of the model is to minimize the total manufacturing costs, subject to the requirement that the guaranteed orders be met. As indicated previously, the deviations below the secondary demand goals are dealt with by defining ''shortfall'' variables with an associated cost. This cost represents a penalty for not having the item in inventory when it is required.

A description of the constraints and the objective function for the model is presented below.

Constraints

Guaranteed orders: Each customer's order for each product is assigned to a single supplier. (This is a multiple-choice constraint.)

Secondary orders: For each product the total amount of secondary demand assigned plus the shortfall must equal the total demand goal (target).

Raw material capacities: The amount of each type of raw material used at a supply source cannot exceed the amount available.

Manufacturing capacities: At each supply source the capacity for each type of production process cannot be exceeded.

Individual product capacities: The amount of product produced at a site cannot exceed that site's capacity for the product.

Group capacities: The total production for a group of similar products at a site cannot exceed that site's capacity for the group of products.

Objective Function

The objective is to minimize the sum of (1) the manufacturing cost for guaranteed orders, (2) the manufacturing cost for secondary orders, and (3) the penalty cost for unsatisfied secondary demand.

Model Solution

It is unreasonable to expect to obtain an optimal solution for a problem of this complexity. Furthermore, the methodology for handling the secondary demand means that an ''optimum'' is of questionable interpretation. What is needed is a ''good'' feasible mixed-integer solution. This is one of the advantages of the branch-and-bound solution procedure. If an integer solution is found whose value is within a few percent of the value of the lower bound given by the LP Relaxation, room for improvement is obviously small.

The solution procedure used is to make a sequence of runs, each beginning where the previous one terminated. Each run allows at most 40 linear programming evaluations (boundings), though many more variables will usually be set to some integer value (branched on). In almost every case the first such run, which includes finding the linear programming relaxation solution, produces a solution satisfactory to the user.

A fairly typical problem has about 800 constraints, 2000 *0–1* assignment variables for the guaranteed orders, and 500 continuous variables associated with the secondary orders. This model is solved using Ketron's MPSIII system. The computer time consumed in producing a solution is approximately 6 minutes on an IBM 3033. Almost half of this time, however, is used to generate the model, optimize the linear programming relaxation, and produce extensive solution reports.

Implementation Notes

In large-scale applications such as this, considerable systems work is involved in generating the data for the model and the managerial reports. Special data processing languages are often available to ease the programming burden of these phases. The DATAFORM language facility of MPSIII is used to generate the data for this model and to prepare the reports.

In this application it is necessary to make a completely separate preprocessing run to check for internal consistency and errors in the data. Only when the data appear logically error-free is the model generated and solved. Although tedious, this kind of preprocessing effort is critical for mixed-integer models, since the cost of solving the wrong model can be significant. Furthermore, in some cases the data preprocessing step permits the size of the model to be reduced. Such a reduction is possible in this application when a demand for a product has only one legitimate source. The computational benefits of such reductions can be substantial.

Question

1. It is mentioned that an "optimum" is of questionable interpretation. Discuss what is meant by this statement. Does it mean that any feasible solution is acceptable?

CHAPTER

13

Project Management: PERT/CPM

In many situations managers assume the responsibility for planning, scheduling, and controlling projects that consist of numerous separate jobs or tasks performed by a variety of departments, individuals, etc. Often these projects are so large and/or complex that the manager cannot possibly keep all the information pertaining to the plan, schedule, and progress of the project in his or her head. In these situations the techniques of PERT (*Program Evaluation and Review Technique*) and CPM (*Critical Path Method*) have proved to be extremely valuable in assisting managers in carrying out their project management responsibilities.

PERT and CPM have been used to plan, schedule, and control a wide variety of projects, such as

1. Research and development of new products and processes
2. Construction of plants, buildings, highways
3. Maintenance of large and complex equipment
4. Design and installation of new systems

In projects such as these, project managers must schedule and coordinate the various jobs or activities so that the entire project is completed on time. A complicating factor in carrying out this task is the interdependence of the activities; for example, some activities depend on the completion of other activities before they can be started. When we realize that projects can have as many as several thousand specific activities, we see why project managers look for procedures that will help them answer questions such as the following:

1. What is the total time to complete the project?
2. What are the scheduled start and finish dates for each activity?
3. Which activities are "critical" and must be completed *exactly* as scheduled in order to keep the project on schedule?
4. How long can "noncritical" activities be delayed before they cause a delay in the total project?

As you will see, PERT and CPM can be used to help answer the above questions.

While PERT and CPM have the same general purpose and utilize much of the same terminology, the techniques were actually developed independently. PERT was introduced in the late 1950s specifically for planning, scheduling, and controlling the Polaris missile project. Since many jobs or activities associated with the Polaris missile project had never been attempted previously, it was difficult to predict the time to complete the various jobs or activities. Consequently, PERT was developed with an objective of being able to handle uncertainties in activity completion times.

On the other hand, CPM was developed primarily for scheduling and controlling industrial projects where job or activity times were considered known. CPM offered the option of reducing activity times by adding more workers and/or resources, usually at an increased cost. Thus a distinguishing feature of CPM was that it enabled time and cost trade-offs for the various activities in the project.

In today's usage the distinction between PERT and CPM as two separate techniques has largely disappeared. Modern project planning, scheduling, and controlling procedures have essentially combined the features of PERT and CPM.

13.1

PERT/CPM NETWORKS

The first step in the PERT/CPM project scheduling process is to determine the jobs, or *activities*, that make up the project. As a simple illustration involving the process of buying a small business, consider the list of four activities shown in Table 13.1. The development of an accurate list of activities such as this is a key step in any project. Since we will be planning the entire project and estimating the project completion time based on the activity list, incorrect specification of activities will lead to inaccurate schedules. We will assume that a careful analysis has been completed for the example problem and that Table 13.1 lists all activities for the small business project.

Table 13.1
Activity List for the Example Project of Buying a Small Business

Activity	Description	Immediate Predecessors
A	Develop a list of sources for financing	—
B	Analyze the financial records of the business	—
C	Develop a business plan (e.g., sales projections, cash flow projections, etc.)	B
D	Submit a proposal to a lending institution	A, C

Note that Table 13.1 also contains a column labeled ''Immediate Predecessors.'' The *immediate predecessors* for a particular activity are the activities that, when completed, enable the start of the activity. For example, the information in Table 13.1 tells us we can start work on activities *A* and *B* anytime, since neither of these activities depends on the completion of prior activities. However, activity *C* cannot be started until activity *B* has been completed, and activity *D* cannot be started until both activities *A* and *C* have been completed. As you will see, the immediate predecessors must be known for each activity in order to describe the interdependencies among the activities in the project.

In Figure 13.1 we have drawn a network that not only depicts the activities listed in Table 13.1 but also portrays the predecessor relationships among the activities. This graphical representation is referred to as the PERT/CPM network for the project. The activities are shown on the branches, or arcs, of the network. The circles, or nodes, of

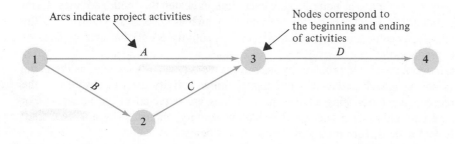

Figure 13.1
PERT/CPM Network for the Example Project of Buying a Small Business

the network correspond to the beginning and ending of the activities. The completion of all the activities that lead into a node is referred to as an *event*. For example, node 2 corresponds to the event that activity *B* has been completed, and node 3 corresponds to the event that both activities *A* and *C* have been completed.

Let us now attempt to develop the network for a project having the following activities and immediate predecessors:

Activity	Immediate Predecessors
A	—
B	—
C	*B*
D	*A, C*
E	*C*
F	*C*
G	*D, E, F*

A portion of the PERT/CPM network that could be used for the first four activities is as follows:

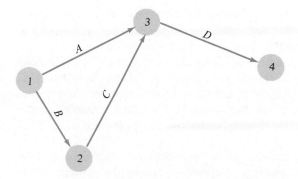

This portion of the network causes no particular problem for activity D, since it shows activities A and C as the correct immediate predecessors. However, when we attempt to add activity E to the network, we encounter a problem. At first we might attempt to show activity E beginning at node 3. However, this indicates that both activities A and C are the immediate predecessors for activity E, which is incorrect. Referring to the original activity schedule for the project, we see that activity E only has activity C as its immediate predecessor.

We can avoid the above problem by inserting a *dummy activity*, which, as the name implies, is not an actual activity but rather a fictitious activity used to ensure that the proper precedence relationships among the activities are depicted in the network. For example, we can add node 5 and insert a dummy activity, indicated by a dashed line, from node 5 to node 3, forming the network shown below.

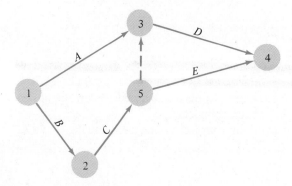

With the above change in the network, activity E starting at node 5 has the correct predecessor of only activity C. The dummy activity does not have a time requirement

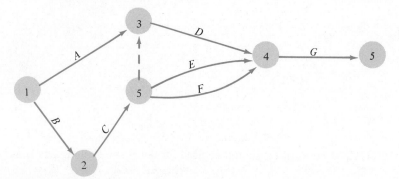

but is used merely to maintain the proper precedence relationships in the network. Note that the insertion of the dummy activity also correctly shows activities A and C as the immediate predecessors for activity D.

The seven-activity network could now be drawn as shown at the bottom of page 522. Note how the network correctly identifies activities D, E, and F as the immediate predecessors for activity G. However, note that activities E and F both start at node 5 and end at node 4. This situation causes problems for certain computer programs that use starting and ending nodes to identify the activities in a PERT/CPM network. In these programs the computer procedure would recognize activities E and F as the same activity, since they have the same starting and ending nodes. When this condition occurs, dummy activities can be added to a network to make sure that two or more activities do not have the same starting and ending nodes. The use of node 7 and a dummy activity as shown below eliminates this problem for activities E and F.

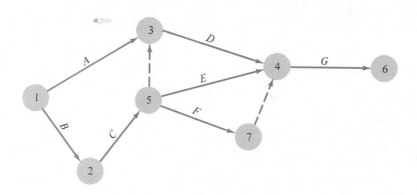

Dummy activities can be used to identify precedence relationships correctly as well as to eliminate the possible confusion of two or more activities having the same starting and ending nodes. Although dummy activities may not be required for all PERT/CPM networks, larger and/or more complex projects may require several dummy activities in order to depict the project network properly.

13.2

PROJECT SCHEDULING WITH PERT/CPM

The owner of the Western Hills Shopping Center is considering modernizing and expanding the current 32-business shopping complex. Financing for the expansion has been arranged through a private investor. If the expansion project is undertaken, the owner hopes to add 8 to 10 new businesses or tenants to the shopping complex.

The specific activities that make up the expansion project are listed in Table 13.2. Note that the list includes the immediate predecessor for each activity as well as the number of weeks required to complete the activity. The PERT/CPM network for the project is shown in Figure 13.2. Check for yourself to see that the network does in fact maintain the immediate predecessor relationships shown in Table 13.2.

Information in Table 13.2 indicates that the total time required to complete all activities in the shopping center expansion project is 51 weeks. However, we can see from the network (Figure 13.2) that several of the activities can be conducted simulta-

Table 13.2
Activity List for the Western Hills Shopping Center Expansion Project

Activity	Activity Description	Immediate Predecessor	Completion Time (weeks)
A	Prepare architectural drawings of planned expansion	—	5
B	Identify potential new tenants	—	6
C	Develop prospectus for tenants	A	4
D	Select contractor	A	3
E	Prepare building permits	A	1
F	Obtain approval for building permits	E	4
G	Construction	D, F	14
H	Finalize contracts with tenants	B, C	12
I	Tenants move in	G, H	2
		Total	51

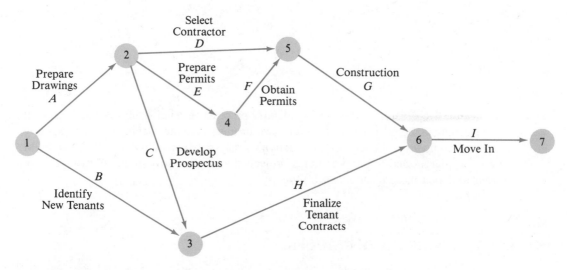

Figure 13.2
PERT/CPM Network for the Western Hills Shopping Center Expansion Project

neously (A and B, for example). Being able to work on two or more activities at the same time will shorten the total project completion time to less than 51 weeks. However, the required project completion time is not available directly from the data in Table 13.2.

In order to facilitate the PERT/CPM computations that we will be making, the project network has been redrawn as shown in Figure 13.3. Note that each activity letter is written above and each activity time is written below the corresponding arc.

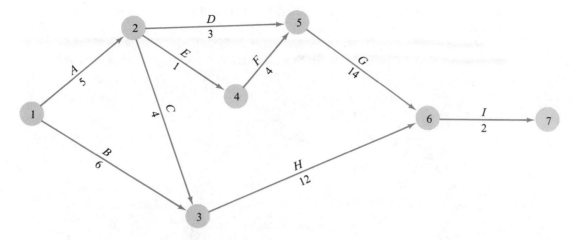

Figure 13.3
Western Hills Shopping Center Project Network with Activity Times

The Critical Path

Once we have the project network and the activity times, we are ready to proceed with the calculations necessary to determine the total time required to complete the project. In addition, we will use the results of the calculations to develop a detailed start and finish schedule for each activity.

In order to determine the project completion time we will have to analyze the network and identify what is called its *critical path*. A *path* is a sequence of connected activities that leads from the starting node (1) to the completion node (7). The connected activities defined by nodes 1–2–3–6–7 form a path consisting of activities *A, C, H,* and *I.* Nodes 1–2–5–6–7 define the path associated with activities *A, D, G,* and *I.* Since *all* paths must be traversed in order to complete the project, we need to analyze the amount of time the various paths require. In particular, we will be interested in the longest path through the network. Since all other paths are shorter in duration, the longest path determines the total time or duration of the project. If activities on the longest path are delayed, the entire project will be delayed. Thus the longest path activities are the *critical activities* of the project, and the longest path is called the *critical path* of the network. If managers wish to reduce the total project time, they will have to reduce the length of the critical path by shortening the duration of the critical activities. The following discussion presents a step-by-step procedure, or algorithm, for finding the critical path of a project network.

Starting at the network's origin (node 1) and using a starting time of 0, compute an *earliest start* and *earliest finish* time for each activity in the network. Let

$$\text{ES} = \text{earliest start time for a particular activity}$$
$$\text{EF} = \text{earliest finish time for a particular activity}$$
$$t = \text{expected activity time for the activity}$$

The following expression can be used to find the earliest finish time for a given activity:

$$\text{EF} = \text{ES} + t \qquad (13.1)$$

For example, for activity A, ES = 0 and t = 5; thus the earliest finish time for activity A is EF = 0 + 5 = 5.

We will write the earliest start and earliest finish times directly on the network in brackets next to the letter of the activity. Using activity A as an example, we have

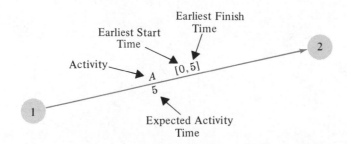

Since activities leaving a node cannot be started until *all* immediately preceding activities have been completed, the following rule can be used to determine the earliest start times for activities:

> **Earliest Start Time Rule:**
> The earliest start time for an activity leaving a particular node is equal to the *largest* of the earliest finish times for all activities entering the node.

In applying this rule to a portion of the network involving activities A, B, C, and H, we obtain the following:

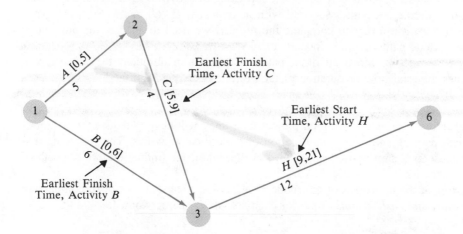

Note that in applying the earliest start time rule for activity C, which leaves node 2, we first recognized that activity A is the only activity entering node 2. Since the earliest finish time for activity A is 5, the earliest start time for activity C is 5. Thus the earliest finish time for activity C must be EF = ES + t = 5 + 4 = 9.

The above diagram also shows that the earliest finish time for activity B is 6. Applying the earliest start time rule for activity H, we see that the earliest start time for this activity must be equal to the largest of the earliest finish times for the two activities that enter node 3, activities *B* and *C*. Thus the earliest start time for activity *H* is 9, and the earliest finish time for activity *H* is EF = ES + t = 9 + 12 = 21.

Proceeding in a *forward pass* through the network, we can establish the earliest start time and then the earliest finish time for each activity. The Western Hills Shopping Center PERT/CPM network, with the ES and EF values for each activity, is shown in Figure 13.4. Note that the earliest finish time for activity *I*, the last activity, is 26 weeks. Thus the earliest completion time for the entire project is 26 weeks.

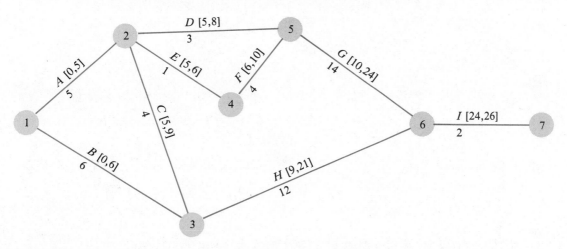

Figure 13.4
Western Hills Shopping Center Project with Earliest Start Times and Earliest Finish Times Shown above the Activity Arcs

We now continue the algorithm for finding the critical path by making a *backward pass* calculation. Beginning at the completion node (node 7) and using a latest finish time of 26 for activity *I*, we trace back through the network computing a *latest start* and *latest finish* time for each activity. Let

LS = latest start time for a particular activity

LF = latest finish time for a particular activity

The following expression can be used to find the latest start time for a given activity:

$$LS = LF - t \qquad (13.2)$$

Given LF = 26 and t = 2 for activity *I*, the latest start time for this activity can be computed as LS = 26 − 2 = 24.

The following rule is necessary in order to determine the latest finish time for any activity in the network:

> **Latest Finish Time Rule:**
> The latest finish time for an activity entering a particular node is equal to the *smallest* of the latest start times for all activities leaving the node.

Logically, the above rule states that the latest time an activity can be finished is equal to the earliest (smallest) value for the latest start time of following activities. The complete network with the LS and LF backward pass calculations is shown in Figure 13.5. The latest start and latest finish times for the activities are written in brackets directly below the earliest start and earliest finish times.

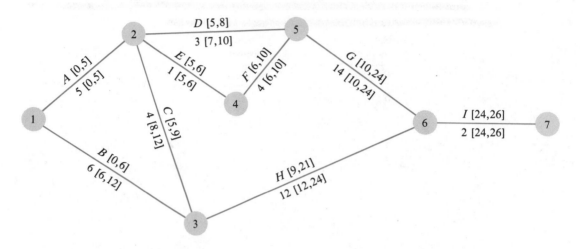

Figure 13.5
Western Hills Shopping Center Project with Latest Start Times and Latest Finish Times Shown below the Activity Arcs

Note the application of the latest finish time rule for activity A, which enters node 2. The latest finish time for activity A (LF = 5) is the smallest of the latest start times for the activities that leave node 2; that is, the smallest LS value for activities C (LS = 8), E (LS = 5), and D (LS = 7) is 5.

After obtaining the start and finish activity times as summarized in Figure 13.5, we can find the amount of slack or free time associated with each of the activities. *Slack* is defined as the length of time an activity can be delayed without affecting the completion date for the entire project. The amount of slack for each activity is computed as follows:

$$\text{Slack} = \text{LS} - \text{ES} = \text{LF} - \text{EF} \tag{13.3}$$

For example, we see that the slack associated with activity C is LS − ES = 8 − 5 = 3 weeks. This means that activity C can be delayed up to 3 weeks (start anywhere between weeks 5 and 8) and the entire project can still be completed in 26 weeks. Thus activity C is not a critical activity and is not part of the critical path. Using equation (13.3), we see that the slack associated with activity E is LS − ES = 5 − 5 = 0. Thus activity E has no slack time and must be held to the 5-week start time schedule. Since activity E cannot be delayed without affecting the entire project, it is a critical activity and is on the critical path. In general, the critical path activities are the activities with zero slack.

The start and finish times shown on the network in Figure 13.5 provide a detailed schedule for all activities. That is, from Figure 13.5 we know the earliest and latest start and finish times for the activities. Putting this information in tabular form provides the activity schedule shown in Table 13.3. Note that by computing the slack associated with each activity, we see that activities A, E, F, G, and I each have zero slack; hence these activities form the critical path in the shopping center expansion network. Note that Table 13.3 also shows the slack or delay that can be tolerated for the noncritical activities before these activities will cause a project delay.

Table 13.3
Activity Schedule for the Western Hills Shopping Center Expansion Project

Activity	Earliest Start (ES)	Latest Start (LS)	Earliest Finish (EF)	Latest Finish (LF)	Slack (LS − ES)	Critical Activity
A	0	0	5	5	0	Yes
B	0	6	6	12	6	
C	5	8	9	12	3	
D	5	7	8	10	2	
E	5	5	6	6	0	Yes
F	6	6	10	10	0	Yes
G	10	10	24	24	0	Yes
H	9	12	21	24	3	
I	24	24	26	26	0	Yes

Contributions of PERT/CPM

Previously we stated that project managers look for procedures that will help answer many important questions regarding the planning, scheduling, and controlling of projects. Let us reconsider these questions in light of the information the PERT/CPM network and critical path calculations have provided about the Western Hills Shopping Center expansion project.

1. What is the total time to complete the project?
   Answer: PERT/CPM has shown that the project can be completed in 26 weeks if the individual activities are completed on schedule.
2. What are the scheduled start and completion times for each activity?
   Answer: PERT/CPM has provided the detailed activity schedule that shows the earliest start, latest start, earliest finish, and latest finish times for each activity (Table 13.3).
3. Which activities are "critical" and must be completed *exactly* as scheduled in order to keep the project on schedule?
   Answer: PERT/CPM has identified the five activities—A, E, F, G, and I—as the critical activities for the project.
4. How long can "noncritical" activities be delayed before they cause a delay in the completion time for the project?
   Answer: PERT/CPM has identified the slack time available for all activities as shown in Table 13.3.

The PERT/CPM module of *The Management Scientist* computer software package could have been used to develop the activity schedule and critical path for the Western Hills Shopping Center project. Data input for the module includes the immediate predecessors and activity completion times as shown in Table 13.2. Output from the module is the activity schedule as shown in Table 13.3. The module also identifies the critical path A–E–F–G–I and the project completion time of 26 weeks. Only a few minutes were required to enter the data and generate the output.

ACTIVITY	EARLIEST START	LATEST START	EARLIEST FINISH	LATEST FINISH	SLACK	CRITICAL ACTIVITY
A	0	0	5	5	0	YES
B	0	6	6	12	6	
C	5	8	9	12	3	
D	5	7	8	10	2	
E	5	5	6	6	0	YES
F	6	6	10	10	0	YES
G	10	10	24	24	0	YES
H	9	12	21	24	3	
I	24	24	26	26	0	YES

CRITICAL PATH: A–E–F–G–I

PROJECT COMPLETION TIME = 26

Figure 13.6
Activity Schedule for the Western Hills Shopping Center Project Using *The Management Scientist* Software Package

Summary of the PERT/CPM Critical Path Procedure

Before leaving this section, let us summarize the PERT/CPM critical path procedure that can be used to plan, schedule, and control projects.

Step 1 Develop a list of activities that make up the project.

Step 2 Determine the immediate predecessor activities for each activity in the project.

Step 3 Estimate the completion time for each activity.

Step 4 Draw a network depicting the activities and immediate predecessors listed in steps 1 and 2.

Step 5 Using the network and the activity time estimates, determine the earliest start time and the earliest finish time for each activity by making a forward pass through the network. The earliest finish time for the last activity in the project identifies the completion time for the entire project.

Step 6 Using the project completion time identified in step 5 as the latest finish time for the last activity, make a backward pass through the network to identify the latest start time and latest finish time for each activity.

| Step 7 | Use the difference between the latest start time and the earliest start time for each activity to identify the slack time available for the activity.

| Step 8 | The critical path activities are the activities with zero slack.

| Step 9 | Use the information from steps 5 and 6 to develop a detailed activity schedule for the project.

13.3

PROJECT SCHEDULING WITH UNCERTAIN ACTIVITY TIMES

In this section we consider the details of project scheduling for a problem involving the research and development of a new product. Because many of the activities in this project have never been previously attempted, the project manager wants to identify and account for the uncertainties in the activity times. Let us show how project scheduling can be conducted with uncertain activity times.

The Daugherty Porta-Vac Project

The H. S. Daugherty Company has manufactured industrial vacuum cleaning systems for a number of years. Recently a member of the company's new-product research team submitted a report suggesting that the company consider manufacturing a cordless vacuum cleaner that could be powered by a rechargeable battery. The vacuum cleaner, referred to as a Porta-Vac, could contribute to Daugherty's expansion into the household market. Management hopes that the new product can be manufactured at a reasonable cost and that its portability and no-cord convenience will make it extremely attractive.

Daugherty's management would like to initiate a project to study the feasibility of proceeding with the Porta-Vac idea. The end result of the feasibility study will be a report recommending the action to be taken for the new product. In order to complete the feasibility study, information must be obtained from the firm's research and development (R&D), product testing, manufacturing, cost estimating, and market research groups. How long do you think this feasibility study will take? When should you tell the product testing group to schedule its work? Obviously, we do not have enough information to answer these questions at this time. In the following discussion we will show how to answer these questions and how to provide the complete schedule and control information for the project.

Again, the first step in the project scheduling process is to determine all the activities that make up the project as well as the immediate predecessors for each activity. For the Porta-Vac project, these data are shown in Table 13.4.

The PERT/CPM network for the Porta-Vac project is shown in Figure 13.7. Check for yourself to see that the network does in fact maintain the immediate predecessor relationships shown in Table 13.4.

Uncertain Activity Times

Once we have established a network for the project, we will need information on the time required to complete each activity. For repeat projects, such as construction and/or maintenance projects, managers may have the experience and historical data necessary

Table 13.4
Activity List for the Daugherty Porta-Vac Project

Activity	Description	Immediate Predecessors
A	R&D product design	—
B	Plan market research	—
C	Routing (manufacturing engineering)	A
D	Build prototype model	A
E	Prepare marketing brochure	A
F	Cost estimates (industrial engineering)	C
G	Preliminary product testing	D
H	Market survey	B, E
I	Pricing and forecast report	H
J	Final report	F, G, I

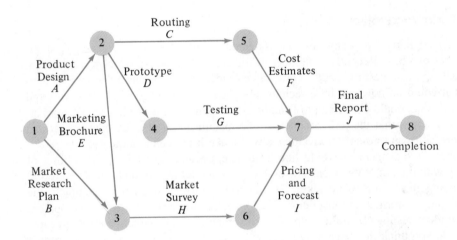

Figure 13.7
Network for the Porta-Vac Project

to provide accurate activity time estimates. However, for new or unique projects, activity time estimation may be significantly more difficult. In fact, in many cases activity times are uncertain and are perhaps best described by a range of possible values rather than one specific activity time estimate. In these instances the uncertain activity times are treated as random variables with associated probability distributions. As a result, probability statements will be provided about the project meeting specific completion dates.

In order to incorporate uncertain activity times into the analysis, we will need to obtain three time estimates for each activity. The three estimates are

Optimistic time (a): The activity time if everything progresses in an ideal manner
Most probable time (m): The most likely activity time under normal conditions
Pessimistic time (b): The activity time if we encounter significant delays

The three estimates enable the manager to specify the most likely activity time and then express the uncertainty by providing time estimates ranging from the best possible (optimistic) time to the worst possible (pessimistic) time.

As an illustration of the PERT/CPM procedure with uncertain activity times, let us consider the optimistic, most probable, and pessimistic time estimates for the Porta-Vac activities as presented in Table 13.5.

Table 13.5
Optimistic, Most Probable, and Pessimistic Activity Time
Estimates (in weeks) for the Porta-Vac Project

Activity	Optimistic (a)	Most Probable (m)	Pessimistic (b)
A	4	5	12
B	1	1.5	5
C	2	3	4
D	3	4	11
E	2	3	4
F	1.5	2	2.5
G	1.5	3	4.5
H	2.5	3.5	7.5
I	1.5	2	2.5
J	1	2	3

Using activity A as an example, we see that this activity will require from 4 weeks (optimistic) to 12 weeks (pessimistic), with the most likely time 5 weeks. If the activity could be repeated a large number of times, what would be the average time for the activity? This average or *expected activity time* (t) can be determined from the following formula:

$$t = \frac{a + 4m + b}{6} \tag{13.4}$$

For activity A we have an estimated average or expected time of

$$t_A = \frac{4 + 4(5) + 12}{6} = \frac{36}{6} = 6 \text{ weeks}$$

With uncertain activity times we can use the common statistical measure of the *variance* to describe the dispersion or variability in the activity time values. The variance of the activity time is given by the following formula[1]:

$$\sigma^2 = \left(\frac{b - a}{6}\right)^2 \tag{13.5}$$

---

[1]The variance equation is based on the notion that a standard deviation is approximately ⅙ of the difference between the extreme values of the distribution: $(b - a)/6$. The variance is simply the square of the standard deviation.

As you can see, the difference between the pessimistic (*b*) and optimistic (*a*) time estimates greatly affects the value of the variance. Large differences in these two values reflects a high degree of uncertainty in the activity time. Accordingly, the variance given by equation (13.5) will be large. Using equation (13.5), we see that the measure of uncertainty— that is, the variance—of activity *A*, denoted σ_A^2, is

$$\sigma_A^2 = \left(\frac{12 - 4}{6}\right)^2 = \left(\frac{8}{6}\right)^2 = 1.78$$

Equations (13.4) and (13.5) are based on the assumption that the uncertainty in activity times can be described by a *beta probability distribution*.[2] With this assumption the probability distribution for the time to complete activity *A* is as shown in Figure 13.8. Using equations (13.4) and (13.5) and the data in Table 13.5, the expected times and variances for all of the Porta-Vac activities are as summarized in Table 13.6.

A network depicting the Porta-Vac project with expected activity times is shown in Figure 13.9. Note that above each arc we have written the letter of the corresponding activity, and directly under the arc we have written the expected time for the activity.

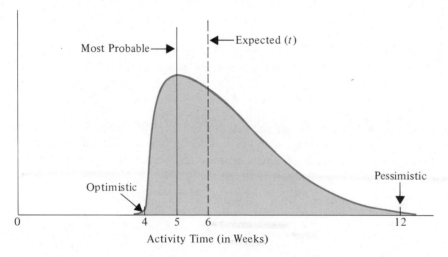

Figure 13.8
Activity Time Distribution for Product Design Activity *A* of the Porta-Vac Project

The Critical Path

Once we have the network and the expected activity times, we are ready to proceed with the critical path calculations necessary to determine the expected project completion time and a detailed activity schedule. In the critical path calculations we will treat the expected activity times (Table 13.6) as the *fixed length* or *known duration* of each activity. As a result, we can use the critical path calculation procedure introduced in Section 13.2 to find the critical path for the Porta-Vac project. After the critical activities and the expected

[2]In order for the equations for *t* and σ^2 to be exact, additional assumptions are required about the parameters of the beta probability distribution. However, even when these additional assumptions are not made, the equations still tend to provide very good and useful approximations of *t* and σ^2.

Table 13.6
Expected Times and Variances for the Porta-Vac
Activities

Activity	Expected Time (in weeks)	Variance
A	6	1.78
B	2	0.44
C	3	0.11
D	5	1.78
E	3	0.11
F	2	0.03
G	3	0.25
H	4	0.69
I	2	0.03
J	2	0.11

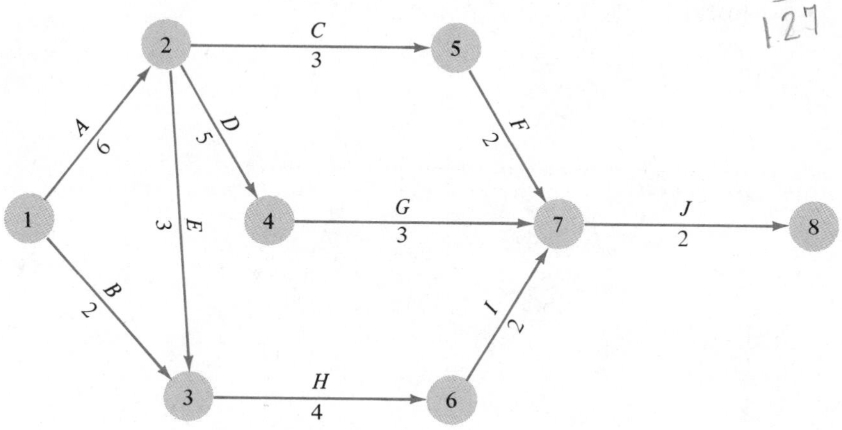

Handwritten notes in right margin:

1.78^2
$+ 1.78$
.25
.11
3.92

#16   A D G J
6 5 3 2 = 16

A C F J
6 3 2 2 = 13

1.78
.11
.03
.11
2.03

B H I J
2 4 2 2 = 10
.44
.69
.03
.11
1.27

Figure 13.9
Porta-Vac Project Network with Expected Activity Times

project completion time have been determined, we will analyze the effect of the activity time variability.

Proceeding with a forward pass through the network shown in Figure 13.9, we can establish the earliest start (ES) and earliest finish (EF) times for each activity. The PERT/CPM network with the ES and EF values is shown in Figure 13.10. Note that the earliest finish time for activity *J*, the last activity, is 17 weeks. Thus the expected completion time for the entire project is 17 weeks. Next we continue with the procedure for finding the critical path by making a backward pass through the network. The backward pass provides the latest start (LS) and latest finish (LF) times shown in Figure 13.11.

The start and finish times shown in Figure 13.11 provide the detailed schedule for all activities. Putting this information in tabular form provides the activity schedule shown in Table 13.7. Note that the slack time = (LS − ES) is also shown for each activity. The activities with zero slack show that activities *A, E, H, I,* and *J* form the critical path for the Porta-Vac project network.

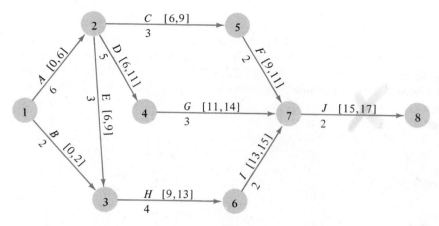

Figure 13.10
Porta-Vac Network with Earliest Start and Earliest Finish Times Shown above Activity Arcs

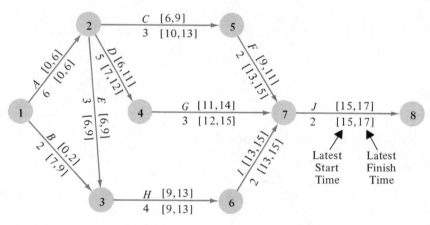

Figure 13.11
Porta-Vac Network with Latest Start and Latest Finish Times Shown below Activity Arcs

Table 13.7
Activity Schedule (in weeks) for the Porta-Vac Project

Activity	Earliest Start (ES)	Latest Start (LS)	Earliest Finish (EF)	Latest Finish (LF)	Slack (LS − ES)	Critical Activity
A	0	0	6	6	0	Yes
B	0	7	2	9	7	
C	6	10	9	13	4	
D	6	7	11	12	1	
E	6	6	9	9	0	Yes
F	9	13	11	15	4	
G	11	12	14	15	1	
H	9	9	13	13	0	Yes
I	13	13	15	15	0	Yes
J	15	15	17	17	0	Yes

Variability in the Project Completion Time

In carrying out the critical path calculations, we treated the activity times as fixed at their expected values; we are now ready to consider the uncertainty in the activity times and determine the effect this uncertainty or variability has on the project completion date. Recall that the critical path determines the duration of the entire project. For the Porta-Vac project the critical path of $A-E-H-I-J$ resulted in an expected project completion time of 17 weeks.

Just as the critical path activities govern the expected project completion time, variation in critical path activities can cause variation in the project completion time. Variation in noncritical path activities will ordinarily have no effect on the project completion time because of the slack time associated with these activities. However, if a noncritical activity were delayed long enough to expend all its slack time, then that activity would become part of a new critical path, and further delays would extend the project completion time. Variability leading to a longer than expected total time for the critical path activities will always extend the project completion time. Let us use the variance in the critical path activities to determine the variance in the project completion time.

If we let T denote the project completion time, then T, which is determined by the critical activities $A-E-H-I-J$ in the Porta-Vac problem, has the expected value of

$$E(T) = t_A + t_E + t_H + t_I + t_J$$
$$= 6 + 3 + 4 + 2 + 2 = 17 \text{ weeks}$$

where t_A, t_E, t_H, t_I, and t_J are the expected completion times for the critical path activities.

Similarly, the variance in the project completion time is given by the sum of the variances of the critical path activities. Thus the variance for the Porta-Vac project completion time is given by

$$\text{Var}(T) = \sigma_A^2 + \sigma_E^2 + \sigma_H^2 + \sigma_I^2 + \sigma_J^2$$
$$= 1.78 + 0.11 + 0.69 + 0.03 + 0.11 = 2.72$$

where σ_A^2, σ_E^2, σ_H^2, σ_I^2, and σ_J^2 are the variances of the critical path activities.

The above computation of var (T) is based on the assumption that the activity times are independent. If two or more activities are dependent, the formula provides only an approximation to the variance of the project completion time. The closer the activities are to being independent, the better is the approximation.

Since we know that the standard deviation is the square root of the variance, we can compute the standard deviation σ for the Porta-Vac project completion time as follows:

$$\sigma = \sqrt{2.72} = 1.65$$

A final assumption, that the distribution of the project completion time T follows a normal or bell-shaped distribution,[3] allows us to draw the distribution shown in Figure 13.12. With this distribution we can compute the probability of meeting a specified project completion date. For example, suppose that management has allotted 20 weeks

[3]The use of the normal distribution as an approximation is based on the central limit theorem, which indicates that the sum of independent activity times follows a normal distribution as the number of activities becomes large.

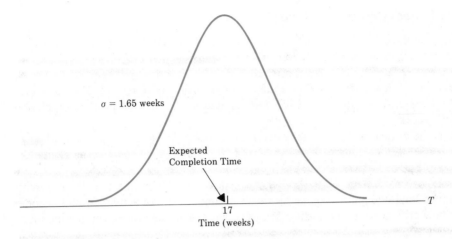

Figure 13.12
Normal Distribution of the Project Completion Time for the Porta-Vac Project

for the Porta-Vac project. What is the probability that we will meet the 20-week deadline? Using the normal distribution from Figure 13.12, we are asking for the probability that $T \leq 20$. This is shown graphically as the shaded area in Figure 13.13. The z value for the normal distribution at $T = 20$ is given by

$$z = \frac{20 - 17}{1.65} = 1.82$$

Using $z = 1.82$ and the tables for the normal distribution (see Appendix C), we see that the probability of the project meeting the 20-week deadline is $0.4656 + 0.5000 = 0.9656$. Thus while activity time variability may cause the project to exceed the 17-week expected duration, there is an excellent chance that the project will be completed before the 20-week deadline. Similar probability calculations can be made for other project deadline alternatives.

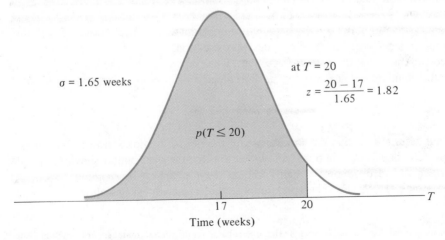

Figure 13.13
Probability of a Porta-Vac Project Completion Date prior to the 20-Week Deadline

Thus we see that a PERT/CPM project scheduling procedure can be used to schedule projects with uncertain activity times. A three-time estimate procedure for each activity (optimistic time, most likely time, and pessimistic time) enables the computation of an expected time and a variance for each activity. Using the expected time as the fixed time, the critical activities and critical path for the project can be found using the procedure presented in Section 13.2. The sum of the expected times of critical path activities provides the expected project completion time. The sum of the variances of critical path activities provides the variance in the project completion time. Using the normal probability distribution assumption for the project completion time, standard procedures from probability can be used to compute the probability of the project being completed by a specific date.

13.4

CONSIDERING TIME-COST TRADE-OFFS

The original developers of the CPM approach to project scheduling provided the project manager with the capability of adding resources to selected activities in an attempt to reduce activity—and thus project—completion times. Since added resources such as more workers, overtime, and so on generally increase project costs, the decision to reduce activity times must take into consideration the additional cost involved. In effect, the project manager has to make a decision that involves trading off decreased activity time against increased project cost.

Table 13.8 defines a two-machine maintenance project consisting of five activities. Since management has had substantial experience with similar projects, the maintenance activities times are considered known; hence a single time estimate is provided for each activity. The network for this project is shown in Figure 13.14.

Table 13.8
Activity List for a Two-Machine Maintenance Project

Activity		Immediate Predecessor	Expected Time (in days)
A	Overhaul machine I	—	7
B	Adjust machine I	A	3
C	Overhaul machine II	—	6
D	Adjust machine II	C	3
E	Test system	B, D	2

Critical path calculations for the maintenance project network are computed following the procedure we used to find the critical path in both the Western Hills Shopping Center expansion and the Porta-Vac networks. Making the forward pass and backward pass calculations for the network in Figure 13.14, we can obtain the activity schedule shown in Table 13.9. As you can see, the zero slack times, and thus the critical path, are associated with activities $A–B–E$ or nodes 1–2–4–5. The length of the critical path, and thus the project, is 12 days.

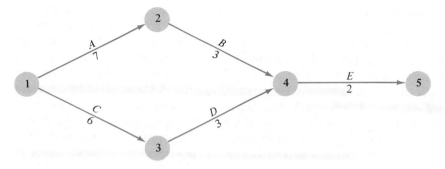

Figure 13.14
Network of a Two-Machine Maintenance Project

Table 13.9
Activity Schedule for the Maintenance Project

Activity	Earliest Start (ES)	Latest Start (LS)	Earliest Finish (EF)	Latest Finish (LF)	Slack (LS − ES)	Critical Activity
A	0	0	7	7	0	Yes
B	7	7	10	10	0	Yes
C	0	1	6	7	1	
D	6	7	9	10	1	
E	10	10	12	12	0	Yes

Crashing Activity Times

Now suppose that the current production levels make it imperative for the maintenance project to be completed within 2 weeks, or 10 working days. By looking at the length of the critical path of the network (12 days), we realize that it is impossible to meet the project completion date unless we can shorten selected activity times. This shortening of activity times, which usually can be achieved by adding resources such as labor or overtime, is referred to as *crashing* the activity times. However, since the added resources associated with crashing activity times usually result in added project costs, we will want to identify the activities that cost least to crash and then crash those activities only the amount necessary to meet the desired project completion time.

In order to determine just where and how much to crash activity times, we will need information on how much each activity can be crashed and how much the crashing process costs. Possibly the best way to accomplish this is to ask management for the following information on each activity:

1. Estimated activity cost under the normal or expected activity time
2. Activity completion time under maximum crashing (that is, shortest possible activity time)
3. Estimated activity cost under maximum crashing

Let

$$\tau_j = \text{normal time for activity } j$$

$$\tau_j' = \text{time for activity } j \text{ under maximum crashing}$$

$$M_j = \text{maximum possible reduction in time for activity } j \text{ due}$$
to maximum crashing

With both τ_j and τ_j' known, we can compute M_j as follows:

$$M_j = \tau_j - \tau_j' \tag{13.6}$$

Next let C_j denote the normal cost for activity j and C_j' denote the cost for activity j under maximum crashing. Thus on a per-unit time basis (for example, per day), the crashing cost K_j for each activity is given by

$$K_j = \frac{C_j' - C_j}{M_j} \tag{13.7}$$

For example, if activity A has a normal activity time of 7 days at a cost of $C_A = \$500$ and a maximum crash activity time of 4 days at a cost of $C_A' = \$800$, equations (13.6) and (13.7) show that activity A can be crashed a maximum of

$$M_A = 7 - 4 = 3 \text{ days}$$

at a crashing cost of

$$K_A = \frac{C_A' - C_A}{M_A} = \frac{800 - 500}{3} = \frac{300}{3} = \$100 \text{ per day}$$

We will make the assumption that any portion or fraction of the activity crash time can be achieved for a corresponding portion of the activity crashing cost. For example, if we decided to crash activity A by only $1\frac{1}{2}$ days, we would assume that this could be accomplished with an added cost of $1\frac{1}{2}(\$100) = \$150$, which results in a total activity cost of $\$500 + \$150 = \$650$. Figure 13.15 shows the graph of the time–cost relationship for activity A. The complete normal and crash activity data for the maintenance project are given in Table 13.10.

Now the question is: Which activities would you crash, and how much should these activities be crashed in order to meet the 10-day project completion deadline at minimum cost? Your first reaction to this question is possibly to consider crashing the critical path activities A, B, or E. Activity A has the lowest crashing costs of the three, and crashing this activity by 2 days will reduce the A–B–E path to the desired 10 days. While this is correct, be careful: As you crash the current critical path activities, other paths may become critical. Thus you will need to check the critical path in the revised network and perhaps either identify additional activities to crash or modify your initial crashing decision. While in a small network you may be able to use this trial-and-error approach to making crashing decisions, in larger networks you will need a mathematical procedure in order to arrive at the optimal decision. The following discussion shows how linear programming can be used to solve the network crashing problem.

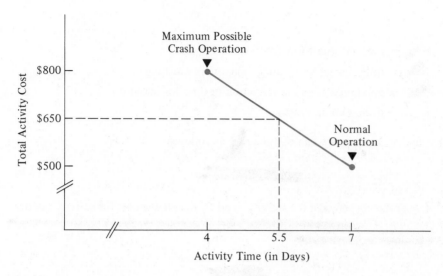

Figure 13.15
Time–Cost Relationship for Activity A

Table 13.10
Normal and Crash Activity Data for the Maintenance Project

Activity	Normal Time	Crash Time	Total Normal Cost C_j	Total Crash Cost C_j'	Maximum Crash Days M_j	Crash Cost per Day $K_j = \dfrac{C_j' - C_j}{M_j}$
A	7	4	$500	$800	3	$100
B	3	2	200	350	1	150
C	6	4	500	900	2	200
D	3	1	200	500	2	150
E	2	1	300	550	1	250
			$1700	$3100		

A Linear Programming Model for Crashing Decisions

While several solution procedures exist for the crashing procedure, the following linear programming model is one approach used to help make crashing decisions. First recall that an event refers to the completion of all the activities that lead into a node. Since we have five nodes or events in the maintenance project example, we need five decision variables to identify the time of occurrence for each event. In addition, we will need five decision variables to represent the amount of crash time used for each of the five activities. Thus we define the following decision variables:

$$x_i = \text{time of occurrence of event } i \qquad i = 1, 2, 3, 4, 5$$
$$y_j = \text{amount of crash time used for activity } j \qquad j = A, B, C, D, E$$

Since the total normal time project cost is fixed at $1700 (see Table 13.10), we can minimize the total project cost (normal cost plus crash cost) simply by minimizing the crashing costs. Thus the linear programming objective function becomes

$$\min \sum_j K_j y_j \qquad (13.8)$$

or

$$\min 100y_A + 150y_B + 200y_C + 150y_D + 250y_E \qquad (13.9)$$

where K_j is the crash cost for activity j, $j = A, B, C, D, E$, on a per-unit time basis.[4]

The constraints on the model involve describing the network, limiting the activity crash times, and meeting the desired project completion time. Of these, the constraints used to describe the network are perhaps the most difficult. These constraints are based on the following conditions:

1. The time of occurrence of event i (x_i) must be greater than or equal to the activity completion time for all activities leading into the node or event.
2. An activity start time is equal to the occurrence time of its preceding node or event.
3. An activity time is equal to its normal time less the length of time it is crashed.

Using an event occurrence time of zero at node 1 ($x_1 = 0$), we can create the following set of network description constraints:

Event 2:

$$x_2 \geq \tau_A - y_A + 0$$

Occurrence	Actual time	Start time
time for event 2	for activity A	for activity A ($x_1 = 0$)

or

$$x_2 + y_A \geq 7 \qquad (13.10)$$

Event 3:

$$x_3 \geq \tau_C - y_C + 0$$

or

$$x_3 + y_C \geq 6 \qquad (13.11)$$

Since two activities enter event or node 4, we have the following two constraints:

Event 4:

$$x_4 \geq \tau_B - y_B + x_2$$
$$x_4 \geq \tau_D - y_D + x_3$$

[4]Note that the x_i variables indicating event occurrences do not result in costs; thus they have zero coefficients in the objective function.

or

$$-x_2 + x_4 + y_B \geq 3 \qquad (13.12)$$
$$-x_3 + x_4 + y_D \geq 3 \qquad (13.13)$$

Event 5:

$$x_5 \geq \tau_E - y_E + x_4$$

or

$$-x_4 + x_5 + y_E \geq 2 \qquad (13.14)$$

The five constraints (13.10) to (13.14) are necessary to describe the network. The maximum allowable crash time constraints are

$$y_A \leq 3 \qquad (13.15)$$
$$y_B \leq 1 \qquad (13.16)$$
$$y_C \leq 2 \qquad (13.17)$$
$$y_D \leq 2 \qquad (13.18)$$
$$y_E \leq 1 \qquad (13.19)$$

and the desired project completion of 10 days provides another constraint:

$$x_5 \leq 10 \qquad (13.20)$$

Adding the nonnegativity restrictions and solving the 9-variable, 11-constraint (13.10) to (13.20) linear programming model provides the following solution:

$$
\begin{array}{ll}
x_2 = 5 & y_A = 2 \\
x_3 = 6 & y_B = 0 \\
x_4 = 8 & y_C = 0 \\
x_5 = 10 & y_D = 1 \\
& y_E = 0
\end{array}
$$

Objective function = \$350

The solution values of $y_A = 2$ and $y_D = 1$ tell us that activity A must be crashed 2 days (\$200) and activity D must be crashed 1 day (\$150) in order to meet the 10-day project completion deadline. Because of this crashing, the time for activity A will be reduced to $7 - 2 = 5$ days, while the time for activity D will be reduced to $3 - 1 = 2$ days. The total project cost (normal cost plus crashing cost) will be \$1700 + \$200 + \$150 = \$2050. To generate the new activity schedule under crashing, we use the crashed activity times and repeat the critical path calculations for the network. Doing this provides the activity schedule shown in Table 13.11. Note that in the final solution all activities are critical. Resolving the linear programming model with alternate project completion times [constraint (13.20)] will show the project manager the costs associated with crashing the project to meet alternate deadlines.

Table 13.11
New Activity Schedule for the Maintenance Project after Crashing Activities
A and D

Activity	Time after Crashing	ES	LS	EF	LF	Slack
A	5	0	0	5	5	0
B	3	5	5	8	8	0
C	6	0	0	6	6	0
D	2	6	6	8	8	0
E	2	8	8	10	10	0

13.5

PERT/COST

As you have seen, PERT/CPM concentrates on the *time* aspect of a project and provides information that can be used to schedule and control individual activities so that the entire project is completed on time. While project time and the meeting of a scheduled completion date are primary considerations for almost every project, there are many situations in which the *cost* associated with the project is just as important as time. In this section we show how the technique referred to as *PERT/Cost* can be used to help plan, schedule, and control project costs. The ultimate objective of a PERT/Cost system is to provide information that can be used to maintain project costs within a specified budget.

Planning and Scheduling Project Costs

The budgeting process for a project usually involves identifying all costs associated with the project and then developing a schedule or forecast of when the costs are expected to occur. Then, at various stages of project completion, the actual project costs incurred can be compared to the scheduled or budgeted costs. If actual costs are exceeding budgeted costs, corrective action may be taken to keep costs within the budget.

The first step in a PERT/Cost control system is to divide the entire project into components that are convenient in terms of measuring and controlling costs. While a PERT/CPM network may already show detailed activities for the project, we may find that these activities are too detailed for conveniently controlling project costs. In such cases related activities that are under the control of one department, subcontractor, etc., are often grouped together to form what are referred to as *work packages*. By identifying costs of each work package, a project manager can use a PERT/Cost system to help plan, schedule, and control project costs.

Since the projects we discuss in this chapter have a relatively small number of activities, we will find it convenient to define work packages as having only one activity. Thus in our discussion of the PERT/Cost technique we will be treating each activity as a separate work package. Realize, however, that in large and complex projects we would almost always group related activities so that a cost control system could be developed for a more reasonable number of work packages.

In order to illustrate the PERT/Cost technique, let us consider the research and development project network shown in Figure 13.16. We are assuming that each activity

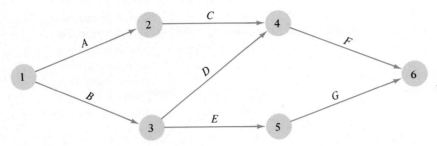

Figure 13.16
A Project Network

is an acceptable work package and that a detailed cost analysis has been made on an activity basis. The activity cost estimates, along with the expected activity times, are shown in Table 13.12. In using the PERT/Cost technique we will be assuming that activities (work packages) are defined such that costs occur at a constant rate over the duration of the activity. For example, activity B, which shows an estimated cost of $30,000 and an expected 3-month duration, is assumed to have a cost rate of $30,000/3 = $10,000 per month. The cost rates for all activities are provided in Table 13.12. Note that the total estimated or budgeted cost for the project is $87,000.

Table 13.12
Activity Time and Cost Estimates

Activity	Expected Time (months)	Budgeted or Estimated Cost	Budgeted Cost per Month
A	2	$10,000	$ 5,000
B	3	30,000	10,000
C	1	3,000	3,000
D	3	6,000	2,000
E	2	20,000	10,000
F	2	10,000	5,000
G	1	8,000	8,000
Total project budget		$87,000	

Using the expected activity times, we can compute the critical path for the project. A summary of the critical path calculations and the resulting activity schedule is shown in Table 13.13. Activities B, D, and F determine the critical path and provide an expected project duration of 8 months.

We are now ready to develop a budget for the project that will show when costs should occur during the 8-month project duration. First let us assume that all activities begin at their earliest possible start time. Using the monthly activity cost rates shown in Table 13.12 and the earliest start times, we can prepare the month-by-month cost forecast as shown in Table 13.14. For example, using the earliest start time for activity A as 0, we expect activity A, which has a 2-month duration, to show a cost of $5000 in each of the first 2 months of the project. By similarly using the earliest start time and monthly cost rate for each activity, we are able to complete Table 13.14 as shown. Note that by summing the costs in each column we obtain the total cost anticipated for each month of the project. Finally, by accumulating the monthly costs, we can show the budgeted total cost schedule, provided that all activities are started at the *earliest* starting times.

Table 13.13
Activity Schedule

Activity	Earliest Start (ES)	Latest Start (LS)	Earliest Finish (EF)	Latest Finish (LF)	Slack	Critical Activity
A	0	3	2	5	3	
B	0	0	3	3	0	Yes
C	2	5	3	6	3	
D	3	3	6	6	0	Yes
E	3	5	5	7	2	
F	6	6	8	8	0	Yes
G	5	7	6	8	2	

Table 13.14
Budgeted Costs for an Earliest Starting Time Schedule ($\$ \times 10^3$)

Activity	Month 1	2	3	4	5	6	7	8
A	5	5						
B	10	10	10					
C			3					
D				2	2	2		
E				10	10			
F							5	5
G						8		
Monthly cost	15	15	13	12	12	10	5	5
Total project cost	15	30	43	55	67	77	82	87

Table 13.15 shows the budgeted total cost schedule when all activities are started at the *latest* starting times.

Provided the project progresses on its PERT/CPM time schedule, each activity will be started somewhere between its earliest and latest starting times. This implies that the total project costs should occur at levels between the earliest start and latest start cost schedules. For example, using the data in Tables 13.14 and 13.15, we see that by month 3, total project costs should be between $30,000 (latest starting time schedule) and $43,000 (earliest starting time schedule). Thus at month 3 a total project cost between $30,000 and $43,000 would be expected.

In Figure 13.17 we show the forecasted total project costs for both the earliest and latest starting time schedules. The shaded region between the two cost curves shows the possible budgets for the project. If the project manager is willing to commit activities to specific starting times, a specific project cost forecast or budget can be prepared. However, based on the above analysis we know that such a budget will have to be in the feasible region shown in Figure 13.17.

Table 13.15
Budgeted Costs for a Latest Starting Time Schedule ($ × 10³)

Activity	Month 1	2	3	4	5	6	7	8
A				5	5			
B	10	10	10					
C						3		
D				2	2	2		
E						10	10	
F							5	5
G								8
Monthly cost	10	10	10	7	7	15	15	13
Total project cost	10	20	30	37	44	59	74	87

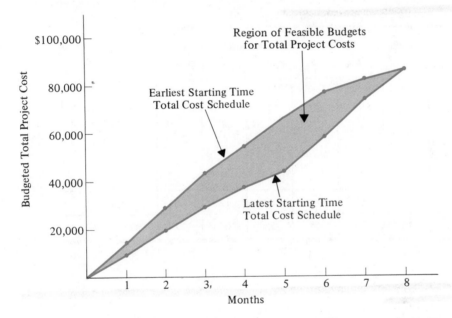

Figure 13.17
Feasible Budgets for Total Project Costs

Controlling Project Costs

The information that we have developed thus far is helpful in terms of planning and scheduling total project costs. However, if we are going to have an effective cost control system we will need to identify costs on a much more detailed basis. For example, information that the project's actual total cost is exceeding the budgeted total cost will be of little value unless we can identify the activity or group of activities that are causing the cost overruns.

The PERT/Cost system provides the desired cost control by budgeting and then recording actual costs on an activity (i.e., work package) basis. Periodically throughout the project's duration, actual costs for all completed and in-process activities are compared with the appropriate budgeted costs. The project manager is then provided with up-to-date information on the cost status of each activity. If at any point in time actual costs exceed budgeted costs, a cost overrun has occurred. On the other hand, if actual costs are less than the budgeted costs, we have a condition referred to as a cost underrun. By identifying the sources of cost overruns and cost underruns, the manager can take corrective action where necessary. Note that the budgeted or estimated activity costs for the R&D project network of Figure 13.16 were shown in Table 13.12.

Now at any point during the project's duration the manager can use a PERT/Cost procedure to obtain an activity cost status report by collecting the following information for *each activity*:

1. Actual cost to date
2. Percent completion to date

A PERT/Cost system will require periodic—perhaps biweekly or monthly—collection of the above information. Let us suppose that we are at the end of the fourth month of the project and have the actual cost and percent completion data for each activity, as shown in Table 13.16. This current status information shows that activities A and B have been completed, activities C, D, and E are in process, and activities F and G have not yet been started.

Table 13.16
Activity Cost and Percent Completion Data at the End of Month 4

Activity	Actual Cost	Percent Completion
A	$12,000	100
B	30,000	100
C	1,000	50
D	2,000	33
E	10,000	25
F	0	0
G	0	0
Total	$55,000	

In order to prepare a cost status report we will need to compute the value for all work completed to date. Let

$$V_i = \text{value of work completed for activity } i$$
$$p_i = \text{percent completion for activity } i$$
$$B_i = \text{budget for activity } i$$

The following relationship is used to find the value of work completed for each activity:

$$V_i = \left(\frac{p_i}{100}\right)B \tag{13.21}$$

Using the budget costs from Table 13.12, the values of work completed for activities A and C are as follows[5]:

$$V_A = (^{100}\!/_{100})(\$10{,}000) = \$10{,}000$$

$$V_C = (^{50}\!/_{100})(\$3000) = \$1500$$

Cost overruns and cost underruns can now be found by comparing the actual cost of each activity with its appropriate budget value. Let

AC_i = actual cost to date for activity i

D_i = difference in actual cost and budgeted value for activity i

We have

$$D_i = AC_i - V_i \qquad (13.22)$$

A positive D_i indicates the activity has a cost *overrun*, while a negative D_i indicates a cost *underrun*. $D_i = 0$ indicates that actual costs are in agreement with the budgeted costs. For example,

$$D_A = AC_A - V_A = \$12{,}000 - \$10{,}000 = \$2000$$

shows that activity A, which has already been completed, has a \$2000 cost overrun. However, activity C, with $D_C = \$1000 - \$1500 = -\$500$, is currently showing a cost underrun, or savings, of \$500. A complete cost status report such as the one shown in Table 13.17 can now be prepared for the project manager.

Table 13.17
Project Cost Status Report at the End of Month 4

Activity	Actual Cost (AC)	Budgeted Value $[V = (p/100)B]$	Differences (D)
A	\$12,000	\$10,000	\$2,000
B	30,000	30,000	0
C	1,000	1,500	−500
D	2,000	2,000	0
E	10,000	5,000	5,000
F	0	0	0
G	0	0	0
Totals	\$55,000	\$48,500	\$6,500

↗
Total project cost
overrun to date

[5]Equation (13.21) and the succeeding calculations are based on the PERT/Cost assumption that activity costs occur at a constant rate over the duration of the activity.

This cost report shows the project manager that the costs to date are $6500 over the estimated or budgeted costs. On a percentage basis, we would say the project is experiencing a ($6,500/$48,500) × 100 = 13.4% cost overrun, which for most projects is a serious situation. By checking each activity, we see that activities A and E are causing the cost overrun. Since activity A has been completed, its cost overrun cannot be corrected; however, activity E is in process and is only 25% complete. Thus activity E should be reviewed immediately. Corrective action for activity E can help to bring actual costs closer to the budgeted costs. The manager may also want to consider cost reduction possibilities for activities C, D, F, and G in order to keep the total project cost within the budget.

While the PERT/Cost procedure described above can be an effective cost control system, it is not without possible drawbacks and implementation problems. First, the activity-by-activity cost recording system can require significant clerical effort, especially for firms with large and/or numerous projects. Thus the personnel and other costs associated with maintaining a PERT/Cost system may offset some of the advantages. Second, questions can arise as to how costs should be allocated to activities or work packages. Overhead, indirect, and even material costs can cause cost allocations and measurement problems. Third, and perhaps most critical, is the fact that PERT/Cost requires a system of cost recording and control that is significantly different from most cost accounting systems. Firms using departments or other organizational units as cost centers will need a substantially revised accounting system to handle the PERT/Cost activity-oriented system. Problems of modifying accounting procedures and/or carrying dual accounting systems are not trivial matters.

Summary

In this chapter we have introduced PERT/CPM and PERT/Cost as procedures designed to assist in the project planning, scheduling, and control process. The key to these project management techniques is to develop a list of activities and their activity precedence relationships. Then, using activity time data, the critical path and the associated critical path activities can be identified. In the process an activity schedule showing the earliest start time, the earliest finish time, the latest start time, the latest finish time, and the slack for each activity can be identified.

We showed how we can include capabilities for handling uncertain activity times and how this information can be used to provide a probability statement about the chances of the project being completed in a specified period of time. Crashing was introduced as a procedure for reducing activity times to meet project completion deadlines. A linear programming model can be used to make the crashing decisions that minimize the cost of reducing the project completion time.

In the final section of this chapter we described how the PERT/Cost technique can be used to help plan, schedule, and control project costs. Because of the numerous computations associated with planning, updating, and revising PERT/CPM and PERT/Cost networks, computer programs are frequently used to implement these project management techniques.

A summary of some of the key steps in any project management task follows:

1. Make a clear statement of the objectives of the project, specifically identifying what is to be accomplished.

2. Make a list of all activities and their immediate predecessors. Provide estimates of the activity times by either specifying the expected time directly or using the optimistic, most likely, and pessimistic time estimates to compute an expected time.
3. Develop the network for the project.
4. Perform the critical path computations to develop an activity schedule for the project, and identify the critical path activities.
5. Make resource allocations and crashing decisions as necessary to achieve the desired project completion date.
6. Be sure someone is responsible for each activity in the project and is working to see that activities are completed as scheduled.
7. Control the project by monitoring actual performance, taking corrective action, and replanning where necessary.

Glossary

Program Evaluation and Review Technique (PERT)   A network-based project management procedure.

Critical Path Method (CPM)   A network-based project management procedure.

Activities   Specific jobs or tasks that are components of a project. These are represented by arcs in a PERT/CPM network.

Immediate predecessors   The activities that must immediately precede a given activity.

Event   An event occurs when *all* the activities leading into a node have been completed.

Dummy activity   A fictitious activity with zero activity time used to maintain activity precedence requirements in a PERT/CPM network.

Path   A sequence of activities (arcs) connecting the first node and the last node of a network.

Critical activities   The activities on the critical path.

Critical path   The longest path in a project management (PERT/CPM) network. The time it takes to traverse this path is the project completion time.

Earliest start time   The earliest time at which an activity may begin.

Earliest finish time   The earliest time at which an activity may be completed.

Forward pass   A calculation procedure moving forward through the network that determines the earliest start and earliest finish times for each activity.

Backward pass   A calculation procedure moving backward through the network that determines the latest start and latest finish times for each activity.

Latest start time   The latest time at which an activity may begin without delaying the complete project.

Latest finish time   The latest time at which an activity may be completed without delaying the complete project.

Slack   The length of time an activity can be delayed without affecting the project completion time.

Optimistic time   An activity time estimate based on the assumption that the activity will progress in an ideal manner.

Most probable time   An activity time estimate for the most likely activity time.

Pessimistic time   An activity time estimate based on the assumption that the most unfavorable conditions occur.

Expected activity time   The average activity time.

Beta probability distribution   A probability distribution used to describe activity times.

Crashing   The process of reducing an activity time by adding resources and hence usually cost.

PERT/Cost   A technique designed to assist in the planning, scheduling, and controlling of project costs.

Work package   A natural grouping of interrelated project activities for purposes of cost control. A work package is a unit of cost control in a PERT/Cost system.

Problems

1. The Mohawk Discount Store chain is designing a management training program for individuals at its corporate headquarters. The company would like to design the program so that the trainees can complete it as quickly as possible. There are important precedence relationships that must be maintained between assignments or activities in the program. For example, a trainee cannot serve as an assistant to the store manager until the trainee has obtained experience in the credit department and at least one sales department. The activities shown below are the assignments that must be completed by each trainee in the program:

Activity	Immediate Predecessor
A	—
B	—
C	A
D	A, B
E	A, B
F	C
G	D, F
H	E, G

Construct a PERT/CPM network for this problem. Do not attempt to perform any further analysis.

2. Consider the PERT/CPM network shown below.

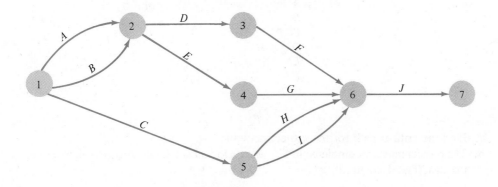

a. Add the dummy activities that will eliminate the problem of activities having the same starting and ending nodes.

b. Add dummy activities that will satisfy the following immediate predecessor requirements:

Activity	Immediate Predecessor
H	B, C
I	B, C
G	D, E

3. Construct a PERT/CPM network for a project having the following activities:

Activity	Immediate Predecessor
A	—
B	—
C	A
D	A
E	C, B
F	C, B
G	D, E

The project is completed when both activities *F* and *G* are completed.

4. Assume that the project in problem 3 has the following activity times:

Activity	Time (months)
A	4
B	6
C	2
D	6
E	3
F	3
G	5

a. Find the critical path for the project network.

b. The project must be completed in $1\frac{1}{2}$ years. Do you anticipate difficulty in meeting the deadline? Explain.

5. Management Decision Systems (MDS) is a consulting company specializing in the development of decision support systems. MDS has just obtained the contract to develop a computer system to assist the management of a large company in formulating its capital expenditure plan. The project leader has developed the following list of activities and immediate predecessors:

Activity	Immediate Predecessor
A	—
B	—
C	—
D	B
E	A
F	B
G	C, D
H	B, E
I	F, G
J	H

Construct a PERT/CPM network for this problem.

6. Consider the following project network (the times shown are in weeks):

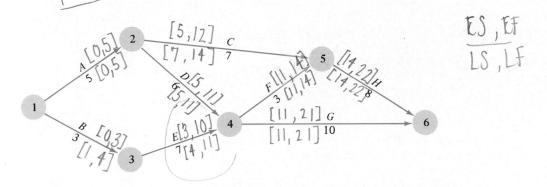

ES, EF
LS, LF

a. Identify the critical path. *A - D - F - H*
b. How long will it take to complete this project? *22*
c. Can activity D be delayed without delaying the entire project? If so, how many weeks? *No, CRITICAL ACTIVITY*
d. Can activity C be delayed without delaying the entire project? If so, how many weeks? *2 WKS (7-5)*
e. What is the schedule for activity E (that is, start and finish times)? *OK*

7. A project involving the installation of a computer system consists of eight activities. The immediate predecessors and activity times in weeks are as follows:

Activity	Immediate Predecessor	Time
A	—	3
B	—	6
C	A	2
D	B, C	5
E	D	4
F	E	3
G	B, C	9
H	F, G	3

a. Draw the PERT/CPM network for this project.

b. What are the critical path activities?

c. What is the project completion time?

8. Colonial State College is considering building a new multipurpose athletic complex on campus. The complex would provide a new gymnasium for intercollegiate basketball games. In addition, it would provide expanded office space, classrooms, and intramural facilities. The activities that would have to be undertaken before beginning construction are shown below. Activity times are stated in weeks.

Activity	Description	Immediate Predecessor	Time
A	Survey building site	—	6
B	Develop initial design	—	8
C	Obtain board approval	A, B	12
D	Select architect	C	4
E	Establish budget	C	6
F	Finalize design	D, E	15
G	Obtain financing	E	12
H	Hire contractor	F, G	8

a. Develop a PERT/CPM network for this project.

b. Identify the critical path.

c. Develop a detailed schedule for all activities in the project.

d. Does it appear reasonable that construction of the athletic complex could begin 1 year after the decision to begin the project with the site survey and initial design plans? What is the completion time for the project?

9. Hamilton County Parks is planning to develop a new park and recreational area on a recently purchased 100-acre tract. Activities making up the park development project include clearing playground and picnic areas, road construction, shelter house construction, picnic equipment purchases, and so on. The PERT/CPM network being used to assist in the planning, scheduling, and controlling of this project is as follows:

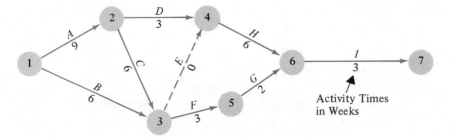

a. What is the critical path for this network?

b. Show the activity schedule and slack for each activity.

c. The park commissioner would like to open the park to the public within 6 months from the time the work on the project is started. Does this opening date appear feasible? Explain.

10. The following estimates of activity times (days) are available for a small project:

Activity	Optimistic	Most Probable	Pessimistic
A	4	5	6
B	8	9	10
C	7	7.5	11
D	7	9	10
E	6	7	9
F	5	6	7

$E(T)$ $E(V\!AR)$

a. Compute the expected activity completion times and the variance for each activity.

b. The critical path consists of activities B–D–F. Compute the expected project completion time and the variance.

11. The project of building a backyard swimming pool consists of nine major activities. The activities and their immediate predecessors are shown below. Develop the PERT/ CPM network for this project.

Activity	Immediate Predecessors
A	—
B	—
C	A, B
D	A, B
E	B
F	C
G	D
H	D, F
I	E, G, H

12. Assume that the activity time estimates in days for the swimming pool construction project from problem 11 are as follows:

Activity	Optimistic	Most Probable	Pessimistic
A	3	5	6
B	2	4	6
C	5	6	7
D	7	9	10
E	2	4	6
F	1	2	3
G	5	8	10
H	6	8	10
I	3	4	5

   a. What are the critical path activities?
   b. What is the expected time to complete the project?
   c. What is the probability that the project can be completed in 25 working days or less?

13. Suppose that the following estimates of activity times (weeks) were provided for the network shown in problem 6:

Activity	Optimistic	Most Probable	Pessimistic
A	4	5	6
B	2.5	3	3.5
C	6	7	8
D	5	5.5	9
E	5	7	9
F	2	3	4
G	8	10	12
H	6	7	14

What is the probability that the project will be completed within
   a. 21 weeks?
   b. 22 weeks?
   c. 25 weeks?

14. Consider the project network given below:

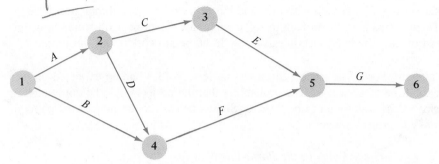

The appropriate managers have made estimates of the optimistic, most probable, and pessimistic times (in days) for completion of the activities. These times are as follows:

Activity	Optimistic a	Most Probable m	Pessimistic b
A	5	6	7
B	5	12	13
C	6	8	10
D	4	10	10
E	5	6	13
F	7	7	10
G	4	7	10

a. Find the critical path.
b. How much slack time, if any, is there for activity *C*?
c. Determine the expected project completion time and the variance.
d. Find the probability that the project will be completed in 30 days or less.

15. Doug Casey is in charge of planning and coordinating next spring's sales management training program for his company. Doug has listed the following activity information for this project:

Activity	Description	Immediate Predecessors	Times (Weeks) Optimistic	Most Probable	Pessimistic
A	Plan topic	—	1.5	2	2.5
B	Obtain speakers	A	2	2.5	6
C	List meeting locations	—	1	2	3
D	Select location	C	1.5	2	2.5
E	Speaker travel plans	B, D	0.5	1	1.5
F	Final check with speakers	E	1	2	3
G	Prepare and mail brochure	B, D	3	3.5	7
H	Take reservations	G	3	4	5
I	Last-minute details	F, H	1.5	2	2.5

a. Show the PERT/CPM network for this project.
b. Prepare the activity schedule for this project.
c. What are the critical path activities and the expected project completion time?
d. If Doug wants a 0.99 probability of completing the project on time, how far ahead of the scheduled meeting date should he begin working on the project?

16. The Daugherty Porta-Vac project discussed in Section 13.3 had an expected project completion time of 17 weeks. The probability that the project could be completed in 20 weeks or less was found to be 0.9656. Shown below are the noncritical paths in the Porta-Vac project network.

Other Paths in the Porta-Vac Network

A–D–G–J
A–C–F–J
B–H–I–J.

a. Using the information in Table 13.6, compute the expected time and variance for each of the above paths.
b. Compute the probability that each path will be completed in the desired 20-week period.
c. Why is the computation of the probability of completing a project based on the analysis of the critical path? In what case, if any, would it be desirable to make the probability computation for a noncritical path?

17. Refer to the Porta-Vac project network shown in Figure 13.7. Suppose that Daugherty's management revises the activity time estimates as follows:

Activity	Optimistic	Most Probable	Pessimistic
A	3	7	11
B	2	2.5	6
C	2	3	4
D	6	7	14
E	2	3	4
F	2.5	3·	3.5
G	2.5	4	5.5
H	4.5	5.5	9.5
I	1	2	3
J	1	2	3

a. Compute the expected time and variance for each activity.
b. Show the new detailed activity schedule.
c. What are the critical path activities?
d. What is the expected project completion time?
e. What is the new probability that the project will be completed before the 20-week deadline?

18. The manager of the Oak Hills Swimming Club is planning the club's swimming team program. The first team practice is scheduled for May 1. The activities, their immediate predecessors, and the activity time estimates in weeks are as follows:

	Activity	Immediate Predecessor	Optimistic Time	Most Probable Time	Pessimistic Time
A.	Meet with board	—	1	1	2
B.	Hire coaches	A	4	6	8
C.	Reserve pool	A	2	4	6
D.	Announce program	B, C	1	2	3
E.	Meet with coaches	B	2	3	4
F.	Order team suits	A	1	2	3
G.	Register swimmers	D	1	2	3
H.	Collect fees	G	1	2	3
I.	Plan first practice	E, H, F	1	1	1

a. Show the PERT/CPM network for this project.
b. Develop an activity schedule for the project.
c. What are the critical path activities and what is the expected project completion time?
d. If the club manager plans to start the project on February 1, what is the probability that the swimming program will be ready by the scheduled May 1 date (13 weeks)? Should the manager begin planning the swimming program prior to February 1?

19. The product development group at Landon Corporation has been working on a new computer software product that has the potential to capture a large market share. Through outside sources, Landon's management has learned that a competitor is working to bring a similar product to the market. As a result Landon's top management has increased its pressure on the product development group. The group's leader has turned to PERT/CPM as an aid to the scheduling of the activities remaining before the new product can be brought to the market. The PERT/CPM network developed is shown below:

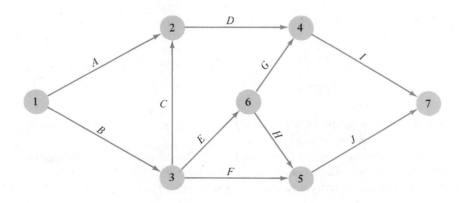

The activity time estimates in weeks are given below:

Activity	Optimistic	Most Probable	Pessimistic
A	3	4	5
B	3	3.5	7
C	4	5	6
D	2	3	4
E	6	10	14
F	7.5	8.5	12.5
G	4.5	6	7.5
H	5	6	13
I	2	2.5	6
J	4	5	6

a. Develop an activity schedule for this project and identify the critical path activities.

b. What is the probability that the project will be completed so that Landon Corporation may introduce the new product within 25 weeks? 30 weeks?

20. Using the computer installation project referred to in problem 7, assume that the project has to be completed in 16 weeks. Crashing of the project is necessary. Relevant information is shown below.

Activity	Normal Time	Crash Time	Normal Cost ($)	Crash Cost ($)
A	3	1	900	1700
B	6	3	2000	4000
C	2	1	500	1000
D	5	3	1800	2400
E	4	3	1500	1850
F	3	1	3000	3900
G	9	4	8000	9800
H	3	2	1000	2000

a. Formulate a linear programming model that can be used to make the crashing decisions for the above network.

b. Solve the linear programming model and make the minimum-cost crashing decisions. What is the added cost of meeting the 16-week completion time?

c. Develop a complete activity schedule using the crashed activity times.

21. Consider the following network with activity times shown in days:

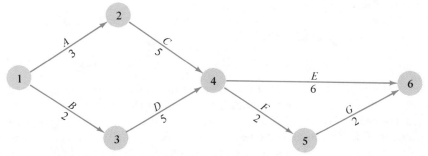

The crash data for this project are as follows:

Activity	Normal Time	Crash Time	Total Normal Cost ($)	Total Crash Cost ($)
A	3	2	800	1400
B	2	1	1200	1900
C	5	3	2000	2800
D	5	3	1500	2300
E	6	4	1800	2800
F	2	1	600	1000
G	2	1	500	1000

a. Find the critical path and the expected project duration using normal times.
b. What is the total project cost using the normal times?

22. Refer to problem 21. Assume that management desires a 12-day project completion time.
  a. Formulate a linear programming model that can be used to assist with the crashing decisions.
  b. What are the activities that should be crashed?
  c. What is the total project cost for the 12-day completion time?

23. Assume that the following crash data are available for the project described in problem 4:

Activity	Normal Time	Crash Time	Total Normal Cost ($ × 10³)	Total Crash Cost ($ × 10³)
A	4	2	50	70
B	6	3	40	55
C	2	1	20	24
D	6	4	100	130
E	3	2	50	60
F	3	3	25	25
G	5	3	60	75

  a. Show a linear programming model that could be used to make the crash decisions if the project has to be completed in T months.
  b. If $T = 12$ months, what activities should be crashed, what is the crashing cost, and what are the critical activities?

24. Office Automation, Inc. has developed a proposal for introducing a new computerized office system that will improve word processing and interoffice communications for a particular company. Contained in the proposal is a list of activities that must be accomplished in order to complete the new office system project. Information about the activities is shown below. Times are in weeks and costs are in thousands of dollars.

	Activity	Immediate Predecessors	Normal Time	Crash Time	Normal Cost	Crash Cost
A.	Plan needs	—	10	8	30	70
B.	Order equipment	A	8	6	120	150
C.	Install equipment	B	10	7	100	160
D.	Set up training lab	A	7	6	40	50
E.	Training course	D	10	8	50	75
F.	Testing system	C, E	3	3	60	—

  a. Show the network for the project.
  b. Develop an activity schedule for the project using normal times.
  c. What are the critical path activities and what is the expected project completion time?
  d. Assume that the company wishes to complete the project in 26 weeks. What crashing decisions would be recommended in order to meet the completion date at the least possible cost? Work through the network and attempt to make the crashing decisions by inspection.
  e. Develop an activity schedule for the crashed project.
  f. What is the added project cost to meet the 26-week completion time?

25. Because Landon Corporation (see problem 19) is being pressured to complete the product development project at the earliest possible date, the project leader has requested an evaluation of the possibility of crashing the project.
  a. Develop a linear programming model that could be used to help in making the crashing decisions.
  b. What information would have to be provided before the linear programming model could be implemented?

26. For the Daugherty Porta-Vac project shown in Figure 13.7, suppose that expected activity costs are as follows:

Activity	Expected Cost ($ \times 10^3$)
A	90
B	16
C	3
D	100
E	6
F	2
G	60
H	20
I	4
J	2

Develop a total cost budget based on both an earliest start and a latest start schedule. Show the graph of feasible budgets for the total project cost.

27. Using the Daugherty Porta-Vac project cost data given in problem 26, prepare a PERT/Cost analysis for each of the following three points in time. For each case, show the percent overrun or underrun for the project to date and indicate any corrective action that should be undertaken. *Note:* If an activity is not listed below, assume that it has not been started.

a. At the end of the fifth week:

Activity	Actual Cost ($ \times 10^3$)	Percent Completion
A	62	80
B	6	50

b. At the end of the 10th week:

Activity	Actual Cost ($ \times 10^3$)	Percent Completion
A	85	100
B	16	100
C	1	33
D	100	80
E	4	100
H	10	25

c. At the end of the 15th week:

Activity	Actual Cost ($ × 10³)	Percent Completion
A	85	
B	16	
C	3	
D	105	
E	4	100
F	3	
G	55	
H	25	
I	4	

28. The two-machine maintenance project discussed in Section 13.4 is shown below:

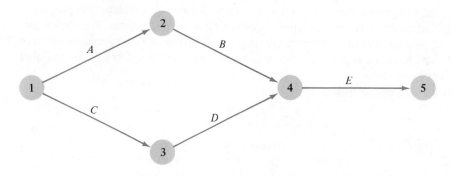

The recommended crashed schedule is shown in Table 13.11. Final times and costs for the project are as follows:

Activity	Expected Time (days)	Cost ($)
A	5	700
B	3	200
C	6	500
D	2	350
E	2	300
Total		2050

a. Show the graph of feasible budgets for the project's total cost. Does this represent an unusual feasible budget region? Explain.

b. Suppose that at the start of day 8 we find the following activity status report:

Activity	Actual Cost ($)	Percent Completion
A	800	100
B	100	67
C	450	100
D	250	50
E	0	0

In terms of both time and cost, is the project on schedule? What action is recommended?

29. A firm is modifying its warehouse operation with the installation of an automated stock handling system. Specific activities include redesigning the warehouse layout, installing the new equipment, testing the new equipment, etc. The project management network is shown below:

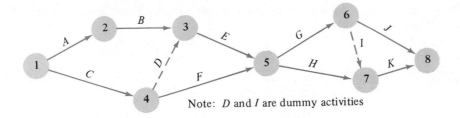

Note: *D* and *I* are dummy activities

Pertinent time and cost data are as follows:

Activity	Expected Time (weeks)	Variance	Budgeted Cost ($)
A	3	0.3	6,000
B	2	0.5	4,000
C	8	2.0	16,000
D	0	0.0	0
E	6	1.0	18,000
F	4	0.2	20,000
G	5	0.4	15,000
H	1	0.1	2,000
I	0	0.0	0
J	5	1.0	5,000
K	6	0.6	12,000

a. Develop an activity schedule for the project.
   (1) What is the critical path?
   (2) What is the expected completion time?
   (3) What is the probability of meeting a desired 26-week completion time?

b. Develop a PERT/Cost budget for total project costs over the project's duration. What should the range be for expenditures after 12 weeks of the project?

30. Refer to the network in problem 29. Suppose that after 12 weeks of operation the following data are available on all completed and in-process activities:

Activity	Actual Cost ($)	Percent Completion
A	5,000	100
B	4,000	100
C	18,000	100
E	9,000	50
F	18,000	75

Is the project in control based on both time and cost considerations? What corrective action, if any, is desirable?

Case Problem
Warehouse Expansion

R. C. Coleman distributes a variety of food products sold through grocery store and supermarket outlets. The company receives orders directly from the individual outlets, with a typical order requesting the delivery of several cases of anywhere from 20 to 50 different products. Under the company's current warehouse operation, warehouse clerks dispatch order-picking personnel to fill each order and have the goods moved to the warehouse shipping area. Because of the high labor costs and relatively low productivity of hand order-picking, the company has decided to automate the warehouse operation by installing a computer-controlled order-picking system, along with a conveyor system for moving goods from storage to the warehouse shipping area.

R. C. Coleman's director of material management has been named the project manager in charge of the automated warehouse system. After consulting with members of the engineering staff and warehouse management personnel, the director has compiled a list of activities associated with the project. The optimistic, most probable, and pessimistic times in weeks have also been provided for each activity.

Activity	Description	Immediate Predecessors
A	Determine equipment needs	—
B	Obtain vendor proposals	—
C	Select vendor	A, B
D	Order system	C
E	Design new warehouse layout	C
F	Layout warehouse	E
G	Design computer interface	C
H	Interface computer	D, F, G
I	Install system	D, F
J	Train system operators	H
K	Test system	I, J

Managerial Report

Develop a report that presents the activity schedule and expected project completion time for the warehouse expansion project. Include a PERT/CPM network of the project in the report. In addition, take into consideration the following information and include a discussion of each issue raised in the report.

| | **Activity Times** | | |
Activity	Optimistic	Most Probable	Pessimistic
A	4	6	8
B	6	8	16
C	2	4	6
D	8	10	24
E	7	10	13
F	4	6	8
G	4	6	20
H	4	6	8
I	4	6	14
J	3	4	5
K	2	4	6

a. R. C. Coleman's top management has established a required 40-week completion time for the project. Can this completion time be achieved? Include probability information in your discussion. What recommendations do you have if the 40-week completion time is required?

b. Suppose that management requests that activity times be shortened in order to provide an 80% chance of meeting the 40-week completion time. Assuming the variance in the project completion time is the same as you found in part (a), how much should the expected project completion time be shortened in order to achieve the goal of providing an 80% chance of completion within 40 weeks?

c. Using the expected activity times as the normal times and the following crashing information, determine the activity crashing decisions and revised activity schedule for the warehouse expansion project.

Activity	Normal Cost	Crashed Activity Time	Crash Cost
A	1,000	4	1,900
B	1,000	7	1,800
C	1,500	2	2,700
D	2,000	8	3,200
E	5,000	7	8,000
F	3,000	4	4,100
G	8,000	5	10,250
H	5,000	4	6,400
I	10,000	4	12,400
J	4,000	3	4,400
K	5,000	3	5,500

Quantitative Methods in Practice

Seasongood & Mayer
Cincinnati, Ohio

Seasongood & Mayer, established in 1887, is an investment securities firm that engages in the following areas of municipal finance:

1. Underwriting new issues of municipal bonds
2. Trading—for example, acting as a market maker for the buying and selling of previously issued bonds
3. Investment banking—that is, the process of obtaining money from the capital markets at the lowest possible cost

The major applications of management science at Seasongood & Mayer are in the investment banking area. One particular application involved the use of PERT/CPM in the introduction of a $31 million hospital revenue bond issue.

Scheduling the Introduction of a Bond Issue

In any major building project there are certain common steps:

1. Defining the project
2. Determining the cost of the project
3. Financing the project

The role of the investment banker in building projects is to develop a method of financing that will result in the owner receiving the necessary funds in a timely manner. In a hospital building project such as the one we will be discussing, the typical method of financing is tax-free hospital revenue bonds.

The construction cost for the building project is an important factor in determining the best approach to financing. Normally, the construction cost is based on a bid submitted by a contractor or a construction manager. However, this cost is usually guaranteed only for a specified period of time, such as 60 to 90 days. The major function of the hospital's investment banker is to arrange the timing of the financing in such a way that the proceeds of the bond issue can be made available within the time limit of the guaranteed-price construction bid. Since most hospitals must have the proceeds of their permanent long-term financing in hand prior to committing to major construction contracts, the investment banker plays a very significant role.

Table A13.1
Activities for the Providence Hospital Project

Activity	Time Required (weeks)	Description of Activity	Immediate Predecessor(s)
A	4	Drafting and distribution of legal documents	—
B	3	Preparation and distribution of unaudited financial statements of hospital	—
C	2	Draft and distribution of hospital history, description of services, and existing facilities for Preliminary Official Statement (POS)	—
D	8	Draft and distribution of demand portion of feasibility study	—
E	4	Review (additions/deletions) and approval as to form of legal documents	A
F	1	Review (additions/deletions) and approval of history, etc., for POS	C
G	4	Review (additions/deletions) and approval of demand portion of feasibility study	D
H	2	Draft and distribution of financial portion (as to form) of feasibility study	E, G
I	2	Drafting and distribution of plan of financing and all pertinent facts relevant to the bond transaction for POS	E
J	0.5	Review and approval of unaudited financial statements	B
K	20	Firm price received for cost of project	—
L	1	Review (additions/deletions), approval, and completion of financial portion of feasibility study	H, K
M	1	Draft of POS completed	F, I, J, L
N	0.14	All material sent to bond rating services	M
O	0.28	POS printed and distributed to all interested parties	M
P	1	Presentation to bond rating services (Standard & Poor's, Moody's)	N
Q	1	Bond rating received	P
R	2	Marketing of bonds	O, Q
S	0*	Purchase Contract executed	R
T	0.14	Final Official Statement authorized and completed, legal documents completed	S
U	3	Fulfillment of all terms and conditions of Purchase Contract	S
V	0*	Bond proceeds available to hospital	T, U
W	0*	Hospital's ability to sign construction contract	T, U

*Occurs instantaneously.

To arrange for the financing, the investment banker must coordinate the activities of hospital attorneys, the bond counsel, and so on. The cooperation of all parties and the coordination of project activities are best achieved if everyone recognizes the interdependency of the activities and the necessity of completing individual tasks in a timely manner. Seasongood & Mayer has found PERT/CPM to be useful in scheduling and coordinating such a project.

As managing underwriter for a $31,050,000 issue of Hospital Facilities Revenue Bonds for Providence Hospital in Hamilton County, Ohio (December 1980), Seasongood & Mayer utilized a critical path analysis to coordinate and schedule the project financing activities. Descriptions of the activities, times required, and immediate predecessors are given in Table A13.1. The complete network is shown in Figure A13.1. The critical path activities $K-L-M-N-P-Q-R-S-U-W$ resulted in a scheduled project completion time of 29.14 weeks; thus the funds for the project are received approximately 64 days after the receipt of a firm construction price. Specific schedules showing start and finish times for all activities were used to keep the entire project on schedule. The use of PERT/CPM was instrumental in helping Seasongood & Mayer obtain financing for this project within the time specified in the construction bid.

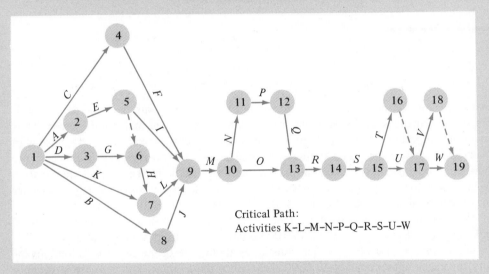

Figure A13.1
Seasongood & Mayer PERT/CPM Network for the Providence Hospital Project

Questions

1. What is the role of the investment banker in building projects?
2. For the hospital project described, what is the primary objective of the investment banker?
3. Perform the critical path calculations for the network shown in Figure A13.1. Is there more than one critical path? Discuss.

CHAPTER

14

Inventory Models

Inventory can be defined as idle goods or materials that are waiting to be used. For most companies the expense associated with financing and maintaining inventory is a substantial part of the cost of doing business. In large companies, especially those with many and/or expensive products, the costs associated with raw material, in-process, and finished goods inventories can run into the millions of dollars. To gain an appreciation of how inventory costs arise and what managers can do to control them, let us consider the situation faced by the R & B Beverage Company. R & B Beverage is a distributor of beer, wine, and soft-drink products in central Ohio. From a main warehouse located in Columbus, R & B supplies nearly 1000 retail stores with beverage products.

R & B's beer inventory, which constitutes about 40% of the company's total inventory, averages approximately 50,000 cases. Since the average cost per case is roughly $5, R & B estimates the value of its beer inventory to be $250,000.

There are a number of costs associated with maintaining or carrying inventory. Taken together, these costs are referred to as the *inventory holding cost*. First, there is the cost of financing. If money is borrowed to maintain the inventory investment, an interest charge is incurred. If the firm's own money is used, there is an opportunity cost associated with not being able to use the money for other investments. In either case, a financing charge exists in the form of an interest cost for the capital tied up in inventory. This *cost of capital* is usually expressed as a percentage of the amount invested. Since R & B estimates its cost of capital at an annual rate of 18%, this portion of the inventory cost is 0.18($250,000) = $45,000 per year.

There are a number of other costs, such as insurance, taxes, breakage, pilferage, and warehouse overhead, that are part of the inventory holding cost. R & B estimates these other costs at an annual rate of approximately 7% of the value of the inventory. Thus total inventory holding cost for the R & B beer inventory is 25% of its value, or 0.25 ($250,000) = $62,500 per year. When we consider that the beer constitutes only about

40% of R & B's total inventory, we can begin to see that the inventory holding cost is a major expense for the R & B Beverage Company.

Managers are faced with the dual problems of maintaining sufficient inventory to meet demand for goods and at the same time incurring the lowest possible inventory holding cost. Basically, managers attempt to solve these problems by making the best possible decisions with respect to the following:

1. How much should be ordered when the inventory for a given item is replenished?
2. When should the inventory for a given item be replenished?

The purpose of this chapter is to show how quantitative models can assist in making the above decisions. While there are many similarities in all inventory systems, each system also has unique characteristics that prevent the application of one or two general inventory models to all situations. We will first consider *deterministic* inventory models, in which it is reasonable to assume that the demand for the item occurs at a known and constant rate. Later we will consider *probabilistic* inventory models, where the demand for the item is uncertain and can be described only in probabilistic terms. In the final section of the chapter we describe the inventory procedure referred to as *material requirements planning* or MRP. This approach to inventory management is well suited for raw materials, subassemblies, and components whose demand is dependent on the demand for final products in the inventory system.

14.1

ECONOMIC ORDER QUANTITY (EOQ) MODEL

The best known and most fundamental inventory model is the *economic order quantity (EOQ) model*. This model is applicable when the demand for the item has a constant, or nearly constant, rate and when the entire quantity ordered arrives in the inventory at one point in time. The *constant demand rate* condition means simply that the same number of units are taken from inventory each period of time, such as 5 units every day, 25 units every week, 100 units every 4-week period, and so on.

Let us see how the EOQ model can be applied by the R & B Beverage Company. R & B's warehouse manager has conducted a preliminary analysis of overall inventory costs and has decided to do a detailed study of one product for the purpose of establishing the *how-much*-to-order and *when*-to-order decision rules that will result in the lowest possible inventory cost for the product. The manager has selected R & B's number-one selling beer, Bub, for this study. Historical sales data for Bub show that a constant demand rate of 104,000 cases per year is a reasonable approximation for inventory planning purposes.

The how-much-to-order decision involves selecting an order quantity that draws a compromise between (1) keeping small inventories and ordering frequently and (2) keeping large inventories and ordering infrequently. The first alternative would result in undesirably high ordering costs, while the second alternative would result in undesirably high inventory holding costs. In order to find an optimal compromise between these conflicting alternatives, let us develop a mathematical model that will show the total cost[1] as the sum of the inventory holding cost and the ordering cost.

---

[1]While quantative analysts typically refer to "total cost" models for inventory systems, often these models describe only the total *variable* or total *relevant* costs for the decision being considered. Costs that are not affected by the how-much-to-order decision are considered fixed or constant and are not included in the model.

Inventory holding cost is the cost that is dependent on the size of the inventory; that is, a larger inventory requires a larger inventory holding cost. Since R & B estimates its annual inventory holding cost to be 25% of the value of the inventory, and since the cost of one case of Bub beer is $5, the cost of holding or carrying one case of Bub beer in inventory for 1 year is 0.25($5) = $1.25. Note that defining the inventory holding cost as a percentage of value of the product is convenient because it is easily transferable to other products. For example, a case of Carle's Red Ribbon Beer ($4.20/case) would have an annual inventory holding cost of 0.25($4.20) = $1.05 per case.

The next step in the inventory analysis is to determine the *ordering cost*—the cost of placing an order. For R & B the largest portion of this cost involves the salaries of the purchasers. An analysis of the purchasing process showed that a purchaser spends approximately 45 minutes preparing and processing an order for Bub beer. This amount of time is required regardless of the number of cases ordered. With a wage rate and fringe benefit cost for purchasers of $16 per hour, the labor portion of the ordering cost is $12. Making allowances for paper, postage, telephone, transportation, and receiving costs at $8 per order, the manager estimates that the cost of ordering is $20 per order. That is, R & B is paying $20 per order regardless of the quantity requested in the order.

The demand, the inventory holding cost, and the ordering cost are the three items that must be determined prior to the use of the EOQ model. Since they have been developed for the R & B example, let us see how they are used to develop a total cost model. We begin by defining Q to be the order quantity. Thus the *how-much-to-order* decision involves finding the value of Q which will minimize the sum of annual inventory holding and annual ordering costs.

The inventory level for Bub will have a maximum value of Q units when the order of size Q is received from the supplier. R & B will then satisfy customer demand from inventory until the inventory is depleted, at which time another shipment of Q units will be received. With the assumption of a constant demand rate, the sketch of the inventory level for Bub beer is shown in Figure 14.1. Note that the sketch indicates that the average

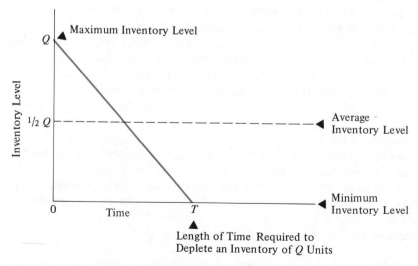

Figure 14.1
Sketch of the Inventory Level for Bub Beer

inventory level is ½ Q. This should appear reasonable since the maximum inventory level is Q, the minimum is 0, and the inventory level declines at a constant rate.

Figure 14.1 shows the inventory pattern during one cycle of length T. As time goes on, this pattern will repeat. This repeating inventory pattern is shown in Figure 14.2. If the average inventory during each cycle is ½ Q, the average inventory level over any number of cycles is also ½ Q. Thus, as long as the time period involved contains an integral number of cycles, the average inventory for the period will be ½ Q.

The annual inventory holding cost can be calculated using the average inventory level. That is, we can calculate the annual inventory holding cost by multiplying the average inventory by the cost of carrying one unit in inventory for a year.

Let

$$I = \text{annual inventory carrying charge (25\% for R \& B)}$$
$$C = \text{unit cost of the inventory item (\$5 for Bub beer)}$$

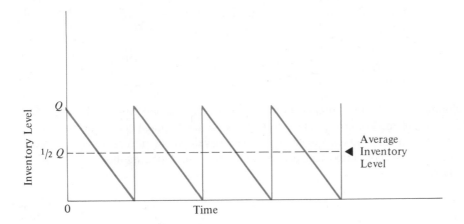

Figure 14.2
Inventory Pattern for the EOQ Inventory Decision Model

The cost of holding one unit in inventory for the year, denoted by C_h, is given by $C_h = IC$, which for Bub is 0.25($5) = $1.25. Thus the general equation for annual inventory holding cost is as follows:

$$\text{Annual inventory holding cost} = \left(\begin{array}{c}\text{average}\\\text{inventory}\end{array}\right)\left(\begin{array}{c}\text{annual holding}\\\text{cost}\\\text{per unit}\end{array}\right)$$

$$= \frac{1}{2}QC_h \qquad (14.1)$$

To complete the total cost model, we must now include the annual ordering cost. Our goal is to express this cost in terms of the order quantity Q. The first question is, how many orders will be placed during the year? Let D denote the annual demand for the product (for R & B, $D = 104{,}000$ cases per year). We know that by ordering Q

units each time we order, we will have to place D/Q orders per year. If C_0 is the cost of placing one order, the general expression for the annual ordering cost is as follows:

$$\text{Annual ordering cost} = \begin{pmatrix} \text{number of} \\ \text{orders} \\ \text{per year} \end{pmatrix} \begin{pmatrix} \text{cost} \\ \text{per} \\ \text{order} \end{pmatrix}$$

$$= \left(\frac{D}{Q}\right)C_0 \qquad (14.2)$$

Thus the total annual cost—annual inventory holding cost plus annual ordering cost—can be expressed as follows:

$$\text{TC} = \frac{1}{2} QC_h + \frac{D}{Q} C_0 \qquad (14.3)$$

Using the Bub beer data, the total cost model with $C_h = \$1.25$, $C_0 = \$20$, and $D = 104,000$ becomes

$$\text{TC} = \frac{1}{2} Q(1.25) + \frac{104,000}{Q} (20) = 0.625 \, Q + \frac{2,080,000}{Q} \qquad (14.4)$$

The development of the above total cost model has gone a long way toward helping solve the inventory problem. We now are able to express the total annual cost as a function of the decision to be made: *how much* to order. The development of a realistic total cost model is perhaps the most important part of applying quantitative methods to inventory decision making.

The How-Much-to-Order Decison

The next step, for Bub beer, is to find the order quantity Q that does in fact minimize the total cost as stated in equation (14.4). Using a trial-and-error approach we can compute the total cost for several possible order quantities. As a starting point, let us consider $Q = 8000$. The total annual cost is

$$\text{TC} = 0.625 \, (8000) + \frac{2,080,000}{8000} = 5260$$

A trial order quantity of 5000 gives

$$\text{TC} = 0.625 \, (5000) + \frac{2,080,000}{5000} = 3541$$

The results using several other trial order quantities are shown in Table 14.1. As can be seen, the lowest-cost solution is around 2000 units. Graphs of the inventory holding, ordering, and total costs are shown in Figure 14.3.

Table 14.1
Inventory Holding and Ordering Costs for Various Order Quantities of Bub Beer

Order Quantity	Annual Inventory Holding Cost	Annual Ordering Cost	Annual Total Cost
5000	$3125	$ 416	$3541
4000	2500	520	3020
3000	1875	693	2568
2000	1250	1040	2290
1000	625	2080	2705

The advantage of the trial-and-error approach is that it is straightforward and provides the total cost for a number of possible order quantity decisions. The disadvantage of this approach, however, is that, even though it provides a good approximation, it does not provide the exact minimum-cost order quantity.

Refer to Figure 14.3. The order quantity that minimizes total cost is denoted by Q^*. Using differential calculus, it can be shown (see Appendix 14.1) that the value of Q^* that minimizes the total cost is given by

$$Q^* = \sqrt{\frac{2DC_0}{C_h}} \tag{14.5}$$

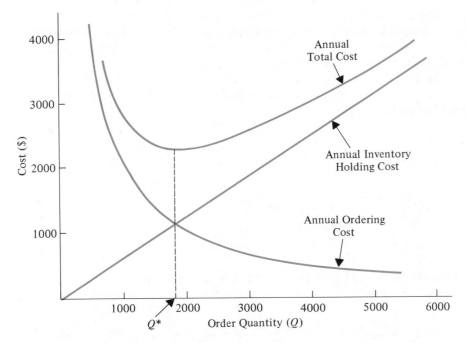

Figure 14.3
Graph of Annual Inventory Holding, Ordering, and Total Cost for Bub Beer

Using equation (14.5), the minimum-total-cost order quantity for Bub beer can be found.

$$Q^* = \sqrt{\frac{2(104,000)20}{1.25}} = \sqrt{3,328,000} = 1824$$

The use of an order quantity of 1824 in equation (14.4) shows that the minimum-cost inventory policy for Bub beer has a total annual cost of $2280. Note that the economic order quantity, Q^*, has balanced the annual inventory holding cost and the annual ordering cost. Check for yourself to see that these costs are equal.[2] Problem 2 at the end of the chapter will ask you to show that annual inventory holding cost and annual ordering cost are always equal for the EOQ model.

The When-To-Order Decision

Determining how much to order, Q^*, is only part of the process of selecting an inventory policy. We must also specify *when* orders should be placed. The objective is to place each order so that the order quantity, Q^*, arrives exactly when the inventory level reaches zero. For the purpose of specifying when to place an order, it is useful to define the notion of inventory position. *Inventory position* is the inventory on hand plus all amounts previously ordered but not yet received. In other words, inventory position is the amount on hand plus the amount on order.

Suppose that the manufacturer of Bub beer guarantees a 2-day delivery on any order placed. Assuming 250 working days per year, the daily demand for Bub beer is the annual demand of 104,000 cases divided by 250. Daily demand = 104,000/250 = 416 cases. With the 2-day delivery time, we would expect (416 cases per day)(2 days) = 832 cases to be sold during the time it takes an order to reach the R & B warehouse. Using inventory terminology, the 2-day delivery period is referred to as the *lead time* for an order, and the 832 cases of demand anticipated during the lead time is referred to as the *lead time demand*. Thus R & B should order a new shipment of Bub beer whenever the inventory position reaches 832 cases.

For inventory systems using the constant demand rate assumption and a constant lead time, the *reorder point* is the same as the lead time demand. The general expression for the reorder point is

$$r = dm \tag{14.6}$$

where

$$r = \text{reorder point}$$
$$d = \text{demand per day}$$
$$m = \text{lead time for a new order in days}$$

In some situations, lead time demand and thus the reorder point may be greater than the economic order quantity, Q^*. In these cases there will be at least one order outstanding

---

[2]Actually, Q^* from equation (14.5) is 1824.28, but since we cannot order fractional cases of beer, a Q^* of 1824 is shown. This value of Q^* may cause a few cents deviation between the two costs. If Q^* is used at its exact value, the annual inventory holding and annual ordering costs will be equal at $1140.18 per year.

when a new order is placed. For example, suppose that the lead time for Bub beer had been 5 days. Lead time demand would then be (416 cases per day)(5 days) = 2080 cases. The reorder point, $r = 2080$, indicates that a new order should be placed whenever the inventory position reaches 2080 cases. Using the economic order quantity of 1824 cases, we see that an inventory position of 2080 occurs when there is an order of 1824 cases already outstanding and the on-hand inventory level reaches $2080 - 1824 = 256$ cases.[3]

The period between orders is referred to as the *cycle time*. Previously [see equation (14.2)] we defined D/Q as the number of orders that will be placed during a year. Thus $D/Q^* = 104,000/1,824 = 57$ is the number of orders R & B will place for Bub each year. If R & B places 57 orders over 250 working days, they will order approximately every $250/57 = 4.4$ working days. Thus the cycle time is computed to be 4.4 working days. The general expression[4] for a cycle time of T days is given by

$$T = \frac{250}{D/Q^*} = \frac{250Q^*}{D} \tag{14.7}$$

Computer Models for Inventory Decisions

Like many other quantitative methods, inventory models can be programmed and made available to inventory managers through the use of computers. The inventory models module of *The Management Scientist* computer software package contains solution procedures for the six different inventory models discussed in this chapter. Using the economic order quantity option of the module, the computer output for the Bub beer inventory policy is shown in Figure 14.4. Our previously computed economic order quantity of

```
                    INVENTORY POLICY
                    ***************
```

OPTIMAL ORDER QUANTITY	1,824.28
ANNUAL INVENTORY HOLDING COST	$1,140.18
ANNUAL ORDERING COST	$1,140.18
TOTAL ANNUAL COST	$2,280.35
MAXIMUM INVENTORY LEVEL	1,824.28
AVERAGE INVENTORY LEVEL	912.14
REORDER POINT	832.00
NUMBER OF ORDERS PER YEAR	57.01
CYCLE TIME (DAYS)	4.39

Figure 14.4
Optimal Inventory Policy for Bub Beer as Computed by *The Management Scientist* Software Package

[3]Some prefer to state the reorder point in terms of inventory on hand instead of inventory position. In the above example, the 2080-case reorder point expressed in terms of inventory position would be replaced by a 256-case reorder point expressed in terms of inventory on hand. The microcomputer software accompanying this text, *The Management Scientist*, computes the reorder point in terms of inventory on hand.

[4]This general expression for cycle time is based on 250 working days per year. If the firm operated 300 working days per year, the cycle time would be given by $T = 300Q^*/D$.

$Q^* = 1824$ provides the minimum-cost inventory policy. The reorder point is shown to be 832. Additional information is provided, including total annual cost, maximum inventory level, average inventory level, number of orders per year, and cycle time. Thus the output provides order quantity and reorder point decision recommendations as well as a variety of additional information that should be helpful to the inventory manager.

Sensitivity Analysis in the EOQ Model

Even though substantial time may have been spent in arriving at the inventory carrying charge (25%) and the cost per order ($20), we should realize that these figures are at best good estimates. Thus we may want to consider how much the recommended order quantity would change if the estimated carrying charge and ordering cost had been different. To determine this, we can calculate the recommended order quantity under several different cost conditions; Table 14.2 shows the minimum-total-cost order quantity for several possibilities. As you can see from the table, the value of Q^* appears relatively stable, even with some variations in the cost estimates. Based on these results it appears that the best order quantity for Bub is somewhere around 1700 to 2000 units. If operated properly, the total cost for the Bub inventory system should be close to $2200 to $2300 per year. We also note that there is very little risk associated with implementing the calculated order quantity of 1824.

Table 14.2
Optimal Order Quantities for Several Cost Possibilities

Possible Inventory Carrying Charge (%)	Possible Cost per Order ($)	Optimal Order Quantity (Q^*)	Projected Total Cost ($)	
			Using Q^*	Using $Q = 1824$
24	19	1815	2178	2178
24	21	1908	2289	2292
26	19	1744	2267	2269
26	21	1833	2383	2383

From the above analysis we would say that the EOQ model is insensitive to small variations or errors in the cost estimates. This is a property of EOQ models in general, which indicates that if we have at least reasonable estimates of the inventory holding cost and the ordering cost, we can expect to obtain a good approximation of the true minimum cost order quantity.

The Manager's Use of the EOQ Model

The EOQ model results in a recommended order quantity of 1824 cases and a reorder point of 832 cases. Is this the final decision, or should the manager's judgment enter into the establishment of the final inventory policy? Although the model has provided a good order quantity recommendation, it may not have taken into account all aspects of the inventory situation. As a result, the manager may want to modify the final order quantity recommendation to meet the unique circumstances of the inventory situation. In this case the manager felt that it would be desirable to increase the order quantity from 1824 units to 2080 units to have an order quantity equal to 5 working days' demand. By doing so, R & B can maintain a weekly inventory cycle.

The warehouse manager also realized that the EOQ model was based on the constant demand rate assumption. While this is a good approximation, we must also recognize that sometimes the demand might vary. If a reorder point of 832 units is used, we would be expecting an 832-unit demand during the lead time and the new order to arrive exactly when the inventory level reaches zero. Such close timing would leave little room for error, and the scheduling of arrivals would be very critical if stockouts were to be avoided. To protect against shortages due to higher-than-expected demands or slightly delayed incoming orders, the manager recommended a 1000-unit reorder point. Thus under normal conditions R & B will order 2080 cases of Bub whenever the current inventory reaches 1000 units. During the expected 2-day lead time 832 cases should be demanded, and thus 168 cases should be in inventory when an order arrives. The extra 168 cases serves as a safety precaution against higher-than-expected demand or a delayed incoming order. In general, the amount by which the reorder point exceeds the expected lead time demand is referred to as *safety stock*.

The decisions to adjust the order quantity and reorder point were purely judgment decisions and were not necessarily made with a minimum cost objective in mind. However, they are examples of how managerial judgment might interface with the inventory decision model to arrive at a sound inventory policy. The final decision of $Q = 2080$ and $r = 1000$ results in a total annual cost of $2510.[5]

How Has the EOQ Decision Model Helped?

The EOQ model has objectively included inventory holding costs and ordering costs and, with the aid of some management judgment, has led to a low-cost inventory policy. In addition, the general optimal order quantity model, equation (14.5), is potentially applicable to other R & B products. For example, Red Ribbon beer ($4.20/case), which has an ordering cost of $20.00, a constant demand rate of 62,400 cases/year, and a 2-day lead time, has a recommended order quantity of

$$Q^* = \sqrt{\frac{2(62,400)(20.00)}{(0.25)(4.20)}} = 1542 \text{ cases}$$

Further analysis will show a recommended reorder point of 499 cases and a total annual cost of $1619.

We will now investigate additional inventory decision models that are designed to make *how-much-* and *when*-to-order decisions for other types of inventory systems.

14.2

ECONOMIC PRODUCTION LOT SIZE MODEL

The following inventory decision model is similar to the EOQ model in that we are attempting to determine *how much* we should order and *when* the order should be placed.

---

[5]Using equation (14.4), a Q of 2080 units resulted in a total cost of $2300. The additional safety stock inventory of 168 units increases the average inventory by 168 units, since it is on hand all year long. Thus the inventory carrying charge is increased by 1.25(168) = $210, and the total cost of the revised policy is $2300 + $210 = $2510.

Again we will make the assumption of a constant demand rate. However, instead of the goods arriving at the warehouse in a shipment of size Q^* as assumed in the EOQ model, we will assume that units are supplied to inventory at a constant rate over several days or several weeks. The *constant supply rate* assumption implies that the same number of units is supplied to inventory each period of time (for example, 10 units every day, 50 units every week, and so on). This model is designed for production situations in which, once an order is placed, production begins and a constant number of units is added to inventory each day until the production run has been completed.

If we have a production system that produces 50 units per day and we decide to schedule 10 days of production, we have a $50(10) = 500$-unit *production lot size*. In general, if we let Q indicate the production lot size, the approach to the inventory decisions will be similar to the EOQ model; that is, we will attempt to build an inventory holding and ordering cost model that expresses the total annual cost as a function of the production lot size. Then we will attempt to find the production lot size that minimizes the total cost.

One other condition that should be mentioned is that the model will apply only to situations where the production rate is greater than the demand rate. Stated more simply, the production system must be able to satisfy the demand. For instance, if the constant demand rate is 2000 units per week, the production rate must be at least 2000 units per week in order to satisfy demand.

Since we will assume that the production rate exceeds the demand rate, each day during a production run we will be producing more units than we ship. Thus we will put the excess production into inventory, resulting in a gradual inventory buildup during the production period. When the production run is completed, the inventory will show a gradual decline until a new production run is started. The inventory pattern for this system is shown in Figure 14.5.

As in the EOQ model, we are now dealing with two costs, the inventory holding cost and the ordering cost. While the inventory holding cost is identical to our definition in the EOQ model, the interpretation of the ordering cost is slightly different. In fact, in a production situation the ordering cost is more correctly referred to as production setup cost. This cost, which includes hours of labor, material, and lost production costs incurred

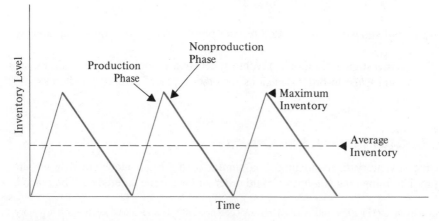

Figure 14.5
Inventory Pattern for the Production Lot Size Inventory Model

while preparing the production system for operation, is a fixed cost that occurs for every production run, regardless of the production lot size.

The Total Cost Model

Let us begin building the production lot size model by writing the annual inventory holding cost in terms of the production lot size, Q. Again, the approach will be to develop an expression for average inventory and then establish the holding cost associated with the average inventory level.

We saw in the EOQ model that the average inventory was simply one-half the maximum inventory or $\frac{1}{2} Q$. Since Figure 14.5 shows a constant inventory buildup rate during the production run and a constant inventory depletion rate during the nonproduction period, the average inventory for the production lot size model will also be one-half of the maximum inventory level. However, in this inventory system the production lot size Q does not go into inventory at one point in time, and thus the inventory level never reaches a level of Q units.

Let us see how we can compute the maximum inventory level. First we define the following symbols:

$$d = \text{daily demand rate for the product}$$
$$p = \text{daily production rate for the product}$$
$$t = \text{number of days for a production run}$$

Since we are assuming that p is larger than d, the excess production each day is $p - d$, which is the daily rate of inventory buildup. If we run production for t days and place $p - d$ units in inventory each day, the inventory level at the end of the production run will be $(p - d)t$. From Figure 14.5 we can see that the inventory level at the end of the production run is also the maximum inventory level. Thus

$$\text{Maximum inventory} = (p - d)t \qquad (14.8)$$

If we know we are producing a production lot size of Q units at a daily production rate of p units, then $Q = pt$, and the length of the production run t must be

$$t = \frac{Q}{p} \text{ days} \qquad (14.9)$$

Thus

$$\text{Maximum inventory} = (p - d)t = (p - d)\left(\frac{Q}{p}\right)$$
$$= \left(1 - \frac{d}{p}\right) Q \qquad (14.10)$$

The average inventory, which is one-half of the maximum inventory, is given by

$$\text{Average inventory} = \frac{1}{2}\left(1 - \frac{d}{p}\right) Q \qquad (14.11)$$

With an annual inventory holding cost of C_h per unit, the general equation for annual inventory holding cost is as follows:

$$\begin{pmatrix} \text{Annual inventory} \\ \text{holding cost} \end{pmatrix} = \begin{pmatrix} \text{average} \\ \text{inventory} \end{pmatrix} \begin{pmatrix} \text{annual holding} \\ \text{cost} \\ \text{per unit} \end{pmatrix}$$

$$= \frac{1}{2}\left(1 - \frac{d}{p}\right) QC_h \tag{14.12}$$

If D is the annual demand for the product and C_0 is the setup cost for a production run, then the total annual setup cost, which takes the place of the total annual ordering cost in the EOQ model, is as follows:

$$\text{Annual setup cost} = \begin{pmatrix} \text{number of production} \\ \text{runs per year} \end{pmatrix} \begin{pmatrix} \text{setup cost} \\ \text{per run} \end{pmatrix}$$

$$= \frac{D}{Q} C_0 \tag{14.13}$$

Thus the total annual cost (TC) model is

$$\text{TC} = \frac{1}{2}\left(1 - \frac{d}{p}\right) QC_h + \frac{D}{Q} C_0 \tag{14.14}$$

Assuming 250 working days per year, we can write daily demand d in terms of annual demand D as follows:

$$d = \frac{D}{250}$$

Now let P denote the annual production for the product if it were produced every day. Then

$$P = 250p \quad \text{and} \quad p = \frac{P}{250}$$

Thus[6]

$$\frac{d}{p} = \frac{D/250}{P/250} = \frac{D}{P}$$

Therefore we can write the total annual cost as follows:

$$\text{TC} = \frac{1}{2}\left(1 - \frac{D}{P}\right) QC_h + \frac{D}{Q} C_0 \tag{14.15}$$

---

[6]The ratio $d/p = D/P$ regardless of the number of days of operation; 250 days was used here merely as an illustration.

Equations (14.14) and (14.15) are equivalent. However, equation (14.15) may be used more frequently, since an *annual* cost model tends to make the analyst think in terms of collecting *annual* demand D and *annual* production P data rather than daily rate data.

Finding the Economic Production Lot Size

Given the estimates of the inventory holding cost C_h, setup cost C_0, annual demand D, and annual production rate P, we could use a trial-and-error approach to compute the total annual cost for various production lot sizes Q. However, this is not necessary; we can use the minimum-cost formula for Q^* that has been developed using differential calculus (see Appendix 14.2). The equation is as follows:

$$Q^* = \sqrt{\frac{2DC_0}{(1 - D/P)C_h}} \qquad (14.16)$$

An Example. Beauty Bar Soap is produced on a production line that has an annual capacity of 60,000 cases. The annual demand is estimated at 26,000 cases, with the demand rate essentially constant throughout the year. The cleaning, preparation, and setup of the production line costs $135.00. The manufacturing cost per case is $4.50, and annual inventory holding cost is figured at a 24% rate. Thus $C_h = IC = 0.24(\$4.50) = \$1.08$. What is the recommended production lot size?

Using equation (14.16) we have

$$Q^* = \sqrt{\frac{2(26,000)(135)}{(1 - 26,000/60,000)(1.08)}} = \sqrt{\frac{7,020,000}{0.612}} = 3387$$

The total annual cost using equation (14.15) and $Q^* = 3387$ is $2073.

Other relevant data include a 5-day lead time to schedule and set up a production run. With 250 working day per year, the lead time demand is $(26,000/250)(5 \text{ days}) = 520$ cases. Thus a reorder point of 520 cases is recommended. Using equation (14.7), we see that the cycle time of $T = [(250)(3,387)]/26,000 = 32.6$ indicates that a production run will need to be scheduled about every 32 to 33 days. Certainly the manager will want to review the model recommendations. Adjusting the recommended $Q^* = 3387$ to a slightly different value and/or adding safety stock may be desirable.

14.3

AN INVENTORY MODEL WITH PLANNED SHORTAGES

In many inventory situations a shortage or stockout—a demand that cannot be supplied from inventory—is undesirable and should be avoided if at all possible. However, there are other situations in which it may be desirable—from an economic point of view—to plan for and allow shortages. In practice these types of situations are most commonly found where the value per unit of the inventory is very high and hence the inventory holding cost is high. An example of this type of situation is a new-car dealer's inventory. It is not uncommon for a dealer not to have the specific car you want in stock. However, if you are willing to wait a few weeks, the dealer can usually order a car for you.

The model developed in this section allows the type of shortage known as a *backorder*. In a backorder situation an assumption is made that when a customer places an order and discovers that the supplier is out of stock, the customer does not withdraw the order. Rather, the customer waits until the next shipment arrives, and then the order is filled. Frequently the waiting period in backordering situations will be relatively short and, by promising the customer top priority and immediate delivery when the goods become available, companies are often able to convince customers to wait for the order. In these cases the backorder assumption is valid. If for a particular product a firm finds that a shortage causes the customer to withdraw the order and a lost sale results, the backorder model would not be the appropriate inventory model.

Using the backorder assumption for shortages, we will develop an extension to the EOQ model presented in Section 14.1. The EOQ model assumptions of the goods arriving in inventory all at one time and a constant demand rate for the product will be used. If we let S indicate the amount of the shortage or the number of backorders that have accumulated when a new shipment of size Q is received, then the inventory system for the backorder case has the following characteristics:

1. With S backorders existing when a new shipment of size Q arrives, the S backorders will be shipped to the appropriate customers immediately and the remaining $Q - S$ units will be placed in inventory.
2. $Q - S$ will be the maximum inventory level.
3. The inventory cycle of T days will be divided into two distinct phases: t_1 days when inventory is on hand and orders are filled as they occur, and t_2 days when there are stockouts and all orders are placed on backorder.

The inventory pattern for this model, where negative inventory represents the number of backorders, is shown in Figure 14.6.

With the inventory pattern now defined, we should be able to proceed with the basic step of all inventory models: namely, the development of a total cost expression. For the inventory model with backorders we will encounter the usual inventory holding cost and ordering cost. In addition, we will incur a backorder cost in terms of the labor and special

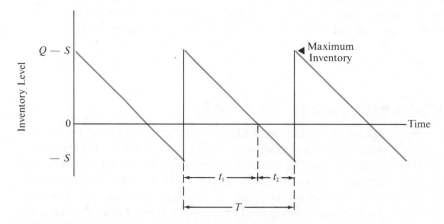

Figure 14.6
Inventory Pattern for an Inventory Model with Backorders

delivery costs directly associated with the handling of the backorders. Another portion of the backorder cost can be expressed as a loss of goodwill with customers due to the fact that customers will have to wait for their orders. Since the *goodwill cost* depends on how long the customer has to wait, it is customary to adopt the convention of expressing all backorder costs in terms of how much it costs to have a unit on backorder for a stated period of time. This method of costing backorders on a time basis is similar to the method we have used to compute the inventory holding cost.

Using this method for costing backorders, we can compute a total annual cost of backorders once the average backorder level and the backorder cost per unit per unit time are known.

Admittedly, the backorder cost rate (especially the goodwill cost) is difficult to determine in practice. However, noting that EOQ models are rather insensitive to the cost estimates (see Table 14.2), we should feel confident that reasonable estimates of the backorder cost will lead to a good approximation of the overall minimum-cost inventory policy.

Let us begin the development of a total cost model by showing how to calculate the inventory holding cost. First we use a small hypothetical example to suggest a procedure for computing the average inventory level. If we have an average inventory of 2 units for 3 days and no inventory on the fourth day, what is the average inventory level over the 4-day period? It is

$$\frac{2 \text{ units (3 days)} + 0 \text{ units (1 day)}}{4 \text{ days}} = \frac{6}{4} = 1.5 \text{ units}$$

Refer to Figure 14.6. You can see that the above situation is exactly what happens in the backorder model. With a maximum inventory of $Q - S$ units, the t_1 days we have inventory on hand will have an average inventory of $(Q - S)/2$. No inventory is carried for the t_2 days in which we experience backorders. Thus over the total cycle time of $T = t_1 + t_2$ days, we can compute the average inventory level as follows:

$$\text{Average inventory level} = \frac{\frac{1}{2}(Q - S) t_1 + 0t_2}{t_1 + t_2} = \frac{\frac{1}{2}(Q - S) t_1}{T} \qquad (14.17)$$

Can we find other ways of expressing t_1 and T? Since we know that the maximum inventory is $Q - S$ and that d represents the constant daily demand, we have

$$t_1 = \frac{Q - S}{d} \text{ days} \qquad (14.18)$$

That is, the maximum inventory level of $Q - S$ units will be used up in $(Q - S)/d$ days. Since Q units are ordered and shipped each cycle, we know that the length of a cycle must be

$$T = \frac{Q}{d} \text{ days} \qquad (14.19)$$

Using equations (14.18) and (14.19) with equation (14.17), we can write the following:

$$\text{Average inventory level} = \frac{\frac{1}{2}(Q - S)[(Q - S)/d]}{Q/d} = \frac{(Q - S)^2}{2Q} \quad (14.20)$$

Thus the average inventory level is expressed in terms of two inventory decisions, how much we order (Q) and the maximum number of backorders we will allow (S).

The formula for the annual number of orders placed under this model is identical to that for the EOQ model. With D representing the annual demand, we have

$$\text{Annual number of orders} = \frac{D}{Q} \quad (14.21)$$

The next step is to develop an expression for the average backorder level. Since there is a maximum of S backorders, we can use the same logic that we used to establish average inventory to find the average number of backorders. We have an average number of backorders during the period t_2 of $\frac{1}{2}$ the maximum number of backorders or $\frac{1}{2} S$. Since we do not have any backorders during the t_1 days we have inventory, we can calculate the average backorder level in a manner similar to equation (14.17). Using this approach, we have

$$\text{Average backorder level} = \frac{0 t_1 + (S/2)t_2}{T} = \frac{(S/2)t_2}{T} \quad (14.22)$$

Since we let the maximum number of backorders reach an amount S at a daily rate of d, the length of the backorder portion of the inventory cycle is

$$t_2 = \frac{S}{d} \quad (14.23)$$

Using equations (14.23) and (14.19) in equation (14.22), we have

$$\text{Average backorder level} = \frac{(S/2)(S/d)}{Q/d} = \frac{S^2}{2Q} \quad (14.24)$$

Let

$$C_h = \text{cost to maintain one unit in inventory for 1 year}$$
$$C_0 = \text{cost per order}$$
$$C_b = \text{cost to maintain one unit on backorder for 1 year}$$

The total annual cost (TC) for the inventory model with backorders becomes

$$\text{TC} = \frac{(Q - S)^2}{2Q} C_h + \frac{D}{Q} C_0 + \frac{S^2}{2Q} C_b \quad (14.25)$$

Given the cost estimates C_h, C_0, and C_b and the annual demand D, we can determine the minimum-cost values for the inventory decisions, Q and S. With two decision components a trial-and-error approach, while valid, becomes cumbersome. Using calculus, quantitative analysts have established the following minimum-cost formulas for the order quantity Q^* and the planned backorders S^*:

$$Q^* = \sqrt{\frac{2DC_0}{C_h} \left(\frac{C_h + C_b}{C_b} \right)} \qquad (14.26)$$

and

$$S^* = Q^* \left(\frac{C_h}{C_h + C_b} \right) \qquad (14.27)$$

An Example. Suppose that the Higley Radio Components Company has a product for which the assumptions of the inventory model with backorders are valid. Information obtained by the company is as follows:

$$D = 2000 \text{ units per year}$$
$$I = 20\% \text{ per year}$$
$$C = \$50 \text{ per unit}$$
$$C_h = IC = \$10 \text{ per unit per year}$$
$$C_0 = \$25 \text{ per order}$$

The company is considering the possibility of allowing some backorders to occur for the product. The annual unit backorder cost has been estimated to be $30 per unit per year. Using equations (14.26) and (14.27), we have

$$Q^* = \sqrt{\frac{2(2000)(25)}{10} \left(\frac{10 + 30}{30} \right)} = \sqrt{10,000(^{40}\!/_{30})} = 115$$

and

$$S^* = 115 \left(\frac{10}{10 + 30} \right) = 115(^{10}\!/_{40}) = 29$$

If this solution is implemented, the system will operate with the following properties:

$$\text{Maximum inventory} = Q - S = 115 - 29 = 86$$

$$\text{Cycle time} = T = \frac{Q}{D} (250) = 14.4 \text{ working days}$$

The total annual cost is computed as follows:

$$\text{Inventory holding cost} = \frac{(86)^2}{2(115)} (10) = \$322$$

$$\text{Ordering cost} = \frac{2000}{115} (25) = \$435$$

$$\text{Backorder cost} = \frac{(29)^2}{2(115)}(30) \qquad = \$110$$

$$\text{Total annual cost} = 322 + 435 + 110 = \$867$$

If the company had chosen to prohibit backorders and had adopted the regular EOQ model, the recommended inventory decision would have been

$$Q^* = \sqrt{\frac{2DC_0}{C_h}} = \sqrt{\frac{2(2000)(25)}{10}} = 100$$

This order quantity would have resulted in a total annual cost of $1000. Thus in this example, allowing backorders is projecting a $1000 - $867 = $133 or 13.3% savings in cost from the no-stockout EOQ model. The above comparison and conclusion are based on the assumption that the backorder model (no lost sales) with an annual cost per backordered unit of $30 is a valid model for the actual inventory situation. If the company has strong fears that stockouts might lead to lost sales, then the above savings might not be enough to warrant switching to an inventory policy that allowed for planned shortages.

14.4

QUANTITY DISCOUNTS FOR THE EOQ MODEL

Quantity discounts occur in numerous businesses and industries where suppliers provide an incentive for large purchase quantities by offering lower unit costs when items are purchased in larger lots or quantities. In this section we show how the EOQ model can be used when quantity discounts are offered.

Assume that we have a product where the basic EOQ model is applicable, but instead of a fixed unit cost, the supplier quotes the following discount schedule:

Discount Category	Order Size	Discount	Unit Cost
1	0 to 999	0%	$5.00
2	1000 to 2499	3%	$4.85
3	2500 and over	5%	$4.75

The 5% discount for the 2500-unit minimum order quantity looks tempting; however, realizing that higher order quantities result in higher inventory-carrying costs, we should prepare a thorough cost analysis before making a final inventory policy recommendation.

Suppose that the data and cost analysis show an inventory carrying charge of 20% per year, ordering costs of $49 per order, and an annual demand of 5000 units; what order quantity should we select? The following three-step procedure shows the calculations necessary to make this decision. In our preliminary calculations we will use Q_1 to indicate the order quantity for discount category 1, Q_2 for discount category 2, and Q_3 for discount category 3.

Step 1 For each discount category, compute a Q^* using the EOQ formula for the unit cost associated with the discount category.

Recall that the EOQ model provides $Q^* = \sqrt{2DC_0/C_h}$. In this case, for the three discount categories we obtain

$$Q_1^* = \sqrt{\frac{2(5000)49}{(0.20)(5.00)}} = 700$$

$$Q_2^* = \sqrt{\frac{2(5000)49}{(0.20)(4.85)}} = 711$$

$$Q_3^* = \sqrt{\frac{2(5000)49}{(0.20(4.75)}} = 718$$

Since the only differences in the EOQ formulas are slight differences in the inventory holding cost, the economic order quantities resulting from this step will be approximately the same. However, these order quantities will not usually all be of the size necessary to qualify for the discount price assumed. In the above case, both Q_2^* and Q_3^* are insufficient order quantities to obtain their assumed discounted costs of \$4.85 and \$4.75, respectively. For those order quantities for which the assumed price is incorrect, the following procedure must then be used.

Step 2 For those Q^*'s that are too small to qualify for the assumed discount price, adjust the order quantity upward to the nearest order quantity that will allow the product to be purchased at the assumed price.

In our example this causes us to set

$$Q_2^* = 1000$$

and

$$Q_3^* = 2500$$

If a calculated Q^* for a given discount price is large enough to qualify for a bigger discount, that value of Q^* cannot lead to an optimal solution. While the reason may not be obvious, it does turn out to be a property of the EOQ quantity discount model. Problem 23 at the end of the chapter will ask you to show that this property is true.

In the previous inventory models considered, we ignored the annual purchase cost of the item because it was constant and never affected by the inventory-order policy decision. However, in the quantity discount model, total annual purchase cost depends on the order quantity decision and the associated unit cost. Thus annual purchase cost (annual demand D × unit cost C) is included in the total cost model as shown below:

$$TC = \frac{Q}{2} C_h + \frac{D}{Q} C_0 + DC \tag{14.28}$$

Using this total cost model we can determine the optimal order quantity for the EOQ discount model in step 3 below.

Step 3   For each of the order quantities resulting from step 1 and step 2, compute the total annual cost using the unit price from the appropriate discount category and equation (14.28). The order quantity yielding the minimum total annual cost is the optimal order quantity.

The step 3 calculations for the example problem are summarized in Table 14.3. As you can see, a decision to order 1000 units at the 3% discount rate yields the minimum cost solution. While the 2500-unit order quantity would result in a 5% discount, its excessive inventory holding cost makes it the second best solution.

Table 14.3
Total Annual Cost Calculations for the EOQ Quantity Discount Model

Discount Category	Unit Cost	Order Quantity	Annual Inventory Cost	Annual Ordering Cost	Annual Purchase Cost	Total Annual Cost
1	$5.00	700	$ 350	$350	$25,000	$25,700
2	$4.85	1000	$ 485	$245	$24,250	$24,980
3	$4.75	2500	$1188	$ 98	$23,750	$25,036

14.5

ORDER QUANTITY–REORDER POINT MODELS WITH PROBABILISTIC DEMAND

In this section we consider the situation where the demand for the inventory item is uncertain and can be expressed only in probabilistic terms. Since the mathematical sophistication required for an exact formulation of a probabilistic inventory model is beyond the scope of this text, we will restrict the discussion to a probabilistic model where a heuristic procedure can be used to obtain good, workable inventory decisions. While the solution procedure can only be expected to provide approximations of the optimal inventory decisions, it has been found to yield very good decisions in many practical situations.

Let us consider the inventory problem of Dabco Industrial Lighting Distributors. Dabco purchases a special high-intensity light bulb for industrial lighting systems from a well-known light bulb manufacturer. Dabco would like a recommendation on how much to order and when to order so that a low-cost inventory policy can be realized. Pertinent facts are that ordering costs are $12 per order, one bulb costs $6, and Dabco uses a 20% annual holding cost rate for its inventory ($C_h = 0.20 \times 6 = \$1.20$). Dabco, which has over 1000 different customers, experiences a *probabilistic demand* in that the number of units shipped will vary considerably from day to day and from week to week. While demand is not known specifically, historical sales data indicate that an annual demand of 8000 bulbs, while not exact, can be used as a good estimate of the anticipated annual volume.

The How-Much-to-Order Decision

Although we are in a probabilistic demand situation, we have an estimate of the expected annual demand, of 8000 units. As an approximation of the best order quantity, we can apply the EOQ model with the expected annual demand D. In Dabco's case,

$$Q^* = \sqrt{\frac{2DC_0}{C_h}} = \sqrt{\frac{2(8000)(12)}{(1.20)}} = 400 \text{ units}$$

When we studied the sensitivity of the EOQ models, we learned that the total cost of operating an inventory system was relatively insensitive to order quantities that were in the neighborhood of Q^*. Using this knowledge, we expect 400 units per order to be a good approximation of the optimal order quantity. Even if annual demand were as low as 7000 units or as high as 9000 units, an order quantity of 400 units should be a relatively good low-cost order size. Thus, given our best estimate of annual demand at 8000 units, we will use $Q^* = 400$.

We have established the 400-unit order quantity by ignoring the fact that demand is probabilistic. Using $Q^* = 400$, Dabco can anticipate placing approximately $D/Q^* = 8000/400 = 20$ orders per year with an average of approximately $250/20 = 12.5$ working days between orders.

The When-to-Order Decision

We now want to establish a when-to-order decision rule or reorder point that will trigger the ordering process. Further pertinent data indicate that it takes a lead time of 5 working days for Dabco to receive a new supply of light bulbs from the manufacturer. With lead time demand of $(8000/250)(5 \text{ days}) = 160$ units, you might first suggest a 160-unit reorder point. However, it now becomes extremely important to consider the probability of demand. If 160 is the lead time demand, and if the demands are symmetrically distributed about 160, then lead time demand will be more than 160 units roughly 50% of the time.

When the demand during the 5-day lead time exceeds 160 units, Dabco will experience a shortage or stockout. Thus with a reorder point of 160 units, approximately 50% of the time (10 of the 20 orders a year), Dabco will be short of bulbs before the new supply arrives. This shortage rate would most likely be viewed as unacceptable. In order to determine a reorder point with a reasonably low likelihood or probability of a stockout, it is necessary to establish a probability distribution for the lead time demand and analyze stockout probabilities.

Using historical data, the *lead time demand distribution* for Dabco's light bulbs is assumed to be a normal distribution with a mean of 160 units and a standard deviation of 25 units. This distribution is shown in Figure 14.7. While the normal distribution of lead time demand is used in the Dabco problem, any demand probability distribution is acceptable. By collecting historical data on actual demands during the lead time period, an analyst should be able to determine if the normal distribution or some other probability distribution is the most realistic representation of the lead time demand distribution.

Given the lead time demand probability distribution, we can now determine how the reorder point r affects the probability of a stockout. Since stockouts occur whenever the demand during the lead time exceeds the reorder point, we can find the probability of a

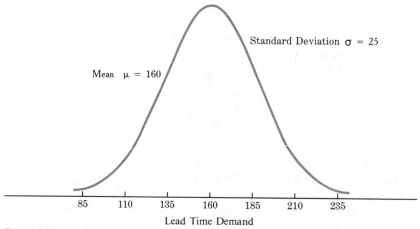

Figure 14.7
Distribution of Demand during the Lead Time for Dabco

stockout by using the lead time demand distribution to compute the probability of demand exceeding r.

We could now approach the when-to-order problem by defining a cost per stockout and then attempting to include this cost in a total-cost equation. However, a more practical approach is to ask the manager to define an acceptable *service level*, where the service level refers to the average number of stockouts we are willing to allow per year.

Suppose in this case that Dabco management is willing to tolerate an average of one stockout per year. Since $Q^* = 400$ indicates that Dabco will place 20 orders per year, this implies that management is willing to allow demand during lead time to exceed the reorder point one time in 20, or 5% of the time. This suggests that the reorder point r can be found by using the lead time demand distribution to find the value of r for which there is only a 5% chance of having a lead time demand exceeding it. This situation is shown graphically in Figure 14.8.

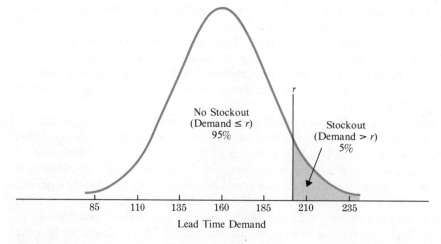

Figure 14.8
Reorder Point r that Allows a 5% Chance of Stockout for Dabco Light Bulbs

From the normal distribution tables in Appendix C, we see that an r value that is 1.645 standard deviations above the mean will allow stockouts during lead time 5% of the time. Therefore, for the assumed normal distribution for lead time demand with $\mu = 160$ and $\sigma = 25$, the reorder point r is determined by

$$r = 160 + 1.645(25) = 201$$

If a normal distribution is used for lead time demand, the general equation for r is

$$r = \mu + z\sigma \qquad (14.29)$$

where z is the number of standard deviations necessary to obtain the acceptable stockout probability.

Thus the recommended inventory decisions are to order 400 units whenever the inventory level reaches the reorder point of 201. Since the mean or expected demand during the lead time is 160 units, the $201 - 160 = 41$ units serve as a safety stock that absorbs higher-than-usual demand during the lead time. Roughly 95% of the time the 201 units will be able to satisfy demand during the lead time. The anticipated annual cost for this system is as follows:

Ordering cost	$(D/Q)C_0 = (8000/400)12$	$= \$240.00$
Holding cost—normal inventory	$(Q/2)C_h = (400/2)(1.20)$	$= \$240.00$
Holding cost—safety stock	$(41)C_h \quad = 41(1.20)$	$= \underline{\$\ 49.20}$
		$\$529.20$

If Dabco could have assumed that a known, constant demand rate of 8000 units per year existed for the light bulbs, a $Q^* = 400$, $r = 160$, and total annual cost of \$480 would have been optimal. When demand is uncertain and can only be expressed in probabilistic terms, a larger annual total cost can be expected. The larger cost occurs in the form of a larger inventory holding cost due to the fact that more inventory must be maintained in order to limit stockouts. For Dabco this additional inventory or safety stock was 41 units with an additional annual inventory holding cost of \$49.20.

14.6

SINGLE-PERIOD INVENTORY MODELS

In the previous treatment of inventory problems we assumed that the inventory system operates continuously and that we will have many repeating cycles or periods. Furthermore, we assumed that the inventory may be carried for one or more repeat periods and that we will be placing repeat orders for the product in the future. The *single-period inventory model* refers to inventory situations in which *one* order is placed for the product; at the end of the period the product has either sold out or there is a surplus of unsold items which will be sold for a salvage value. The single-period models occur in situations involving seasonal or perishable items that cannot be carried in inventory and sold in future periods. Seasonal clothing (such as bathing suits, winter coats) are typically handled in a single-period manner. In these situations a buyer places one preseason order for each item and then experiences a stockout or holds a clearance sale on the surplus stock at the end of the season. No items are carried in inventory and sold the following year. Newspapers are another example of a product that is ordered one time and is either sold or not sold during the single period. While newspapers are ordered daily, they cannot be carried in inventory and sold in later periods. Thus newspaper orders may be treated as a sequence of single-period models; that is, each day or period is separate, and a single-period inventory decision must be made each period (day). Since we order only once for the period, the only inventory decision we must make is *how much* of the product to order at the start of the period. Because newspaper sales is an excellent example of a single-period situation, the single-period inventory problem is sometimes referred to as the *newsboy problem.*

Obviously, if the demand were known for a single-period inventory situation, the solution would be easy: We would simply order the amount we knew would be demanded. However, in most single-period models the exact demand is not known. In fact, forecasts may show that demand can have a wide variety of values. If we are going to analyze this type of inventory decision problem in a quantitative manner, we will need information about the probabilities associated with the various demand possibilities. Thus the single-period model is another type of probabilistic demand model.

Let us consider a single-period inventory model that could be used to make a how-much-to-order decision for the Johnson Shoe Company. The buyer for the Johnson Shoe Company has decided to order a shoe for men that has just been shown at a buyers' meeting in New York City. The shoe will be part of the company's spring–summer promotion and will be sold through nine retail stores in the Chicago area. Since the shoe is designed for spring and summer months, it cannot be expected to sell in the fall. Johnson plans to hold a special August clearance sale in an attempt to sell all shoes that have not been sold by July 31. The shoes cost $40 per pair and retail for $60 per pair. At the sale price of $30 per pair, it is expected that all surplus shoes can be sold during the August sale. If you were the buyer for the Johnson Shoe Company, how many pairs of the shoes would you order?

An obvious question at this time is, what are the possible levels of demand for the shoe? We will need this information in order to answer the question of how much to order. Let us suppose that the uniform probability distribution shown in Figure 14.9 can be used to describe the demand for the size 10D shoes. In particular, note that the range

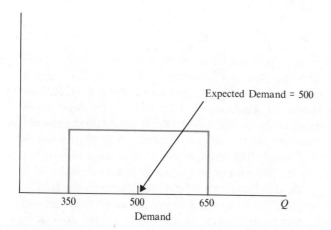

Figure 14.9
Uniform Probability Distribution of Demand for the Johnson Shoe Company Size 10D Shoes

of demand is from 350 to 650 pairs of shoes with an average or expected demand of 500 pairs of shoes.

Let us show how the method of marginal analysis, introduced in Section 4.9, can be used to determine the optimal order quantity for a single-period inventory model. Marginal analysis addresses the how-much-to-order question by comparing the cost or loss of *ordering one additional unit* with the cost or loss of *not ordering one additional unit*. The costs involved are defined as follows:

c_o = the cost per unit of *overestimating* demand; this cost represents the loss of ordering one additional unit and finding that it cannot be sold.

c_u = the cost per unit of *underestimating* demand; this cost represents the opportunity loss of not ordering one additional unit and finding that it could have been sold.

As shown in Section 4.9, the optimal order quantity (Q^*) using marginal analysis satisfies the following expression:

$$P(\text{demand} \leq Q^*) = \frac{c_u}{c_u + c_o} \tag{14.30}$$

In the Johnson Shoe Company example, the company will incur the cost of overestimating demand whenever it orders too much and has to sell the extra shoes during the August sale. Thus the cost per unit of overestimating demand is equal to the purchase cost per unit minus the August sales price per unit; that is, $c_o = \$40 - \$30 = \$10$. In other words, Johnson will lose \$10 for each pair of shoes that it orders over the quantity demanded. The cost of underestimating demand is the lost profit (opportunity loss) due to the fact that a pair of shoes that could have been sold was not available in inventory. Thus the per-unit cost of underestimating demand is the difference between the regular selling price per unit and the purchase cost per unit; that is, $c_u = \$60 - \$40 = \$20$. Thus equation (14.30) shows that the optimal order size for Johnson shoes must satisfy the following condition:

$$P(\text{demand} \leq Q^*) = \frac{c_u}{c_u + c_o} = \frac{20}{20 + 10} = \frac{20}{30} = \frac{2}{3}$$

We can find the optimal order quantity Q^* by referring to the assumed probability distribution shown in Figure 14.9 and finding the value of Q that will provide P (demand $\leq Q^*$) = $2/3$. In order to do this, we note that in the uniform distribution the probability is evenly distributed over the range from 350 to 650 pairs of shoes. Thus we can satisfy the expression for Q^* by moving two-thirds of the way from 350 to 650. Since this is a range of $650 - 350 = 300$, we move 200 units from 350 toward 650. Doing so provides the optimal order quantity of 550 pairs of size 10D shoes.

We note that in equation (14.30) the value of $c_u/(c_u + c_o)$ will be equal to 0.50 whenever $c_u = c_o$; in this case we select an order quantity corresponding to the median of the probability distribution of demand. With this choice it is just as likely to have a stockout as a surplus. This makes sense since the costs are equal. Whenever $c_u < c_o$, equation (14.30) leads to the choice of an order quantity more likely to be less than demand; hence a higher risk of a stockout is present. However, for the Johnson Shoe example, $c_u > c_o$ and the optimal order quantity leads to a higher risk of a surplus. This can be seen from the fact that the order quantity is 50 pairs of shoes over the expected demand of 500 pairs of shoes. Thus the optimal order quantity for Johnson has a probability of a stockout of ⅓ and a probability of a surplus of ⅔. This is what we should have expected, since $c_u = 20$ is greater than $c_o = 10$.

In the Johnson Shoe Company example a uniform probability distribution was used to describe the demand for the size 10D shoes. However, any probability distribution of demand may be used for the single-period inventory model. Using the cost of overestimation and underestimation, equation (14.30) can be used to find the location of Q^* in any appropriate demand probability distribution. For example, suppose that a normal probability distribution with a mean of 500 and a standard deviation of 100 had been a better description of the demand distribution for the size 10D shoes. This probability distribution is shown in Figure 14.10. With $c_u = \$20$ and $c_o = \$10$ as previously computed, equation (14.30) still shows that the optimal order quantity Q^* must satisfy the requirement that $P(\text{demand} \leq Q^*) = ⅔$. We simply use the table of areas under the normal curve (Appendix C) to find the Q^* where this condition is satisfied.

Referring to Figure 14.11, $P(\text{demand} \leq Q^*) = ⅔$ requires a 0.1667 area, or probability, between the mean demand of 500 and the optimal order quantity Q^*. From Appendix C we see that the 0.1667 area under the normal curve occurs at $z = 0.43$ standard deviation above the mean. With the mean or expected demand given by $\mu = 500$ and the standard deviation given by $\sigma = 100$, we have

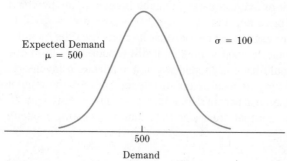

Expected Demand
$\mu = 500$

$\sigma = 100$

500

Demand

Figure 14.10
Normal Probability Distribution of Demand for the Johnson Shoe Company Size 10D Shoes

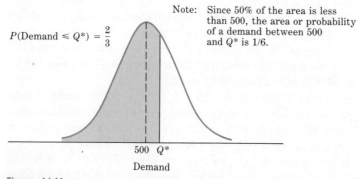

$P(\text{Demand} \leq Q^*) = \dfrac{2}{3}$

Note: Since 50% of the area is less than 500, the area or probability of a demand between 500 and Q^* is 1/6.

500 Q^*

Demand

Figure 14.11
Probability Distribution of Demand for the Johnson Shoe Company Showing the Location of the Optimal Order Quantity Q^*

$$Q^* = \mu + 0.43\sigma$$
$$= 500 + 0.43(100) = 543$$

Thus, with the assumed normal probability of demand, Johnson should order 543 pairs of the size 10D shoes in anticipation of customer orders.

In any probabilistic inventory model, the assumption about the probability distribution of demand is critical and can affect the recommended inventory decision. Equation (14.30), which provides the critical probability value, $P(\text{demand} \leq Q^*)$, can be applied to any demand probability distribution. Thus, in using quantitative approaches to inventory decision problems with probabilistic demand, we must exercise care in selecting the probability distribution that is the best approximation of reality.

14.7

MATERIAL REQUIREMENTS PLANNING

The inventory models we have discussed thus far have been found to be most appropriate for managing the inventories of finished goods. Finished goods are characterized as having *independent* demands, which may be forecast. In this section we focus on the planning and controlling of manufacturing inventories such as raw materials, components, and subassemblies. The demand for these types of items is *dependent* on the amounts of finished goods that are scheduled to be produced and can be *calculated* from the forecasts and scheduled production of finished goods. A technique that can be used to manage dependent-demand inventories is called *material requirements planning*, MRP.

Dependent Demand and the MRP Concept

Let us consider a finished product with one component part in order to illustrate dependent demand and the MRP concept. The demand for the finished product consists of many independent demands from many customers. Since these demands occur somewhat randomly, the demand rate is often fairly constant and the assumptions of the production lot size model are reasonable. The inventory level for the finished product is shown at the top of Figure 14.12. Assume that the single component is purchased from an outside supplier. When production of the finished product is initiated (point A on the time axis), the component parts are withdrawn from inventory in order to meet the manufacturing needs. The inventory level of the component part is shown at the bottom of Figure 14.12. When the component inventory level falls below its reorder point, an order for the component is placed with the supplier. The shipment is received at point B and the component inventory is replenished. However, note that the component is not needed again until the next production run for the finished product, which is scheduled to occur at point C. Clearly, the investment in the component inventory from points B to C is unnecessary. We can eliminate this unnecessary component inventory by "backing up" from point C according to the purchase lead time so that the components will arrive just at time C. This situation is illustrated in Figure 14.13. Note that the component inventory level and corresponding inventory investment is less in Figure 14.13 than it is in Figure 14.12.

The philosophy of ordering component inventory depending on the demand and production needs of other items is the approach followed by MRP. When operating properly, the MRP system will reduce inventory investment, improve work flow, reduce

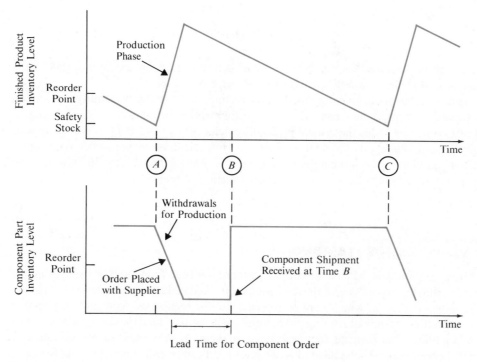

Figure 14.12
Finished Product and Component Part Inventory Levels without an MRP System

the shortage of materials and components, and help achieve more reliable delivery schedules.

Information System for MRP

What makes the MRP process difficult to implement is that many finished products consist of dozens or hundreds of parts, many of which are in turn dependent on other parts. Therefore, there must be accurate data and a reliable computer information system to perform the many calculations that will be required for MRP.

Material requirements planning calculations begin with the *master production schedule*, which states the number of units of each finished product to be produced each time period. With the information in the master production schedule, we can begin to determine when the various components that make up the final products must be available. Thus the next step will be to identify the list of components that are required by the products. This information is available from the *bill of materials* (BOM).

The BOM is a structured parts list; however, it differs from an ordinary parts list in that it shows the hierarchical relationship between the finished product and its various components. An example of a BOM for the Spiecker Company is shown in Figure 14.14. This figure shows the bill of materials for a 14-inch snowblower. The finished product is shown at the top of the hierarchy (called level 0). It consists of one main housing assembly, one wheel assembly, one engine assembly, and one handle assembly. If we consider the BOM as a "family tree," then the 14-inch snowblower is the "parent" item

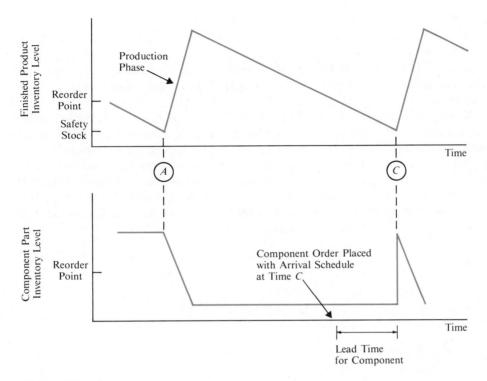

Figure 14.13
Finished Product and Component Part Inventory Levels with an MRP System

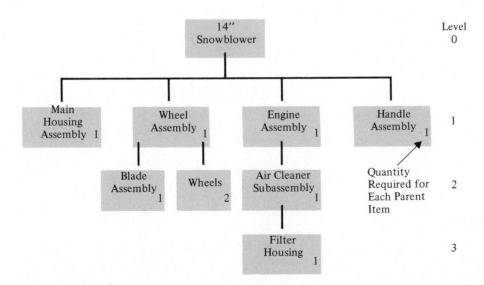

Figure 14.14
Bill of Materials for the Spiecker 14-inch Snowblower

for each of these assemblies. These assemblies, in turn, are parent items for all the components included in them. Thus the wheel assembly is the parent item of one blade assembly and two wheels. In general, items at level k are parent items for components at level $k + 1$. From the BOM we can determine exactly how many components are needed in order to produce the quantity of finished products stated in the master production schedule.

A schematic diagram of an MRP information system is given in Figure 14.15. Forecasts and orders are used to develop the master production schedule. The master production schedule, BOM, and current inventory files are the inputs needed to begin the MRP computations. The outputs from the MRP system are the requirements for each item in the BOM along with the dates each item is needed. This information is used to plan order releases for production and purchasing. In order to illustrate how these calculations are performed, let us consider an MRP system for the Spiecker snowblower example.

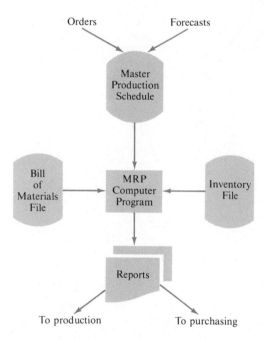

Figure 14.15
An MRP Computer System

MRP Calculations

In MRP terminology, the time periods are called *buckets* and are usually 1 week in length. Small buckets, such as 1 week, are good for scheduling production over a short time horizon but may be too precise for long-range planning. Often, larger buckets are used as the planning horizon gets larger. However, for the Spiecker Manufacturing problem, we assume that all buckets are 1 week in length.

The master production schedule calls for the final assembly of 1250 units of the 14-inch snowblower during week 21 of the current planning period. The assembly lead time is 1 week; thus, to meet this schedule, the four main assemblies in the bill of materials must be completed no later than the end of week 20. We now examine the production and inventory-control aspects for the engine assembly in detail, concentrating on how the MRP approach can be applied. Relevant data regarding the number of units in inventory and lead time are given in Table 14.4.

Table 14.4
Inventory on Hand and Lead Time for the Spiecker Manufacturing Example

Component	Units in Inventory	Lead Time (weeks)
Engine assembly	450	4
Air cleaner subassembly	250	1
Filter housing	500	2

Before the advent of MRP, the net requirement for each component was often found using the following formula:

$$\begin{array}{c}\text{Net component}\\\text{requirement}\end{array} = \left(\begin{array}{c}\text{number of components}\\\text{required to meet}\\\text{demand for}\\\text{finished good}\end{array}\right) - \left(\begin{array}{c}\text{number of}\\\text{components}\\\text{in inventory}\end{array}\right)$$

Thus the net requirements based on 1250 snowblowers are calculated as follows:

Components	Number of Components Required to Meet Demand for 1250 Snowblowers	−	Number in Inventory	=	Net Requirement
Engines	1250	−	450	=	800
Air cleaners	1250	−	250	=	1000
Filter housings	1250	−	500	=	750

However, note that this approach does not recognize the nature of dependent demand; for example, the number of filter housings required is dependent on the number of air cleaners produced, and so on.

The approach to determining net requirements whenever a dependent demand situation exists is

$$\begin{array}{c}\text{Net component}\\\text{requirement}\end{array} = \left(\begin{array}{c}\text{gross component}\\\text{requirement}\end{array}\right) - \left(\begin{array}{c}\text{scheduled}\\\text{receipts}\end{array}\right) - \left(\begin{array}{c}\text{number of}\\\text{components}\\\text{in inventory}\end{array}\right)$$

where the gross component requirement is the quantity of the component needed to support production at the next higher level of assembly. For example, the gross component requirement for the filter housing is the number of filter housings required to meet the net requirement for the air cleaner subassembly; the gross component requirement for the air cleaner subassembly is the number of air cleaners needed to meet the net requirement for the engine assembly; and so on. Let us see how these requirements can be computed for Spiecker Manufacturing. (We assume, for simplicity, that scheduled receipts are zero.)

Quantity of snowblowers to be produced:	1250
Gross requirements, engines:	1250
Less engines in inventory:	450
Net requirements, engines:	800 ← Engines
Gross requirements, air cleaners:	800
Less air cleaners in inventory:	250
Net requirements, air cleaners:	550 ← Air cleaners
Gross requirements, filter housings:	550
Less filter housings in inventory:	500
Net requirements, filter housings:	50 ← Filter housings

While the net requirements for engines under the MRP approach is still 800 units, note how MRP has used the dependent-demand information to show that fewer air cleaners and filter housings will be needed. In addition to considering dependent demand in the determination of net requirements for components, an MRP system also determines when the net requirements are needed. MRP handles this aspect of production and inventory control using the *time-phasing* concept. By starting with the time that the finished product must be completed, we can work backward in order to determine when an order for each component must be placed. For example, the time-phasing calculations for the Spiecker snowblower problem might appear as follows:

	Week
Complete order for engines:	20
Minus lead time for engines:	4
Place an order for engines:	16 ← Order engines
Complete order for air cleaners:	16
Minus lead time for air cleaners:	1
Place an order for air cleaners:	15 ← Order air cleaners
Complete order for filter housings:	15
Minus lead time for filter housings:	2
Place an order for filter housings:	13 ← Order filter housings

The components are scheduled so that they are made available only when required for the next higher level of assembly. Similar calculations can be made for all the other components of the snowblower, and if the bill of materials is exploded into detailed part requirements, a complete schedule for shop orders and purchase requisitions is available.

Until the development of large-scale computers, the sheer volume of calculations prohibited the implementation of an MRP system. For example, even in our small illustration, you can begin to appreciate the complexity involved in keeping track of the production and inventory status for every component. Fortunately, because of modern computer technology, we find that what was an unmanageable problem for earlier manual approaches can now be handled routinely by an MRP system.

Summary

In this chapter we have presented some of the approaches quantitative analysts use when developing models that will assist managers in establishing low-cost inventory policies. We first considered cases where the demand for the product occurs at a stable or constant rate. In analyzing these inventory systems, total cost models were developed that include ordering costs, inventory holding costs, and, in some cases, backordering costs. Then minimum-cost formulas for the order quantity Q were presented. A reorder point r can be established by considering the lead time demand for the item.

In addition, we discussed inventory decision models where a constant demand could not be assumed, and thus demand was described by a probability distribution. A critical issue with probabilistic demand models is obtaining a probability distribution that most realistically approximates demand for the item. A solution procedure was presented for approximating the order quantity and reorder point decisions. In addition, a solution procedure was presented for the single-period probabilistic inventory model.

We pointed out that the approaches referred to above are most applicable for controlling finished goods inventory. For manufacturing inventories, where dependent demand exists, methods such as MRP offer significant advantages.

With an increasing emphasis on lowering costs and improving productivity, the continued use of quantitative models for optimal inventory decisions, as well as the development of new methods of inventory management, can be expected. A recent development that evolved from the Japanese approach to material management and control is known as *just-in-time* (JIT). JIT is based on the goal of producing or delivering parts and material only when and where they are needed. It has been shown in practice that the JIT approach results in less inventory investment, reduces scrap, provides higher quality, and, in general, elicits improved productivity. Although a full discussion of JIT is beyond the scope of this text, further information can be found in a variety of texts dealing with modern techniques of production and operations management.

In closing this chapter we reemphasize that inventory and inventory systems can be an expensive phase of a firm's operation. It is of utmost economic importance for managers to be aware of the cost of inventory systems and to make the best possible operating policy decisions for the inventory system. Inventory decision models, as presented in this chapter, can help managers to develop good inventory policies.

Glossary

Inventory holding cost   The cost associated with maintaining an inventory investment: cost of the capital investment in the inventory, insurance, taxes, warehouse overhead, and so on. This cost may be stated as a percentage of the inventory investment or a cost per unit.

Cost of capital   The cost a firm incurs, usually interest payments on borrowed funds or dividend payments on stocks, in order to obtain capital for investment. The cost of capital, which may be stated as an annual percentage rate, is part of the holding cost associated with maintaining inventory.

Economic order quantity (EOQ)   The order quantity that minimizes the total inventory cost in the most fundamental inventory model.

Constant demand rate   An assumption of many inventory models that states that the same number of units are taken from inventory in each period of time.

Ordering cost   The cost (salaries, paper, transportation, and so on) associated with placing an order for an item.

Inventory position   Inventory on hand plus inventory on order.

Lead time   The time between the placing of an order and its receipt in the inventory system.

Lead time demand   The number of units demanded during the lead time period.

Reorder point   The inventory position when a new order should be placed.

Cycle time   The length of time between the placing of two consecutive orders.

Safety stock   Inventory maintained in order to reduce the number of stockouts resulting from higher-than-expected demand during the lead time.

Constant supply rate   The situation in which the inventory is built up at a constant rate over a period of time. This assumption applies to the production lot size model of this chapter.

Backorder   The receipt of an order for a product when there are no units on hand in inventory. These backorders become shortages, which are eventually satisfied when a new supply of the product becomes available.

Goodwill cost   A cost associated with a backorder, a lost sale, or any form of stockout or unsatisfied demand. This cost may be used to reflect the loss of future profits due to the fact that a customer experienced an unsatisfied demand.

Quantity discounts   Discounts or lower unit costs offered by a manufacturer when a customer purchases larger quantities of the product.

Probabilistic demand   Situations in which demand for the inventory item is not known exactly and probabilities must be used to describe the demand alternatives for the item.

Lead time demand distribution   In probabilistic inventory models, the distribution of demand that occurs during the lead time period.

Service level   The average number of stockouts we are willing to allow per year.

Single-period inventory models   Inventory models in which it is assumed that only one order is placed for the product, and at the end of the period the item has either sold out or there is a surplus of unsold items that will be sold for a salvage value.

Dependent demand   The demand for one component depends on the demand for another component.

Material requirements planning (MRP)   A computerized inventory management system whose function is to schedule production and control the level of inventory for components with dependent demand.

Master production schedule   A statement of how many finished items are to be produced and when.

Bill of materials   A structured parts list that shows the manner in which the product is actually put together.

Time phasing   Adding the dimension of time to inventory status data in an MRP environment.

Problems

1. Suppose that R & B Beverage Company has a soft-drink product that has a constant annual demand rate of 3600 cases. A case of the soft drink costs R & B $3. Ordering costs are $20 per order and inventory holding costs are charged at 25% of the cost per unit. There are 250 working days per year and the lead time is 5 days. Identify the following aspects of the inventory policy.
   a. Economic order quantity
   b. Reorder point
   c. Cycle time
   d. Total annual cost

2. A general property of the EOQ inventory model is that total inventory holding and total ordering costs are equal or balanced at the optimal solution. Use the data in problem 1 to show that this result is observed for this problem. Use equations (14.1), (14.2), and (14.4) to show in general that total inventory holding costs and total ordering costs are equal whenever $Q*$ is used.

3. The reorder point [see equation (14.6)] is defined as the lead time demand for the item. In cases of long lead times, the lead time demand and thus the reorder point may exceed the economic order quantity $Q*$. In such cases the inventory position will not equal the inventory on hand when an order is placed and the reorder point may either be expressed in terms of inventory position or inventory on hand. Consider the economic order quantity model with $D = 5000$, $C_o = \$32$, $C_h = \$2$, and 250 working days per year. Identify the reorder point in terms of inventory position and in terms of inventory on hand for each of the following lead times.
   a. 5 days
   b. 15 days
   c. 25 days
   d. 45 days

4. The XYZ Company purchases a component used in the manufacture of automobile generators directly from the supplier. XYZ's generator production operation, which is operated at a constant rate, will require 1000 components per month throughout the year (12,000 units annually). Assume ordering costs are $25 per order, unit cost is $2.50 per component, and annual inventory holding costs are charged at 20%. There are 250 working days per year and the lead time is 5 days. Answer the following inventory policy questions for XYZ.
   a. What is the EOQ for this component?
   b. What is the reorder point?
   c. What is the cycle time?
   d. What are the total annual inventory holding and ordering costs associated with your recommended EOQ?

5. Suppose that XYZ's management in problem 4 likes the operational efficiency of ordering in quantities of 1000 units and ordering once each month. How much more expensive would this policy be than your EOQ recommendation? Would you recommend in favor of the 1000-unit order quantity? Explain. What would the reorder point be if the 1000-unit quantity were acceptable?

6. Tele-Reco is a new specialty store that sells television sets, videotape recorders, video games, and other television-related products. A new Japanese-manufactured videotape recorder costs Tele-Reco $600 per unit. Tele-Reco's inventory carrying cost is figured at an annual rate of 22%. Ordering costs are estimated to be $70 per order.
    a. If demand for the new videotape recorder is expected to be constant with a rate of 20 units per month, what is the recommended order quantity for the videotape recorder?
    b. What are the estimated annual inventory holding and ordering costs associated with this product?
    c. How many orders will be placed per year?
    d. With 250 working days per year, what is the cycle time for this product?

7. A large distributor of oil-well drilling equipment has operated over the past 2 years with EOQ policies based on an annual inventory carrying charge of 22%. Under the EOQ policy, a particular product has been ordered with a $Q^* = 80$. A recent evaluation of carrying costs shows that because of an increase in the interest rate associated with bank loans, the inventory carrying charge should be 27%.
    a. What is the new economic order quantity for the product?
    b. Develop a general expression showing how the economic order quantity changes when the inventory carrying cost is changed from I to I'.

8. Nation-Wide Bus Lines is proud of its 6-week bus driver training program that it conducts for all new Nation-Wide drivers. A 6-week training program costs Nation-Wide $22,000 for instructors, equipment, and so on, and is independent of the number of new drivers in the class as long as the class size remains less than or equal to 35. The Nation-Wide training program must provide the company with approximately five new fully trained drivers per month. After completing the training program, new drivers are paid $1600 per month but do not work until a full-time driver position is open. Nation-Wide views the $1600 per month paid to each idle new driver as a holding cost necessary to maintain a supply of newly trained drivers available for immediate service. Viewing new drivers as inventory-type units, how large should the training classes be in order to minimize Nation-Wide's total annual training and new driver idle-time costs? How many training classes should the company hold each year? What is the total annual cost associated with your recommendation?

9. Cress Electronic Products manufactures components used in the automotive industry. Cress purchases parts for use in its manufacturing operation from a variety of different suppliers. One particular supplier provides a part where the assumptions of the EOQ model are realistic. The annual demand is 5000 units. Ordering costs are $80 per order and inventory carrying costs are figured at an annual rate of 25%.
    a. If the cost of the part is $20 per unit, what is the economic order quantity?
    b. Assume 250 days of operation per year. If the lead time for an order is 12 days, what is the reorder point?
    c. If the lead time for the part is 7 weeks (35 days), what is the reorder point?
    d. What is the reorder point for part (c) if the reorder point is expressed in terms of inventory on hand rather than inventory position?

10. All-Star Bat Manufacturing, Inc. supplies baseball bats to major and minor league baseball teams. After an initial order in January, demand over the 6-month baseball season is approximately constant at 1000 bats per month. Assuming that the bat production process can handle up to 4000 bats per month, the bat production setup

costs are $150 per setup, the production cost is $10 per bat, and assuming that All-Star uses a 2% monthly inventory holding cost, what production lot size would you recommend to meet the demand during the baseball season? If All-Star operates 20 days per month, how often will the production process operate, and what is the length of a production run?

11. Assume that a production line operates such that the production lot size model of Section 14.2 is applicable. Given $D = 6400$ units per year, $C_0 = \$100$, and $C_h = \$2$ per unit per year, compute the minimum-cost production lot size for each of the following production rates:
   a. 8000 units per year
   b. 10,000 units per year
   c. 32,000 units per year
   d. 100,000 units per year
   Compute the EOQ recommended lot size using equation (14.5). What two observations can you make about the relationship between the EOQ model and the production lot size model?

12. Assume that you are reviewing the production lot size decision associated with a production operation where $P = 8000$ units per year, $D = 2000$ units per year, $C_0 = \$300$, and $C_h = \$1.60$ per unit per year. Also assume that current practice calls for production runs of 500 units every 3 months. Would you recommend changing the current production lot size? Why or why not? How much could be saved by converting to your production lot size recommendation?

13. Wilson Publishing Company produces books for the retail market. Demand for a current book is expected to occur at a constant annual rate of 7200 copies. The cost of one copy of the book is $14.50. Inventory holding costs are based on an 18% annual rate, and production setup costs are $150 per setup. The equipment the book is produced on has an annual production volume of 25,000 copies. There are 250 working days per year and the lead time for a production run is 15 days. Use the production lot size model to compute the following values:
   a. Minimum-cost production lot size
   b. Number of production runs per year
   c. Cycle time
   d. Length of a production run
   e. Maximum inventory level
   f. Total annual cost
   g. Reorder point

14. A well-known manufacturer of several brands of toothpaste uses the production lot size model to determine production quantities for its various products. The product known as Extra White is currently being produced in production lot sizes of 5000 units. The length of the production run for this quantity is 10 days. Because of a recent shortage of a particular raw material, the supplier of the material has announced a cost increase that will be passed along to the manufacturer of Extra White. Current estimates are that the new raw material cost will increase the manufacturing cost of the toothpaste products by 23% per unit. What will be the effect of this price increase on the production lot sizes for Extra White?

15. Suppose that the XYZ Company of problem 4, with $D = 12,000$ units per year, $C_h = (2.50)(0.20) = \$0.50$, and $C_0 = \$25$, decided to operate with a backorder

inventory policy. Backorder costs are estimated to be $5 per unit per year. Identify the following:

a. Minimum-cost order quantity
b. Maximum number of backorders
c. Maximum inventory level
d. Cycle time
e. Total annual cost

16. Assuming 250 days of operation per year and a lead time of 5 days, what is the reorder point for the XYZ Company in problem 15? Show the general formula for the reorder point for the EOQ model with backorders. In general, is the reorder point when backorders are allowed greater than or less than the reorder point when backorders are not allowed? Explain.

17. A manager of an inventory system believes that inventory models are important decision-making aids. While often using an EOQ policy, the manager has never considered a backorder model because of the assumption that backorders were "bad" and should be avoided. However, with upper management's continued pressure for cost reduction, you have been asked to analyze the economics of a backordering policy for some products that can possibly be backordered. For a specific product with $D = 800$ units per year, $C_0 = \$150$, $C_h = \$3$, and $C_b = \$20$, what is the economic difference in the EOQ and the planned shortage or backorder model? If the manager adds constraints that no more than 25% of the units can be backordered and that no customer will have to wait more than 15 days for an order, should the backorder inventory policy be adopted? Assume 250 working days per year.

18. If the lead time for new orders is 20 days for the inventory system discussed in problem 17, find the reorder point for both the EOQ and the backorder models.

19. The A&M Hobby Shop carries a line of radio-controlled model racing cars. Demand for the cars is assumed to be constant at a rate of 40 cars per month. The cars cost $60 each, and ordering costs are approximately $15 per order, regardless of the order size. Inventory carrying costs are 20% annually.

a. Determine the economic order quantity and total annual cost under the assumption that no backorders are permitted.
b. Using a $45 per unit per year backorder cost, determine the minimum-cost inventory policy and total annual cost for the model racing cars.
c. What is the maximum number of days a customer would have to wait for a backorder under the policy in part (b)? Assume that the Hobby Shop is open for business 300 days per year.
d. Would you recommend a no-backorder or a backorder inventory policy for this product? Explain.
e. If the lead time is 6 days, what is the reorder point for both the no-backorder and backorder inventory policies?

20. Assume that the following quantity discount schedule is appropriate:

Order Size	Discount	Unit Cost
0 to 49	0%	$30.00
50 to 99	5%	$28.50
100 or more	10%	$27.00

If annual demand is 120 units, ordering cost is $20 per order, and annual inventory carrying cost is 25%, what order quantity would you recommend?

21. Apply the EOQ model to the following quantity discount situation:

Discount Category	Order Size	Discount	Unit Cost
1	0 to 99	0%	$10.00
2	100 or more	3%	$ 9.70

$D = 500$ units per year, $C_0 = \$40$, and an annual inventory holding cost of 20% are given. What order quantity do you recommend?

22. Keith Shoe Stores carries a basic black dress shoe for men that sells at an approximate constant rate of 500 pairs of shoes every 3 months. Keith's current buying policy is to order 500 pairs each time an order is placed. It costs Keith $30 to place an order. Inventory carrying costs have an annual rate of 20%. With the order quantity of 500, Keith obtains the shoes at the lowest possible unit cost of $28 per pair. Other quantity discounts offered by the manufacturer are as follows:

Order Quantity	Price per Pair
0–99	$36
100–199	$32
200–299	$30
300 or more	$28

What is the minimum cost order quantity for the shoes? What are the annual savings of your inventory policy over the policy currently being used by Keith?

23. In the EOQ model with quantity discounts we stated that if the Q^* for a price category is larger than necessary to qualify for the category price, the category cannot be optimal. Use the two discount categories in problem 21 to show that this is true. That

is, plot the total cost curves for the two categories and show that if the category 2 minimum cost Q is an acceptable solution, we do not have to consider category 1.

24. Floyd Distributors, Inc. provides a variety of auto parts to small local garages. Floyd purchases parts from manufacturers according to the EOQ model and then ships the parts from a regional warehouse direct to its customers. For a particular type of muffler, Floyd's EOQ analysis recommends orders with $Q^* = 25$ to satisfy an annual demand of 200 mufflers. There are 250 working days per year and the lead time averages 15 days.
    a. What is the reorder point if Floyd assumes a constant demand rate?
    b. Suppose that an analysis of Floyd's muffler demand shows that the lead time demand follows a normal distribution with $\mu = 12$ and $\sigma = 2.5$. If Floyd's management can tolerate one stockout per year, what is the revised reorder point?
    c. What is the safety stock for part (b)? If $C_h = \$5$/unit/year, what is the extra cost due to the uncertainty of demand?

25. For Floyd Distributors in problem 24, we were given $Q^* = 25$, $D = 200$, $C_h = \$5$, and a normal lead time demand distribution with $\mu = 12$ and $\sigma = 2.5$.
    a. What is Floyd's reorder point if the firm is willing to tolerate two stockouts during the year?
    b. What is Floyd's reorder point if the firm wants to restrict the probability of a stockout on any one cycle to at most 1%?
    c. What are the safety stock levels and the annual safety stock costs for the reorder points found in parts (a) and (b)?

26. A product with an annual demand of 1000 units has $C_0 = \$25.50$ and $C_h = \$8$. The demand exhibits some variability such that the lead time demand follows a normal distribution with $\mu = 25$ and $\sigma = 5$.
    a. What is the recommended order quantity?
    b. What are the reorder point and safety stock if the firm desires at most a 2% probability of stockout on any given order cycle?
    c. If a manager sets the reorder point at 30, what is the probability of a stockout on any given order cycle? How many times would you expect to stockout during the year if this reorder point were used?

27. The B&S Novelty and Craft Shop in Bennington, Vermont, sells a variety of quality handmade items to tourists. B&S will sell 300 hand-carved miniature replicas of a Colonial soldier each year, but the demand pattern during the year is uncertain. The replicas sell for $20 each, and B&S uses a 15% annual inventory holding cost rate. Ordering costs are $5 per order, and demand during the lead time follows a normal distribution with $\mu = 15$ and $\sigma = 6$.
    a. What is the recommended order quantity?
    b. If B&S is willing to accept a stockout roughly twice a year, what reorder point would you recommend? What is the probability that B&S will have a stockout in any one order cycle?
    c. What are the safety stock and annual safety stock costs for this product?

28. The J&B Card Shop sells calendars with different Colonial pictures shown for each month. The once-a-year order for each year's calendar arrives in September. From past experience the September-to-July demand for the calendars can be approximated by a normal distribution with $\mu = 500$ and $\sigma = 120$. The calendars cost $1.50 each, and J&B sells them for $3 each.

a. If J&B throws out all unsold calendars at the end of July (that is, salvage value is zero), how many calendars should be ordered?

b. If J&B reduces the calendar price to $1 at the end of July and can sell all surplus calendars at this price, how many calendars should be ordered?

29. The Gilbert Air-Conditioning Company is considering the purchase of a special shipment of portable air conditioners manufactured in Japan. Each unit will cost Gilbert $80 and it will be sold for $125. Gilbert does not want to carry surplus air conditioners over until the following year. Thus all supplies will be sold to a wholesaler, who has agreed to take all surplus units for $50 per unit. Assume that the air conditioner demand has a normal distribution with $\mu = 20$ and $\sigma = 8$.

 a. What is the recommended order quantity?

 b. What is the probability that Gilbert will sell all units it orders?

30. A popular newsstand in a large metropolitan area is attempting to determine how many copies of the Sunday paper it should purchase each week. Demand for the newspaper on Sundays can be approximated by a normal distribution with $\mu = 450$ and $\sigma = 100$. The newspaper costs the newsstand 35¢ a copy and sells for 50¢ a copy. The newsstand does not receive any value from surplus papers and thus absorbs a 100% loss on all unsold papers.

 a. How many copies of the Sunday paper should be purchased each week?

 b. What is the probability that the newsstand will have a stockout?

 c. The manager of the newsstand is concerned about the newsstand's image if the probability of stockout is high. The customers often purchase other items after coming to the newsstand for the Sunday paper. Frequent stockouts would cause customers to go to another newsstand. The manager agrees that a 50¢ loss of goodwill cost should be assigned to any stockout. What are the new recommended order quantity and the new probability of a stockout?

31. A perishable dairy product is ordered daily at a particular supermarket. The product, which costs $1.19 per unit, sells for $1.65 per unit. If units are unsold at the end of the day, the supplier takes them back at a rebate of $1 per unit. Assume that daily demand is approximately normally distributed with $\mu = 150$ and $\sigma = 30$.

 a. What is your recommended daily order quantity for the supermarket?

 b. What is the probability that the supermarket will sell all the units it orders?

 c. In problems such as these, why would the supplier offer a rebate as high as $1? For example, why not offer a nominal rebate of, say, 25¢ per unit? What happens to the supermarket order quantity as the rebate is reduced?

32. A retail outlet sells a seasonal product for $10 per unit. The cost of the product is $8 per unit. All units not sold during the regular season are sold for half the retail price in an end-of-season clearance sale. Assume that demand for the product is uniformly distributed between 200 and 800.

 a. What is the recommended order quantity?

 b. What is the probability that at least some customers will ask to purchase the product after the outlet is sold out? That is, what is the probability of a stockout using your order quantity in part (a)?

 c. Suppose the owner's policy is that in order to keep customers happy and returning to the store later, stockouts should be avoided if at all possible. What is your recommended order quantity if you get the owner to agree to a 0.15 probability of stockout?

d. Using your answer to part (c), what is the goodwill cost you are assigning to a stockout?

33. Consider the Spiecker Manufacturing example of Section 14.7. Determine the net requirements for the engine assembly, the air cleaner subassembly, and the filter housing if the number of units in inventory were 2000, 1500, and 1000, respectively. Assume that 5000 units of the 14-inch snowblower are required in week 21.

34. For the Spiecker Manufacturing example of Section 14.7, determine the effect on time phasing if lead times were 10 for the engine assembly, 3 for the air cleaner subassembly, and 5 for the filter housing.

35. C & D Lawn Products manufactures a rotary spreader for applying fertilizer. A portion of the bill of materials is shown below:

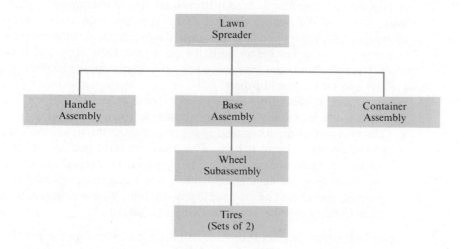

If 3000 lawn spreaders are needed to satisfy a customer's order, determine the net requirements for the base assembly, wheel subassembly, and tires (sets of two). Assume that 1000 base assemblies, 1500 wheel subassemblies, and 800 tires (sets of two) are currently in inventory.

36. In problem 35, assume that the lead time for the base assembly, wheel subassembly, and tires are 2 weeks, 4 weeks, and 5 weeks, respectively. If all components must be completed no later than week 15 of the current production period, determine when orders must be placed to meet the production schedule.

Case Problem
A Make-or-Buy Analysis

Wagner Fabricating Company is reviewing the economic feasibility of manufacturing a part that it currently purchases from a supplier. Forecasted annual demand for the part is 3200 units. Wagner operates 250 days per year.

Wagner's financial analysts have established a cost of capital of 14% on the use of funds for investments within the company. In addition, over the past year $600,000 has been the average investment in the company's inventory. Accounting information shows that a total of $24,000 was spent on taxes and insurance related to the company's inventory. In addition, it has been estimated that $9000 was lost due to inventory shrinkage, which included damaged goods as well as pilferage. A remaining $15,000 was spent on warehouse overhead, including utility expenses for heating and lighting.

An analysis of the purchasing operation shows that approximately 2 hours are required to process and coordinate an order for the part regardless of the quantity ordered. Purchasing salaries average $28 per hour, including employee benefits. In addition, a detailed analysis of 125 orders showed that $2375 was spent on telephone, paper, and postage directly related to the ordering process.

A 5-day lead time is required to obtain the part from the supplier. An analysis of demand during the lead time shows that lead time demand is approximately normally distributed with a mean of 64 units and a standard deviation of 10 units. Service level guidelines indicate that one stockout per year is acceptable.

Currently the company has a contract to purchase the part from a supplier at a cost of $18 per unit. However, over the past few months, the company's production capacity has been expanded. As a result, excess capacity is now available in certain production departments and the company is considering the alternative of producing the parts itself.

Forecasted utilization of equipment shows that production capacity will be available for the part being considered. The production capacity is available at the rate of 1000 units per month, with up to 5 months of production time available. It is felt that with a 2-week lead time, schedules can be arranged so that the part can be produced whenever needed. The demand during the 2-week lead time is approximately normally distributed with a mean of 128 units and a standard deviation of 20 units. Production costs are expected to be $17 per part.

A concern of management is that setup costs will be significant. The total cost of labor and lost production time is estimated to be $50 per hour, and it will take a full 8-hour shift to set up the equipment for producing the part.

Managerial Report

Develop a report for management of Wagner Fabricating that will address the question of whether the company should continue to purchase the part from the supplier or should begin to produce the part itself. Include the following factors in your report:

1. An analysis of the inventory holding cost, including the appropriate annual inventory holding cost rate.

2. An analysis of ordering costs, including the appropriate cost per order from the supplier.

3. An analysis of setup costs for the production operation.

4. A development of the inventory policy for the following two alternatives:
   a. Ordering a fixed quantity Q from the supplier
   b. Ordering a fixed quantity Q from in-plant production

5. Include the following in the policies of 4(a) and 4(b) above:
   a. The quantity Q
   b. The number of order or production runs per year
   c. The cycle time
   d. The reorder point
   e. The amount of safety stock
   f. The expected maximum inventory level
   g. The average inventory level
   h. The total annual inventory holding cost
   i. The total annual ordering cost
   j. The total annual cost of the units purchased or manufactured
   k. The total annual cost of the purchase policy and the total annual cost of the production policy

6. Make a recommendation as to whether the company should purchase or manufacture the part. What is the saving associated with your recommendation as compared with the other alternative?

APPENDIX 14.1

DEVELOPMENT OF THE OPTIMAL ORDER QUANTITY (Q*) FOR THE EOQ MODEL

Given equation (14.3) as the general total annual cost formula for the EOQ model,

$$TC = \frac{1}{2} QC_h + \frac{D}{Q} C_0 \tag{14.3}$$

we can find the order quantity Q that minimizes the total cost by setting the derivative, dTC/dQ, equal to zero and solving for Q^*.

$$\frac{dTC}{dQ} = \frac{1}{2} C_h - \frac{D}{Q^2} C_0 = 0$$

$$\frac{1}{2} C_h = \frac{D}{Q^2} C_0$$

$$C_h Q^2 = 2DC_0$$

$$Q^2 = \frac{2DC_0}{C_h}$$

Hence

$$Q^* = \sqrt{\frac{2DC_0}{C_h}} \tag{14.5}$$

The second derivative is

$$\frac{d^2TC}{dQ^2} = \frac{2D}{Q^3} C_0$$

Since the value of the second derivative is greater than zero for D, C_0, and Q greater than zero, Q^* from equation (14.5) is in fact the minimum-cost solution.

APPENDIX 14.2

DEVELOPMENT OF THE OPTIMAL LOT SIZE (Q*) FOR THE PRODUCTION LOT SIZE MODEL

Given equation (14.15) as the total annual cost formula for the production lot size model,

$$TC = \frac{1}{2} \left(1 - \frac{D}{P} \right) QC_h + \frac{D}{Q} C_0 \tag{14.15}$$

we can find the order quantity Q that minimizes the total cost by setting the derivative, dTC/dQ, equal to zero and solving for $Q*$.

$$\frac{dTC}{dQ} = \frac{1}{2}\left(1 - \frac{D}{P}\right)C_h - \frac{D}{Q^2}C_0 = 0$$

Solving for $Q*$ we have

$$\frac{1}{2}\left(1 - \frac{D}{P}\right)C_h = \frac{D}{Q^2}C_0$$

$$\left(1 - \frac{D}{P}\right)C_hQ^2 = 2DC_0$$

$$Q^2 = \frac{2DC_0}{(1 - D/P)C_h}$$

Hence

$$Q* = \sqrt{\frac{2DC_0}{(1 - D/P)C_h}} \tag{14.16}$$

The second derivative is

$$\frac{d^2TC}{dQ^2} = \frac{2DC_0}{Q^3}$$

Since the value of the second derivative is greater than zero for D, C_0, and Q greater than zero, $Q*$ from equation (14.16) is a minimum-cost solution.

Quantitative Methods
in Practice

Informatics General Corporation*
Woodland Hills, California

Informatics General Corporation was formed in 1962 as a computer software company. Today it has offices located throughout the United States and in several foreign countries. Informatics has concentrated its business activities in three areas:

1. Software products—selling computer software packages
2. Information processing—selling computer time-sharing services and turnkey systems
3. Professional services—providing consultants, computer programmers, and other trained personnel

The application that follows describes the use of an Informatics system known as DISTRIBUTION IV. This computerized system has been used for effective inventory management and merchandise distribution in several of Informatics' client companies.

An Inventory Management Application

Medi-$ave Pharmacies, part of National Medical Enterprises, distributes prescription and over-the-counter merchandise to drugstores across the United States. The company was experiencing profitability problems stemming from a very rapid growth rate. The total number of distribution outlets had climbed to 86, and the company was handling more than 7000 items in its inventory.

To improve bottom-line profits, Medi-$ave attacked the problem of poorly controlled expansion by working toward resource concentration. The company moved away from small-chain-store distribution and began to develop a business base with leased pharmacy departments in major discount stores.

One of the key factors in making the resource concentration strategy successful was to meticulously control the flow of goods from inventory to drug outlets. To achieve tight inventory control, Medi-$ave installed the merchandise management reporting system called DISTRIBUTION IV. DISTRIBUTION IV is a computerized information system developed for the wholesale and retail distribution industry by Informatics General

*The authors are indebted to Carol Hays of Informatics General Corporation for providing this application.

Corporation. With the DISTRIBUTION IV system, Medi-$ave generates as many as 500 different reports, which provide all types of inventory status information. Many of these reports not only provide raw information, they also analyze it. For instance, DISTRIBUTION IV generates "picking" reports that give instructions to warehouse workers as each merchandise order is received. The picking report tells the worker exactly where to find the merchandise by aisle and bin location. "Screened" picking reports instruct the worker on how many items to draw from that location. For example, a report might list an order for five bottles of aspirin, show that only three bottles are in inventory, and then instruct the worker to pick all three bottles.

Medi-$ave also uses a billing system report that issues billings at the retail rate for each store. These billings come from store-by-store statements that show the number of items ordered and the number shipped, and they include a supply of retail price stickers.

An inventory management system issues reports on low stock, dead items, and items with excessive demand. These are examples of raw information reports that are analyzed by an inventory manager. The reports can be issued in any number of variations—by department, by age of inventory, by dollar amount in inventory—and the variation is selectable at any time.

Medi-$ave also analyzes its stock by velocity code. Velocity codes define the typical demand and movement of certain types of stock. For instance, an item coded "A" is ordered regularly and usually in large amounts, "B"-coded items have less movement than "A" items, and "C" items less movement than "B" items. Velocity code reports provide information on the amount of time each coded item remains in stock, helping to determine reorder rates.

The scientific buying module of DISTRIBUTION IV is an example of analytical reporting. Records on the history of activity levels for each item in inventory are analyzed and recommendations on purchases are made based on past demand. An objective of this scientific buying module is to make the inventory replenishment decisions in such a fashion that the contribution margin on inventory investment is maximized. What has evolved is a system known as "cycle time max." Under this system, 80–85% of the inventory replenishment orders are placed at a specified point in time. With such an ordering policy, larger orders are placed, resulting in quantity discounts and other concessions from suppliers.

The 15–20% of the inventory items that are not under the "cycle time max" system are handled by the scientific buying module on an exception basis. These items are generally the high-volume items that require standard order quantity and reorder level rules based on inventory carrying and ordering costs.

All of the reports provided by the DISTRIBUTION IV system have helped Medi-$ave to achieve tight controls on methods of inventory. Prescription merchandise is now shipped from the Medi-$ave warehouse in Baton Rouge, Louisiana, to all stores 5 days a week. Over-the-counter merchandise is shipped once every 2 weeks. Stores place their orders at prearranged times each day through direct order entry devices. At the same time, management information on store sales, number of prescriptions, purchases for the day, and bank deposits are also transmitted to the Medi-$ave headquarters.

With the new reporting system, Medi-$ave has been able to track the gross margin return on investment for every inventoried item and every vendor. Consequently, Medi-$ave has decided to concentrate on leased pharmacy departments of discount stores, minimizing activity with free-standing drugstores. In addition, the discount stores themselves stock health and beauty aids, allowing Medi-$ave to eliminate these items from its own inventory.

As a result of Medi-$ave's strategy, the total number of outlets was cut from 86 to 64. Inventory was reduced from 7000 items to 4500. These efforts have had positive effects on profit figures for Medi-$ave. Over the 5 years the company has conducted the program, profits have increased by 35.3%, and return on investment for the most recent year was up by 16.1%.

Sales per square foot are $286, as compared with the National Association of Chain Drug Stores (NACDS) reported national median of $158, and Medi-$ave now has a net pretax profit-to-sales ratio of 3.6% (versus the NACDS median of 2.3%).

The DISTRIBUTION IV merchandise management system was first introduced by Informatics in 1971. Today it is being used for the inventory control and management of over one million items.

Questions

1. What was the major problem of Medi-$ave pharmacies that led to the installation of DISTRIBUTION IV?
2. What is the purpose of the "picking" reports that are generated by the DISTRIBUTION IV system?
3. Describe the primary objective of the scientific buying module of DISTRIBUTION IV.
4. What are the major benefits Medi-$ave realized through the use of a merchandise management reporting system?

CHAPTER

15

Computer Simulation

The quantitative methods presented in the other chapters of this text emphasize the formulation and solution of a mathematical model of the system under study. Frequently the "solution" process employs an analytical procedure that identifies an optimal solution for the model. Although this process of formulating and solving a mathematical model has been successfully applied in many practical situations, there are other systems that are so complex they cannot be modeled and solved in this manner. Computer *simulation* has proved to be a valuable approach in these instances.

As with all models, the purpose of a computer simulation model is to provide a representation of a real system. Great care is usually taken to ensure that the simulation model is descriptive of the real system. Then, through a series of computer runs, or experiments, we study the behavior of the simulation model. The operating characteristics of the simulation model are then used to make inferences about the operating characteristics of the real system. The more representative the simulation model is of the real system, the better the inferences will be.

The surveys of current uses of quantitative techniques referred to in Chapter 1 indicate that computer simulation is one of the most popular and frequently used problem-solving tools. Some of the reasons why computer simulation is so widely used are the following.

1. Computer simulation can be used to obtain good solutions to problems that are too complex to be solved with procedures such as linear programming or inventory models.
2. The simulation approach is relatively easy to explain and understand. As a result, management confidence is increased, and consequently acceptance of the technique is more easily obtained.

3. Computer manufacturers have developed extensive software packages consisting of specialized simulation programming languages, thus facilitating use by analysts.

4. Simulation is a very flexible technique that can be applied to a wide variety of situations. For example, the technique has been used to describe the behavior of production systems, financial systems, inventory systems, waiting-line systems, and so on.

In this chapter we introduce the concepts and procedures of computer simulation by studying how the approach can be applied to a waiting-line system and to an inventory system. Analytic techniques for these problems are presented in Chapters 14 and 16. The analytic techniques should be used when the mathematical model is not too complex and the underlying assumptions are satisfied. In other cases the simulation approach, as described in this chapter, is a viable alternative.

15.1

COUNTY BEVERAGE DRIVE-THRU

County Beverage Drive-Thru, Inc. is a company that is building a chain of beverage supply stores throughout an area in northern Illinois. The stores are designed to enable customers to pick up beverages, snacks, and party supplies without getting out of their cars. A typical store design is shown in Figure 15.1. A service lane runs through the middle of the store, and soft drinks, beer, and other supplies are stored at various locations along both sides of the service lane. When a customer drives into the store, the store clerk takes the order, fills the order, and collects the money. The customer remains in the car while receiving service. When additional customers arrive at the store, they wait in a line outside the store until the preceding customer's order is complete. Then the next customer in line drives into the store for service.

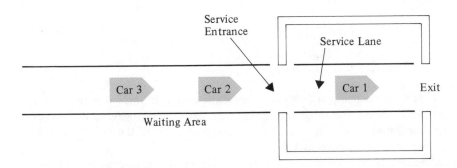

Figure 15.1
Layout of County Beverage Drive-Thru

The County Beverage Drive-Thru operation is an example of a *waiting-line* or *queueing system*. This particular waiting-line configuration has one service lane and is therefore referred to as a *single-channel waiting line*. If we are willing to assume that the number of cars arriving at the store has a Poisson probability distribution and that the length of time that the customer is actually in the store (service time) has an exponential probability distribution, the mathematical models presented in the next chapter can be used to study this waiting-line system. However, for the County Beverage Drive-Thru we are not willing to make these assumptions; thus we will be using computer simulation to study the operation of the store.

The specific situation we will simulate is a new store that will be located near a major shopping center. Construction of the store will not begin for approximately 3 months. County Beverage's president has requested planning information on the projected operation of the store, including estimates of the number of customers served, profitability of the store, and the number of lost sales due to long waiting lines.

In modeling the system we will study the store's operation in terms of what happens during time periods of 3 minutes each. That is, we will count the number of customer arrivals, count the number of customers lost, and determine whether or not a customer is being serviced during each 3-minute interval. A simulation model that increments time in fixed intervals is referred to as a *fixed-time simulation model*.[1]

Based on a study of traffic flow, the company has estimated that the probability distribution of customer arrivals is as shown in Table 15.1. This probability distribution is believed to be representative of the number of arrivals during the peak business period occurring in the late afternoon and early evening. As the data show, there is a 0.19 probability of no customers arriving during a given 3-minute period, a 0.39 probability of one customer arriving during the same 3-minute period, and so on.

Table 15.1
Probability Distribution for the Number of Customers Arriving at the County Beverage Drive-Thru during a 3-Minute Period

Number of Customers Arriving	Probability
0	0.19
1	0.39
2	0.19
3	0.15
4	0.08
	1.00

Sales records from the company's other stores show customer variability in terms of the size of the order placed. For three classes of order size (small, medium, and large), the probability for the various order sizes, the average time to fill the orders, and the average profit per order are shown in Table 15.2.

As an additional operating condition, experience with other company stores indicates that customers will wait for service only if there are less than four cars in the waiting line. If a customer arrives and there are already four cars in the waiting area, the customer will drive off. This failure to enter the waiting line is referred to as *balking* and results in a lost customer and a lost profit.

---

[1] Simulation models that increment time based on the occurrence of the next event (time of next arrival, time of next service, and so on) are referred to as *next-event simulation models*. Next-event simulation models will not be discussed in detail in this text.

Table 15.2
Order Size Data for the County Beverage Drive-Thru

Order Size	Probability	Time to Fill Order	Average Profit
Small	0.39	3 minutes	$0.75
Medium	0.50	6 minutes	$1.50
Large	<u>0.11</u>	9 minutes	$3.00
	1.00		

Simulation of Customer Arrivals

Before developing the complete simulation model, let us concentrate on simulating the number of customers that arrive at the store during any 3-minute period. In simulating the customer arrival process for County Beverage we will also be demonstrating how the probabilistic component of a real-world process or system is modeled.

The technique used to simulate customer arrivals is based on the use of random numbers. Almost everyone who has been exposed to simple random sampling and basic statistics is familiar with tables of random digits or random numbers.[2] We have included a table of random numbers in Appendix E. Twenty random numbers from the first line of this table are as follows:

$$63271 \quad 59986 \quad 71744 \quad 51102$$

The specific digit appearing in a given position is a random selection of the digits 0, 1, 2, . . . , 9, with each digit having an equal chance of selection. The grouping of the numbers in sets of five is simply for the convenience of making the table easier to read.

Suppose that we select random numbers from our table in sets of two digits. There are 100 two-digit random numbers from 00 to 99, with each two-digit random number having a $1/100 = 0.01$ chance of occurring. While we could select two-digit random numbers from any part of the random number table, suppose we start by using the first row of random numbers from Appendix E. The first 10 two-digit random numbers are

$$63 \quad 27 \quad 15 \quad 99 \quad 86 \quad 71 \quad 74 \quad 45 \quad 11 \quad 02$$

Now let us see how we can simulate the number of customers arriving in a 3-minute period by associating a given number of arrivals with each of the 100 two-digit random numbers. For example, let us consider the possibility of no customers arriving during a 3-minute interval. The probability distribution in Table 15.1 shows this event to have a 0.19 probability. Since each two-digit random number has a 0.01 probability of occurrence, we can let 19 of the 100 possible two-digit random numbers correspond to no customers arriving. Any 19 numbers from 00 to 99 will do, but for convenience we associate the arrival of 0 customers with the first 19 two-digit numbers: 00, 01, 02, 03, . . . , 18. Thus any time one of these two-digit numbers is observed in a random selection, we will say that no customers arrived during that period. Since the numbers 00 to 18 include 19% of the possible two-digit random numbers, we expect the arrival of no customers for any given 3-minute interval to have a probability of 0.19.

[2]See, for example, *A Million Random Digits with 100,000 Normal Deviates*, Rand Corporation, 1983.

Now consider the possibility of one customer arriving during a 3-minute period, an event that has a 0.39 probability of occurring (see Table 15.1). Letting 39 of the 100 two-digit numbers (such as 19, 20, 21, 22, . . . , 57) correspond to a simulated arrival of one customer will provide a 0.39 probability for one customer arrival. Continuing to assign the number of customers arriving to sets of two-digit numbers according to the probability distribution shown in Table 15.1 results in the sets of random numbers and customer arrival assignments shown in Table 15.3.

Table 15.3
Random Number Assignments for the Number of Customers Arriving at the County Beverage Drive-Thru during a 3-Minute Time Period

Number of Customers	Associated Two-Digit Random Numbers	Interval Description	Probability
0	00, 01, . . . , 18	00 but less than 19	0.19
1	19, 20, . . . , 57	19 but less than 58	0.39
2	58, 59, . . . , 76	58 but less than 77	0.19
3	77, 78, . . . , 91	77 but less than 92	0.15
4	92, 93, . . . , 99	92 but less than 100	0.08

Using Table 15.3 and the two-digit random numbers in the first row of Appendix E (63, 27, 15, 99, 86, . . .), we can simulate the number of customers arriving during the 3-minute periods. The results for 10 such 3-minute periods, or ½ hour of store operation, are shown in Table 15.4. The first two-digit random number, 63, is in the interval 58 to 76; thus according to Table 15.3 this corresponds to two customers arriving during the first 3-minute period. The second random number, 27, is in the interval 19 to 57; thus the number of simulated customer arrivals during the second period is one, and so on.

Table 15.4
Simulated Customer Arrivals for Ten 3-Minute Periods at the County Beverage Drive-Thru

Period	Random Number	Simulated Customer Arrivals
1	63	2
2	27	1
3	15	0
4	99	4
5	86	3
6	71	2
7	74	2
8	45	1
9	11	0
10	02	0
	Total	15

By selecting a two-digit random number for each 3-minute period, we can simulate the number of customer arrivals during that period. In doing so, the simulated probability distribution for the number of customer arrivals is the same as the given probability distribution shown in Table 15.1. In this manner, the simulation of customer arrivals has the same characteristics as the specified distribution of customer arrivals. A simulation that uses a random number procedure to generate probabilistic inputs such as the number of customer arrivals is referred to as a *Monte Carlo simulation*.

For any simulation model it is relatively easy to apply the above random number procedure to simulate values of a random variable. First develop a table similar to Table 15.3 by associating an interval of random numbers with each possible value of the random variable. In doing so, be sure that the probability of selecting a random number from each interval is the same as the actual probability associated with the value of the random variable. Then each time a value of the random variable is needed, we simply select a new random number and use the corresponding interval of random numbers to find the value of the random variable. Using a similar procedure, we see that the random number intervals given in Table 15.5 can be used to simulate order sizes for customers stopping at the County Beverage Drive-Thru.

Table 15.5
Random Number Assignments for the Order Size of Customers at the County Beverage Drive-Thru

Order Size	Associated Two-Digit Random Numbers	Interval Description	Probability
Small	00, 01, . . . , 38	00 but less than 39	0.39
Medium	39, 40, . . . , 88	39 but less than 89	0.50
Large	89, 90, . . . , 99	89 but less than 100	0.11

A Simulation Model for County Beverage Drive-Thru

Now that we know how to simulate the number of customers arriving and the customer order size, let us proceed with the development of the logic for the County Beverage simulation model. We will develop the model in a step-by-step manner. In doing so, we will carry out the necessary calculations to demonstrate how the simulation process works.

Whenever we need to generate a value for the number of customers arriving and/or the order size, we will use the random numbers from row 10 of Appendix E. Tables 15.3 and 15.5 will be used to determine the corresponding number of customer arrivals and the order sizes. For convenience, the first five two-digit random numbers from row 10 are reproduced here:

$$81 \quad 62 \quad 83 \quad 61 \quad 00$$

In developing the logic and mathematical relationships for the simulation model, we follow the logic and relationships of the actual operation as closely as possible. To demonstrate the simulation process, we begin with an idle or empty store and simulate what happens for each of the first three periods. Try to follow the logic of the model and see if you agree with the statements under the column labeled "Things That Happen."

Period 1 (see Figure 15.2)

Random Number	Things That Happen
81	Three cars arrive for service; thus the first car, identified as car 1, gets immediate service.
62	Car 1 places a medium order and hence will not finish service until the end of period 2 (6 minutes).
	Cars 2 and 3 still want service and consequently are in the waiting line.

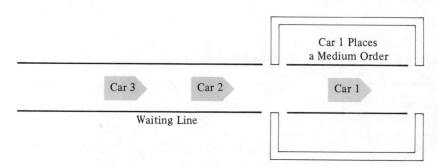

Figure 15.2
Status of the Operation for the First 3-Minute Simulation Period

Period 2 (see Figure 15.3)

Random Number	Things That Happen
83	Three more cars, identified as cars 4, 5, and 6, arrive for service.
	The Drive-Thru is still busy serving the customer from period 1; thus a total of five cars (two waiting plus three new customers) are wanting service this period.
	Too many cars are attempting to get service; hence one customer (car 6) will be lost and four cars will remain in the waiting line.
	Car 1 completes service at the end of this period; a profit of $1.50 is recorded.

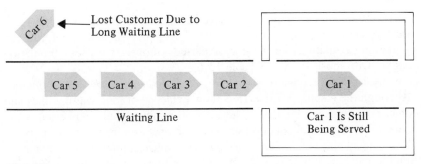

Figure 15.3
Status of the Operation for the Second 3-Minute Simulation Period

Period 3 (see Figure 15.4)

Random Number	Things That Happen
61	Two more cars, identified as cars 7 and 8, arrive for service.
	The service area is free at the beginning of the period, since the customer from period 1 (car 1) has completed service and left the Drive-Thru.
	One car from the waiting line (car 2) begins service, leaving five cars still wanting service; hence one customer (car 8) will be lost and four cars will remain in the waiting line.
00	The customer in car 2 places a small order; thus car 2 will finish service at the end of this period. Total profit as of the end of this period will be \$1.50 (car 1) + \$0.75 (car 2) = \$2.25.

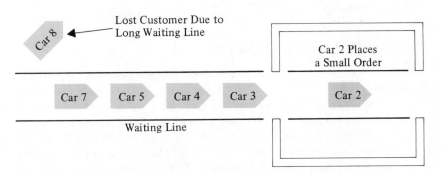

Figure 15.4
Status of the Operation for the Third 3-Minute Simulation Period

The flowchart of the simulation model we have been using is shown in Figure 15.5. Continue to use the random numbers from row 10 of Appendix E and see if you can conduct the simulation calculations for the first 10 periods of operation. Your simulation results should agree with those shown in Table 15.6.

At this point we have succeeded in simulating 10 periods, or a total of 30 minutes of operation. Although the results in Table 15.6 show evidence of long waiting lines and high lost customer rates (eight in the first ½ hour), a 30-minute simulation period is too short a time frame to draw general conclusions about the operation of the store. In order to take full advantage of the simulation procedure, we must continue to simulate the store's operation for many more time periods. But even for this relatively small simulation problem, continuing the hand simulation computations as we have been doing is unrealistic, if not practically impossible. Thus we will look to the computer to provide the computational assistance necessary to conduct the simulation process.

Computer Simulation: Generating Pseudorandom Numbers

If a computer procedure is going to be used to perform the simulation calculations, we will need a way for the computer to generate random numbers and values for the probabilistic components of the model. While the computer could be programmed to store random number tables and then follow the procedure outlined previously, the computer storage space required would result in an inefficient use of computer resources. For this reason, computer simulations make use of mathematical formulas that generate numbers which, for all practical purposes, have the same properties as the numbers selected from random number tables. These numbers are called *pseudorandom numbers*. In computer simulations pseudorandom numbers are used in exactly the same way as we used the random numbers selected from random number tables in our hand simulation.

Most mathematical formulas designed to generate pseudorandom numbers produce numbers from 0 up to but not including 1. Thus we must modify our approach in order to simulate the number of customer arrivals and the order size. We must now associate an interval of pseudorandom numbers with each number of arrivals so that the probability of generating a pseudorandom number in the interval will be equal to the probability of the corresponding number of arrivals. Table 15.7 shows how this would be done for the number of cars arriving at the County Beverage Drive-Thru. Note that Table 15.7 shows a pseudorandom number less than 0.19 corresponds to no arrivals, a pseudorandom number greater than or equal to 0.19 but less than 0.58 corresponds to one arrival, and so on. Table 15.8 provides the pseudorandom number intervals that can be used to simulate the order sizes for County Beverage customers.

Computer Simulation: Computer Program and Results

A computer *simulator* is a computer program written to conduct simulation computations. In order to simulate the operation of the County Beverage Drive-Thru, we need to develop a computer program containing the logic shown in Figure 15.5. Such a program would perform the calculations and keep track of the simulation results in a form similar to that shown in Table 15.6. Figure 15.6 shows a computer program written in the BASIC language that will simulate the County Beverage operation. This particular program was developed for and run on an IBM Personal Computer. For relatively small simulation models, the use of the BASIC language and a microcomputer is a realistic approach to conducting a simulation of a particular system.

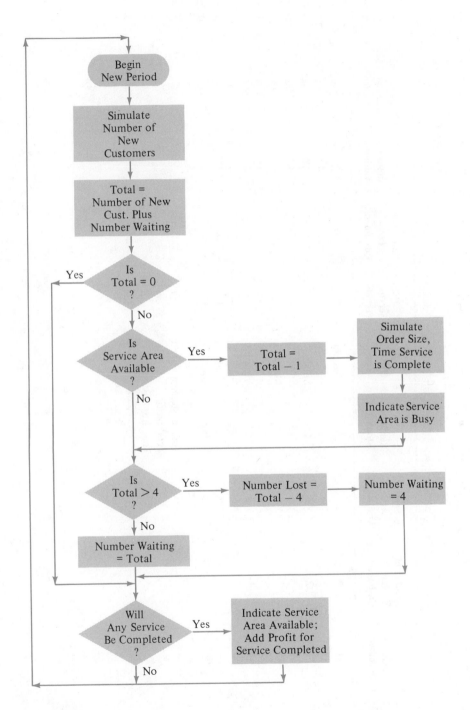

Figure 15.5
Flowchart of the County Beverage Drive-Thru Simulation Model

Table 15.6
Simulation Results from Ten 3-Minute Periods of Operation for the County Beverage Drive-Thru

Period	Random Number	Number of New Customers	Is Service Area Available?	Random Number	Order Size	Service Periods	Number of Lost Customers	Number Waiting	Was Service Completed This Period?	Profit
1	81	3	Yes	62	Medium	2	0	2	No	—
2	83	3	No	—	—	—	1	4	Yes	$1.50
3	61	2	Yes	00	Small	1	1	4	Yes	0.75
4	39	1	Yes	25	Small	1	0	4	Yes	0.75
5	45	1	Yes	68	Medium	2	0	4	No	—
6	35	1	No	—	—	—	1	4	Yes	1.50
7	37	1	Yes	63	Medium	2	0	4	No	—
8	60	2	No	—	—	—	2	4	Yes	1.50
9	24	1	Yes	21	Small	1	0	4	Yes	0.75
10	98	4	Yes	06	Small	1	3	4	Yes	0.75

Total customers served   7
Total profit $7.50
Total lost customers   8

Table 15.7
Pseudorandom Number Intervals and the Associated Number of Customers Arriving at the County Beverage Drive-Thru

Interval of Pseudorandom Numbers	Simulated Customer Arrivals	Probability
0.00 but less than 0.19	0	0.19
0.19 but less than 0.58	1	0.39
0.58 but less than 0.77	2	0.19
0.77 but less than 0.92	3	0.15
0.92 but less than 1.00	4	0.08
		1.00

Table 15.8
Pseudorandom Number Intervals and the Associated Order Sizes for County Beverage Customers

Interval of Pseudorandom Numbers	Simulated Order Size	Probability
0.00 but less than 0.39	Small	0.39
0.39 but less than 0.89	Medium	0.50
0.89 but less than 1.00	Large	0.11
		1.00

Results from the computer simulation are shown in Table 15.9. The store's operation was simulated for a total of 30 hours (600 time periods). Based on the simulation results, we are able to make the following observations about the behavior of the system:

1. 365 customers were serviced during the 30 hours of simulated operation. However, 575 customers (61.2%) were lost because of long waiting lines.
2. The average profit was $16.28 per hour or $1.34 per car serviced ($488.25/365 = $1.34).
3. The biggest problem with the store's operation appears to be the number of lost customers (an average of 19.17 per hour). An estimate of the average dollar loss per hour due to lost customers is 19.17 ($1.34 per car) = $25.69.

Table 15.9
Computer Simulation Results for 30 Hours of Operation

Item of Interest	Total	Percent	Hourly Average
Number served	365	38.8	12.17
Number lost	575	61.2	19.17
Profit	$488.25	—	$16.28

```
10 RANDOMIZE
20 REM
30 REM   THIS PROGRAM SIMULATES THE OPERATION OF THE
40 REM   COUNTY BEVERAGE DRIVE-THRU
50 REM
60 WORKING$ = "NO"
70 HOUR = 0
80 NUMBER.WAITING = 0
90 FINISH = 0
100 TOTAL.SERVED = 0
110 TOTAL.PROFIT = 0
120 TOTAL.LOST = 0
130 HOUR = HOUR + 1
135 TIME = 0
140 IF FINISH >= 20 THEN FINISH = FINISH - 20
150 REM
160 REM   SIMULATE THE NUMBER OF CARS ARRIVING IN A TIME PERIOD
170 REM
180 TIME = TIME + 1
190 X = RND(1)
200 IF X < .19 THEN NEW.CARS = 0
210 IF X >= .19 AND X < .58 THEN NEW.CARS = 1
220 IF X >= .58 AND X < .77 THEN NEW.CARS = 2
230 IF X >= .77 AND X < .92 THEN NEW.CARS = 3
240 IF X >= .92 THEN NEW.CARS = 4
250 TOTAL.IN.LINE = NUMBER.WAITING + NEW.CARS
260 IF TOTAL.IN.LINE = 0 THEN GOTO 500
270 IF WORKING$ = "YES" THEN GOTO 400
280 TOTAL.IN.LINE = TOTAL.IN.LINE - 1
290 REM
300 REM   SIMULATE THE ORDER SIZE FOR THEN NEXT CAR TO BE SERVICED
310 REM
320 X = RND(1)
330 IF X < .39 THEN LENGTH = 1
340 IF X >= .39 AND X < .89 THEN LENGTH = 2
350 IF X >= .89 THEN LENGTH = 3
360 FINISH = TIME + LENGTH - 1
370 WORKING$ = "YES"
380 REM
390 REM   CALCULATE THE NUMBER OF LOST CUSTOMERS AND THE NUMBER WAITING
400 REM
410 IF TOTAL.IN.LINE > 4 THEN GOTO 440
420 NUMBER.WAITING = TOTAL.IN.LINE
430 GOTO 500
440 LOST.CUSTOMERS = TOTAL.IN.LINE - 4
450 NUMBER.WAITING = 4
460 TOTAL.LOST = TOTAL.LOST + LOST.CUSTOMERS
470 REM
480 REM   RELEASE A CAR COMPLETING SERVICE AND RECORD THE PROFIT
490 REM
500 IF FINISH > TIME THEN GOTO 180
510 IF LENGTH = 1 THEN PROFIT = .75
520 IF LENGTH = 2 THEN PROFIT = 1.5
530 IF LENGTH = 3 THEN PROFIT = 3
540 TOTAL.PROFIT = TOTAL.PROFIT + PROFIT
550 TOTAL.SERVED = TOTAL.SERVED + 1
560 WORKING$ = "NO"
570 REM
580 REM   SIMULATION RUN OF 20 TIME PERIODS PER HOUR
590 REM
600 IF TIME < 20 THEN GOTO 180
620 IF HOUR < 30 THEN GOTO 130
630 REM
640 REM   WRITE THE SUMMARY RESULTS FOR THE SIMULATION RUN
650 REM
670 AVERAGE.SERVED = TOTAL.SERVED / 30
680 PERCENT.SERVED = TOTAL.SERVED / (TOTAL.SERVED + TOTAL.LOST) * 100
682 TS = TOTAL.SERVED
684 AV = AVERAGE.SERVED
686 PS = PERCENT.SERVED
690 AVERAGE.LOST = TOTAL.LOST / 30
700 PERCENT.LOST = 100 - PERCENT.SERVED
702 TL = TOTAL.LOST
```

Figure 15.6
BASIC Program for Simulation of the County Beverage Drive-Thru

```
704 AL = AVERAGE.LOST
706 PL = PERCENT.LOST
710 AVERAGE.PROFIT = TOTAL.PROFIT / 30
712 TP = TOTAL.PROFIT
714 AP = AVERAGE.PROFIT
718 CLS
720 PRINT
730 PRINT
740 PRINT TAB(8); "ITEM OF INTEREST"; TAB(29); "TOTAL"; TAB(41); "PERCENT";
745 PRINT TAB(55); "AVERAGE"
750 PRINT
755 PRINT
760 PRINT TAB(10); "NUMBER SERVED";
770 PRINT USING "     ######       ###.#      ######.##"; TS, PS, AV
780 PRINT
790 PRINT TAB(10); "NUMBER LOST   ";
800 PRINT USING "       ####       ###.#        ####.##"; TL, PL, AL
810 PRINT
820 PRINT TAB(10); "PROFIT        ";
830 PRINT USING "  ######.##                   #####.##"; TP, AP
840 END
```

Figure 15.6 *continued*

Recall for a moment that a primary objective of simulation is to describe the behavior of a real system. In the County Beverage Drive-Thru simulation this is exactly what we have done. We have not determined an optimal solution or decision for the store; we have simply simulated what could happen in 30 hours of actual operation of the Drive-Thru. If the actual operation behaves as the simulation model indicates, County Beverage will have a significant waiting-line problem with a sizable lost profit.

15.2

COUNTY BEVERAGE DRIVE-THRU: ADDITIONAL SIMULATION RESULTS

The primary conclusion from the simulation results presented in Section 15.1 for the County Beverage operation is that the store cannot handle the amount of business that is anticipated. Undoubtedly, County Beverage management would like to explore alternative operating policies that might improve service and hence company profits. Certainly, the addition of a second store clerk should help the performance of the system. In addition, since construction of the building has not begun, management could consider a possible redesign of the store. Thus the following two operating policies and store layouts are being considered.

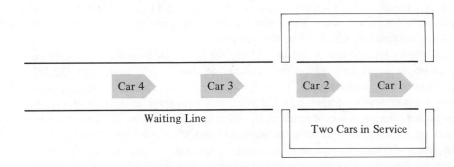

Figure 15.7
Proposed Design, System *A*, for the County Beverage Drive-Thru

System A (see Figure 15.7)

Two clerks will operate the store during the peak business period. Two cars will be permitted into the store area for servicing at the same time. Bottlenecks may still occur because both cars must use the same lane. If the second car completes service before the first car, it will have to wait for the first car to complete service before it can leave the store. Also, if the first car finishes service first, it can leave the store, but a new customer cannot enter the store until the car in the second position has its order filled.

System B (see Figure 15.8)

Two clerks will operate the store during the peak period. The service lane of the store will be widened to permit two cars to be serviced simultaneously, with each car being permitted to leave the store as soon as it is finished. Waiting cars move into the store as soon as either lane opens up.

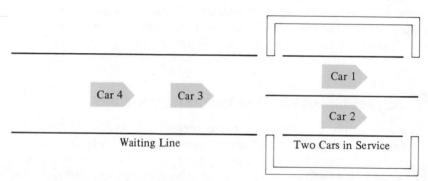

Figure 15.8
Proposed Design, System B, for the County Beverage Drive-Thru

In order to help the company determine which system should be adopted, simulation models were developed for both systems. Tables 15.10 and 15.11 show the results of 30 hours of simulation for each system. These simulation results provide critical information to the individual responsible for the final design decision.

System A shows an average profit of $27.88 per hour, an increase of $11.60 per hour over the original one-lane, one-server system. However, 302 customers (32.8%) were lost because of long waiting lines. Although system B shows a higher average profit ($34.48) and a lower lost customer rate (15.9%), the advantage of system B may be offset by the added construction cost required to widen the service lane. The final decision may still take more study, but the simulation results provide important information for the decision maker. Perhaps a creative person could come up with an idea for modifying the single-service-lane operation to increase the number of cars served and still avoid the costly two-lane construction. If such an idea occurs, a simulation model could be developed to evaluate its effectiveness.

Table 15.10
Computer Simulation Results for 30 Hours of Operation at the County Beverage Drive-Thru under System *A*

Item of Interest	Total	Percent	Hourly Average
Number served	618	67.2	20.60
Number lost	302	32.8	10.07
Profit	$836.25	—	$27.88

Table 15.11
Computer Simulation Results for 30 Hours of Operation at the County Beverage Drive-Thru under System *B*

Item of Interest	Total	Percent	Hourly Average
Number served	785	84.1	26.17
Number lost	148	15.9	4.93
Profit	$1034.25	—	$34.48

15.3

SOME PRACTICAL CONSIDERATIONS

Let us now describe some other aspects of simulation that are encountered in almost every simulation study.

Selecting a Simulation Language

In developing the computer program or simulator, a decision must be made as to the computer language that will be used. General-purpose programming languages such as BASIC, FORTRAN, Pascal, and PL/1 can be used to develop the computer programs. However, as simulation applications and interest have increased, users as well as computer manufacturers have recognized that most computer simulations have many common features: Values of random variables must be generated from probability distributions; tables are needed to keep track of simulation results; and so on. Thus special programming languages have been developed to enable analysts and programmers to describe more easily simulation models in computer form.

Some of the more common simulation languages in use today are GPSS, SIMSCRIPT, DYNAMO, GASP, and SLAM. These special simulation languages frequently have automatic or built-in time indicators, simplified procedures for generating probabilistic components, and automatic collection and printout of statistical results. One programming statement of a simulation language often performs the computation and record keeping that would require several BASIC, FORTRAN, PASCAL, or PL/1 statements to duplicate. There are complete textbooks devoted to a discussion of the use of computer languages in simulation, and the interested reader can refer to one of the references listed at the end of this text.

Validation

An important step in any simulation study is the validation of the simulation model. Validation involves verifying that the simulation model accurately represents the real-world system it is designed to simulate. Models that do not adequately reflect the behavior of the real system cannot be expected to provide worthwhile information. Thus, before implementing any simulation results, the analyst must be sure that a thorough job of model validation has been done.

If the simulation model applies to a system currently in operation, the simulation results can be compared with the current and past behavior of the system in order to determine the validity of the model. The procedure usually followed is to run the simulation model using an actual set of past observations. In this way the output of the simulation model can be compared directly with the behavior of the actual system. Any major difference in the results is indicative of problems in the model.

Another approach to model validation is to have the overall model reviewed by people who are most familiar with the operation of the real system. This review is subjective in nature, with the appropriate individuals evaluating the reasonableness of the simulation model and the simulation results.

In addition, careful attention should also be paid to the programming of the simulation model. Even if the model is formulated correctly, improper programming of the model can lead to inaccurate results. Standard quality control steps and good programming practice can be the best safeguards against this type of error.

A further check in the validation procedure is to compare the simulated distributions for the probabilistic components with the corresponding distributions in the real system. For example, in the County Beverage study the probability distribution for the number of cars arriving in a three-minute period was considered known and was an important input for the simulation model. Recall that the simulation results shown in Table 15.9 were based on 30 hours of simulated operation. Since each hour has 20 three-minute periods, the total simulation contained 30(20) = 600 three-minute periods. Thus if the simulation model is correctly simulating the number of customers arriving at the store, the relative frequencies of the number of cars arriving should approximate the probability distribution for the real system as shown in Table 15.1.

Table 15.12 shows the relative frequencies for the number of customers that arrived during the 600 three-minute periods in the simulation run. A comparison of the simulated distribution and the actual probability distribution from Table 15.1 shows no major differences. Thus we conclude that the number of customer arrivals is being simulated correctly.[3] A similar comparison of the actual and simulated distributions for the size of the customer orders resulted in the conclusion that the model was valid in terms of its simulation of this probabilistic component.

Start-up Problems

Most simulation studies are concerned with the operation of a system during its normal, or *steady-state*, condition. In the County Beverage example the firm is interested in what happens during a "normal" hour of operation. Recall, however, that when we started

---

[3]Standard statistical procedures, such as the chi-square goodness-of-fit test, can be performed to test whether or not the results observed are representative of those expected. The use of such tests is described in most standard statistics texts. For example, see D. R. Anderson, D. J. Sweeney, and T. A. Williams, *Statistics for Business and Economics*, 3d ed. St. Paul, Minn.: West Publishing Company, 1987.

Table 15.12
Model Validation Step Showing a Comparison of the Simulated Relative Frequencies and the Actual Probability Distribution for the Number of Customer Arrivals at the County Beverage Drive-Thru

Number of Customer Arrivals	Number of Simulated Periods Having This Number of Arrivals	Simulated Relative Frequencies	Actual Probabilities (See Table 15.1)
0	124	0.207	0.19
1	229	0.382	0.39
2	104	0.173	0.19
3	86	0.143	0.15
4	57	0.095	0.08
Totals	600	1.000	1.00

the simulation calculations we assumed that no cars were waiting and that no cars were being served. Therefore data collected during the first part of the simulation can be expected to differ from the data collected during time intervals later in the simulation. The usual way to avoid start-up difficulties is to run the simulation model for a specified time period without collecting any data. The length of this start-up period must be sufficient for the system to have stabilized. Data are then collected on the system after it has reached a stable, or steady-state, condition. For the County Beverage simulation, the first hour of operation was considered a start-up period. The data for the 30 hours of simulation reported in Table 15.9 are the simulation results for hours 2 through 31.

Statistical Considerations

The results of any simulation run actually represent a sample. For example, the simulation results in Table 15.9 can be viewed as a sample of 30 hours of operation. Thus $16.28 is an estimate of the average hourly profit for the County Beverage operation. The important thing to keep in mind is that different values for average hourly profit would be observed if the simulation was run again using a different sequence of random numbers. To illustrate this, we ran two additional simulations each for 30 hours of operation. The results are as follows:

	Simulation 1	Simulation 2	Simulation 3
Number served	365	361	356
Number lost	575	558	622
Average hourly profit	$16.28	$16.13	$16.10

Although different results are obtained in each case, by running the simulations for long periods, most analysts are willing to use the values obtained from the original simulation run to estimate the true mean value of interest.

Determining the best statistical approach to estimating the value of some quantity (such as hourly profit) is not a simple problem. A complete study of this issue would require a background in the area of statistics referred to as experimental design. Consequently, the interested reader is referred to one of the more advanced texts in simulation listed at the end of the text.

15.4

AN INVENTORY SIMULATION MODEL

In this section we present a simulation model of an inventory system being operated by an auto supply company. While we are interested in understanding how the inventory system operates, we are also interested in making decisions concerning the reorder point and order quantity for a particular inventory item. By designing a set of experiments, we will simulate the operation of the inventory system for a variety of reorder point and order quantity alternatives. Upon completion of the experiments with the simulation model, we should be able to select a good reorder point and order quantity for the item.

Art's Auto Supplies, Inc. is a specialty auto supplies store that carries over 1000 items in inventory. Although the store's manager has used inventory models to determine how much to order and when to order for most of the products, the manager has become especially concerned about the inventory problem for a deluxe tool cabinet. Demand for the cabinets has been relatively low but subject to some variability. While on approximately one-half of the days the store is open for business no one orders a cabinet, about 1 day per month three or four orders occur. If variable demand were the only source of uncertainty, the store manager believes that the order quantity and reorder point decisions could be based on an inventory model, perhaps similar to the inventory model discussed in Section 14.1. However, the tool cabinet inventory problem is further complicated by the fact that the lead time—the time between order placement and order arrival—also varies. Historically the length of the lead time has been anywhere between 1 and 5 days. These lead times have caused the store to run out of inventory on several occasions. Orders received during the out-of-stock period have caused lost sales. Thus, given this situation, the store manager would like to establish order quantity and reorder point decisions that minimize total relevant inventory costs—that is, ordering, holding, and stockout or shortage costs.

After an analysis of delivery charges and other costs associated with each order, the store manager was able to estimate the order cost at $20 per order. An analysis of interest, insurance, and other inventory carrying costs led to an estimate for the holding cost of $0.10 per unit per day. Finally, the shortage cost was estimated to be $50 per unit. The total cost of the system is given by the sum of the ordering cost, the holding cost, and the shortage cost. The objective is to find the order quantity and reorder point combination that will result in the lowest possible total cost.

A first step in the simulation approach to this problem is to develop a model that can be used to simulate the total costs corresponding to a specific order size and reorder point. Then, using this model, the two decision variables can be varied systematically in order to determine what appears to be the lowest-cost combination. Let us see what is involved in developing such a model to carry out a 1-day simulation of the inventory process.

Assume that a specific reorder point and order quantity have already been selected. We must begin each day of the simulation by checking whether any inventory that had been ordered has just arrived. If so, the current inventory on hand must be increased by the quantity of goods received. Note that this assumes that orders are received and inventory on hand is updated at the start of each day. If this assumption is not appropriate, a different model, perhaps calling for goods to be received at the end of the day, would have to be developed.

Next our simulator must generate a value for the daily demand from the appropriate probability distribution. If there is sufficient inventory on hand to meet the daily demand, the inventory on hand will be decreased by the amount of the daily demand. If, however, inventory on hand is not sufficient to satisfy all the demand, we will satisfy as much of the demand as possible. The inventory will then be zero, and a shortage cost will be computed for all unsatisfied demand. In using this procedure we are assuming that if a customer orders more cabinets than the store has in inventory, the customer will take what is available and shop elsewhere for the remainder of the order. With another auto supply store only two blocks away, the store manager is sure that unsatisfied demand will result in lost sales, and a $50 goodwill cost for each shortage is appropriate.

After the daily order has been processed, the next step is to determine if the ending inventory has reached the reorder point and a new order should be placed. However, prior to placing a new order, we must check to see if the most recent order is outstanding and should be arriving shortly. If so, we do not place another order.[4] Otherwise an order is placed and the company incurs an ordering cost. If a new order is placed, a lead time must be randomly generated to reflect the time between the placement and the receipt of the goods.

Finally, an inventory holding cost, which is $0.10 for each unit in the daily ending inventory, is computed. The sum of the shortage costs, ordering costs, and inventory holding costs becomes the total daily cost for the simulation. Performing the above sequence of operations would complete 1 day of simulation. Figure 15.9 depicts this daily simulation process for the deluxe tool-cabinet inventory operation.

The daily simulation process should be repeated for as many days as are necessary to obtain meaningful results. The output from the simulation will show the total cost involved in using one particular order quantity and reorder point combination. By simulating the inventory operation with different order quantity–reorder point combinations, we can compare total operating costs and select the apparent "best" order quantity and reorder point decisions for the deluxe tool cabinets.

Suppose that the store has a complete set of records showing the demand for the deluxe tool cabinets for the past year (300 days). Furthermore, suppose that the records also show the number of days between placement and receipt of each order over the same period. Table 15.13 shows the frequency and relative frequency distributions for demand, and Table 15.14 shows the frequency and relative frequency distributions for lead time.

In order to carry out the simulation steps depicted in Figure 15.9, we must develop the procedure for generating values from the demand and lead time distributions. As before, we will associate with each value of the random variable an interval of pseudorandom numbers such that the probability of generating a pseudorandom number in that interval is the same as the relative frequency of the associated demand and lead time. The intervals of pseudorandom numbers are shown in Tables 15.15 and 15.16.

To appreciate how the simulation method works for this problem, we will follow a 10-day simulation of the process. Let us assume that the store manager wants to determine

---

[4]We are assuming that it will never be necessary to have two orders outstanding simultaneously. However, in other simulation models, having several orders outstanding may be an entirely appropriate assumption.

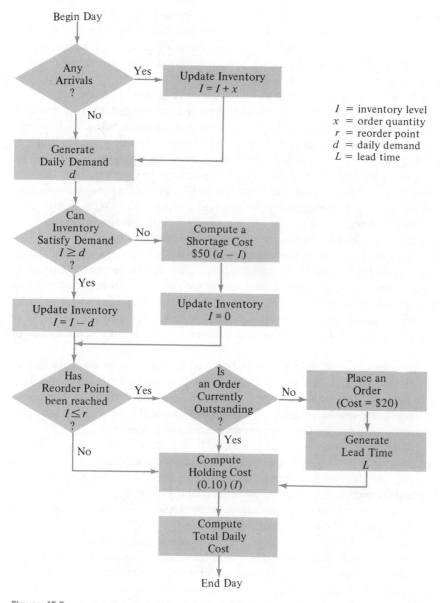

Figure 15.9
Flowchart of the Simulation of 1 Day of Operation for the Art's Auto Supplies Inventory System

the effect of using an order quantity of 5 units with a reorder point of 3 units. For purposes of starting the simulation, let us assume that we have a beginning inventory of 5 units at the start of day 1 of our 10-day simulation.

Refer to the flowchart in Figure 15.9. The first step is to check to see if any shipments have arrived. Since this is the first day of the simulation, we assume no arrivals, and generate the daily demand for day 1. Let us assume that we use a computer to generate pseudorandom numbers between 0 and 0.999 · · · and that the first number generated is

Table 15.13
Frequency and Relative Frequency Distributions for Demand in Art's Auto
Supplies Problem

Demand (units)	Frequency (days)	Relative Frequency
0	150	0.50
1	75	0.25
2	45	0.15
3	15	0.05
4	15	0.05
	300	1.00

Table 15.14
Frequency and Relative Frequency Distributions for Lead Time in Art's
Auto Supplies Problem

Lead Time (days)	Frequency (days)	Relative Frequency
1	6	0.20
2	3	0.10
3	12	0.40
4	6	0.20
5	3	0.10
	30	1.00

Table 15.15
Pseudorandom Numbers and Associated Daily Demands for Art's Auto Supplies Problem

Daily Demand	Relative Frequency	Interval of Pseudorandom Numbers	Probability of Selecting a Pseudorandom Number in Interval
0	0.50	0.00 but less than 0.50	0.50
1	0.25	0.50 but less than 0.75	0.25
2	0.15	0.75 but less than 0.90	0.15
3	0.05	0.90 but less than 0.95	0.05
4	0.05	0.95 but less than 1.00	0.05
	1.00		1.00

0.093. From Table 15.15 we see that this pseudorandom number corresponds to a demand of 0 units. Note that we have no shortage costs to compute, since the inventory on hand (5 units) is greater than the reorder point (3 units); and, we do not place an order. The holding costs for day 1 are computed to be ($0.10)5, or $0.50. With no shortages and

Table 15.16

Pseudorandom Number Intervals and Associated Lead Times for Art's Auto Supplies Problem

Lead Time (days)	Relative Frequency	Interval of Pseudorandom Numbers	Probability of Selecting a Pseudorandom Number in Interval
1	0.20	0.00 but less than 0.20	0.20
2	0.10	0.20 but less than 0.30	0.10
3	0.40	0.30 but less than 0.70	0.40
4	0.20	0.70 but less than 0.90	0.20
5	0.10	0.90 but less than 1.00	0.10
	1.00		1.00

Table 15.17

Computer Simulation Results for 10 Days of Operation of Art's Auto Supplies with an Order Quantity of 5 and Reorder Point of 3

Day	Beg Inv	Units Rec'd	Rndm Num	Units Demd	End Inv	Rndm Num	Lead Time	Holding Cost ($)	Order Cost ($)	Short Cost ($)	Total Cost ($)
1	5	0	0.093	0	5			0.50	0.00	0.00	0.50
2	5	0	0.681	1	4			0.40	0.00	0.00	0.40
3	4	0	0.292	0	4			0.40	0.00	0.00	0.40
4	4	0	0.528	1	3	0.620	3	0.30	20.00	0.00	20.30
5	3	0	0.866	2	1			0.10	0.00	0.00	0.10
6	1	0	0.975	4	0			0.00	0.00	150.00	150.00
7	0	5	0.622	1	4			0.40	0.00	0.00	0.40
8	4	0	0.819	2	2	0.939	5	0.20	20.00	0.00	20.20
9	2	0	0.373	0	2			0.20	0.00	0.00	0.20
10	2	0	0.353	0	2			0.20	0.00	0.00	0.20
					Average cost for 10 simulated days			0.27	4.00	15.00	19.27

no ordering, the total cost for day 1 is just the holding cost of $0.50. Continuing the simulation in this manner, we obtained the computer-generated results shown in Table 15.17.

At the start of day 4 the beginning inventory was 4 units. The random number selected to generate daily demand was 0.528; thus a daily demand of 1 unit was generated. As a result, the ending inventory dropped to 3 units and an order for 5 units was placed. Generating another random number, in this case 0.620, indicates (see Table 15.16) a lead time of 3 days, which means that the new order will be available on day 7. The day 4 costs are ($0.10)3 = $0.30 for the inventory holding cost and $20.00 for the ordering cost. Since there is no shortage cost, the total cost for the day is $20.30. The figures at the bottom of Table 15.17 provide the average holding cost, average ordering cost, average shortage cost, and average total cost for the 10-day simulation. Prior to drawing any firm conclusions based on these limited simulation results, we should run the simulation for many more days. Also we will want to test many other order quantity–reorder point combinations.

A computer programmer could develop a computer simulation program or simulator that would enable the store to explore a variety of order quantities and reorder points for a large number of simulated days. In Table 15.18 we present output from a simulator that was developed to solve inventory problems such as the auto supplies problem. In this simulator the decision maker has the option of selecting a variety of order quantities and reorder points. For purposes of illustration, the computer simulation output is shown for simulations with order quantities of from 5 units to 50 units in increments of 5 and for reorder points of from 1 to 10 in increments of one. A total of 1000 days is represented in the simulation of each order quantity–reorder point combination.

Table 15.18
Simulated Average Daily Cost for 1000 Days of Art's Auto Supplies Inventory Problem

Reorder Point	Order Quantity									
	5	10	15	20	25	30	35	40	45	50
1	14.35	8.30	6.58	5.20	5.35	4.16	3.30	4.42	3.98	5.22
2	11.51	5.93	5.46	3.92	3.91	3.44	2.96	3.69	3.62	3.71
3	9.34	5.64	3.37	3.01	3.03	2.84	3.96	3.29	2.90	3.07
4	6.90	4.12	3.47	2.78	3.14	2.79	3.29	3.25	3.37	3.42
5	5.41	3.31	2.85	2.42	2.61	3.24	3.25	2.93	3.18	3.22
6	4.72	2.75	2.69	2.60	2.39	2.74	2.93	3.06	3.13	3.34
7	4.72	2.85	2.52	2.60	2.76	2.71	3.06	2.99	3.02	3.28
8	5.50	2.89	2.66	2.50	2.62	2.75	2.99	3.05	3.33	3.56
9	4.36	3.11	2.62	2.62	2.66	2.77	3.05	3.18	3.34	3.49
10	4.68	3.05	2.75	2.72	2.80	2.85	3.18	3.28	3.31	3.72

We see that the results of this computer simulation indicate that the lowest-cost solution occurs at an order quantity of 25 units and a reorder point of 6 units; in this case the resulting average total cost is $2.39 per day. After studying these results, the store manager might wish to explore other order quantities near the apparent "best" order quantity of 25. In Table 15.19 the results of varying the order quantity from 21 to 30 (in increments of 1) and reorder points from 4 to 8 are shown. The smallest simulated average total cost of $2.33 now occurs when the order quantity is 22 units and the reorder point is 6 units. Note, however, that in this second set of simulation experiments the previously best order quantity of 25 units and reorder point of 6 units has a total cost of $2.75 per day. Since different random numbers were used in the two simulations, different total costs are to be expected. The selection of the "best" order quantity and reorder point is now up to the analyst. What decisions would you make? While you might want to run more or longer simulations, the simulation data of Tables 15.18 and 15.19 indicate that good solutions apparently exist with order quantities around 20 to 25 units and reorder points around 6 or 7 units. Thus, while simulation has not guaranteed an optimal solution, it has enabled us to identify apparent low-cost or "near-optimal" decisions for the inventory problem. The final decision for an order quantity and reorder point will be based on the store manager's preference from among the good or "near-optimal" solutions.

Table 15.19
Simulated Average Daily Cost for 1000 Days of Art's Auto Supplies Inventory Problem

Reorder Point	Order Quantity									
	21	22	23	24	25	26	27	28	29	30
4	2.94	3.02	3.13	2.74	2.89	2.56	2.74	3.07	2.67	3.24
5	2.59	2.58	2.84	2.70	2.66	2.59	2.88	2.57	2.48	2.75
6	2.55	2.33	2.87	2.35	2.75	2.45	2.81	2.79	2.61	2.60
7	2.52	2.45	2.47	2.51	2.57	2.62	2.61	2.63	2.62	2.67
8	2.50	2.69	2.48	2.49	2.63	2.57	2.63	2.69	2.69	2.71

15.5

ADVANTAGES AND DISADVANTAGES OF COMPUTER SIMULATION

A primary advantage of computer simulation is that it is applicable in complex cases where analytical procedures cannot be employed. For example, the County Beverage waiting-line system and the Art's Auto Supply inventory system were sufficiently complex that the analytical approaches discussed in other chapters of this text do not apply. That is, the forms of the probability distributions involved do not satisfy the assumptions of the analytical models. In general, as the number of probabilistic components in the system becomes larger, the more likely it is that simulation will be the best approach.

Another advantage of the simulation approach is that the simulation model and simulator provide a convenient experimental laboratory. Once the computer program has been developed, it is usually relatively easy to experiment with the model. For example, if we wanted to know the effect of an increase in shortage cost on the recommended solution to our inventory problem, we could have simply changed the shortage cost input value and rerun the simulation. The effect of experimental changes in other inputs, such as the probability distributions of customer arrivals, lead time, and so on, could also be investigated.

Simulation is not without its disadvantages. One obvious disadvantage is that someone must develop the computer program. For large simulation projects this is usually a substantial undertaking. Hence one should certainly not attempt to develop a simulation model unless the potential gains promise to outweigh the costs of model development. This disadvantage has been reduced with the development of computer simulation languages such as GPSS, SIMSCRIPT, and SLAM (available on microcomputers). The use of these languages often leads to considerable savings in time and money as the computer program or simulator is developed.

Another disadvantage of simulation is that it does not guarantee an optimal solution to a problem. One usually selects those values of the decision variables to test in the model that have a good chance of being near the optimal solution. However, since it is usually too costly to try all values of the decision variables, and since different simulation runs may provide different results, there is no guarantee that the best simulation solution found is the overall optimal solution. Nonetheless, the danger of obtaining bad solutions is slight if good judgment is exercised in developing and running the simulation model. The decision maker usually has a good idea of reasonable values to try for the decision variables, and it is usually possible to run the simulation long enough to identify the apparent best decisions.

Summary

In this chapter we have seen how two different problems could be analyzed and solved using computer simulation. Based on these two simulation models, we can make the following general observations about the simulation approach:

1. Simulation is most appropriate when the problem is too complex or difficult to solve using another quantitative technique.
2. A model must be developed to represent the various relationships existing in the problem situation.
3. A process involving random numbers must be used to generate values for the probabilistic components in the model.
4. A bookkeeping procedure must be developed to keep track of what is happening in the simulation process (see Table 15.6).
5. Because of the numerous calculations required in most simulations, a computer program or simulator is required.
6. The simulation process must be conducted for many days or periods in order to establish the long-run averages for the decision alternatives or other variables in the system.

Simulation should not be thought of as a technique for finding optimal solutions to problems. However, once a simulation model has been developed, a quantitative analyst may vary certain key design parameters and observe the effect on the output of the computer runs. Through a series of experiments with the simulation model good values may be selected for the key design parameters of the system. In the County Beverage problem, simulation experiments helped to identify the two-lane design as the one yielding the highest average hourly profit. In the simulation of Art's Auto Supply the simulation experiments helped identify an order quantity of 22 and a reorder level of 6 as a good low-cost inventory policy. Thus through these two examples we have shown how simulation experiments can be used to provide information on how to improve the performance of a system.

In both problems studied in this chapter, the probabilistic components resulted from discrete probability distributions; the random variables involved could take on only a finite number of values. In many situations probabilistic components are encountered that follow continuous distributions such as the normal or exponential probability distributions. The basic simulation approach we have developed in this chapter is still appropriate for these situations. The only difference concerns the method of generating random values from the appropriate continuous probability distributions.

Glossary

Simulation   A technique used to describe the behavior of a real-world system over time. Most often this technique employs a computer program to perform the simulation computations.

Monte Carlo simulation   Simulations that use a random number procedure to create values for the probabilistic components.

Pseudorandom numbers   Computer-generated numbers developed from mathematical expressions that have the properties of random numbers.

Simulator   The computer program written to perform the simulation calculations.

Problems

Most of the problems in this section are designed to enable you to perform simulations with hand calculations. To keep the calculations reasonable, we will ask you to consider only a few decision alternatives and relatively short periods of simulation. While this should give you a good understanding of the simulation process, the simulation results will not be sufficient for you to make final conclusions or decisions about the problem situation. If you have access to a computer, we suggest that you develop a computer simulation model for some of the problems. Then, by using the model to test several decision alternatives over a much longer simulated period of time, you will be able to obtain the desired decision-making information.

1. A retail store has experienced the following historical daily demand for a particular product:

Sales (units)	Frequency (days)
0	4
1	6
2	14
3	12
4	7
5	5
6	2
Total	50

a. Develop a relative frequency distribution for the above data.

b. Use the random numbers from row 4 of Appendix E to simulate daily sales for a 10-day period. This row begins with the random numbers 46276 87453 44790.

2. A study was conducted in order to investigate the number of cars arriving at the drive-in window of Community Savings Bank. The following data were collected for 100 randomly selected 5-minute intervals.

Number of Arrivals	Number of Occurrences
0	12
1	24
2	37
3	19
4	8
Total	100

a. Develop a relative frequency distribution for the above data.

b. Use random numbers 08, 61, and 22 to simulate the number of customers that arrive between 9:00 A.M. and 9:15 A.M. on a given day.

3. Decca Industries has experienced the following weekly absenteeism frequency over the past 20 weeks:

Number of Employees Absent	Frequency
1	2
2	4
3	7
4	3
5	2
6	2
Total	20

a. Develop a relative frequency distribution for the above data.
b. Use random numbers to simulate weekly absenteeism for a 15-week period.

4. Given below are 50 weeks of historical sales data for cars sold by Domoy Motors, Inc., a new-car dealer in Newton, Ohio.

Number of Sales	Number of Weeks
0	2
1	5
2	8
3	22
4	10
5	3
Total	50

a. Develop the relative frequency distribution for these data.
b. Use a random number procedure to simulate weekly automobile sales for a 12-week period.

5. Charlestown Electric Company is building a new generator for its Mount Washington plant. Even with good maintenance procedures, the generator will have periodic failures or breakdowns. Historical figures for similar generators indicate that the relative frequency of failures during a year is as follows:

Number of Failures	Relative Frequency
0	0.80
1	0.15
2	0.04
3	0.01

Assume that the useful lifetime of the generator is 25 years. Use simulation to estimate the number of breakdowns that will occur in the 25 years of operation. Is it common to have five or more consecutive years of operation without a failure?

6. Use row 15 of Appendix E beginning with 20711 and 55609 to simulate 15 minutes of operation for the County Beverage Drive-Thru application presented in Section 15.1. Show your simulation results in the format of Table 15.6.

7. A service technician for a major photocopier company is trained to service two models of copier: the X100 and the Y200. Approximately 60% of the technician's service calls are for the X100, and 40% are for the Y200. The service time distributions for the two models are as follows:

X100		Y200	
Time (minutes)	Relative Frequency	Time (minutes)	Relative Frequency
25	0.50	20	0.40
30	0.25	25	0.40
35	0.15	30	0.10
40	0.10	35	0.10

a. Show the random number intervals that can be used to simulate the type of machine to be serviced and the length of the service time for each model.
b. Simulate 20 service calls. What is the total service time the technician spends on the 20 calls?

8. Bushnell's Sand and Gravel (BSG) is a small firm that supplies sand, gravel, and topsoil to contractors and landscaping firms. BSG maintains an inventory of high-quality screened topsoil that is used to supply the weekly orders for two companies: Bath Landscaping Service and Pittsford Lawn Care, Inc. The problem BSG has is to determine how many cubic yards of screened topsoil to have in inventory at the beginning of each week in order to satisfy the needs of both its customers. BSG would like to select the lowest possible inventory level that would have a 0.95 probability of satisfying the combined weekly orders from both customers. The demand distributions for the two customers are as follows:

	Weekly Demand	Relative Frequency
Bath Landscaping	10	0.20
	15	0.35
	20	0.30
	25	0.10
	30	0.05
Pittsford Lawn Care	30	0.20
	40	0.40
	50	0.30
	60	0.10

Simulate 20 weeks of operation for beginning inventories of 70 and of 80 cubic yards. Based on your limited simulation results, how many cubic yards should BSG maintain in inventory? Discuss what you would want to do in a full-scale simulation of this problem.

9. Paula Williams is currently completing the design for a movie theater to be located in Big Flats, New York. Paula is in the planning stage of determining the number of customers the theater should accommodate. Based on experience with five other theaters over the past 8 years, Paula estimates that the nightly attendance will range from 100 to 500 with the relative frequencies shown below:

Approximate Number of Customers	Relative Frequency
100	0.10
200	0.25
300	0.40
400	0.15
500	0.10

a. Simulate 20 nights of attendance for theater capacities of 300, 400, and 500.

b. In the 20 nights of simulated operation, how many demands of 300 would you have expected? Did you observe this many in your simulation? Should you have? Explain.

10. A door-to-door magazine salesperson has the following historical sales record. If the salesperson talks to the woman of the house, there is a 15% chance of making a sale. Furthermore, if the salesperson convinces the woman of the house to purchase some magazines, the relative frequency distribution for the number of the subscriptions ordered is as follows:

Number of Subscriptions	Relative Frequency
1	0.60
2	0.30
3	0.10

On the other hand, if the man of the house answers the door, the salesperson's chances of making a sale are 25%. In addition, the relative frequency distribution for the number of subscriptions ordered is as follows:

Number of Subscriptions	Relative Frequency
1	0.10
2	0.40
3	0.30
4	0.20

The salesperson has found that no one answers the door at about 30% of the houses contacted. However, of the people who do answer the door, 80% are women and 20% are men. The salesperson's profit is $2 for each subscription sold.

a. Prepare a simulation model flowchart (see Figure 15.5) for this problem. The output of the model should be the total profit the salesperson makes from calling on N houses.

b. Simulate this problem and show the house-by-house results for 25 calls. What is the total profit projected for the 25 calls?

c. Based on your results from part (b), how many subscriptions should the salesperson expect to sell by calling on 100 houses per day? What is the salesperson's expected daily profit?

11. A project has four activities (A, B, C, and D) that must be completed sequentially in order to complete the project. The probability distribution for the time required to complete each of the activities is as follows:

Activity	Activity Times (weeks)	Probability
A	5	0.25
	6	0.30
	7	0.30
	8	0.15
B	3	0.20
	5	0.55
	7	0.25
C	10	0.10
	12	0.25
	14	0.40
	16	0.20
	18	0.05
D	8	0.60
	10	0.40

a. Use a random number procedure to simulate the completion time for each activity. Sum the activity times to establish a completion time for the entire project.

b. Use the simulation procedure developed in part (a) to simulate 20 completions of this project. Show the distribution of completion times and estimate the probability that the project can be completed in 35 weeks or less.

12. A New York City corner newsstand orders 250 copies of *The New York Times* daily. Primarily due to weather conditions, the demand for newspapers varies from day to day. The probability distribution of the demand for newspapers is as follows:

Number of Newspapers	Probability
150	0.10
175	0.30
200	0.30
225	0.20
250	0.10

The newsstand makes a 15-cent profit on every paper sold, but it loses 10 cents on every paper unsold by the end of the day. Use 10 days of simulated results to determine whether the newsstand should order 200, 225, or 250 papers per day. What is the average daily profit that the newsstand can anticipate based on your recommendation?

13. For the Art's Auto Supplies problem in Section 15.4, develop a 10-day simulation when the following demand distribution is assumed:

Demand	Relative Frequency
0	0.25
1	0.50
2	0.15
3	0.05
4	0.05

Using an order quantity of 5 and a reorder point of 3, show your results in the format of Table 15.17.

14. Bristol Bikes, Inc. would like to develop an order quantity and reorder point policy that would minimize the total costs associated with the company's inventory of exercise bikes. The relative frequency distribution for retail demand on a weekly basis is as follows:

Demand	Probability
0	0.20
1	0.50
2	0.10
3	0.10
4	0.05
5	0.05

The relative frequency distribution for lead time is as follows:

Lead Time (weeks)	Relative Frequency
1	0.10
2	0.25
3	0.60
4	0.05

The inventory holding costs are $1 per unit per week, the ordering cost is $20 per order, the shortage cost is $25 per unit, and the beginning inventory is 7 units. Using an order quantity of 12 and a reorder point of 5, simulate 10 weeks of operation of this inventory system.

15. Stollar's Bakery Shop would like to determine how many 10-inch white cakes should be produced each day in order to maximize profits. The production costs are $2.50 per cake, and the selling price is $4.50. Any cakes that are not sold at the end of the day are sold for $1.50 to a local store that specializes in day-old goods. Assume that the bakery has available the following data showing the daily demand during the past month (20 days of operation):

Daily Demand	Frequency (number of days observed)
0	1
1	2
2	1
3	2
4	3
5	6
6	3
7	1
8	1
Total	20

Develop a 10-day simulation for production sizes ranging from one to eight cakes per day. Use the following random numbers to generate daily demand:

| 48 | 12 | 77 | 24 | 32 | 43 | 96 | 03 | 62 | 77 |

What appears to be the best production size?

16. Domoy Motors, Inc. purchases a certain model automobile for $5778. In order to finance the purchase of cars of this model, Domoy must pay an 18% annual interest rate on borrowed capital. This interest rate amounts to approximately $20 per car per week. Orders for additional cars can be placed each week, but a minimum order size of five cars is required on any given order. It currently takes 3 weeks to receive a new shipment of cars after the order is placed. The cost of placing an order is $50. If Domoy runs out of cars in inventory, a shortage cost of $300 per car is incurred. Currently Domoy has 20 cars of this model in inventory. Historical data showing the weekly demand were given in problem 4.

    a. Assuming an order quantity of 15 cars and a reorder point of 10 cars, perform a 12-week simulation of Domoy's operation. Use the first 12 two-digit random numbers from row 2 of Appendix E beginning with the number 88547. Show your simulation results in the format of Table 15.17.

    b. Write a computer program to simulate weekly sales at Domoy Motors. Use the program to determine the order policy that appears to minimize Domoy's overall costs.

17. A firm with a national chain of hotels and motels is interested in learning where individuals prefer to stay when on business trips. Three competing hotel and motel chains are included in the study. They are the Marimont Inn, the Harrison Inn, and the Hinton Hotel. The study found that where an individual stays on one trip is a good predictor of where the individual will stay the next trip. However, the study showed that sometimes individuals switch from one chain to another. The probabilities of staying at each chain are shown below. For example, if an individual stayed at the Marimont Inn on one trip, there is a 0.70 probability of staying at the Marimont Inn the next trip, a 0.10 probability of staying at the Harrison Inn the next trip, and a 0.20 probability of staying at the Hinton Hotel the next trip. Similar probability values are shown for individuals staying at the Harrison Inn and Hinton Hotel on a particular trip.

Currently Staying at	Probability of Staying the Next Trip at		
	Marimont	Harrison	Hinton
Marimont	0.70	0.10	0.20
Harrison	0.20	0.60	0.20
Hinton	0.15	0.05	0.80

    a. Show the random number assignments that can be used to simulate the next visit for an individual currently staying at the Marimont, Harrison, and Hinton chains.

b. Develop a flowchart that describes the simulation process for simulating where an individual will stay during a series of business trips.

c. Assume that an individual most recently stayed at the Marimont Inn. Simulate where the individual would stay on the next 50 business trips. What percentage of time will the person select each chain? Which appears to be the most popular chain?

d. Repeat the simulation in part (c) starting with an individual most recently staying at the Harrison Inn. Repeat part (c) again with the individual most recently staying at the Hinton Inn. Which is the most popular chain based on these simulation results?

18. Shown below is the probability distribution for the number of pins a bowler obtains on a first ball.

Number of Pins	Probability
6	0.02
7	0.08
8	0.20
9	0.30
10	0.40

The probability table showing the number of pins obtained on a second ball is as follows:

If Number of Pins on First Ball is	Number of Pins on Second Ball				
	0	1	2	3	4
6	0.01	0.03	0.20	0.26	0.50
7	0.04	0.10	0.36	0.50	
8	0.05	0.25	0.70		
9	0.15	0.85			

a. Using the above information, simulate a game of bowling. What is the bowler's score?

b. Develop a simulation program for this problem and simulate several games of bowling. What is an estimate of the bowler's average score?

19. Mount Washington Garage sells regular and unleaded gasoline. Pump 1, a self-service facility, is used by customers who want to pump their own gas. Pump 2, a full-service facility, is used by customers who are willing to pay a higher cost per gallon in order to have an attendant pump the gas, check the oil, and so on. Both pumps can service one car at a time. Based on past data, the owner of the garage estimates that 70% of the customers select the self-service pump and 30% want full service. The arrival

rate of cars for each minute of operation is given by the following probability distribution:

Number of Arrivals in 1 Minute of Operation	Probability
0	0.10
1	0.20
2	0.35
3	0.30
4	0.05
	1.00

The time to service a car, which depends on whether the self-service or full-service facility is used, is given by the following probability distribution:

Self-Service Pump		Full-Service Pump	
Service Time (minutes)	Probability	Service Time (minutes)	Probability
2	0.10	3	0.20
3	0.20	4	0.30
4	0.60	5	0.35
5	0.10	6	0.10
	1.00	7	0.05
			1.00

Study the operation of the system for 10 minutes using simulation. As part of your analysis, consider the following types of questions. What is the average number of cars waiting for service per minute at both facilities? What is the average amount of time a car must wait for service? Prepare a brief report for Mount Washington Garage that describes your analysis and any conclusions.

20. A medical consulting firm has been asked to determine the facilities required in the x-ray laboratory of a new hospital. In particular, the firm should provide recommendations on the number of x-ray units for the laboratory. How could computer simulation assist in reaching a good decision? What factors would you consider in a simulation model of this problem?

21. Consider a medium-sized community that currently has only one fire station. You have been hired by the city manager to assist in the determination of the best location for a second fire station. What would be your objective for this problem? Explain how computer simulation might be used to evaluate alternative locations and help identify the best location.

22. A bus company is considering adding a new 10-stop route to its operation. The bus will be scheduled to complete the route once each hour. If the company has determined the approximate demand distribution for each location, discuss how simulation might be used to project the hourly profit associated with the new route. If the company can assign a regular bus or a more economical minibus to this route, discuss how simulation might help make this decision. Note that with the minibus the company's management is concerned about being unable to pick up customers if the bus is already carrying its maximum number of riders.

Case Problem
Machine Repair

Jerry Masters, president of Pacific Plastics, Inc. (PPI), has become concerned with reports that downtime for PPI's plastic injection-molding machines has been increasing. The downtime for a machine includes the time the machine must wait for a repair service technician to arrive after a breakdown plus the actual repair time. Currently PPI has three plastic injection-molding machines, which are repaired by one service technician. However, because of an increase in business, PPI is considering the purchase of three additional machines. Jerry is concerned that with the additional machines the downtime problem will increase.

An analysis of historical data shows that the probability of each machine breaking down during 1 hour of operation is 0.10. In addition, the distribution of the repair time for a machine that breaks down is as follows:

Repair Time (hours)	Probability
1	0.20
2	0.35
3	0.25
4	0.15
5	0.05

The loss in revenue associated with a machine being down for 1 hour is $100. PPI pays its service technician $22 per hour, and it is believed that additional service technicians can be hired at the same wage rate.

In reviewing the breakdown problem, Jerry decided that the best way to learn about the machine repair operation would be to simulate the performance of the system. In considering the potential use of simulation, Jerry indicated that PPI must deal with the two conflicting sources of cost: the cost of the service technician(s) and the cost of machine downtime. He indicated that PPI could minimize salaries by employing only one service technician. On the other hand, PPI could minimize the cost of machine downtime by hiring so many service technicians that a machine could be serviced immediately after a breakdown.

Jerry would like you to develop a simulation model of the machine repair operation and use it to determine how many service technicians PPI should employ in order to minimize its total cost. When developing the simulation model, you can assume that if a machine has a breakdown, the breakdown can be treated as occurring at the beginning of the hour of operation. Thus, if a machine were to break down in hour 4, it would be considered to break down at the beginning of the hour. If 1 hour was spent waiting for a service technician and the length of time required to service the machine were 2 hours, the machine would be down during hours 4, 5, and 6, then be ready for operation at the beginning of hour 7. You can also assume that the probability of any machine breakdown is independent of the breakdown of any other machine, and that the service times are also independent of other service times.

Managerial Report

Prepare a report that discusses the general development of the simulation model, the conclusions that you plan to draw by using the model, and any recommendations that you have regarding the best decision for PPI. Include the following:

1. List the information the simulation model should generate so that the decision can be made about the desired number of service technicians.
2. Set up a flowchart of the machine repair operation for one machine and one service technician.
3. Use a random number table and hand computations to demonstrate the simulation of the machine repair operation with three machines and one service technician. Use a table similar to Table 15.6 to summarize 10 hours of simulation results.
4. Develop a computer simulation model for the machine repair operation when PPI expands to six machines. Use your simulation results to make a recommendation about the number of service technicians that PPI should employ.

Quantitative Methods in Practice

Champion International Corporation*

New York, New York

Champion International Corporation is one of the largest forest products companies in the world, employing over 41,000 people in the United States, Canada, and Brazil. Champion manages over 3 million acres of timberlands in the United States. Its objective is to maximize the return of this timber base by converting trees into three basic product groups: (1) building materials, such as lumber and plywood; (2) white paper products, including printing and writing grades of white paper; (3) brown paper products, such as linerboard and corrugated containers. Given the highly competitive markets within the forest products industry, survival dictates that Champion must maintain its position as a low-cost producer of quality products. This requires an ambitious capital program to improve the timber base and to build additional modern, cost-effective timber-conversion facilities.

Quantitative Analysis

The quantitative analysis function at Champion International Corporation is organizationally structured within the corporate planning department and operates as an internal consulting service within the company. Approximately 40% of the project activity is involved with facility and production planning, 30% with physical distribution, 20% with process improvement, and 10% with capital budgeting. The primary techniques used are mathematical programming (e.g., linear programming), simulation, and statistical analyses.

A Simulation Application

An integrated pulp and paper mill is a facility in which wood chips and chemicals are processed in order to produce paper products or dried pulp. To begin with, wood chips are cooked and bleached in the pulp mill; the resulting pulp is piped directly into storage tanks, as shown in Figure A15.1. From the storage tanks the pulp is sent to either the

---

*The authors are indebted to Bill Griggs and Walter Foody of Champion International for providing this application.

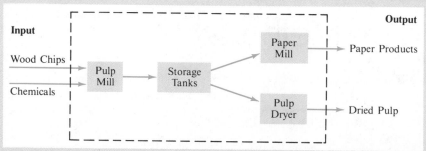

Figure A15.1
The Champion Integrated Pulp and Paper Mill Facility

paper mill or a dryer. In the paper mill the pulp is routed to one or more paper machines, which produce the finished paper products. Alternatively, the pulp is sent to a dryer, and the dried pulp is then sold to other paper mills that do not have the capability of producing their own pulp. The total system, referred to as an integrated pulp and paper mill, is a large facility costing several hundred million dollars.

One of Champion's major pulp and paper facilities consists of a pulp mill, three paper machines, and a dryer. As the facility developed, it was found that the pulp mill could produce more pulp than the combination of paper machines and the dryer could use. A study was undertaken to determine whether it would be worthwhile to invest in improvements that would increase the capacity of the dryer. One of the first questions to be answered in the study was: How much additional pulp could be produced and dried, given each possible capacity increase for the dryer?

A simple approach to this question is to look at average flows. For example, the pulp mill has a capacity of 940 tons[†] per day (TPD), the three paper machines together average 650 TPD of pulp use, and the dryer can handle 200 TPD. Based on average flows for each ton of increased dryer capacity, we can produce one more ton of pulp in the pulp mill. Note, however, that this is true only until the capacity of the dryer reaches 290 TPD, after which further improvements to the dryer will have no benefit.

The average flow analysis is inadequate because it ignores the day-to-day deviations from the average. That is, all of the equipment in the mill is subject to downtime and to variations in efficiency. For example, suppose that on one day the pulp mill is inoperable for more than the average length of time and on the same day the paper machines are experiencing less than the usual downtime. In this case there will be very little pulp available for the dryer, regardless of its capacity. This lack of pulp will not "average out" on days when the opposite conditions occur, since there will be far more pulp available than the pulp dryer can handle. Consequently, the pulp storage tanks will become full, and the pulp mill will have to shut down.

Based on the above analysis, we can conclude that in order not to reduce the production on the paper machines the ratio of additional pulp production to the increase in dryer capacity will be less than 1. Since the benefits of any investment in the dryer are directly proportional to this ratio, a simulation was undertaken in order to estimate this ratio as precisely as possible. The simulation model that was developed had the following components:

Pulp mill   The pulp mill was assumed to have an average production rate of 1044 TPD when it is operating, with an average of 10% downtime. The actual downtime

---

[†]All numerical values have been modified to protect proprietary information.

used in the model in each time period simulated was drawn randomly from a sample of actual downtimes experienced by the pulp mill over several months. Thus, one day the pulp mill might be down 2% of the time, the next day 20%, etc.

Paper machine The rate of pulp flow to the paper machines in a time period is a function of the particular type of paper being made and the amount of downtime on the paper machines. In the simulation, the rate of pulp flow was input to the model based on a typical schedule of types of paper to be made. The downtime for each machine was drawn from a sample of actual downtimes.

Pulp dryer In each run of the model, downtime on the dryer was drawn from a sample of actual downtimes. The capacity of the dryer was set at different levels in different runs.

Storage tanks The connecting link between the pulp mill, the paper machines, and the dryer is the pulp storage tanks. In the model all pulp produced by the pulp mill is added to the inventory in these tanks. All pulp drawn by the dryer and paper machines is subtracted from this inventory. If the storage tanks are empty, the model must shut down the paper machines. If the tanks are full, the pulp mill must be shut down. The actual rate at which the dryer is operated at any moment must be set by the model (as it is in reality) to try to keep the storage tanks from becoming "too empty or too full."

Results

A PL/1 computer program was developed to simulate the above process. The simulation program was run at various levels of dryer capacity. The simulation results showed that for every TPD of additional pulp capacity, approximately 0.8 TPD of additional pulp could actually be dried without reducing the production of the paper machines. This number was then used by management in comparing the costs and benefits of the capital investment necessary to increase the pulp dryer capacity. Note that if the "average basis" analysis had been used, the benefits of the project would have been overstated by 25%.

Questions

1. Briefly describe the function of an integrated pulp and paper facility.
2. What is the primary reason why Champion conducted a study of its integrated pulp and paper facility?
3. Why is an analysis of average flows inadequate in studying the current operation?
4. Describe how you might use a sample of actual downtimes for the pulp mill in order to simulate its operation.
5. What were the advantages of using a simulation model of the pulp and paper mill facility?

CHAPTER

16

Waiting-Line Models

Everyone has experienced situations such as waiting in a line at a supermarket checkout counter, waiting in a line at a teller window of a bank, or waiting in a line of cars at a traffic light. In these and many other situations, *waiting* time is undesirable for all parties concerned. For instance, the customer in a supermarket checkout line can become very annoyed by excessive waiting times. If the manager of the supermarket is concerned about the existence of long waiting lines, one obvious solution would be to add more checkout counters. The added service capability should provide better service and correspondingly shorter customer waiting lines. However, additional supermarket checkout counters will lead to greater costs in terms of additional personnel, equipment, and space requirements. The supermarket waiting-line problem requires the manager to balance the benefits of better service with the added costs involved.

Quantitative models have been developed to help managers understand and make better decisions concerning the operation of waiting lines. *Queueing theory* is the term used to refer to the study of waiting lines. The waiting line is referred to as the *queue*. Thus, in the supermarket example, customers in the waiting line could have been referred to as customers in the queue.

For a given waiting-line system, waiting-line models may be used to identify *operating characteristics*, such as

1. The percentage of time or probability that the service facilities are idle
2. The probability of a specific number of units (customers) in the system[1]
3. The average number of units in the waiting line
4. The average number of units in the system
5. The average time a unit spends in the waiting line

[1]The system includes the waiting line and the service facility.

6. The average time a unit spends in the system (waiting time plus service time)

7. The probability that an arriving unit has to wait for service

Managers who are provided with the above information are better equipped to make decisions that balance desirable service levels with service costs.

In this chapter we will discuss how analytical and simulation models of waiting lines can assist in developing good decisions for waiting-line problems. As an illustration of an application of a waiting-line model, let us consider the problem that Schips, Inc. is presently having with the truck dock at the company's Western Hills store.

16.1

THE SCHIPS, INC. TRUCK DOCK PROBLEM

Schips, Inc. is a large department store chain that has six branch stores located throughout the city. The company's Western Hills store, which was built some years ago, has recently been experiencing some problems in its receiving and shipping department because of the substantial growth in the branch's sales volume. Unfortunately, the store's truck dock was designed to handle only one truck at a time, and the branch's increased business volume has led to a bottleneck in the truck dock area. At times the branch manager has observed as many as five Schips trucks waiting to be loaded or unloaded. As a result, the manager would like to consider various alternatives for improving the operation of the truck dock and reducing the truck waiting times.

One alternative the manager is considering is to speed up the loading/unloading operation by installing a conveyor system at the truck dock. As another alternative, the manager is considering adding a second truck dock so that two trucks can be loaded and/or unloaded simultaneously.

What should the manager do in order to improve the operation of the truck dock? Obviously, more information is needed before a course of action can be taken. While the alternatives being considered should reduce the truck waiting times, they may also increase the cost of operating the dock. Thus the manager will want to know how each alternative will affect both the waiting times and the cost of operating the dock before making a final decision. Let us see how a waiting-line model of the truck dock operation can assist the manager in making this decision.

The Single-Channel Waiting Line

Schip's current receiving and shipping operation is an example of a *single-channel waiting line*. By this we mean that each truck entering the system must pass through *one* channel— the one truck dock—in order to complete the loading and/or unloading process. The trucks form a waiting line and wait for the truck dock to become available. A diagram of the Schips single-channel waiting line is shown in Figure 16.1

In order to develop a waiting-line model for the truck dock operation we will need to identify some important characteristics of the system: (1) the arrival distribution for the trucks; (2) the service time distribution for the truck loading and unloading operation; and (3) the waiting line or queue discipline for the trucks.

Arrival Distribution

Defining the arrival distribution for a waiting line involves determining how many units arrive and the pattern of arrivals over a given period of time. For example, in the Schips

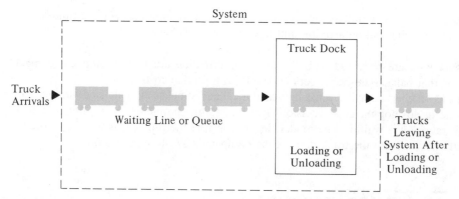

Figure 16.1
Diagram of Schips Single-Channel Truck Dock Waiting Line

waiting-line problem we will be interested in determining the number of trucks that arrive at the truck dock in a 1-hour period. Since the number of trucks arriving varies from hour to hour, we will need to define a probability distribution that describes the truck arrivals.

For many waiting lines, the arrivals appear to have a *random pattern*; that is, each arrival is independent of other arrivals and we cannot predict when an arrival will occur. In such cases, quantitative analysts have found that the *Poisson probability distribution*, discussed in Chapter 3, provides a good description of the arrival pattern.

Using the Poisson probability distribution,[2] the probability of x arrivals in a specific time period is defined as follows:

$$f(x) = \frac{\lambda^x e^{-\lambda}}{x!} \qquad \text{for } x = 0, 1, 2, \ldots \qquad (16.1)$$

where

x = number of arrivals in the time period
λ = average or expected number of arrivals for the time period
e = 2.71828

Values of $e^{-\lambda}$ are provided in Table 16.1 and in Appendix D.

In the Schips loading dock problem, truck arrivals occur at an average rate of 3 trucks per hour ($\lambda = 3$). Thus we can use the following Poisson distribution to compute the probability of x truck arrivals in an hour:

$$f(x) = \frac{\lambda^x e^{-\lambda}}{x!} = \frac{3^x e^{-3}}{x!} \qquad (16.2)$$

[2]The term $x!$, referred to as x *factorial*, is defined as $x! = x(x-1)(x-2) \ldots (2)(1)$. For example, $5! = (5)(4)(3)(2)(1) = 120$. For the special case of $x = 0$, $0! = 1$ by definition.

Table 16.1 can be used to verify that $e^{-3} = 0.0498$. Thus the probabilities for 0, 1, and 2 trucks arriving in an hour are as follows:

$$P(x = 0 \text{ trucks}) = f(0) = \frac{3^0 e^{-3}}{0!} = e^{-3} = 0.0498$$

$$P(x = 1 \text{ truck}) = f(1) = \frac{3^1 e^{-3}}{1!} = 3e^{-3} = 3(0.0498) = 0.1494$$

$$P(x = 2 \text{ trucks}) = f(2) = \frac{3^2 e^{-3}}{2!} = \frac{9e^{-3}}{2} = \frac{9(0.0498)}{2} = 0.2241$$

Table 16.1
Values of $e^{-\lambda}$

λ	$e^{-\lambda}$	λ	$e^{-\lambda}$
0.0	1.0000	3.3	0.0369
0.1	0.9048	3.4	0.0334
0.2	0.8187	3.5	0.0302
0.3	0.7408	3.6	0.0273
0.4	0.6703	3.7	0.0247
0.5	0.6065	3.8	0.0224
0.6	0.5488	3.9	0.0202
0.7	0.4966	4.0	0.0183
0.8	0.4493	4.1	0.0166
0.9	0.4066	4.2	0.0150
1.0	0.3679	4.3	0.0136
1.1	0.3329	4.4	0.0123
1.2	0.3012	4.5	0.0111
1.3	0.2725	4.6	0.0101
1.4	0.2466	4.7	0.0091
1.5	0.2231	4.8	0.0082
1.6	0.2019	4.9	0.0074
1.7	0.1827	5.0	0.0067
1.8	0.1653	5.1	0.0061
1.9	0.1496	5.2	0.0055
2.0	0.1353	5.3	0.0050
2.1	0.1225	5.4	0.0045
2.2	0.1108	5.5	0.0041
2.3	0.1003	5.6	0.0037
2.4	0.0907	5.7	0.0033
2.5	0.0821	5.8	0.0030
2.6	0.0743	5.9	0.0027
2.7	0.0672	6.0	0.0025
2.8	0.0608	7.0	0.0009
2.9	0.0550	8.0	0.000335
3.0	0.0498	9.0	0.000123
3.1	0.0450	10.0	0.000045
3.2	0.0408		

Thus we see that the probability of no trucks arriving in a 1-hour period is 0.0498, the probability of exactly one truck arriving in a 1-hour period is 0.1494, and the probability of exactly two trucks arriving in a 1-hour period is 0.2241. Continuing the probability calculations for other values of x will provide additional probability information about the number of truck arrivals during a 1-hour period. Figure 16.2 shows a graphical summary of the arrival probabilities for Schips trucks based on the assumption of a Poisson arrival distribution.

In the analysis that follows we will use the Poisson distribution to describe the truck arrivals for Schips. You will see that the assumption of a Poisson arrival distribution will help simplify the analysis of the waiting-line problem. In practice you would want to record the actual number of arrivals per time period for several days or weeks and compare the frequency distribution of the observed number of arrivals to the Poisson distribution to see if the Poisson distribution is a good approximation of the arrival distribution for the trucks.

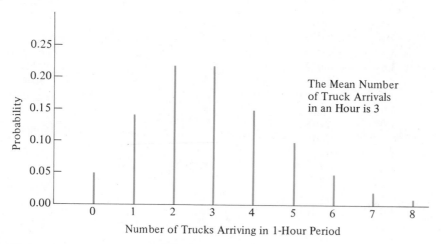

Figure 16.2
Poisson Distribution of Truck Arrivals for Schips

Service Time Distribution

A service time probability distribution is needed to describe how long it takes to load or unload (that is, service) a truck once the loading or unloading operation begins. Since the trucks carry different quantities of different items, the loading and unloading service times will vary from truck to truck. Quantitative analysts have found that the *exponential probability distribution*, discussed in Chapter 3, often provides a good description of a service time distribution.

With an exponential service time distribution, *the probability of a unit completing service within a specific period of time, t,* is given by

$$P(\text{service time} \le t) = 1 - e^{-\mu t} \qquad (16.3)$$

where

μ = average or expected number of units that the service facility can service per unit of time

Suppose that after collecting data on loading and unloading times for Schips trucks, we find that when working continuously the truck dock can service an average of four trucks per hour. Then, using $\mu = 4$, the probability of a unit completing service within t hours [see equation (16.3)] is as follows:

$$P(\text{service time} \leq t) = 1 - e^{-4t}$$

Using this equation and values from Table 16.1, we can compute the probability that a truck is loaded and/or unloaded (serviced) within any specified time t. For example,

$$P(\text{service time} \leq 0.1 \text{ hours}) = 1 - e^{-4(0.1)} = 1 - e^{-0.4} = 1 - 0.6703 = 0.3297$$
$$P(\text{service time} \leq 0.3 \text{ hours}) = 1 - e^{-4(0.3)} = 1 - e^{-1.2} = 1 - 0.3012 = 0.6988$$
$$P(\text{service time} \leq 0.5 \text{ hours}) = 1 - e^{-4(0.5)} = 1 - e^{-2.0} = 1 - 0.1353 = 0.8647$$

Thus, using the exponential distribution, we would expect 32.97% of the trucks to be serviced in $t = 0.1$ hour or less (6 minutes), 69.88% in $t = 0.3$ hour or less (18 minutes), and 86.47% in $t = 0.5$ hour or less (30 minutes). Figure 16.3 shows graphically the probability that t hours or less will be required to service a Schips truck.

In the analysis of a specific waiting line you will want to collect data on actual service times to see if the exponential distribution assumption is appropriate. For the Schips problem, we will assume that it has already been determined that the exponential distribution is the most appropriate representation of the service times.

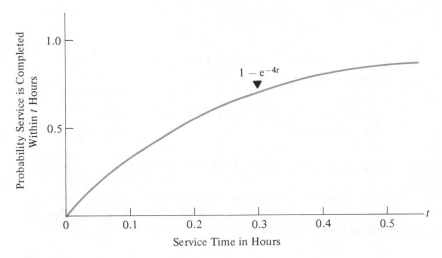

Figure 16.3
Probability That a Schips Truck Will Be Serviced in t Hours or Less

Queue Discipline

In describing a waiting line we must define the manner in which the waiting units are ordered for service. For the Schips, Inc. problem, and in general for most customer-oriented waiting lines, the waiting units are ordered on a *first-come, first-served* basis, which is referred to as a FCFS queue discipline. When people wait in line for an elevator, it is usually the last one in line who is the first one serviced (that is, first to leave the elevator). Other types of queue disciplines assign priorities to the waiting units and service the unit with the highest priority first. We will restrict our attention to waiting lines with a FCFS queue discipline.

16.2

THE SINGLE-CHANNEL WAITING-LINE MODEL WITH POISSON ARRIVALS AND EXPONENTIAL SERVICE TIMES

The waiting-line model presented in this section can be applied to waiting lines where the following assumptions or conditions exist:

1. The waiting line has a single channel.
2. The pattern of arrivals follows a Poisson probability distribution.
3. The service times follow an exponential probability distribution.
4. The queue discipline is first-come, first-served (FCFS).

Since we have assumed that the above conditions are applicable to the Schips problem, we will show how this waiting-line model can be used to analyze the truck dock operation.

The quantitative methodology used in the development of most waiting-line models is rather complex. However, our purpose in this chapter is not to provide a theoretical development. Rather we restrict our presentation to showing how the operating characteristics of a waiting-line model can be determined and how this information can be applied to problems such as the one encountered at Schips, Inc.

Let us begin by reviewing the following notation:

$$\lambda = \text{expected number of arrivals per time period}$$
$$\text{(mean arrival rate)}$$

$$\mu = \text{expected number of services possible per time period}$$
$$\text{(mean service rate)}$$

For the Schips problem we have already concluded that $\lambda = 3$ trucks per hour and $\mu = 4$ trucks per hour.

Using the assumptions of Poisson arrivals and exponential service times, quantitative analysts have developed the following expressions, which define the operating characteristics of a single-channel waiting line[3]:

---

[3]These equations apply to the *steady-state* operation of a waiting line, which occurs after a start-up or transient period.

1. The probability that the service facility is idle (that is, the probability of 0 units in the system):

$$P_0 = \left(1 - \frac{\lambda}{\mu}\right) \qquad (16.4)$$

2. The probability of n units in the system:

$$P_n = \left(\frac{\lambda}{\mu}\right)^n P_0 \qquad (16.5)$$

3. The average number of units waiting for service:

$$L_q = \frac{\lambda^2}{\mu(\mu - \lambda)} \qquad (16.6)$$

4. The average number of units in the system:

$$L = L_q + \frac{\lambda}{\mu} \qquad (16.7)$$

5. The average time a unit spends waiting for service:

$$W_q = \frac{L_q}{\lambda} \qquad (16.8)$$

6. The average time a unit spends in the system (waiting time plus service time):

$$W = W_q + \frac{1}{\mu} \qquad (16.9)$$

7. The probability that an arriving unit has to wait for service:

$$P_w = \frac{\lambda}{\mu} \qquad (16.10)$$

The values of the mean arrival rate λ and the mean service rate μ are clearly important components in the above formulas. From equation (16.10) we see that the ratio of these two values, λ/μ, is simply the probability that an arriving unit has to wait because the server is busy. Thus λ/μ is often referred to as the *utilization factor* for the waiting line.

The formulas for determining the operating characteristics of a single-channel waiting line presented in equations (16.4) to (16.10) are applicable only when the utilization factor $\lambda/\mu < 1$. This condition occurs when the mean service rate μ is greater than the mean arrival rate λ, and hence the service rate is sufficient to process or service all arrivals.

Returning to the Schips truck dock problem, we see that with $\lambda = 3$ trucks per hour, $\mu = 4$ trucks per hour, and $\lambda/\mu = \frac{3}{4}$, we can use equations (16.4) to (16.10) to determine the operating characteristics of the loading dock operation. This is done as follows:

$$P_0 = \left(1 - \frac{\lambda}{\mu}\right) = \left(1 - \frac{3}{4}\right) = 0.25$$

$$L_q = \frac{\lambda^2}{\mu(\mu - \lambda)} = \frac{3^2}{4(4 - 3)} = 2.25 \text{ trucks}$$

$$L = L_q + \frac{\lambda}{\mu} = 2.25 + \frac{3}{4} = 3 \text{ trucks}$$

$$W_q = \frac{L_q}{\lambda} = \frac{2.25}{3} = 0.75 \text{ hour per truck}$$

$$W = W_q + \frac{1}{\mu} = 0.75 + \frac{1}{4} = 1 \text{ hour per truck}$$

$$P_w = \frac{\lambda}{\mu} = \frac{3}{4} = 0.75$$

By looking at the above data for the waiting line, we can learn several important things about the operation of the truck dock. In particular, the fact that trucks wait an average of $W_q = 0.75$ hour or 45 minutes before being loaded or unloaded appears excessive and undesirable. In addition, the facts that the average number of trucks waiting for service is $L_q = 2.25$ trucks and that 75% of the arriving trucks ($P_w = 0.75$) have to wait for service are indicators that something should be done to improve the efficiency of the truck dock operation.

Before we continue with the Schips truck dock problem, let us review how the use of the single-channel waiting-line model has contributed to our understanding of the truck dock operation. We began the discussion of the Schips problem by pointing out that the branch manager had become aware of the fact that an increase in business volume was leading to a bottleneck in the truck dock area. However, the manager did not have detailed information readily available concerning operating characteristics, such as the average number of trucks waiting for service, the average time trucks wait for service, the percent of arriving trucks that have to wait for service, and so on. Thus the contribution of the single-channel waiting-line model is that if the assumptions are satisfied, formulas are available for computing a variety of operating characteristics for the system. In the case of Poisson arrivals and exponential service times, the formulas are based on the mean arrival rate, λ, and the mean service rate, μ.

In general, waiting-line models provide descriptive information about the operating characteristics of the waiting-line system. If a manager or decision maker wishes to implement changes in the design of a waiting line, a waiting-line model and its formulas can be used to predict the operating characteristics that will result from the changed design. In this sense, waiting-line models provide important and helpful information that assists the decision maker in designing waiting-line systems.

The Management Scientist software package can be used to provide the operating characteristics for waiting-line systems with Poisson arrivals and exponential service times. The computer output for the Schips truck dock problem is shown in Figure 16.4.

Improving the Service Rate for Schips Truck Dock

Assume that after reviewing the operating characteristics provided by the waiting-line model, the branch manager has concluded that improvements in the truck dock operation

```
SUMMARY OF A 1 CHANNEL WAITING LINE WITH
******************************************

      MEAN NUMBER OF ARRIVALS = 3

      MEAN NUMBER OF SERVICES = 4

THE PROBABILITY THAT THE CHANNEL IS IDLE             0.2500

THE AVERAGE NUMBER OF UNITS WAITING FOR SERVICE      2.2500

THE AVERAGE NUMBER OF UNITS IN THE SYSTEM            3.0000

THE AVERAGE TIME A UNIT SPENDS WAITING FOR SERVICE   0.7500

THE AVERAGE TIME A UNIT SPENDS IN THE SYSTEM         1.0000

THE PROBABILITY THAT AN ARRIVING UNIT HAS TO WAIT    0.7500
```

Figure 16.4
The Management Scientist Computer Output for the Schips Truck Dock Problem

are necessary. While the manager cannot change the arrival rate of $\lambda = 3$ trucks per hour, the manager may be able to suggest changes in the system that will enable the truck dock to service an average of more than 4 trucks per hour. The value of the waiting line model is that if the manager can identify an alternative design that will increase the service rate to, say, $\mu = 6$ trucks per hour, the waiting-line model with $\lambda = 3$ and $\mu = 6$ can be used to identify the operating characteristics of the new system. In this way the manager can determine how an improved service rate will affect the performance of the waiting-line system.

Let us assume that in an effort to improve the operation of the truck dock the branch manager is considering the use of a conveyor system to speed up the loading/unloading process. Table 16.2 was prepared to help the manager better understand the potential benefits of improving the service rate. In particular, note that as the mean service rate increases, the average waiting time per truck, the average number of trucks waiting, and the probability of an arriving truck having to wait all improve. For example, if installing the conveyor system will increase the service rate to $\mu = 6$ trucks per hour, Table 16.2 shows that the average time a truck spends in the system can be reduced from 1 hour to 0.3333 hours, or 20 minutes. In addition, we see that the probability of a truck having to wait for service would be reduced from 0.70 to 0.50.

In evaluating a specific proposal for a conveyor system, the manager can use the projected service rate μ and the information in Table 16.2 to determine what improvements

Table 16.2
Waiting-Line System Characteristics for the Schips Truck Dock Problem

Mean Service Rate μ, Trucks per Hour	4	6	8	10
Probability that the dock is idle, P_0	0.25	0.5	0.625	0.7
Average number of trucks waiting, L_q	2.25	0.5	0.225	0.1286
Average number of trucks in system, L	3	1	0.6	0.4286
Average time a truck spends waiting, W_q, hours	0.75	0.1667	0.075	0.0429
Average time a truck spends in system, W, hours	1	0.3333	0.2	0.1429
Probability that an arriving truck has to wait for service, P_w	0.75	0.5	0.375	0.3

can be anticipated in the truck dock operation. The added cost of any proposed change can be compared with the corresponding benefits to help the manager determine whether or not the specific proposal is worthwhile.

16.3

THE MULTIPLE-CHANNEL WAITING-LINE MODEL WITH POISSON ARRIVALS AND EXPONENTIAL SERVICE TIMES

A logical extension of the single-channel waiting line is the *multiple-channel waiting line*. By multiple-channel waiting lines we mean that two or more channels or service locations are present. Although items arriving for service wait in a single waiting line, they move to the first available channel to be serviced. The Schips truck dock problem involved a single channel. However, a multiple-channel waiting-line model could be applied if the branch manager implemented an expansion of the dock area such that two trucks could be loaded and/or unloaded simultaneously. The trucks arriving for service would form a waiting line and wait for either of the two service areas or channels to become available. A diagram of the Schips two-channel waiting-line system is shown in Figure 16.5.

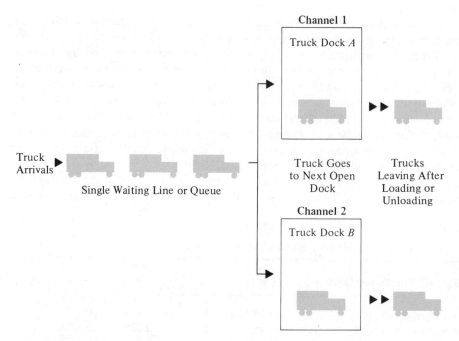

Figure 16.5
Diagram of Schips Two-Channel Truck Dock Waiting Line

In this section we present formulas that can be used to compute various operating characteristics for a multiple-channel waiting line. The model we will use can be applied to situations where the following assumptions are met:

1. The waiting line has two or more identical channels.
2. The arrivals are Poisson with a *mean arrival rate* of λ.
3. The service times have an exponential distribution.
4. The *mean service rate* μ is the same for each channel.
5. The arrivals wait in a single waiting line and then move to the first open channel for service.
6. The queue discipline is first-come, first-served (FCFS).

Using these assumptions, quantitative analysts have developed formulas for determining the operating characteristics of the multiple-channel waiting line.

Let

$$k = \text{number of channels}$$
$$\lambda = \text{mean arrival rate for the system}$$
$$\mu = \text{mean service rate for } each \text{ channel}$$

The following equations apply to multiple-channel waiting lines for which the overall mean service rate, $k\mu$, is greater than the mean arrival rate, λ; in such cases, the service rate is sufficient to process or service all arrivals.

1. The probability that all k service channels are idle (that is, the probability of zero units in the system):

$$P_0 = \cfrac{1}{\left[\displaystyle\sum_{n=0}^{k-1} \frac{(\lambda/\mu)^n}{n!} \right] + \frac{(\lambda/\mu)^k}{(k-1)!} \frac{\mu}{k\mu - \lambda}} \qquad (16.11)$$

2. The probability of n units in the system:

$$P_n = \frac{(\lambda/\mu)^n}{k! \, k^{n-k}} P_0 \qquad \text{for } n > k \qquad (16.12)$$

$$P_n = \frac{(\lambda/\mu)^n}{n!} P_0 \qquad \text{for } 0 \le n \le k \qquad (16.13)$$

3. The average number of units waiting for service:

$$L_q = \frac{(\lambda/\mu)^k \lambda \mu}{(k-1)!(k\mu - \lambda)^2} P_0 \qquad (16.14)$$

4. The average number of units in the system:

$$L = L_q + \frac{\lambda}{\mu} \qquad (16.15)$$

5. The average time a unit spends waiting for service:

$$W_q = \frac{L_q}{\lambda} \qquad (16.16)$$

6. The average time a unit spends in the system (waiting time + service time):

$$W = W_q + \frac{1}{\mu} \tag{16.17}$$

7. The probability that an arriving unit has to wait for service:

$$P_w = \frac{1}{k!} \left(\frac{\lambda}{\mu} \right)^k \frac{k\mu}{k\mu - \lambda} P_0 \tag{16.18}$$

While the equations describing the operating characteristics of a multiple-channel waiting line with Poisson arrivals and exponential service times are somewhat more complex than the single-channel equations, they provide the same information and are used exactly as we used the results from the single-channel model. To simplify the use of equations (16.11)–(16.18), Table 16.3 shows values of P_0 for selected values of λ/μ; note that the values provided correspond to cases for which $k\mu > \lambda$ and hence the service rate is sufficient to service all arrivals.

As an illustration of the multiple-channel waiting-line model, let us return to the Schips truck dock problem. Suppose the manager wishes to consider the desirability of expanding the loading dock area to provide space to load and/or unload two trucks simultaneously. If this were done, Schips would have a two-channel waiting line. What are the operating characteristics of this two-channel system?

We can answer this question by applying equations (16.11) to (16.18) specifically for the two-channel ($k = 2$) waiting line. Using $\lambda = 3$ trucks per hour and $\mu = 4$ trucks per hour for each channel, we have the following operating characteristics:

$$P_0 = 0.4545 \qquad \text{(From Table 16.3 for } \lambda/\mu = .75 \text{ and } k = 2\text{)}$$

$$L_q = \frac{(\sqrt[3]{4})^2 3(4)}{(1)!(8 - 3)^2} (0.4545) = 0.1227 \text{ truck}$$

$$L = 0.1227 + \frac{3}{4} = 0.8727 \text{ truck}$$

$$W_q = \frac{0.1227}{3} = 0.0409 \text{ hour}$$

$$W = 0.0409 + \frac{1}{4} = 0.2909 \text{ hour}$$

$$P_w = \frac{1}{2!} \left(\frac{3}{4} \right)^2 \frac{2(4)}{(2(4) - 3)} (0.4545) = 0.2045$$

Shown below are some of the operating characteristics of the two-channel truck dock operation as compared with the single-channel system discussed in Section 16.2.

1. The average time a truck is at the dock (waiting time plus service time) is reduced from 1 hour to $W = 0.2909$ hour, or 17.45 minutes).
2. The average length of the waiting line is reduced from 2.25 trucks to $L_q = 0.1227$ truck.

3. The average time a truck waits for service is reduced from 45 minutes to $W_q = 0.0409$ hour, or 2.45 minutes.

4. The probability of a truck having to wait for service is reduced from 0.75 to $P_w = 0.2045$.

The advantages are clear. The two-channel system will greatly improve the operating characteristics of the waiting line. However, before implementing the two-dock system, the manager will undoubtedly want to consider the economic aspects of such a change.

Table 16.3
Values of P_0 for Multiple-Channel Waiting Lines with Poisson Arrivals and Exponential Service Times

Ratio λ/μ	Number of Channels (k)			
	2	3	4	5
0.15	0.8605	0.8607	0.8607	0.8607
0.20	0.8182	0.8187	0.8187	0.8187
0.25	0.7778	0.7788	0.7788	0.7788
0.30	0.7391	0.7407	0.7408	0.7408
0.35	0.7021	0.7046	0.7047	0.7047
0.40	0.6667	0.6701	0.6703	0.6703
0.45	0.6327	0.6373	0.6376	0.6376
0.50	0.6000	0.6061	0.6065	0.6065
0.55	0.5686	0.5763	0.5769	0.5769
0.60	0.5385	0.5479	0.5487	0.5488
0.65	0.5094	0.5209	0.5219	0.5220
0.70	0.4815	0.4952	0.4965	0.4966
0.75	0.4545	0.4706	0.4722	0.4724
0.80	0.4286	0.4472	0.4491	0.4493
0.85	0.4035	0.4248	0.4271	0.4274
0.90	0.3793	0.4035	0.4062	0.4065
0.95	0.3559	0.3831	0.3863	0.3867
1.00	0.3333	0.3636	0.3673	0.3678
1.20	0.2500	0.2941	0.3002	0.3011
1.40	0.1765	0.2360	0.2449	0.2463
1.60	0.1111	0.1872	0.1993	0.2014
1.80	0.0526	0.1460	0.1616	0.1646
2.00		0.1111	0.1304	0.1343
2.20		0.0815	0.1046	0.1094
2.40		0.0562	0.0831	0.0889
2.60		0.0345	0.0651	0.0721
2.80		0.0160	0.0521	0.0581
3.00			0.0377	0.0466
3.20			0.0273	0.0372
3.40			0.0186	0.0293
3.60			0.0113	0.0228
3.80			0.0051	0.0174
4.00				0.0130
4.20				0.0093
4.40				0.0063
4.60				0.0038
4.80				0.0017

16.4

ECONOMIC ANALYSIS OF WAITING LINES

As we have shown, waiting-line models can be used to determine operating characteristics of a waiting-line system. In the economic analysis of waiting lines we will seek to use the information provided by the waiting-line model to develop a cost model for the waiting line under study. Then we will use the cost model to help the manager balance the cost of waiting for service with the cost of providing the service.

In developing a cost model for the Schips truck dock problem, we will want to consider the cost of waiting for the trucks, both in the waiting line and while being serviced at the dock, and the cost of the truck dock service. We can develop a mathematical model that will enable us to compare the costs of Schips single-channel and two-channel truck dock operations as follows:

Let

$$c_1 = \text{hourly cost for each truck}$$
$$L = \text{average number of trucks in the system}$$
$$c_2 = \text{hourly cost for each channel}$$
$$k = \text{number of channels}$$

Then

$$\text{Total truck cost/hour} = c_1 L$$
$$\text{Total channel cost/hour} = c_2 k$$
$$\text{Total cost per hour} = c_1 L + c_2 k \tag{16.19}$$

By evaluating the above total cost model for the one- and two-channel systems, we will be able to obtain cost information helpful in making the decision regarding the truck dock operation. For example, suppose that the Schips trucks are operated at a cost of $c_1 = \$25$ per hour and that the dock cost is $c_2 = \$30$ per hour for each channel in operation. Table 16.4 summarizes the costs associated with the Schips truck dock alternatives. These cost projections tell us that the hourly costs will be reduced by $\$105 - 81.82 = \$23.18$ per hour in changing to the two-channel system. This is a 22% reduction in costs resulting from an improved truck dock operation. Assuming an annual operation of 40 hours per week for 52 weeks a year, this hourly saving results in a total savings of $(40)(52)(\$23.18) = \$48,214.40$ per year. Although the manager must now consider the cost of expanding the operation to the two-channel system, the projected savings of $\$48,214.40$ per year makes the two-channel operation an attractive alternative.

As a final comment concerning the use of economic analysis in waiting-line situations, we note that in the Schips truck dock problem the expenses associated with both the customer (trucks) and the server (docks) are being paid by the company. In cases such as this, where the customer and the server have common interests, balancing the cost of offering the service with the cost of waiting for the service is generally not too difficult. However, in many other waiting-line situations the customer and server do not share common interests. For example, in a supermarket customers generally prefer more check-

Table 16.4
Total Hourly Cost Summary for the Schips Truck Dock Problem

System	Average Number of Trucks in System	Total Truck Cost/Hour	Number of Channels	Total Channel Cost/Hour	Total Cost/Hour
Single-channel	3.00	($25)3.00 = $75	1	($30)1 = $30	$105.00
Two-channel	0.8727	($25)0.8727 = $21.82	2	($30)2 = $60	$ 81.82

out counters than fewer checkout counters because this will shorten the time they have to wait. The fact that the cost of providing more checkout counters might be very expensive is usually of little concern to the customer. On the other hand, from the point of view of the supermarket, it may be very difficult to assign a monetary value to the cost of customer waiting time. Thus, whenever the customer and the server do not share common interests, it may be difficult to estimate the cost of waiting. In such cases the decision maker may wish to specify a desired service goal such as a reasonable average waiting time, a reasonable probability of waiting a specified length of time, and so on. The results of the waiting-line model may then be used to determine the system design that will achieve the desired service goal.

16.5

OTHER WAITING-LINE MODELS

In this chapter you have been exposed to single-channel and multiple-channel waiting lines with Poisson arrivals and exponential service times. However, many variations of these specific systems exist in actual waiting-line situations. Quantitative analysts have analyzed a wide variety of possible waiting lines and developed general expressions for average customer waiting time, average number of customers in the system, percent of the time servers are idle, and other operating characteristics of the system. Specifically, models are available covering some of the following types of waiting-line situations:

1. Arrivals other than Poisson
2. Service times other than exponential
3. Arrivals in bulk quantities rather than one at a time
4. Limited or finite waiting lines, called *truncated queues*
5. Mean arrival and mean service rates that vary with the number of the units waiting for service
6. Queue disciplines other than first-come, first-served
7. Sequential waiting lines, where units pass through a fixed sequence or series of servers

D. G. Kendall suggested a special notation for classifying waiting-line models. The Kendall system is a shorthand notation for identifying the waiting-line model being considered. While the Kendall notation cannot completely describe all waiting-line configurations, it has been adopted as a common method for classifying the arrival distribution, service time distribution, and number of parallel servers in a waiting-line system. The three-symbol Kendall notation is as follows:

_____ / _____ / _____

code indicating	code indicating	number of
arrival distribution	service time	parallel servers
	distribution	or channels

With M being the code for both the Poisson arrival distribution and also the exponential service time distribution, the single-channel waiting line discussed in Section 16.2 is the $M/M/1$ waiting-line model. The two-channel system of Section 16.3 is an example of the $M/M/2$ model. Several other arrival and service time distributions are possible and are denoted by other code letters.

With many models of waiting lines available, a decision maker with a specific waiting-line problem should attempt to identify a model that closely approximates the specific problem; that is, the decision maker should attempt to identify a model with an arrival distribution, service time distribution, number of servers, queue discipline, and so on that closely approximates the actual situation. Even with the numerous waiting-line models in existence, many practical waiting-line problems are so complex that quantitative analysts have been unable to develop the analytical expressions necessary to determine the operating characteristics. If the decision maker is unable to find an analytical model applicable to the specific waiting line, a computer simulation model of the problem may be used to develop the necessary operating characteristics.

16.6

SIMULATION OF WAITING LINES

Computer simulation models offer an attractive alternative to the use of mathematical models when studying the behavior and operating characteristics of waiting lines. In Chapter 15 we saw how a simulation model could be used to study the waiting-line situation at the County Beverage Drive-Thru. The attractiveness of computer simulation models rests primarily with their versatility. Although we pointed out that mathematical models have been developed for waiting-line situations that differ from the Poisson-exponential systems described in this chapter, the complexity and diversity of waiting lines often prohibits an analyst from finding an existing model that fits the specific situation being studied. Even when models that appear to be good approximations of the problem can be identified, the mathematics of the models are often so complex that many practitioners are unable to determine whether the models are applicable or not. Thus a computer simulation model of a waiting-line problem offers another approach to studying waiting-line situations.

Let us consider a deviation from the assumptions that enabled us to utilize existing mathematical models for the Schips truck dock waiting line. One key assumption was that the service times in the Schips problem were essentially random *and* independent of all other conditions. This enabled us to use the same exponential distribution and mean service rate for all trucks. Let us suppose that the Schips truck dock crew does not work independently of the number of trucks waiting to be serviced. That is, suppose that management has observed that as the length of the waiting line increases, the rate at which the dock crew loads and unloads also increases. Thus our previous assumption that service times are always distributed exponentially with a mean service rate of 4 trucks per hour would not reflect the actual situation. Hence, while the decision maker might still elect to use the Poisson-exponential model as a rough approximation, it may be desirable to develop a computer simulation model that attempts to account for the varying work rates of the crew.

Also recall that the waiting-line models in this chapter employ a first-come, first-served queue discipline. Suppose that the branch manager wanted to evaluate the policy of having delivery trucks loaded before unloading incoming shipments from the central warehouse. How would the waiting times and operating costs be affected by this policy? We cannot answer this question with a waiting-line model that assumes a first-come, first-served queue discipline. However, a computer simulation model could be used to test this new priority policy.

Finally, suppose that we collected actual arrival and service time data for the Schips trucks for a 2-week period and found that arrivals did not follow a Poisson distribution and the service times did not follow an exponential distribution. We might try to identify the general distributions that these data follow and attempt to identify an existing waiting-line model based on these distributions. However, if an existing model cannot be found or if the arrivals and/or service times do not follow any recognizable probability distribution, we could input the observed relative frequency data for the arrival and service times into a simulation model and use computer simulation to generate the operating characteristics of the truck dock.

Although we have mentioned only a few specific changes in the characteristics of the Schips waiting-line problem, it should be apparent that many other possibilities could be considered. Again, this is where computer simulation starts to become especially attractive as a solution procedure. Instead of using an existing waiting-line model that is perhaps a poor approximation of the waiting line being studied, we develop a computer simulation model that more closely reflects the true characteristics of the waiting line.

Summary

Waiting-line problems occur in a variety of practical situations in which customers or other units may wait for service. Waiting-line models have been developed that provide information regarding waiting times, idle time, number of units waiting, and other operating characteristics of a waiting line. This information, along with cost data, may be used to balance the benefits of improved service with the cost necessary to improve the service.

In this chapter we have presented models for single-channel and multiple-channel waiting lines with Poisson arrivals and exponential service times. In addition, we pointed out that models exist that are applicable in a variety of other waiting-line situations. However, a computer simulation model of the waiting line is recommended if the assumptions of existing waiting-line models do not closely approximate the specific problem under study.

Glossary

Queueing theory A term for the body of knowledge dealing with waiting lines.
Queue A waiting line.
Single-channel waiting line A waiting line with only one service facility.

Poisson probability distribution   A probability distribution used to describe the random arrival pattern for some waiting lines.

Exponential probability distribution   A probability distribution used to describe the pattern of service times for some waiting lines.

Multiple-channel waiting line   A waiting line with two or more parallel identical service facilities.

Mean arrival rate   The expected number of customers or units arriving or entering the system in a given period of time.

Mean service rate   The expected number of customers or units that can be serviced by one server in a given period of time.

Problems

The following waiting-line problems are all based on the assumptions of Poisson arrivals and exponential service times.

1. The reference desk of a large library receives requests for assistance at a mean rate of 10 requests per hour. Assuming that the reference desk has a mean service rate of 12 requests per hour, consider the following questions.
   a. What is the probability that the reference desk is idle?
   b. What is the average number of requests that will be waiting for service?
   c. What is the average waiting time plus service time for a request for assistance?
   d. What is the utilization factor for the reference desk?

2. Trucks using a single-channel loading dock have a mean arrival rate of 12 per day. The loading/unloading rate is 18 per day.
   a. What is the probability that the truck dock will be idle?
   b. What is the average number of trucks waiting for service?
   c. What is the average time a truck waits for the loading or unloading service?
   d. What is the probability that a new arrival will have to wait?

3. A mail-order nursery specializes in European beech trees. New orders, which are processed by a single shipping clerk, have a mean arrival rate of 6 per day and a mean service rate of 8 per day.
   a. What is the average time that an order spends in the queue waiting for the clerk to begin service?
   b. What is the average time that an order spends in the system?

4. For the Schips single-channel waiting line, assume that the mean arrival rate is four trucks per hour and the mean service rate for the channel is five trucks per hour.
   a. What is the probability that the truck dock will be idle?
   b. What is the average number of trucks in the queue?
   c. What is the average number of trucks in the system?
   d. What is the average time a truck spends in the queue waiting for service?
   e. What is the average time a truck spends in the system?
   f. What is the probability that an arriving truck will have to wait?
   g. Does this waiting line provide more or less service than the original Schips dock operation (see Table 16.2)?

5. Marty's Barber Shop has one barber. Customers arrive at a rate of 2.2 per hour, and haircuts are given at an average rate of five customers per hour.
   a. What is the probability that the barber is idle?
   b. What is the probability that one customer is receiving a haircut and no one is waiting?
   c. What is the probability that one customer is receiving a haircut and one customer is waiting?
   d. What is the probability that one customer is receiving a haircut and two customers are waiting?
   e. What is the probability that more than two customers are waiting?
   f. What is the average time a customer waits for service?

6. Trosper Tire Company has decided to hire a new mechanic to handle all tire changes for customers ordering a new set of tires. Two mechanics are available for the job. One mechanic has limited experience and can be hired for $7 per hour. It is expected that this mechanic can service an average of three customers per hour. A mechanic with several years of experience is also being considered for the job. This mechanic can service an average of four customers per hour, but must be paid $10 per hour. Assume that customers arrive at the Trosper garage at the rate of two per hour.
   a. Compute waiting-line operating characteristics for each mechanic.
   b. If the company assigns a customer waiting cost of $15 per hour, which mechanic provides the lower operating cost?

7. Agan Interior Design provides home and office decorating assistance for its customers. In normal operation an average of 2.5 customers arrive per hour. One design consultant is available to answer customer questions and make product recommendations. The consultant averages 10 minutes with each customer.
   a. Compute operating characteristics for the customer waiting line.
   b. Service goals dictate that an arriving customer should not wait for service more than an average of 5 minutes. Is this goal being met? What action do you recommend?
   c. If the consultant can reduce the average time spent per customer to 8 minutes, will the service goal be met?

8. Pete's Market is a small local grocery store with only one checkout counter. Assume that shoppers arrive at the checkout lane at an average rate of 15 customers per hour and that the average order takes 3 minutes to ring up and bag. What information would you develop for Pete to aid him in analyzing the current operation? If Pete does not want the average time waiting for service to exceed 5 minutes, what would you tell Pete about the current system?

9. In problem 8 you analyzed the checkout waiting line for Pete's Market. After reviewing the analysis, Pete felt it would be desirable to hire a full-time person to assist in the checkout operation. Pete believed that if the new employee assisted the checkout cashier, average service time could be reduced to 2 minutes. However, Pete was also considering installing a second checkout lane, which could be operated by the new person. This second alternative would provide a two-channel system with the average service time of 3 minutes for each server. Should Pete use the new employee to assist on the current checkout counter or operate a second counter? Justify your recommendation.

10. Keuka Park Savings and Loan currently has one drive-in teller window. The arrival of cars occurs at a mean rate of 10 cars per hour. The mean service rate is 12 cars per hour.
    a. What is the probability that the service facility will be idle?
    b. If you were to drive up to the facility, what is the expected number of cars you would see waiting and being serviced?
    c. What is the average time waiting for service?
    d. What is the probability an arriving car has to wait?
    e. As a potential customer of the system, would you be satisfied with the above waiting-line characteristics? How do you think management could go about assessing the feelings of its customers with respect to the operation of the current system?

11. In order to improve the service to the customer, Keuka Park Savings and Loan wants to investigate the effect of a second drive-in teller window. Assume a mean arrival rate of 10 cars per hour. In addition, assume a mean service rate of 12 cars per hour for each drive-in window. What effect would the addition of a new teller window have on the system? Does this system appear acceptable?

12. Fore and Aft Marina is a newly planned marina that will be located on the Ohio River near Madison, Indiana. Assume that Fore and Aft decides to build one docking facility and that a mean arrival rate of 5 boats per hour and a mean service rate of 10 boats per hour are expected. Consider the following questions:
    a. What is the probability that the boat dock will be idle?
    b. What is the average number of boats that will be waiting for service?
    c. What is the average time a boat will spend waiting for service?
    d. What is the average time a boat will spend at the dock?
    e. If you were the management of Fore and Aft Marina, would you be satisfied with the service level your system would be providing?

13. Management of the Fore and Aft Marina project in problem 12 wants to investigate the possibility of adding a second dock. Assume a mean arrival rate of 5 boats per hour for the marina and a mean service rate of 10 boats per hour for each channel.
    a. What is the probability that the boat dock will be idle?
    b. What is the average number of boats that will be waiting for service?
    c. What is the average time a boat will spend waiting for service?
    d. What is the average time a boat will spend at the dock?
    e. If you were the management of Fore and Aft Marina, would you be satisfied with the service level your system would be providing?

14. The City Beverage Drive-Thru is considering a two-channel system. Cars arrive at the beverage store at the mean rate of 6 per hour. The service rate for each channel is 10 per hour.
    a. What is the probability that both channels are idle?
    b. What is the average number of cars waiting for service?
    c. What is the average time waiting for service?
    d. What is the average time in the system?
    e. What is the probability of having to wait for service?

15. Consider a two-channel waiting line with a mean arrival rate for the system of 50 per hour and a mean service rate of 75 per hour for each channel.
    a. What is the probability that both channels are idle?

b. What is the average number of cars waiting for service?

c. What is the average time waiting for service?

d. What is the average time in the system?

e. What is the probability of having to wait for service?

16. For a two-channel waiting line with a mean arrival rate of 14 per hour and a mean service rate of 10 per hour per channel, determine the probability that an arrival has to wait. What is the probability of waiting if the system is expanded to three channels?

17. Big Al's Quickie Car Wash has two wash areas. Each area can wash 15 cars per hour. Cars arrive at the carwash at the rate of 15 cars per hour on the average, join the waiting line, and select the next open wash area when it becomes available.

   a. What is the average time waiting for a wash area?

   b. What is the probability that a customer who arrives at the carwash will have to wait?

   c. As a customer of Big Al's Quickie Car Wash, do you think the service of the system favors the customer? If you were Al, what would your attitude be relative to this service level?

18. Refer to the Agan Interior Design situation in problem 7. Agan would like to evaluate two alternatives:

   (1) Use one consultant with an average service time of 8 minutes per customer.

   (2) Expand to two consultants, each of whom has an average service time of 10 minutes per customer.

   If the consultants are paid $16 per hour and the customer waiting time is valued at $25 per hour, should Agan expand to the two-design-consultant system? Explain.

19. A fast-food franchise is currently operating a drive-up window. Orders are placed at an intercom station at the back of the parking lot. After placing an order, the customer pulls up and waits in line at the drive-up window until the cars in front have been served. By hiring a second person to help take and fill orders, management is hoping to improve customer service.

   With one person filling orders, the average service time for a drive-up customer is 2 minutes; with a second person working, the average service time can be reduced to 1 minute, 15 seconds. Note that the drive-up window operation with two people is still a single-channel waiting line. However, with the addition of the second person, the average service time can be decreased. Cars arrive at the rate of 24 per hour.

   a. Determine the average waiting time in the queue when only one person is working the drive-up window.

   b. With only one person working the drive-up window, what percentage of time will that person not be occupied serving customers?

   c. Determine the average waiting time when two people are working at the drive-up window.

   d. With two persons working the drive-up window, what percentage of time will no one be occupied serving drive-up customers?

   e. Would you recommend hiring a second person to work the drive-up window? Justify your answer.

20. Refer to problem 19. Space is available to install a second drive-up window adjacent to the first. Management is considering adding such a window. One person will be assigned to serve customers at each window.

   a. Determine the average customer waiting time for this two-channel system.

    b. What percentage of the time will both windows be idle?

    c. Which design would you recommend for providing service at the drive-up window? One attendant at one window? Two attendants at one window? Two attendants and two windows with one attendant at each window?

21. All-National Insurance handles customer telephone claims at its central office. Between the hours of 10:00 A.M. and noon, telephone calls arrive at the rate of 12 per hour. One or more agents are assigned to the telephone claim service, depending on the anticipated call volume. Each agent can process an average of eight telephone claims per hour. If all agents are busy when a telephone call arrives, the customer receives a recorded message that says an agent will be available shortly. Waiting calls are answered in the order in which they are received. Company guidelines are that on average the calling customers should not have to wait more than 1 minute before an agent becomes available. How many agents are needed between the hours of 10:00 A.M. and noon? Determine the waiting-line characteristics for the system you recommend.

22. In Sections 16.3 and 16.4 we determined the operating characteristics and prepared an economic analysis of the Schips problem using a two-channel waiting line. Our waiting-line model assumed that each channel operated with a mean service rate of four trucks per hour. Suppose that in actual operation of the truck dock the four-trucks-per-hour service rate per channel is appropriate when two trucks are being loaded/unloaded simultaneously. However, when only one truck is in the dock area, all dock workers are assigned to it. Thus, when only one truck is present, the service rate is temporarily increased. The formulas presented in Section 16.3 are not applicable to this new situation, since the service rate varies depending on the situation. This is a case in which a simulation model of the waiting line would be helpful.

    a. Discuss in a step-by-step fashion how you would develop a simulation model to determine the operating characteristics for this waiting-line system.

    b. What type of output would you like to have as a result of the simulation?

    c. Do you anticipate that the cost model would show this approach to be better or worse than the two-channel system considered in Section 16.3? Explain.

Case Problem
Airline Reservations

Regional Airlines is establishing a new phone system for handling flight reservations. During the 10:00 A.M.–11:00 A.M. time period, past data show that calls to the ticket agents occur at an average rate of one call every 4.28 minutes. In addition, service time data indicate that an average of 3 minutes will be required to process a call. If a customer calls and the ticket agents are busy, a recorded message tells the customer that the call is being held in the order received and that a ticket agent will be available shortly; the customer will be asked to wait until an agent is free.

Regional Airline's management feels that offering an efficient telephone reservation system is an important part of establishing an image as a service-oriented carrier and, if properly implemented, the system will increase business. However, management also is aware of the fact that a busy or overloaded system with long waiting times may result in negative customer reaction to the point that Regional might even lose business. The cost per hour for a ticket reservation agent is $20. Thus management wants to provide good service, but does not want to overstaff the telephone reservation operation with more agents than are necessary.

At a planning meeting Regional's management team agreed that an acceptable service goal is to immediately answer and process at least 85% of the incoming calls. During the planning meeting, Regional's vice-president of administration pointed out that the historical data show that the average service rate by the agent is faster than the average arrival rate of the telephone calls. His conclusion is that one agent should be able to handle the telephone reservations and still have some idle time. The vice-president of marketing disagreed and felt the company should use at least two agents.

Managerial Report

Prepare a report for Regional Airlines, analyzing the telephone reservation operation. Include the following information in your report:

1. A detailed analysis of the operating characteristics of the reservation system with one ticket agent as proposed by the vice-president of administration.
2. A detailed analysis of the operating characteristics of the ticket reservation system based on your recommendation regarding the number of reservation agents Regional should use.
3. The telephone arrival data presented above are for the 10:00 A.M.–11:00 A.M time period; however, the arrival rate of incoming calls is expected to change from hour to hour. Describe how your waiting-line analysis could be used to develop a ticket agent staffing plan that would enable the company to provide different levels of staffing for the ticket reservation system at different times during the day. Indicate the information that you would need to develop this staffing plan.

Quantitative Methods in Practice

Goodyear Tire & Rubber Company*
Akron, Ohio

The Goodyear Tire & Rubber Company had its beginning in an old, converted strawboard factory in 1898. Its first product was bicycle tires. Since 1926 it has been the world's largest rubber company and one of the nation's leading industrial corporations.

Although tires are Goodyear's biggest single product line, the company has become a highly diversified corporate enterprise. The company's product line has changed from the original bicycle tires, carriage tires, and horseshoe pads to tires of all types, chemicals, industrial rubber products, defense products, packaging films, foam cushioning, shoe soles and heels, flooring and counter tops, metal rims and wheels, aircraft brakes and wheels, aerospace products, and atomic energy.

Goodyear has more than 129 production facilities—about half in the United States, half overseas—and approximately 155,000 employees. Its sales and distribution operations cover virtually all areas of the free world. Corporate headquarters are in Akron, Ohio.

Familiar to millions of people are the company airships, named the *Enterprise, Columbia*, and *America*, which are stationed in the United States, and the *Europa*, which is stationed in Europe. These airships are made by Goodyear Aerospace Corporation, a subsidiary of The Goodyear Tire & Rubber Company.

Quantitative Methods at Goodyear

Goodyear has many departments that make use of quantitative methods for decision making. Most analyses are performed by one of the computer programming departments under the guidance of a user (client) department. These computer programming departments are involved in a variety of applications from routine data collection and systems maintenance to queueing analysis. For example, one department is responsible for maintaining a system that gathers records of orders and sales; another department is responsible for forecasting and assisting production schedulers; and a third department is responsible for quality control. The waiting-line (queueing) application discussed in the remainder

---

*The authors are indebted to Dr. Walt Fenske of The Goodyear Tire & Rubber Company for providing this application.

of this presentation was the responsibility of yet another department. Many of the applications performed by the departments are interrelated, and one department will often use data generated by another department.

A Waiting-Line Application

The application discussed involves a system for dispatching maintenance personnel to fix machines. Under the then-current manual system, whenever a machine needed repair, a production supervisor used a phone intercom system to call an individual referred to as a dispatcher. The dispatcher recorded the information provided by the production supervisor on cards. Then, whenever maintenance personnel called the dispatcher to request a new assignment, the information on these cards was used by the dispatcher to tell the maintenance personnel which machine should be repaired.

Due primarily to a need to develop a computerized database that could be analyzed to improve the maintenance function, Goodyear decided to replace the manual system with a computer-controlled system. In the computer-controlled system the dispatcher function is performed by a person called a coordinator. The function of the coordinator is to enter service information when received into the computer using a remote computer terminal. The need for more information to be entered causes the coordinator's task to be more time consuming than the dispatcher's function in the old system. However, the computer-controlled system offers many potential advantages in other areas because of the wide variety of information entered by the coordinator.

A waiting-line model was used in designing the computer-controlled system. The problem to be solved was to determine how many coordinators (and consequently, remote computer terminals) were needed. If there are not enough coordinators, production supervisors and maintenance personnel will have difficulty reaching a coordinator. If the computer system is to be a success, people trying to reach the coordinator should not have long waits. However, if there are too many coordinators, excessive coordinator and computer terminal expenses will be incurred. Some of the questions that had to be answered were the following:

1. What percentage of the time will the coordinator be busy?
2. What is the maximum number of people waiting to reach the coordinator?
3. What is the average time spent waiting to reach the coordinator?
4. How many calls does the coordinator receive?
5. How many callers have to wait longer than 4 minutes to reach the coordinator?
6. How many callers do not have to wait to reach the coordinator?

These questions suggest that the design of the new system may be aided by use of a waiting-line model. In a waiting-line model of this situation, the coordinators are the servers, and the people waiting to talk to the coordinators constitute the waiting line. Thus, if one coordinator is used, the model is a single-channel waiting-line model. Otherwise it is a multiple-channel waiting-line model.

The complexity of the proposed computer system can best be understood by considering the four types of arrivals that must be handled. The first type of arrival is a call received from a production supervisor stating that a machine needs repair. At this time a *work order is initiated*. The second type of arrival is a call from a maintenance person stating that the repair work is being started; this is referred to as placing the *work order in process*. The third type of arrival, referred to as *completing a work order*, is a call from a maintenance person stating that the repair work has been completed. The fourth type of arrival is any other type of call. Note that each work order generates three calls to the coordinator.

For this problem the arrivals were known to differ from the Poisson distribution. In addition, there were a number of other complicating factors that precluded the use of the waiting-line models introduced in this chapter. However, a simulation model of the system, built on many of the basic waiting-line principles in this chapter, was implemented. The General Purpose Simulation System (GPSS) was the programming language used for the simulation model.

Computer simulation runs were performed for a system with one coordinator and a system with two coordinators. In the one-coordinator system the simulation runs showed that the coordinator would be busy about 69% of the time and that the average waiting time to reach the coordinator would be 4.9 minutes. The average waiting time for the one-coordinator system was considered to be much too high.

For the two-coordinator system the simulation results indicated that each coordinator would be busy approximately 35% of the time. However, the average waiting time to reach a coordinator dropped to 42 seconds. In fact, it was found that a call would get through immediately about 90% of the time. Since management believed that these times were reasonable, the system was designed to have two coordinators and two remote computer terminals.

Questions

1. What is the primary reason that Goodyear decided to replace the manual system with a computer-controlled system?
2. What factors in this application led to the use of a simulation model rather than an analytical model of the waiting line?

CHAPTER

17

Multicriteria Decision Problems

In previous chapters we have introduced quantitative procedures designed to help managers make better decisions. For example, in decision analysis (Chapter 4) we showed how optimal strategies can be developed when a decision maker is faced with several decision alternatives and an uncertain or risk-filled pattern of future events. Recall, however, that the decision analysis techniques we presented were used for problem situations in which the decision alternatives were evaluated with respect to a single output measure or criterion such as profit, cost, or time. In studying linear programming (Chapters 7–10) we saw how models involving a linear objective function and a set of linear constraints could be used to maximize or minimize the value of a criterion such as profit, cost, return on investment, advertising effectiveness, and so on. If we continue to review each of the other quantitative methods discussed thus far, we will find that the underlying objective in each case is to identify the decision that is best for the selected criterion.

In this chapter we present quantitative approaches that are appropriate for situations in which the decision maker desires to consider multiple criteria in arriving at the overall best decision. For example, consider a company that is involved in selecting a location for a new manufacturing plant. Since the cost of land and construction may vary from location to location, one criterion in selecting the best site would be the total cost involved in building the plant; if this were the sole criterion of interest, management would simply select the location where the land cost plus the construction cost is minimized. Before making any decision, however, management might also want to consider additional criteria such as the availability of transportation from the plant to the firm's distribution centers, the attractiveness of the proposed location in terms of hiring and retaining employees, energy costs at the proposed site, and state and local taxes. In situations such as this, the complexity of the problem increases since one location can be more desirable from the perspective of one criterion and less desirable from the perspective of one or more of the other criteria.

To introduce the topic of multicriteria decision making we will first consider a technique referred to as *goal programming*. This procedure was developed to handle multiple-criteria situations within the general framework of linear programming. The other approach we will consider, referred to as the *analytic hierarchy process*, permits the inclusion of subjective factors in arriving at a recommended decision. In this approach the decision maker must provide judgments about the relative importance of each of the decision criteria and then specify a preference for each decision alternative relative to each criterion; the output is a prioritized ranking indicating the overall preference for each of the decision alternatives.

17.1

GOAL PROGRAMMING

Linear programming problems are limited to a single objective, such as the maximization of profit or the minimization of cost. However, on occasion, managers or decision makers face problem situations in which more than one objective exists. Goal programming has been developed as a procedure for handling multiple-objective situations. In goal programming each objective is viewed as a "goal." Then, given the usual resource limitations, or constraints, the manager attempts to develop decisions that provide the "best" solution in terms of coming as close as possible to reaching all goals.

The Basic Goal Programming Model

To understand the goal programming approach, let us consider a problem faced by McKenna Office Supplies, Inc. McKenna's management establishes monthly performance goals for its sales force. While each individual on the sales force has a sales volume quota for the month, McKenna also specifies goals, or quotas, for the types of customers contacted. McKenna's customer contact strategy for next month calls for the sales force to make 200 contacts with customers who have previously purchased supplies from the firm. In addition, the strategy calls for 120 contacts of new customers. The purpose of this latter quota or goal is to ensure that the sales force is continuing to investigate new sources of sales.

Making allowances for travel and waiting time, as well as for demonstration and direct sales time, McKenna has allocated 2 hours of sales force effort to each contact of a previous customer. New customer contacts tend to take longer and require 3 hours per contact. For the upcoming month, McKenna projects a maximum of 640 hours of sales force time available for both previous and new customer contacts.

You might first think of the 200 previous customer contacts and the 120 new customer contacts as constraints, but we will view them as objectives, or goals. The question is, does McKenna have sufficient sales force resources to achieve both of these customer contact goals? The goals of 200 previous customer contacts and 120 new customer contacts require a total of $2(200) + 3(120) = 760$ hours. Since only 640 hours of sales force time are available, McKenna cannot satisfy both goals simultaneously. This is the type of situation for which the goal programming approach was developed.

Let us proceed with a goal programming formulation to help resolve McKenna's problem. An important first step in goal programming is to state each goal explicitly. For the McKenna Office Supplies problem the goals can be stated as follows:

Goal 1: Reach 200 previous customers.
Goal 2: Reach 120 new customers.

Note that each goal has a stated target value: 200 and 120 in the McKenna example. This is a property of all goal programming models. That is, rather than stating objectives in terms of maximizing some quantity, the objectives or goals are expressed in terms of reaching a desired quantity or target value for each goal.

Once we have listed the goals with appropriate target values, we can proceed with the development of the model. The next step is to write each goal or objective in the form of a constraint. Considering the first goal of reaching 200 previous customers and letting

$$x_1 = \text{number of previous customers contacted}$$

we could write the previous customer contact goal as

$$1x_1 = 200$$

However, the above constraint would require meeting the previous customer goal exactly, which we have seen may not be possible. Thus we add deviation variables that reflect the amount the solution deviates from the stated goal. For example, for the previous-customer contact goal we would add the following deviation variables:

$$d_1^+ = \text{number of previous customer contacts over the desired 200}$$

$$d_1^- = \text{number of previous customer contacts under the desired 200}$$

This notation associates the letter d with the deviation from the goal. A superscript of plus or minus is used to indicate whether the solution exceeds or falls below the stated goal. Including the deviation variables, we write the previous customer contact goal as

$$1x_1 = 200 + 1d_1^+ - 1d_1^-$$

Thus these deviation variables allow us to miss the goal and still obtain a feasible solution. For example, if $x_1 = 220$ in the final solution, d_1^+ would be 20 to reflect the overachievement of the goal by 20 contacts; d_1^- in this case would be zero. If $x_1 = 175$, then $d_1^- = 25$ and $d_1^+ = 0$ in order to reflect that $x_1 = 175$ is 25 contacts short of the 200 goal. Rewriting this constraint with all the variables on the left-hand side, the constraint for the 200 previous customer contact goal is

$$1x_1 - 1d_1^+ + 1d_1^- = 200$$

The next step is to develop a similar constraint in order to reflect the second goal of reaching 120 new customers. Letting

$$x_2 = \text{number of new customers contacted}$$
$$d_2^+ = \text{number of new customer contacts over the desired 120}$$
$$d_2^- = \text{number of new customer contacts under the desired 120}$$

the constraint for the new customer goal is

$$1x_2 - 1d_2^+ + 1d_2^- = 120$$

The sales force availability constraint can be handled just as in previous linear programming models. Doing so, we obtain

$$2x_1 + 3x_2 \leq 640$$

We now have three constraints and six decision variables, which combine to reflect the two goals and the one resource constraint. If we can now develop an objective function, we will have a goal programming model with six variables and three constraints. What is the appropriate objective function?

Note that if the deviation variables could be reduced to zero, we would satisfy the goals exactly. However, even if the deviation variables cannot be reduced to zero, we can at least reduce them to their minimum possible values. Since small values for the deviation variables imply small deviations from the goals, the objective function in goal programming calls for minimizing the weighted sum of the deviation variables. The deviation variables portion of the objective function for McKenna's problem can be written as follows:

$$\min \quad 0d_1^+ + 1d_1^- + 0d_2^+ + 1d_2^-$$

Note that d_1^+ and d_2^+, which correspond to an overachievement of goals, have been given zero weights or coefficients. The reason for this is that there is no penalty for overachieving the two goals. On the other hand, the d_1^- and d_2^- variables have both been given weights of 1, indicating that management attaches equal importance to deviations from the two goals. Since the firm's overall objective is to minimize the combined underachievement of the two goals, the complete goal programming model can be written as follows:

$$\min \quad 0x_1 + 0x_2 + 0d_1^+ + 1d_1^- + 0d_2^+ + 1d_2^-$$
$$\text{s.t.}$$
$$1x_1 \qquad\quad - 1d_1^+ + 1d_1^- \qquad\qquad\qquad = 200$$
$$1x_2 \qquad\qquad\qquad - 1d_2^+ + 1d_2^- = 120$$
$$2x_1 + 3x_2 \qquad\qquad\qquad\qquad\qquad \leq 640$$
$$x_1, x_2, d_1^+, d_1^-, d_2^+, d_2^- \geq 0$$

Since the above model is a linear program, we can use LINDO/PC to obtain the optimal solution shown below (see Figure 17.1, where D1MI represents d_1^-, D1PL represents d_1^+, and so on)

```
            OBJECTIVE FUNCTION VALUE

    1)          40.0000000

        VARIABLE         VALUE              REDUCED COST
          D1MI          .000000               .333333
          D2MI        40.000000               .000000
            X1       200.000000               .000000
          D1PL          .000000               .666667
            X2        80.000000               .000000
          D2PL          .000000              1.000000
```

Figure 17.1
Solution to McKenna Company Goal Programming Problem Using LINDO/PC

$$x_1 = 200$$
$$x_2 = 80$$
$$d_1^+ = 0$$
$$d_1^- = 0$$
$$d_2^+ = 0$$
$$d_2^- = 40$$

We see that the previous customer contact goal is reached while the new customer contact goal is underachieved by $d_2^- = 40$.

With the goal programming approach to the McKenna problem in mind, let us summarize the characteristics common to the basic goal programming model:

1. Each goal appears in a separate constraint, with the right-hand-side value indicating the target value for the goal.
2. Deviation variables d_i^+ and d_i^- are included for each goal in order to reflect the possible overachievement or underachievement of the goal.
3. Other constraints, reflecting resource capacities or other restrictions, are included just as they would be in any linear programming model.
4. The objective function requires minimizing the weighted sum of the deviation variables. Coefficients (weights) for the deviation variables in the objective function reflect the relative "cost" or "penalty" for each unit deviation from the corresponding goal's target value. Zero coefficients mean that the corresponding deviations from the target values carry no penalty.

In order to appreciate some of the flexibility offered by the goal programming model, note that in the goal programming model of the McKenna problem we assigned a weight (coefficient) of 1 to a one-unit underachievement of each goal (d_1^- and d_2^-). This implied that a one-unit underachievement of one goal was just as undesirable as a one-unit underachievement of the other goal. However, suppose that McKenna's management was very much concerned about contacting new customers in order to provide growth in future sales. In fact, suppose that on a per-unit basis, management felt the new customer contacts were twice as important as the previous customer contacts. The changed relative importance of the two goals can be reflected by altering the weights or coefficients for the deviation variables in the objective function. This reevaluation of the importance of new customer contacts could be expressed with the following objective function:

$$\text{min} \quad 0x_1 + 0x_2 + 0d_1^+ + 1d_1^- + 0d_2^+ + 2d_2^-$$

Using the same three constraints and the revised objective function, the following goal programming solution is obtained:

$$x_1 = 140$$
$$x_2 = 120$$
$$d_1^+ = 0$$
$$d_1^- = 60$$
$$d_2^+ = 0$$
$$d_2^- = 0$$

The increased importance of goal 2 now leads to reaching the new customer goal while underachieving the previous customer goal by $d_1^- = 60$.

Priority Levels for Goals

A further extension of goal programming provides the capability of specifying different priority levels for each of the goals or objectives. This extension is valuable in situations where one goal is so much more important than the others that the decision maker is unwilling to "trade off" satisfaction of the one goal for any amount of deviation from another goal. In the current version of the McKenna problem, while we might select different objective function coefficients, or weights, to reflect the relative importance of the goals, the problem contained only one priority level since the objective function and constraints permitted trading off the satisfaction of one goal for the satisfaction of the other.

In goal programming problems with priority levels, first-priority (P_1) goals are treated in an objective function much like the one used in the McKenna problem. Second-priority (P_2) goals are considered only after the priority level 1 goals are reached. An objective function containing P_2 goals is then used. The solution is revised under the P_2 goal objective function as long as it does not cause a reduction in achievement of the P_1 goals. In this extension of goal programming, P_1 goals are considered first, the P_2 goals second, the P_3 goals third, and so on. At each stage a solution revision can be made as long as it causes no reduction in achievement of the higher priority goals.

17.2

THE ANALYTIC HIERARCHY PROCESS

The analytic hierarchy process (AHP), developed by Thomas L. Saaty,[1] is designed to solve complex problems involving multiple criteria. The process requires the decision

[1] Saaty, Thomas L., *The Analytic Hierarchy Process*, New York, McGraw-Hill, 1980.

maker to provide judgments about the relative importance of each of the criteria and then to specify a preference for each decision alternative relative to each criterion. The output of the AHP is a prioritized ranking indicating the overall preference for each of the decision alternatives.

In order to introduce the AHP, we consider the problem faced by Dave Payne. Dave is planning to purchase a new car. After a preliminary analysis of the makes and models available, Dave has narrowed the list of decision alternatives to three cars, which we will refer to as car A, car B, and car C. Table 17.1 provides a summary of the information Dave has collected regarding these cars.

Table 17.1
Information for the Car-Selection Example

	Car A	Car B	Car C
Price	$13,100	$11,200	$9500
MPG	18	23	29
Interior	Deluxe	Above average	Standard
Body	4-door midsize	2-door sport	2-door compact
Radio	AM/FM, tape	AM/FM	AM
Engine	6-cylinder	4-cylinder turbo	4-cylinder

Based on the information in Table 17.1—as well as his own personal feelings resulting from driving each car—Dave decided that there were several criteria that he needed to consider in making the purchase decision. After some thought, he selected purchase price, miles per gallon (MPG), comfort, and style as the four criteria to be considered. Quantitative data regarding the purchase price and MPG criteria are provided directly in Table 17.1. However, measures of comfort and style cannot be specified so easily. Dave will need to consider factors such as car interior, type of radio, ease of entry and exit, seat-adjustment features, etc., in order to determine the comfort level for each car. The style criterion will need to be measured in terms of Dave's subjective evaluation of each car.

Even when we deal with a criterion as easily measured as purchase price, however, subjectivity becomes an issue whenever a particular decision maker indicates his or her personal preferences. For instance, car A costs $3600 more than car C; this difference might represent a great deal of money to one person but not very much money to another person. Thus whether car A is considered extremely more expensive than car C or only moderately more expensive than car C is a subjective judgment that will depend primarily on the financial status of the person making the comparison. An advantage of the AHP is that it is designed to handle situations such as this, in which the subjective judgments of individuals constitute an important part of the decision process.

Developing the Hierarchy

The first step in the AHP is to develop a graphical representation of the problem in terms of the *overall goal*, the *criteria*, and the *decision alternatives*. Such a graph depicts the *hierarchy* for the problem. Figure 17.2 shows the hierarchy for the car-selection problem. Note that the first level of the hierarchy shows that the overall goal is to select the best car. At the second level, we see that the four criteria (purchase price, MPG, comfort,

Overall Goal:

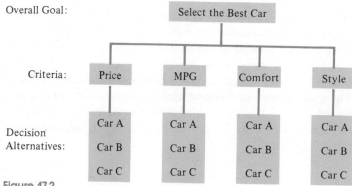

Figure 17.2
Hierarchy for the Car-Selection Problem

and style) will contribute to the achievement of the overall goal. Finally, at the third level, we see that each decision alternative (car A, car B, and car C) can contribute to each criterion in a unique way.

The approach AHP takes is to have the decision maker specify his or her judgments about the relative importance of each criterion in terms of its contribution to the achievement of the overall goal. At the next level, the AHP asks the decision maker to indicate a preference or priority for each decision alternative in terms of how it contributes to each criterion. For example, in the car-selection problem, Dave will need to specify his judgment about the relative importance of each of the four criteria. He will also need to indicate his preference for each of the three cars relative to each criterion. Given the information on relative importance and preferences, a mathematical process is used to synthesize the information and provide a priority ranking of the three cars in terms of their overall preference.

17.3

ESTABLISHING PRIORITIES USING THE AHP

In this section we will show how the AHP utilizes pairwise comparisons to establish priority measures for both the criteria and decision alternatives. The sets of priorities that need to be determined in the car-selection problem are as follows:

1. The priorities of the four criteria in terms of the overall goal
2. The priorities of the three cars in terms of the purchase-price criterion
3. The priorities of the three cars in terms of the MPG criterion
4. The priorities of the three cars in terms of the comfort criterion
5. The priorities of the three cars in terms of the style criterion

In the following discussion we will demonstrate how to establish priorities for the three cars in terms of the *comfort* criterion. The other sets of priorities can be determined in a similar fashion.

Pairwise Comparisons

Pairwise comparisons are fundamental building blocks of the AHP. In establishing the priorities for the three cars in terms of comfort, we will ask Dave to state a preference for the comfort of the cars when the cars are considered two at a time (pairwise). That is, Dave will be asked to compare the comfort of car A to car B, car A to car C, and car B to car C in three separate comparisons.

The AHP employs an underlying scale with values from 1 to 9 to score the relative preferences for two items. Table 17.2 provides the numerical scores recommended for the verbal preferences expressed by the decision maker. Research and experience has confirmed the 9-unit scale as a reasonable basis for discriminating between the preferences for two items.

Table 17.2
Pairwise Comparison Scale for the AHP Preferences

Verbal Judgment of Preference	Numerical Rating
Extremely preferred	9
Very strongly to extremely	8
Very strongly preferred	7
Strongly to very strongly	6
Strongly preferred	5
Moderately to strongly	4
Moderately preferred	3
Equally to moderately	2
Equally preferred	1

In the car-selection example, suppose that Dave has compared the comforts of car A with car B and is convinced that car A is more comfortable. Dave is then asked to state his preference for the comfort of car A compared to car B using one of the verbal descriptions shown in Table 17.2. If he believes that car A is *moderately* preferred to car B, a value of 3 is utilized in the AHP; if he believes that car A is *strongly* preferred, a value of 5 is utilized; if he believes that car A is *very strongly* preferred, a value of 7 is utilized; if he believes that car A is *extremely* preferred, a value of 9 is utilized. Values of 2, 4, 6, and 8 are the intermediate values for the scale. A value of 1 is reserved for the case where the two items are judged to be *equally* preferred.

Suppose that when asked his preference between cars A and B with respect to the comfort criterion, Dave states that car A is between equally and moderately more preferred than car B; the numerical measure that reflects this judgment is 2. Dave is then asked to provide his preference between car A and car C. Suppose in this case he states that car A is very strongly to extremely more preferred than car C; this corresponds to a numerical rating of 8. Finally, Dave is asked to state his preference for car B compared to car C. Suppose in this case he indicates that car B is strongly to very strongly preferred to car C; the AHP would assign a numerical rating of 6.

The Pairwise Comparison Matrix

In order to develop the priorities for the three cars in terms of the comfort criterion, we need to develop a matrix of the pairwise comparison scores. Since three cars are being considered, the pairwise comparison matrix will consist of three rows and three columns. Shown is a portion of the *pairwise comparison matrix* based on the preferences Dave has specified.

Comfort	Car A	Car B	Car C
Car A		2	8
Car B			6
Car C			

Note: In the pairwise comparison matrix, the value in row i and column j is the measure of preference of the car in row i when compared to the car in column j.

We see that the value in the matrix that corresponds to comparing car A with car B is 2, the value that corresponds to comparing car A with car C is 8, and the value that corresponds to comparing car B with car C is 6.

In order to determine the remaining entries in the pairwise comparison matrix, first note that when we compare any car against itself, the judgment must be that they are equally preferred. Thus, using the scale shown in Table 17.2, the rating of car A compared to car A, car B compared to car B, and car C compared to car C must be 1. Hence the AHP assigns a 1 to all elements on the diagonal of the pairwise comparison matrix.

Given these entries, all that remains is to determine the rating for car B compared to car A, car C compared to car A, and car C compared to car B. Obviously, we could follow the same procedure and ask Dave to provide his preferences for these pairwise comparisons. However, since we already know that Dave has rated his preference for car A compared to car B as 2, there is no need for him to make another pairwise comparison with these two cars. In fact, we will conclude that the preference rating for car B when compared to car A is simply the reciprocal of the preference rating for car A when compared to car B: $\frac{1}{2}$. To see intuitively why the reciprocal can be used, note that the preference value of 2 is interpreted as indicating that car A is twice as preferable as car B. Thus it follows that car B must be one-half as preferable as car A. Using this logic the AHP obtains the preference rating of car B compared to car A by computing the reciprocal of the rating of car A compared to car B. Using this inverse, or reciprocal, relationship, we find that the rating of car C compared to car A is $\frac{1}{8}$ and the rating of car C compared to car B is $\frac{1}{6}$. Using these numerical values of preference, the complete pairwise comparison matrix for the comfort criterion is shown in Table 17.3.

Table 17.3
Pairwise Comparison Matrix Showing Preferences for the Three
Cars in Terms of Comfort

Comfort	Car A	Car B	Car C
Car A	1	2	8
Car B	$\frac{1}{2}$	1	6
Car C	$\frac{1}{8}$	$\frac{1}{6}$	1

Synthesis

Once the matrix of pairwise comparisons has been developed, we can calculate what is called the *priority* of each of the elements being compared. For example, we would now like to use the pairwise comparison information in Table 17.3 to estimate the relative priority for each of the cars in terms of the comfort criterion. This part of the AHP is referred to as *synthesization*.

The exact mathematical procedure required to perform this synthesization involves the computation of eigenvalues and eigenvectors and is beyond the scope of this text. However, the following three-step procedure provides a good approximation of the synthesized priorities.

Procedure for Synthesizing Judgments

Step 1   Sum the values in each column of the pairwise comparison matrix.

Step 2   Divide each element in the pairwise comparison matrix by its column total; the resulting matrix is referred to as the *normalized pairwise comparison matrix*.

Step 3   Compute the average of the elements in each row of the normalized matrix; these averages provide an estimate of the relative priorities of the elements being compared.

To see how the synthesization process works for our example problem, we carry out the procedure using the pairwise comparison matrix shown in Table 17.3. The three steps are as follows.

Step 1   Sum the values in each column.

Comfort	Car A	Car B	Car C
Car A	1	2	8
Car B	½	1	6
Car C	⅛	⅙	1
Column totals	$^{13}/_8$	$^{19}/_6$	15

Step 2   Divide each element of the matrix by its column total.

Comfort	Car A	Car B	Car C
Car A	$^{8}/_{13}$	$^{12}/_{19}$	$^{8}/_{15}$
Car B	$^{4}/_{13}$	$^{6}/_{19}$	$^{6}/_{15}$
Car C	$^{1}/_{13}$	$^{1}/_{19}$	$^{1}/_{15}$

Note that all columns in the normalized pairwise comparison matrix now have a sum of 1.

Step 3   Average the elements in each row. (The values in the normalized pairwise comparison matrix have been converted to decimal form.)

Comfort	Car A	Car B	Car C	Row Avg.
Car A	0.615	0.632	0.533	0.593
Car B	0.308	0.316	0.400	0.341
Car C	0.077	0.053	0.067	0.066
			Total	1.000

This synthesis provides the relative priorities for the three cars with respect to the comfort criterion. Thus we see that, considering comfort, the most preferred car is car A (with a priority of 0.593). Car B (with a priority of 0.341) is second, followed by car C (with a priority of 0.066). The priority vector showing the relative priorities of car A, car B, and car C with respect to the comfort criterion is written as follows:

$$\begin{bmatrix} 0.593 \\ 0.341 \\ 0.066 \end{bmatrix}$$

Consistency

A key step in the AHP is the establishment of priorities through the use of the pairwise comparison procedure just described. An important consideration in terms of the quality of the ultimate decision relates to the *consistency* of judgments that the decision maker demonstrated during the series of pairwise comparisons. For example, consider a situation involving the comparison of three job offers with respect to the salary criterion. Suppose that the following pairwise comparison matrix was developed.

Salary	Job 1	Job 2	Job 3
Job 1	1	2	8
Job 2	1/2	1	3
Job 3	1/8	1/3	1

The interpretation of the preference scores is that the preference for job 1 is twice the preference for job 2, and the preference for job 2 is three times the preference for job 3. Using these two pieces of information we would logically conclude that the preference for job 1 should be $2 \times 3 = 6$ times the preference for job 3. The fact that the pairwise comparison matrix showed a preference of 8 instead of 6 indicates that some lack of consistency exists in the pairwise comparisons.

However, before we become too concerned about a lack of consistency in the pairwise comparisons, realize that perfect consistency is very difficult to achieve and that some lack of consistency is expected to exist in almost any set of pairwise comparisons. To handle the consistency question, the AHP provides a method for measuring the degree of consistency among the pairwise judgments provided by the decision maker. If the degree of consistency is acceptable, the decision process can continue. However, if the degree of consistency is unacceptable, the decision maker should reconsider and possibly revise the pairwise comparison judgments before proceeding with the analysis.

The AHP provides a measure of the consistency of pairwise comparison judgments by computing a *consistency ratio*. This ratio is designed in such a way that values of the ratio exceeding 0.10 are indicative of inconsistent judgments; in such cases the decision maker would probably want to reconsider and revise the original values in the pairwise comparison matrix. Values of the consistency ratio of 0.10 or less are considered to indicate a reasonable level of consistency in the pairwise comparisons.

Although the exact mathematical computation of the consistency ratio is beyond the scope of this text, an approximation of the ratio can be obtained. We will illustrate this computational procedure for the car-selection problem by considering Dave's pairwise comparisons for the comfort criterion. The steps of the computational procedure are described and demonstrated next.

Estimating the Consistency Ratio

Step 1 Multiply each value in the first column of the pairwise comparison matrix by the relative priority of the first item considered; multiply each value in the second column of the matrix by the relative priority of the second item considered; multiply each value in the third column of the matrix by the relative priority of the third item considered. Sum the values across the rows to obtain a vector of values labeled "weighted sum." This computation for the car-selection example is

$$0.593\begin{bmatrix}1\\\frac{1}{2}\\\frac{1}{8}\end{bmatrix} + 0.341\begin{bmatrix}2\\1\\\frac{1}{6}\end{bmatrix} + 0.066\begin{bmatrix}8\\6\\1\end{bmatrix} = \begin{bmatrix}0.593\\0.297\\0.074\end{bmatrix} + \begin{bmatrix}0.682\\0.341\\0.057\end{bmatrix} + \begin{bmatrix}0.528\\0.396\\0.066\end{bmatrix} = \begin{matrix}\text{Weighted}\\\text{Sum Vector}\\\begin{bmatrix}1.803\\1.034\\0.197\end{bmatrix}\end{matrix}$$

Step 2 Divide the elements of the vector of weighted sums obtained in step 1 by the corresponding priority value. For the car-selection example, we obtain

$$\frac{1.803}{0.593} = 3.040$$

$$\frac{1.034}{0.341} = 3.032$$

$$\frac{0.197}{0.066} = 2.985$$

Step 3 Compute the average of the values computed in step 2; this average is denoted by λ_{max}. For the car-selection example, we obtain

$$\lambda_{max} = \frac{(3.040 + 3.032 + 2.985)}{3} = 3.019$$

Step 4 Compute the consistency index (CI), which is defined as follows:

$$CI = \frac{\lambda_{max} - n}{n - 1}$$

where

$$n = \text{number of items being compared}$$

For the car-selection example with $n = 3$, we obtain

$$CI = \frac{3.019 - 3}{2} = 0.010$$

Step 5 Compute the consistency ratio (CR), which is defined as follows:

$$CR = \frac{CI}{RI}$$

where RI, the random index, is the consistency index of a randomly generated pairwise comparison matrix. It can be shown that RI depends on the number of elements being compared and takes on the following values:

n	RI
3	0.58
4	0.90
5	1.12
6	1.24
7	1.32
8	1.41

Thus for our car-selection example with $n = 3$ and RI $= 0.58$, we obtain the following consistency ratio:

$$CR = \frac{0.010}{0.58} = 0.017$$

As mentioned previously, a consistency ratio of 0.10 or less is considered acceptable. Since our example shows a consistency ratio of 0.017, the degree of consistency exhibited in the pairwise comparison matrix for comfort is acceptable.

Other Pairwise Comparisons for the Car-Selection Example

In continuing with the AHP analysis of the car-selection problem, we need to use the pairwise comparison procedure to determine the priorities of the three cars in terms of the purchase price, MPG, and style criteria. This requires that Dave express pairwise comparison preferences for the cars, considering each of these criteria one at a time. Assume that this has been done and that Dave's preferences are summarized in the pairwise comparison matrices shown in Table 17.4.

The interpretation of the numerical values in Table 17.4 is the same as the interpretation of the preference values we observed for the comfort criterion. For example, consider the comparison of car A and car B in terms of the purchase price criterion. Car B ($11,200) is considered more preferable than car A ($13,100). In fact, the pairwise comparison matrix shows Dave's preference for car B is three times greater than his preference for car A in terms of purchase price. Similarly, car A is only $\frac{1}{3}$ as preferred as car B. Recall that the pairwise comparison matrix is set up to show the preference of the item in row i when compared to the item in column j.

Following the same synthesis procedure that we used for the comfort criterion, the priority vectors for these criteria can be computed. The result of this synthesis is shown in Table 17.5.

Table 17.4
Pairwise Comparison Matrices for Price, MPG, and Style for the Car-Selection Example

Price	Car A	Car B	Car C
Car A	1	$\frac{1}{3}$	$\frac{1}{4}$
Car B	3	1	$\frac{1}{2}$
Car C	4	2	1

MPG	Car A	Car B	Car C
Car A	1	$\frac{1}{4}$	$\frac{1}{6}$
Car B	4	1	$\frac{1}{3}$
Car C	6	3	1

Style	Car A	Car B	Car C
Car A	1	$\frac{1}{3}$	4
Car B	3	1	7
Car C	$\frac{1}{4}$	$\frac{1}{7}$	1

Table 17.5
Priority Vectors for Price, MPG, and Style

Price	MPG	Style
$\begin{bmatrix} 0.123 \\ 0.320 \\ 0.557 \end{bmatrix}$	$\begin{bmatrix} 0.087 \\ 0.274 \\ 0.639 \end{bmatrix}$	$\begin{bmatrix} 0.265 \\ 0.655 \\ 0.080 \end{bmatrix}$

In interpreting these priorities we see that car C is the most preferable in terms of purchase price (0.557) and miles per gallon (0.639). Car B is the most preferable in terms of style (0.655). No car is the most preferred with respect to all criteria. Thus, before a final decision can be made, we must assess the relative importance of the criteria.

In addition to the pairwise comparisons for the decision alternatives, we must use the same pairwise comparison procedure to set priorities for all four criteria in terms of the importance of each in contributing toward the overall goal of selecting the best car. To develop this final pairwise comparison matrix, Dave would have to specify how important he thought each criterion was compared to each of the other criteria. In order to do this, six pairwise judgments have to be made: purchase price compared to MPG; purchase price compared to comfort; purchase price compared to style; MPG compared to comfort; MPG compared to style; and comfort compared to style. For example, in the pairwise comparison of the purchase price and MPG criteria, Dave indicated that purchase price was *moderately* more important than MPG. Using the AHP 9-point numerical rating scale (see Table 17.2), a value of 3 was recorded to show the higher importance of the purchase-price criterion. The summary of the pairwise comparison preferences for the four criteria is shown in Table 17.6.

Table 17.6
Pairwise Comparison Matrix for the Four Criteria in the Car-Selection Problem

Criterion	Price	MPG	Comfort	Style
Price	1	3	2	2
MPG	$\frac{1}{3}$	1	$\frac{1}{4}$	$\frac{1}{4}$
Comfort	$\frac{1}{2}$	4	1	$\frac{1}{2}$
Style	$\frac{1}{2}$	4	2	1

The synthesization process described earlier in this section can now be used to convert the pairwise comparison information into the priorities for the overall goal, as shown:

$$\text{Priorities for the Overall Goal}$$

$$\begin{matrix} \text{Price} \\ \text{MPG} \\ \text{Comfort} \\ \text{Style} \end{matrix} \begin{bmatrix} 0.398 \\ 0.085 \\ 0.218 \\ 0.299 \end{bmatrix}$$

From this priority vector we see that the purchase price (0.398) has been identified as the highest priority or most important criterion in the car-selection decision. Style (0.299) and comfort (0.218) rank next in importance. Miles per gallon (0.085) is a relatively unimportant criterion in terms of the overall goal of selecting the best car. In the next section we show how the AHP uses the priority information generated in this section to develop an overall priority ranking for the three cars.

17.4

USING THE AHP TO DEVELOP AN OVERALL PRIORITY RANKING

In the previous section we showed how a pairwise comparison matrix can be used to develop a prioritized ranking of the items being compared. In this section we show how the criterion priorities and the priorities of each decision alternative relative to each criterion can be combined to develop an overall priority ranking of the decision alternatives. Table 17.7 contains a matrix that summarizes the priorities for each car in terms of each criterion as computed in Section 17.2. We will refer to this matrix as the *priority matrix*.

The procedure used to compute the overall priorities for each decision alternative can be best understood if we think of the priority for each criterion as a weight that

Table 17.7
The Priority Matrix for the Car-Selection Problem

	Criterion	Price	MPG	Comfort	Style
	Car A	0.123	0.087	0.593	0.265
Alternative	**Car B**	0.320	0.274	0.341	0.655
	Car C	0.557	0.639	0.066	0.080

reflects its importance. The overall priority for each decision alternative is obtained by summing the product of the criterion priority times the priority of the decision alternative with respect to that criterion. Recall that the criterion priorities were found to be 0.398 for purchase price, 0.085 for MPG, 0.218 for comfort, and 0.299 for style. Thus the computation of the overall priority for car A is as follows:

$$\text{Overall car A priority} = 0.398(0.123) + 0.085(0.087) + 0.218(0.593)$$
$$+ 0.299(0.265)$$
$$= 0.265$$

Repeating this calculation for cars B and C provides their overall priorities as follows:

$$\text{Overall car B priority} = 0.398(0.320) + 0.085(0.274) + 0.218(0.341)$$
$$+ 0.299(0.655)$$
$$= 0.421$$

$$\text{Overall car C priority} = 0.398(0.557) + 0.085(0.639) + 0.218(0.066)$$
$$+ 0.299(0.080)$$
$$= 0.314$$

Ranking these priority values, we have the following AHP ranking of the decision alternatives:

Alternative	Priority
Car B	0.421
Car C	0.314
Car A	0.265
Total	1.000

These results provide a basis for Dave to make a decision regarding the purchase of a car. Based on the AHP priorities, Dave should select car B. Whether or not Dave actually decides to purchase car B based on the AHP analysis is still his decision to make. If Dave believes that the judgments that he has made regarding the importance of the criteria and his preferences for the cars in terms of the criteria are valid, then the AHP priorities show that car B is the preferred car. Whether or not Dave actually decides to purchase car B may not be as important as the additional understanding of the problem that he has obtained as a result of performing the analysis required by the AHP. This in itself may be as helpful to Dave as the actual decision recommendation that has been obtained.

17.5

USING EXPERT CHOICE TO IMPLEMENT THE AHP

Expert Choice (EC), a software pckage marketed by Decision Support Software, provides a user-friendly procedure for implementing the AHP on a microcomputer. In this section we provide an introduction to this software package by showing how it can be used to compute the priorities for the car selection problem.

Expert Choice enables the user simply to construct a graphical representation of the hierarchy. For example, to create the hierarchy for the car-selection example, the user selects the option to develop a new application; what appears on the computer's monitor is a request to define the overall goal. After the user defines the overall goal, a rectangular box, or node, appears on the screen, with the goal description written directly above it. The user selects the EDIT command and then the INSERT option; another rectangular box or node appears below the goal node, and the user now types the name of a criterion, which will be entered inside the box. This process continues until all four criterion nodes have been specified. Figure 17.3 shows the partial hierarchy appearing on the computer screen after the four criterion have been specified.

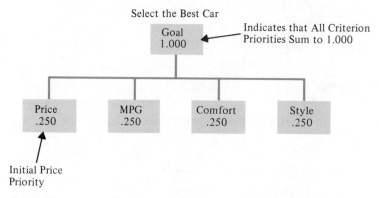

Figure 17.3
Partial Hierarchy Showing Criterion with Initial Priorities Equal to 0.250

In Figure 17.3 we see that in addition to the names of each criterion, the criterion nodes also contain the decimal value 0.250. This value represents the initial weight, or priority, given to each criterion at the start of the *EC* session. The user can now continue the process of using the EDIT command with the INSERT option to define the decision alternative nodes associated with each of the criterion nodes. In Figure 17.4 we show the result of defining the decision alternative nodes for the price criterion; note that since there are three alternatives, the initial priorities are set at 0.333. A similar set of decision alternatives are then identified for each of the other three criteria.

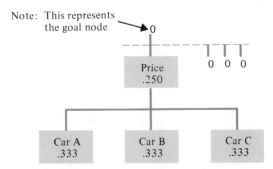

Note: This represents the goal node

Figure 17.4
Partial Hierarchy Showing Price Criterion with Initial Priorities for Cars A, B, and C equal to 0.333

Once the user has developed the complete hierarchy for the problem, he or she can focus on any particular part of the hierarchy through the use of the REDRAW command. In fact, to show the detail displayed in Figure 17.4, all we did was to point to the price node (using the arrows on the keyboard's numeric key pad) and then type R for redraw. Our intent here is not to attempt to show you how to use *EC* but merely to let you develop some appreciation for the ease in which the analysis can be performed using this software package.

Now that the hierarchy has been input to *EC*, we are ready to begin developing the pairwise comparisons needed to establish priorities for the decision alternatives. In order to illustrate the type of approach used, we moved back to the goal node with *EC* and then selected the COMPARE command by typing C. After selecting the option to make comparisons based on the importance of the decision criteria, the *EC* system begins to go through the pairwise comparison analysis.

One portion of this analysis, which shows the approach used by *EC* to establish the comparative importance between the purchase price and MPG criteria, is shown in Figure 17.5. Note that this figure indicates to the *EC* system that price is moderately more important than MPG. This process continues until all the entries in the pairwise comparison matrix for criteria have been developed. The synthesization process is then performed to compute the priorities for the criteria; Figure 17.6 shows the priorities that were obtained after synthesization.

The process of entering pairwise preferences for the cars relative to each of the criteria was then performed in a similar manner. The overall decision was then arrived at by entering the command S, which is an abbreviation for synthesizing; this command is used only when we have entered all the data for the pairwise comparison matrices and want to obtain an overall prioritization of the decision alternatives. Figure 17.7 shows the results obtained. Note that the results indicate that the final priority for car B, the most preferable, is 0.422.

The *EC* system is much more powerful and comprehensive than our brief introduction can begin to show. It is a very helpful software package in performing the multiple-criteria decision analysis of the AHP. In addition to providing the overall priorities for the decision alternatives, *EC* has the capability of doing "what if" types of analyses, where the decision maker can begin to learn how the overall priorities for the decision alternative are affected by changes in the preference input data.

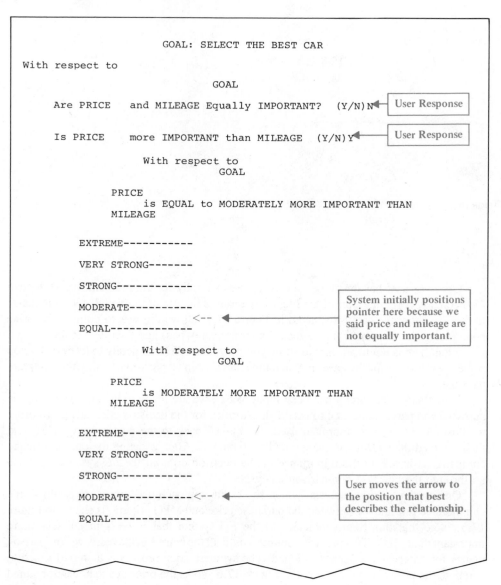

Figure 17.5
Determining the Rating for the Price and MPG Pairwise Comparison

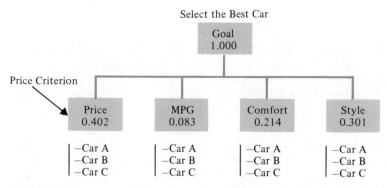

Select the Best Car

Price Criterion

Figure 17.6
The Hierarchy Showing Priorities after Synthesization for the Criteria

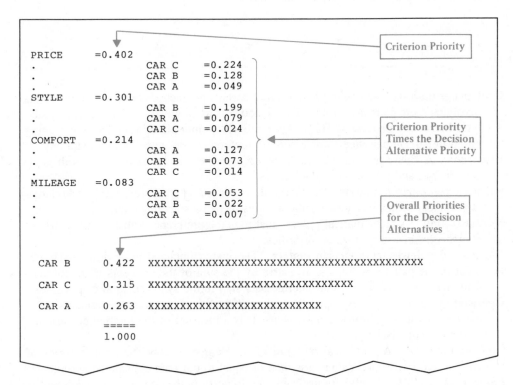

Figure 17.7
Final Results of Using the AHP for the Car-Selection Example

Summary

In this chapter we have shown how goal programming can be used to solve problems with multiple objectives within the linear programming framework. The basic goal programming model treats each goal as a constraint and is designed to minimize the deviations from the goals. General linear programming computer codes can be used to solve this basic goal programming model; it is even possible to apply different weights to the different goals to reflect their relative importance. Finally, we mentioned the case of preemptive priorities as an extension of goal programming that is useful when a manager is not willing to trade off achievement of one goal for achievement of another.

We also presented an approach to multiple-criteria decision making known as the analytic hierarchy process (AHP). We showed that a key part of the AHP is the development of judgments concerning the relative importance of, or preference for, the elements being compared. A consistency ratio is computed to determine the degree of consistency exhibited by the decision maker in making the pairwise comparisons. Values of the consistency ratio less than or equal to 0.10 are considered acceptable.

Once the set of all pairwise comparisons has been developed, a process referred to as synthesization is used to determine the priorities for the elements being compared. The final step of the AHP process is a further synthesization, in which the priority levels established for the decision alternatives relative to each criterion are multiplied by the priority levels reflecting the importance of the criteria themselves; the sum of these products over all the criteria is the overall priority level for the decision alternative. The chapter concluded with a brief introduction to *Expert Choice*, a software package designed to perform the computational steps of the AHP.

Glossary

Goal programming A linear programming-based approach developed for problems involving more than one criteria. The objective is to minimize deviations from goals.

Analytic hierarchy process (AHP) An approach to multiple-criteria decision making based in part on pairwise comparisons of preference for elements in a hierarchy.

Hierarchy A figure that shows the levels of a problem in terms of the overall goal, the criteria, and the decision alternatives.

Pairwise comparison matrix A matrix that consists of the preference, or relative importance, scores provided during a series of pairwise comparisons.

Synthesization A mathematical process that uses the preference values in the pairwise comparison matrix to develop priorities.

Normalized pairwise comparison matrix The matrix obtained by dividing each element of the pairwise comparison matrix by the sum of the elements in its column. This matrix is computed as an intermediate step in the synthesization of priorities.

Consistency A concept developed to assess the quality of preference judgments made during a series of pairwise comparisons. It is a measure of the internal consistency of these comparisons.

Consistency ratio A numerical measure of the degree of consistency in a series of pairwise comparisons. Values less than or equal to 0.10 are considered acceptable.

Expert Choice (EC) A software package used to perform the computations required by the analytic hierarchy process.

Problems

1. Recall the RMC linear programming problem introduced in Chapter 7. In that problem, three raw materials are blended to produce two products: a fuel additive and a solvent base. Each ton of fuel additive is a mixture of $2/5$ ton of material 1 and $3/5$ ton of material 3. A ton of solvent base is a mixture of $1/2$ ton of·material 1, $1/5$ ton of material 2, and $3/10$ ton of material 3. RMC's production is constrained by a limited availability of the three raw materials. For the current production period RMC has the following quantities of each raw material: material 1, 20 tons; material 2, 5 tons; material 3, 21 tons. Assume that management would like to achieve the following production goals:

   Goal 1:   Produce 30 tons of fuel additive.
   Goal 2:   Produce 15 tons of solvent base.

   a. Is it possible for management to achieve both goals given the amounts of each material available? Explain.
   b. Formulate and solve a goal programming model to determine the optimal product mix. Assume that both goals are equally important to management.
   c. If goal 1 is twice as important as goal 2, what is the optimal product mix? What situation might exist in order for goal 1 to be twice as important as goal 2?

2. Michigan Motor Corporation (MMC) has just introduced a new luxury touring sedan. As part of the promotional campaign the marketing department has decided to send personalized invitations to test drive the new sedans to two target groups: (1) current owners of a MMC luxury automobile and (2) owners of luxury cars manufactured by one of MMC's competitors. Based on previous experience with this type of advertising, MMC estimates that 25% of the customers contacted from group 1 and 10% of the customers contacted from group 2 will test drive the new sedan. As part of this campaign MMC has set the following two goals:

   Goal 1:   10,000 customers from group 1 should test drive the new sedan.
   Goal 2:   5,000 customers from group 2 should test drive the new sedan.

   The cost to send a personalized invitation to each customer is estimated to be $1 per letter, and management has established a budget of $70,000 to cover the expenses associated with sending out the invitations.
   a. Can MMC reach both of their goals given the current budget?
   b. Assuming that both goals are equally important, formulate a goal programming model of the MMC problem.
   c. Solve the model formulated in part (b) in order to determine the best solution possible.
   d. If management believes that contacting customers from group 2 is twice as important as contacting customers from group 1, what should MMC do?

3. Investment Advisors, Inc. must develop an investment portfolio for a new client. As an initial investment strategy, the new client would like to restrict the portfolio to a mix of the following stocks:

Stock	Price/Share	Estimated Annual Return/Share	Risk Index/Share
U.S. Oil	$25	$3	0.50
Hub Properties	$50	$5	0.25

The risk index is a rating of the relative risk of the two investment alternatives. For the given data, U.S. Oil is judged to be the riskier investment. By constraining the total risk for the portfolio, the investment firm avoids placing excessive amounts of the portfolio in potentially high-return but also high-risk investments.

a. Consider the following constraints: (1) $80,000 is available to invest; (2) an upper limit of 700 has been set for the total risk index of all investments; (3) an upper limit has been set of 1000 shares of the more risky U.S. Oil stock. Formulate and solve a linear programming model in order to determine how many shares of each stock should be purchased in order to maximize the total annual return.

b. Suppose that the client has indicated that there are two goals associated with the investment: (1) receive an annual return of $10,000 and (2) maintain a total risk index of all investments of 700. Treating the $80,000 dollars available and the 1000-shares restriction for U.S. Oil as fixed constraints, formulate a goal programming model that could be used to develop the best investment strategy.

c. Solve the goal programming model formulated in part (b) and compare your recommendations with the solution developed in part (a).

4. The L. Young & Sons Manufacturing Company produces two products, which have the following profit and resource requirement characteristics:

	Product 1	Product 2
Profit/unit	$4	$2
Dept. A hours/unit	1	1
Dept. B hours/unit	2	5

Last month's production schedule used 350 hours of labor in department A and 1000 hours of labor in department B.

Young's management has been experiencing work force morale and labor union problems during the past 6 months because of monthly departmental workload fluctuations. New hirings, layoffs, and interdepartmental transfers have been common because the firm has not attempted to stabilize departmental workload requirements.

Management would like to develop a production schedule for the coming month that will minimize deviations from the goals of maintaining department A workload at 350 hours and department B workload at 1000 hours.

a. Management has specified that a minimum of $1300 profit must be earned. Formulate and solve a goal programming model that will lead to minimum work force fluctuations subject to satisfying the profit requirement.

b. Suppose the firm ignores the workload fluctuations and considers the 350 hours in department A and the 1000 hours in department B as the maximum available.

Formulate and solve a linear programming problem to maximize profit subject to these constraints.

c. Compare the approaches taken in parts (a) and (b). Discuss which approach you favor and tell why.

5. Morley Company is attempting to determine the best location for a new machine in an existing layout of three machines. The existing machines are located at the following x_1, x_2 coordinates on the shop floor:

$$\text{Machine 1:} \quad x_1 = 1, \ x_2 = 7$$
$$\text{Machine 2:} \quad x_1 = 5, \ x_2 = 9$$
$$\text{Machine 3:} \quad x_1 = 6, \ x_2 = 2$$

a. Develop a goal programming model that can be solved to minimize the total distance of the new machine from the three existing machines. The distance is to be measured rectangularly. For example (see below), if the location of the new machine is ($x_1 = 3$, $x_2 = 5$), it is considered to be a distance of 4 units from machine 1. *Hint:* In the goal programming formulation, let

$$x_1 = \text{first coordinate of the new machine location}$$
$$x_2 = \text{second coordinate of the new machine location}$$
$$d_i^+ = \text{amount by which the } x_1 \text{ coordinate of the new machine}$$
$$\text{exceeds the } x_1 \text{ coordinate of machine } i. \ (i = 1, 2, 3)$$
$$d_i^- = \text{amount by which the } x_1 \text{ coordinate of machine } i$$
$$\text{exceeds the } x_1 \text{ coordinate of the new machine} \ (i = 1, 2, 3)$$
$$e_i^+ = \text{amount by which the } x_2 \text{ coordinate of the new machine}$$
$$\text{exceeds the } x_2 \text{ coordinate of machine } i \ (i = 1, 2, 3)$$

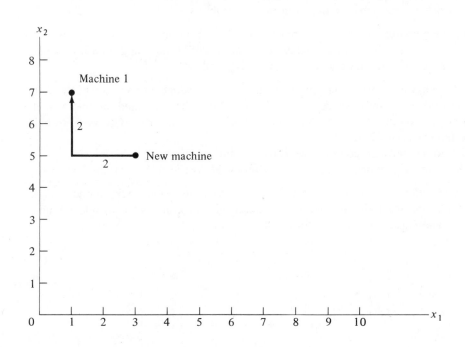

$e_i^- =$ amount by which the x_2 coordinate of machine i
exceeds the x_2 coordinate of the new machine $(i = 1, 2, 3)$

b. What is the optimal location for the new machine? (See art on page 717)

6. A fast-food chain is attempting to determine the best location for a new outlet. Management would like to determine the best location for drawing customers from three population centers. Letting (x_1, x_2) represent the map coordinates of the three population centers, we can show their locations as follows:

Population center 1: $x_1 = 2, \ x_2 = 8$
Population center 2: $x_1 = 6, \ x_2 = 6$
Population center 3: $x_1 = 1, \ x_2 = 1$

If the new outlet is located at coordinates $(x_1 = 3, x_2 = 2)$, then it is a distance of $(3 - 1) + (2 - 1) = 3$ miles from population center 3 (distance is measured as the sum of the east–west and north–south differences in coordinates).

a. Formulate and solve a goal programming model to determine what location for the new outlet will minimize the total distance from the three population centers. (*Hint:* Let x_1, x_2 represent the coordinates of the new location.)

b. Population center 1 is four times as large as center 3, and center 2 is twice as large as center 3. The firm feels that the importance of locating near a population center is proportional to its population. Develop and solve a new goal programming model where the weights on the deviations reflect this importance.

7. Using the pairwise comparison matrix for the price criterion as shown in Table 17.4, verify that the priorities after synthesization are 0.123, 0.320, and 0.557. Compute the consistency ratio and comment on its acceptability.

8. Using the pairwise comparison matrix for the MPG criterion as shown in Table 17.4, verify that the priorities after synthesization are 0.087, 0.274, and 0.639. Compute the consistency ratio and comment on its acceptability.

9. Using the pairwise comparison matrix for the style criterion as shown in Table 17.4, verify that the priorities after synthesization are 0.265, 0.655, and 0.080. Compute the consistency ratio and comment on its acceptability.

10. Dan Joseph was considering entering one of two graduate schools of business to pursue studies for an MBA degree. When asked how he compared the two schools with respect to reputation, he responded that school A was strongly to very strongly preferred over school B.

a. Set up the pairwise comparison matrix for this problem.
b. Determine the priorities for the two schools relative to this criterion.

11. An organization was considering relocating its corporate headquarters to one of three possible cities. The following pairwise comparison matrix shows the president's judgments regarding the desirability for the three cities:

	City 1	City 2	City 3
City 1	1	5	7
City 2	$1/5$	1	3
City 3	$1/7$	$1/3$	1

a. Determine the priorities for the three cities.

b. Is the president consistent in terms of the judgments provided? Explain.

12. The following pairwise comparison matrix contains the judgments of an individual regarding the fairness of two proposed tax programs, A and B:

	A	B
A	1	3
B	⅓	1

a. Determine the priorities for the two programs.

b. Are the individual's judgments consistent? Explain.

13. An individual was asked to compare three soft drinks with respect to flavor. The following judgments were obtained:

A is moderately more preferable than B.
A is equally to moderately more preferable than C.
B is strongly more preferable than C.

a. Set up the pairwise comparison matrix for this problem.

b. Determine the priorities for soft drinks with respect to the flavor criterion.

c. Compute the consistency ratio. Are the individual's judgments consistent? Explain.

14. Refer to problem 13. Suppose that the individual had provided the following judgments instead of those given in problem 13:

A is strongly more preferable than C.
B is equally to moderately more preferable than A.
B is strongly more preferable than C.

Answer parts (a), (b), and (c) as stated in problem 13.

15. The national sales director for Jones Office Supplies needs to determine the best location for the next national sales meeting. Three locations have been proposed: Dallas, San Francisco, and New York. One criterion considered important in the decision is the desirability of the location in terms of restaurants, entertainment, and so on. The national sales manager provided the following judgments with regard to this criterion:

New York is very strongly more preferred than Dallas.
New York is moderately more preferred than San Francisco.
San Francisco is moderately to strongly more preferred than Dallas.

a. Set up the pairwise comparison matrix for this problem.

b. Determine the priorities for the desirability criterion.

c. Compute the consistency ratio. Are the sales manager's judgments consistent? Explain.

16. A study comparing four personal computers resulted in the following pairwise comparison matrix for the performance criterion:

Computer

		1	**2**	**3**	**4**
	1	1	3	7	$\frac{1}{3}$
Computer	**2**	$\frac{1}{3}$	1	4	$\frac{1}{4}$
	3	$\frac{1}{7}$	$\frac{1}{4}$	1	$\frac{1}{6}$
	4	3	4	6	1

a. Determine the priorities for the four computers relative to the performance criterion.

b. Compute the consistency ratio. Are the judgments regarding performance consistent? Explain.

17. An individual was interested in determining in which of two stocks, Central Computing Company (CCC) or Software Research, Inc. (SRI), to invest. The criteria thought to be most relevant in making the decision are the potential yield of the stock and the risk associated with the investment. The pairwise comparison matrices for this problem are as follows:

Criterion	Yield	Risk
Yield	1	2
Risk	$\frac{1}{2}$	1

Yield	CCI	SRI
CCI	1	3
SRI	$\frac{1}{3}$	1

Risk	CCI	SRI
CCI	1	$\frac{1}{2}$
SRI	2	1

a. Draw the hierarchy for this problem.

b. Compute the priorities for each of the pairwise comparison matrices.

c. Determine the overall priority for the two investments.

18. The vice-president of Harling Equipment needs to select a new director of marketing. The two possible candidates are Bill Jacobs and Sue Martin, and the criteria thought to be most relevant in the selection are leadership ability (L), personal skills (P), and administrative skills (A). The following pairwise comparison matrices were obtained:

Criterion	L	P	A
L	1	$\frac{1}{3}$	$\frac{1}{4}$
P	3	1	2
A	4	$\frac{1}{2}$	1

Leadership	Jacobs	Martin
Jacobs	1	4
Martin	$\frac{1}{4}$	1

Personal	Jacobs	Martin
Jacobs	1	$\frac{1}{3}$
Martin	3	1

Administrative	Jacobs	Martin
Jacobs	1	2
Martin	$\frac{1}{2}$	1

a. Draw the hierarchy for this decision problem.

b. Compute the priorities for each of the pairwise comparison matrices.

c. Determine an overall priority for each of the candidates.

19. A woman considering the purchase of a custom sound stereo system for her car looked at three different systems that varied in terms of price (P), sound quality (Q), and FM reception (FM). The following pairwise consistency matrices were developed:

Criterion	P	Q	FM
P	1	3	4
Q	$\frac{1}{3}$	1	3
FM	$\frac{1}{4}$	$\frac{1}{3}$	1

Price	A	B	C
A	1	4	2
B	$\frac{1}{4}$	1	$\frac{1}{3}$
C	$\frac{1}{2}$	3	1

Quality	A	B	C
A	1	$\frac{1}{2}$	$\frac{1}{4}$
B	2	1	$\frac{1}{3}$
C	4	3	1

FM Reception	A	B	C
A	1	4	2
B	$\frac{1}{4}$	1	1
C	$\frac{1}{2}$	1	1

a. Draw the hierarchy for this decision problem.

b. Compute the priorities for each of the pairwise comparison matrices.

c. Determine an overall priority for each of the systems.

EPILOGUE

Quantitative Methods and Computer-Based Information Systems

The purpose of this text has been to provide an understanding of the role of quantitative methods in the decision-making process. We have described many of the quantitative methods that have been developed over the years, explained how they work, and showed how they can be applied and interpreted by the decision maker. The purpose of the Epilogue is to discuss the impact of computer-based information systems on the decision-making process and to explore the interaction between such systems and the quantitative methods introduced in this text.

Our discussion will focus on two types of computer-based information systems: decision support systems (DSS) and expert systems (ES). We will see that these systems frequently make use of the models developed in this text; as a result, the development of such systems can benefit from the joint efforts of quantitative analysts and information system specialists.

DECISION SUPPORT SYSTEMS: AN OVERVIEW

A decision support system is a computer-based information system designed to provide support for a decision process. As a foundation for understanding the role of decision support systems in the decision-making process, we will consider a taxonomy of managerial activity developed by Robert Anthony[1] and a classification for decision making proposed by Herbert Simon.[2]

In Anthony's taxonomy, three categories are used to classify the purpose of management activity:

[1]Anthony, R. N., *Planning and Control Systems: A Framework for Analysis*, Boston, Harvard University Graduate School of Business Administration, 1965.
[2]Simon, H. A., *The New Science of Management Decision*, rev. ed., New York, Harper & Row, 1977.

1. Strategic planning: ". . . the process of deciding on objectives of the organization, on changes in these objectives, on the resources used to attain these objectives, and on the policies that are to govern the acquisition, use, and disposition of these resources."[3]
2. Management control: ". . . the process by which managers assure that resources are obtained and used effectively and efficiently in the accomplishment of the organization's objectives."[4]
3. Operational control: ". . . the process of assuring that specific tasks are carried out effectively and efficiently."[5]

Because the activities associated with these three categories are sufficiently different, many organizations have tailored their computer-based information systems to the level of management involvement.

In studying decision making, Herbert Simon equates the job of management with the process of decision making. According to Simon, decision-making problems exist along a continuum ranging from programmed or structured decisions to nonprogrammed or unstructured decisions. A decision is structured if it is repetitive and routine in nature, and a clearly defined procedure or algorithm can be developed to arrive at the decision. Thus, in the context of the quantitative methods we have explored in this text, an inventory decision for which the standard EOQ model is applicable is an example of a structured decision. Unstructured decisions require novel and unusually consequential approaches for their solution. There are no cut-and-dried methods for handling these types of problems, because they haven't been encountered before, because their precise nature and structure is elusive or complex, or because they are so important that they deserve custom-tailored treatment.[6] Personal judgment plays a predominant role in determining which alternative will be selected in these situations. Situations involving unstructured decisions typically involve extensive information searches where several possible alternatives are identified and where each alternative may vary in terms of desirability with respect to one or more attributes. An example of an unstructured decision is the hiring decision an organization faces when seeking a new chief executive officer.

Decisions that do not fall at the extremes of the continuum described by Simon are referred to as semistructured. Although these types of decisions may involve the use of well-structured procedures, the results of the well-structured analyses must be evaluated and considered in terms of the decision maker's own judgment.

The perceived structure of a decision often changes over time as a decision maker develops a better understanding of a problem and the procedure for solving it. Decisions that were originally unstructured begin to take on the characteristics of more structured decisions as the decision maker begins to identify aspects of the decision process that can be handled routinely and with formalized activity.

A Framework for Computer-Based Information Systems

Reflecting on the ideas of Anthony and Simon, two different ways of looking at managerial activity within any organization emerge; Anthony's classification is based on the purpose of the management activity, and Simon's is based on the type of decision that needs to

[3]Anthony, op. cit., p. 24.
[4]Anthony, op. cit., p. 27.
[5]Anthony, op. cit., p. 69.
[6]Simon, op. cit., p. 46.

be made. By combining these two conceptual viewpoints, Gorry and Scott Morton[7] proposed a useful framework from which to view computer-based information systems; Figure E.1 illustrates this framework.

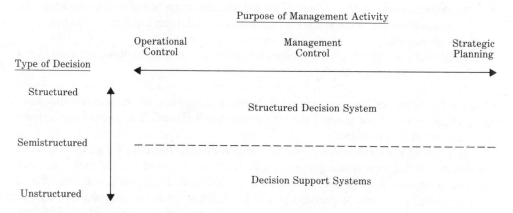

Figure E.1
A Framework for Computer-Based Information Systems

Referring to Figure E.1, we see that Gorry and Scott Morton define systems developed for situations below the dashed line as decision support systems (DSS). Using this taxonomy, a DSS is defined as a computer-based system designed to support managers at every level of the organization in solving problems ranging from those involving semistructured decisions to those involving unstructured decisions.

Although there is yet no consensus in the field of information systems on what a DSS is, the approach advocated by Gorry and Scott Morton does provide a sufficient working definition; thus, it is the viewpoint we will accept throughout the remainder of the Epilogue.

Although our focus is on decision support systems, it seems appropriate to consider the role of management information systems (MIS) within this framework. Turban[8] states that the purpose of a MIS is ". . . to retrieve, extract, and integrate data from various sources in order to provide timely information necessary for managerial decision making. MIS have been most successful in providing information for routine, structured, and anticipated types of decisions." Gorry and Scott Morton's viewpoint is that in practice the area labeled "Structured Decision Systems" in Figure E.1 encompasses most of what has been called MIS; thus, their position is consistent with Turban's definition. We subscribe to a commonly held position that the scope of MIS really encompasses all of Gorry and Scott Morton's taxonomy; thus, DSS is a subset of MIS.

Characteristics of Decision Support Systems

The previous discussion noted some of the characteristics of DSS; the following list provides a summary of these characteristics and additional items common to most, but not necessarily all, DSS:

---

[7]Gory, G. Anthony, and Michael S. Scott Morton, "A Framework for Management Information Systems," *Sloan Management Review*, Fall 1971, pp. 55–70.
[8]Turban, Efraim, *Decision Support and Expert Systems*, New York, Macmillan, 1988, p. 5.

1. DSS provide support to decision makers faced with semistructured or unstructured problems.
2. Support is provided for decisions made at every level of an organization.
3. DSS are designed to facilitate decision processes as opposed to making clerical transaction processing more efficient; thus, effectiveness and not efficiency is the focus.
4. DSS are able to respond quickly to the changing needs of the decision maker.
5. DSS should support rather than automate decision making.
6. DSS should be easy for the decision maker to use.

It is not surprising, then, that decision support systems take on a variety of forms. In some cases the DSS will contain a mathematical model that provides a decision maker with recommended courses of action—for example, a large-scale linear programming system designed to be used as a decision aid for production scheduling. In other cases the decision support system may involve a sophisticated hardware/software system that simply provides easy and rapid access to information contained in a database.

Components of Decision Support Systems

Most decision support systems contain the following four basic subsystems:

1. An interactive capability that enables the decision maker to communicate directly with the system.
2. A data management system that makes it possible to extract necessary information from both internal and external databases.
3. A modeling subsystem that includes financial, statistical, and quantitative models. The modeling subsystem permits the decision maker to interact with the quantitative models by inputting parameters and tailoring situations to specific decision-making needs.
4. An output generator with graphics capability that provides the decision maker with the capability to ask ''what if'' questions and obtain output in easily interpretable form.

These four subsystems make up the software part of the DSS. However, a unique characteristic of DSS, as compared to previous computer-based information systems, is that the decision maker or user is also considered to be a component of the DSS. Turban points out that ''. . . some of the unique contributions of DSS are derived from the interaction between the computer and the decision maker.''[9] We will have more to say about this aspect later, when we discuss the impact of personal computers.

E.2

APPLICATIONS OF DECISION SUPPORT SYSTEMS

Many of the applications (''Quantitative Methods in Practice'') provided at the end of selected chapters of this text describe systems that can be called decision support systems. For example, the Optimal Decision Systems application at the end of Chapter 11 involves a DSS for scheduling a fleet of trucks. To better understand the concept of DSS, let us

[9]Ibid., p. 76.

consider some of the details associated with that system and another DSS designed for portfolio management.

A DSS for Truck Fleet Scheduling

The scheduling process developed by Optimal Decision Systems begins with the DSS generating a schedule and displaying it on the dispatcher's computer screen. The schedule provided shows the complete assignment of all drivers to all loads (at the various plants) for the day's operation. The dispatcher reviews the solution and then makes modifications to the daily model, based on a variety of factors. High-priority loads that have been assigned to common carriers may be reassigned to company trucks. Loads may be switched to accommodate driver preferences. The dispatcher tries to balance driver workloads; if a driver has a difficult assignment one day, the dispatcher tries not to give that driver a heavy load the next day. The dispatcher might also, after consulting the plants, assign different pickup times in hopes of improving the schedule.

The DSS employs a quantitative model to optimize the schedules. After the dispatcher has modified the network model to accommodate the above considerations, a new solution is generated by the DSS. The new solution is displayed on the CRT, and the dispatcher reviews it to see if any further modifications are necessary. When the dispatcher is satisfied, the process is terminated and the schedule implemented. Experience with the DSS has shown that usually two or three iterations are required before the dispatcher is satisfied with the schedule. Figure E.2 depicts the use of this decision support system by the dispatcher.

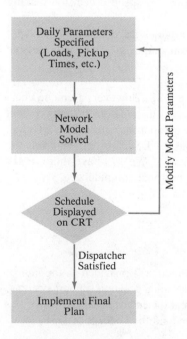

Figure E.2
Decision Support System for Truck Fleet Scheduling

A DSS for Portfolio Management

Keen and Scott Morton[10] describe a DSS to assist portfolio managers. The system is called Portfolio Management System (PMS) and was initially designed by T. P. Gerrity.[11] PMS is a decision support system designed for use by investment managers in the trust departments of banks. It is an interactive system that is designed to provide decision-making support for managing portfolios.

A command language is provided with PMS to assist portfolio managers in interacting with the system. Some of the capabilities of the DSS are as follows:

1. The user can request a display of the contents of a portfolio.
2. Portfolio values and other information, such as price–earnings ratios, etc., can be requested.
3. Graphs and figures can be constructed.
4. Portfolios satisfying certain conditions can be identified.
5. Hypothetical portfolios can be created and evaluated.

The PMS is an example of a DSS for an unstructured problem. No recommended solutions (such as with the DSS for truck fleet scheduling) are presented. It is designed to help with the portfolio management process, but there are no specific criteria. Indeed, a variety of uses have been found for the system with different managers selecting different uses. Some found the system an aid in making cash management decisions, while others found it most helpful in providing a variety of information for interacting with customers.

E.3
THE IMPACT OF PERSONAL COMPUTERS

The rapid expansion of the use of personal computers in business has resulted in an increasing number of personal computer-based decision support systems. This is especially true for decision support systems designed to support personal decision making, that is, decision-making situations for which a single decision maker has the responsibility and the authority to make and implement the decision.

For example, consider a situation in which the branch managers of a large bank have the authority to make personal loans of up to $100,000 based on an analysis of the loan application and an interview with the loan applicant. It might be difficult for one branch manager to convince his or her superiors to invest in the development of a decision support system that could support a particular branch manager in deciding whether or not to make a loan. However, if the individual had access to a personal computer, and either he/she or someone else on his/her staff had some programming experience, a custom-designed system could be developed for a modest investment in time and money.

Decision support systems that are designed to support the needs of primarily one decision maker, that are limited in scope, and that were developed to be put into use as quickly as possible are often referred to as *ad hoc* or *quick-hit* DSS. For example, a system developed to support the decision needs of one of the branch managers in making

[10]Keen, Peter G. W., and Michael S. Scott Morton, *Decision Support Systems: An Organizational Perspective*, Reading, Mass., Addison-Wesley, 1978.
[11]Gerrity, T. P., Jr., "The Design of Man-Machine Decision Systems: An Application to Portfolio Management," *Sloan Management Review*, Vol. 12, No. 2, 1971, pp. 59–75.

loan decisions would be classified as an *ad hoc* DSS. The primary reason why many organizations are beginning to encourage and support the development of *ad hoc* DSS is that they have found that such systems have a higher success rate than larger systems designed for more general use. This is attributable to the fact that it is substantially more difficult to develop a system that will satisfy the needs of many different decision makers than it is to develop a system to meet the needs of just one decision maker.

Lucas[12] describes a situation involving a major service company with offices in the United States and Europe. To help the vice-chairman of the board of directors determine the possible effect of an employee stock ownership plan, the information systems manager wrote a BASIC program consisting of about 40 lines of code; the program showed the impact of the stock ownership plan over a period of 30 years. When the results were presented to the executive committee, the plan was adopted.

Sullivan and Secrest[13] describe the development of another *ad hoc* decision support system; it was designed to aid production planning at the Dairyman's Cooperative Creamery Association in Tulare, California. The system uses an interactive user-friendly linear programming model coded in BASIC and designed to run on a CompuPro microcomputer. The system was developed for a total cost, including hardware and design, of less than $15,000. This system is typical of many of the personal computer-based DSS that utilize quantitative methods such as linear programming.

Many *ad hoc* decision support systems are designed and developed by the user. Thus the availability of software packages that provide easy-to-use interactive capability has increased the use of personal computers in developing decision support systems.

In an article in *The Wall Street Journal*,[14] William Bulkeley describes a feed-mixing system developed by Agricultural Software Consultants, Inc. in Kingsville, Texas. The system asks the farmer or feed mill operator to enter costs and nutritional requirements and then uses a linear programming blending model to develop the optimal product mix. In another application a nursing administrator at Grant Hospital of Chicago used "What's Best!," a linear programming tool developed for personal computers by General Optimization, Inc. to develop monthly schedules for 300 nurses; the estimated cost savings were approximately $80,000 per month.

The development of decision support tools such as those described indicates a bright and exciting future for the role of personal computers in the design, development, and implementation of decision support systems.

E.4

EXPERT SYSTEMS

Recent applications in the field of artificial intelligence have had many important successes. Among the most significant of these has been the development of new computer systems known as expert or knowledge-based systems. These programs are designed to represent and apply factual knowledge of specific areas of expertise to solve problems.[15]

---

[12]Lucas, H. C., Jr., *Implementation: The Key to Successful Information Systems*, New York, Columbia University Press, 1981.

[13]Sullivan, Robert S., and Stephen C. Secrest, "A Simple Optimization DSS for Production Planning at Dairyman's Cooperative Creamery Association," *Interfaces*, Vol. 15, No. 5, pp. 46–53.

[14]Bulkeley, William M., "The Right Mix: New Software Makes the Choice Much Easier," *The Wall Street Journal*, March 27, 1987.

[15]Hayes-Roth, Frederick, Donald A. Waterman, and Douglas B. Lenat, eds., *Building Expert Systems*, Reading, Mass., Addison-Wesley, 1983.

Expert systems (ES) are computer-based systems that offer advice or solutions in particular problem areas. The output of these systems (i.e., advice or solutions) is comparable to that which would be offered by a human expert in a given problem area. Some of the typical applications of expert systems have been in medical diagnosis, credit analysis and approval, insurance policy and rate selection, automobile and computer repair, circuit design and layout, and weather forecasting.

Components of an Expert System

The architecture of an expert system includes three components: a knowledge base, an inference engine, and a user interface. The knowledge base contains facts and other representations of knowledge, usually in the form of IF. . .THEN. . . rules. It is the place where the expertise of the system resides. The inference engine is a program that evaluates information in the knowledge base and applies it to whatever problem the expert system is addressing. It determines which rules and facts (i.e., which knowledge) will be considered, and in which order they will be considered. It is the active or thinking part of the system.

The user interface is the component that allows the system and its users to communicate with each other. Users introduce new data or new knowledge to the system using the interface, and the system communicates with users through it. It also allows the expert system to ''explain'' to the user how it came to arrive at a particular conclusion.

Recent Software Developments

Expert systems are just beginning to realize their potential. One major reason for this is that until just recently, they have not been economically feasible. For example, it cost millions of dollars and took several years of work effort to implement most of the expert systems developed prior to the late 1980s. Recent developments in the expert systems field, however, have resulted in technology that has lowered the cost to develop an expert system. Smaller, less sophisticated systems can now be developed with the help of expert system ''shells.''

An expert system shell is a software product that already has an inference engine and many elements of a user interface built in place. The user of a shell merely describes the knowledge the system is to work with and provides some details about the user interface. With this new technology, expert system developers can focus on building the knowledge base. This makes it possible to develop relatively inexpensive expert systems that support applications involving relatively small amounts of knowledge. These systems work with knowledge bases having only a few hundred rules in place; in contrast, the XCON expert system, a system developed by the Digital Equipment Corporation to develop computer configurations, contains over 3000 rules!

The Future of ES and Its Relationship to DSS

Expert systems represent a direct application of research in the field of artificial intelligence. Proponents of ES argue that they can help a decision maker solve complex problems that previously required a human expert. Although there is some controversy in the field of decision support sytems as to whether an ES is really a DSS, there is no doubt that the expert systems that have been developed are capable of simulating the reasoning process of human experts, can apply rules of thumb based on experience, and can recommend the best course of action from a list of alternatives. DSS that combine expert system capabilities with quantitative methods, such as those discussed in this text, offer very exciting potential for those individuals concerned with improving the decision-making process.

Summary

Not all decision support systems make use of quantitative methods. But many DSS are based heavily on the mathematical models and solution procedures developed by quantitative analysts. The DSS for truck fleet scheduling, described in ''Quantitative Methods in Practice'' at the end of Chapter 11 and discussed in this epilogue, makes extensive use of quantitative methods. The same is true of the decision support system described in ''Quantitative Methods in Practice'' at the end of Chapter 12; it makes use of a mixed integer programming model to assign customer orders to sources of supply.

Decision support systems and expert systems are showing promise of being vehicles for integrating the efforts of quantitative analysts and information system specialists. The potential exists for decision support systems to have a major impact on future managerial decision processes. We are enthusiastic about this potential and anticipate a larger combined role for quantitative methods, decision support systems, and expert systems in the organizations of the future.

Appendixes

Entries in the table give the probability of x successes in n trials of a binomial experiment, where p is the probability of a success on one trial. For example, with $n = 6$ trials and $p = 0.40$, the probability of $x = 2$ successes is 0.3110.

n	x	0.05	0.10	0.15	0.20	0.25	0.30	0.35	0.40	0.45	0.50
1	0	0.9500	0.9000	0.8500	0.8000	0.7500	0.7000	0.6500	0.6000	0.5500	0.5000
	1	0.0500	0.1000	0.1500	0.2000	0.2500	0.3000	0.3500	0.4000	0.4500	0.5000
2	0	0.9025	0.8100	0.7225	0.6400	0.5625	0.4900	0.4225	0.3600	0.3025	0.2500
	1	0.0950	0.1800	0.2550	0.3200	0.3750	0.4200	0.4550	0.4800	0.4950	0.5000
	2	0.0025	0.0100	0.0225	0.0400	0.0625	0.0900	0.1225	0.1600	0.2025	0.2500
3	0	0.8574	0.7290	0.6141	0.5120	0.4219	0.3430	0.2746	0.2160	0.1664	0.1250
	1	0.1354	0.2430	0.3251	0.3840	0.4219	0.4410	0.4436	0.4320	0.4084	0.3750
	2	0.0071	0.0270	0.0574	0.0960	0.1406	0.1890	0.2389	0.2880	0.3341	0.3750
	3	0.0001	0.0010	0.0034	0.0080	0.0156	0.0270	0.0429	0.0640	0.0911	0.1250
4	0	0.8145	0.6561	0.5220	0.4096	0.3164	0.2401	0.1785	0.1296	0.0915	0.0625
	1	0.1715	0.2916	0.3685	0.4096	0.4219	0.4116	0.3845	0.3456	0.2995	0.2500
	2	0.0135	0.0486	0.0975	0.1536	0.2109	0.2646	0.3105	0.3456	0.3675	0.3750
	3	0.0005	0.0036	0.0115	0.0256	0.0469	0.0756	0.1115	0.1536	0.2005	0.2500
	4	0.0000	0.0001	0.0005	0.0016	0.0039	0.0081	0.0150	0.0256	0.0410	0.0625
5	0	0.7738	0.5905	0.4437	0.3277	0.2373	0.1681	0.1160	0.0778	0.0503	0.0312
	1	0.2036	0.3280	0.3915	0.4096	0.3955	0.3602	0.3124	0.2592	0.2059	0.1562
	2	0.0214	0.0729	0.1382	0.2048	0.2637	0.3087	0.3364	0.3456	0.3369	0.3125
	3	0.0011	0.0081	0.0244	0.0512	0.0879	0.1323	0.1811	0.2304	0.2757	0.3125
	4	0.0000	0.0004	0.0022	0.0064	0.0146	0.0284	0.0488	0.0768	0.1128	0.1562
	5	0.0000	0.0000	0.0001	0.0003	0.0010	0.0024	0.0053	0.0102	0.0185	0.0312
6	0	0.7351	0.5314	0.3771	0.2621	0.1780	0.1176	0.0754	0.0467	0.0277	0.0156
	1	0.2321	0.3543	0.3993	0.3932	0.3560	0.3025	0.2437	0.1866	0.1359	0.0938
	2	0.0305	0.0984	0.1762	0.2458	0.2966	0.3241	0.3280	0.3110	0.2780	0.2344
	3	0.0021	0.0146	0.0415	0.0819	0.1318	0.1852	0.2355	0.2765	0.3032	0.3125
	4	0.0001	0.0012	0.0055	0.0154	0.0330	0.0595	0.0951	0.1382	0.1861	0.2344
	5	0.0000	0.0001	0.0004	0.0015	0.0044	0.0102	0.0205	0.0369	0.0609	0.0938
	6	0.0000	0.0000	0.0000	0.0001	0.0002	0.0007	0.0018	0.0041	0.0083	0.0156

From *Handbook of Probability and Statistics with Tables* by Burington and May. Copyright 1970 by McGraw-Hill, Inc. Used with permission of McGraw-Hill Book Company.

Binomial Probabilities *(Continued)*

n	x	0.05	0.10	0.15	0.20	0.25	0.30	0.35	0.40	0.45	0.50
7	0	0.6983	0.4783	0.3206	0.2097	0.1335	0.0824	0.0490	0.0280	0.0152	0.0078
	1	0.2573	0.3720	0.3960	0.3670	0.3115	0.2471	0.1848	0.1306	0.0872	0.0547
	2	0.0406	0.1240	0.2097	0.2753	0.3115	0.3177	0.2985	0.2613	0.2140	0.1641
	3	0.0036	0.0230	0.0617	0.1147	0.1730	0.2269	0.2679	0.2903	0.2918	0.2734
	4	0.0002	0.0026	0.0109	0.0287	0.0577	0.0972	0.1442	0.1935	0.2388	0.2734
	5	0.0000	0.0002	0.0012	0.0043	0.0115	0.0250	0.0466	0.0774	0.1172	0.1641
	6	0.0000	0.0000	0.0001	0.0004	0.0013	0.0036	0.0084	0.0172	0.0320	0.0547
	7	0.0000	0.0000	0.0000	0.0000	0.0001	0.0002	0.0006	0.0016	0.0037	0.0078
8	0	0.6634	0.4305	0.2725	0.1678	0.1001	0.0576	0.0319	0.0168	0.0084	0.0039
	1	0.2793	0.3826	0.3847	0.3355	0.2670	0.1977	0.1373	0.0896	0.0548	0.0312
	2	0.0515	0.1488	0.2376	0.2936	0.3115	0.2965	0.2587	0.2090	0.1569	0.1094
	3	0.0054	0.0331	0.0839	0.1468	0.2076	0.2541	0.2786	0.2787	0.2568	0.2188
	4	0.0004	0.0046	0.0185	0.0459	0.0865	0.1361	0.1875	0.2322	0.2627	0.2734
	5	0.0000	0.0004	0.0026	0.0092	0.0231	0.0467	0.0808	0.1239	0.1719	0.2188
	6	0.0000	0.0000	0.0002	0.0011	0.0038	0.0100	0.0217	0.0413	0.0703	0.1094
	7	0.0000	0.0000	0.0000	0.0001	0.0004	0.0012	0.0033	0.0079	0.0164	0.0312
	8	0.0000	0.0000	0.0000	0.0000	0.0000	0.0001	0.0002	0.0007	0.0017	0.0039
9	0	0.6302	0.3874	0.2316	0.1342	0.0751	0.0404	0.0207	0.0101	0.0046	0.0020
	1	0.2985	0.3874	0.3679	0.3020	0.2253	0.1556	0.1004	0.0605	0.0339	0.0176
	2	0.0629	0.1722	0.2597	0.3020	0.3003	0.2668	0.2162	0.1612	0.1110	0.0703
	3	0.0077	0.0446	0.1069	0.1762	0.2336	0.2668	0.2716	0.2508	0.2119	0.1641
	4	0.0006	0.0074	0.0283	0.0661	0.1168	0.1715	0.2194	0.2508	0.2600	0.2461
	5	0.0000	0.0008	0.0050	0.0165	0.0389	0.0735	0.1181	0.1672	0.2128	0.2461
	6	0.0000	0.0001	0.0006	0.0028	0.0087	0.0210	0.0424	0.0743	0.1160	0.1641
	7	0.0000	0.0000	0.0000	0.0003	0.0012	0.0039	0.0098	0.0212	0.0407	0.0703
	8	0.0000	0.0000	0.0000	0.0000	0.0001	0.0004	0.0013	0.0035	0.0083	0.0176
	9	0.0000	0.0000	0.0000	0.0000	0.0000	0.0000	0.0001	0.0003	0.0008	0.0020
10	0	0.5987	0.3487	0.1969	0.1074	0.0563	0.0282	0.0135	0.0060	0.0025	0.0010
	1	0.3151	0.3874	0.3474	0.2684	0.1877	0.1211	0.0725	0.0403	0.0207	0.0098
	2	0.0746	0.1937	0.2759	0.3020	0.2816	0.2335	0.1757	0.1209	0.0763	0.0439
	3	0.0105	0.0574	0.1298	0.2013	0.2503	0.2668	0.2522	0.2150	0.1665	0.1172
	4	0.0010	0.0112	0.0401	0.0881	0.1460	0.2001	0.2377	0.2508	0.2384	0.2051
	5	0.0001	0.0015	0.0085	0.0264	0.0584	0.1029	0.1536	0.2007	0.2340	0.2461
	6	0.0000	0.0001	0.0012	0.0055	0.0162	0.0368	0.0689	0.1115	0.1596	0.2051
	7	0.0000	0.0000	0.0001	0.0008	0.0031	0.0090	0.0212	0.0425	0.0746	0.1172
	8	0.0000	0.0000	0.0000	0.0001	0.0004	0.0014	0.0043	0.0106	0.0229	0.0439
	9	0.0000	0.0000	0.0000	0.0000	0.0000	0.0001	0.0005	0.0016	0.0042	0.0098
	10	0.0000	0.0000	0.0000	0.0000	0.0000	0.0000	0.0000	0.0001	0.0003	0.0010
11	0	0.5688	0.3138	0.1673	0.0859	0.0422	0.0198	0.0088	0.0036	0.0014	0.0005
	1	0.3293	0.3835	0.3248	0.2362	0.1549	0.0932	0.0518	0.0266	0.0125	0.0054
	2	0.0867	0.2131	0.2866	0.2953	0.2581	0.1998	0.1395	0.0887	0.0513	0.0269
	3	0.0137	0.0710	0.1517	0.2215	0.2581	0.2568	0.2254	0.1774	0.1259	0.0806
	4	0.0014	0.0158	0.0536	0.1107	0.1721	0.2201	0.2428	0.2365	0.2060	0.1611

Binomial Probabilities *(Continued)*

							p				
n	x	0.05	0.10	0.15	0.20	0.25	0.30	0.35	0.40	0.45	0.50
	5	0.0001	0.0025	0.0132	0.0388	0.0803	0.1321	0.1830	0.2207	0.2360	0.2256
	6	0.0000	0.0003	0.0023	0.0097	0.0268	0.0566	0.0985	0.1471	0.1931	0.2256
	7	0.0000	0.0000	0.0003	0.0017	0.0064	0.0173	0.0379	0.0701	0.1128	0.1611
	8	0.0000	0.0000	0.0000	0.0002	0.0011	0.0037	0.0102	0.0234	0.0462	0.0806
	9	0.0000	0.0000	0.0000	0.0000	0.0001	0.0005	0.0018	0.0052	0.0126	0.0269
	10	0.0000	0.0000	0.0000	0.0000	0.0000	0.0000	0.0002	0.0007	0.0021	0.0054
	11	0.0000	0.0000	0.0000	0.0000	0.0000	0.0000	0.0000	0.0000	0.0002	0.0005
12	0	0.5404	0.2824	0.1422	0.0687	0.0317	0.0138	0.0057	0.0022	0.0008	0.0002
	1	0.3413	0.3766	0.3012	0.2062	0.1267	0.0712	0.0368	0.0174	0.0075	0.0029
	2	0.0988	0.2301	0.2924	0.2835	0.2323	0.1678	0.1088	0.0639	0.0339	0.0161
	3	0.0173	0.0853	0.1720	0.2362	0.2581	0.2397	0.1954	0.1419	0.0923	0.0537
	4	0.0021	0.0213	0.0683	0.1329	0.1936	0.2311	0.2367	0.2128	0.1700	0.1208
	5	0.0002	0.0038	0.0193	0.0532	0.1032	0.1585	0.2039	0.2270	0.2225	0.1934
	6	0.0000	0.0005	0.0040	0.0155	0.0401	0.0792	0.1281	0.1766	0.2124	0.2256
	7	0.0000	0.0000	0.0006	0.0033	0.0115	0.0291	0.0591	0.1009	0.1489	0.1934
	8	0.0000	0.0000	0.0001	0.0005	0.0024	0.0078	0.0199	0.0420	0.0762	0.1208
	9	0.0000	0.0000	0.0000	0.0001	0.0004	0.0015	0.0048	0.0125	0.0277	0.0537
	10	0.0000	0.0000	0.0000	0.0000	0.0000	0.0002	0.0008	0.0025	0.0068	0.0161
	11	0.0000	0.0000	0.0000	0.0000	0.0000	0.0000	0.0001	0.0003	0.0010	0.0029
	12	0.0000	0.0000	0.0000	0.0000	0.0000	0.0000	0.0000	0.0000	0.0001	0.0002
13	0	0.5133	0.2542	0.1209	0.0550	0.0238	0.0097	0.0037	0.0013	0.0004	0.0001
	1	0.3512	0.3672	0.2774	0.1787	0.1029	0.0540	0.0259	0.0113	0.0045	0.0016
	2	0.1109	0.2448	0.2937	0.2680	0.2059	0.1388	0.0836	0.0453	0.0220	0.0095
	3	0.0214	0.0997	0.1900	0.2457	0.2517	0.2181	0.1651	0.1107	0.0660	0.0349
	4	0.0028	0.0277	0.0838	0.1535	0.2097	0.2337	0.2222	0.1845	0.1350	0.0873
	5	0.0003	0.0055	0.0266	0.0691	0.1258	0.1803	0.2154	0.2214	0.1989	0.1571
	6	0.0000	0.0008	0.0063	0.0230	0.0559	0.1030	0.1546	0.1968	0.2169	0.2095
	7	0.0000	0.0001	0.0011	0.0058	0.0186	0.0442	0.0833	0.1312	0.1775	0.2095
	8	0.0000	0.0000	0.0001	0.0011	0.0047	0.0142	0.0336	0.0656	0.1089	0.1571
	9	0.0000	0.0000	0.0000	0.0001	0.0009	0.0034	0.0101	0.0243	0.0495	0.0873
	10	0.0000	0.0000	0.0000	0.0000	0.0001	0.0006	0.0022	0.0065	0.0162	0.0349
	11	0.0000	0.0000	0.0000	0.0000	0.0000	0.0001	0.0003	0.0012	0.0036	0.0095
	12	0.0000	0.0000	0.0000	0.0000	0.0000	0.0000	0.0000	0.0001	0.0005	0.0016
	13	0.0000	0.0000	0.0000	0.0000	0.0000	0.0000	0.0000	0.0000	0.0000	0.0001
14	0	0.4877	0.2288	0.1028	0.0440	0.0178	0.0068	0.0024	0.0008	0.0002	0.0001
	1	0.3593	0.3559	0.2539	0.1539	0.0832	0.0407	0.0181	0.0073	0.0027	0.0009
	2	0.1229	0.2570	0.2912	0.2501	0.1802	0.1134	0.0634	0.0317	0.0141	0.0056
	3	0.0259	0.1142	0.2056	0.2501	0.2402	0.1943	0.1366	0.0845	0.0462	0.0222
	4	0.0037	0.0349	0.0998	0.1720	0.2202	0.2290	0.2022	0.1549	0.1040	0.0611
	5	0.0004	0.0078	0.0352	0.0860	0.1468	0.1963	0.2178	0.2066	0.1701	0.1222
	6	0.0000	0.0013	0.0093	0.0322	0.0734	0.1262	0.1759	0.2066	0.2088	0.1833
	7	0.0000	0.0002	0.0019	0.0092	0.0280	0.0618	0.1082	0.1574	0.1952	0.2095

Binomial Probabilities *(Continued)*

						p					
n	x	0.05	0.10	0.15	0.20	0.25	0.30	0.35	0.40	0.45	0.50
	8	0.0000	0.0000	0.0003	0.0020	0.0082	0.0232	0.0510	0.0918	0.1398	0.1833
	9	0.0000	0.0000	0.0000	0.0003	0.0018	0.0066	0.0183	0.0408	0.0762	0.1222
	10	0.0000	0.0000	0.0000	0.0000	0.0003	0.0014	0.0049	0.0136	0.0312	0.0611
	11	0.0000	0.0000	0.0000	0.0000	0.0000	0.0002	0.0010	0.0033	0.0093	0.0222
	12	0.0000	0.0000	0.0000	0.0000	0.0000	0.0000	0.0001	0.0005	0.0019	0.0056
	13	0.0000	0.0000	0.0000	0.0000	0.0000	0.0000	0.0000	0.0001	0.0002	0.0009
	14	0.0000	0.0000	0.0000	0.0000	0.0000	0.0000	0.0000	0.0000	0.0000	0.0001
15	0	0.4633	0.2059	0.0874	0.0352	0.0134	0.0047	0.0016	0.0005	0.0001	0.0000
	1	0.3658	0.3432	0.2312	0.1319	0.0668	0.0305	0.0126	0.0047	0.0016	0.0005
	2	0.1348	0.2669	0.2856	0.2309	0.1559	0.0916	0.0476	0.0219	0.0090	0.0032
	3	0.0307	0.1285	0.2184	0.2501	0.2252	0.1700	0.1110	0.0634	0.0318	0.0139
	4	0.0049	0.0428	0.1156	0.1876	0.2252	0.2186	0.1792	0.1268	0.0780	0.0417
	5	0.0006	0.0105	0.0449	0.1032	0.1651	0.2061	0.2123	0.1859	0.1404	0.0916
	6	0.0000	0.0019	0.0132	0.0430	0.0917	0.1472	0.1906	0.2066	0.1914	0.1527
	7	0.0000	0.0003	0.0030	0.0138	0.0393	0.0811	0.1319	0.1771	0.2013	0.1964
	8	0.0000	0.0000	0.0005	0.0035	0.0131	0.0348	0.0710	0.1181	0.1647	0.1964
	9	0.0000	0.0000	0.0001	0.0007	0.0034	0.0116	0.0298	0.0612	0.1048	0.1527
	10	0.0000	0.0000	0.0000	0.0001	0.0007	0.0030	0.0096	0.0245	0.0515	0.0916
	11	0.0000	0.0000	0.0000	0.0000	0.0001	0.0006	0.0024	0.0074	0.0191	0.0417
	12	0.0000	0.0000	0.0000	0.0000	0.0000	0.0001	0.0004	0.0016	0.0052	0.0139
	13	0.0000	0.0000	0.0000	0.0000	0.0000	0.0000	0.0001	0.0003	0.0010	0.0032
	14	0.0000	0.0000	0.0000	0.0000	0.0000	0.0000	0.0000	0.0000	0.0001	0.0005
	15	0.0000	0.0000	0.0000	0.0000	0.0000	0.0000	0.0000	0.0000	0.0000	0.0000
16	0	0.4401	0.1853	0.0743	0.0281	0.0100	0.0033	0.0010	0.0003	0.0001	0.0000
	1	0.3706	0.3294	0.2097	0.1126	0.0535	0.0228	0.0087	0.0030	0.0009	0.0002
	2	0.1463	0.2745	0.2775	0.2111	0.1336	0.0732	0.0353	0.0150	0.0056	0.0018
	3	0.0359	0.1423	0.2285	0.2463	0.2079	0.1465	0.0888	0.0468	0.0215	0.0085
	4	0.0061	0.0514	0.1311	0.2001	0.2252	0.2040	0.1553	0.1014	0.0572	0.0278
	5	0.0008	0.0137	0.0555	0.1201	0.1802	0.2099	0.2008	0.1623	0.1123	0.0667
	6	0.0001	0.0028	0.0180	0.0550	0.1101	0.1649	0.1982	0.1983	0.1684	0.1222
	7	0.0000	0.0004	0.0045	0.0197	0.0524	0.1010	0.1524	0.1889	0.1969	0.1746
	8	0.0000	0.0001	0.0009	0.0055	0.0197	0.0487	0.0923	0.1417	0.1812	0.1964
	9	0.0000	0.0000	0.0001	0.0012	0.0058	0.0185	0.0442	0.0840	0.1318	0.1746
	10	0.0000	0.0000	0.0000	0.0002	0.0014	0.0056	0.0167	0.0392	0.0755	0.1222
	11	0.0000	0.0000	0.0000	0.0000	0.0002	0.0013	0.0049	0.0142	0.0337	0.0667
	12	0.0000	0.0000	0.0000	0.0000	0.0000	0.0002	0.0011	0.0040	0.0115	0.0278
	13	0.0000	0.0000	0.0000	0.0000	0.0000	0.0000	0.0002	0.0008	0.0029	0.0085
	14	0.0000	0.0000	0.0000	0.0000	0.0000	0.0000	0.0000	0.0001	0.0005	0.0018
	15	0.0000	0.0000	0.0000	0.0000	0.0000	0.0000	0.0000	0.0000	0.0001	0.0002
	16	0.0000	0.0000	0.0000	0.0000	0.0000	0.0000	0.0000	0.0000	0.0000	0.0000
17	0	0.4181	0.1668	0.0631	0.0225	0.0075	0.0023	0.0007	0.0002	0.0000	0.0000
	1	0.3741	0.3150	0.1893	0.0957	0.0426	0.0169	0.0060	0.0019	0.0005	0.0001

Binomial Probabilities *(Continued)*

							p				
n	*x*	0.05	0.10	0.15	0.20	0.25	0.30	0.35	0.40	0.45	0.50
	2	0.1575	0.2800	0.2673	0.1914	0.1136	0.0581	0.0260	0.0102	0.0035	0.0010
	3	0.0415	0.1556	0.2359	0.2393	0.1893	0.1245	0.0701	0.0341	0.0144	0.0052
	4	0.0076	0.0605	0.1457	0.2093	0.2209	0.1868	0.1320	0.0796	0.0411	0.0182
	5	0.0010	0.0175	0.0668	0.1361	0.1914	0.2081	0.1849	0.1379	0.0875	0.0472
	6	0.0001	0.0039	0.0236	0.0680	0.1276	0.1784	0.1991	0.1839	0.1432	0.0944
	7	0.0000	0.0007	0.0065	0.0267	0.0668	0.1201	0.1685	0.1927	0.1841	0.1484
	8	0.0000	0.0001	0.0014	0.0084	0.0279	0.0644	0.1134	0.1606	0.1883	0.1855
	9	0.0000	0.0000	0.0003	0.0021	0.0093	0.0276	0.0611	0.1070	0.1540	0.1855
17	10	0.0000	0.0000	0.0000	0.0004	0.0025	0.0095	0.0263	0.0571	0.1008	0.1484
	11	0.0000	0.0000	0.0000	0.0001	0.0005	0.0026	0.0090	0.0242	0.0525	0.0944
	12	0.0000	0.0000	0.0000	0.0000	0.0001	0.0006	0.0024	0.0081	0.0215	0.0472
	13	0.0000	0.0000	0.0000	0.0000	0.0000	0.0001	0.0005	0.0021	0.0068	0.0182
	14	0.0000	0.0000	0.0000	0.0000	0.0000	0.0000	0.0001	0.0004	0.0016	0.0052
	15	0.0000	0.0000	0.0000	0.0000	0.0000	0.0000	0.0000	0.0001	0.0003	0.0010
	16	0.0000	0.0000	0.0000	0.0000	0.0000	0.0000	0.0000	0.0000	0.0000	0.0001
	17	0.0000	0.0000	0.0000	0.0000	0.0000	0.0000	0.0000	0.0000	0.0000	0.0000
18	0	0.3972	0.1501	0.0536	0.0180	0.0056	0.0016	0.0004	0.0001	0.0000	0.0000
	1	0.3763	0.3002	0.1704	0.0811	0.0338	0.0126	0.0042	0.0012	0.0003	0.0001
	2	0.1683	0.2835	0.2556	0.1723	0.0958	0.0458	0.0190	0.0069	0.0022	0.0006
	3	0.0473	0.1680	0.2406	0.2297	0.1704	0.1046	0.0547	0.0246	0.0095	0.0031
	4	0.0093	0.0700	0.1592	0.2153	0.2130	0.1681	0.1104	0.0614	0.0291	0.0117
	5	0.0014	0.0218	0.0787	0.1507	0.1988	0.2017	0.1664	0.1146	0.0666	0.0327
	6	0.0002	0.0052	0.0301	0.0816	0.1436	0.1873	0.1941	0.1655	0.1181	0.0708
	7	0.0000	0.0010	0.0091	0.0350	0.0820	0.1376	0.1792	0.1892	0.1657	0.1214
	8	0.0000	0.0002	0.0022	0.0120	0.0376	0.0811	0.1327	0.1734	0.1864	0.1669
	9	0.0000	0.0000	0.0004	0.0033	0.0139	0.0386	0.0794	0.1284	0.1694	0.1855
	10	0.0000	0.0000	0.0001	0.0008	0.0042	0.0149	0.0385	0.0771	0.1248	0.1669
	11	0.0000	0.0000	0.0000	0.0001	0.0010	0.0046	0.0151	0.0374	0.0742	0.1214
	12	0.0000	0.0000	0.0000	0.0000	0.0002	0.0012	0.0047	0.0145	0.0354	0.0708
	13	0.0000	0.0000	0.0000	0.0000	0.0000	0.0002	0.0012	0.0045	0.0134	0.0327
	14	0.0000	0.0000	0.0000	0.0000	0.0000	0.0000	0.0002	0.0011	0.0039	0.0117
	15	0.0000	0.0000	0.0000	0.0000	0.0000	0.0000	0.0000	0.0002	0.0009	0.0031
	16	0.0000	0.0000	0.0000	0.0000	0.0000	0.0000	0.0000	0.0000	0.0001	0.0006
	17	0.0000	0.0000	0.0000	0.0000	0.0000	0.0000	0.0000	0.0000	0.0000	0.0001
	18	0.0000	0.0000	0.0000	0.0000	0.0000	0.0000	0.0000	0.0000	0.0000	0.0000
19	0	0.3774	0.1351	0.0456	0.0144	0.0042	0.0011	0.0003	0.0001	0.0000	0.0000
	1	0.3774	0.2852	0.1529	0.0685	0.0268	0.0093	0.0029	0.0008	0.0002	0.0000
	2	0.1787	0.2852	0.2428	0.1540	0.0803	0.0358	0.0138	0.0046	0.0013	0.0003
	3	0.0533	0.1796	0.2428	0.2182	0.1517	0.0869	0.0422	0.0175	0.0062	0.0018
	4	0.0112	0.0798	0.1714	0.2182	0.2023	0.1491	0.0909	0.0467	0.0203	0.0074
	5	0.0018	0.0266	0.0907	0.1636	0.2023	0.1916	0.1468	0.0933	0.0497	0.0222
	6	0.0002	0.0069	0.0374	0.0955	0.1574	0.1916	0.1844	0.1451	0.0949	0.0518
	7	0.0000	0.0014	0.0122	0.0443	0.0974	0.1525	0.1844	0.1797	0.1443	0.0961

Binomial Probabilities *(Continued)*

n	x	0.05	0.10	0.15	0.20	0.25	0.30	0.35	0.40	0.45	0.50
	8	0.0000	0.0002	0.0032	0.0166	0.0487	0.0981	0.1489	0.1797	0.1771	0.1442
	9	0.0000	0.0000	0.0007	0.0051	0.0198	0.0514	0.0980	0.1464	0.1771	0.1762
	10	0.0000	0.0000	0.0001	0.0013	0.0066	0.0220	0.0528	0.0976	0.1449	0.1762
	11	0.0000	0.0000	0.0000	0.0003	0.0018	0.0077	0.0233	0.0532	0.0970	0.1442
	12	0.0000	0.0000	0.0000	0.0000	0.0004	0.0022	0.0083	0.0237	0.0529	0.0961
	13	0.0000	0.0000	0.0000	0.0000	0.0001	0.0005	0.0024	0.0085	0.0233	0.0518
	14	0.0000	0.0000	0.0000	0.0000	0.0000	0.0001	0.0006	0.0024	0.0082	0.0222
19	15	0.0000	0.0000	0.0000	0.0000	0.0000	0.0000	0.0001	0.0005	0.0022	0.0074
	16	0.0000	0.0000	0.0000	0.0000	0.0000	0.0000	0.0000	0.0001	0.0005	0.0018
	17	0.0000	0.0000	0.0000	0.0000	0.0000	0.0000	0.0000	0.0000	0.0001	0.0003
	18	0.0000	0.0000	0.0000	0.0000	0.0000	0.0000	0.0000	0.0000	0.0000	0.0000
	19	0.0000	0.0000	0.0000	0.0000	0.0000	0.0000	0.0000	0.0000	0.0000	0.0000
20	0	0.3585	0.1216	0.0388	0.0115	0.0032	0.0008	0.0002	0.0000	0.0000	0.0000
	1	0.3774	0.2702	0.1368	0.0576	0.0211	0.0068	0.0020	0.0005	0.0001	0.0000
	2	0.1887	0.2852	0.2293	0.1369	0.0669	0.0278	0.0100	0.0031	0.0008	0.0002
	3	0.0596	0.1901	0.2428	0.2054	0.1339	0.0716	0.0323	0.0123	0.0040	0.0011
	4	0.0133	0.0898	0.1821	0.2182	0.1897	0.1304	0.0738	0.0350	0.0139	0.0046
	5	0.0022	0.0319	0.1028	0.1746	0.2023	0.1789	0.1272	0.0746	0.0365	0.0148
	6	0.0003	0.0089	0.0454	0.1091	0.1686	0.1916	0.1712	0.1244	0.0746	0.0370
	7	0.0000	0.0020	0.0160	0.0545	0.1124	0.1643	0.1844	0.1659	0.1221	0.0739
	8	0.0000	0.0004	0.0046	0.0222	0.0609	0.1144	0.1614	0.1797	0.1623	0.1201
	9	0.0000	0.0001	0.0011	0.0074	0.0271	0.0654	0.1158	0.1597	0.1771	0.1602
	10	0.0000	0.0000	0.0002	0.0020	0.0099	0.0308	0.0686	0.1171	0.1593	0.1762
	11	0.0000	0.0000	0.0000	0.0005	0.0030	0.0120	0.0336	0.0710	0.1185	0.1602
	12	0.0000	0.0000	0.0000	0.0001	0.0008	0.0039	0.0136	0.0355	0.0727	0.1201
	13	0.0000	0.0000	0.0000	0.0000	0.0002	0.0010	0.0045	0.0146	0.0366	0.0739
	14	0.0000	0.0000	0.0000	0.0000	0.0000	0.0002	0.0012	0.0049	0.0150	0.0370
	15	0.0000	0.0000	0.0000	0.0000	0.0000	0.0000	0.0003	0.0013	0.0049	0.0148
	16	0.0000	0.0000	0.0000	0.0000	0.0000	0.0000	0.0000	0.0003	0.0013	0.0046
	17	0.0000	0.0000	0.0000	0.0000	0.0000	0.0000	0.0000	0.0000	0.0002	0.0011
	18	0.0000	0.0000	0.0000	0.0000	0.0000	0.0000	0.0000	0.0000	0.0000	0.0002
	19	0.0000	0.0000	0.0000	0.0000	0.0000	0.0000	0.0000	0.0000	0.0000	0.0000
	20	0.0000	0.0000	0.0000	0.0000	0.0000	0.0000	0.0000	0.0000	0.0000	0.0000

Appendix B   Poisson Probabilities

Entries in the table give the probability of x occurrences for a Poisson process with a mean λ. For example, when $\lambda = 2.5$, the probability of $x = 4$ occurrences is 0.1336.

					λ					
x	0.1	0.2	0.3	0.4	0.5	0.6	0.7	0.8	0.9	1.0
0	0.9048	0.8187	0.7408	0.6703	0.6065	0.5488	0.4966	0.4493	0.4066	0.3679
1	0.0905	0.1637	0.2222	0.2681	0.3033	0.3293	0.3476	0.3595	0.3659	0.3679
2	0.0045	0.0164	0.0333	0.0536	0.0758	0.0988	0.1217	0.1438	0.1647	0.1839
3	0.0002	0.0011	0.0033	0.0072	0.0126	0.0198	0.0284	0.0383	0.0494	0.0613
4	0.0000	0.0001	0.0002	0.0007	0.0016	0.0030	0.0050	0.0077	0.0111	0.0153
5	0.0000	0.0000	0.0000	0.0001	0.0002	0.0004	0.0007	0.0012	0.0020	0.0031
6	0.0000	0.0000	0.0000	0.0000	0.0000	0.0000	0.0001	0.0002	0.0003	0.0005
7	0.0000	0.0000	0.0000	0.0000	0.0000	0.0000	0.0000	0.0000	0.0000	0.0001

					λ					
x	1.1	1.2	1.3	1.4	1.5	1.6	1.7	1.8	1.9	2.0
0	0.3329	0.3012	0.2725	0.2466	0.2231	0.2019	0.1827	0.1653	0.1496	0.1353
1	0.3662	0.3614	0.3543	0.3452	0.3347	0.3230	0.3106	0.2975	0.2842	0.2707
2	0.2014	0.2169	0.2303	0.2417	0.2510	0.2584	0.2640	0.2678	0.2700	0.2707
3	0.0738	0.0867	0.0998	0.1128	0.1255	0.1378	0.1496	0.1607	0.1710	0.1804
4	0.0203	0.0260	0.0324	0.0395	0.0471	0.0551	0.0636	0.0723	0.0812	0.0902
5	0.0045	0.0062	0.0084	0.0111	0.0141	0.0176	0.0216	0.0260	0.0309	0.0361
6	0.0008	0.0012	0.0018	0.0026	0.0035	0.0047	0.0061	0.0078	0.0098	0.0120
7	0.0001	0.0002	0.0003	0.0005	0.0008	0.0011	0.0015	0.0020	0.0027	0.0034
8	0.0000	0.0000	0.0001	0.0001	0.0001	0.0002	0.0003	0.0005	0.0006	0.0009
9	0.0000	0.0000	0.0000	0.0000	0.0000	0.0000	0.0001	0.0001	0.0001	0.0002

					λ					
x	2.1	2.2	2.3	2.4	2.5	2.6	2.7	2.8	2.9	3.0
0	0.1225	0.1108	0.1003	0.0907	0.0821	0.0743	0.0672	0.0608	0.0550	0.0498
1	0.2572	0.2438	0.2306	0.2177	0.2052	0.1931	0.1815	0.1703	0.1596	0.1494
2	0.2700	0.2681	0.2652	0.2613	0.2565	0.2510	0.2450	0.2384	0.2314	0.2240
3	0.1890	0.1966	0.2033	0.2090	0.2138	0.2176	0.2205	0.2225	0.2237	0.2240
4	0.0992	0.1082	0.1169	0.1254	0.1336	0.1414	0.1488	0.1557	0.1622	0.1680
5	0.0417	0.0476	0.0538	0.0602	0.0668	0.0735	0.0804	0.0872	0.0940	0.1008
6	0.0146	0.0174	0.0206	0.0241	0.0278	0.0319	0.0362	0.0407	0.0455	0.0540
7	0.0044	0.0055	0.0068	0.0083	0.0099	0.0118	0.0139	0.0163	0.0188	0.0216
8	0.0011	0.0015	0.0019	0.0025	0.0031	0.0038	0.0047	0.0057	0.0068	0.0081
9	0.0003	0.0004	0.0005	0.0007	0.0009	0.0011	0.0014	0.0018	0.0022	0.0027
10	0.0001	0.0001	0.0001	0.0002	0.0002	0.0003	0.0004	0.0005	0.0006	0.0008
11	0.0000	0.0000	0.0000	0.0000	0.0000	0.0001	0.0001	0.0001	0.0002	0.0002
12	0.0000	0.0000	0.0000	0.0000	0.0000	0.0000	0.0000	0.0000	0.0000	0.0001

From *Handbook of Probability and Statistics with Tables*, by Burington and May. Copyright 1970 by McGraw-Hill, Inc. Used with permission of McGraw-Hill Book Company.

Poisson Probabilities *(Continued)*

					λ					
x	3.1	3.2	3.3	3.4	3.5	3.6	3.7	3.8	3.9	4.0
0	0.0450	0.0408	0.0369	0.0344	0.0302	0.0273	0.0247	0.0224	0.0202	0.0183
1	0.1397	0.1304	0.1217	0.1135	0.1057	0.0984	0.0915	0.0850	0.0789	0.0733
2	0.2165	0.2087	0.2008	0.1929	0.1850	0.1771	0.1692	0.1615	0.1539	0.1465
3	0.2237	0.2226	0.2209	0.2186	0.2158	0.2125	0.2087	0.2046	0.2001	0.1954
4	0.1734	0.1781	0.1823	0.1858	0.1888	0.1912	0.1931	0.1944	0.1951	0.1954
5	0.1075	0.1140	0.1203	0.1264	0.1322	0.1377	0.1429	0.1477	0.1522	0.1563
6	0.0555	0.0608	0.0662	0.0716	0.0771	0.0826	0.0881	0.0936	0.0989	0.1042
7	0.0246	0.0278	0.0312	0.0348	0.0385	0.0425	0.0466	0.0508	0.0551	0.0595
8	0.0095	0.0111	0.0129	0.0148	0.0169	0.0191	0.0215	0.0241	0.0269	0.0298
9	0.0033	0.0040	0.0047	0.0056	0.0066	0.0076	0.0089	0.0102	0.0116	0.0132
10	0.0010	0.0013	0.0016	0.0019	0.0023	0.0028	0.0033	0.0039	0.0045	0.0053
11	0.0003	0.0004	0.0005	0.0006	0.0007	0.0009	0.0011	0.0013	0.0016	0.0019
12	0.0001	0.0001	0.0001	0.0002	0.0002	0.0003	0.0003	0.0004	0.0005	0.0006
13	0.0000	0.0000	0.0000	0.0000	0.0001	0.0001	0.0001	0.0001	0.0002	0.0002
14	0.0000	0.0000	0.0000	0.0000	0.0000	0.0000	0.0000	0.0000	0.0000	0.0001

					λ					
x	4.1	4.2	4.3	4.4	4.5	4.6	4.7	4.8	4.9	5.0
0	0.0166	0.0150	0.0136	0.0123	0.0111	0.0101	0.0091	0.0082	0.0074	0.0067
1	0.0679	0.0630	0.0583	0.0540	0.0500	0.0462	0.0427	0.0395	0.0365	0.0337
2	0.1393	0.1323	0.1254	0.1188	0.1125	0.1063	0.1005	0.0948	0.0894	0.0842
3	0.1904	0.1852	0.1798	0.1743	0.1687	0.1631	0.1574	0.1517	0.1460	0.1404
4	0.1951	0.1944	0.1933	0.1917	0.1898	0.1875	0.1849	0.1820	0.1789	0.1755
5	0.1600	0.1633	0.1662	0.1687	0.1708	0.1725	0.1738	0.1747	0.1753	0.1755
6	0.1093	0.1143	0.1191	0.1237	0.1281	0.1323	0.1362	0.1398	0.1432	0.1462
7	0.0640	0.0686	0.0732	0.0778	0.0824	0.0869	0.0914	0.0959	0.1002	0.1044
8	0.0328	0.0360	0.0393	0.0428	0.0463	0.0500	0.0537	0.0575	0.0614	0.0653
9	0.0150	0.0168	0.0188	0.0209	0.0232	0.0255	0.0280	0.0307	0.0334	0.0363
10	0.0061	0.0071	0.0081	0.0092	0.0104	0.0118	0.0132	0.0147	0.0164	0.0181
11	0.0023	0.0027	0.0032	0.0037	0.0043	0.0049	0.0056	0.0064	0.0073	0.0082
12	0.0008	0.0009	0.0011	0.0014	0.0016	0.0019	0.0022	0.0026	0.0030	0.0034
13	0.0002	0.0003	0.0004	0.0005	0.0006	0.0007	0.0008	0.0009	0.0011	0.0013
14	0.0001	0.0001	0.0001	0.0001	0.0002	0.0002	0.0003	0.0003	0.0004	0.0005
15	0.0000	0.0000	0.0000	0.0000	0.0001	0.0001	0.0001	0.0001	0.0001	0.0002

					λ					
x	5.1	5.2	5.3	5.4	5.5	5.6	5.7	5.8	5.9	6.0
0	0.0061	0.0055	0.0050	0.0045	0.0041	0.0037	0.0033	0.0030	0.0027	0.0025
1	0.0311	0.0287	0.0265	0.0244	0.0225	0.0207	0.0191	0.0176	0.0162	0.0149
2	0.0793	0.0746	0.0701	0.0659	0.0618	0.0580	0.0544	0.0509	0.0477	0.0446
3	0.1348	0.1293	0.1239	0.1185	0.1133	0.1082	0.1033	0.0985	0.0938	0.0892
4	0.1719	0.1681	0.1641	0.1600	0.1558	0.1515	0.1472	0.1428	0.1383	0.1339

Poisson Probabilities *(Continued)*

						λ				
x	5.1	5.2	5.3	5.4	5.5	5.6	5.7	5.8	5.9	6.0
5	0.1753	0.1748	0.1740	0.1728	0.1714	0.1697	0.1678	0.1656	0.1632	0.1606
6	0.1490	0.1515	0.1537	0.1555	0.1571	0.1587	0.1594	0.1601	0.1605	0.1606
7	0.1086	0.1125	0.1163	0.1200	0.1234	0.1267	0.1298	0.1326	0.1353	0.1377
8	0.0692	0.0731	0.0771	0.0810	0.0849	0.0887	0.0925	0.0962	0.0998	0.1033
9	0.0392	0.0423	0.0454	0.0486	0.0519	0.0552	0.0586	0.0620	0.0654	0.0688
10	0.0200	0.0220	0.0241	0.0262	0.0285	0.0309	0.0334	0.0359	0.0386	0.0413
11	0.0093	0.0104	0.0116	0.0129	0.0143	0.0157	0.0173	0.0190	0.0207	0.0225
12	0.0039	0.0045	0.0051	0.0058	0.0065	0.0073	0.0082	0.0092	0.0102	0.0113
13	0.0015	0.0018	0.0021	0.0024	0.0028	0.0032	0.0036	0.0041	0.0046	0.0052
14	0.0006	0.0007	0.0008	0.0009	0.0011	0.0013	0.0015	0.0017	0.0019	0.0022
15	0.0002	0.0002	0.0003	0.0003	0.0004	0.0005	0.0006	0.0007	0.0008	0.0009
16	0.0001	0.0001	0.0001	0.0001	0.0001	0.0002	0.0002	0.0002	0.0003	0.0003
17	0.0000	0.0000	0.0000	0.0000	0.0000	0.0001	0.0001	0.0001	0.0001	0.0001

						λ				
x	6.1	6.2	6.3	6.4	6.5	6.6	6.7	6.8	6.9	7.0
0	0.0022	0.0020	0.0018	0.0017	0.0015	0.0014	0.0012	0.0011	0.0010	0.0009
1	0.0137	0.0126	0.0116	0.0106	0.0098	0.0090	0.0082	0.0076	0.0070	0.0064
2	0.0417	0.0390	0.0364	0.0340	0.0318	0.0296	0.0276	0.0258	0.0240	0.0223
3	0.0848	0.0806	0.0765	0.0726	0.0688	0.0652	0.0617	0.0584	0.0552	0.0521
4	0.1294	0.1249	0.1205	0.1162	0.1118	0.1076	0.1034	0.0992	0.0952	0.0912
5	0.1579	0.1549	0.1519	0.1487	0.1454	0.1420	0.1385	0.1349	0.1314	0.1277
6	0.1605	0.1601	0.1595	0.1586	0.1575	0.1562	0.1546	0.1529	0.1511	0.1490
7	0.1399	0.1418	0.1435	0.1450	0.1462	0.1472	0.1480	0.1486	0.1489	0.1490
8	0.1066	0.1099	0.1130	0.1160	0.1188	0.1215	0.1240	0.1263	0.1284	0.1304
9	0.0723	0.0757	0.0791	0.0825	0.0858	0.0891	0.0923	0.0954	0.0985	0.1014
10	0.0441	0.0469	0.0498	0.0528	0.0558	0.0588	0.0618	0.0649	0.0679	0.0710
11	0.0245	0.0265	0.0285	0.0307	0.0330	0.0353	0.0377	0.0401	0.0426	0.0452
12	0.0124	0.0137	0.0150	0.0164	0.0179	0.0194	0.0210	0.0227	0.0245	0.0264
13	0.0058	0.0065	0.0073	0.0081	0.0089	0.0098	0.0108	0.0119	0.0130	0.0142
14	0.0025	0.0029	0.0033	0.0037	0.0041	0.0046	0.0052	0.0058	0.0064	0.0071
15	0.0010	0.0012	0.0014	0.0016	0.0018	0.0020	0.0023	0.0025	0.0029	0.0033
16	0.0004	0.0005	0.0005	0.0006	0.0007	0.0008	0.0010	0.0011	0.0013	0.0014
17	0.0001	0.0002	0.0002	0.0002	0.0003	0.0003	0.0004	0.0004	0.0005	0.0006
18	0.0000	0.0001	0.0001	0.0001	0.0001	0.0001	0.0001	0.0002	0.0002	0.0002
19	0.0000	0.0000	0.0000	0.0000	0.0000	0.0000	0.0000	0.0001	0.0001	0.0001

						λ				
x	7.1	7.2	7.3	7.4	7.5	7.6	7.7	7.8	7.9	8.0
0	0.0008	0.0007	0.0007	0.0006	0.0006	0.0005	0.0005	0.0004	0.0004	0.0003
1	0.0059	0.0054	0.0049	0.0045	0.0041	0.0038	0.0035	0.0032	0.0029	0.0027
2	0.0208	0.0194	0.0180	0.0167	0.0156	0.0145	0.0134	0.0125	0.0116	0.0107

Poisson Probabilities *(Continued)*

	λ									
x	7.1	7.2	7.3	7.4	7.5	7.6	7.7	7.8	7.9	8.0
3	0.0492	0.0464	0.0438	0.0413	0.0389	0.0366	0.0345	0.0324	0.0305	0.0286
4	0.0874	0.0836	0.0799	0.0764	0.0729	0.0696	0.0663	0.0632	0.0602	0.0573
5	0.1241	0.1204	0.1167	0.1130	0.1094	0.1057	0.1021	0.0986	0.0951	0.0916
6	0.1468	0.1445	0.1420	0.1394	0.1367	0.1339	0.1311	0.1282	0.1252	0.1221
7	0.1489	0.1486	0.1481	0.1474	0.1465	0.1454	0.1442	0.1428	0.1413	0.1396
8	0.1321	0.1337	0.1351	0.1363	0.1373	0.1382	0.1388	0.1392	0.1395	0.1396
9	0.1042	0.1070	0.1096	0.1121	0.1144	0.1167	0.1187	0.1207	0.1224	0.1241
10	0.0740	0.0770	0.0800	0.0829	0.0858	0.0887	0.0914	0.0941	0.0967	0.0993
11	0.0478	0.0504	0.0531	0.0558	0.0585	0.0613	0.0640	0.0667	0.0695	0.0722
12	0.0283	0.0303	0.0323	0.0344	0.0366	0.0388	0.0411	0.0434	0.0457	0.0481
13	0.0154	0.0168	0.0181	0.0196	0.0211	0.0227	0.0243	0.0260	0.0278	0.0296
14	0.0078	0.0086	0.0095	0.0104	0.0113	0.0123	0.0134	0.0145	0.0157	0.0169
15	0.0037	0.0041	0.0046	0.0051	0.0057	0.0062	0.0069	0.0075	0.0083	0.0090
16	0.0016	0.0019	0.0021	0.0024	0.0026	0.0030	0.0033	0.0037	0.0041	0.0045
17	0.0007	0.0008	0.0009	0.0010	0.0012	0.0013	0.0015	0.0017	0.0019	0.0021
18	0.0003	0.0003	0.0004	0.0004	0.0005	0.0006	0.0006	0.0007	0.0008	0.0009
19	0.0001	0.0001	0.0001	0.0002	0.0002	0.0002	0.0003	0.0003	0.0003	0.0004
20	0.0000	0.0000	0.0001	0.0001	0.0001	0.0001	0.0001	0.0001	0.0001	0.0002
21	0.0000	0.0000	0.0000	0.0000	0.0000	0.0000	0.0000	0.0000	0.0001	0.0001

	λ									
x	8.1	8.2	8.3	8.4	8.5	8.6	8.7	8.8	8.9	9.0
0	0.0003	0.0003	0.0002	0.0002	0.0002	0.0002	0.0002	0.0002	0.0001	0.0001
1	0.0025	0.0023	0.0021	0.0019	0.0017	0.0016	0.0014	0.0013	0.0012	0.0011
2	0.0100	0.0092	0.0086	0.0079	0.0074	0.0068	0.0063	0.0058	0.0054	0.0050
3	0.0269	0.0252	0.0237	0.0222	0.0208	0.0195	0.0183	0.0171	0.0160	0.0150
4	0.0544	0.0517	0.0491	0.0466	0.0443	0.0420	0.0398	0.0377	0.0357	0.0337
5	0.0882	0.0849	0.0816	0.0784	0.0752	0.0722	0.0692	0.0663	0.0635	0.0607
6	0.1191	0.1160	0.1128	0.1097	0.1066	0.1034	0.1003	0.0972	0.0941	0.0911
7	0.1378	0.1358	0.1338	0.1317	0.1294	0.1271	0.1247	0.1222	0.1197	0.1171
8	0.1395	0.1392	0.1388	0.1382	0.1375	0.1366	0.1356	0.1344	0.1332	0.1318
9	0.1256	0.1269	0.1280	0.1290	0.1299	0.1306	0.1311	0.1315	0.1317	0.1318
10	0.1017	0.1040	0.1063	0.1084	0.1104	0.1123	0.1140	0.1157	0.1172	0.1186
11	0.0749	0.0776	0.0802	0.0828	0.0853	0.0878	0.0902	0.0925	0.0948	0.0970
12	0.0505	0.0530	0.0555	0.0579	0.0604	0.0629	0.0654	0.0679	0.0703	0.0728
13	0.0315	0.0334	0.0354	0.0374	0.0395	0.0416	0.0438	0.0459	0.0481	0.0504
14	0.0182	0.0196	0.0210	0.0225	0.0240	0.0256	0.0272	0.0289	0.0306	0.0324
15	0.0098	0.0107	0.0116	0.0126	0.0136	0.0147	0.0158	0.0169	0.0182	0.1094
16	0.0050	0.0055	0.0060	0.0066	0.0072	0.0079	0.0086	0.0093	0.0101	0.0109
17	0.0024	0.0026	0.0029	0.0033	0.0036	0.0040	0.0044	0.0048	0.0053	0.0058
18	0.0011	0.0012	0.0014	0.0015	0.0017	0.0019	0.0021	0.0024	0.0026	0.0029
19	0.0005	0.0005	0.0006	0.0007	0.0008	0.0009	0.0010	0.0011	0.0012	0.0014

Poisson Probabilities *(Continued)*

						λ				
x	8.1	8.2	8.3	8.4	8.5	8.6	8.7	8.8	8.9	9.0
20	0.0002	0.0002	0.0002	0.0003	0.0003	0.0004	0.0004	0.0005	0.0005	0.0006
21	0.0001	0.0001	0.0001	0.0001	0.0001	0.0002	0.0002	0.0002	0.0002	0.0003
22	0.0000	0.0000	0.0000	0.0000	0.0001	0.0001	0.0001	0.0001	0.0001	0.0001

						λ				
x	9.1	9.2	9.3	9.4	9.5	9.6	9.7	9.8	9.9	10
0	0.0001	0.0001	0.0001	0.0001	0.0001	0.0001	0.0001	0.0001	0.0001	0.0000
1	0.0010	0.0009	0.0009	0.0008	0.0007	0.0007	0.0006	0.0005	0.0005	0.0005
2	0.0046	0.0043	0.0040	0.0037	0.0034	0.0031	0.0029	0.0027	0.0025	0.0023
3	0.0140	0.0131	0.0123	0.0115	0.0107	0.0100	0.0093	0.0087	0.0081	0.0076
4	0.0319	0.0302	0.0285	0.0269	0.0254	0.0240	0.0226	0.0213	0.0201	0.0189
5	0.0581	0.0555	0.0530	0.0506	0.0483	0.0460	0.0439	0.0418	0.0398	0.0378
6	0.0881	0.0851	0.0822	0.0793	0.0764	0.0736	0.0709	0.0682	0.0656	0.0631
7	0.1145	0.1118	0.1091	0.1064	0.1037	0.1010	0.0982	0.0955	0.0928	0.0901
8	0.1302	0.1286	0.1269	0.1251	0.1232	0.1212	0.1191	0.1170	0.1148	0.1126
9	0.1317	0.1315	0.1311	0.1306	0.1300	0.1293	0.1284	0.1274	0.1263	0.1251
10	0.1198	0.1210	0.1219	0.1228	0.1235	0.1241	0.1245	0.1249	0.1250	0.1251
11	0.0991	0.1012	0.1031	0.1049	0.1067	0.1083	0.1098	0.1112	0.1125	0.1137
12	0.0752	0.0776	0.0799	0.0822	0.0844	0.0866	0.0888	0.0908	0.0928	0.0948
13	0.0526	0.0549	0.0572	0.0594	0.0617	0.0640	0.0662	0.0685	0.0707	0.0729
14	0.0342	0.0361	0.0380	0.0399	0.0419	0.0439	0.0459	0.0479	0.0500	0.0521
15	0.0208	0.0221	0.0235	0.0250	0.0265	0.0281	0.0297	0.0313	0.0330	0.0347
16	0.0118	0.0127	0.0137	0.0147	0.0157	0.0168	0.0180	0.0192	0.0204	0.0217
17	0.0063	0.0069	0.0075	0.0081	0.0088	0.0095	0.0103	0.0111	0.0119	0.0128
18	0.0032	0.0035	0.0039	0.0042	0.0046	0.0051	0.0055	0.0060	0.0065	0.0071
19	0.0015	0.0017	0.0019	0.0021	0.0023	0.0026	0.0028	0.0031	0.0034	0.0027
20	0.0007	0.0008	0.0009	0.0010	0.0011	0.0012	0.0014	0.0015	0.0017	0.0019
21	0.0003	0.0003	0.0004	0.0004	0.0005	0.0006	0.0006	0.0007	0.0008	0.0009
22	0.0001	0.0001	0.0002	0.0002	0.0002	0.0002	0.0003	0.0003	0.0004	0.0004
23	0.0000	0.0001	0.0001	0.0001	0.0001	0.0001	0.0001	0.0001	0.0002	0.0002
24	0.0000	0.0000	0.0000	0.0000	0.0000	0.0000	0.0000	0.0001	0.0001	0.0001

						λ				
x	11	12	13	14	15	16	17	18	19	20
0	0.0000	0.0000	0.0000	0.0000	0.0000	0.0000	0.0000	0.0000	0.0000	0.0000
1	0.0002	0.0001	0.0000	0.0000	0.0000	0.0000	0.0000	0.0000	0.0000	0.0000
2	0.0010	0.0004	0.0002	0.0001	0.0000	0.0000	0.0000	0.0000	0.0000	0.0000
3	0.0037	0.0018	0.0008	0.0004	0.0002	0.0001	0.0000	0.0000	0.0000	0.0000
4	0.0102	0.0053	0.0027	0.0013	0.0006	0.0003	0.0001	0.0001	0.0000	0.0000
5	0.0224	0.0127	0.0070	0.0037	0.0019	0.0010	0.0005	0.0002	0.0001	0.0001
6	0.0411	0.0255	0.0152	0.0087	0.0048	0.0026	0.0014	0.0007	0.0004	0.0002
7	0.0646	0.0437	0.0281	0.0174	0.0104	0.0060	0.0034	0.0018	0.0010	0.0005
8	0.0888	0.0655	0.0457	0.0304	0.0194	0.0120	0.0072	0.0042	0.0024	0.0013

Poisson Probabilities *(Continued)*

					λ					
x	11	12	13	14	15	16	17	18	19	20
9	0.1085	0.0874	0.0661	0.0473	0.0324	0.0213	0.0135	0.0083	0.0050	0.0029
10	0.1194	0.1048	0.0859	0.0663	0.0486	0.0341	0.0230	0.0150	0.0095	0.0058
11	0.1194	0.1144	0.1015	0.0844	0.0663	0.0496	0.0355	0.0245	0.0164	0.0106
12	0.1094	0.1144	0.1099	0.0984	0.0829	0.0661	0.0504	0.0368	0.0259	0.0176
13	0.0926	0.1056	0.1099	0.1060	0.0956	0.0814	0.0658	0.0509	0.0378	0.0271
14	0.0728	0.0905	0.1021	0.1060	0.1024	0.0930	0.0800	0.0655	0.0514	0.0387
15	0.0534	0.0724	0.0885	0.0989	0.1024	0.0992	0.0906	0.0786	0.0650	0.0516
16	0.0367	0.0543	0.0719	0.0866	0.0960	0.0992	0.0963	0.0884	0.0772	0.0646
17	0.0237	0.0383	0.0550	0.0713	0.0847	0.0934	0.0963	0.0936	0.0863	0.0760
18	0.0145	0.0256	0.0397	0.0554	0.0706	0.0830	0.0909	0.0936	0.0911	0.0844
19	0.0084	0.0161	0.0272	0.0409	0.0557	0.0699	0.0814	0.0887	0.0911	0.0888
20	0.0046	0.0097	0.0177	0.0286	0.0418	0.0559	0.0692	0.0798	0.0866	0.0888
21	0.0024	0.0055	0.0109	0.0191	0.0299	0.0426	0.0560	0.0684	0.0783	0.0846
22	0.0012	0.0030	0.0065	0.0121	0.0204	0.0310	0.0433	0.0560	0.0676	0.0769
23	0.0006	0.0016	0.0037	0.0074	0.0133	0.0216	0.0320	0.0438	0.0559	0.0669
24	0.0003	0.0008	0.0020	0.0043	0.0083	0.0144	0.0226	0.0328	0.0442	0.0557
25	0.0001	0.0004	0.0010	0.0024	0.0050	0.0092	0.0154	0.0237	0.0336	0.0446
26	0.0000	0.0002	0.0005	0.0013	0.0029	0.0057	0.0101	0.0164	0.0246	0.0343
27	0.0000	0.0001	0.0002	0.0007	0.0016	0.0034	0.0063	0.0109	0.0173	0.0254
28	0.0000	0.0000	0.0001	0.0003	0.0009	0.0019	0.0038	0.0070	0.0117	0.0181
29	0.0000	0.0000	0.0001	0.0002	0.0004	0.0011	0.0023	0.0044	0.0077	0.0125
30	0.0000	0.0000	0.0000	0.0001	0.0002	0.0006	0.0013	0.0026	0.0049	0.0083
31	0.0000	0.0000	0.0000	0.0000	0.0001	0.0003	0.0007	0.0015	0.0030	0.0054
32	0.0000	0.0000	0.0000	0.0000	0.0001	0.0001	0.0004	0.0009	0.0018	0.0034
33	0.0000	0.0000	0.0000	0.0000	0.0000	0.0001	0.0002	0.0005	0.0010	0.0020
34	0.0000	0.0000	0.0000	0.0000	0.0000	0.0000	0.0001	0.0002	0.0006	0.0012
35	0.0000	0.0000	0.0000	0.0000	0.0000	0.0000	0.0000	0.0001	0.0003	0.0007
36	0.0000	0.0000	0.0000	0.0000	0.0000	0.0000	0.0000	0.0001	0.0002	0.0004
37	0.0000	0.0000	0.0000	0.0000	0.0000	0.0000	0.0000	0.0000	0.0001	0.0002
38	0.0000	0.0000	0.0000	0.0000	0.0000	0.0000	0.0000	0.0000	0.0000	0.0001
39	0.0000	0.0000	0.0000	0.0000	0.0000	0.0000	0.0000	0.0000	0.0000	0.0001

Appendix C Areas for the Standard Normal Distribution

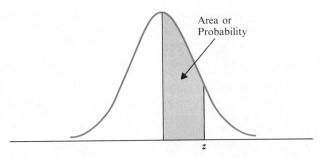

Area or
Probability

z

Entries in the table give the area under the curve between the mean and z standard deviations above the mean. For example, for $z = 1.25$, the area under the curve between the mean and z is 0.3944.

z	0.00	0.01	0.02	0.03	0.04	0.05	0.06	0.07	0.08	0.09
0.0	0.0000	0.0040	0.0080	0.0120	0.0160	0.0199	0.0239	0.0279	0.0319	0.0359
0.1	0.0398	0.0438	0.0478	0.0517	0.0557	0.0596	0.0636	0.0675	0.0714	0.0753
0.2	0.0793	0.0832	0.0871	0.0910	0.0948	0.0987	0.1026	0.1064	0.1103	0.1141
0.3	0.1179	0.1217	0.1255	0.1293	0.1331	0.1368	0.1406	0.1443	0.1480	0.1517
0.4	0.1554	0.1591	0.1628	0.1664	0.1700	0.1736	0.1772	0.1808	0.1844	0.1879
0.5	0.1915	0.1950	0.1985	0.2019	0.2054	0.2088	0.2123	0.2157	0.2190	0.2224
0.6	0.2257	0.2291	0.2324	0.2357	0.2389	0.2422	0.2454	0.2486	0.2518	0.2549
0.7	0.2580	0.2612	0.2642	0.2673	0.2704	0.2734	0.2764	0.2794	0.2823	0.2852
0.8	0.2881	0.2910	0.2939	0.2967	0.2995	0.3023	0.3051	0.3078	0.3106	0.3133
0.9	0.3159	0.3186	0.3212	0.3238	0.3264	0.3289	0.3315	0.3340	0.3365	0.3389
1.0	0.3413	0.3438	0.3461	0.3485	0.3508	0.3531	0.3554	0.3577	0.3599	0.3621
1.1	0.3643	0.3665	0.3686	0.3708	0.3729	0.3749	0.3770	0.3790	0.3810	0.3830
1.2	0.3849	0.3869	0.3888	0.3907	0.3925	0.3944	0.3962	0.3980	0.3997	0.4015
1.3	0.4032	0.4049	0.4066	0.4082	0.4099	0.4115	0.4131	0.4147	0.4162	0.4177
1.4	0.4192	0.4207	0.4222	0.4236	0.4251	0.4265	0.4279	0.4292	0.4306	0.4319
1.5	0.4332	0.4345	0.4357	0.4370	0.4382	0.4394	0.4406	0.4418	0.4429	0.4441
1.6	0.4452	0.4463	0.4474	0.4484	0.4495	0.4505	0.4515	0.4525	0.4535	0.4545
1.7	0.4554	0.4564	0.4573	0.4582	0.4591	0.4599	0.4608	0.4616	0.4625	0.4633
1.8	0.4641	0.4649	0.4656	0.4664	0.4671	0.4678	0.4686	0.4693	0.4699	0.4706
1.9	0.4713	0.4719	0.4726	0.4732	0.4738	0.4744	0.4750	0.4756	0.4761	0.4767
2.0	0.4772	0.4778	0.4783	0.4788	0.4793	0.4798	0.4803	0.4808	0.4812	0.4817
2.1	0.4821	0.4826	0.4830	0.4834	0.4838	0.4842	0.4846	0.4850	0.4854	0.4857
2.2	0.4861	0.4864	0.4868	0.4871	0.4875	0.4878	0.4881	0.4884	0.4887	0.4890
2.3	0.4893	0.4896	0.4898	0.4901	0.4904	0.4906	0.4909	0.4911	0.4913	0.4916
2.4	0.4918	0.4920	0.4922	0.4925	0.4927	0.4929	0.4931	0.4932	0.4934	0.4936
2.5	0.4938	0.4940	0.4941	0.4943	0.4945	0.4946	0.4948	0.4949	0.4951	0.4952
2.6	0.4953	0.4955	0.4956	0.4957	0.4959	0.4960	0.4961	0.4962	0.4963	0.4964
2.7	0.4965	0.4966	0.4967	0.4968	0.4969	0.4970	0.4971	0.4972	0.4973	0.4974
2.8	0.4974	0.4975	0.4976	0.4977	0.4977	0.4978	0.4979	0.4979	0.4980	0.4981
2.9	0.4981	0.4982	0.4982	0.4983	0.4984	0.4984	0.4985	0.4985	0.4986	0.4986
3.0	0.4986	0.4987	0.4987	0.4988	0.4988	0.4989	0.4989	0.4989	0.4990	0.4990

Appendix D   Values of $e^{-\lambda}$

λ	$e^{-\lambda}$	λ	$e^{-\lambda}$
0.0	1.0000	3.3	0.0369
0.1	0.9048	3.4	0.0334
0.2	0.8187	3.5	0.0302
0.3	0.7408	3.6	0.0273
0.4	0.6703	3.7	0.0247
0.5	0.6065	3.8	0.0224
0.6	0.5488	3.9	0.0202
0.7	0.4966	4.0	0.0183
0.8	0.4493	4.1	0.0166
0.9	0.4066	4.2	0.0150
1.0	0.3679	4.3	0.0136
1.1	0.3329	4.4	0.0123
1.2	0.3012	4.5	0.0111
1.3	0.2725	4.6	0.0101
1.4	0.2466	4.7	0.0091
1.5	0.2231	4.8	0.0082
1.6	0.2019	4.9	0.0074
1.7	0.1827	5.0	0.0067
1.8	0.1653	5.1	0.0061
1.9	0.1496	5.2	0.0055
2.0	0.1353	5.3	0.0050
2.1	0.1225	5.4	0.0045
2.2	0.1108	5.5	0.0041
2.3	0.1003	5.6	0.0037
2.4	0.0907	5.7	0.0033
2.5	0.0821	5.8	0.0030
2.6	0.0743	5.9	0.0027
2.7	0.0672	6.0	0.0025
2.8	0.0608	7.0	0.0009
2.9	0.0550	8.0	0.000335
3.0	0.0498	9.0	0.000123
3.1	0.0450	10.0	0.000045
3.2	0.0408		

Appendix E   Random Digits

63271	59986	71744	51102	15141	80714	58683	93108	13554	79945
88547	09896	95436	79115	08303	01041	20030	63754	08459	28364
55957	57243	83865	09911	19761	66535	40102	26646	60147	15702
46276	87453	44790	67122	45573	84358	21625	16999	13385	22782
55363	07449	34835	15290	76616	67191	12777	21861	68689	03263
69393	92785	49902	58447	42048	30378	87618	26933	40640	16281
13186	29431	88190	04588	38733	81290	89541	70290	40113	08243
17726	28652	56836	78351	47327	18518	92222	55201	27340	10493
36520	64465	05550	30157	82242	29520	69753	72602	23756	54935
81628	36100	39254	56835	37636	02421	98063	89641	64953	99337
84649	48968	75215	75498	49539	74240	03466	49292	36401	45525
63291	11618	12613	75055	43915	26488	41116	64531	56827	30825
70502	53225	03655	05915	37140	57051	48393	91322	25653	06543
06426	24771	59935	49801	11082	66762	94477	02494	88215	27191
20711	55609	29430	70165	45406	78484	31639	52009	18873	96927
41990	70538	77191	25860	55204	73417	83920	69468	74972	38712
72452	36618	76298	26678	89334	33938	95567	29380	75906	91807
37042	40318	57099	10528	09925	89773	41335	96244	29002	46453
53766	52875	15987	46962	67342	77592	57651	95508	80033	69828
90585	58955	53122	16025	84299	53310	67380	84249	25348	04332
32001	96293	37203	64516	51530	37069	40261	61374	05815	06714
62606	64324	46354	72157	67248	20135	49804	09226	64419	29457
10078	28073	85389	50324	14500	15562	64165	06125	71353	77669
91561	46145	24177	15294	10061	98124	75732	00815	83452	97355
13091	98112	53959	79607	52244	63303	10413	63839	74762	50289
73864	83014	72457	22682	03033	61714	88173	90835	00634	85169
66668	25467	48894	51043	02365	91726	09365	63167	95264	45643
84745	41042	29493	01836	09044	51926	43630	63470	76508	14194
48068	26805	94595	47907	13357	38412	33318	26098	82782	42851
54310	96175	97594	88616	42035	38093	36745	56702	40644	83514
14877	33095	10924	58013	61439	21882	42059	24177	58739	60170
78295	23179	02771	43464	59061	71411	05697	67194	30495	21157
67524	02865	39593	54278	04237	92441	26602	63835	38032	94770
58268	57219	68124	73455	83236	08710	04284	55005	84171	42596
97158	28672	50685	01181	24262	19427	52106	34308	73685	74246
04230	16831	69085	30802	65559	09205	71829	06489	85650	38707
94879	56606	30401	02602	57658	70091	54986	41394	60437	03195
71446	15232	66715	26385	91518	70566	02888	79941	39684	54315
32886	05644	79316	09819	00813	88407	17461	73925	53037	91904
62048	33711	25290	21526	02223	75947	66466	06232	10913	75336

Reproduced with permission from The Rand Corporation, *A Million Random Digits*, New York, The Free Press, 1955 and 1983.

References and Bibliography

The Role and Nature of Quantitative Methods (Chapter 1)

Churchman, C. W., R. L. Ackoff, and E. L. Arnoff, *Introduction to Operations Research*, New York, John Wiley & Sons, 1957.

Forgionne, G. A., "Corporate Management Science Activities: An Update," *Interfaces*, Vol. 13, No. 3, 1983, pp. 20–23.

Gaither, N., "The Adoption of Operations Research Techniques by Manufacturing Organizations," *Decision Sciences*, Vol. 6, No. 4, 1975, pp. 797–813.

Grayson, C. J., Jr., "Management Science and Business Practice," *Harvard Business Review*, Vol. 51, 1973, pp. 41–48.

Hillier, F., and G. J. Lieberman, *Introduction to Operations Research*, 4th ed., San Francisco, Holden-Day, 1986.

Ledbetter, W., and J. Cox, "Are OR Techniques Being Used?," *Industrial Engineering*, Vol. 9, 1977, pp. 19–21.

Radnor, M., and R. D. Neal, "The Progress of Management Science Activities in Large U.S. Industrial Corporations," *Operations Research*, Vol. 21, 1973, pp. 427–450.

Shannon, R. E., S. S. Long, and B. P. Buckles, "Operations Research Methodologies in Industrial Engineering: A Survey," *AIIE Transactions*, Vol. 12, No. 4, 1980, pp. 364–367.

Thomas, G., and J. DaCosta, "A Sample Survey of Corporate Operations Research," *Interfaces*, August 1979.

Thomas, G., and M. Mitchell, "OR in the U.S. Marine Corps: A Characterization," *Interfaces*, June 1983.

Probability (Chapters 2–3)

Feller, W., *An Introduction to Probability Theory and Its Applications*, Vol. I, 3rd ed., New York, John Wiley & Sons, 1968.

Feller, W., *An Introduction to Probability Theory and Its Applications*, Vol. II, 2nd ed., New York, John Wiley & Sons, 1971.

Hoel, P. G., S. C. Port, and C. J. Stone, *Introduction to Probability Theory*, Boston, Houghton Mifflin, 1971.

Parzen, E., *Modern Probability Theory and Its Applications*, New York, John Wiley & Sons, 1960.

Zehna, P. W., *Probability Distributions and Statistics*, Boston, Allyn & Bacon, 1970.

Decision Analysis (Chapters 4–5)

Bunn, D., *Applied Decision Analysis*, New York, McGraw-Hill, 1984.

Chernoff, H., and L. E. Moses, *Elementary Decision Theory*, New York, John Wiley & Sons, 1959.

Keeney, R. L., and H. Raiffa, *Decisions with Multiple Objectives: Preferences and Value Trade Offs*, New York, John Wiley & Sons, 1976.

Raiffa, H., *Decision Analysis*, Reading, Mass., Addison-Wesley, 1968.

Schlaifer, R., *Analysis of Decisions under Uncertainty*, New York, McGraw-Hill, 1969.

Winkler, R. L., *An Introduction to Bayesian Inference and Decision*, New York, Holt, Rinehart & Winston, 1972.

Winkler, R. L., and W. L. Hays, *Statistics: Probability, Inference and Decision*, 2nd ed., New York, Holt, Rinehart & Winston, 1975.

Forecasting (Chapter 6)

Bowerman, B. L., and R. T. O'Connell, *Forecasting and Time Series*, North Scituate, Mass., Duxbury Press, 1979.

Box, G. E. P., and G. M. Jenkins, *Time Series Analysis: Forecasting and Control*, rev. ed., San Francisco, Holden-Day, 1976.

Gilchrist, W. G., *Statistical Forecasting*, New York, John Wiley & Sons, 1976.

Hanke, J. E., and A. G. Reitsch, *Business Forecasting*, 2nd ed., Boston, Allyn & Bacon, 1986.

Makridakis, S., S. C. Wheelwright, and Victor E. McGee, *Forecasting: Methods and Applications*, 2nd ed., New York, John Wiley & Sons, 1983.

Nelson, C. R., *Applied Time Series Analysis*, San Francisco, Holden-Day, 1973.

Thomopoulos, N. T., *Applied Forecasting Methods*, Englewood Cliffs, N.J., Prentice-Hall, 1980.

Wheelwright, S. C., and S. Makridakis, *Forecasting Models for Management*, 4th ed., New York, John Wiley & Sons, 1985.

Linear Programming, Transportation, Assignment, and Transshipment Problems (Chapters 7 to 11)

Anderson, D. R., D. J. Sweeney, and T. A. Williams, *Linear Programming for Decision Making*, St. Paul, Minn., West Publishing, 1974.

Bazarra, M. S., and J. J. Jarvis, *Linear Programming and Network Flows*, New York, John Wiley & Sons, 1977.

Bradley, S. P., A. C. Hax, and T. L. Magnanti, *Applied Mathematical Programming*, Reading, Mass., Addison-Wesley, 1977.

Charnes, A., and W. W. Cooper, *Management Models and Industrial Applications of Linear Programming*, New York, John Wiley & Sons, 1961.

Charnes, A., W. W. Cooper, J. K. DeVoe, D. B. Learner, and W. Remecke, "A Goal Programming Model for Media Planning," *Management Science*, Vol. 14, No. 8, April 1968, pp. B423–B430.

Daellenbach, Hans G., and J. Bell, *User's Guide to Linear Programming*, Englewood Cliffs, N.J., Prentice-Hall, 1970.

Dantzig, G. B., *Linear Programming and Extensions*, Princeton, N.J., Princeton University Press, 1963.

Gass, S., *Linear Programming*, 4th ed., New York, McGraw-Hill, 1975.

Hillier, F., and G. J. Lieberman, *Introduction to Operations Research*, 4th ed., San Francisco, Holden-Day, 1986.

Hooker, J. N., "Karmarkar's Linear Programming Algorithm," *Interfaces*, Vol. 16, No. 4, 1986, pp. 75–90.

Ijiri, Y., *Management Goals and Accounting for Control*, Chicago, Rand McNally, 1965.

Lee, S. M., *Goal Programming for Decision Analysis*, Philadelphia, Auerbach, 1972.

Phillips, D. T., A. Ravindran, and J. J. Solberg, *Operations Research: Principles and Practice*, 2nd ed., New York, John Wiley & Sons, 1987.

Schrage, L., *Linear, Integer, and Quadratic Programming with LINDO*, Palo Alto, Calif., Scientific Press, 1986.

Schrage, L., *User's Manual for Linear, Integer, and Quadratic Programming with LINDO*, Redwood City, Calif., Scientific Press, 1987.

Wagner, H., *Principles of Operations Research with Applications to Managerial Decisions*, 2nd ed., Englewood Cliffs, N.J., Prentice-Hall, 1975.

Integer Linear Programming (Chapter 12)

Garfinkel, R. S., and G. L. Nemhauser, *Integer Programming*, New York, John Wiley & Sons, 1972.

Plane, D. R., and C. McMillan, *Discrete Optimization*, Englewood Cliffs, N.J., Prentice-Hall, 1971.

Salkin, H. M., *Integer Programming*, Reading, Mass., Addison-Wesley, 1975.

Zionts, Stanley, *Linear and Integer Programming*, Englewood Cliffs, N.J., Prentice-Hall, 1974.

PERT/CPM (Chapter 13)

Evarts, H. F., *Introduction to PERT*, Boston, Allyn & Bacon, 1964.

Moder, J. J., and C. R. Phillips, *Project Management with CPM and PERT*, 2nd ed., New York, Van Nostrand, 1970.

Wagner, H., *Principles of Operations Research with Applications to Managerial Decisions*, 2nd ed., Englewood Cliffs, N.J., Prentice-Hall, 1975.

Wiest, J., and F. Levy, *Management Guide to PERT/CPM*, 2nd ed., Englewood Cliffs, N.J., Prentice-Hall, 1977.

Inventory Models (Chapter 14)

Buffa, E. S., and W. Taubert, *Production-Inventory Systems: Planning and Control*, 3rd ed., Homewood, Ill., Richard D. Irwin, 1979.

Davis, E. W., *Case Studies in Material Requirements Planning*, Washington, D.C., APICS, 1978.

Greene, J. H., *Production and Inventory Control Handbook*, New York, McGraw-Hill, 1970.

Hadley, G., and T. M. Whitin, *Analysis of Inventory Systems*, Englewood Cliffs, N.J., Prentice-Hall, 1963.

Hillier, F., and G. J. Lieberman, *Introduction to Operations Research*, 4th ed., San Francisco, Holden-Day, 1986.

Naddor, E., *Inventory Systems*, New York, John Wiley & Sons, 1966.

Orlicky, J., *Material Requirements Planning*, New York, McGraw-Hill, 1975.

Plossl, G. W., *Manufacturing Control: The Last Frontier for Profits*, Reston, Va., Reston, 1973.

Starr, M., and D. Miller, *Inventory Control: Theory and Practice*, Englewood Cliffs, N.J., Prentice-Hall, 1962.

Stockton, R. S., *Basic Inventory Systems: Concepts and Analysis*, Boston, Allyn & Bacon, 1965.

Wagner, H., *Principles of Operations Research with Applications to Managerial Decisions*, 2nd ed., Englewood Cliffs, N.J., Prentice-Hall, 1975.

Wight, O. W., *Production and Inventory Management in the Computer Age*, Boston, Cahners Books, 1974.

Computer Simulation (Chapter 15)

Christy, D. P., and H. J. Watson, "The Application of Simulation: A Survey of Industry Practice," *Interfaces*, October 1983.

Emshoff, J. R., and R. L. Sisson, *Design and Use of Computer Simulation Models*, New York, Macmillan, 1970.

Fishman, George S., *Principles of Discrete Event Simulation*, New York, John Wiley & Sons, 1978.

Greenberg, S., *GPSS Primer*, New York, John Wiley & Sons, 1972.

Maisel, H., and G. Gnugnoli, *Simulation of Discrete Stochastic Systems*, Chicago, SRA, 1972.

Naylor, T. H., *Computer Simulation Experiments with Models of Economic Systems*, New York, John Wiley & Sons, 1971.

Naylor, T. H., J. L. Balintfy, D. S. Burdick, and K. Chu, *Computer Simulation Techniques*, New York, John Wiley & Sons, 1968.

Schmidt, J. W., and R. E. Taylor, *Simulation and Analysis of Industrial Systems*, Homewood, Ill., Richard D. Irwin, 1970.

Waiting Lines (Chapter 16)

Bhat, U. N., *Elements of Applied Stochastic Processes*, New York, John Wiley & Sons, 1972.

Cooper, R. B., *Introduction to Queueing Theory*, New York, Macmillan, 1972.

Cox, D. R., and W. L. Smith, *Queues*, New York, John Wiley & Sons, 1965.

Gross, D., and C. M. Harris, *Fundamentals of Queueing Theory*, New York, John Wiley & Sons, 1974.

Hillier, F., and G. J. Lieberman, *Introduction to Operations Research*. 4th ed., San Francisco, Holden-Day, 1986.

Newell, G. F., *Applications of Queueing Theory*, London, Chapman & Hall, 1971.

Multicriteria Decision Problems (Chapter 17)

Charnes, A., W. W. Cooper, J. K. DeVoe, D. B. Learner, and W. Remecke, "A Goal Programming Model for Media Planning," *Management Science*, Vol. 14, No. 8, April 1968, pp. B423–B430.

Ignizio, J. P., *Goal Programming and Extensions*, Lexington, Mass., Lexington Books, 1976.

Ijiri, Y., *Management Goals and Accounting for Control*, Chicago, Rand McNally, 1965.

Lee, S. M., *Goal Programming for Decision Analysis*, Philadelphia, Auerback, 1972.

Saaty, T. L., *The Analytic Hierarchy Process*, New York, McGraw-Hill, 1980.

Saaty, T. L., *Decision Making for Leaders*, Belmont, Calif., Lifetime Learning Publications, 1982.

Quantitative Methods and Computer-Based Information Systems (Epilogue)

Alter, Steven, *Decision Support Systems: Current Practice and Continuing Challenges*, Reading, Mass., Addison-Wesley, 1980.

Blanning, R. W., "What is Happening in DSS?" *Interfaces*, October 1983.

Davis, Gordon B., *Management Information Systems: Conceptual Foundations, Structure and Development*, New York, McGraw-Hill, 1974.

Donovan, J. J., "Database System Approach to Management Decision Support," *ACM Transactions on Database Systems*, Vol. 1, No. 4, December 1976, pp. 344–369.

Fordyce, K., P. Norden, and G. Sullivan, "Review of Expert Systems for the Management Science Practitioner," *Interfaces*, Vol. 17, No. 2, 1987, pp. 64–77.

Gerrity, T. P., Jr., "The Design of Man-Machine Decision Systems: An Application to Portfolio Management," *Sloan Management Review*, Vol. 12, No. 2, 1971, pp. 59–75.

Hicks, James O., *Management Information Systems: A User Perspective*, 2nd ed., St. Paul, Minn., West Publishing, 1987.

Keen, Peter G. W., and Scott Morton, Michael S., *Decision Support Systems: An Organizational Perspective*, Reading, Mass., Addison-Wesley, 1978.

Mann, R. I., and H. J. Watson, "A Contingency Model for User Involvement in DSS Development," *MIS Quarterly*, March 1984.

Moore, Jeffery H., and Chang, Michael G., "Design of Decision Support Systems," *Data Base*, September/November 1980, pp. 8–14.

Scott, Jim, "The Management Science Opportunity: A Systems Development Viewpoint," presentation at the Society for Management Information Systems Annual Conference in Washington, D.C., September 1978.

Waterman, Donald A., *A Guide to Expert Systems*, Reading, Mass., Addison-Wesley, 1986.

Watson, H. J., and M. Hill, "Decision Support Systems or What Didn't Happen with MIS," *Interfaces*, October 1983.

Answers to Even-Numbered Problems

Chapter 1

2. **a.** The problem is relatively large and complex
   b. Because of potential lost sales, poor schedules may be costly
   c. The problem is a new one and no one has the experience to rely solely on managerial judgment
   d. The problem is repetitive and requires weekly decisions

4. **a.** iconic—scale model of a new plant or building; memorial statues; scale model racing cars
   b. analog—barometer, altimeter
   c. mathematical—inventory cost equation, cost-volume models, profit-volume models

6. **a.** max $10x_1 + 5x_2$
   s.t.
   $$5x_1 + 2x_2 \leq 40$$
   $$x_1 \geq 0$$
   $$x_2 \geq 0$$

   b. Controllable inputs: production quantities x_1 and x_2
   Uncontrollable inputs: unit profits of \$10 and \$5
   labor usage of 5 and 2 hours
   40 hours of labor available

   d. $x_1 = 0$ and $x_2 = 20$; Profit = \$100

8. | If $a =$ | Optimal Solution x | Projected Profit |
   |---|---|---|
   | 3 | $13\frac{1}{3}$ | \$133 |
   | 4 | 10 | \$100 |
   | 5 | 8 | \$ 80 |
   | 6 | $6\frac{2}{3}$ | \$ 67 |

   Since the value of a is stochastic and cannot be stated with certainty, the optimal solution x and the projected profit cannot be known with certainty

10. Let $d =$ distance in miles (one-way)
    $m =$ miles per gallon
    $c =$ cost per gallon

$$\text{Total Cost} = \frac{2d}{m}c$$

To make this a deterministic model, you must be willing to treat m and c as known and not subject to variation

12. **a.** For $p = 20$, $x = 600$ units
       For $p = 70$, $x = 100$ units
    b. Total Revenue $= 800p - 10p^2$
    c. If $p =$ Total Revenue

If $p =$	Total Revenue
$30	$15,000
$40	$16,000 (max revenue at $p = \$40$)
$50	$15,000

    d. For $p = 40$, $x = 400$ units
       Total Revenue $= \$16,000$

14. **a.** $s_j = s_{j-1} + x_j - d_j$
       or $s_j - s_{j-1} - x_j + d_j = 0$
    b. $x_j \le C_j$
    c. $s_j \ge I_j$

16. **a.** $C(x) = 250,000 + 4.5x$
       $R(x) = 28x$
       $P(x) = 23.5x - 250,000$
    b. Break even occurs when $P(x) = 0$ with $x = 10,638$ copies
    c. The projected profit is $P(x) = \$102,500$

18. **a.** $C(x) = 4000 - 4.4x$
       $R(x) = 10x$
       $P(x) = 5.6x - 4000$
    b. $1600
    c. Yes; $3150

Chapter 2

2. **a.** Six; $S = \{0, 1, 2, 3, 4, 5\}$
   b. Relative frequency method
      $P(0) = .12$, $P(1) = .24$, $P(2) = .30$, $P(3) = .20$, $P(4) = .10$ and
      $P(5) = .04$

4. **a.** .05
   b. .20
   c. .55

6. **a.** .80, .40, .30
   b. .90
   c. .10

8. **a.** .30; yes
   b. .20; advertisement should help increase the market share

10. a.

	Smoker	Nonsmoker	Total
Heart Disease	.10	.08	.18
No Heart Disease	.20	.62	.82
Total	.30	.70	1.00

b. .10

c. $P(H) = .18$; $P(\overline{H}) = .82$; 18% have heart disease
$P(S) = .30$; $P(\overline{S}) = .70$; 30% are smokers

d. .33

e. .11

f. No; $P(H|S) \neq P(H)$

g. Higher probability of heart disease among smokers

12. a. .30, .50, .20

b. No; $P(A \cap B) \neq 0$

c. .40

d. No; $P(A \mid B) \neq P(A)$

e. Commercial has positive effect

14. a.

	Son Attended	Son Did Not Attend	Total
Father Attended	.2250	.0875	.3125
Father Did Not Attend	.2750	.4125	.6875
Total	.5000	.5000	1.0000

b. P(Father Attended) $= .3125$
P(Son Attended) $= .5000$

c. .72

d. .40

e. No; P(Son Attended $\mid$ Father Attended) $\neq P$(Son Attended)

16. a. .25, .40

b. .10

c. .25

d. Independent events; training program has no effect

18. a. .20

b. .35

c. .65

20. .625

22. a. .60

c. .75, .25

24. .21; Yes, call back

26. a. A_2; .23, .46 and .31

b. .0065

Chapter 3

2. **a.** 0.45
   b. 2.45
   c. 2.05, 1.43

4. **a.**

x	$f(x)$
5	$^{18}/_{38}$
-5	$^{20}/_{38}$

   b. $-\$0.26$
   c. 24.93
   d. $-\$26.00$

6. **a.** Medium-Scale 145 (preferred)
      Large-Scale 140
   b. Medium-Scale 2725 (preferred)
      Large-Scale 12,400

8. **a.** 0.0198
   b. 0.9510
   c. 2
   d. 1.4071

10. **a.** 0.0324, 0.2952, 0.6724
    b. 0.1936, 0.4928, 0.3136

12. **a.** 0.2240
    b. 0.5768

14. **a.** 0.1396
    b. 0.1954

16. **a.** 0.000045
    b. 0.010245
    c. 0.0821
    d. 0.9179

18. **a.** $f(x) = \frac{1}{20}$ $70 \leq x \leq 90$
    b. 0.25
    c. 0.40
    d. zero since x is continuous

20. **a.** $f(x) = \frac{1}{10}$ $30 \leq x \leq 40$
    b. 0.20
    c. 37 minutes

22. **a.** 0.0475
    b. 0.0099
    c. 0.7938
    d. $796.75

24. **a.** 0.3830
    b. 0.0359
    c. 0.3821 (38.21%)

26. **a.** 0.7745
    b. 36.32 days
    c. 0.1894 (18.94%)

28. **a.** 0.4592
    b. 0.0301
    c. 3976

30. **a.** 0.7769
    b. 0.5488
    c. 0.4396

32. **a.** 0.2592
    b. 0.4512
    c. 0.1920
    d. 0.2231

34. **a.** 0.6321
    b. 0.1353

Chapter 4

2. **a.** d_1; $EV(d_1) = 11.3$
   b. d_4; $EV(d_4) = 9.5$

4. **a.** d_1; $EV(d_1) = 28$
   b. d_2 if $p < 0.75$; d_1 if $p > 0.75$;
      d_1, d_2, or d_3 if $p = 0.75$
   c. EV may not be the best approach

6. **a.** $d_1 =$ St. Louis; $EV(d_1) = 2000$
   b. d_1 if $p < 0.67$; d_2 if $p > 0.67$;
      d_1 or d_2 if $p = 0.67$
   c. EVPI $= \$200$

8. **a.** Optimistic–d_3; conservative–d_1;   minimax regret–d_2
   b. d_2; $EV(d_2) = 500$
   c. EVPI $= 195$

10. **b.** $d_1 =$ invest; $EV(d_1) = \$700$

12. **a.** $d_2 =$ purchase; $EV(d_2) = 40.25$
    b. EVPI $= \$9000$

14. **a.**

	$s_1 = 100$	$s_2 = 200$	$s_3 = 300$
$d_1 = 100$	500	200	-100
$d_2 = 200$	-500	1000	700
$d_3 = 300$	-1500	0	1500

    b. d_3; $EV(d_3) = 600$
    c. EVPI $= \$600$

16. **a.**

	s_1	s_2	s_3	s_4
d_1	\$250	\$250	\$250	\$250
d_2	\$ 0	\$125	\$250	\$375

    b. $d_2 =$ no inspection; $EV(d_2) = \$206.25$

18. **a.** d_1; $EV(d_1) = 14$
    b. d_3 if $p < 0.59$; d_1 if $p > 0.59$;
       d_1 or d_3 if $p = 0.59$
    c. EVPI = 2
    d. d_3; $EV(d_3) = 13.8068$

20. **a.** d_2; $EV(d_2) = 280$
    b. EVSI = 12
    c. EVPI = 60
    d. 20%

22. **a.** If I_1 then d_2
        If I_2 then d_2 $\Big\}$ EV = \$538.50
        If I_3 then d_3
    b. EVSI = \$38,500
    c. EVPI = \$195,000; 19.7%

24. **a.** d_3; $EV(d_3) = 720$
    b. d_1; $EV(d_1) = 300$

26. **b.** If I_1 then d_1
        If I_2 then d_1 $\Big\}$ EV = 26.65
        If I_3 then d_2
    c. 60.0%

28. **a.** Yes; EV(fund) = \$64,210.62
    b. No; EV(do not fund) = 0
    c. If I_1 then d_1
        If I_2 then d_2 $\Big\}$ EV = \$12,200
        If I_3 then d_3
    d. EVSI = \$12,200; 45.2%

30. **a.** If I_1 then d_1
        If I_2 then d_1 $\Big\}$ EV = 2000
    b. $P(s_1 \mid I_1) = 0.57$
    c. 0%

32. $Q^* = 27,520$ copies

34. **a.** $Q^* = 220$
    b. $Q^* = 247$

Chapter 5

2. **a.** d_2; $EV(d_2) = \$5,000$
   b. p = probability of a \$0 cost
         $1 - p$ = probability of a \$200,000 cost
   c. d_1; $EV(d_1) = 9.9$
   d. expected utility approach

4. **a.** Route B; EV = 58.5
   b. p = probability of a 45 minute travel time
         $1 - p$ = probability of a 90 minute travel time
   c. Route A; EV = 7.6; risk avoider strategy

6. $A - d_1$; $B - d_2$; $C - d_2$

8. **a.**

	Win	Lose
Bet	350	−10
Do not bet	0	0

   b. d_2
   c. risk takers
   d. Between 0 and 0.26

10. **a.** Western; EV = 26%
   b. p = probability of a 40% show
      $1 - p$ = probability of a 15% show
   c. Musical; risk taker

Chapter 6

2. **a.** Forecast for week 4 = 19.33; forecast for week 12 = 17.83
   b. 11.49; prefer the unweighted

4. **a.** $F_{13} = 0.2Y_{12} + 0.16Y_{11} + 0.128Y_{10} + 0.1024Y_9 + 0.08192Y_8 + 0.32768F_8$
   b. The more recent data receives the greater weight. The moving averages method weights the last n data values equally

6. 0.3 is better

8. $F_{11} = 0.2(21) + 0.8(20.08) = 20.26$

10. $T_t = 28{,}800 + 421.429t$

12. **a.** A linear trend appears to exist
   b. $T_t = 19.993 + 1.774t$; $1.77 per unit per year

14. $T_8 = 197.714 + 6.821(8) = 252.28$
   $T_9 = 197.714 + 6.821(9) = 259.10$

16. **a.** Yes
   b. $Y_t = 22.857 + 15.536t$
   c. 147.15

18.

Month	Index
1	0.707
2	0.777
3	0.827
4	0.966
5	1.016
6	1.305
7	1.494
8	1.225
9	0.976
10	0.986
11	0.936
12	0.787

20. **a.**

Quarter	Index
1	1.271
2	0.613
3	0.498
4	1.619

  b. Quarter 4; This seems reasonable

22. **a.** $T_t = -0.345 + 0.995t$
  b. 20.55, 21.55, 22.54, 23.54
  c. 26.10, 13.15, 11.27, 38.13

24. **a.** $\hat{y} = 37.666 - 3.222x$
  b. \$3444

Chapter 7

6. $x_1 = 100$, $x_2 = 50$, $z = 750$

10. $x_1 = {}^{12}\!/_7$, $x_2 = {}^{15}\!/_7$, $z = {}^{69}\!/_7$

12. **a.** $x_1 = 2$, $x_2 = 2$, $z = 10$
  b. Yes, constraint 2

14. **a.** $x_1 = 0$, $x_2 = 540$
  b. Inspection & Packaging and $x_1 \geq 0$

16. **a.** One possibility is $90x_1 + 30x_2$
  b. $x_1 = 35$ $x_2 = 0$

18. **a.** max $25x_1 + 30x_2$
  s.t.
$$
\begin{aligned}
1.5x_1 + 3x_2 &\leq 450 \\
2x_1 + x_2 &\leq 350 \\
.25x_1 + .25x_2 &\leq 50 \\
x_1, x_2 &\geq 0
\end{aligned}
$$

  b. $x_1 = 100$, $x_2 = 100$, $z = 5500$
  c.

Dept.	Prod. Time	Slack
A	450	0
B	300	50
C	50	0

20. $x_1 = 800$, $x_2 = 1200$, $z = 8400$

22. **a.** 250 gallons of product 1, 100 gallons of product 2
  b. \$800
  c. 125 gallons of product 1

24.

Extreme Point	z	Slack or Surplus
$x_1 = 250$, $x_2 = 100$	800	$s_1 = 125$, $s_2 = 0$, $s_3 = 0$
$x_1 = 125$, $x_2 = 225$	925	$s_1 = 0$, $s_2 = 0$, $s_3 = 125$
$x_1 = 125$, $x_2 = 350$	1300	$s_1 = 0$, $s_2 = 125$, $s_3 = 0$

26. $x_1 = 12$, $x_2 = 3$, $z = 63$

28. $x_1 = 6$, $x_2 = 10$, cost $=$ \$.54 per can

30. **a.**
$$\max \quad x_1 + 1.5x_2 + 0s_1 + 0s_2 + 0s_3 + 0s_4$$
s.t.
$$
\begin{aligned}
x_1 + \quad x_2 + s_1 \qquad\qquad\qquad\qquad &= 150 \\
\tfrac{1}{4}x_1 + \tfrac{1}{2}x_2 \qquad\quad + s_2 \qquad\qquad\quad &= 50 \\
x_1 \qquad\qquad\qquad\quad - s_3 \qquad\quad &= 50 \\
x_2 \qquad\qquad\qquad\quad - s_4 &= 25
\end{aligned}
$$
$$x_1, x_2, s_1, s_2, s_3, s_4 \geq 0$$

b. $s_1 = 0$, $s_2 = 0$, $s_3 = 50$, $s_4 = 25$

c. Dough and Topping are the binding constraints

32. **a.**
$$\max \quad 100x_1 + 200x_2$$
s.t.
$$
\begin{aligned}
x_1 + \quad x_2 &\leq 500 \\
x_1 \qquad\quad &\leq 200 \\
2x_1 + \quad 6x_2 &\leq 1200
\end{aligned}
$$
$$x_1, x_2 \geq 0$$

b. Add a slack variable to each constraint

c. $x_1 = 200$, $x_2 = 133\frac{1}{3}$, $z = 46{,}666$

d. $(x_1 = 0, x_2 = 0)$, $(x_1 = 200, x_2 = 0)$, $(x_1 = 200, x_2 = 133\frac{1}{3})$, $(x_1 = 0, x_2 = 200)$

e. Labor hours

34. **b.** $(x_1 = 5, x_2 = 4)$, $(x_1 = 2, x_2 = 4)$

c. $x_1 = 2$, $x_2 = 4$, $z = 10$

36. Add a slack variable to each constraint

38. **b.** $x_1 = \frac{20}{3}$, $x_2 = \frac{8}{3}$, $z = 30\frac{2}{3}$

c. $s_1 = \frac{28}{3}$, $s_2 = 0$, $s_3 = 0$

40. Infeasible

42. **a.** $x_1 = \frac{30}{16}$, $x_2 = \frac{30}{16}$, $z = \frac{60}{16}$

b. $x_1 = 0$, $x_2 = 3$, $z = 6$

c. $1x_1 + \frac{5}{3}x_2$

44. Alternate optimal solutions

46. **d.** $x_1 = 50$, $x_2 = 30$, value $= 90$

Chapter 8

2. Solution: $x_1 = 527.5$, $x_2 = 270.75$
   Shadow price $= 4.375$

4. **a.** Constraint 1: 1.5, Constraint 2: 0
   b. Same as shadow prices

6. **a.** Constraint 1: .333, Constraint 2: .333, Constraint 3: 0
   b. Constraint 1: $-.333$, Constraint 2: $-.333$, Constraint 3: 0

8. **a.** Optimal solution: $x_1 = 9$, $x_2 = 4$
   b. Constraint 2: 0, Constraint 3: .0769

10. **a.** $x_1 = 0$, $x_2 = 10$
    b. Same as for problem 7: $x_1 = 7$, $x_2 = 7$

12. **a.** $4 \leq c_1 \leq 12.0012$ $3.333 \leq c_2 \leq 10$
    c.

Min RHS	Max RHS
725.0038	∞
133.320	399.9999
75.00	134.9982

   d. 560.012

14. **a.** more than \$7.00
    b. more than \$3.50
    c. None

16. **a.** $x_1 = 30$, $x_2 = 25$ minimum production cost = \$55
    b. $.5 \leq c_1 < \infty$ $0.0 \leq c_2 \leq 2$
    c. $-.50$, $-.50$, 0.00
    d. $.50$, $.50$, 0.00
    e. Increase by 2.50
    f.

Min RHS	Max RHS
70.0	∞
0.0	40.0
$-\infty$	25.0

18. **a.** $x_1 = 0$, $x_2 = 25$, $x_3 = 125$, $x_4 = 0$; value = 525
    b. Ones for machines A and C
    c. machine B
    d. Yes

20. **a.** $x_1 = 7.297$, $x_2 = 0.000$, $x_3 = 1.892$; value = 139.7297
    b. Constraints 2 and 3
    c. 0.000, -3.405, -4.432
    d. 0.000, 3.405, 4.432
    e. Constraint 3 from 20 to 19

22. **a.** All-Pro: 1000, College: 0, High School: 250
    b. Sewing and minimum production of the All-Pro model
    d. $-\infty < c_1 \leq 5$, $-\infty < c_2 \leq 5$, $4.0 \leq c_3 < \infty$

24. **a.** $x_1 = 600$, $x_2 = 700$, $x_3 = 200$
    b. $-\infty < c_1 \leq 9.0$, $5.33 \leq c_2 \leq 9.0$, $6.00 \leq c_3 < \infty$
    c.

Constraint	Min RHS	Max RHS
1	4400	7440
2	6300	∞
3	100	900
4	600	∞
5	700	∞
6	514.28571	1000

   d. Nothing
   e. No

Chapter 9

2. **a.**

Advertisement	Number	Budget Allocation
television	4	$ 8,000
radio	14	4,200
newspaper	10	6,000
		$18,200

    Audience $= 1,052,000$

  b. Approximately 5130

4. **a.** $x_1 = 77.89$, $x_2 = 63.16$, $z = \$3,284.21$
  b. Dept. A \$15.79, Dept. B \$47.37
  c. $x_1 = 87.21$, $x_2 = 65.12$, $z = \$3,341.34$
    Dept. A 10 hours, Dept. B 3.2 hours

6. **a.** $x_1 = 500$, $x_2 = 300$, $x_3 = 200$, $z = \$550$
  b. \$0.55
  c. Aroma 75, Taste 84.4
  d. \$0.60

8. 50 units of product 1
   0 units of product 2
  300 hours dept. A, 600 hours dept. B

10.

	Modern Line	Old Line
1	500	0
2	300	400

    Cost $= \$3850$

12.

	Mfr.	Purchase
Base	3750	1250
Cartridge	5000	0
Handle	3750	1250

    Cost $= \$11,875$

  b. Depts. A and B; add only to A
  c. Only 25 hours can be used

14. $x_1 =$ number of 10-inch rolls processed by cutting alternative i
  a. $x_1 = 0$, $x_2 = 125$, $x_3 = 500$, $x_4 = 1500$, $x_5 = 0$, $x_6 = 0$, $x_7 = 0$;
    2125 rolls with waste of 750 inches
  b. 2500 rolls with no waste; however, $1\frac{1}{2}$ inch size is overproduced by 3000 units

16. **a.** 5 super, 2 regular, and 3 econotankers
    Total cost \$583,000; monthly operating cost \$4650

18. $x_1 = 48$, $x_2 = 96$, $z = 456$
  Assembler times: 480, 480 and 456

20. **a.** Marginal $= 0.6$; average $= .079$; diminishing marginal returns have set in

Chapter 10

2. $x_1 = 5$, $x_2 = 1$, $x_3 = 4$

4. **b.**

$$\max \quad 5x_1 + 20x_2 + 25x_3 + 0s_1 + 0s_2 + 0s_3$$

s.t.

$$
\begin{aligned}
2x_1 + x_2 \quad\quad + s_1 \quad\quad\quad\quad\quad &= 40 \\
2x_2 + x_3 \quad\quad + s_2 \quad\quad &= 30 \\
3x_1 \quad\quad - \tfrac{1}{2}x_3 \quad\quad\quad\quad + s_3 &= 15
\end{aligned}
$$

$$x_1, x_2, x_3, s_1, s_2, s_3 \geq 0$$

   c. Initial basis: s_1, s_2, s_3. It is the origin
   d. 0
   e. x_3 enters and s_2 will leave
   f. 30 units of x_3
   g. $x_1 = 10$, $x_2 = 0$, $x_3 = 30$, $s_1 = 20$, $s_2 = 0$, $s_3 = 0$

6. Coefficients of slack variables equal 1 and all RHS's ≥ 0

8. **a.** $x_1 = 540$, $x_2 = 252$
   b. $7668
   c. 630, 480, 708, 117
   d. 0, 120, 0, 18

10. Sequence: $(x_1 = 0, x_2 = 0)$, $(x_1 = 6, x_2 = 0)$, $(x_1 = 4.2, x_2 = 3.6)$

12. Corresponds to basic variables that will decrease

14. Next solution would be infeasible

16. 30 Deskpros and 12 Portables

18. **a.** 0, 50, 75
    b. $s_1 = 50$, $s_2 = 0$, $s_3 = 30$, $s_4 = 0$
    c. Grade B grapes and labor hours

22. $x_1 = 9$, $x_2 = 2$, $x_3 = \tfrac{1}{2}$; $z = 41.5$

24. **a.** $x_1 = 250$, $x_2 = 100$ cost $= 800$
    c. 2
    d. 1

26. John: 480 cases of Incentive
    Brenda: 480 cases of Temptation
    Red: 800 cases of Temptation

28. Alternate optima: $x_1 = 4$, $x_2 = 4$ and $x_1 = 8$, $x_2 = 0$

30. Alternate optima: $x_1 = 4$, $x_2 = 0$, $x_3 = 0$ and $x_1 = 0$, $x_2 = 0$, $x_3 = 8$

32. Infeasible

34. **b.** $x_1 = 300$, $x_2 = 420$, $s_2 = 100$, $s_3 = 128$. s_3 enters, s_4 leaves

36. Infeasible

38. a. $0 \leq b_1 \leq 12$ $2 \leq b_2 \leq 6$ $4.5 \leq b_3 < \infty$
   b. $1\frac{7}{8}$
   c. $7\frac{1}{2}$
   d. 0

40. a. $495.6 \leq b_1 \leq 682.36$
   b. $480 \leq b_2 < \infty$
   c. $580 \leq b_3 \leq 900$
   d. $117 \leq b_4 < \infty$
   e. Cutting and Dyeing, Finishing

42. a. 131.25
   b. No decrease
   c. 262.5

44. a. $x_3 = 15$, $x_4 = 8\frac{1}{3}$
   b. $2 \leq c_3 < \infty$
   c. New solution: $x_1 = 10$, $x_4 = 8\frac{1}{3}$
   d. $-\infty < c_2 \leq 4\frac{1}{2}$
   e. No effect

46. a. $24 \leq c_1 \leq 64$
   b. $31.25 \leq c_2 \leq 83.33$
   c. Same optimal solution. New value $= 1380$
   d. New solution: $x_1 = 16\frac{2}{3}$, $x_2 = 20$, value $= 1133.33$

Chapter 11

2. a. The model consists of $3 \leq$ constraints and $3 =$ constraints; the objective function
   is
$$\min \quad 20x_{11} + 16x_{12} + 24x_{13} + 10x_{21} + 10x_{22} + 8x_{23} +$$
$$12x_{31} + 18x_{32} + 10x_{33}$$
   b. Change to maximization objective function
   c. $P_1 - W_2 : 300$ $P_2 - W_1 : 100$ $P_2 - W_2 : 100$
   $P_2 - W_3 : 300$ $P_3 - W_1 : 100$

4. b. Detroit - Atlanta   100
   St. Louis - Atlanta   100
   St. Louis - Houston   200
   Denver - Boston   300
          Total cost: $3900
   c. Add $x_{11} = 100$
   d. Delete x_{31} and x_{22}

6. a. $O_1 - D_1 : 150$ $O_1 - D_2 : 100$ $O_2 - D_2 : 100$
   $O_2 - D_3 : 50$ $O_3 - D_3 : 100$
   b. $O_1 - D_1 : 150$ $O_1 - D_2 : 50$ $O_1 - D_3 : 50$
   $O_2 - D_2 : 150$ $O_3 - D_3 : 100$
   c. $O_1 - D_1 : 50$ $O_1 - D_2 : 50$ $O_1 - D_3 : 150$
   $O_2 - D_2 : 150$ $O_3 - D_1 : 100$

8. Clifton Springs - D_2 4000
 Clifton Springs - D_4 1000
 Danville - D_1 2000
 Danville - D_4 1000
      Customer 2 is 1000 short
      Customer 3 is 3000 short

10. **a.** Product A: 300 on I,   1200 on II,   500 on III
      Product B: 500 on III
      Product C: 1200 on I
 b. Yes   Product A: 1500 on I,   500 on III
        Product B: 500 on III
        Product C: 1200 on II

12. **a.** Total time $= 64$
 b. Jackson—2; Ellis—1; Smith—3

14. **a.** Optimal solution: Bostock—Southwest,
        Miller—Northwest
      Value $= 184$

16. **a.** Toy—2   Auto Parts—4
      Housewares—3   Record—1
      Profit $= 61$

18. 1—B 2—C
    3—A 4—D Total time $= 74$ hours

20. 1—A,   2—E,   3—B, 4—D, 5—C; value $= 12$

22. 1—D,   2—C,   3—B,   4—A; value $= 505$ miles

24. **b.**

Variable	Value
x_{13}	400
x_{14}	0
x_{15}	0
x_{23}	350
x_{24}	0
x_{25}	250
x_{34}	750
x_{35}	0

Value $= 7500$

c. add $x_{34} \leq 500$; the new optimal solution is:

Variable	Value
x_{13}	400
x_{14}	0
x_{15}	0
x_{23}	100
x_{24}	250
x_{25}	250
x_{34}	500
x_{35}	0

Value $= 7750$

26. **c.**

Variable	Value
x_{14}	400
x_{15}	0
x_{24}	450
x_{25}	0
x_{34}	0
x_{35}	350
x_{46}	0
x_{47}	500
x_{48}	300
x_{49}	50
x_{56}	200
x_{57}	0
x_{58}	0
x_{59}	150

Value = 16,150

Chapter 12

2. **b.** $x_1 = 1.43$, $x_2 = 4.29$; its value is 41.47
   $x_1 = 1$, $x_2 = 4$; its value is 37
   c. Not the same: $x_1 = 0$, $x_2 = 5$; its value is 40

4. **a.** Rounded down solution: $x_1 = 3$, $x_2 = 0$; its value is 30
   Lower bound = 30, upper bound is 36.7 (actually an upper bound of 36)
   b. $x_1 = 3$, $x_2 = 2$; its value is 36
   c. LP relaxation: $x_1 = 0$, $x_2 = 5.71$; its value is 34.26
   Rounding down: $x_1 = 0$, $x_2 = 5$ with value 30
   Upper bound = 34.26, lower bound = 30
   Optimal integer: $x_1 = 0$, $x_2 = 5$; its value is 30

6. **b.** $x_1 = 1.96$, $x_2 = 5.48$; its value is 7.44
   Upper bound = 7.44, lower bound = 6.96
   c. $x_1 = 1.29$, $x_2 = 6$; its value is 7.29

8. **b.** Locate a PPB in Ashland county

12. **a.** $x_1 + x_3 + x_5 + x_6 = 2$
    b. $x_3 - x_5 = 0$
    c. $x_1 + x_4 = 1$
    d. $x_4 \leq x_1$ $\quad$ $x_4 \leq x_3$
    e. $x_4 \leq x_1$ $\quad$ $x_4 \leq x_3$ $\quad$ $x_4 \geq x_1 + x_3 - 1$

14. **a.** County 11
    b. Counties 3 and 11
    c. 642,000 customers can be served, 1,058,000 cannot

Chapter 13

2. b.

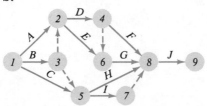

4. a. A–D–G
   b. No; Time = 15 months

6. a. A–D–F–H
   b. 22 weeks
   c. No, it is a critical activity
   d. Yes, 2 weeks
   e. ES = 3, LS = 4, EF = 10, LF = 11

8. b. B–C–E–F–H
   d. Yes; Time = 49 weeks

10. a.

Activity	Time	Variance
A	5.00	0.11
B	9.00	0.11
C	8.00	0.44
D	8.83	0.25
E	7.17	0.25
F	6.00	0.11

   b. 23.83, 0.47

12. a. A–D–H–I
   b. 25.66 days
   c. 0.2578

14. a. A–D–F–G
   b. 1.5 days
   c. 29.5, 2.36
   d. 0.6293

16. a.

$E(T)$	Variance
16	3.92
13	2.03
10	1.27

   b. 0.9783, approximately 1.00, approximately 1.00

18. c. A–B–D–G–H–I, 14.17 weeks
   d. Yes, P(13 weeks completion) = 0.0951

20. b. Crash B(1 week), D(2 weeks), E(1 week), F(1 week), G(1 week)
      Total Cost = $2427
   c. All activities are critical

22. b. Crash C(1 day) and E(1 day)
   c. $9300

24. **c.** A–B–C–F, 31 weeks
    d. Crash A(2 weeks), B(2 weeks), C(1 week), D(1 week), E(1 week)
    e. All activities are critical
    f. $112,500

26.

Activity	Cost/Week
A	15
B	8
C	1
D	20
E	2
F	1
G	20
H	5
I	2
J	1

28. **b.** 6% overrun; followup on activity D

30. Corrective action desired
    Activity E—one week behind
    Activity F—$3000 cost overrun

Chapter 14

2. $164.32 for each; Total Cost = $328.64

4. **a.** 1095.45
   b. 240
   c. 22.82 days
   d. $273.86 for each; Total Cost = $547.72

6. **a.** 15.95
   b. $2106
   c. 15.04
   d. 16.62 days

8. $Q^* = 11.73$, use 12 classes
   5 classes per year
   $225,200 for 12 classes

10. $Q^* = 1414.21$
    $T = 28.28$ days
    Production runs of 7.07 days

12. $Q^* = 1000$ Total Cost = $1200
    Yes, the change saves $300 per year

14. New $Q^* = 4509$

16. 135.55; $r = dm - S$; less than

18. 64, 24.44

20. $Q^* = 100$; Total Cost = $3,601.50

22. $Q^* = 300$;   Savings = \$480

24. **a.** 12
    b. 15
    c. 3 units; \$15

26. **a.** 79.84
    b. $r = 35$; Safety Stock = 10
    c. 0.1587; 2 stockouts per year

28. **a.** 500
    b. 580.4

30. **a.** 397
    b. 0.70
    c. 489, 0.35

32. **a.** 440
    b. 0.60
    c. 7.10
    d. $c_u = \$17$; Goodwill Cost = \$15

34. Order 10 engines
    Order 7 air cleaners
    Order 2 filter housings

36. Order 13 bases
    Order 9 wheels
    Order 4 tires

Chapter 15

2.
Number of Arrivals	Relative Frequency	Random Numbers
0	.12	00–11
1	.24	12–35
2	.37	36–72
3	.19	73–91
4	.08	92–99

Time Period	Arriving Customers
9:00–9:05 A.M.	0
9:05–9:10 A.M.	2
9:10–9:15 A.M.	1

4. **a.** .04, .10, .16, .44, .20, .06
   b. Intervals of random numbers are 00–03, 04–13, 14–29, 30–73, 74–93, 94–99

6. 3 customers served; total profit = \$3.75

8. Use 80 since 70 should not satisfy demand 95% of the time

10. **b.** Simulation results vary near a value of \$10.85
    c. Simulation results vary near 21–22 subscriptions and a daily profit of \$42 to \$45

12. Profit values should be near the \$24 to \$28 range
    Simulation results vary but order sizes of 200 or 225 should be preferred

14. Ten week simulation results vary considerably depending upon the occurrence of shortages

16. Average weekly total cost = $202.50

Chapter 16

2. **a.** 0.3333
   b. 1.3333
   c. 0.1111 hours (6.67 minutes)
   d. 0.6667

4. **a.** 0.20
   b. 3.2
   c. 4
   d. 0.8 hours
   e. 1 hour
   f. 0.80

6. **a.**

	$\mu = 3$	$\mu = 4$
L_q	1.3333	0.50
L	2.0000	1.00
W_q	0.6667	0.25
W	1.0000	0.50
P_w	0.6667	0.50

   b. New $37; Experience $25
   Hire experienced

8. Service needs improvement
   Average number waiting = 2.25
   Average time waiting for service = 9 minutes

10. **a.** 0.1667
    b. 5
    c. 0.4167 hours (25 minutes)
    d. 0.8333

12. **a.** 0.50
    b. 0.50
    c. 0.1 hours (6 minutes)
    d. 0.2 hours (12 minutes)

14. **a.** 0.5385
    b. 0.0593
    c. 0.6593
    d. 0.0099 hours (.59 minutes)
    e. 0.1099 hours (6.59 minutes)

16. 0.5765, 0.2024

18. One with $\mu = 7.5$, $L = 0.50$, $28.50
    Two with $\mu = 6$, $L = 0.4356$, $42.89
    Use one consultant

20. **a.** 0.0063 hours (.38 minutes)
    b. 0.4286
    c. 2 channels (.38 minute wait)
       1 channel (1.25 minute wait)

Chapter 17

2. **a.** No
   c. 40,000 letters mailed to group 1 and 30,000 letters mailed to group 2; this solution will reach 10,000 group 1 customers and 3,000 group 2 customers
   d. 20,000 letters mailed to group 1 and 50,000 letters mailed to group 2

4. **a.** 281.25 units of product 1 and 87.50 units of product 2; profit = \$1300
   b. 350–product 1; 0–product 2; profit = \$1400
   c. Favor approach in part (**a**)

6. **a.** $x_1 = 2$, $x_2 = 6$
   b. $x_1 = 2$, $x_2 = 8$

8. CR = .05; acceptable

10. **a.**

	A	B
A	1	6
B	1/6	1

   b. .857, .143

12. **a.** .75, .25
    b. Cannot be inconsistent

14. **a.**

	A	B	C
A	1	1/2	5
B	2	1	5
C	1/5	1/5	1

   b. .354, .556, .091
   c. CR = .047; acceptable

16. **a.** .292, .140, .053, .515
    b. CR = .084; acceptable

18. **b.** .128, .512, .360
    c. Jacobs: .471
       Martin: .529

Index